Contents

- **III** Distance table
- **IV** Route planning maps
- **VIII** Key to road map symbols
- **1** Key to road map pages
- **2** Road maps of Great Britain at 10 miles to 1 inch
- **33** Key to city plan and approach map symbols
- **34** City plans and **NAVIGATOR**® approach maps

34 Aberdeen	72 Glasgow	118 Oxford
35 Aberystwyth	74 Gloucester	119 Perth
36 Ashford	75 Grimsby	120 Peterborough
37 Ayr	76 Hanley	121 Plymouth
38 Bangor	77 Harrogate	122 Poole
39 Barrow-in-Furness	78 Haywards Heath	123 Portsmouth
40 Bath	79 Hull	124 Preston
41 Berwick-upon-Tweed	80 Inverness	125 Reading
42 Birmingham	81 Ipswich	126 St Andrews
44 Blackpool	82 Kendal	127 Salisbury
45 Bournemouth	83 King's Lynn	128 Scarborough
46 Bradford	84 Lancaster	129 Shrewsbury
47 Brighton	85 Leicester	130 Sheffield
48 Bristol	86 Leeds	132 Southampton
50 Bury St Edmunds	88 Lewes	133 Southend-on-Sea
51 Cambridge	89 Lincoln	134 Stirling
52 Cardiff	90 Liverpool	135 Stoke
54 Canterbury	92 Llandudno	136 Stratford-upon-Avon
55 Carlisle	93 Llanelli	137 Sunderland
56 Chelmsford	94 London	138 Swansea
57 Cheltenham	102 Luton	139 Swindon
58 Chester	103 Macclesfield	140 Taunton
59 Chichester	104 Manchester	141 Telford
60 Colchester	106 Maidstone	142 Torquay
61 Coventry	107 Merthyr Tydfil	143 Truro
62 Croydon	108 Middlesbrough	144 Wick
63 Derby	109 Milton Keynes	145 Winchester
64 Dorchester	110 Newcastle-upon-Tyne	146 Windsor
65 Dumfries	112 Newport	147 Wolverhampton
66 Dundee	113 Newquay	148 Worcester
67 Durham	114 Northampton	149 Wrexham
68 Edinburgh	115 Norwich	150 York
70 Exeter	116 Nottingham	
71 Fort William	117 Oban	

- **151** Index to road maps

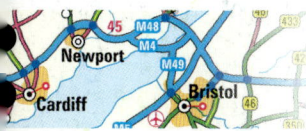

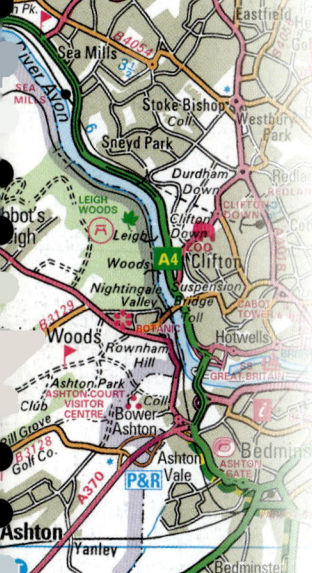

First published in 2004 by
Philip's, a division of
Octopus Publishing Group Ltd,
2–4 Heron Quays, London E14 4JP

www.philips-maps.co.uk

Second edition 2006
First impression 2006

ISBN-10 0-540-08923-0
ISBN-13 978-0-540-08923-9

Cartography by Philip's
Copyright © 2006 Philip's

This product includes mapping data licenced from Ordnance Survey®, with the permission of the Controller of Her Majesty's Stationery Office. © Crown copyright 2006. All rights reserved. Licence number 100011710

All rights reserved. Apart from any fair dealing for the purpose of private study, research, criticism or review, as permitted under the Copyright Designs and Patents Act, 1988, no part of this publication may be reproduced, stored in a retrieval system, or transmitted in any form or by any means, electronic, electrical, chemical, mechanical, optical, photocopying, recording, or otherwise, without prior written permission.
All enquiries should be addressed to the Publisher.

To the best of the Publisher's knowledge, the information in this atlas was correct at the time of going to press. No responsibility can be accepted for any errors or their consequences.

The representation in this atlas of any road, drive or track is no evidence of the existence of a right of way.

Information for Tourist Attractions in England shown on the mapping supplied by the British Tourist Authority / English Tourist Board.

Information for National Parks, Areas of Outstanding Natural Beauty, National Trails and Country Parks in Wales supplied by the Countryside Council for Wales.

Data for Regional parks, Long Distance Footpaths and Country Parks in Scotland provided by Scottish National Heritage.

Information for National Parks, Areas of Outstanding Natural Beauty, National Trails and Country Parks in England supplied by the Countryside Agency.

Information for canal bridge numbers supplied by GEOprojects (UK) Ltd.

Printed by Toppan, China

Photographic acknowledgements

Aberdeen – Doug Houghton / Alamy • **Aberystwyth** – The Photolibrary Wales / Alamy • **Ashford** – Image Advertising • **Ayr** – Ayrshire and Arran Tourist Board • **Bangor** – Rob Rayworth / Alamy • **Barrow-in-Furness** – David Crausby / Alamy • **Bath** – James Hughes • **Berwick-upon-Tweed** – Jim Gibson / Alamy • **Birmingham** – Birmingham City Council • **Blackpool** – Chris Parker • **Bournemouth** – Bournemouth Borough Council • **Bradford** – Bradford Council • **Brighton** – Leonardo Media BV • **Bristol** – James Hughes • **Bury St Edmunds** – East of England Tourist Board • **Cambridge** – East of England Tourist Board • **Cardiff** – James Hughes; The Photolibrary Wales / Alamy • **Canterbury** – Canterbury City Council • **Carlisle** – Leslie Garland Picture Library / Alamy • **Chelmsford** - East of England Tourist Board • **Cheltenham** – Cheltenham Tourism / David Sellman • **Chester** – Iconotec / Alamy • **Chichester** – James Hughes • **Colchester** – Colchester Image Library • **Coventry** – CV One Ltd • **Croydon** – Croydon Design • **Derby** – Derby City Council • **Dorchester** – Rolf Richardson / Alamy • **Dumfries** – Allan Devlin • **Dundee** – Doug Houghton / Alamy • **Durham** – James Hughes • **Edinburgh** – Michael Juno / Alamy • **Exeter** – James Hughes • **Fort William** – The Highlands of Scotland Tourist Board • **Glasgow** – Greater Glasgow and Clyde Valley Tourist Board • **Gloucester** – James Hughes • **Grimsby** – North East Lincolnshire Council • **Hanley** – Stoke-on-Trent City Council • **Harrogate** – Harrogate International Centre • **Haywards Heath** – Robert Harding Picture Library Ltd / Alamy • **Hull** – Hull City Council • **Inverness** – The Highland Council • **Ipswich** – Ipswich Borough Council • **Kendal** – South Lakeland District Council • **King's Lynn** – Borough Council of King's Lynn and West Norfolk • **Lancaster** – Lancaster City Council • **Leicester** – Aerofilms / Alamy • **Leeds** – David Lyons / Alamy • **Lewes** – Lewes District Council • **Lincoln** – Hideo Kurihara / Alamy • **Liverpool** – The Mersey Partnership • **Llandudno** – Rob Rayworth / Alamy • **Llanelli** – Carmarthenshire County Council • **London** – Image State / Alamy; James Hughes; Coaster / Alamy • **Luton** – Popperfoto / Alamy • **Macclesfield** – Macclesfield Borough Council • **Manchester** – North West Tourist Board • **Maidstone** – Worldwide Picture Library / Alamy • **Merthyr Tydfil** – Lyndon Beddoe / Alamy • **Middlesbrough** – Leslie Garland Picture Library / Alamy • **Milton Keynes** – Justin Kase / Alamy • **Newcastle-upon-Tyne** – Andrew Siddens / Alamy • **Newport** – James Hughes • **Newquay** – Restormel Borough Council • **Northampton** – David Gould / Alamy • **Norwich** – East of England Tourist Board • **Nottingham** – Joe Fox / Alamy • **Oban** – Worldwide Picture Library / Alamy • **Oxford** – Tourism South East • **Perth** – Worldwide Picture Library / Alamy • **Peterborough** – East of England Tourist Board • **Plymouth** – James Hughes • **Poole** – Poole Tourism • **Portsmouth** – Worldwide Picture Library / Alamy **Preston** – Lancashire Tourism Partnership • **Reading** – Boating Images Photo Library / Alamy **St Andrews** – Kingdom of Fife Tourist Board • **Salisbury** – James Hughes • **Scarborough** – Scarborough Borough Council • **Shrewsbury** – Shropshire Tourism • **Sheffield** - Elmtree Images / Alamy • **Southampton** – Peter Titmuss / Alamy • **Southend** – David Burton / Alamy **Stirling** – David Sanger Photography / Alamy • **Stoke** - Rolf Richardson / Alamy • **Stratford-upon-Avon** – James Kerr / Alamy • **Sunderland** – Geoffrey Morgan / Alamy • **Swansea** – James Hughes • **Swindon** – Justin Kase / Alamy • **Taunton** – James Hughes • **Telford** – Borough of Telford and Wrekin • **Torquay** – English Riviera Tourist Board • **Truro** – James Hughes • **Wick** – P Tomkins / Visit Scotland / Scottish Viewpoint • **Winchester** – James Hughes • **Windsor** – Royal Borough of Windsor and Maidenhead • **Wolverhampton** – Wolverhampton City Council • **Worcester** – James Hughes **Wrexham** – Wrexham County Borough Council • **York** – James Hughes

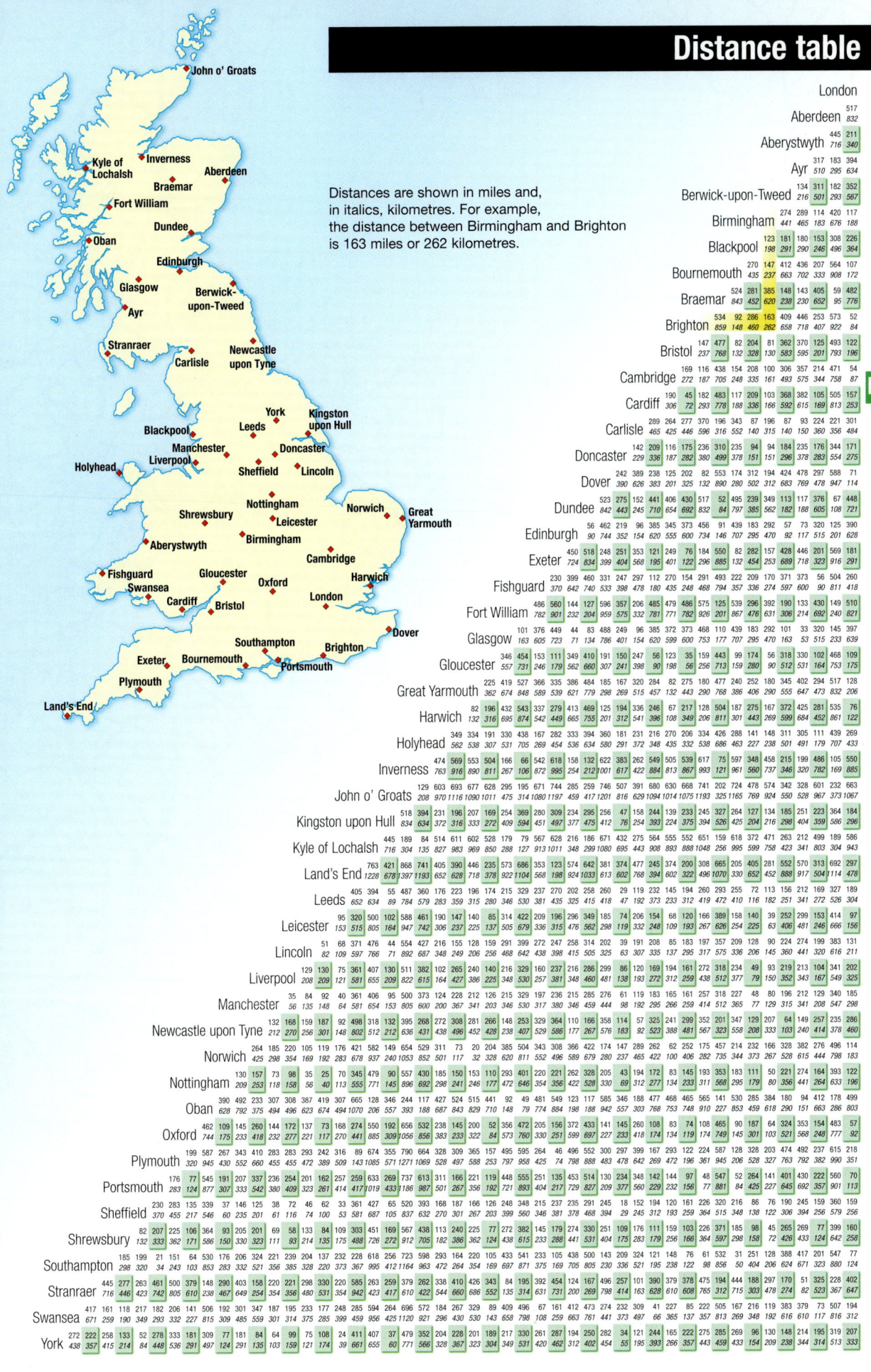

VI

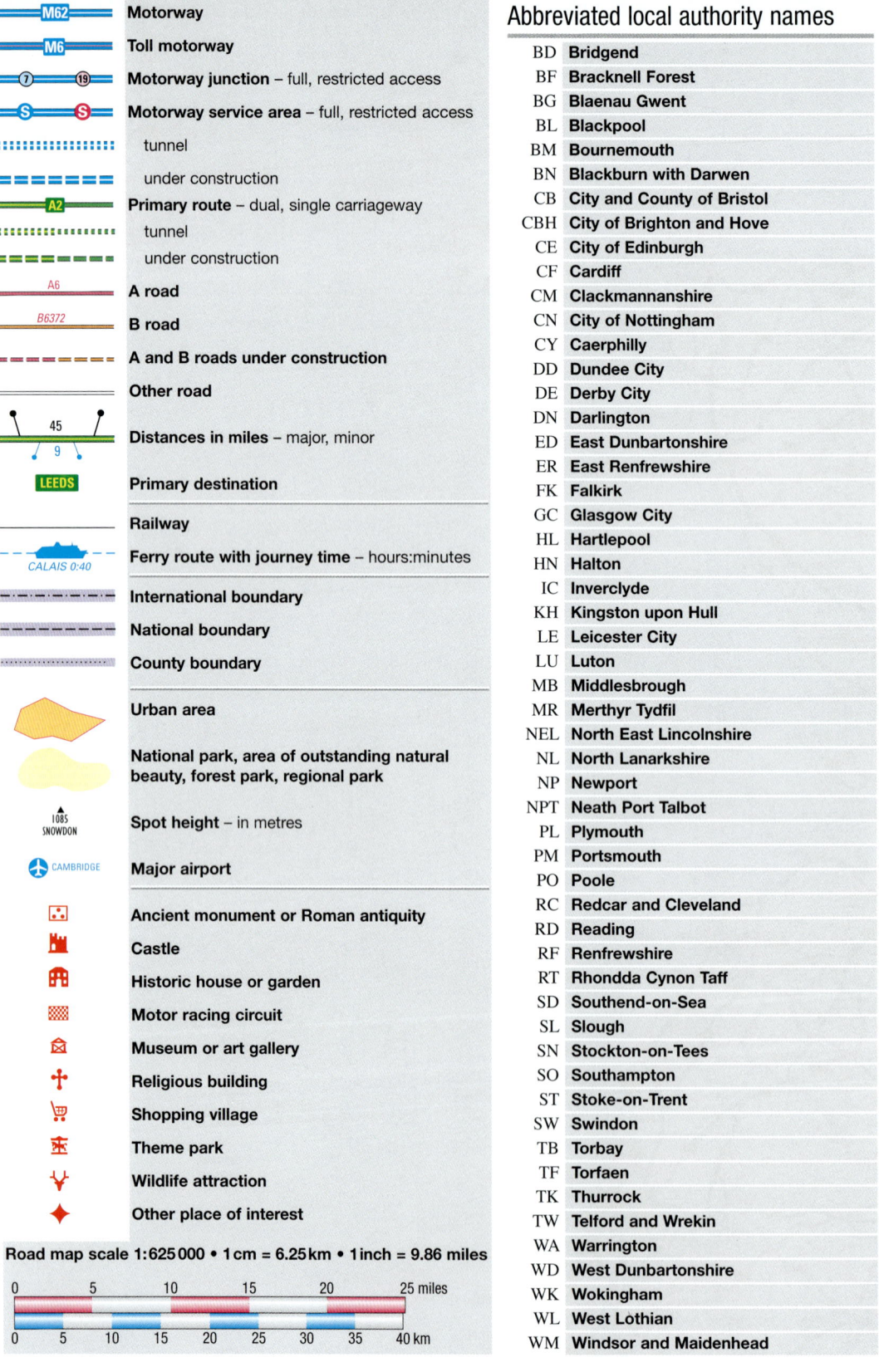

Key to road map pages

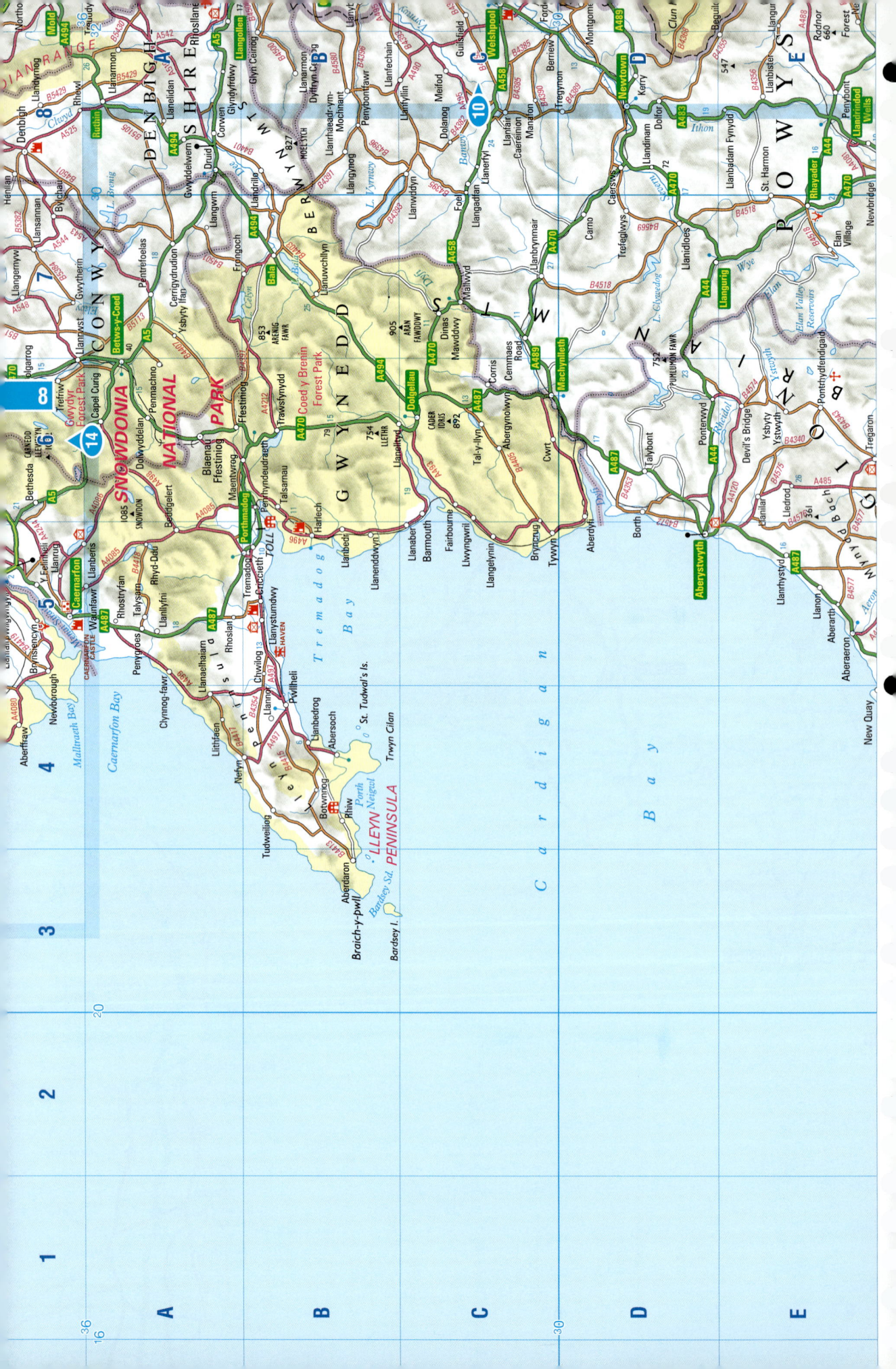

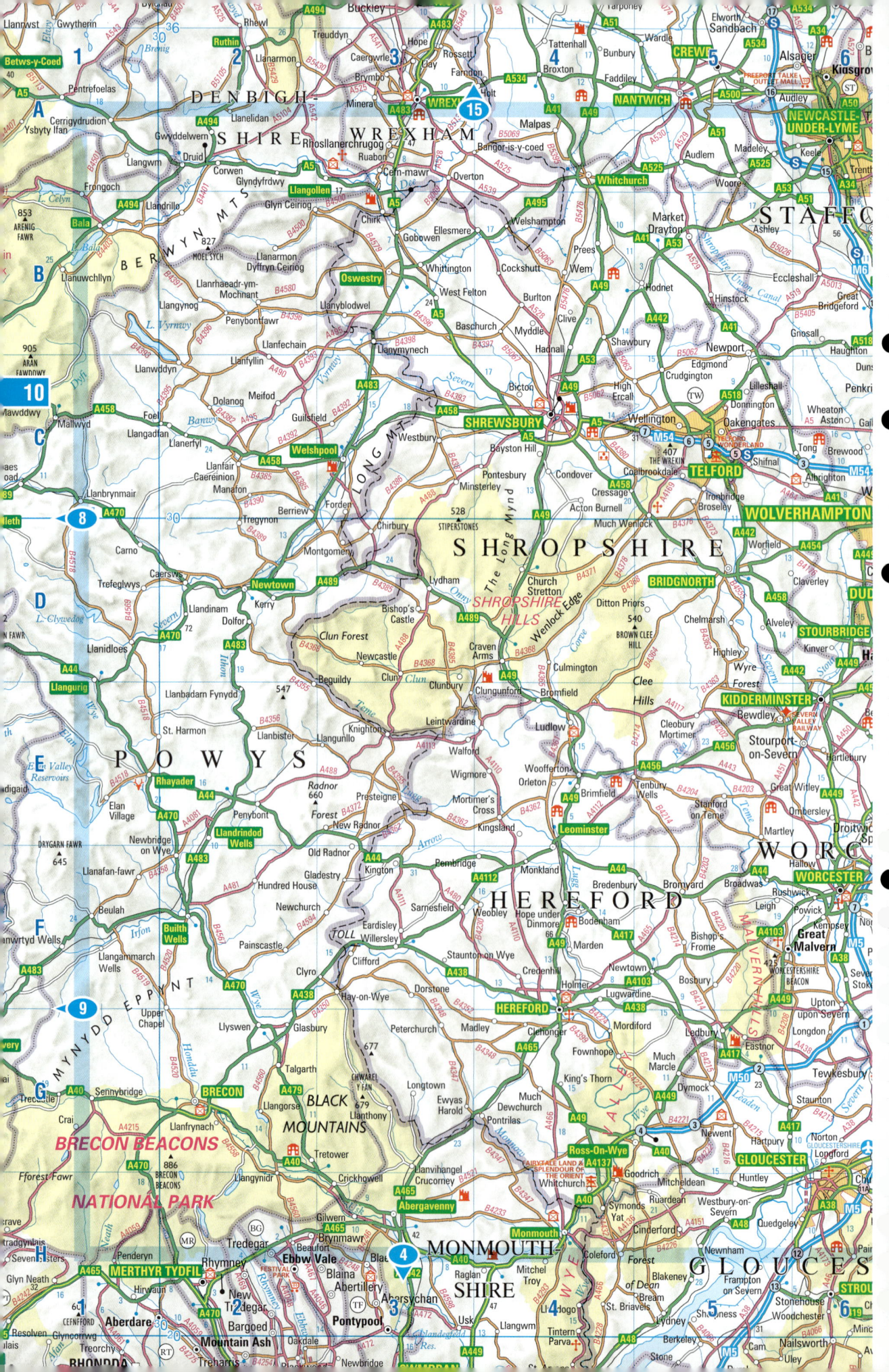

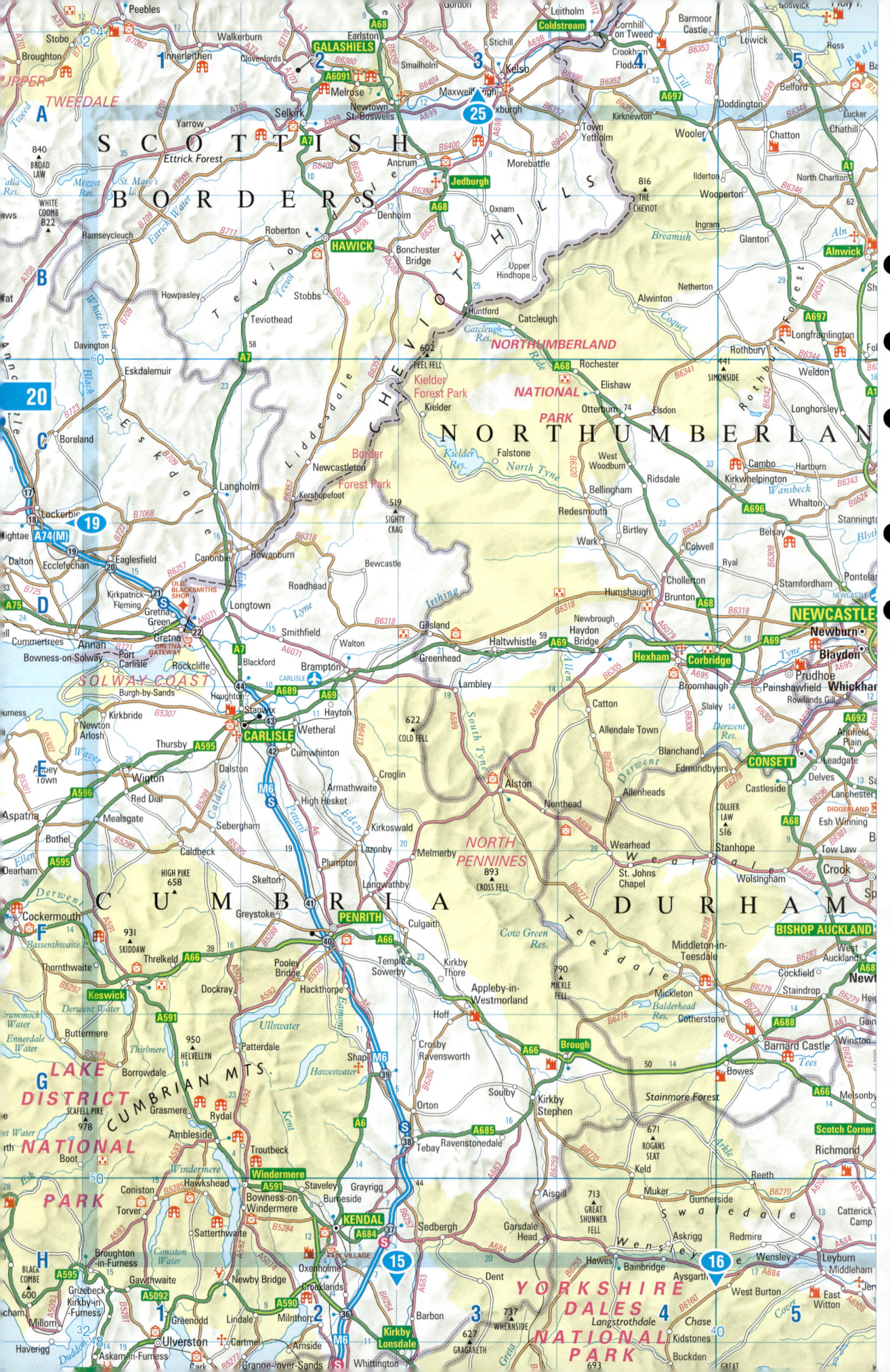

6
7
8
9
10
A
B
C
D
E
F
G
H
31
24
25
ABERDEENSHIRE
BUCHAN
FORMARTINE
STRATHBOGIE
GARIOCH
MAR
KINCARDINE
BRAES OF ANGUS
ANGUS
ABERDEEN CITY
HOWE OF THE MEARNS
Glen Esk
FRASERBURGH
PETERHEAD
ABERDEEN
ELGIN
Lossiemouth
Findochty
Portknockie
Cullen
Portsoy
Buckie
Garmouth
Portgordon
Lhanbryde
Fochabers
Craibstone
Fordyce
Banff
Macduff
Gardenstown
Troup Hd.
Pennan
Rosehearty
Kinnairds Hd.
Inverallochy
St. Combs
Rathen
New Aberdour
Rattray Hd.
Crimond
Strichen
New Pitsligo
Newbyth
Weachyburn
Aberchirder
Cuminestown
Turriff
Newmill
Mulben
Keith
Rothes
Craigellachie
Charlestown of Aberlour
Dufftown
Marypark
840 BEN RINNES
Glenlivet
Laggan
Huntly
Fortrie
Badenscoth
New Deer
Maud
Old Deer
Mintlaw
Longside
St. Fergus
Buchan Ness
Boddam
Hatton
Cruden Bay
Methlick
Fyvie
Rothienorman
Tarves
Ellon
Hackley Head
Newburgh
Colpy
Insch
Kennethmont
Rhynie
Ardwell
Cabrach
Tomnavoulin
722 THE BUCK
Oldmeldrum
Inverurie
Lumsden
Tullynessle
Badenyon
803 CARN MOR
Strathdon
Cock Bridge
Alford
Kemnay
Monymusk
Newmachar
Kintore
Dyce
Balmedie
ABERDEEN (DYCE)
KIRKWALL 6:00
LERWICK 14:00
Ordhead
Dunecht
Bankhead
Bucksburn
Bridge of Don
Westhill
Echt
Girdle Ness
Cults
Lumphanan
Torphins
Peterculter
Cove Bay
Tarland
872 MORVEN
Ordie
Aboyne
Crathie
Ballater
Marywell
Banchory
Portlethen
Cammachmore
Strachan
Newtonhill
Muchalls
Stonehaven
Ballochan
938 MT. KEEN
1154 LOCHNAGAR
Spittal of Glenmuick
Auchronie
Auchenblae
Todhead Point
Glendoll Lodge
Clova
Waterhead
Fettercairn
Inverbervie
Laurencekirk
Gourdon
Johnshaven
Rottal
Edzell
Marykirk
St. Cyrus
Kirkton of Glenisla
Backwater Res.
Dykehead
Tannadice
Brechin
Montrose
S. Esk
N. Esk
Dee
Don
Deveron
Ythan
Ugie
Isla
Spey
Spey B.
Urie
Lossie
A90
A96
A95
A98
A97
A947
A920
A952
A950
A981
A948
A975
A944
A93
A939
A941
A957
A92
A937
A935
B9031
B9093
B9170
B9005
B9000
B976
B966
B974
40
42
92
90
80
76

30

1
2
3
4
5
A
B
C
D
E
F
G
H
106
18
20
100
90
Rona
Sule Skerry
Stack Skerry
C. Wrath
Kyle of Durness
Faraid Hd.
Durness
Whiten Hd.
Achiemore
Strathan
Kyle of Tongue
Bettyhill
A836
25
Sheigra
Heilam
A838
28
L. Eriboll
L. Inchard
Kinlochbervie
A838
B801
Eriboll
Tongue
A836
Borgie
18
Rhiconich
KYLE OF TONGUE
L. Laxford
908
FOINAVEN
L. Hope
927
BEN HOPE
763
BEN LOYAL
Handa I.
NORTH-WEST SUTHERLAND
Reay Forest
Strathmore
L. Loyal
Strath Naver
B871
Scourie
A894
Laxford Bridge
721
BEN STACK
L. More
Naver
B871
Eddrachillis Bay
B873
Pt. of Stoer
A838
873
BEN HEE
Altnaharra
L. Naver
L. nan Clar
Kylestrome
Kinloch
Culkein
Drumbeg
Unapool
B869
809
QUINAG
36
961
BEN KLIBRECK
Stoer
ASSYNT
A894
A836
L. Choire
A837
SUTHERLAND
36
L. Assynt
Inchnadamph
Lochinver
998
BEN MORE ASSYNT
28
Rubha Coigeach
Inverkirkaig
Enard B.
847
CANISP
A838
Black Water
ASSYNT-COIGACH
A837
Glen Oykel
Duchally
Loch Shin
Dalnessie
Reiff
Ledmore
Summer Is.
Elphin
Langwell
27
28
Achiltibuie
Lurgainn
A835
Cromalt Hills
Sallachy
Lairg
14
A839
Rogart
Achavraie
COIGACH
16
Lubcroy
Rosehall
Torroble
18
A839
9
10
Strathkanaird
A837
Oykel Bridge
Oykel
Altass
B864
A837
12
Fleet
Greenstone Pt.
Gruinard
L. Broom
Inveran
NORTHERN HIGHLANDS

ORKNEY
HOY & WEST MAINLAND
MAINLAND
CAITHNESS
Mull Head
Papa Westray
Westray
Noup Hd.
Pierowall
Papa Sd.
The North Sound
Midbea
Berst Ness
Rapness
North Ronaldsay
Hollandstoun
Dennis Hd.
N. Ronaldsay
N. Ronaldsay Firth
Burness
Sanday
Start Pt.
Overbister
Kettletoft
Calfsound
Eday Sd.
Store
Sanday Sound
Eday
Veness
Westray Firth
Sacquoy Hd.
Wasbister
Rousay
Brinyan
Egilsay
Eynhallow Sd.
Brough Hd.
The Barony
Twatt
Redland
Dounby
Wyre
Gairsay
Stronsay Firth
Stronsay
Papa Stronsay
Odie
Whitehall
Aith
Rothiesholm
Lamb Hd.
Balfour
Shapinsay
Auskerry
L. of Harray
Voy
Wide Firth
L. of Stenness
Finstown
Shapinsay Sd.
Stromness
Kirkwall
Mull Head
Deer Sound
Deerness
ABERDEEN 6:00
LERWICK 6:00
Gritley
Pt. of Ayre
Copinsay
Orphir
Hoy Sd.
SCRABSTER 1:30
Linksness
Graemsay
St. Mary's
WARD HILL
Old Man of Hoy
Rora Hd.
Rackwick
Scapa Flow
Rose Ness
Burray
Hoy
Flotta
St. Margaret's Hope
Lyness
Longhope
South Ronaldsay
Tor Ness
Hurliness
South Walls
Swona
Burwick
Cleat
Pentland Firth
STROMNESS 1:30
Dunnet Hd.
Stroma
Muckle Skerries
John o' Groats
Duncansby Head
Duncansby
Brough
Mey
Canisbay
Holborn Hd.
Dunnet B.
Strathy Pt.
Scrabster
Thurso
Dunnet
Castletown
Portskerra
Dounreay
Strathy
Melvich
Reay
Freswick
Nybster
Sordale
Sortat
Keiss
L. Calder
Strath Halladale
Halkirk
Hastigrow
Sinclair's B.
Craigtown
Olgrinmore
Reiss
Noss Hd.
Dalhalvaig
Staxigoe
Watten
Wick
Mybster
Forsinain
Forsinard
Thrumster
Achavanich
Ulbster
Halberry Head
Lybster
Latheron
Kinbrace
705
MORVEN
Braemore
Dunbeath
Strath of Kildonan
Altanduino
Kildonan
Berriedale
Ousdale
Ord of Caithness
Helmsdale
628
BEN DHORAIN
L. Brora
Brora
Golspie
A9
A99
A836
A882
A897
B874
B876
B870
A961
A960
A965
A964
A966
A967
A986
B9056
B9057
B9055
B9047
B9052
B9064
B9066
B9068
B9069
B9070
B9063
B9061
B9060
B9059
6
7
8
9
10
A
B
C
D
E
F
G
H
28
29
31
30
38
106
100
90

SHETLAND
Herma Ness
Muckle Flugga
Norwick
Haroldswick
Baltasound
Balta
UNST
Bluemull Sd.
Cullivoe
Uyeasound
Mu Ness
Gutcher
Belmont
Whale Firth
Ramna Stacks
Pt. of Fethaland
Fetlar
Mid Yell
Funzie
Isbister
North Roe
Yell Sound
YELL
Colgrave Sd.
The Snap
The Faither
RONAS HILL 453
Esha Ness
Hillswick
Ulsta
Burravoe
Sullom Voe
Sullom
Lunna Ness
Hamnavoe
Out Skerries
St. Magnus Bay
Muckle Roe
Brae
WHALSAY
Skaw Taing
Whalsay
Vidlin
Papa Stour
Voe
Dury Voe
Symbister
Sd. of Papa
Sandness
Neap
South Nesting B.
Dale
Aith
MAINLAND
Walls
Vaila
LERWICK (TINGWALL)
Gruting Voe
Weisdale Voe
Scord Hd.
Bressay
Easter Skeld
Gunnista
Foula
418
Lerwick
I. of Noss
Scalloway
Kirkabister
SHETLAND
Hamnavoe
Bard Hd.
West Burra
Bressay Sd.
SEYDISFJÖRDUR 30:00
TORSHAVN 12:30
BERGEN 12:00
(May-Sept)
293
Kettla Ness
ABERDEEN 14:00
KIRKWALL 6:00
Hoswick
Mousa
St. Ninian's I.
Northpunds
Scousburgh
Boddam
Fitful Hd.
SUMBURGH
Toab
B. of Quendale
Sumburgh Hd.
Butt of Lewis
Port Nis
Dail bho Dheas
NESS
Cellar Hd.
Borgh
Barabhas
OUTER HEBRIDES
Siabost
Tolastadh bho Thuath
Tolsta Hd.
Carlabhagh
Bac
291 BEN MHOLACH
Gallan Hd.
Great Bernera
Aird Uig
Broad Bay
Port Nan Giuran
Newmarket
Mealabost
EYE PENINSULA
L. Roag
Calanais
Stornoway
Gearraidh na h-Aibhne
STORNOWAY
Pabail
Chicken Hd.
Aird Brenish
575 MEALISVAL
Breanais
Giosla
LEWIS
Crosbost
SOUTH LEWIS,
HARRIS & NORTH UIST
Baile Ailein
Cromor
Scarp
L. Langavat
L. Erisort
ULLAPOOL 2:40
Kintarvie
Seaforth
Grabhair
Kebock Hd.
Fair Isle
Husinish
NORTH HARRIS
Aird a Mhulaidh
Leumrabhagh
L. Shell
Husinish Pt
26
571 BEINN MHOR
27
799 CLISHAM
WESTERN ISLES
Taransay
Ardhasig
Aird Asaig
Tairbeart (Tarbert)
Sd. of Taransay
Sd. of Shiant
Shiant Is.

NAVIGATOR® city approach maps

Motorways

- Junction
- Restricted junction
- Pease Pottage Services
- Toll
- Toll motorway

Primary route – dual, single carriageway, service station
Numbered junctions – full, restricted access
under construction, narrow
Primary destination
A road – dual, single carriageway
under construction, narrow
B road – dual, single carriageway
under construction, narrow
Minor road, drive or track
Ring road
Distance in miles
Tunnel, multi-level junction
Toll, steep gradient – points downhill
National trail – England and Wales
Long distance footpath – Scotland
Railway with station, level crossing, tunnel
Preserved railway with station, tramway
National boundary
County or unitary authority boundary
Car ferry, catamaran
Passenger ferry, catamaran
Hovercraft, freight ferry
Internal ferry – car, passenger
Principal airport, other airport or airfield
Area of outstanding natural beauty – England and Wales; **Forest park**, **National park**, **National scenic area** – Scotland; **Regional park**
Woodland
Beach – sand, shingle
Linear antiquity
Navigable river or canal
Lock, flight of locks, canal bridge number
Viewpoint, motoring organisation phone box
Site and date of battle, spot height – in metres
National nature reserve, national sport venue
Shopping village, park and ride
Caravan site, camping site

✱ Abbey / priory	🎪 Country park – Scotland
🏛 Ancient monument	🐄 County show ground
🐬 Aquarium / dolphinarium	🚜 Farm park
🏛 Art gallery	✿ Garden
🖼 Art collection or museum	⛳ Golf course
🐪 Bird sanctuary or aviary	⚓ Historic ship
🏰 Castle	🏠 House
✝ Cathedral	🏡 House and garden
⛪ Church	🏛 Local museum
🎪 Country park	⚓ Marina

Key to map symbols

City and town plans

- Motorway
- **Primary route** – dual, single carriageway
- **A road** – dual, single carriageway
- **B road** – dual, single carriageway
- Minor through road, one-way street
- Pedestrian roads
- Shopping streets
- Railway with station
- Bank / West St — Underground station, metro station
- City Hall — Tramway with station
- Railway or bus station
- Shopping Precinct / Retail Park
- Park
- H ℗ Hospital, parking,
- Police station, post office, youth hostel

✝ Abbey or cathedral	🏡 House and garden
🏛 Ancient monument	🏛 Museum
🐬 Aquarium	🚂 Preserved railway
🖼 Art gallery	🏛 Roman antiquity
🦜 Bird garden	🌴 Safari park
🏛 Building of public interest	🛒 Shopmobility
🏰 Castle	🎭 Theatre
⛪ Church of interest	*i* Tourist Information Centre open all year
🎬 Cinema	*i* Tourist Information Centre open summer only
✿ Garden	
⚓ Historic ship	🐘 Zoo
🏠 House	◆ Other place of interest

Approach map scale 1:100 000 • 1cm = 1km • 1inch = 1.6 miles

0 — 1 — 2 — 3 — 4 miles
0 — 1 — 2 — 3 — 4 — 5 — 6 kilometres

◆ Maritime or military museum	**Tourist Information Centre**
▓ Motor racing circuit	*i* – open all year
🏛 Museum	*i* – seasonal
Ⓟ Picnic area	⊖ Transport collection
🚂 Preserved railway	★ Viewpoint
🏇 Racecourse	△ Youth hostel
🏛 Roman antiquity	🐘 Zoo
🌴 Safari park	∴ Historic feature or place of interest
🎢 Theme park	◆ Other place of interest

Aberdeen

Known chiefly as the Granite City (granite is still used in all forms of building, even the roads), Aberdeen is the oil capital of Europe and the floral capital of Scotland with 45 parks and two miles of sandy beach. Places of interest include St Machar's and St Andrew's Cathedrals, the Winter Gardens, Provost Skene's House and the university, which was founded in 1495. The shopping hub for north-east Scotland, the city boasts five shopping centres – the Bon Accord, the Academy, St Nicholas, the Trinity and the Galleria, as well as a large indoor Market Hall. There is a good selection of bars and restaurants as well as theatres, music venues and cinemas.

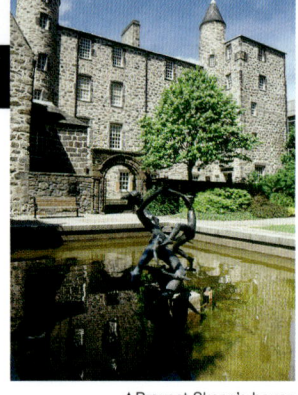

▲ Provost Skene's house

Aberdeen Visitor Centre,
23 Union Street, Aberdeen AB11 5BP
Tel 01224 288828

BBC Radio Scotland 92.4-94.7 FM and 810 AM • **Northsound 1** 96.9 FM
Northsound 2 1035 MW

www.aberdeencity.gov.uk

★ Do not miss

- ★ **Aberdeen Art Gallery,** Schoolhill – Modern Art, Impressionists, Scottish Colourists
- ★ **Aberdeen Maritime Museum,** Shiprow – shipbuilding, fishing industry and North Sea oil
- ★ **Satrosphere,** The Tramsheds, Constitution Street – interactive science and technology museum

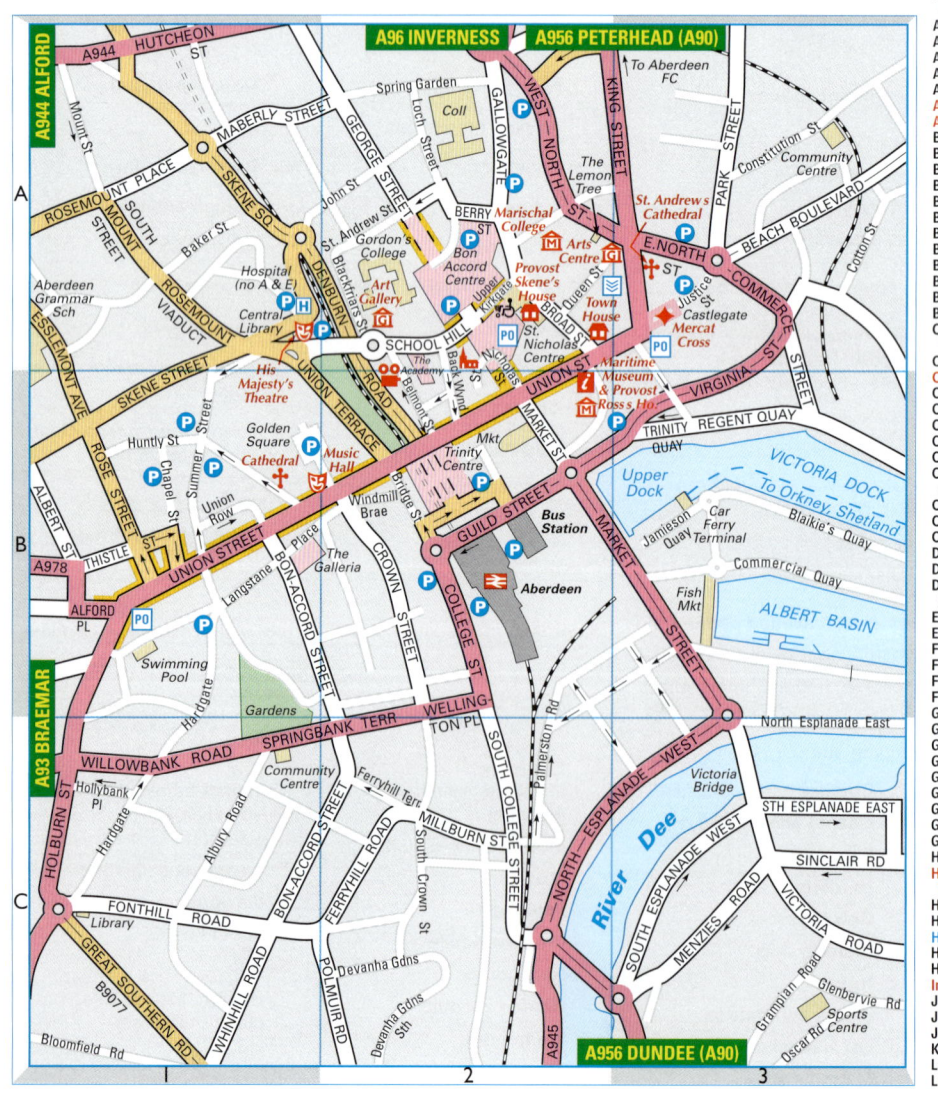

Aberdeen

Aberdeen ⇌	B2
Aberdeen Grammar School	A1
Academy, The	B2
Albert Basin	B3
Albert St	B1
Albury Rd	C1
Alford Pl	B1
Art Gallery	A2
Arts Centre	A2
Back Wynd	A2
Baker St	A1
Beach Blvd	A3
Belmont St	B2
Berry St	A2
Blackfriars St	A2
Blaikie's Quay	B3
Bloomfield Rd	C1
Bon-Accord Ctr	A2
Bon-Accord St	B1
Bridge St	B2
Bus Station	B2
Car Ferry Terminal	B3
Castlegate	A3
Cathedral †	B1
Central Library	A1
Chapel St	B1
College St	B2
Commerce St	A3
Commercial Quay	B3
Community Centre	A3/C1
Constitution St	A3
Cotton St	A3
Crown St	B2
Denburn Rd	A2
Devanha Gdns	C2
Devanha Gdns South	C2
East North St	A3
Esslemont Ave	A1
Ferryhill Rd	C2
Ferryhill Terr	C2
Fish Market	B3
Fonthill Rd	C1
Galleria, The	B1
Gallowgate	A2
George St	A2
Glenbervie Rd	C3
Golden Sq	A1
Gordon's College	A2
Grampian Rd	C3
Gt Southern Rd	C1
Guild St	B2
Hardgate	B1
His Majesty's Theatre	A1
Holburn St	C1
Hollybank Pl	C1
Hospital	B1
Huntly St	B1
Hutcheon St	A1
Information Ctr	B2
Jamieson Quay	B3
John St	A2
Justice St	A3
King St	A2
Langstane Pl	B1
Library	C1
Lemon Tree, The	A2
Loch St	A2
Maberly St	A1
Marischal College	A2
Maritime Museum & Provost Ross's House	B2
Market St	B3
Menzies Rd	C3
Mercat Cross	A3
Millburn St	C2
Miller St	A3
Market	
Market St	B2
Mount St	A1
Music Hall	B1
North Esp East	C3
North Esp West	C2
Oscar Rd	C3
Palmerston Rd	C2
Park St	A3
Police Station	A2
Polmuir Rd	C2
Post Office	A2/A3/B1
Provost Skene's House	A2
Queen St	A2
Regent Quay	B3
Rose St	A1
Rosemount Pl	A1
Rosemount Viaduct	A1
St Andrew St	A2
St Andrew's Cathedral †	A3
St Nicholas Centre	A2
St Nicholas St	A2
School Hill	A2
Sinclair Rd	C3
Skene Sq	A1
Skene St	B1
South College St	C2
South Crown St	C2
South Esp East	C3
South Esp West	C3
South Mount St	A1
Sports Centre	C3
Spring Garden	A2
Springbank Terr	C1
Summer St	B1
Swimming Pool	B1
Thistle St	B1
Town House	A2
Trinity Centre	B2
Trinity Quay	B3
Union Row	B1
Union St	B1
Union Terr	B1
Upper Dock	B3
Upper Kirkgate	A2
Victoria Bridge	C3
Victoria Dock	B3
Victoria Rd	C3
Virginia St	A3
Wellington Pl	C2
West North St	A2
Whinhill Rd	C1
Willowbank Rd	C1
Windmill Brae	B2

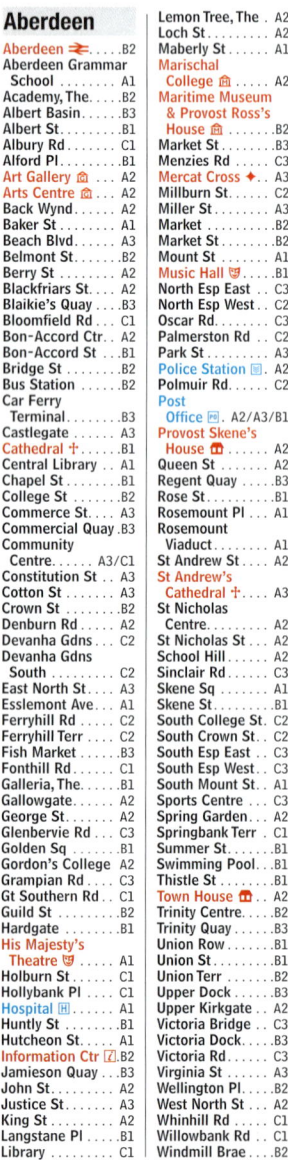

Aberystwyth

Aberystwyth exists on the site of a prehistoric hillfort called Pen Dinas – the earthworks of which are still visible. The town was established more than 700 years ago by charter from Edward I and is now an important seat of learning and the main town and holiday resort of Cardigan Bay with a one-mile-long promenade to rival Brighton. There are many places of interest such as the remains of the castle, Aberystwyth Cliff Railway, the National Library of Wales, Dyfi Furnace, the pier and the marina. There is a regular market on Saturdays and a farmers' market once or twice a month.

▲ The promenade, Aberystwyth

★ Do not miss:

- ★ **Aberystwyth Arts Centre**, Penglais – film, theatre, music, exhibitions
- ★ **Coliseum Gallery Ceredigion Museum**, Terrace Road – historical artefacts
- ★ **Vale of Rheidol Railway**, Park Avenue – a steam railway

Tourist Information Centre,
Lisburne House, Terrace Road,
Aberystwyth SY23 2AG
Tel 01970 612125

BBC Radio Wales 95.3 FM • Radio Ceredigion 96.6, 97.4, 103.3 FM

www.aberystwyth-online.co.uk

Aberystwyth

Name	Grid
Aberystwyth RFC	C3
Aberystwyth Station	B2
Aberystwyth Town Football Ground	B2
Alexandra Rd	B2
Ambulance Station	C3
Baker St	B1
Banadl Rd	B2
Bandstand	A1
Bath St	A2
Boat Landing Stage	A1
Boulevard St Brieuc	C3
Bridge St	B1
Bronglais Hospital	B3
Bryn-y-Mor Rd	A2
Buarth Rd	B2
Bus Station	B2
Cae Ceredig	C3
Cae Melyn	A2
Cae'r'Gog	B3
Cambrian St	B2
Caradoc Rd	B2
Caravan Site	C2
Castle (Remains of)	B1
Castle St	B1
Cattle Market	B2
Cemetary	B3
Ceredigion Museum	A1
Chalybeate St	A1
Cliff Terr	A2
Club House	A2
Commodore	A1
County Court	A2
Crown Buildings	B2
Dan-y-Coed	A3
Dinas Terr	C1
Eastgate	B1
Edge-hill Rd	B2
Elm Tree Ave	B2
Elysian Gr	A2
Felin-y-Mor Rd	C1
Fifth Ave	C2
Fire Station	B1
Glanrafon Terr	B1
Glyndwr Rd	B2
Golf Course	A1
Gray's Inn Rd	B1
Great Darkgate St	B1
Greenfield St	B1
Heol-y-Bryn	A2
High St	B1
Infirmary Rd	A2
Information Ctr	B1
Iorwerth Ave	B3
King St	B1
Lauraplace	B1
Library	B1
Lifeboat Station	C1
Llanbadarn Rd	B3
Loveden Rd	B1
Magistrates Court	A1
Marina	C1
Marine Terr	A1
Market	B1
Mill St	B1
Moor La	B2
National Library of Wales	B3
New Promenade	B1
New St	B1
North Beach	A1
North Parade	B2
North Rd	A2
Northgate St	B2
Parc Natur Penglais	A3
Parc-y-Llyn Retail Park	C3
Park & Ride	B2
Park Ave	B2
Pavillion	B1
Pendinas	C1
Penglais Rd	B3
Penparcau Rd	C1/C2
Penrheidol	C2
Pen-y-Craig	A2
Pen-yr-angor	C1
Pier St	B1
Plas Ave	B3
Plas Helyg	C2
Plascrug Ave	B2/C3
Police Station	C2
Poplar Row	B2
Portland Rd	B2
Portland St	A2
Post Office	B1/B3
Powell Rd	B1
Prospect St	B1
Quay Rd	B1
Queen St	B1
Queen's Ave	A2
Queen's Rd	B1
Riverside Terr	B1
St Davids Rd	B3
St Michael's	B1
School of Art	B2
South Beach	B1
South Rd	B1
Sports Ground	B3
Spring Gdns	C1
Stanley Rd	B2
Swimming Pool & Leisure Centre	C3
Tanybwlch Beach	C1
Tennis Courts	B3
Terrace Rd	B1
The Bar	C1
Town Hall	A2
Trefechan Bridge	B1
Trefor Rd	A2
Trinity Rd	B2
University Campus	B3
University of Wales (Aberystwyth)	B1
Vaenor St	B2
Vale of Rheidol Railway	C3
Victoria Terr	A1
Viewpoint	A2/A3
War Memorial	B1
Y Lanfa	C1

Ashford

A Kent town believed to date back to the Danish invasion of the country in 893. By 1600, it had become a substantial market town, with numerous picturesque medieval and Tudor buildings; local history is traced in the Ashford Borough Museum. Today it's best known as a stopping point on the Eurostar route to the Continent and for its large designer clothes outlet. Nearby attractions include the Agricultural Museum at Brook, the awardwinning South of England Rare Breeds Centre and neighbouring Yonsea Farm, the Woodchurch Village Life Exhibition, Woodchurch Windmill, the Port Lympne Wild Animal Park and Historic Mansion and Gardens, Swanton Hill watermill at Mersham, Church Hill Cottage Gardens at Charing Heath, Beech Court Gardens at Challock, the Romney, Hythe and Dymchurch railway towards the coast, Kipp Cottage Garden at Biddenden Green, and Biddenden Vineyards and Ciderworks. The town is on the doorstep of the North Downs, with its many walks, and activities such as golf, cycling, gliding and fishing.

▲ North Street

Ashford Tourist Information Centre,
18 The Churchyard, Ashford
TN23 1QG Tel 01233 629165

BBC Radio Kent 96.5, 97.6, 104.2 FM • Invicta 96.1 FM

www.ashford.gov.uk

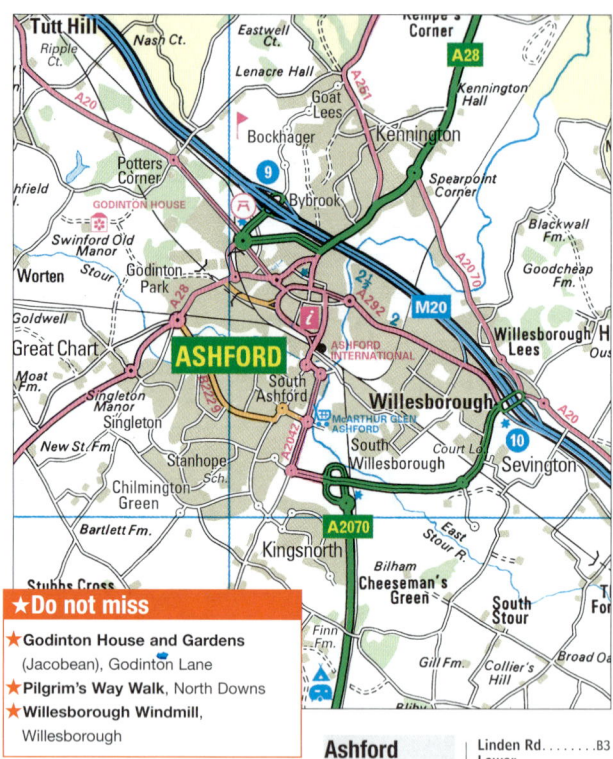

★ Do not miss
- ★ **Godinton House and Gardens** (Jacobean), Godinton Lane
- ★ **Pilgrim's Way Walk**, North Downs
- ★ **Willesborough Windmill**, Willesborough

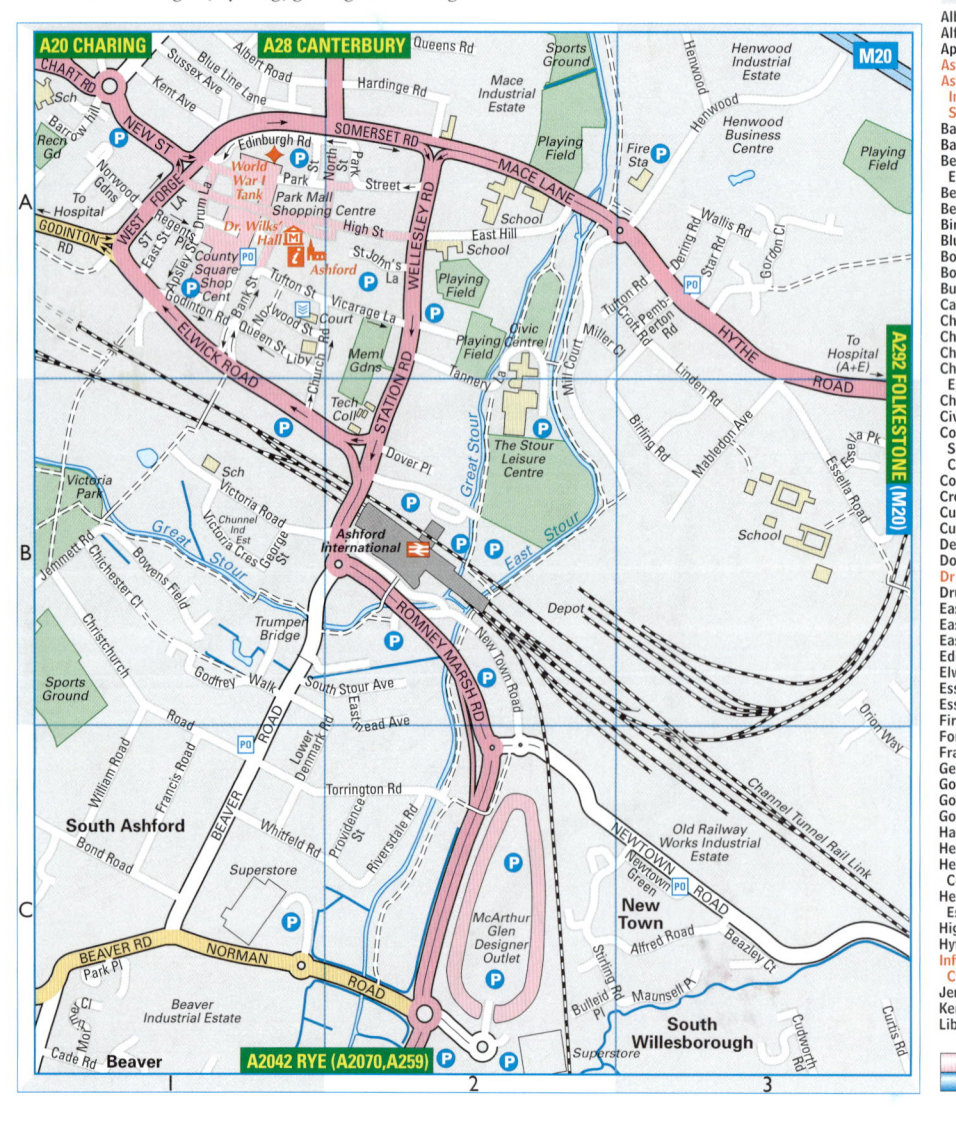

Ashford

Albert Rd	A1
Alfred Rd	C3
Apsley St	A1
Ashford	A1
Ashford International Station	B2
Bank St	A1
Barrow Hill Gdns	A1
Beaver Industrial Estate	C1
Beaver Rd	C1
Beazley Ct	C3
Birling Rd	B3
Blue Line La	A1
Bond Rd	C1
Bowens Field	B1
Bulleid Pl	C2
Cade Rd	C1
Chart Rd	A1
Chichester Cl	B1
Christchurch Rd	B1
Chunnel Industrial Estate	B1
Church Rd	A1
Civic Centre	A2
County Square Shopping Centre	A1
Court	A1
Croft Rd	A3
Cudworth Rd	C3
Curtis Rd	C3
Dering Rd	A3
Dover Pl	B2
Dr Wilks' Hall	A1
Drum La	A1
East Hill	A2
East St	A1
Eastmead Ave	B2
Edinburgh Rd	A1
Elwick Rd	A2
Essella Pk	B3
Essella Rd	B3
Fire Sta	A3
Forge La	A1
Francis Rd	C1
George St	B1
Godfrey Walk	B1
Godinton Rd	A1
Gordon Cl	A3
Hardinge Rd	A2
Henwood	A3
Henwood Business Centre	A3
Henwood Industrial Estate	A3
High St	A1
Hythe Rd	A3
Information Ctr	A1
Jemmett Rd	B1
Kent Ave	A1
Library	A1
Linden Rd	B3
Lower Denmark Rd	C1
Mabledon Ave	B3
Mace Industrial Estate	A2
Mace La	A2
Maunsell Pl	C3
McArthur Glen Designer Outlet	C2
Memorial Gdns	A1
Mill Ct	A1
Miller Cl	A2
Mortimer Cl	C1
New St	A1
Newtown Green	C3
Newtown Rd	B2/C3
Norman Rd	C1
North St	A2
Norwood Gdns	A1
Norwood St	A1
Old Railway Works Industrial Estate	C3
Orion Way	A1
Park Mall Shopping Centre	A1
Park Pl	C1
Park St	A1/A2
Pemberton Rd	A3
Police Station	A1
Post Office	A1/A3/C1
Providence St	C1
Queen St	A1
Queens Rd	A2
Regents Pl	A1
Riversdale Rd	C2
Romney Marsh Rd	B2
St John's La	A1
Somerset Rd	A2
South Stour Ave	B2
Star Rd	A3
Station Rd	B2
Stirling Rd	C2
Stour Leisure Centre, The	B2
Sussex Ave	A1
Tannery La	A2
Technical College	B2
Torrington Rd	C1
Trumper Bridge	B1
Tufton Rd	A3
Tufton St	A1
Vicarage La	A2
Victoria Cres	B1
Victoria Park	B1
Victoria Rd	B1
Wallis Rd	A3
Wellesley Rd	A1
West St	A1
Whitfeld Rd	C1
William Rd	C1
World War I Tank	A1

Ayr

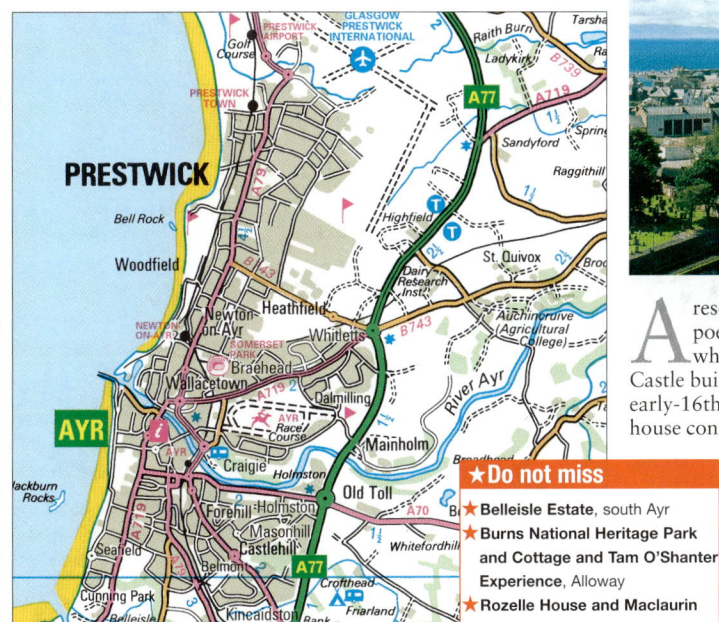

A resort on the west coast of Scotland, the birthplace of poet Robert Burns, with a c.1491 bridge, a 1650s church where Burns was christened, the 15th-century Greenan Castle built on the site of an Iron Age fort, Loudoun Hall, a fine early-16th-century townhouse, Miller's Folly, an observation house converted from a sentinel post on Cromwell's citadel, and the thatched Tam O'Shanter public house. Among the many traditional seaside entertainments and recreational facilities are some long sandy beaches, sea-angling trips, Firth of Clyde cruises aboard the *Waverley* (the world's last seagoing paddlesteamer), a leading racecourse, the Heads of Ayr Farm Park, and Haven Holiday Park. There's a wide range of both specialist and chain shops in its centre.

▲ Ayr with Arran in the distance

★ Do not miss
- ★ **Belleisle Estate**, south Ayr
- ★ **Burns National Heritage Park and Cottage and Tam O'Shanter Experience**, Alloway
- ★ **Rozelle House and Maclaurin Gallery**, south Ayr

Ayr

Ailsa Pl B1	Alloway Pl C1	Auld Kirk B2	Back Main St B2	Bath Pl B1	Boswell Pk B2
Alexandra Terr ... A3	Alloway St C2	Ayr Station C2	Back Peebles St .. A2	Bellevue Cres C1	Britannia Pl A3
Allison St B2	Arran Terr C1	Ayr Academy B1	Barns Cres C1	Bellevue La C1	Bruce Cres B1
Alloway Pk C1	Arthur St B2	Ayr Harbour A1	Barns Pk C1	Beresford La C2	Burns Statue B2
	Ashgrove St B2	Ayr United FC ... A3	Barns Street La .. C1	Beresford Terr ... C2	Bus Sta B2
	Auld Brig B2	Back Hawkhill Ave A3	Barns St C1	Borderline B2	Carrick St C2

Cassillis St B1	Mill Wynd C2	Compass Pier ... A1	Newton-on-Ayr Station A2	Park Terr C1
Cathcart St B1	Miller Rd C1	Content Ave C1	North Harbour St .B1	Pavilion Rd C1
Charlotte St B1	Montgomerie Terr.B1	Content St B2	North Pier A1	Peebles St A2
Citadel Leisure Centre B1	New Bridge B2	Craigie Ave B3	Odeon C2	Philip Sq B2
Citadel Pl B1	New Bridge St ... B2	Craigie Rd B3	Oswald La A1	Police Station ... B2
Civic C3	New Rd A2	Craigie Way B3	Park Circus C1	Post Office ... A2/B2
	Newmarket St ... B2	Cromwell Rd B1	Park Circus La .. C1	Princes Ct A2
		Crown St A2		Queen St B3
		Dalblair Rd C2		Queen's Terr B1
		Dam Park Sports Stadium C3		Racecourse Rd .. C1
		Damside A2		River St B2
		Dongola Rd C3		Riverside Pl B2
		Eglinton Pl B1		Russell Dr A2
		Eglinton Terr B1		St Andrews Church C2
		Elba St B2		St George's Rd .. A3
		Elmbank St A2		Sandgate B1
		Esplanade B1		Savoy Park C1
		Farifield Rd C1		Seabank Rd B2
		Fort St B1		Smith St C2
		Fothringham Rd . C1		Somerset Rd A3
		Fullarton St C1		South Beach Rd . B2
		Gaiety C2		South Harbour St .B1
		Garden St B2		South Pier A1
		George St B2		Strathaye Pl B2
		George's Ave A3		Tam's Brig B1
		Glebe Cres A2		Taylor St B2
		Glebe Rd A2		Town Hall B2
		Gorden Terr B3		Tryfield Pl A3
		Green St B2		Turner's Bridge .. B2
		Green Street La .. A2		Union Ave A3
		Hawkhill Ave A3		Victoria St B3
		Hawkhill Avenue La B3		Victoria Bridge .. C2
		High St B2		Viewfield Rd A3
		Holmston Rd C3		Virginia Gdns ... A2
		Information Ctr .. B1		Waggon Rd A2
		James St B3		Walker Rd A3
		John St B2		Wallace Tower ... B2
		King St B2		Weaver St C1
		Kings Ct B2		Weir Rd A2
		Kyle Centre C2		Wellington La ... C1
		Kyle St C2		Wellington Sq ... C1
		Library B2		West Sanouhar Rd A3
		Limekiln Rd A2		Whitletts Rd B3
		Limonds Wynd .. B2		Wilson St A3
		Loudoun Hall ... B2		York St A1
		Lymburn Pl B3		York Street La ... B1
		Macadam Pl B2		
		Main St B2		
		Mcadam's Monument C1		
		Mccall's Ave A3		
		Mews La B1		
		Mill Brae C3		
		Mill St C2		

ℹ **Ayr Tourist Office**, 22 Sandgate, KA7 1BW   Tel 01292 288688

📻 **BBC Radio Scotland** 92.4–94.7 FM and 810 AM • **West FM** 96.7 FM

🖥 www.south-ayrshire.gov.uk

37

Bangor

▲ Penrhyn Castle

An historic university and cathedral city, one of Wales' oldest, Bangor is first recorded as the site of a monastery built by Bishop Deiniol in about AD 525. The tomb of Welsh prince Owain Gwynned lies in the cathedral, and the city was the starting point for pilgrimages to Bardsey Island. The Museum and Art Gallery details the city's history as a major seaport from which local slate was shipped around the world. Situated across the Menai Strait from Anglesey and offering panoramic views, Bangor has an elaborate Victorian pier and Wales' longest high street, with good shopping facilities. The Gorsedd Circle was used for a previous Eisteddfod.

Bangor Tourist Information Centre,
Town Hall, Deiniol Road, Bangor
LL57 2RE Tel 01248 352786

BBC Radio Wales 94.8 FM
Champion 103.0 FM

www.nwt.co.uk

★ Do not miss
- ★ **Bangor Cathedral**, Cathedral Close
- ★ **Cochwillan Old Hall**, Tal-y-Bont
- ★ **Penrhyn Castle**, east Bangor

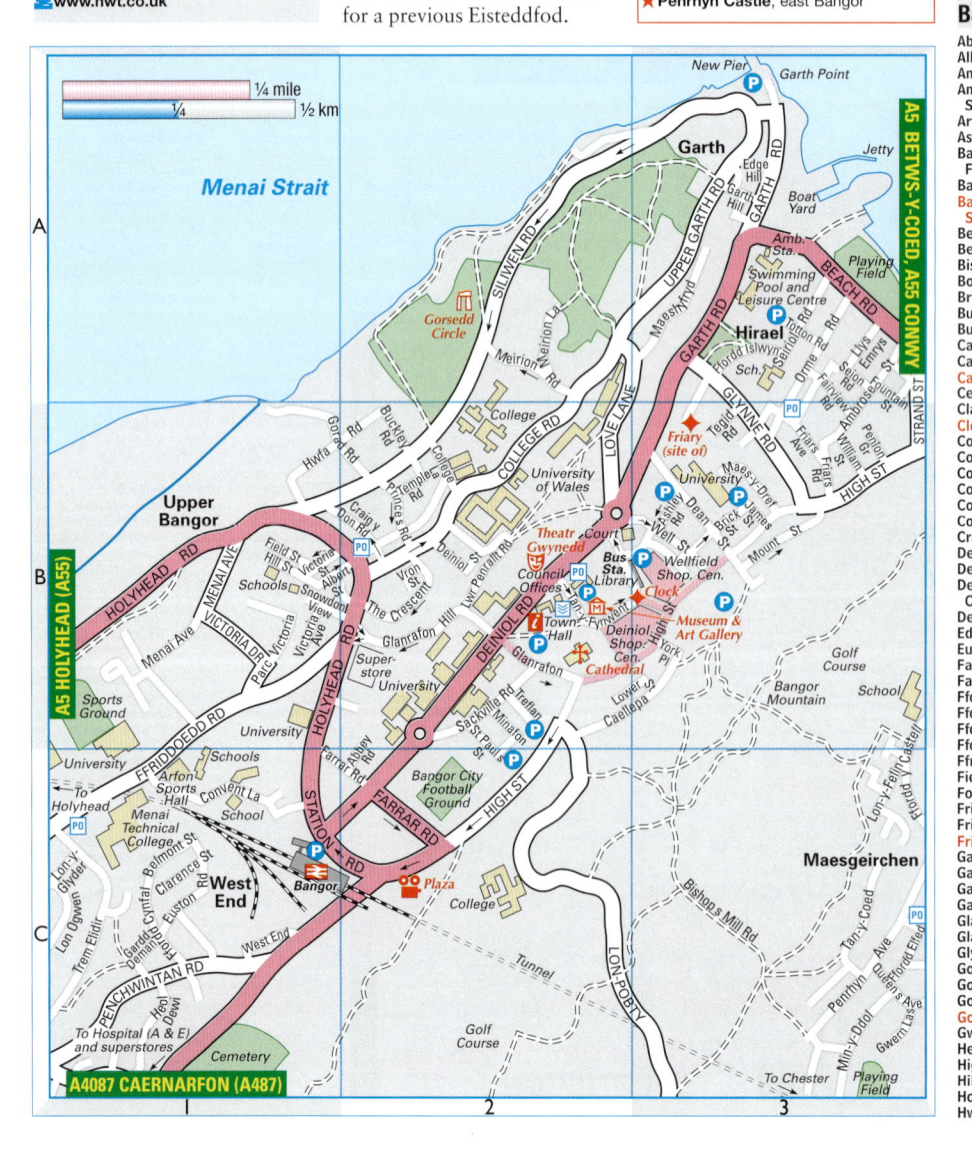

Bangor

Abbey Rd	C2
Albert St	B1
Ambrose St	A3
Ambulance Station	A3
Arfon Sports Hall	C1
Ashley Rd	B3
Bangor City Football Ground	C2
Bangor Mountain	B3
Bangor Station ⛟	C1
Beach Rd	A3
Belmont St	C1
Bishop's Mill Rd	C3
Boat Yard	A3
Brick St	B1
Buckley Rd	B2
Bus Station	B3
Caellepa	B2
Caernarfon Rd	C1
Cathedral ✝	B2
Cemetery	C1
Clarence St	C1
Clock ✦	B3
College	B2/C2
College La	B2
College Rd	B2
Convent La	C1
Council Offices	B2
Court	B2/B3/C1/B2
Craig y Don Rd	B2
Dean St	B3
Deiniol Rd	B2
Deiniol Shopping Centre	B2
Deiniol St	B2
Edge Hill	A3
Euston Rd	C1
Fairview Rd	A3
Farrar Rd	C2
Ffordd Cynfal	C1
Ffordd Elfed	C3
Ffordd Islwyn	A3
Ffordd y Castell	C3
Ffriddoedd Rd	B1
Field St	B1
Fountain St	A3
Friars Ave	B3
Friars Rd	B3
Friary (Site of) ✦	B3
Gardd Deman	C1
Garth Hill	A3
Garth Point	A3
Garth Rd	A3
Glanrafon	B2
Glanrafon Hill	B2
Glynne Rd	B3
Golf Course	B3
Golf Course	C2
Gorad Rd	B1
Gorsedd Circle	A2
Gwern Las	C3
Heol Dewi	C1
High St	B3/C2
Hill St	B1
Holyhead Rd	B1
Hwfa Rd	B1
Information Ctr ℹ	B2
James St	B3
Library	B3
Llys Emrys	A3
Lon Ogwen	C1
Lon-Pobty	B1
Lon-y-Felin	C3
Lon-y-Glyder	C1
Love La	B2
Lower Penrallt Rd	B2
Lower St	B2
Maes-y-Dref	B2
Maeshyfryd	A3
Meirion La	A2
Meirion Rd	A2
Menai Ave	B1
Menai Technical College	C1
Min-y-Ddol	C3
Minafon	B2
Mount St	B3
Museum & Art Gallery	B2
New Pier	A3
Orme Rd	A3
Parc Victoria	B1
Penchwintan Rd	C1
Penlon Gr	B3
Penrhyn Ave	C3
Plaza ✸	C2
Police Station	B2
Post Office	
Prince's Rd	A3
Queen's Ave	C3
Sackville Rd	B2
St Paul's St	B2
Seion Rd	B2
Seiriol Rd	A3
Siliwen Rd	A2
Snowdon View	B1
Sports Ground	B1
Station Rd	C1
Strand St	B2
Swimming Pool & Leisure Centre	A3
Tan-y-Coed	C3
Tan-y-Fynwent	B2
Tegid Rd	B3
Temple Rd	B3
The Crescent	B2
Theatr Gwynedd ✸	B2
Totton Rd	A3
Town Hall	B2
Treflan	B2
Trem Elidir	B2
University of Wales	B2
Upper Garth Rd	A3
Victoria Ave	B1
Victoria Dr	B1
Victoria St	B1
Vron St	B1
Well St	B3
Wellfield Shopping Centre	B2
West End	C1
William St	B1
York Pl	B3

Barrow-in-Furness

A Victorian market town with a proud shipbuilding history, focused around its handsome red sandstone modern Gothic town hall and set within easy reach of several good beaches and against the backdrop of the mountains of the Lake District (20 minutes away). The large indoor market has more than 80 independent stalls selling local produce and more. Nearby are South Lakes Wild Animal Park, a leading conservation zoo, Bardsea Country Park with its woodland areas and picnic areas, Dalton Castle (National Trust), once a courthouse and dungeon for Furness Abbey, two nature reserves on the Isle of Walney and the characterful villages of Askam and Ireleth on the Duddon Estuary. The annual summer Festival of the Sea is one of the best times to visit.

▲ Furness Abbey

Barrow Tourist Information, Duke Street, Barrow-in-Furness LA14 1RR Tel 01229 894784

BBC Radio Cumbria 96.1 FM and 837 AM • **The Bay** 96.9 FM

www.barrowbc.gov.uk

★ Do not miss
★ **Dock Museum**, North Road
★ **Furness Abbey and Custodian's Cottage** (English Heritage), just north of town
★ **Piel Castle** (English Heritage), Piel Island

Barrow-in-Furness

Abbey Rd A3/B2	Hawke St B2	Storey Sq B3	Vernon St B2
Adelaide St A2	Hibbert Rd A2	Strand C3	Vincent St B2
Ainslie St A3	High Level Bridge C2	Sutherland St B3	Walney Rd A1
Albert St A3	High St B2	TA Centre A2	West Gate Rd A2
Allison St B3	Hindpool Park	The Park A3	West View Rd A3
Anson St A2	Retail Park B2	Thwaite St B3	Westmorland St . . A3
Argyle St B3	Hindpool Rd B2	Town Hall B2	Whitehead St A3
Arthur St B3	Holker St A2	Town Quay C3	Wordsworth St . . A2
Ashburner Way . . A1	Hollywood Retail		
Barrow Raiders	& Leisure Park . . B1		
RLFC B1	Hood St A2		
Barrow	Howard St B2		
Station A1	Howe St B2		
Bath St A1/B2	Information Ctr . . . B2		
Bedford Rd A3	Ironworks Rd . . A1/B1		
Bessamer Way . . . A1	James St B3		
Blake St A1/A2	Jubliee Bridge C1		
Bridge Rd C1	Keith St B2		
Buccleuch Dock . C3	Keyes St A2		
Buccleuch Dock	Lancaster St A3		
Rd C2/C3	Lawson St B2		
Buccleuch St B2	Library B2		
Byron St A2	Lincoln St A3		
Calcutta St A1	Longreins Rd A3		
Cameron St C1	Lonsdale St C3		
Carlton Ave A3	Lord St B3		
Cavendish Dock	Lorne Rd B3		
Rd C3	Lyon St A2		
Cavendish St . . B2/B3	Manchester St B2		
Channelside Walk . B1	Market B2		
Channelside	Market St B2		
Haven C1	Marsh St B3		
Chatsworth St A2	Michaelson Rd . . . C2		
Cheltenham St . . . A3	Milton St A2		
Church St B2	Monk St B2		
Clifford St B2	Mount Pleasant . . . B3		
Clive St B1	Nan Tait Centre . . B2		
Collingwood St . . B2	Napier St B2		
Cook St A2	Nelson St B2		
Cornerhouse	North Rd B1		
Retail Park B2	Open Market B2		
Cornwallis St B2	Parade St B2		
Courts A2	Paradise St B3		
Crellin St B3	Park Ave A3		
Cross St C3	Park Dr A3		
Dalkeith St B2	Parker St A2		
Dalton Rd B2/C2	Parry St A2		
Derby St B3	Peter Green Way. . A1		
Devonshire Dock . C2	Phoenix Rd A1		
Dock Museum,	Police Station . . . B2		
The B1	Portland Walk		
Drake St A2	Shopping Centre . B2		
Dryden St B2	Post		
Duke St A1/B2/C2	Office A3/B2/B3		
Duncan St C2	**Princess**		
Dundee St C2	**Selandia** C2		
Dundonald St B2	Raleigh St A2		
Earle St B2	Ramsden St B3		
Emlyn St B2	Rawlinson St B3		
Exmouth St C1	Robert St B2		
Farm St C2	Rodney St B2		
Fell St B2	Rutland St B2		
Fenton St B3	St Patrick's Rd . . . C1		
Ferry Rd C1	Salthouse Rd C3		
Forum 28 . . . . . . B2	School St B3		
Furness College . . B1	Scott St B2		
Glasgow St B3	Settle St A3		
Goldsmith St A2	Shore St B3		
Greengate St B3	Sidney St B2		
Hardwick St A2	Silverdale St B3		
Harrison St B3	Slater St B2		
Hartington St A2	Smeaton St B3		
	Stafford St A3		
	Stanley Rd C1		
	Stark St C3		
	Steel St B1		

Bath

▲ Pulteney Bridge

★ Do not miss
★ **Bath Abbey and Heritage Vaults,** York Street
★ **Roman Baths Museum and Pump Room,** Stall Street
★ **No.1 Royal Crescent** – 18th-century townhouse with period furnishings

A UNESCO World Heritage site on the site of thermal springs, boasting a host of important architectural sites, including the Royal Crescent and the Circus. Historical museums and galleries include the Building of Bath Museum, Museum of Bath at Work, Museum of Costume, Postal Museum, Bath Aqua Theatre of Glass, the William Herschel Museum, the Museum of East Asian Art and the Victoria Art Gallery in the Guildhall. The Theatre Royal is one of the country's oldest and most impressive drama venues and the 18th-century Assembly Rooms are still used for concerts and balls. Jane Austen's life and times are explored in the Jane Austen Centre. Green spaces include the Georgian Garden, the Royal Victoria Park and Prior Park Landscape Garden. The town is a major centre for shopping with specialist shops lining Robert Adam's Pulteney Bridge and plenty of high street shops. As a university town there are many great pubs and restaurants for all tastes. The long-awaited Thermae Bath Spa is scheduled to open in 2006.

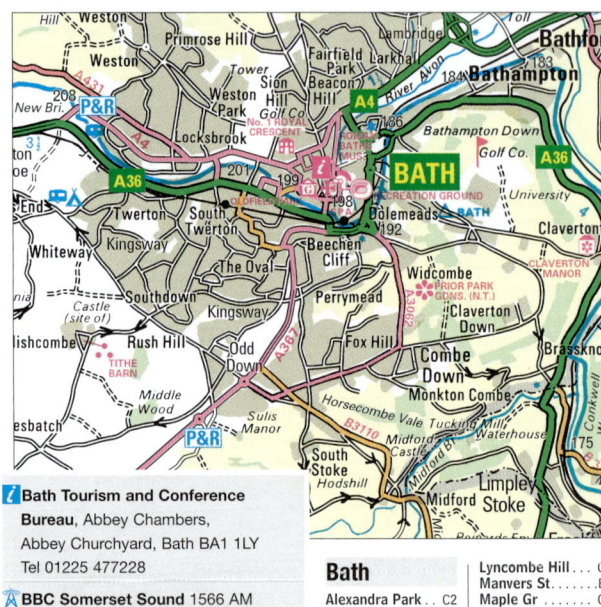

Bath Tourism and Conference Bureau, Abbey Chambers, Abbey Churchyard, Bath BA1 1LY
Tel 01225 477288
BBC Somerset Sound 1566 AM
Bath FM 107.9 FM • Classic Gold 1260 AM • GWR 103.0 FM
www.visitbath.co.uk

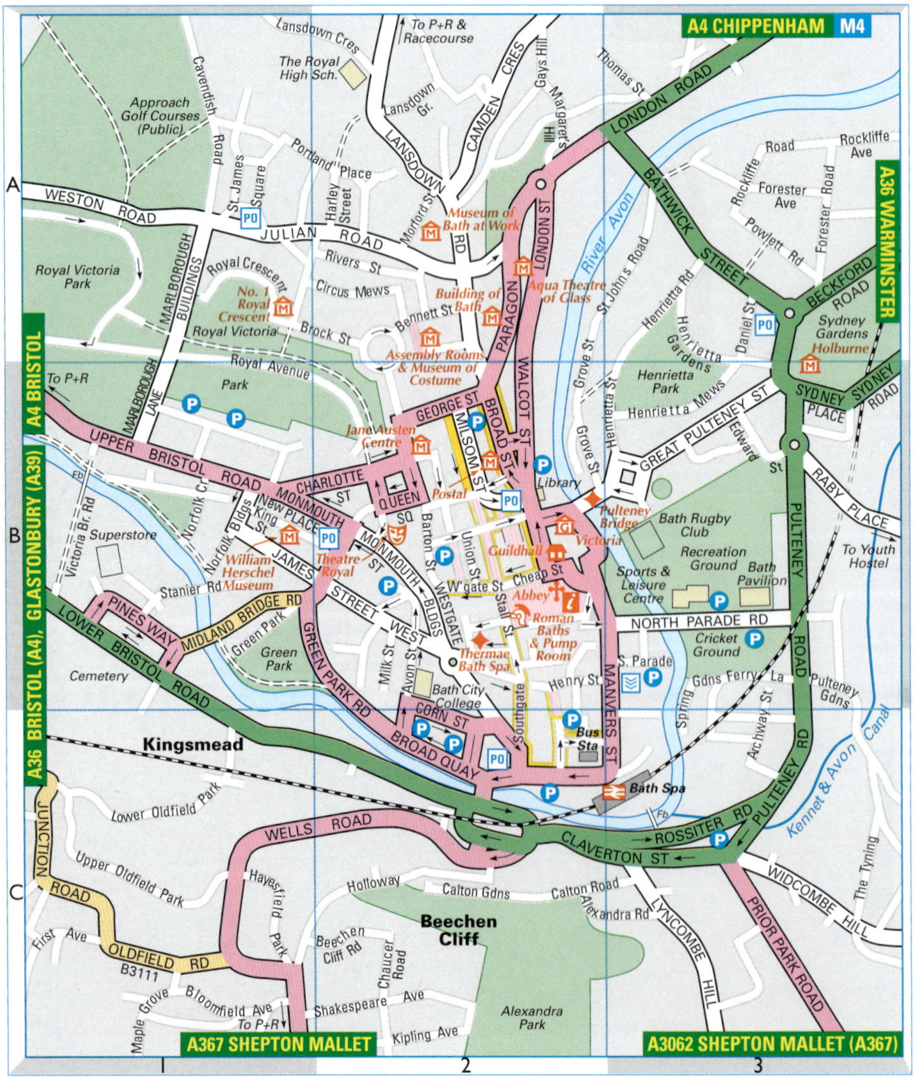

Bath

Alexandra Park	C2	Lyncombe Hill	C3
Alexandra Rd	C2	Manvers St	B3
Approach Golf Courses (Public)	A1	Maple Gr	C1
Aqua Theatre of Glass	A2	Margaret's Hill	A2
Archway St	C3	Marlborough Buildings	A1
Assembly Rooms & Museum of Costume	A2	Marlborough La	B1
Avon St	B2	Midland Bridge Rd	B1
Barton St	B2	Milk St	B2
Bath Abbey	B2	Milsom St	B2
Bath City College	B2	Monmouth St	B2
Bath Pavilion	B3	Morford St	A2
Bath Rugby Club	B3	Museum of Bath at Work	A2
Bath Spa Station	C3	New King St	B1
Bathwick St	A3	No. 1 Royal Crescent	A1
Beechen Cliff Rd	C2	Norfolk Bldgs	A1
Bennett St	A2	Norfolk Cr	B1
Bloomfield Ave	C1	North Parade Rd	B3
Broad Quay	C2	Oldfield Rd	C1
Broad St	B2	Paragon	A2
Brock St	A1	Pines Way	B1
Building of Bath Museum	A2	Police Station	B3
Bus Station	B2	Portland Pl	A2
Calton Gdns	C2	Post Office	A1/A3/B2/C2
Calton Rd	C2	Postal Mus	B2
Camden Cr	A2	Powlett Rd	A3
Cavendish Rd	A1	Prior Park Rd	C3
Cemetery	B1	Pulteney Bridge	B2
Charlotte St	B2	Pulteney Gdns	B3
Chaucer Rd	C2	Pulteney Rd	B3
Cheap St	B2	Queen Sq	B2
Circus Mews	A1	Raby Pl	B3
Claverton St	C2	Recreation Ground	B3
Corn St	C2	Rivers St	A2
Cricket Ground	B3	Rockliffe Ave	A3
Daniel St	A3	Rockliffe Rd	A3
Edward St	A3	Roman Baths & Pump Room	B2
Ferry La	B3	Rossiter Rd	C3
First St	C1	Royal Ave	A1
Forester Ave	A3	Royal Cr	A1
Forester Rd	A3	Royal High School, The	A2
Gays Hill	A2	Royal Victoria Park	A1
George St	B3	St James Sq	A1
Great Pulteney St	B3	St John's Rd	A3
Green Park	B1	Shakespeare Ave	C2
Green Park Rd	B2	Southgate	C2
Grove St	B2	South Pde	B3
Guildhall	B2	Sports & Leisure Centre	B2
Harley St	A2	Spring Gdns	C3
Hayesfield Park	C1	Stall St	B2
Henrietta Gdns	A3	Stanier Rd	B1
Henrietta Mews	B3	Sydney Gdns	A3
Henrietta Park	B3	Sydney Pl	B3
Henrietta Rd	A3	Theatre Royal	B2
Henrietta St	B3	Thermae Bath Spa	B2
Henry St	B2	The Tyning	C3
Holburne Mus	B3	Thomas St	A3
Holloway	C2	Union St	B2
Information Ctr	B2	Upper Bristol Rd	B1
James St West	B1/B2	Upper Oldfield Park	C1
Jane Austen Centre	B2	Victoria Art Gallery	B2
Julian Rd	A1	Victoria Bridge Rd	B1
Junction Rd	C1	Walcot St	B2
Kipling Ave	C1	Wells Rd	C1
Lansdown Cr	A1	Westgate St	B2
Lansdown Gr	A2	Weston Rd	A1
Lansdown Rd	A2	Widcombe Hill	C3
Library	B2	William Herschel Museum	B1
London Rd	A3		
London St	A2		
Lower Bristol Rd	B1		
Lower Oldfield Park	C1		

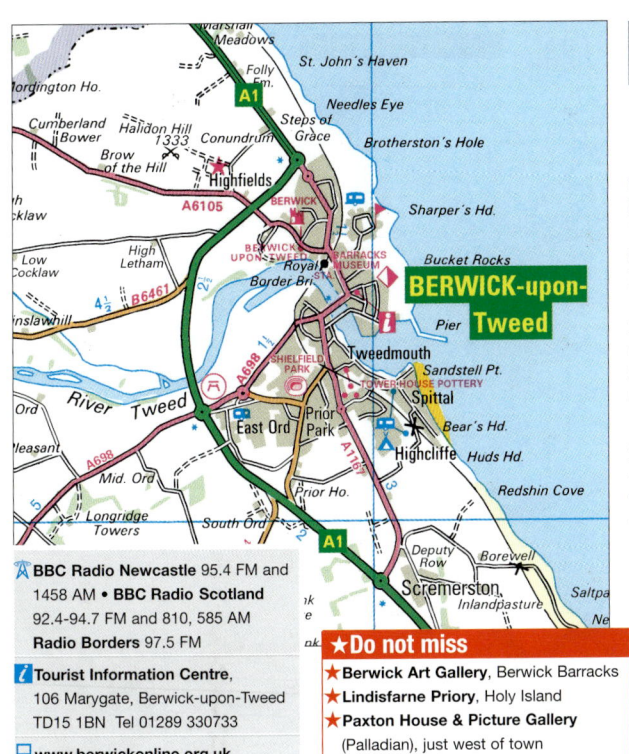

Berwick-upon-Tweed

England's most northerly town, which began life as an Anglo-Saxon settlement and changed hands between the Scottish and English 13 times. It has retained part of its walls, erected by Edward I against Scottish attack in the 14th century (little remains of its border castle), and the 1611 Old Bridge over the Tweed. Set amidst its many attractive Georgian buildings are a mid-18th-century spired town hall and a rare Cromwellian church, Holy Trinity, with some 16th-century Flemish stained glass and a reredos by Lutyens but minus a steeple, tower or church bell. The country's oldest purpose-built barracks now house an art gallery containing part of the Burrell Art Collection, two military museums and local-history displays. Just south of Berwick, Holy Island has a 7th-century priory that was the cradle of Christianity in the north, a Heritage Centre, and a miniature 16th-century castle converted into an Edwardian country house by Lutyens. Nearby you will find 14th-century Etal Castle with an exhibition of border warfare and weaponry, some relating to the Battle of Flodden. The town is also home to many arts and crafts shops. The Maltings arts centre and several pubs provide entertainment.

▲ Berwick Bridge and town walls

BBC Radio Newcastle 95.4 FM and 1458 AM • **BBC Radio Scotland** 92.4–94.7 FM and 810, 585 AM
Radio Borders 97.5 FM

Tourist Information Centre, 106 Marygate, Berwick-upon-Tweed TD15 1BN Tel 01289 330733
www.berwickonline.org.uk

★ **Do not miss**
★ **Berwick Art Gallery**, Berwick Barracks
★ **Lindisfarne Priory**, Holy Island
★ **Paxton House & Picture Gallery** (Palladian), just west of town

Berwick-upon-Tweed

Bank Hill B2
Barracks A3
Bell Tower A3
Bell Tower Pl A3
Berwick Bridge B2
Berwick Infirmary . . . A3
Berwick Rangers F.C. . . C1
Berwick-upon-Tweed . . A2
Billendean Rd C3
Blakewell Gdns B2
Blakewell St B2
Brass Bastion A3
Bridge St B3
Brucegate St A2
Castle (Remains of) . . A2
Castle Terrace A2
Castlegate A2
Chapel St A3
Church Rd C2
Church St A3
Court B3
Coxon's La A3
Cumberland Bastion . . A3
Dean Dr C2
Dock Rd C2/C3
Elizabethan Walls . . . A2/B3
Fire Station B1
Flagstaff Park B3
Football Ground . . . C3
Foul Ford B3
Gallery A3
Golden Sq B2
Golf Course A3
Greenwood C1
Gunpowder Magazine . B3
Hide Hill B3
High Greens A3
Holy Trinity A3
Information Ctr . . . A2
Kiln Hill B2
King's Mount B3
Ladywell Rd C2
Library A3
Lifeboat Station . . . C3
Lord's Mount A3
Lovaine Terrace . . . A2
Low Greens A3
Main Guard B3
Main St B2/C2
Maltings Art Centre, The . B3
Marygate B3
Meg's Mount A2
Middle St C3
Mill St C2
Mount Rd C2
Museum B3
Ness St B3
North Rd A2
Northumberland Ave . . A2
Northumberland Rd . . C2
Ord Dr B1
Osborne Cr B1
Osborne Rd B1
Palace Gr B3
Palace St B3
Palace St East B3
Pier Rd B3
Playing Field C1
Police Station B3
Post Office A2/B2/B2
Prince Edward Rd . . . B2
Prior Rd C2
Quay Walls B3
Railway St A2
Ravensdowne B3
Records Office . . . A3
Riverdene B1
Riverside Rd B3
Royal Border Bridge . . A2
Royal Tweed Bridge . . B2
Russian Gun B3
Scots Gate A2
Scott's Pl A2
Shielfield Park C1
Shielfield Terr C2
Silver St B3
Spittal Quay C3
Superstores C2
The Avenue B3
The Parade A3
Tower Gdns A2
Tower Rd C2
Town Hall B3
Turret Gdns C2
Tweed Dock B3
Tweed St A2
Tweedside Trading Estate . C1
Union Brae B2
Union Park Rd B2
Walkergate A3
Wallace St A3
War Memorial A2
Warkworth Terrace . . A2
Well Close Sq A2
West End B2
West End Pl B1
West End Rd B1
West St B3
West St C3
Windmill Bastion . . . B3
Woolmarket B3

Birthday

Birmingham

Abbey St. A2
Aberdeen St. A1
Acorn Gr. B2
Adams St. A5
Adderley St. C6
Albert St. B4/B5
Albion St. B2
Alcester St. C5
Aldgate Gr. A3
Alexandra
  Theatre C3
All Saint's St. . . . A2
All Saints Rd. . . . A2
Allcock St. C5
Allesley St. A4
Allison St. C5
Alma Cr. B6
Alston Rd. C1
Arcadian Centre . C4
Arthur St. C6
Assay Office B3
Aston
  Expressway . . . A5
Aston Science
  Park B5
Aston St. B4
Avenue Rd. A5
BT Tower B3
Bacchus Rd. A1
Bagot St. B4
Banbury St. B5
Barford Rd. B1
Barford St. C4
Barn St. C5
Barnwell Rd. C6
Barr St. A3
Barrack St. B5
Bartholomew St. . C4
Barwick St. B4
Bath Row. C3
Beaufort Rd. C1
Belmont Row. . . . B5
Benson Rd. A1
Berkley St. C3
Bexhill Gr. C5
Birchall St. C5
Birmingham
  City F.C.
  (St Andrew's) . . C6
Birmingham City
  Hospital
  (A&E) A1
Bishopsgate St. . . C3
Blews St. A4
Bloomsbury St. . . A6
Blucher St. C3
Bordesley St. C4
Bowyer St. C5
Bradburne Way. . A5
Bradford St. C4
Branston St. A3
Brearley St. A4
Brewery St. A4
Bridge St. A3
Bridge St. C3
Bridge St West . . B3
Brindley Dr. B3
Broad St. C3
Broad St UGC . . . C2
Broadway
  Plaza C2
Bromley St. C5
Bromsgrove St. . . C4
Brookfield Rd . . . A1
Browning St. C2
Bryant St. A1
Buckingham St. . A3
Bullring C4
Bull St. B4
Cambridge St. . . . C3
Camden Dr. B3
Camden St. B2
Cannon St. C4
Cardigan St. B5
Carlisle St. A1
Carlyle Rd. C1
Caroline St. B3
Carver St. B2
Cato St. A6
Cato St North . . . A6
Cattell Rd. C6
Cattells Gr. A6
Cawdor Cr. C1
Cecil St. B4
Cemetery A2/B2
Cemetery La A2
Centre Link
  Industrial Estate A6
Charlotte St. B3
Cheapside C4
Chester St. A5
Children's
  Hospital B4
Church St. B4
Claremont Rd. . . . A1
Clarendon Rd. . . . C1
Clark St. C1
Clement St. B3
Clissold St. B2
Cleveland St. C4
Coach Station . . . C5
College St. B2
Colmore Circus . . B4

Colmore Row. . . . B4
Commercial St. . . C3
Constitution Hill . B3
Convention
  Centre. C3
Cope St. B2
Coplow St. B1
Corporation St. . . B4
Council House . . B3
County Court . . . A4
Coveley Gr A2
Coventry Rd. C6
Coventry St C4
Cox St. B3
Crabtree Rd. A2
Cregoe St. C3
Crescent Ave A2
Crescent
  Theatre C3
Cromwell St. A6
Cromwell St. B3
Curzon St. B4
Cuthbert Rd B1
Dale End. B4
Dart St. C6
Dartmouth Circus A4
Dartmouth
  Middleway A4
Dental Hospital . . B4
Deritend C5
Devon St. A6
Devonshire St. . . A1
Digbeth Civic
  Hall C5
Digbeth High St . C4
Dolman St. B5
Dover St. A1
Duchess Rd C2
Duddeston B6
Duddeston
  Manor Rd. B5
Duddeston Mill
  Rd. B6
Duddeston Mill
  Trading Estate. . B6
Dudley Rd. B1
Edgbaston
  Shopping Centre C2
Edmund St. B3
Edward St. B3
Elkington St. A4
Ellen St. A3
Ellis St. C3
Erskine St. B6
Essex St C4
Eyre St B2
Farm Croft A3
Farm St. A2
Fazeley St. B4
Felstead Way. . . . B5
Finstall Cl. B5
Five Ways. C2
Fleet St. B3
Floodgate St. C5
Ford St A2
Fore St. A6
Forster St. B5
Francis Rd C2
Francis St. B5
Frankfort St. A4
Frederick St. B3
Freeth St C1
Freightliner
  Terminal. B6
Garrison La C5
Garrison St. B6
Gas St C3
Geach St. A4
George St B3
George St West . . B3
Gibb St C5
Gillott Rd. B1
Gilby Rd C1
Glover St C5
Goode Ave A2
Goodrick Way . . A6
Gordon St. B6
Graham St. B3
Granville St C3
Gray St C6
Great Barr St. . . . C5
Great Charles St. B3
Great Francis St. . B6
Great Hampton
  Row. A3
Great
  Hampton St . . . A3
Great King St. . . A3
Great Lister St. . . A5
Great Tindal St. . C2
Green La. C5
Green St. C5
Greenway St C6
Grosvenor St
  West C2
Guest Gr. A3
Guild Cl B2
Guildford Dr. A4
Guthrie Cl. A3
Hagley Rd. C1
Hall St. B3
Hampton St A3
Handsworth
  New Rd. A1
Hanley St. B4

Harford St. A3
Harmer Rd. A2
Harold St. C1
Hatchett St A4
Heath Mill La. . . . C5
Heath St. B1
Heath St South . . B1
Heaton St. A2
Heneage St B5
Henrietta St A4
Herbert Rd C6
High St C4
High St C5
Hilden Rd B5
Hill St C4
Hindlow Cl B6
Hingeston St B2
Hippodrome
  Theatre C4
HM Prison A1
Hockley Circus . . A2
Hockley Hill A3
Hockley St A3
Holliday St C3
Holloway Circus . C4
Holloway Head . . C3
Holt St. B5
Hooper St. B1
Horse Fair C4
Hospital St A4
Howard St A3
Howe St. B5
Hubert St. A5
Hunters Rd A2
Hunters Vale A2
Huntly Rd. C2
Hurst St C4
Icknield Port Rd . B1
Icknield Sq. B2
Icknield St. B2
Ikon Gallery C3
Information Ctr . . C3
Inge St. C4
Irving St. C3
Ivy La C6
James Watt
  Queensway B4

Jennens Rd B5
Jewellery
  Quarter A3
Jewellery Quarter
  Museum A3
John Bright St . . . C4
Keeley St C6
Kellett Rd B5
Kent St C4
Kent St North . . . A1
Kenyon St. B3
Key Hill A3
Kilby Ave C2
King Edwards Rd B2
King Edwards Rd B3
Kingston Rd C6
Kirby Rd B1
Ladywood
  Middleway C2
Ladywood Rd. . . . C1
Lancaster St. B4
Landor St. B6
Law Courts B4
Lawford Cl B5
Lawley
  Middleway B5
Ledbury Cl C2
Ledsam St C2
Lees St A1
Legge La. B3
Lennox St A3
Library A6/C3
Library Walk A5
Lighthorne Ave . . B2
Link Rd B3
Lionel St B3
Lister St. B5
Little Ann St. C5
Little Hall Rd A6
Liverpool St C5
Livery St B3
Lodge Rd A1
Lord St A5
Love La. A5
Loveday St. B4
Lower
  Dartmouth St. . . C6

Lower Loveday St. B4
Lower Tower St. . A4
Lower Trinty St . . C5
Ludgate Hill B3
Mailbox Centre
  & BBC. C4
Margaret St B3
Markby Rd A1
Marroway St. . . . B1
Maxstoke St C6
Melvina Rd A6
Meriden St C4
Metropolitan
  (R.C.) B4
Midland St B6
Milk St C5
Mill St A5
Millennium Point . B5
Miller St. A4
Milton St A4
Moat La C4
Montague Rd . . . A5
Montague St C5
Monument Rd . . . C1
Moor Street C4
Moor St
  Queensway . . . C4
Moorsom St A4
Morville St C2
Mosborough Cr. . A3
Moseley St C5
Mott St B3
Museum & Art
  Gallery B3
Musgrave Rd . . . A1
National Indoor
  Arena C3
National Sea Life
  Centre C3
Navigation St. . . . C4
Nechell's Park
  Rd A6
Nechells A6
Nechells
  Parkway A5
Nechells Pl. A5
New Bartholomew
  St. C4

New Canal St. . . . B5
New John St
  West A3
New Spring St. . . B2
New St C2
New Street C4
New Summer St. A4
New Town Row . A4
Newhall Hill B3
Newhall St. B3
Newton St B4
Newtown A4
Noel Rd C1
Norman St A1
Northbrook St . . . B1
Northwood St . . . B3
Norton St A2
Old Crown
  House C5
Old Rep Theatre,
  The B4
Old Snow Hill . . . B4
Oliver Rd C1
Oliver St. A5
Osler St. C1
Oxford St C5
Pallasades
  Centre. C4
Palmer St C5
Paradise Circus . . C3
Paradise St C3
Park Rd A2
Park St. C4
Pavilions Centre . C4
Paxton Rd A1
Peel St A1
Penn St. B5
Pershore St C4
Phillips St A4
Pickford St. C5
Pinfold St C4
Pitsford St B3
Plough &
  Harrow Rd C1
Police
  Station A4/B1/
      B4/C2/C4

Pope St. B2
Portland Rd C1
Post Office
    . . . . A1/A3/A5/B1/
      B5/C1/C2/C3/C5
Preston Rd A1
Price St B4
Princip St B4
Printing House St. A4
Priory
  Queensway. . . . B4
Pritchett St A4
Queensway. B3
Radnor St A2
Railway
  Mosaics B3
Rea St. C4
Regent Pl. B3
Register Office . . C3
Repertory
  Theatre C3
Reservoir Rd C1
Richard St A5
River St. C5
Rocky La A5
Rodney Cl. C1
Roseberry St B2
Rotton Park St. . . B1
Rupert St A5
Ruston St C2
Ryland St C2
St Andrew's
  Industrial
  Estate. C6
St Andrew's Rd . . C6
St Andrew's St. . . C6
St Bolton St C6
St Chads Circus. . B4
St Chads
  Queensway. . . . B4
St Clements Rd . . A5
St George's A3
St James Pl B5
St Marks Cr B2
St Martin's C4
St Paul's B3

St Paul's (Metro
  station) B3
St Paul's Sq B3
St Philip's B4
St Stephen's St . . C3
St Thomas' Peace
  Garden C3
St Vincent St C2
Saltley Rd. A6
Sand Pits Pde . . . C3
Severn St C3
Shadwell St B4
Sheepcote St C2
Shefford Rd A4
Sherborne Rd . . . C2
Shylton's Croft . . C2
Skipton Rd C2
Smallbrook
  Queensway. . . . C4
Smith St A3
Snow Hill B4
Snow Hill
  Queensway. . . . B4
Soho, Benson Rd
  (Metro station) . A1
South Rd A1
Spencer St B3
Spring Hill B2
Staniforth St B4
Station St. C4
Steelhouse La . . . B4
Stephenson St . . . C4
Steward St. B1
Stirling Rd C1
Stour St B2
Suffolk St C3
Summer Hill Rd. . B2
Summer Hill St. . B3
Summer Hill Terr. B2
Summer La. A4
Summer Row . . . B3
Summerfield Cr. . B1
Summerfield
  Park B1
Sutton St C3
Swallow St C3
Sydney Rd C6

Biringham

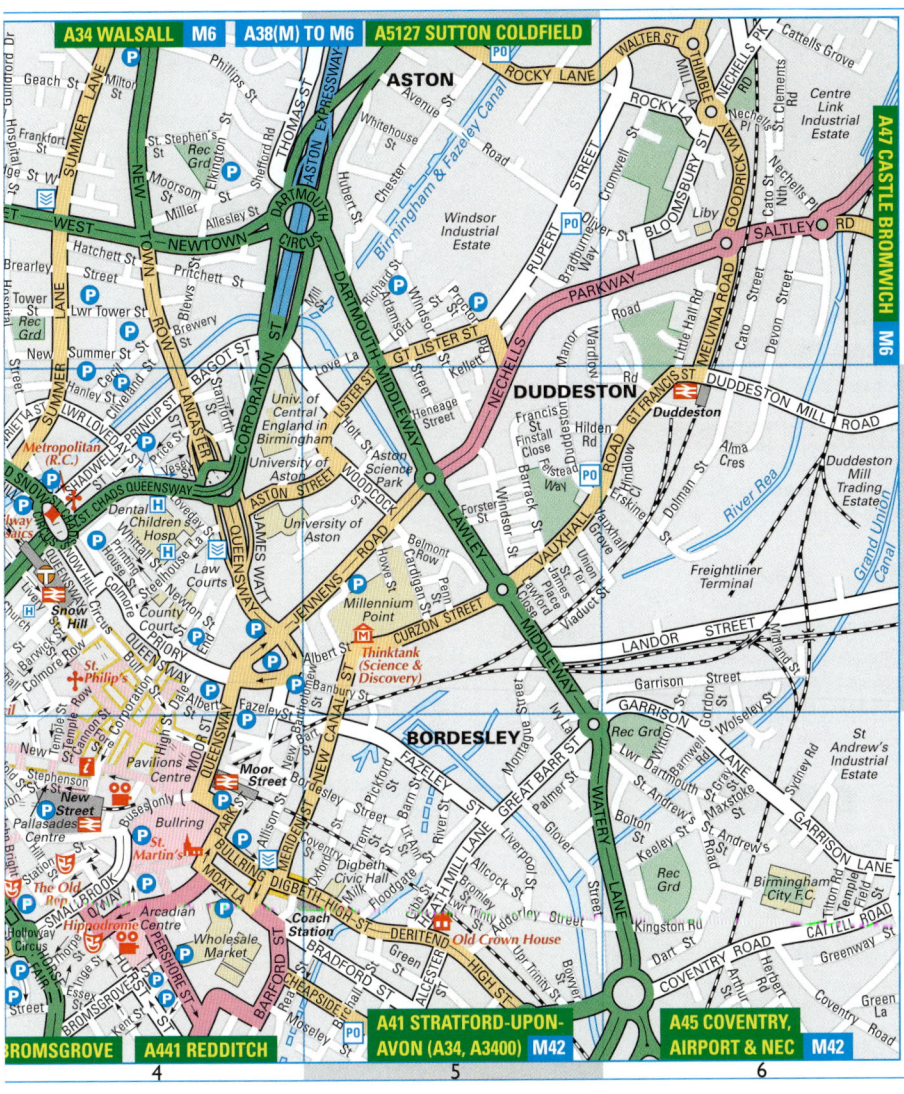

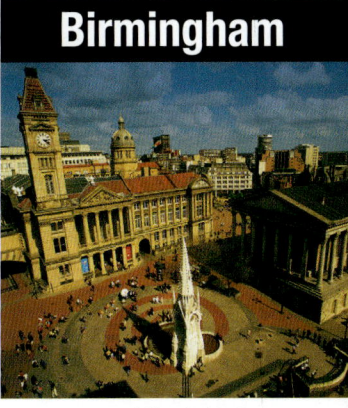

▲ Chamberlain Square

Birmingham has recently undergone major regeneration in the centre with the redevelopment of the Bullring Shopping Centre to house luxury shops and boutiques, restaurants and glass-covered pedestrian streets, and to include the landmark Selfridges building. There are also many different street markets. The extensive canal network has also been improved and there are more acres of parks and open spaces than in any other city in the UK, including the Botanical Gardens in Edgbaston. The Barber Institute of Fine Arts is within University campus. There is a wealth of choice of entertainment, from theatres and cinemas to international cuisine and a fine array of pubs and bars. The city is also known as the capital of Balti – chiefly in the area between the A34 and the A435 to the south of the centre.

43

Symphony Hall	C3
Talbot St	A1
Temple Row	C4
Temple St	C4
Templefield St	C6
Tenby St	B3
Tenby St North	B2
Tennant St	C2
The Crescent	A2
Thimble Mill La	A6
Thinktank (Science & Discovery)	B5
Thomas St	A4
Thorpe St	C4
Tilton Rd	C6
Tower St	A4
Town Hall	C5
Trent St	C5
Turner's Buildings	A1
Unett St	A3
Union Terr	B5
University of Central England in Birmingham	B4
University of Aston	B4/B5
Upper Trinity St	C5
Uxbridge St	A3
Vauxhall Gr	B5
Vauxhall Rd	B5
Vernon Rd	C1
Vesey St	B4
Viaduct St	B5
Victoria Sq	C3
Villa St	A3
Vittoria St	B3
Vyse St	B3
Walter St	A6
Wardlow Rd	A5
Warstone La	B2
Washington St	B3
Water St	B3
Waterworks Rd	C1
Watery La	C5
Well St	A3
Western Rd	B1
Wharf St	A2
Wheeler St	A3
Whitehouse St	A5
Whitmore St	A2
Whittall St	B4
Wholesale Market	C4
Wiggin St	B1
Willes Rd	A1
Windsor Industrial Estate	A5
Windsor St	A5
Windsor St	B5
Winson Green Rd	A1
Witton St	C6
Wolseley St	C6
Woodcock St	B5

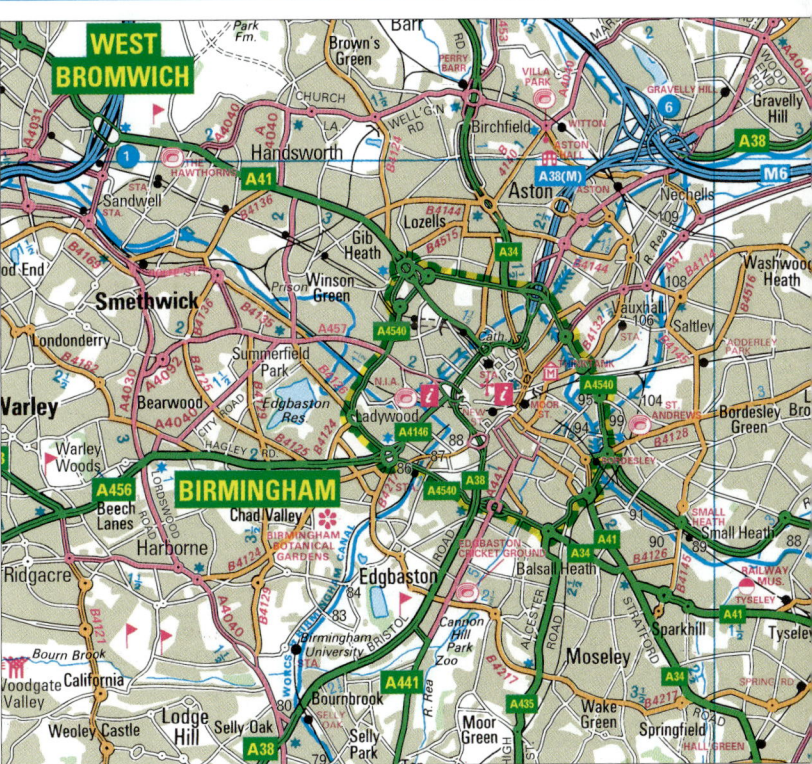

Tourism Centre and Ticketshop,
The Rotunda, 150 New Street,
Birmingham B2 4PA
Tel 0121 202 5099

BBC WM 95.6 FM • **BRMB** 96.4 FM
Heart 100.7 FM • **Saga** 105.7 FM

www.birmingham.gov.uk

★ **Do not miss:**

★ **Birmingham Museum and Art Gallery,** Chamberlain Square – fine art, archaeology, local and industrial history

★ **Millennium Point,** Curzon Street – The Hub, University of the First Age • Thinktank (the Birmingham Museum of Science and Discovery) • Young People's Parliament • IMAX

★ **National Sea Life Centre,** Brindley Place – aquarium

Blackpool

A popular holiday resort since mid-Victorian times, with a 10-mile promenade decorated by the Illuminations for part of the year and along which trams run. The Pleasure Beach has more than 145 rides and attractions, including the tallest, fastest rollercoaster in Europe, and the famous 518ft tower, opened in 1894 and based on the Eiffel Tower, with a circus and ballroom. The town has 3 piers, the 32-acre Zoo Park and Dinosaur Experience, the Lifeboat Station and Visitor Centre, the Model Village and Gardens, Louis Tussaud's Waxworks, and the Sandcastle – one of the UK's largest waterworlds. Green relief is afforded by the Blackpool Countryside Experience, a series of nature walks starting at Stanley Park, and temporary exhibitions are held at the Grundy Art Gallery.

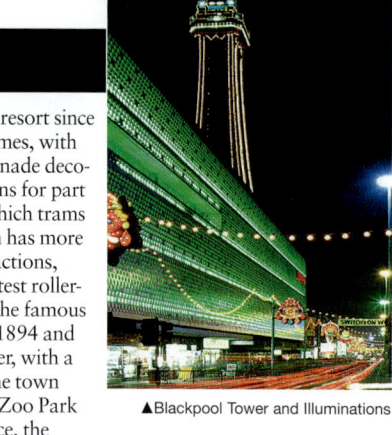

▲ Blackpool Tower and Illuminations

★ Do not miss
- ★ **Blackpool Tower**, The Promenade
- ★ **Sea Life Centre**, The Promenade
- ★ **Stanley Park**, near town centre

Tourist Information Centre,
1 Clifton Street, Blackpool,
Lancashire FY1 1LY   Tel 01253 478222

BBC Radio Lancashire 103.9 FM
Magic 999 AM • **Radio Wave** 96.5 FM • **Rock FM** 97.4 FM

www.visitblackpool.com

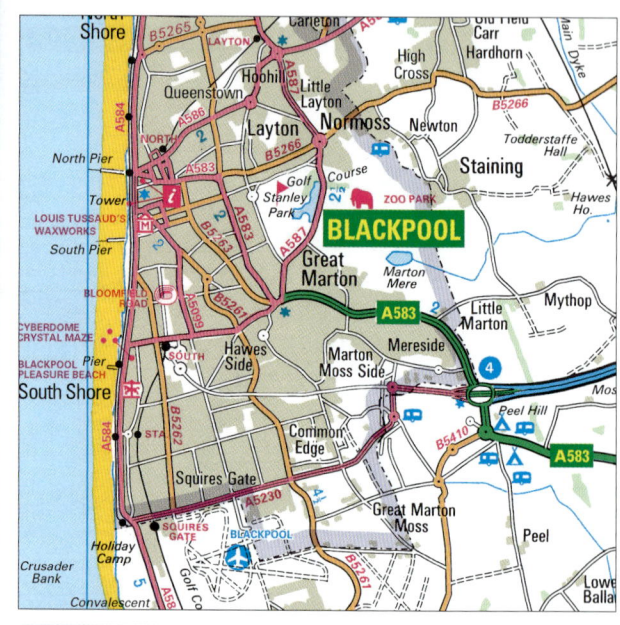

Blackpool

Abingdon St	A1
Addison Cr	A3
Adelaide St	B1
Albert Rd	B2
Alfred St	B2
Ascot Rd	A3
Ashton Rd	C2
Auburn Gr	C3
Bank Hey St	B1
Banks St	A1
Beech Ave	B3
Bela Gr	C2
Belmont Ct	B2
Birley St	A1
Blackpool & Fleetwood Tram	B1
Blackpool F.C.	C2
Blackpool Tower ✦	B1
Blundell St	C1
Bonny St	B1
Breck Rd	A3
Bryan Rd	A3
Buchanan St	A2
Bus Station	A2
Cambridge Rd	A3
Caunce St	A2
Central Pier ✦	C1
Central Pier (Tram stop)	C1
Central Pier Theatre	C1
Chapel St	C1
Charles St	A2
Charnley Rd	B1
Church St	A1
Clifton St	A1
Clinton Ave	B2
Coach Station	C1
Cocker St	A1
Cocker St (Tram stop)	A1
Coleridge Rd	A3
Collingwood Ave	A3
Condor Gr	C3
Cookson St	B1
Coronation St	B1
Corporation St	A1
Courts	B1
Cumberland Ave	B3
Cunliffe Rd	B3
Dale St	C1
Devonshire Rd	A3
Devonshire Sq	A3
Dickson Rd	A2
Elizabeth St	A2
Ferguson Rd	C3
Forest Gate	B3
Foxhall Rd	C1
Foxhall Sq (Tram stop)	C1
Freckleton St	C2
George St	A2
Gloucester Ave	B3
Golden Mile, The	C1
Gorse Rd	B3
Gorton St	A2
Granville Rd	A2
Grasmere Rd	C2
Grosvenor St	A2
Grundy Art Gallery	A1
Harvey Rd	B3
Hornby Rd	B3
Hounds Hill Shopping Centre	B1
Hull Rd	B1
Ibbison Ct	C2
Information Ctr	A1
Kent Rd	C2
Keswick Rd	C2
King St	A2
Knox Gr	C3
Laycock Gate	A3
Layton Rd	A3
Leamington Rd	B2
Leeds Rd	B3
Leicester Rd	B2
Levens Gr	C2
Library	B1
Lifeboat Station	B1
Lincoln Rd	B2
Liverpool Rd	B3
Livingstone Rd	B2
London Rd	A3
Louis Tussaud's Waxworks	B1
Lune Gr	C2
Lytham Rd	C1
Manchester Sq (Tram stop)	C1
Manor Rd	B3
Maple Ave	B3
Market	A2
Market St	A1
Marlboro Rd	B3
Mere Rd	B3
Milbourne St	A2
Newcastle Ave	B3
Newton Dr	A3
North Pier ✦	A1
North Pier Theatre	A1
North Station	A2
Odeon	C2
Olive Gr	B3
Palatine Rd	B2
Park Rd	B2
Peter St	A2
Police Station	B1
Post Office	A1/B2/B3
Princess Pde	A1
Princess St	C1/C2
Promenade	A1/C1
Queen St	A1
Queen Victoria Rd	C2
Raikes Pde	B2
Read's Ave	B2
Regent Rd	B2
Ribble Rd	B2
Rigby Rd	C1
Ripon Rd	B3
St Albans Rd	B3
St Ives Ave	C3
St Vincent Ave	C3
Salisbury Rd	B3
Salthouse Ave	C2
Sands Way	C1
Sea Life Centre	B1
Seaside Way	C1
Selbourne Rd	A2/A3
Sharrow Gr	C3
Somerset Ave	C3
Springfield Rd	A1
South King St	B2
Sutton Pl	B2
Talbot Rd	A1
Talbot Sq (Tram stop)	A1
Thornber Gr	C2
Topping St	A1
Tower (Tram stop)	B1
Town Hall	A1
Tram Depot	C1
Tyldesley Rd	C1
Vance Rd	B1
Victoria St	B1
Victory Rd	A2
Wayman Rd	A3
Westmorland Ave	C2
Whitegate Dr	B3
Winter Gardens Theatre & Opera House	B1
Woodland Gr	B3
Woolman Rd	B2

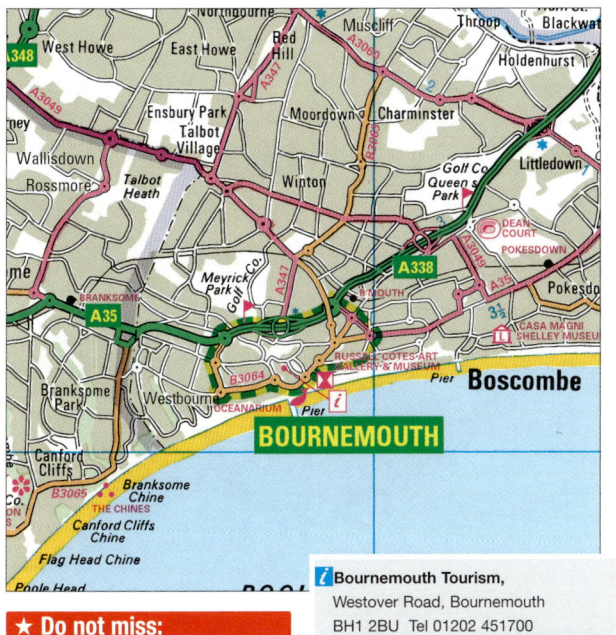

Bournemouth

Bournemouth is known primarily for its seven miles of beaches and also for its parks and gardens and has long been a destination for holidaymakers and people seeking the sea air. There are many diverse attractions available from the Russell-Cotes Art Gallery and Museum to the Bournemouth International Centre, the Oceanarium and the host of gardens. It has a vast array of shops from the high street chains to small independents and boutiques on Westover Road and Old Christchurch Road, plus The Avenue shopping centre on Commercial Road. North of the city are the Wild Things Play Centre and Alice in Wonderland Family Park. The wide range of restaurants, bars and clubs make it a great place for all ages.

▲View from Russell-Cotes

Bournemouth Tourism,
Westover Road, Bournemouth
BH1 2BU Tel 01202 451700

BBC Radio Solent 103.8 FM and 1359 AM • **Classic Gold** 828 AM
Fire 107.6 FM • **2CR FM** 102.3 FM

www.bournemouth.gov.uk

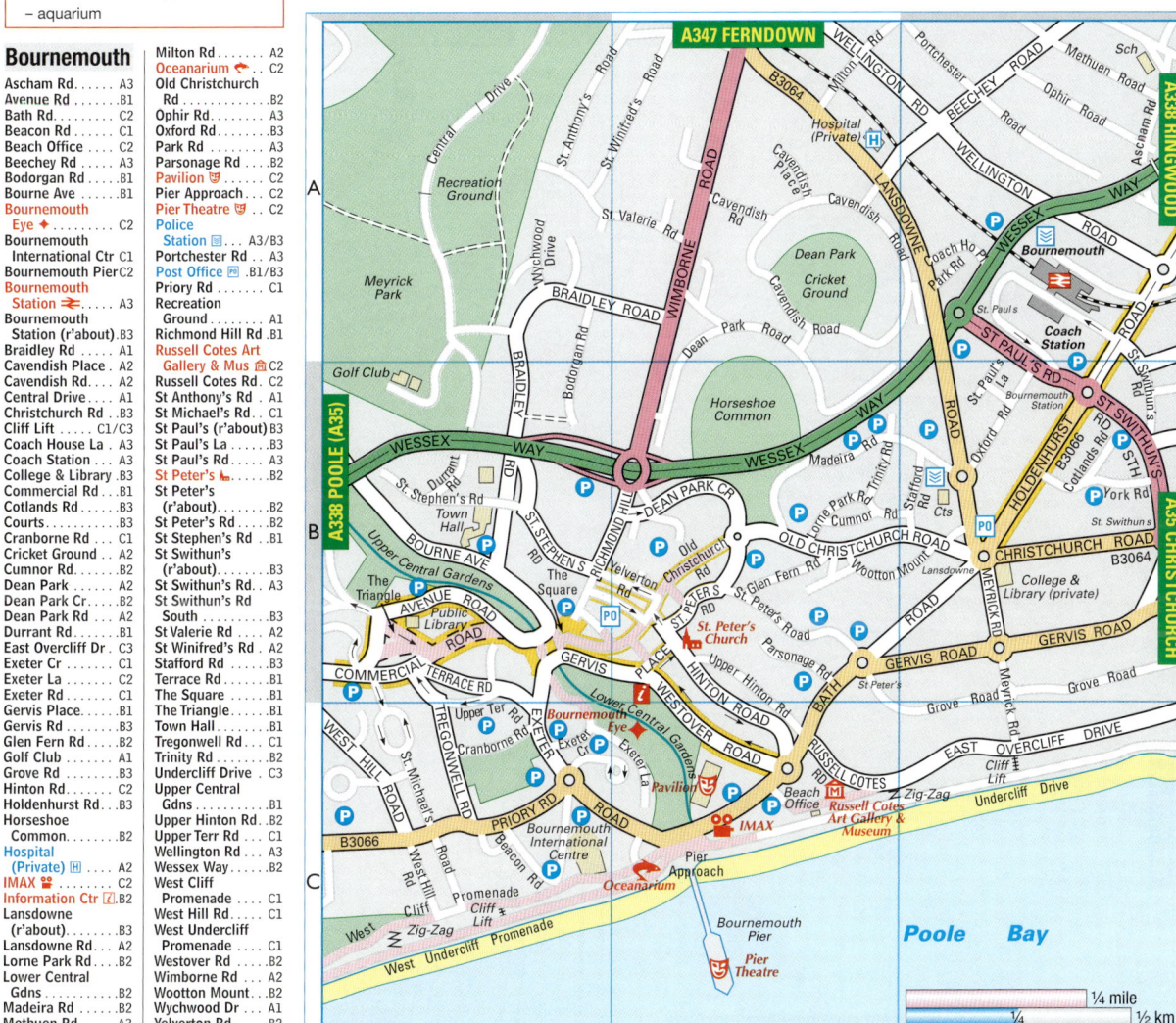

★ Do not miss:
- ★ **Russell-Cotes Art Gallery & Museum**, Russell Cotes Road
- ★ **Bournemouth Eye**, Lower Gardens – tethered balloon flight
- ★ **Oceanarium**, Pier Approach – aquarium

Bournemouth

Street	Grid
Ascham Rd	A3
Avenue Rd	B1
Bath Rd	C2
Beacon Rd	C1
Beach Office	C2
Beechey Rd	A3
Bodorgan Rd	B1
Bourne Ave	B1
Bournemouth Eye ◆	
Bournemouth International Ctr	C1
Bournemouth Pier	C2
Bournemouth Station ≈	A3
Bournemouth Station (r'about)	B3
Braidley Rd	A1
Cavendish Place	A2
Cavendish Rd	A2
Central Drive	A1
Christchurch Rd	B3
Cliff Lift	C1/C3
Coach House La	A1
Coach Station	A3
College & Library	B3
Commercial Rd	B1
Cotlands Rd	B3
Courts	B3
Cranborne Rd	C1
Cricket Ground	A2
Cumnor Rd	B2
Dean Park	A2
Dean Park Cr	B2
Dean Park Rd	A2
Durrant Rd	B1
East Overcliff Dr	C3
Exeter Cr	C2
Exeter La	C2
Exeter Rd	C2
Gervis Place	B1
Gervis Rd	C3
Glen Fern Rd	B2
Golf Club	A1
Grove Rd	C3
Hinton Rd	C2
Holdenhurst Rd	B3
Horseshoe Common	B2
Hospital (Private) H	A2
IMAX	C2
Information Ctr	B2
Lansdowne (r'about)	B3
Lansdowne Rd	B3
Lorne Park Rd	B2
Lower Central Gdns	B2
Madeira Rd	B2
Methuen Rd	A3
Meyrick Park	A1
Meyrick Rd	B3
Milton Rd	A2
Oceanarium ⌖	C2
Old Christchurch Rd	B2
Ophir Rd	A3
Oxford Rd	B3
Park Rd	A3
Parsonage Rd	B2
Pavilion	C2
Pier Approach	C2
Pier Theatre	C2
Police Station	A3/B3
Portchester Rd	A3
Post Office	B1/B3
Priory Rd	C1
Recreation Ground	A1
Richmond Hill Rd	B1
Russell Cotes Art Gallery & Mus	C2
Russell Cotes Rd	C2
St Anthony's Rd	A1
St Michael's Rd	C1
St Paul's (r'about)	B3
St Paul's La	B3
St Paul's Rd	A3
St Peter's ⌖	B2
St Peter's (r'about)	B2
St Peter's Rd	B2
St Stephen's Rd	B1
St Swithun's (r'about)	B3
St Swithun's Rd	A3
St Swithun's Rd South	B3
St Valerie Rd	A2
St Winifred's Rd	A2
Stafford Rd	B3
Terrace Rd	B1
The Square	B1
The Triangle	B1
Town Hall	B1
Tregonwell Rd	C1
Trinity Rd	C1
Undercliff Drive	C3
Upper Central Gdns	B1
Upper Hinton Rd	B2
Upper Terr Rd	C1
Wellington Rd	A3
Wessex Way	B2
West Cliff Promenade	C1
West Hill Rd	C1
West Undercliff Promenade	C1
Westover Rd	B2
Wimborne Rd	A2
Wootton Mount	B2
Wychwood Dr	A1
Yelverton Rd	B1
York Rd	B3
Zig-Zag Walks	C1/C3

Bradford

An ethnically diverse city that grew from a 19th-century rural market town, with a rich industrial heritage as the world's one-time wool capital, still visible in Little Germany, the former merchants' quarter, the impressive Wool Exchange, and the many surrounding mills. The Bradford Industrial Museum & Working Horses re-creates 19th-century life here, while the Colour Museum is a unique venue charting the history, evolution and technology of colour, and the Peace Museum looks at peace history and conflict resolution. The Cartwright Hall Art Gallery and Museum specialises in 19th- and 20th-century British art, plus contemporary South Asian art. Historic buildings include the partly 15th-century cathedral with its William Morris windows, and the 17th-century Bolling Hall manor house. Shops range from high-street standards to Asian shops selling sumptuous fabrics and jewellery, and the newly created Mughal Gardens are based on 16th-19th-century Indian design. At Saltaire's Salt's Mill you'll find Europe's largest collection of works by David Hockney.

▲ Bradford Town Hall

★ Do not miss
- ★ Brontë Birthplace, Thornton
- ★ National Museum of Photography, Film and Television, IMAX
- ★ Saltaire Victorian 'model' industrial village (UNESCO World Heritage Site), Salt's Mill, Saltaire

Bradford Tourist Information Centre, City Hall, Centenary Square, Bradford BD1 1HY Tel 01274 433678

BBC Radio Leeds 92.4, 95.3 FM and 774 AM • Pulse Classic Gold 1278 AM • Sunrise Radio 103.2 FM
The Pulse 97.5 FM

www.visitbradford.com

Bradford

Alhambra ... B2	Listerhills Rd ... B1
Back Ashgrove ... B1	Little Horton La. ... C1
Barkerend Rd. ... A3	Little Horton Gn ... C1
Barnard Rd. ... C3	Longside La ... B1
Barry St ... B2	Lower Kirkgate ... B2
Bolling Rd ... B3	Lumb La ... A1
Bolton Rd ... A3	Manchester Rd ... C2
Bowland St ... A1	Manningham La ... A1
Bradford College ... B1	Manor Row ... A2
Bradford Forster Sq ... B2	Market ... A2/B2
Bradford Interchange ... B3	Market St ... B2
Bradford Playhouse ... B3	Melbourne Place ... C1
Bridge St ... B2	Midland Rd ... A2
Britannia St ... B2	Mill La. ... C2
Broadway ... B2	Morley St ... B1
Burnett St ... B3	Nat. Museum of Photography, Film & Television ... B2
Bus Station ... B3	Nelson St ... B2
Butler St West ... A3	Nesfield St. ... A2
Caledonia St ... C2	New Otley Rd. ... A3
Canal Rd. ... A2	Norcroft St. ... B1
Carlton St ... B1	North Parade ... A2
Cathedral † ... A3	North St ... A3
Centenary Sq. ... B2	North Wing ... A3
Chapel St ... B3	Otley Rd ... A3
Cheapside ... A2	Park Ave ... C1
Church Bank ... B3	Park La ... C1
City Hall ... B2	Park Rd ... C2
City Rd ... A1	Parma St ... C2
Claremont ... B1	Peckover St ... B3
Colour Mus ... B1	Piccadilly ... A2
	Police Station ... B2
	Post Office ... A2/B1/B2/C3
Croft St. ... A1	Princes Way ... B2
Darfield St. ... A1	Prospect St. ... B2
Darley St ... A1	Radwell Drive ... C2
Drewton Rd ... A1	Rawson Rd. ... A1
Drummond Trading Estate ... A1	Rebecca St. ... A1
Dryden St. ... B3	Richmond Rd. ... B1
Dyson St ... A1	Russell St. ... C1
Easby Rd ... C1	St George's Hall ... B2
East Parade ... B3	St Lukes Hospital ... C1
Eldon Pl ... A1	St Mary's ... A3
Filey St ... B3	Shipley Airedale Rd ... A3/B3
Forster Square Retail Park ... A2	Simes St. ... A1
Gallery ... B3	Smith St. ... B1
Garnett St ... B3	Spring Mill St ... B1
Godwin St ... B2	Stott Hill ... A3
Gracechurch St. ... A1	Sunbridge Rd ... A1
Grattan Rd. ... B1	Thornton Rd ... A1
Great Horton Rd ... B1	Trafalgar St ... A2
Grove Terr ... B1	Trinity Rd ... C1
Hall Ings ... B2	Tumbling Hill St ... B1
Hall La ... C3	Tyrrel St ... B2
Hallfield Rd ... A1	University of Bradford ... B1/C1
Hammstrasse ... A2	Usher St ... C3
Harris St. ... B3	Valley Rd ... A2
Holdsworth St. ... A1	Vicar La ... B3
Ice Rink ◆ ... B1	Wakefield Rd ... C3
Information Ctr ... B2	Wapping Rd ... A3
Ivegate ... B2	Westgate ... A1
James St ... B2	White Abbey Rd ... A1
John St ... A2	Wigan Rd ... A1
Kirkgate ... B2	Wilton St ... B1
Kirkgate Centre ... B2	Wood St ... A1
Laisteridge La ... C1	Wool Exchange ... B2
Law Courts ... B3	Worthington St ... A1
Leeds Rd ... B3	
Library ... B1/B2	

Brighton

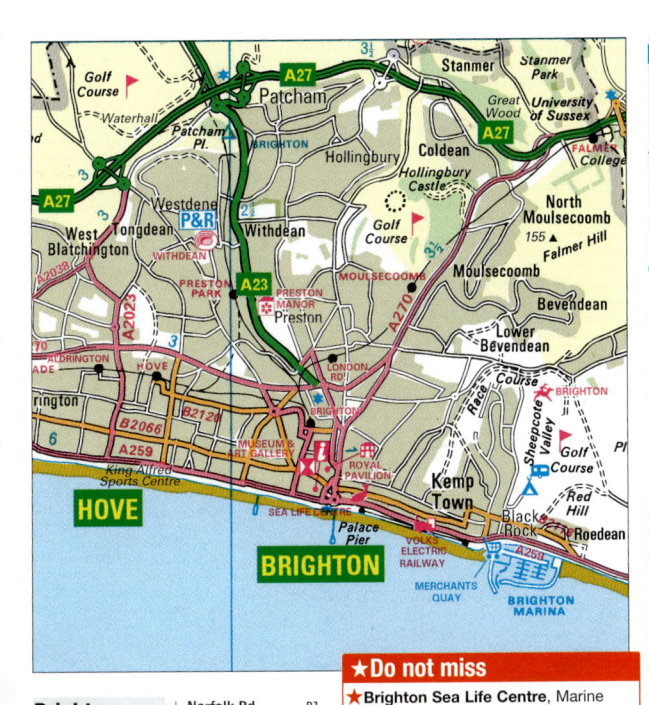

Tourist Information Centre,
10 Bartholomew Square, Brighton
BN1 1JS Tel 0906 711 2255
(50p per minute)

BBC Radio Southern Counties
95.3 FM • **Capital Gold** 945 and
1323 AM • **Juice** 107.2 FM
Southern FM 103.5 FM

www.visitbrighton.com

The Domesday Survey from 1086 shows a population of around 400 in Brighton and a well-established fishing industry. Brighton is now a fashionable, vibrant, cosmopolitan city. Massive investment has transformed the seafront and many of the town's landmarks. Brighton Dome is now a major venue. The Lanes are a network of alleyways with boutiques selling antiques, jewellery and interior design; the North Laine comprises a group of streets between the station and the Pavilion offering an eclectic range of independent clothes and shoe shops, music shops, bars and restaurants. The promenade running along the seafront is a great place for a stroll, or you can take Volks Electric Railway up to the revitalised Brighton Marina, now home to designer outlet shops, restaurants, bars, cinemas and a casino.

◀ Royal Pavilion

★ Do not miss
- ★ **Brighton Sea Life Centre**, Marine Parade – aquarium
- ★ **Palace Pier** – arcades and rides
- ★ **Royal Pavilion**, Pavilion Buildings

Brighton

Addison Rd	A1
Albert Rd	B2
Albion Hill	B3
Albion St	B3
Ann St	A3
Art Gallery & Museum	B3
Baker St	A3
Brighton ≷	A2
Brighton Ctr	C2
Broad St	C3
Buckingham Pl	A2
Buckingham Rd	B2
Cannon Pl	C1
Carlton Hill	B3
Chatham Pl	A1
Cheapside	A3
Church St	B2
Churchill Square Shopping Centre	B2
Clifton Hill	B1
Clifton Pl	B1
Clifton Rd	B1
Clifton Terr	B1
Clock Tower	B2
Clyde Rd	A3
Coach Park	C3
Compton Ave	A2
Davigdor Rd	A1
Denmark Terr	B1
Ditchling Rd	A3
Dome, The	B2
Duke St	B2
Duke's La	C2
Dyke Rd	A1
East St	C2
Edward St	B3
Elmore Rd	B3
Frederick St	B2
Fruit & Veg Market (Wholesale)	B3
Gardner St	B2
Gloucester Pl	B3
Gloucester Rd	B2
Goldsmid Rd	A1
Grand Junction Rd	C2
Grand Pde	B3
Hampton Pl	B1
Hanover Terr	A3
High St	C3
Highdown Rd	A1
Information Ctr	C2
John St	B3
Kemp St	B2
Kensington Pl	A3
Kings Rd	C1
Law Courts	B3
Lewes Rd	A3
Library (temp)	A2
London Rd	A3
Madeira Dr	C3
Marine Pde	C3
Middle St	C2
Montpelier Pl	B1
Montpelier Rd	B1
Montpelier St	B1
New England Rd	A2
New England St	A2
New Rd	B2
Newhaven St	A3
Nizells Ave	A1
Norfolk Rd	B1
Norfolk Terr	B1
North Rd	B2
North St	B2
Old Shoreham Rd	A1
Old Steine	C3
Osmond Rd	A1
Over St	B2
Oxford St	A3
Paddling Pool	C1
Palace Pier	C3
Park Crescent Terr	A3
Police Station	B3
Post Office	A1/A2/A3/B1/B2/B3/C3
Preston Rd	A2
Preston St	B1
Prestonville Rd	A1
Queen's Rd	B2
Regency Sq	C1
Regent St	B2
Richmond Pl	B3
Richmond St	B3
Richmond Terr	A3
Rose Hill Terr	A3
Royal Alexandra Hospital	B2
Royal Pavilion	B2
St Bartholomew's	A2
St James' St	C3
St Nicholas'	B2
St Peter's	A3
Sea Life Centre	C3
Shaftesbury Rd	A3
Sillwood Rd	B1
Sillwood St	B1
Southover St	A3
Spring Gdns	B2
Stanford Rd	A1
Stanley Rd	A3
Sussex St	B3
Sussex Terr	B3
Swimming Pool	B3
Sydney St	B3
Temple Gdns	B1
Terminus Rd	A1
The Lanes	C2
Theatre Royal	B2
Tidy St	B2
Town Hall	C2
Toy & Model Museum	A1
Trafalgar St	B2
Union Rd	A3
University of Brighton	B3
Upper Lewes Rd	A3
Upper North St	B1
Vernon Terr	A1
Viaduct Rd	A3
Victoria Gdns	B3
Victoria Rd	B1
Volk's Electric Railway	C3
West Pier (Closed to the Public)	C1
West St	C2
Western Rd	B1
Whitecross St	B2
York Ave	B1
York Pl	B3

Bristol

▲ Clifton Suspension Bridge

Historic city and seaport, manufacturing centre and university town. Places of interest include the Cathedral, Clifton Suspension Bridge, Maritime Heritage Centre, The Watershed Media Centre and the Bristol Industrial Museum. A major and diverse centre for shopping from Whiteladies Road and Clifton Village designer clothes, art and crafts, antiques, jewellery to St Nicholas Markets' hand-crafted goods and deli foods and the nearby Christmas Steps selling couture clothing, hand-made shoes and musical instruments. Big name shops can be found in Broadmead and the Galleries. There is a great variety of bars and restaurants in the centre of the city and the Clifton area.

★ Do not miss

- ★ **Bristol Zoo Gardens**, Clifton
- ★ **Bristol City Museum and Art Gallery**, Queen's Road
- ★ **At Bristol**, Anchor Road, Harbourside – Explore, Wildwalk, IMAX

Bristol

Acramans Rd C4
Albert Rd C6
Alfred Hill A4
All Saint's St A4
All Saints' B4
Allington Rd C3
Alpha Rd C1
Ambra Vale B1
Ambra Vale East . . B2
Ambrose Rd B2
Amphitheatre C3
Anchor Rd B3
Anvil St B6
Architecture Centre ✦ B4
Argyle Pl B2
Arlington Villas . . . A2
Arnolfini Arts Centre, The ✦ . . . B4
Art Gallery 🏛 . . . A3
Ashton Gate Rd . . . C1
Ashton Rd C1
at-Bristol ✦ B3
Avon Bridge C1
Avon Cr. C1
Avon St. B6
Baldwin St B4
Baltic Wharf C2
Baltic Wharf Leisure Centre & Caravan Park ✦ C2
Barossa Pl C4
Barton Manor B6
Barton Rd B6
Barton Vale B6
Bath Rd B6
Bathurst Basin . . . C4
Bathurst Parade . . C4
Beauley Rd C3
Bedminster Bridge C5
Bedminster Parade C4
Bellevue Cr B2
Bellevue B2
Bellevue Rd B2
Berkeley Pl A2
Berkeley Sq A3
Birch Rd C2
Blackfriars A4
Bond St A5
Braggs La A6
Brandon Hill B3
Brandon Steep . . . B3
Bristol Bridge B5
Bristol Cathedral (CE) ✝ B3
Bristol Grammar School A3
Bristol Harbour Railway 🚂 A4
Bristol Marina C2
Bristol Royal (A&E) 🏥 A4
Bristol Temple Meads Station 🚉 B6
Broad Plain B4
Broad Quay B4
Broad St A4
Broad Weir A5
Broadcasting House A3
Broadmead A5
Brunel Way C1
Brunswick Sq A5
Burton Cl C5
Bus Station A4
Butts Rd B3
Cabot Tower ✦ . . . B3
Caledonia Pl B1
Callowhill Ct A5
Cambridge St C6
Camden Rd A4
Camp Rd A1
Canada Way C2
Cannon St A4
Canon's Rd B3/B4
Canon's Way B3
Cantock's Cl A3
Canynge Rd A1
Canynge Sq A1
Castle Park A5
Castle St A5
Catherine Meade St. C4
Cattle Market Rd . . C6
Charles Pl B1
Charlotte St B3
Charlotte St South . B3
Chatterton House B5
Chatterton Sq B5
Chatterton St C5
Cheese La B5
Children's Hospital 🏥 A4
Christchurch ⛪ . . . A4
Christchurch Rd . . . A1
Christmas Steps ✦ . A4
Church La C5
Church St B5
City Museum 🏛 . . . A3
City of Bristol College B3
Clare St B4
Clarence Rd C5
Cliff Rd C1
Clift House Rd C1
Clifton Cathedral (RC) ✝ A2
Clifton Down Rd . . . A1
Clifton Down A1
Clifton Hill A2
Clifton Park A2
Clifton Park Rd . . . A1
Clifton Rd A2
Cliftonwood Cr B2
Cliftonwood Rd . . . B2
Cliftonwood Terr . . . B2
Clifton Vale B1
Cobblestone Mews A4
College Green B3
College Rd A1
College St B3
Colston Almshouses 🏛 . . . B3
Colston Ave B4
Colston Hall 🎭 . . . B4
Colston Parade . . . C5
Colston St A4
Commercial Rd . . . C4
Commonwealth Museum 🏛 . . . B6
Constitution Hill . . . B2
Cooperage La C2
Corn St B4
Cornwallis Ave B1
Cornwallis Cr B1
Coronation Rd C3
Council House 🏛 . . B3
Countership B5
Courts B4
Create Centre, The ✦ B1
Crosby Row B2
Culver St B3
Cumberland Basin . C1
Cumberland Cl . . . C2
Cumberland Rd . . . C2
Dale St A6
David St A6
Dean La C4
Deanery Rd B3
Denmark St B4
Dowry Sq B1
East St A5
Eaton Cr A1
Elmdale Rd A3
Elton Rd A3
Eugene St A4
Exchange, The & St Nicholas' Mkts 🏛 B4
Fairfax St A5
Fire Station B5
Floating Harbour . . B3
Foster Almshouses 🏛 . . . A4
Frayne Rd C1
Frederick Pl A2
Freeland Pl B1
Frogmore St B3
Fry's Hill A2
Gas La B6
Gasferry Rd C3
General Hospital 🏥 C4
Georgian House 🏛 . . . B3
Glendale B1
Glentworth Rd B2
Gloucester St A1
Goldney Hall B2
Goldney Rd B1
Gordon Rd A2
Granby Hill B1
Grange Rd A1
Great Ann St A6
Great George St . . A4
Great George St . . B3
Great Western Way B6
Green St North . . . B1
Green St South . . . B1
Greenay Bush La . . C2
Greenbank Rd C2
Greville Smyth Park C1
Guildhall 🏛 A4
Guinea St C4
Hamilton Rd C3
Hanbury Rd A2
Hanover Pl C2
Harbour Way B3
Harley Pl A1
Haymarket A5
Hensman's Hill . . . B1
High St B4
Highbury Villas . . . A3
Hill St B3
Hill St C6
Hippodrome 🎭 . . . B4
Hopechapel Hill . . . B1
Horfield Rd A4
Horton St B6
Host St A4
Hotwell Rd B2
Houlton St A6
Howard Rd C1
Ice Rink B3
IMAX Cinema 🎬 . . . B4
Industrial Museum 🏛 C4
Information Ctr 🛈 . . B4
Islington Rd C3
Jacob St A5/A6
Jacob's Wells Rd . . B2
John Carr's Terr . . . A1
John Wesley's Chapel ⛪ A5
Joy Hill B1
Jubilee St B6
Kensington Pl A2
Kilkenny St B6
King St B4
Kingsland Rd B6
Kingston Rd C3
Lamb St A6
Lansdown Rd A2
Lawford St A6
Lawfords Gate A6
Leighton Rd C1
Lewins Mead A4
Lime Rd C1
Little Ann St A6
Little Caroline Pl . . . B1
Little George St . . . B4
Little King St B4
Litfield Rd A1
Llandoger Trow 🏛 . . B4
Lloyds' Building, The C3
Lodge St A4
Lord Mayor's Chapel ⛪ A4
Lower Castle St . . . A5
Lower Church La . . A4
Lower Clifton Hill . . B2
Lower Guinea St . . C4
Lower Lamb St . . . B3
Lower Maudlin St . . A4
Lower Park Rd . . . A1
Lower Sidney St . . C2
Lucky La C4
Lydstep Terr C1
Mall Galleries, The Shopping Ctr . . . A5
Manilla Rd A1
Mardyke Ferry Rd . C2
Maritime Heritage Centre 🏛 C3
Marlborough Hill . . A4
Marlborough St . . . A4
Marsh St B4
Maternity Hospital 🏥 A4
Mead St C5
Meadow St A5
Merchant Dock . . . C2
Merchant St A5
Merchants Rd A1
Merchants Rd C1
Meridian Pl A2
Meridian Vale A2
Merrywood Rd . . . C3
Millard St B1
Milford St C3
Millennium Sq B3
Mitchell La B5
Mortimer Rd A1
Murray Rd C4
Myrtle Rd A3
Narrow Plain B5
Narrow Quay B4
Nelson St A4
New Charlotte St . . C4
New Kingsley Rd . . B6
New Queen St . . . C5
New St A6
Newfoundland St . . A5
Newgate A5
Newton St A6
Norland Rd A1
North St C2
Oakfield Gr A2
Oakfield Pl A2
Oakfield Rd A2
Old Bread St B6
Old Market St A6
Old Park Hill A4
Oldfield Rd B1
Orchard Ave B4
Orchard La B4
Orchard St B4
Osbourne Rd C3
Oxford St B6
Park Pl A2
Park Rd C3
Park Row A3
Park St A3
Passage St B5
Pembroke Gr A2
Pembroke Rd C3
Pembroke Rd A3
Pembroke St A5
Penn St A5
Pennywell Rd A6
Percival Rd A1
Pero's Bridge B4
Perry Rd A4
Pip & Jay ⛪ A5
Plimsoll Bridge . . . B1
Post Office 🏤 . A1/A3/A4/A5/A6/B1/B4/C4/C5
Police Sta A4/A6
Polygon Rd B1
Portland St A1
Portwall La C5
Prewett St C5
Prince St B4
Prince St Bridge . . . C4
Princess St C5
Princess Victoria St B1
Priory Rd A3
Pump La B4
QEH Theatre 🎭 . . A3
Queen Charlotte St B4
Queen Elizabeth Hospital School . . A3
Queen Sq B4
Queen St B5
Queen's Ave A3
Queen's Parade . . . B3
Queen's Rd A3
Raleigh Rd C1
Randall Rd A2
Redcliffe Backs . . . B5
Redcliffe Bridge . . . B4
Redcliffe Hill C5
Redcliffe Parade . . C5
Redcliffe St B5
Redcliffe Way B5
Redcross La A6
Redcross St A6
Redgrave Theatre 🎭 A1
Red Lodge 🏛 A4
Regent St B1
Richmond Hill A2
Richmond Hill Ave . A2
Richmond La A2
Richmond Park Rd . A2
Richmond St C6
Richmond Terr A2
River St A6
Rownham Mead . . B2
Royal Fort Rd A3
Royal Park A2
Royal West of England Academy 🏛 . . . A3
Royal York Cr B1
Royal York Villas . . B1
Rupert St A4
Russ St B6
St Andrew's Walk . . A1
St George's 🎭 . . . B3
St George's Rd . . . B3
St James ⛪ A4
St John's ⛪ A4
St John's Rd C4
St Luke's Rd C5
St Mary Redcliffe ⛪ C5
St Mary's Hospital 🏥 A3
St Matthias Park . . A6
St Michael's Hill . . . A3
St Michael's Park . . A3
St Nicholas St B4
St Paul St A5
St Peter's (Ruin) ⛪ A5

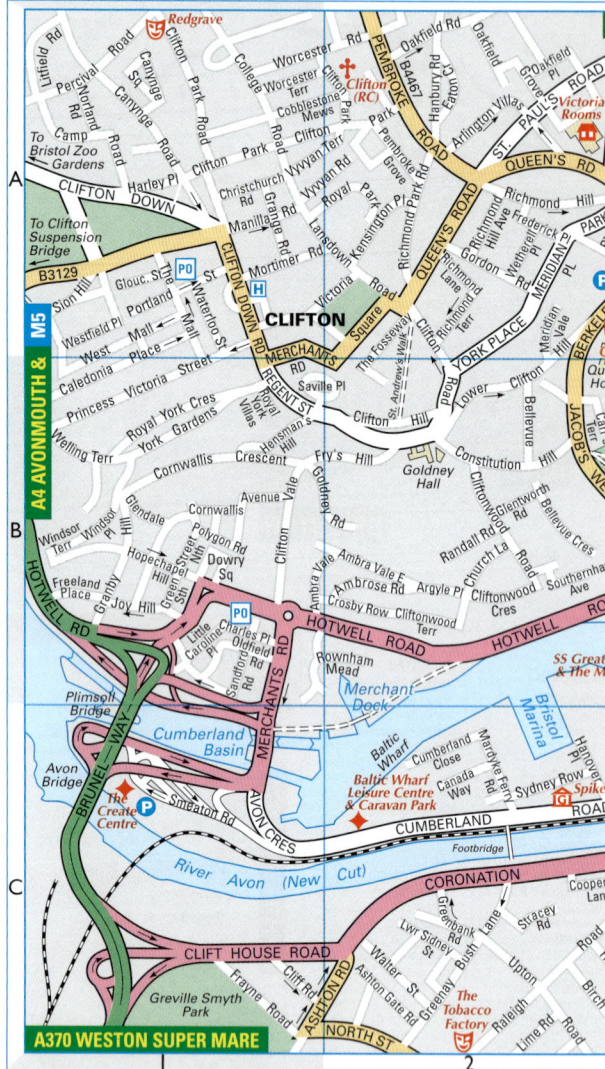

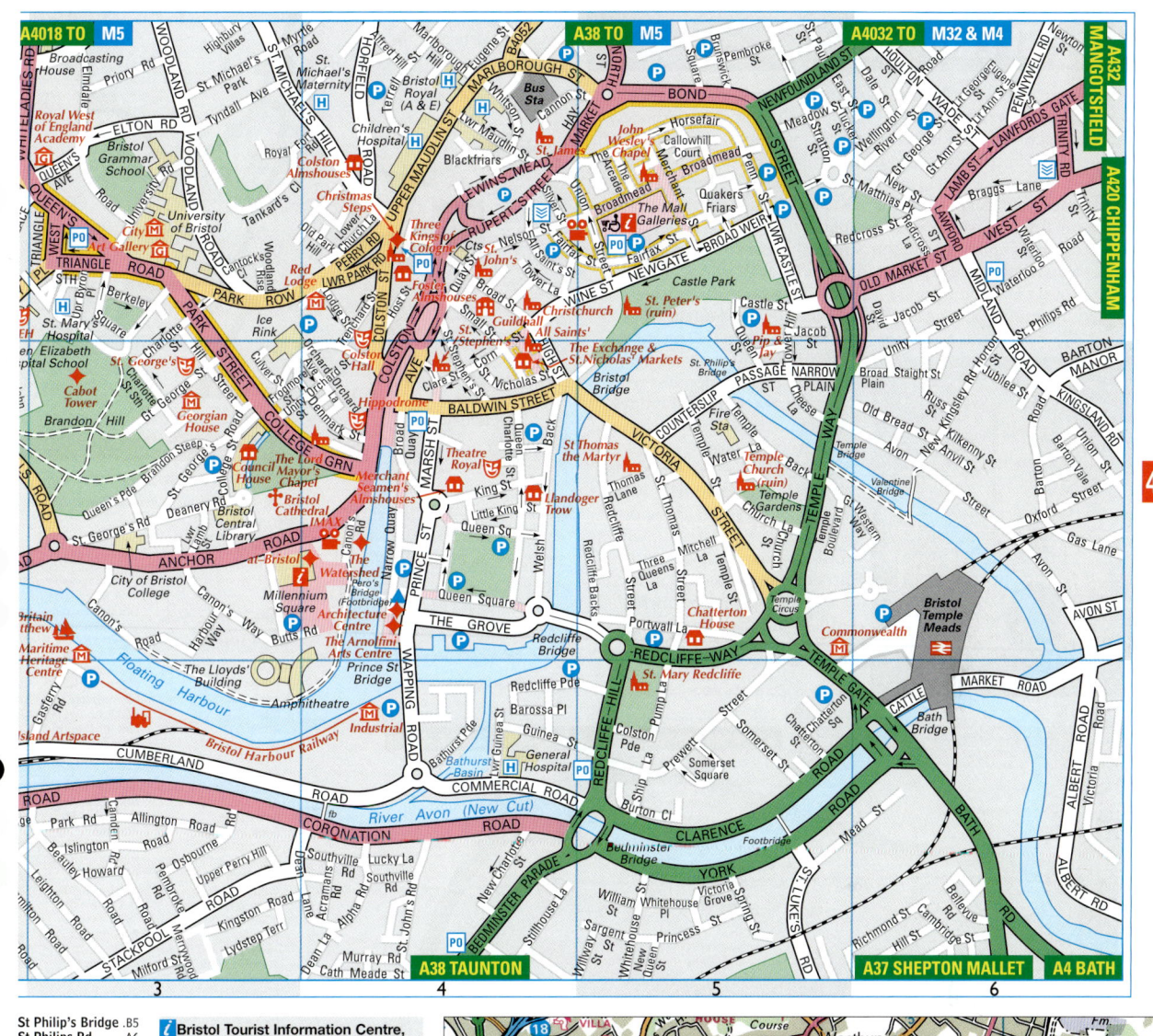

St Philip's Bridge	B5
St Philips Rd	A6
St Stephen's Church	**B4**
St Stephen's St	B4
St Thomas St	B5
St Thomas the Martyr	**B5**
Sandford Rd	B1
Sargent St	C5
Saville Pl	B1
Ship La	C5
Silver St	A4
Sion Hill	A1
Small St	A4
Smeaton Rd	C1
Somerset Sq	C5
Somerset St	C5
Southernhay Ave	B2
Southville Rd	C4
Spike Island Artspace	**C2**
Spring St	C5
SS Great Britain & The Matthew	**C3**
Stackpool Rd	C3
Staight St	B6
Stillhouse La	C4
Stracey Rd	C2
Stratton St	A5
Sydney Row	C2
Tankard's Cl	A3
Temple Back	B5
Temple Blvd	B5
Temple Bridge	B5
Temple Church	**B5**
Temple Gate	C5
Temple St	B5
Temple Way	B5
Terrell St	A4
The Arcade	A5
The Fosseway	A2
The Grove	B4
The Horsefair	A5
The Mall	A1
Theatre Royal	**B4**
Thomas La	B5
Three Kings of Cologne	**A4**
Three Queens La	B5
Tobacco Factory, The	**C2**
Tower Hill	B5
Tower La	A4
Trenchard St	A4
Triangle South	A3
Triangle West	A3
Trinity Rd	A6
Trinity St	A3
Tucker St	A5
Tyndall Ave	A3
Union St	B6
Union St	A5
Unity St	C5
Unity St	B3
Univ of Bristol	A3
University Rd	A3
Upper Maudlin St	A4
Upper Perry Hill	C3
Upper Byron Pl	A3
Upton Rd	C2
Valentine Bridge	B6
Victoria Gr	A1
Victoria Rd	C6
Victoria Rooms	**A2**
Victoria St	B5
Vyvyan Rd	A1
Vyvyan Terr	A1
Wade St	A6
Walter St	C2
Wapping Rd	C4
Water La	B5
Waterloo Rd	A6
Waterloo St	A1
Waterloo St	A6
Watershed, The	**B4**
Welling Terr	B1
Wellington Rd	A6
Welsh Back	B4
West Mall	A1
West St	A6
Westfield Pl	A1
Wetherell Pl	A2
Whitehouse Pl	C5
Whitehouse St	C5
Whiteladies Rd	A1
Whitson St	A4
William St	C5
Willway St	C4
Windsor Pl	B1
Windsor Terr	B1
Wine St	A4
Woodland Rise	A3
Woodland Rd	A3
Worcester Rd	A1
Worcester Terr	A1
YHA	**B4**
York Gdns	B1
York Pl	A2
York Rd	C5

Bristol Tourist Information Centre, The Annexe, Wildscreen Walk, Harbourside, Bristol BS1 5DB
Tel 0117 9260767

BBC Radio Bristol 95.5, 94.9 FM and 1548 AM • **Classic Gold** 1260 AM
GWR 96.3 FM • **Star** 107.3 FM

www.bristol-city.gov.uk

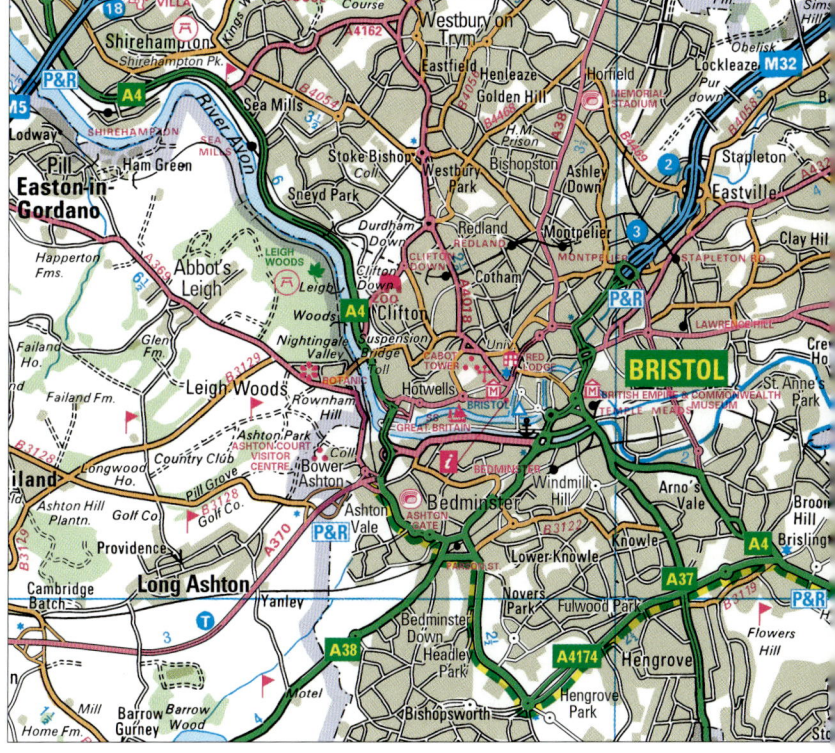

Bury St Edmunds

An attractive market town of Saxon origins that became home to one of medieval Europe's most powerful abbeys, which was founded in 1020 by King Canute and torn down in the mid 16th century: there are still ruins dotted about town. Mary Tudor, sister of Henry VIII, is buried in the sanctuary of the 14th-century St Mary's Church; the 1735 Manor House contains a museum of art, fashion and horology; there's an art gallery in a Robert Adams building; and the National Trust's Angel Corner is a Queen Anne house with the former mayor's parlour. The 16th-century St Edmundsbury is the country's only unfinished cathedral-church, lacking a spire but boasting a Norman tower as a belfry, and the 18th-century Theatre Royal is one of the UK's oldest and smallest working theatres. On Wednesdays and Saturdays the town hosts East Anglia's largest street market. Nearby are the Anglo-Saxon Village in nearby West Stow Country Park, Ickworth House (National Trust), with an 18th-century rotunda and fine art collection, Rede Hall Farm Park, the remains of Ixworth Abbey and the award-winning Lackford Wildfowl Reserve.

◀ Bury St Edmunds Abbey Great Gate

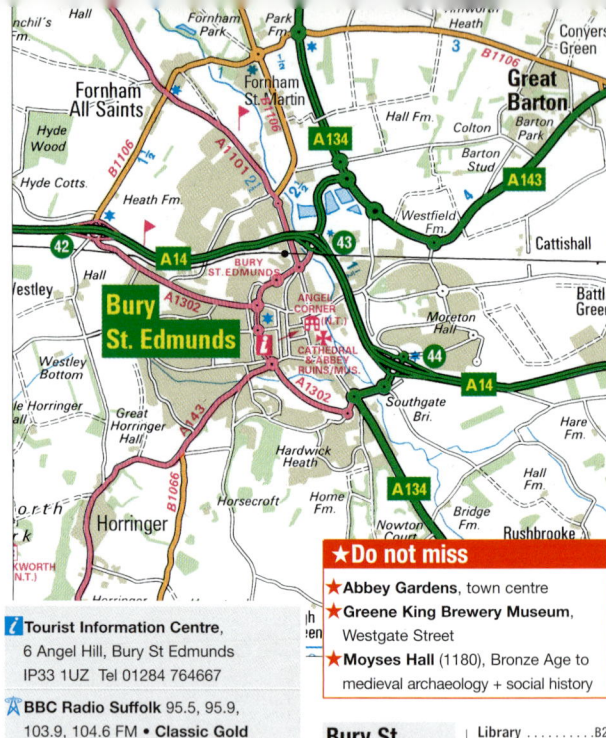

Tourist Information Centre,
6 Angel Hill, Bury St Edmunds
IP33 1UZ Tel 01284 764667

BBC Radio Suffolk 95.5, 95.9, 103.9, 104.6 FM • **Classic Gold Amber** 1170 AM • **SGR** 96.4 FM
Vibe FM 105.0-108.0 FM

www.stedmundsbury.gov.uk

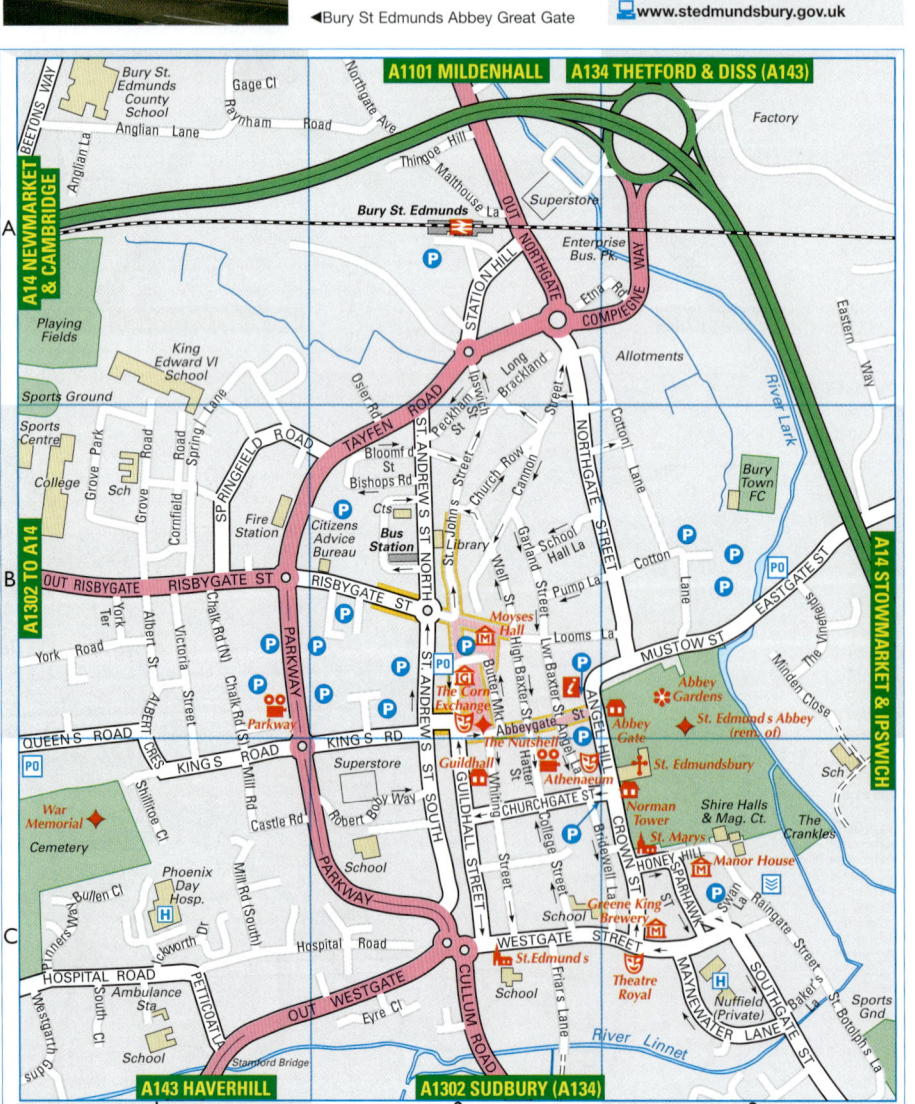

★ Do not miss
- ★ **Abbey Gardens**, town centre
- ★ **Greene King Brewery Museum**, Westgate Street
- ★ **Moyses Hall** (1180), Bronze Age to medieval archaeology + social history

Bury St Edmunds

Abbey Gardens ✿ . . B3	Library B2
Abbey Gate B3	Long Brackland . . A2
Abbeygate St B2	Looms La B2
Albert Cr B1	Lwr Baxter St B2
Albert St B1	Malthouse La A2
Ambulance Sta . . . C1	**Manor House** . . B2
Angel Hill B2	Maynewater La . . . C3
Angel La B2	Mill Rd C1
Anglian Lane A1	Mill Rd (South) . . . C1
Athenaeum C2	Minden Close B3
Baker's La C3	**Moyses Hall** . . . B2
Beetons Way A1	Mustow St B3
Bishops Rd B2	**Norman Tower** . . C2
Bloomfield St B2	Northgate Ave . . . A2
Bridewell La C2	Northgate St B2
Bullen Cl C1	**Nuffield**
Bury St Edmunds	(Private) C1
County School . . A1	**Nutshell, The** . . . B2
Bury St	Osier Rd A2
Edmunds ⇌ . . . A2	Out Northgate . . . A2
Bury Town FC B3	Out Risbygate . . . B1
Bus Station B2	Out Westgate C1
Butter Mkt B2	Parkway B1/C2
Cannon St B2	**Parkway** B1
Castle Rd C1	Peckham St B1
Cemetery C1	Petticoat La C1
Chalk Rd (N) B1	**Phoenix Day**
Chalk Rd (S) B1	Hospital C1
Church Row B2	Pinners Way C1
Churchgate St . . . C2	Police Station . . . C3
Citizens Advice	Post Office . . B2/B3
Bureau B2	Pump La B2
College St C2	Queen's Rd B1
Compiegne Way . . A3	Raingate St C2
Corn Exchange,	Raynham Rd A1
The B2	Risbygate St . . B1/B2
Cornfield Rd B1	Robert Boby Way . . B1
Cotton Lane B3	St Andrew's St
Courts B2	North B2
Crown St C3	St Andrew's St
Cullum St C2	South B2
Eastern Way A3	St Botolph's La . . C3
Eastgate St B3	**St Edmund's Abbey**
Enterprise	(Remains) B3
Business Park . . A2	**St Edmundsbury** ✝ . C2
Etna Rd A2	St John's St B2
Eyre Cl C2	**St Marys** C2
Fire Station B1	School Hall La . . . B2
Friar's Lane C2	Shillitoe Cl C1
Gage Cl A1	Shire Halls &
Garland St B2	Magistrates Ct . . C3
Greene King	South Cl C3
Brewery C3	Southgate St C3
Grove Park B1	Sparhawk St C3
Grove Rd B1	Spring Lane B1
Guildhall C2	Springfield Rd . . . B1
Guildhall St C2	Station Hill A2
Hatter St C2	Swan La C3
High Baxter St . . . B2	Tayfen Rd B1
Honey Hill C3	The Vinefields . . . B3
Hospital Rd . . . C1/C2	**Theatre Royal** 🎭 . . C2
Ickworth Dr C1	Thingoe Hill A2
Information Ctr ℹ . B2	Victoria St C1
Ipswich St B2	**War Memorial** ✦ . C1
King Edward VI	Well St B2
School A1	Westgarth Gdns . . C1
King's Rd C1/B2	Westgate St C2
	Whiting St C2
	York Rd B1
	York Terr B1

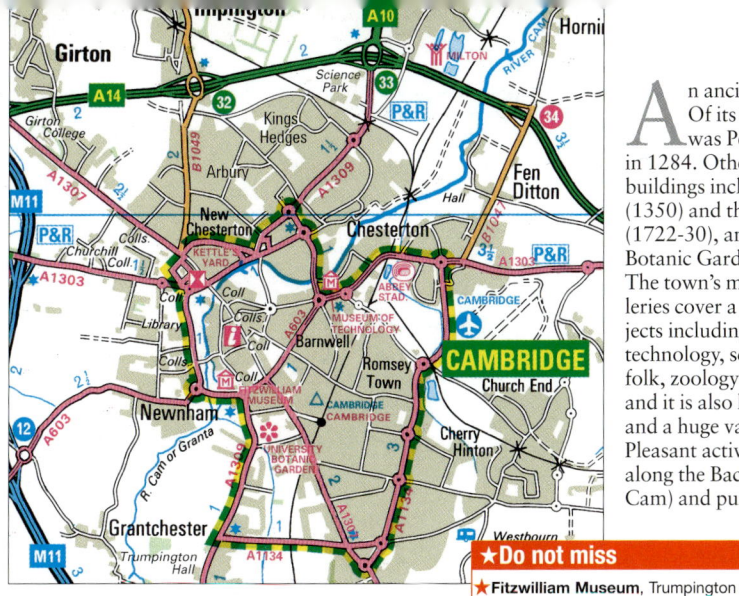

Cambridge

An ancient university town. Of its 31 colleges, the first was Peterhouse, founded in 1284. Other fine university buildings include the Old Schools (1350) and the Senate House (1722-30), and the University Botanic Garden is worth a visit. The town's museums and art galleries cover a wide range of subjects including polar exploration, technology, scientific instruments, folk, zoology and archaeology and it is also home to fine markets and a huge variety of bookshops. Pleasant activities include walking along the Backs (the banks of the Cam) and punting along the river, and there are many cultural activities. Close by are Milton and Wandlebury country parks and the National Trust's Anglesey Abbey.

▲King's College Chapel

★ Do not miss

- **Fitzwilliam Museum**, Trumpington Street – University art collection
- **Kettle's Yard**, Castle Street – gallery of 20th-century and contemporary art
- **King's College Chapel and Choir**, King's Parade

Tourist Information Centre, The Old Library, Wheeler Street, Cambridge CB2 3QB
Tel 0906 5862526 (calls charged at 60p per minute)

BBC Radio Cambridgeshire 96.0 FM and 1026 AM
Q103 103.0 FM • Star 107.9 FM • Vibe FM 105.6 FM

www.cambridge.gov.uk

Cambridge

Abbey Rd A3	King St A2	Tennis Court Rd . . . B2
ADC A2	King's (Coll) B1	The Backs B1
Anglia Polytechnic University B3	King's College Chapel B1	The Fen Causeway C1
Archaeology & Anthropology B2	King's Parade B1	Thompson's La A1
Art Gallery A1	Lensfield Rd C2	Trinity (Coll) B1
Arts Theatre B1	Lion Yard Centre . . . B2	Trinity Hall (Coll) . . . B1
Auckland Rd A3	Little St Mary's La . . B1	Trinity St B1
Bateman St C1	Lyndewod Rd C3	Trumpington Rd . . . C2
B.B.C. C3	Magdalene (Coll) . . . A1	Trumpington St C2
Bene't St B1	Magdalene St A1	Union Rd C2
Bradmore St C3	Maid's Causeway . . A3	Univ Botanic Gardens C2
Bridge St A1	Malcolm St A2	Victoria Ave A2
Broad St B1	Market Hill B1	Victoria St B2
Brookside C2	Market St B1	Warkworth St B3
Brunswick Terr A3	Mathematical Br . . . B1	Warkworth Terr B3
Burleigh St B3	Mawson Rd C3	Wesley Hse (Coll) . . A2
Bus Station B2	Midsummer Com . . . A3	West Rd B1
Butt Green A2	Mill La B1	Westcott Hse (Coll) A2
Cambridge Contemporary Art Gall . . B1	Mill Rd B3	Westminster (Coll) A1
Castle Mound A1	Napier St A3	Whipple B2
Castle St A1	New Square A2	Willis Rd B3
Chesterton La A1	Newmarket Rd A3	Willow Walk A2
Christ's (Coll) B2	Newnham Rd C1	Zoology B2
Christ's Pieces B2	Norfolk St B3	
City Rd B3	Northampton St . . . A1	
Clare (Coll) B1	Norwich St C2	
Clarendon St B2	Orchard St B2	
Coe Fen C2	Panton St C2	
Coronation St C3	Paradise Nature Reserve C1	
Corpus Christi (Coll) B2	Paradise St B3	
Council Offices C3	Park Parade A1	
Cross St C3	Park St A2	
Crusoe Bridge C1	Park Terr B2	
Darwin (Coll) C1	Parker St B2	
Devonshire Rd C3	Parker's Piece B2	
Downing (Coll) B2	Parkside B3	
Downing St B2	Parkside Swimming Pool B3	
Earl St B2	Parsonage St A3	
East Rd B3	Pembroke (Coll) . . . B2	
Eden St B3	Pembroke St B1	
Elizabeth Way A3	Perowne St B3	
Elm St B2	Peterhouse (Coll) . . C1	
Emery St B3	Petty Cury B2	
Emmanuel (Coll) . . . B2	Police Station B3	
Emmanuel Rd B2	Post Office A1/A3/B2/B3/C1/C2/C3	
Emmanuel St B2	Queens' (Coll) B1	
Fair St A3	Queen's La B1	
Fenners (Cambridge Univ C.C.) C3	Queen's Rd B1	
Fire Station B3	Regent St B2	
Fitzroy St B3	Regent Terr B2	
Fitzwilliam Mus C1	Ridley Hall (Coll) . . . C1	
Fitzwilliam St C1	Riverside A3	
Folk Mus A1	Round Church, The A1	
Glisson Rd C3	Russell St C2	
Gonville & Caius (Coll) B1	St Andrew's St B2	
Gonville Place B3	St Benet's B1	
Grafton Centre A3	St Catharine's (Coll) B1	
Gresham Rd C3	St Eligius St C2	
Green St B1	St John's (Coll) A1	
Guest Rd B3	St Mary's B1	
Guildhall B2	St Paul's Rd C3	
Harvey Rd C3	Saxon St C2	
Hills Rd C3	Scott Polar Research Inst & Mus C2	
Hobson St B2	Sedgwick Mus B2	
Hughes Hall (Coll) . . B3	Sheep's Green C1	
Information Ctr B2	Shelly Row A1	
James St A3	Shire Hall A1	
Jesus (Coll) A2	Sidgwick Ave C1	
Jesus Green A2	Sidney St B2	
Jesus La A2	Sidney Sussex (Coll) B2	
Jesus Terr B3	Silver St B1	
John St B3	Station Rd C3	
Kelsey Kerridge Sports Hall B3	Tenison Ave C3	
	Tenison Rd C3	

51

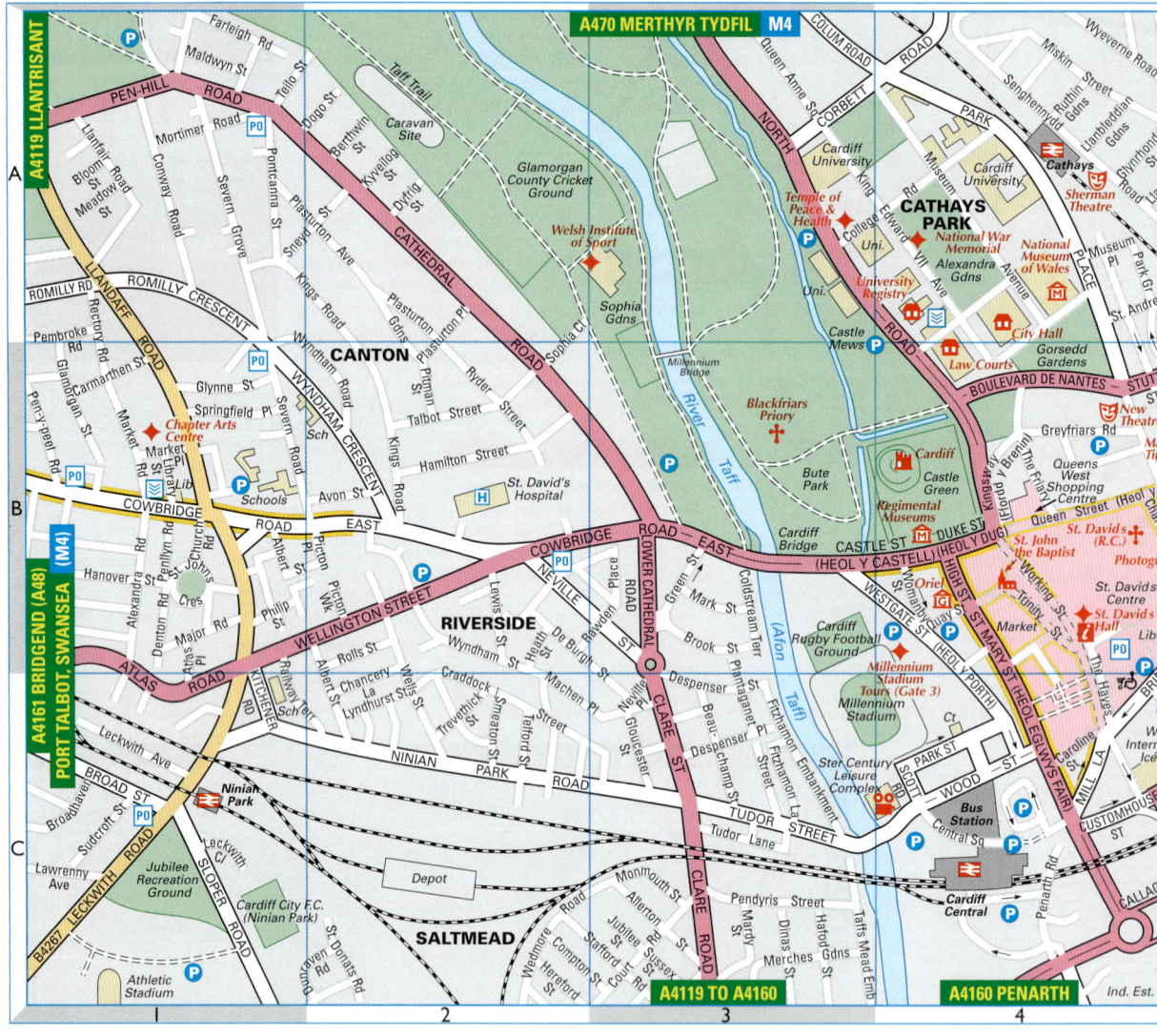

Cardiff/Caerdydd

Name	Grid
Adam St	B5
Adamsdown La	B6
Albert St	B1
Alexandra Gdns	A4
Alexandra Rd	B1
Allerton St	C3
Arran St	A5
Athletic Stadium	C1
Atlas Pl	B1
Atlas Rd	C1
Augusta St	B6
Avon St	B2
Beauchamp St	C3
Bedford St	A5
Berthwin St	A2
Blackfriars Priory ✝	B3
Bloom St	A1
Boulevard De Nantes	B4
Bridge St	B5
Broad St	C1
Broadhaven	C1
Broadway	A6
Brook St	B3
Bus Station	C4
Bute East Dock	C6
Bute Park	B3
Bute St	C4
Bute Terr	C5
Byron St	A5
Callaghan Sq	C4/C5
Capitol Shopping Ctr, The	B5
Caravan Site	A2
Cardiff Bridge	B3
Cardiff Castle ✠	B4
Cardiff Central Station	C4
Cardiff Centre Trading Estate	C5
Cardiff City F.C. (Ninian Park)	C1
Cardiff International Arena ◆	C5
Cardiff Rugby Football Ground	B3
Cardiff Univ	A3/A4/B5
Carmarthen St	B1
Caroline St	C4
Castle Green	C4
Castle Mews	A3
Castle St (Heol y Castell)	B3
Cathays ≷	A4
Cathedral Rd	A3
Celerity Drive	C5
Central Link	C6
Central Sq	C4
Chancery La	C3
Chapter Arts Ctr ◆	B1
Charles St	B5
Church Rd	B1
Churchill Way	B5
City Hall ✠	A4
City Rd	A5
Clare Rd	C3
Clare St	C3
Clifton St	A6
Coburn St	A5
Coldstream Terr	B3
College of Cardiff	A3
College Rd	A3
Colum Rd	A3
Comet St	B6
Compton St	A6
Constellation St	B6
Conway Rd	A1
Copper St	B3
Corbett Rd	B4
Court	C4
Court Rd	C1
Cowbridge Rd East	B1/B2
Craddock St	C2
Craiglee Drive	C6
Cranbrook St	A5
Crofts St	A6
Cumnock Pl	B6
Customhouse St	C4
Cyfartha St	A5
Davis St	B5
De Burgh St	B2
Denton Rd	B1
Despenser Pl	C3
Despenser St	C3
Dinas St	C3
Dogo St	A2
Duke St (Heol y Dug)	B4
Dumfries Pl	B5
Dunraven St	C1
Dyfrig St	A2
East Grove	A5
East Moors Rd	C6
East Tyndall St	C6
Eclipse St	B6
Ellen St	C5
Elm St	A6
Farleigh Rd	A1
Fire Station	B5
Fitzalan Pl	B5
Fitzhamon Emb	C3
Fitzhamon La	C3
Garesfield St	B6
Glamorgan County Cricket Ground	A2
Glamorgan St	B1
Glossop Rd	B6
Gloucester St	C3
Glynne St	B1
Glynrhondda St	A4
Gold St	A6
Gordon Rd	A5
Gorsedd Gdns	B4
Green St	B3
Greyfriars Rd	B4
HM Prison	B5
Hafod St	C3
Hamilton St	B2
Hanover St	B1
Heath St	A2
Herbert St	C5
Hereford St	C2
High St	B4
Howard Pl	B6
Industrial Estate	C5
Information Ctr ℹ	B4
John St	C5
Jubilee Rec Gnd	C1
Jubilee St	C3
King Edward VII Ave	A3
Kings Rd	A1/B2
Kingsway (Ffordd y Brenin)	B4
Kitchener Rd	C1
Knox Rd	B5
Kyveilog St	A2
Law Courts	B4
Lawrenny Ave	C1
Lead St	B6
Leckwith Ave	C1
Leckwith Close	C1
Leckwith Rd	C1
Lewis St	B2
Library	B1/B5
Library St	B1
Lily St	A6
Llanbleddian Gdns	A4
Llandaff Rd	B1
Llanfair Rd	A1
Llantwit St	A4
Lloyd George Ave	C5
Longcross St	B6
Lower Cathedral Rd	B3
Lowther Rd	A5
Lyndhurst St	C2
Machen Pl	C2
Magistrates Court	B5
Major St	B1
Maldwyn St	A1
Mansion House	A5
Mardy St	C3
Mark St	B3
Market	B4
Market Pl	B1
Market St	B1
Martin Tinney 🏛	B5
Mary Ann St	C5
Meadow St	A1
Merches Gdns	C3
Metal St	B6
Meteor St	B6
Mill La	C5
Millennium Bridge	B3
Millennium Stadium	C3
Millennium Stadium Tours (Gate 3) ◆	B4
Milton St	A5
Miskin St	A4
Moira Pl	B6
Moira St	B6
Moira Terr	B6
Monmouth St	C3
Mortimer Rd	A1
Museum Ave	A4
Museum Pl	A4
National Museum of Wales 🏛	A4
National Tennis Centre	C6
National War Memorial ✠	A4
Neville Pl	C3
Neville St	B2
New Theatre ✠	B4
Newport Rd	A6/B5
Newport Rd La	B5
Ninian Park ≷	C1
Ninian Park Rd	C2
North Rd	A3
Northcote La	A5
Northcote St	A5
North Luton Pl	B6
Oakfield St	A6
Ocean Way	C6
Orbit St	A6
Oriel 🏛	B4
Oxford La	A6
Oxford St	A6
Park Grove	A4
Park Pl	A4
Park St	C4
Partridge La	A6
Partridge Rd	A6
Pembroke Rd	A1
Pen-Hill Rd	A1
Pen-y-Peel Rd	B1
Penarth Rd	C4
Pendyris St	C3
Penllyn Rd	B1
Philip St	B1
Photographic Library ✠	B5
Picton Pl	B2
Picton Walk	B2
Piercefield Pl	A6
Pitman St	C2
Plat St	B6
Plantaganet St	C3
Plasnewydd Rd	A5
Plasturton Ave	A1
Plasturton Gdns	A2
Plasturton Pl	A2
Police Station	A4/A6/B1
Pontcanna St	A1
Post Office	A1/A5/A6/B1/B2/B4/B6/C1
Princes St	A6
Quay St	B4
Queen Anne Sq	A3
Queen St (Heol y Frenhines)	B4
Queen St ≷	B5
Queens West Shopping Ctr	B4
Railway Terr	C1
Rawden Pl	B3
Rectory Rd	A1
Regimental Museums	B4
Rhymney St	A5
Richmond Rd	A5
Rolls St	B2
Romilly Cr	A1
Romilly Rd	A1
Rose St	A4
Royal Infirmary H	A6
Russell St	A5
Ruthin Gdns	A4
Ryder St	B2
St Andrews Pl	A4
St David's ✝	B4
St David's Centre	B4
St David's Hall	B4
St David's Hospital H	B2
St Donats Rd	C2
St John The Baptist ✝	B4
St John's Cr	B1
St Mary St (Heol Eglwys Fair)	B4
St Peter's St	A5
Salisbury Rd	A5
Sandon St	B5
Sanquhar St	B6
Schooner Way	C5
Scott Rd	C4
Senghennydd Rd	A4
Severn Green	A1
Severn Rd	A1
Sherman Theatre ✠	A4
Silver St	A6
Sloper Rd	C1
Smeaton St	C2
Sneyd St	A1
Sophia Cl	B2
Sophia Gdns	A3
South Luton Pl	B6
Southey St	A6
Springfield Pl	B1
Stafford Rd	C3
Star St	B6
Station Terr	B5
Stuttgarter Strasse	B4
Sudcroft St	C1
Sun St	B6
Sussex St	C3
System St	B6
Taffs Mead Embankment	C3
Taff Trail	A2
Talbot St	B2
Talworth St	A5
Teal St	A6
Teilo St	A1
Telford St	C1
Temple of Peace & Health ◆	A3
The Friary	B4
The Hayes	B4
The Parade	A5
The Walk	A5
Treharris St	A5
Trevethick St	C1
Trinity St	B4
Tudor La	C3
Tudor St	C3
Tyndall St	C5
UGC Leisure Complex ✠	C5
University Registry	A4
Wales Int. Ice Rink	C4
Wedmore Rd	C2
Wellington St	B2
Wells St	C2
Welsh Institute of Sport ◆	A3
West Green	A5
Westgate St (Heol y Porth)	B4
Windsor Pl	B5
Windsor Rd	C3
Womanby St	B4
Wood St	C4
Wordsworth Ave	A6
Working St	B4
Wyeverne Rd	A4
Wyndham Cr	B1
Wyndham Pl	B2
Wyndham St	B2

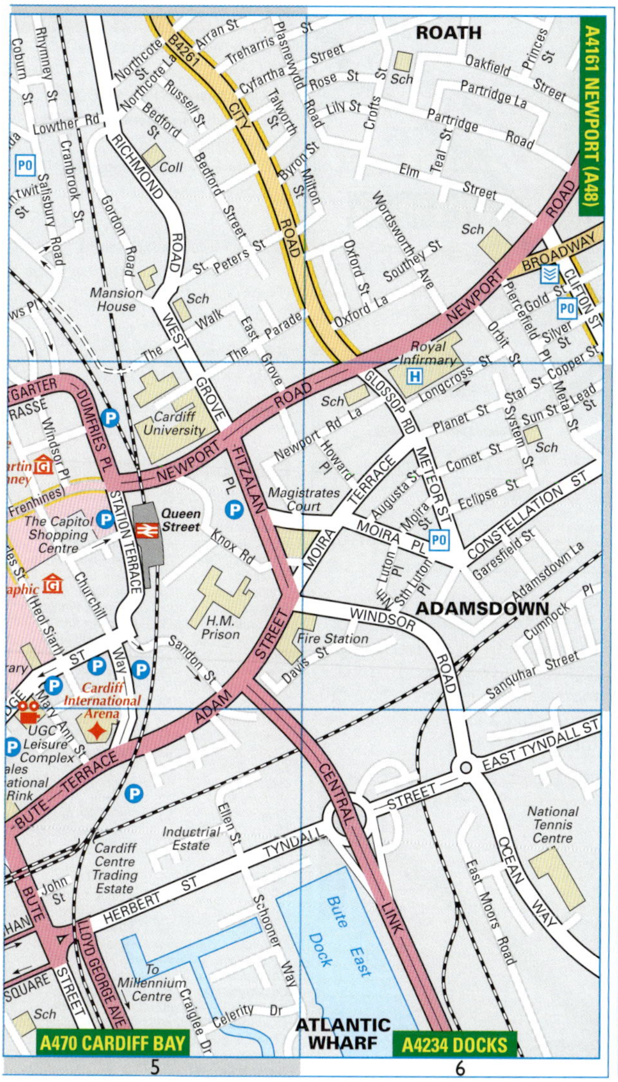

Cardiff

The Welsh capital since 1955, on the site of a fort established by the Romans in AD75, and the subject of large-scale regeneration over the past decade. Highlights include the Castle, with remains from Roman, Norman and medieval buildings and stunning 19th-century interiors and three military museums, the hi-tech Millennium Stadium (Europe's largest covered stadium), and the Techniquest science-discovery centre. The revitalised bay and docklands can be viewed by boat and road-train trips, at the Cardiff Bay Barrage, at the Tube (Cardiff Bay Visitor Centre), and at the Butetown History and Arts Centre. Lively, cosmopolitan and a designated Centre of Culture, the city has a thriving contemporary art scene (including the Wales Millennium Centre), good shops and department stores, and an array of glamorous restaurants and hotels.

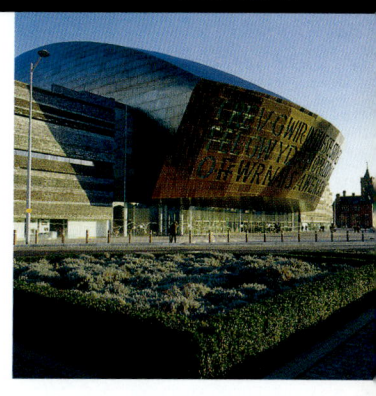

▲The Wales Millennium Centre

Cardiff Gateway Visitor Centre,
The Old Library, The Hayes, Cardiff
CF10 1AH Tel 029 2022 7281

BBC Radio Wales 103.9 FM
Real Radio Wales 105.4 FM
Red Dragon FM 103.2 FM

www.visitcardiff.info

★ Do not miss
- ★ **Cardiff Castle**, Castle Street
- ★ **Museum of Welsh Life**, St Fagans
- ★ **National Museum and Gallery**, Cathays Park

▼The Millennium Stadium

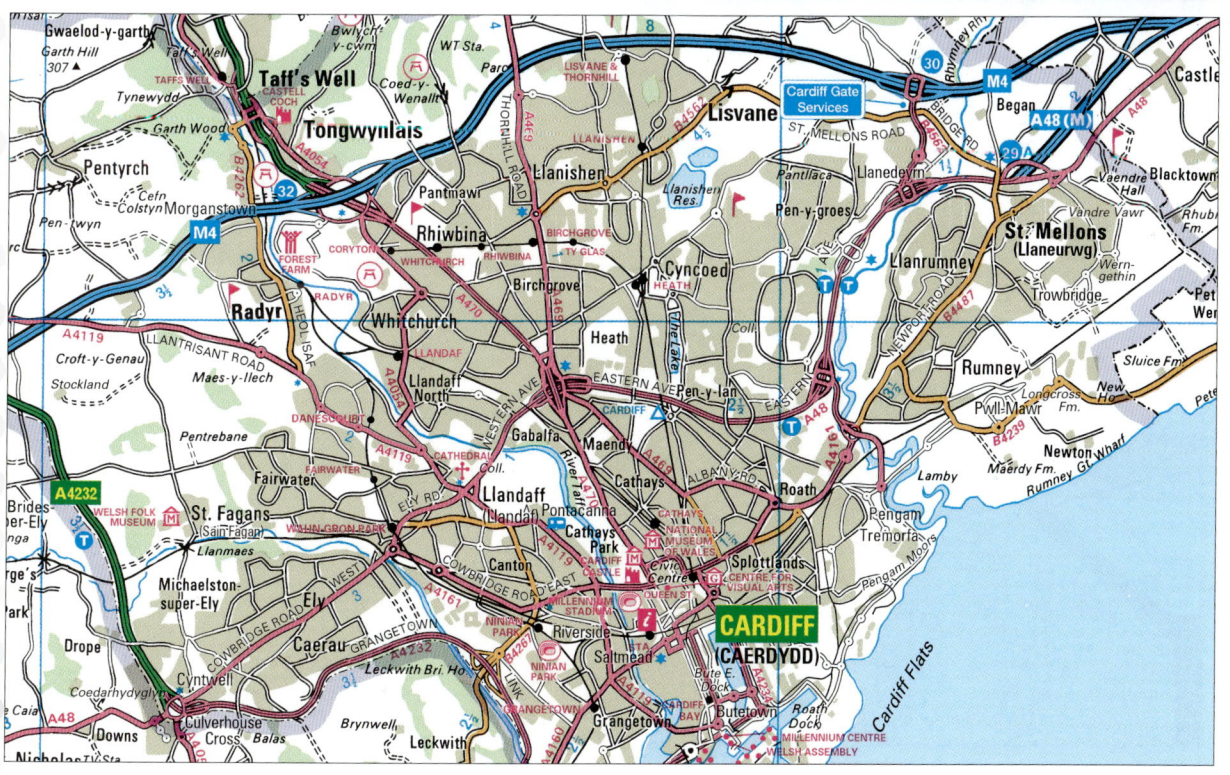

Canterbury

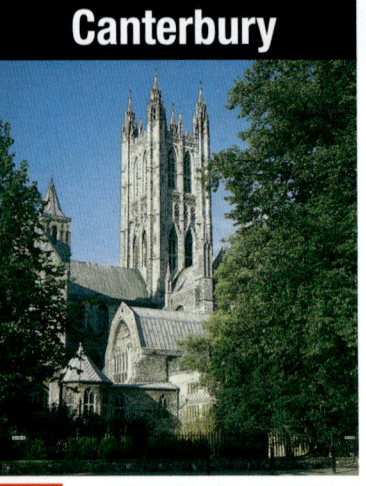

▲ The Cathedral from King's School

The Cathedral, St Martin's Church and St Augustine's Abbey form a UNESCO world heritage site. Places of interest include the Eastbridge Hospital of St Thomas the Martyr, founded in 1190; St Augustine's Abbey, founded in 598; the Norman Keep – also known as Canterbury Castle, West Gate Towers. Other attractions in the town centre include Planet Lazer on St George's Street, the Odeon Cinema and the Marlowe Theatre. Canterbury has a diverse selection of shops from the Marlowe arcade through to St Margaret's Street and Burgate, as well as a twice weekly street market, many of the city's restaurants, pubs and bars can also be found in this area.

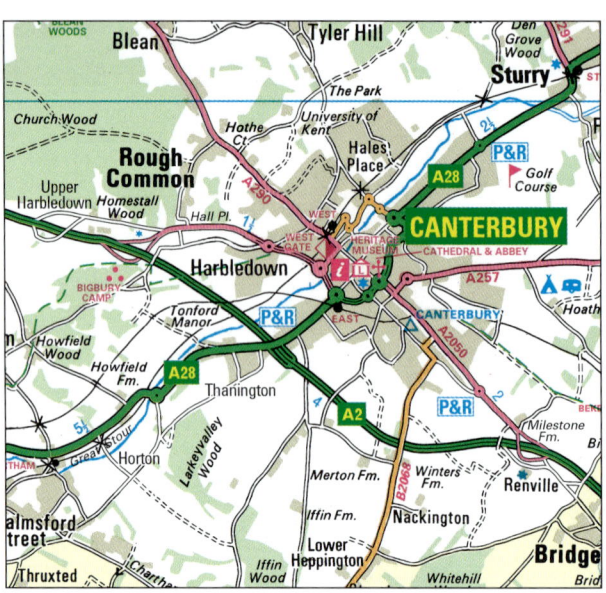

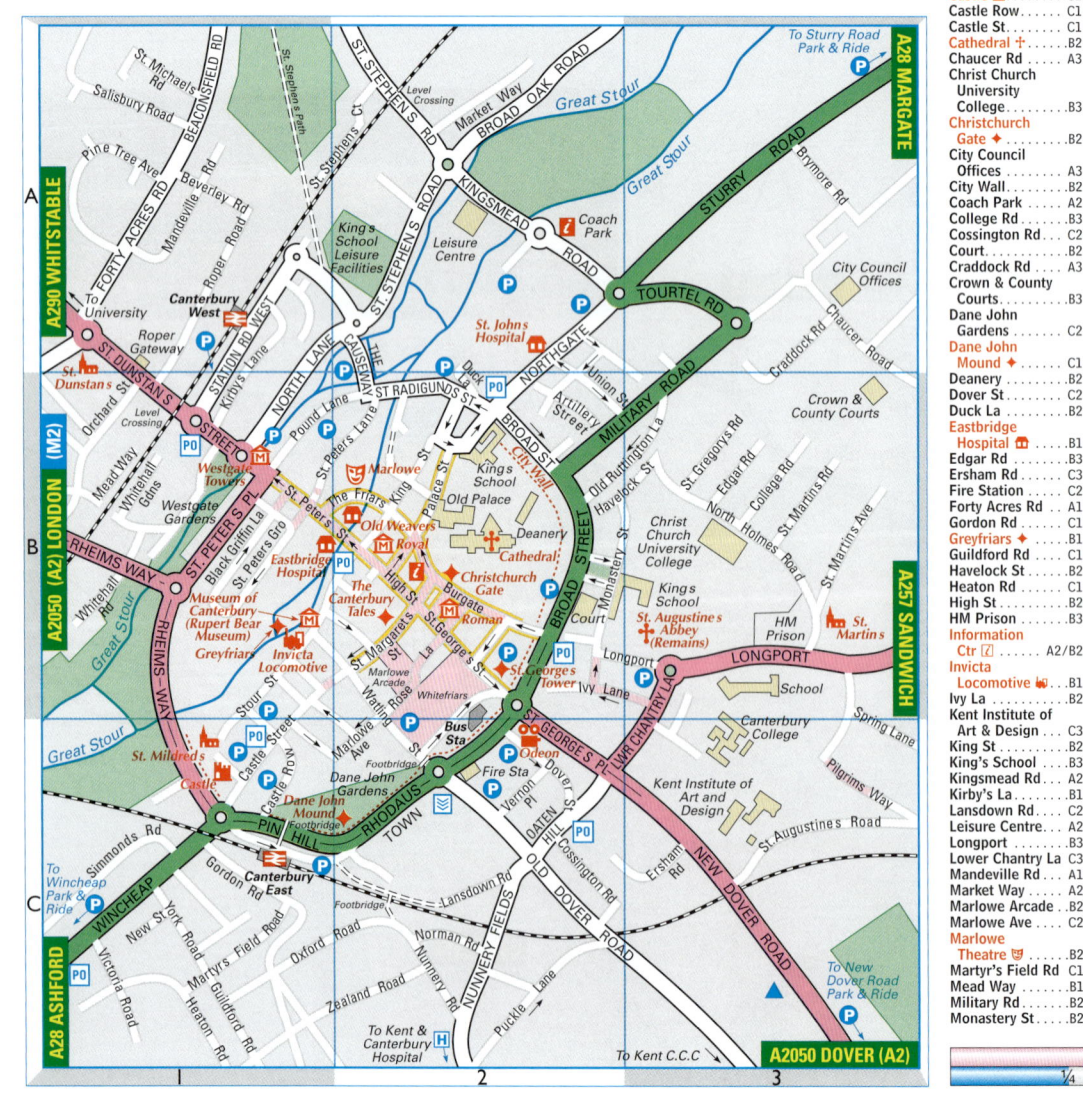

★ Do not miss
- ★ **Canterbury Cathedral**, The Precincts
- ★ **Royal Museum and Art Gallery with Buffs Regimental Museum**, High Street
- ★ **Canterbury Roman Museum**, Butchery Lane

Tourist Information Centre
12/13 Sun Street, The Buttermarket, Canterbury CT1 2HX
Tel 01227 378100

BBC Radio Kent 97.6 FM
KM-fm 106.0 FM

www.canterbury.co.uk

Canterbury

Artillery St B2	Mus of Canterbury (Rupert Bear Museum) B1
Beaconsfield Rd A1	New Dover Rd C3
Beverley Rd A1	New St C1
Black Griffin La B1	Norman Rd C2
Broad Oak Rd A2	North Holmes Rd B3
Broad St B2	North La B1
Brymore Rd A3	Northgate A2
Burgate B2	Nunnery Fields C2
Bus Station C2	Nunnery Rd C2
Canterbury Coll C3	Oaten Hill C2
Canterbury East C1	Odeon Cinema B2
Canterbury Tales, The ◆ B2	Old Dover Rd C3
Canterbury West A1	Old Palace B2
Castle C1	Old Ruttington La B2
Castle Row C1	Old Weavers B2
Castle St C1	Orchard St B1
Cathedral † B2	Oxford Rd C1
Chaucer Rd A3	Palace St B2
Christ Church University College B3	Pilgrims Way C3
Christchurch Gate ◆ B2	Pin Hill C1
City Council Offices A3	Pine Tree Ave A1
City Wall B2	Police Station C2
Coach Park A2	Post Office B1/B2/C1/C2
College Rd B3	Pound La B1
Cossington Rd C2	Puckle La C2
Court B2	Rheims Way B1
Craddock Rd A3	Rhodaus Town C2
Crown & County Courts B3	Roman Mus B2
Dane John Gardens C2	Roper Gateway A1
Dane John Mound ◆ C1	Roper Rd A1
Deanery B2	Rose La B2
Dover St C2	Royal Mus B2
Duck La B2	St Augustine's Abbey (Remains) † B3
Eastbridge Hospital B1	St Augustine's Rd C3
Edgar Rd B3	St Dunstan's A1
Ersham Rd C3	St Dunstan's St A1
Fire Station C2	St George's Pl C2
Forty Acres Rd A1	St George's St B2
Gordon Rd C1	St George's Tower ◆ B2
Greyfriars ◆ B1	St Gregory's Rd B3
Guildford Rd C1	St John's Hospital A2
Havelock St B2	St Margaret's St B2
Heaton Rd C1	St Martin's B3
High St B2	St Martin's Ave B3
HM Prison B3	St Martin's Rd B3
Information Ctr ℹ A2/B2	St Michael's Rd C1
Invicta Locomotive B1	St Mildred's C1
Ivy La B2	St Peter's Gr B1
Kent Institute of Art & Design C3	St Peter's La B2
King St B2	St Peter's Pl B1
King's School B3	St Peter's St B1
Kingsmead Rd A2	St Radigunds St B2
Kirby's La B1	St Stephen's Ct A1
Lansdown Rd C2	St Stephen's Path A1
Leisure Centre A2	St Stephen's Rd A1
Longport B3	Salisbury Rd A1
Lower Chantry La C3	Simmonds Rd C1
Mandeville Rd A1	Spring La C3
Market Way A2	Station Rd West B1
Marlowe Arcade B2	Stour St B1
Marlowe Ave C2	Sturry Rd A3
Marlowe Theatre B2	The Causeway A2
Martyr's Field Rd C1	The Friars B2
Mead Way B1	Tourtel Rd A3
Military Rd B2	Union St B2
Monastery St B2	Vernon Pl C2
	Victoria Rd C1
	Watling St B2
	Westgate Towers B1
	Westgate Gdns B1
	Whitefriars B2
	Whitehall Gdns B1
	Whitehall Rd B1
	Wincheap C1
	York Rd C1
	Zealand Rd C1

¼ mile
½ km

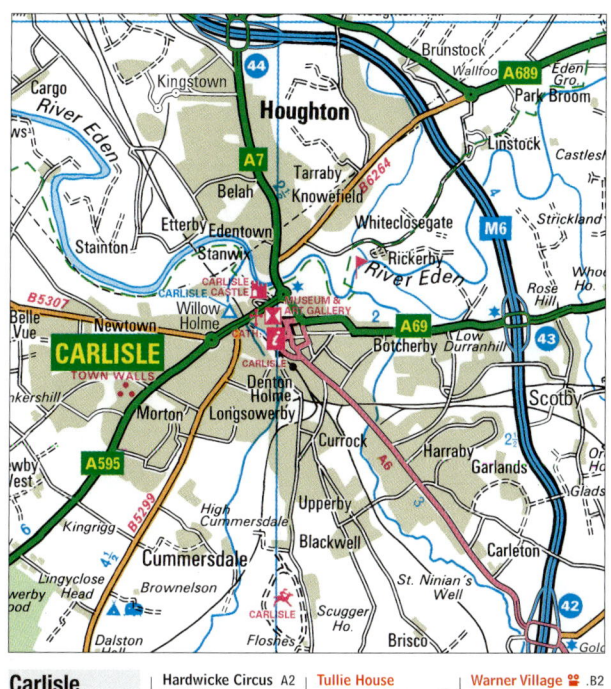

Carlisle

The city is surrounded by much of historical interest with a 900-year-old castle, a cathedral dating back to 1122 and the nearby Birdoswald Roman Fort on Hadrian's Wall. Tullie House Museum and Art Gallery portrays Carlisle's history as a border city as well as displaying traditional and modern artists and the Guildhall Museum, situated in a half-timbered late 14th-century building, features work from the various guildsmen of Carlisle dating to 18th century. A major shopping destination for Cumbria and south west Scotland it includes The Lanes and The Market Hall centres. There is a good range of sports and leisure facilities from golf and birdwatching to watersports and racing, and there are many bars, and restaurants of all cuisines.

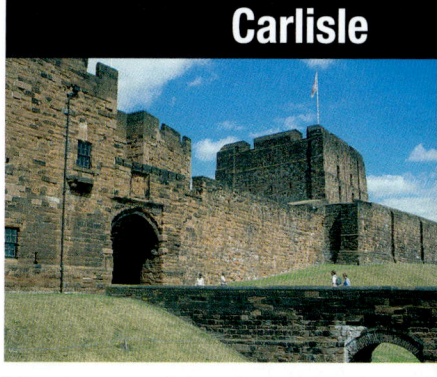

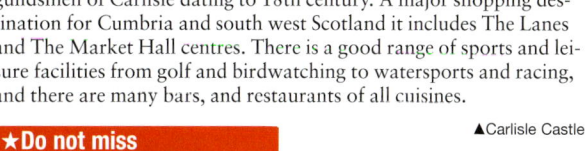

▲ Carlisle Castle

★ Do not miss
- ★ Tullie House Museum and Art Gallery, Castle Street
- ★ Carlisle Cathedral, Castle Street
- ★ Carlisle Castle, Castle Way

i Carlisle Visitor Centre, Old Town Hall, Greenmarket, Carlisle CA3 8JE
Tel 01228 625600

BBC Radio Cumbria 95.6, 96.1, 104.1 FM • CFM Radio 96.4 FM

www.carlisle.gov.uk

Carlisle

Abbey St	A1
Aglionby St	B3
Albion St	C3
Alexander St	C3
AMF Bowl ✦	C2
Annetwell St	A1
Bank St	B2
Bitts Park	A1
Blackfriars St	B2
Blencome St	C1
Blunt St	C1
Botchergate	B2
Boustead's Grassing	C2
Bowman St	B3
Broad St	B3
Bridge St	A1
Brook St	C3
Brunswick St	B2
Bus Station	B2
Caldew Bridge	A1
Caldew St	C1
Carlisle (Citadel) Station	B2
Castle ♜	A1
Castle St	A1
Castle Way	A1
Cathedral ✝	A1
Cecil St	B2
Chapel St	A2
Charles St	B3
Charlotte St	B1
Chatsworth Square	A2
Chiswick St	B2
Citadel, The	B2
City Walls	A1
Civic Centre	A2
Clifton St	C1
Close St	B3
Collingwood St	C1
Colville St	C1
Colville Terr	C1
Court	B2
Court St	B2
Crosby St	B2
Crown St	C2
Currock Rd	C2
Dacre Rd	A1
Dale St	C1
Denton St	C1
Devonshire Walk	A1
Duke's Rd	A2
East Dale St	C1
East Norfolk St	C1
Eden Bridge	A1
Edward St	B3
Elm St	B1
English St	B2
Fire Station	A2
Fisher St	A1
Flower St	C3
Freer St	C1
Fusehill St	B3
Georgian Way	A1
Gloucester Rd	C3
Golf Course	A1
Graham St	C1
Grey St	B3
Guildhall Museum	A2
Halfey's La	B3
Hardwicke Circus	A2
Hart St	B3
Hewson St	C2
Howard Pl	A3
Howe St	B3
Information Ctr *i*	A2
James St	B2
Junction St	B1
King St	B2
Lancaster St	C2
Lanes Shopping Centre	A2/B2
Laserquest ✦	B2
Library	A2/B1
Lime St	B1
Lindisfarne St	C3
Linton St	B3
Lismore Pl	A3
Lismore St	B3
London Rd	C3
Lonsdale ✦	B2
Lonsdale Rd	B2
Lord St	C3
Lorne Cres	B1
Lorne St	B1
Lowther St	B2
Market Hall	A2
Mary St	B2
Memorial Bridge	A3
Metcalfe St	C1
Milbourne St	B1
Myddleton St	B3
Nelson St	C1
Norfolk St	C1
Old Town Hall	A2
Oswald St	C3
Peter St	A2
Petteril St	B3
Police Station ✦	B2
Portland Pl	B2
Portland Sq	B2
Post Office	A2/B2/B3/C1/C3
Princess St	C3
Pugin St	B1
Red Bank Terr	C2
Regent St	C3
Richardson St	C1
Rickerby Park	A3
Rickergate	A2
River St	B3
Rome St	C2
Rydal St	B3
St Cuthbert's	B2
St Cuthbert's La	B2
St James' Park	B1
St James' Rd	C1
St Nicholas St	C3
Sands Centre	A2
Scotch St	A2
Shaddongate	B1
Sheffield St	B1
South Henry St	B3
South John St	C2
South St	B3
Spencer St	B2
Sports Centre	A2
Strand Rd	A2
Swimming Baths	B2
Sybil St	B3
Tait St	B2
Thomas St	B1
Thomson St	C3
Trafalgar St	C1
Tullie House Museum ✦	A1
Tyne St	C3
Viaduct Estate Rd	B1
Victoria Pl	A2/A3
Victoria Viaduct	B2
Warner Village ✦	B2
Warwick Rd	B3
Warwick Sq	B3
Water St	B2
West Walls	B1
Westmorland St	C1

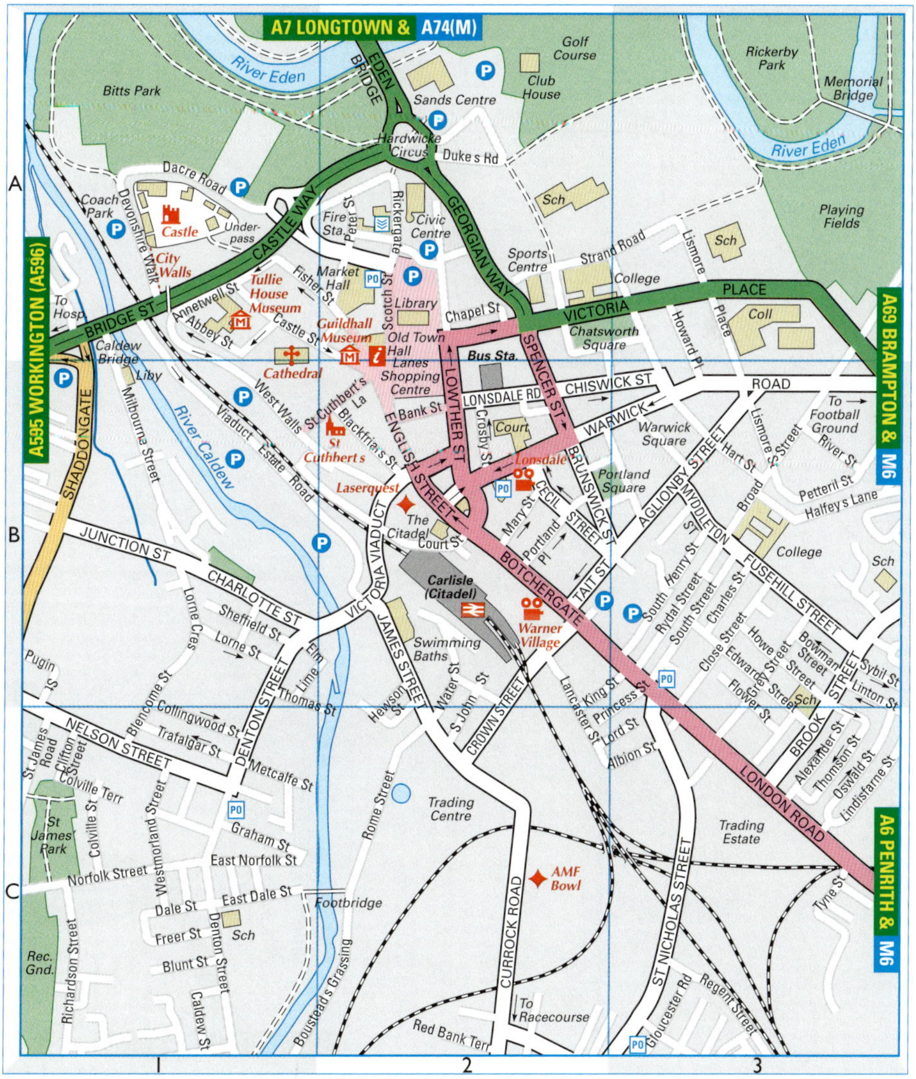

55

Chelmsford

The county town of Essex, Chelmsford has Roman origins and has been home to its main market and assizes since the 12th century. Chelmsford Museum has local and natural history displays, a domestic life and costume gallery and art collections. The small cathedral is one of the country's newest (1914), as well as one of the few to also be a parish church. The town's pedestrianised high street and two large malls make it a prime shopping venue containing both national chain stores and independent shops, while Moulsham Mill is now a crafts and business centre with a number of retail outlets. There are extensive green spaces and riverside walks in the centre, Galleywood Common nature reserve lies to the south and Danbury Country Park is within easy reach.

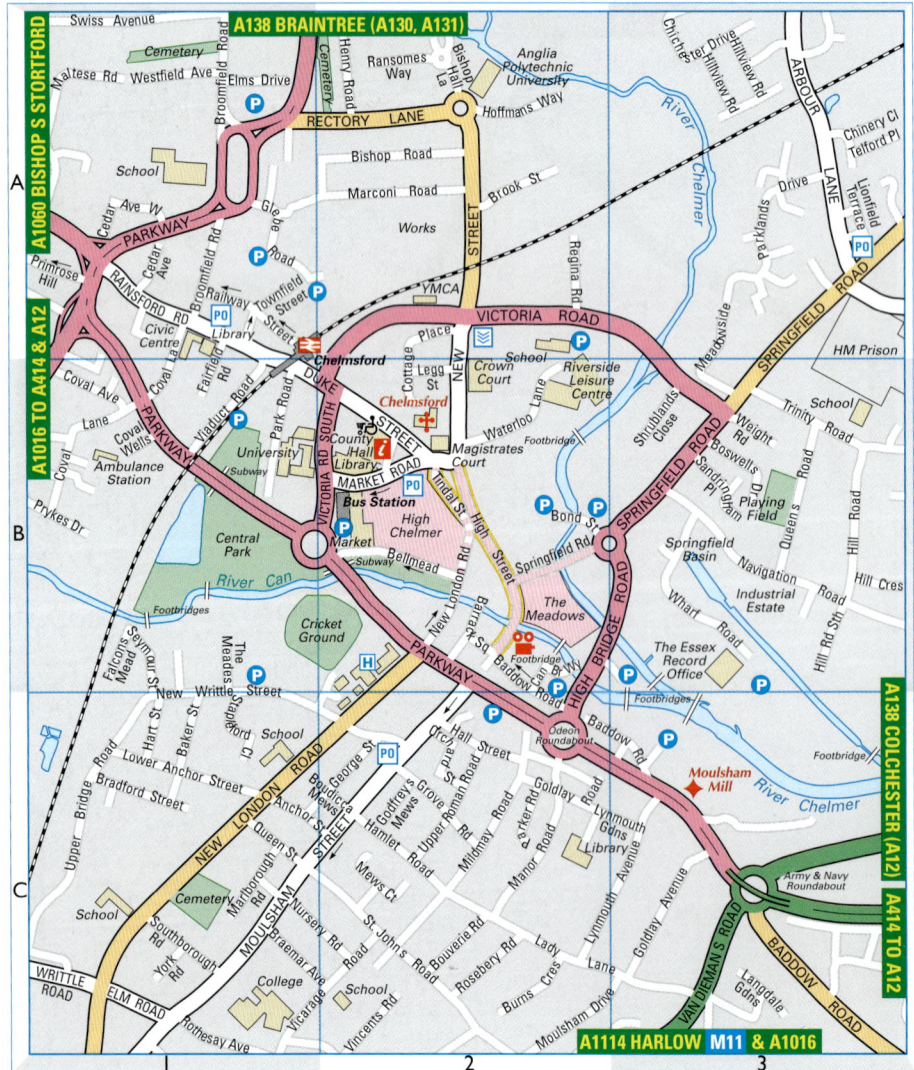

Chelmsford Tourist Information Centre, County Hall, Market Road, Chelmsford CM1 1GG, Tel 01245 283400

BBC **Essex** 103.5 FM
Classic Gold Breeze 1359 AM
Essex FM 96.3, 102.6 FM

www.chelmsfordbc.gov.uk

▲ Chelmsford Cathedral

★ Do not miss

★ **Essex Regiment Museum**, Oaklands Park, Moulsham Street
★ **Hylands House, Gardens and Parkland**, Writtle bypass
★ **Royal Horticultural Society Gardens**, Hyde Hall

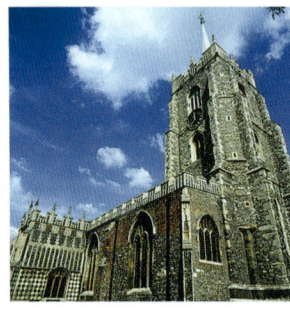

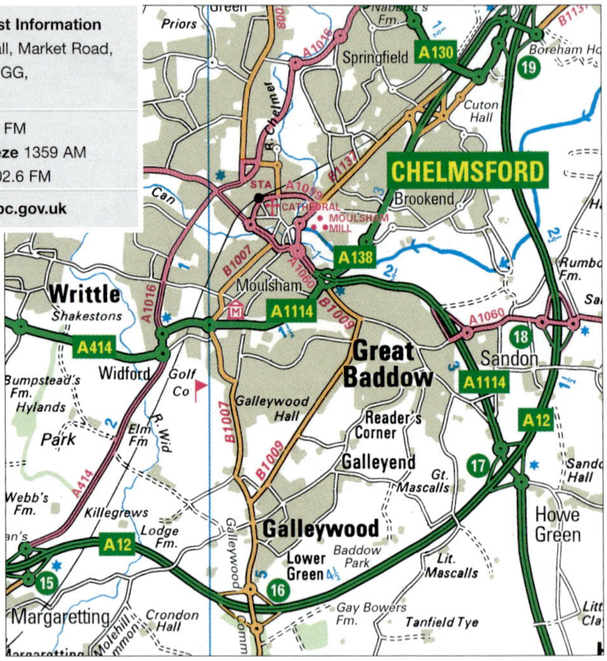

Chelmsford

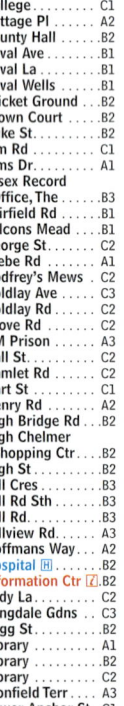

Ambulance Station B1	Anglia Polytechnic University A2	Barrack Sq B2	Boswells Dr B3
Anchor St C1	Arbour La A3	Bellmead B2	Boudicca Mews . . C2
	Baddow Rd . . B2/C3	Bishop Hall La . . A2	Bouverie Rd C2
	Baker St C1	Bishop Rd A2	Bradford St C1
		Bond St B2	Braemar Ave C1
Brook St A2	Market B2
Broomfield Rd . . A1	Market Rd B2
Burns Cres C2	Marlborough Rd . C1
Bus Station B2	Meadows Shopping Ctr, the B2
Can Bridge Way . B2	Meadowside A3
Cedar Ave A1	Mews Ct C2
Cedar Ave W A1	Mildmay Rd C1
Cemetery A1	Moulsham Dr C2
Cemetery A2	Moulsham Mill ✦ . C3
Cemetery B2	Moulsham Rd . C1/C2
Central Park B1	Navigation Rd . . . B3
Chelmsford † . . . B2	New London Rd B2/C1
Chelmsford ⇌ . . A1	New St A2/B2
Chichester Dr . . . A3	New Writtle St . . C1
Chinery Cl A3	Nursery Rd C2
Cinema B2	Orchard St C1
Civic Centre A1	Park Rd B1
College C1	Parker Rd C2
Cottage Pl A2	Parklands Dr A3
County Hall B2	Parkway . . A1/B1/B2
Coval Ave B1	Police Station . . A2
Coval La B1	Post Office A1/A3/B2/C2
Coval Wells B1	Primrose Hill A1
Cricket Ground . . B2	Prykes Dr B1
Crown Court B2	Queen St C1
Duke St B2	Queen's Rd B3
Elm Rd C1	Railway St A1
Elms Dr A1	Rainsford Rd A1
Essex Record Office, The B3	Ransomes Way . . A1
Fairfield Rd B1	Rectory La A2
Falcons Mead . . . B1	Regina Rd A1
George St C2	Riverside Leisure Ctr B2
Glebe Rd A1	Rosebery Rd C2
Godfrey's Mews . C2	Rothesay Ave . . . C1
Goldlay Ave C3	St John's Rd C2
Goldlay Rd C3	Sandringham Pl . . B3
Grove Rd C2	Seymour Rd B1
HM Prison A3	Shrublands Cl . . . B3
Hall St B2	Southborough Rd . C1
Hamlet Rd C2	Springfield Basin . B3
Hart St C1	Springfield Rd A3/B2/B3
Henry Rd A2	Stapleford Cl C1
High Bridge Rd . . B2	Swiss Ave A1
High Chelmer Shopping Ctr . . . B2	Telford Pl A3
High St B2	The Meades B1
Hill Cres B3	Tindal St B2
Hill Rd Sth B3	Townfield St A1
Hill Rd B3	Trinity Rd B3
Hillview Rd A3	University A2
Hoffmans Way . . A2	Upper Bridge Rd . C1
Hospital B2	Upper Roman Rd . C2
Information Ctr . B2	Van Dieman's Rd . C3
Lady La C1	Viaduct Rd B1
Langdale Gdns . . C3	Vicarage Rd C1
Legg St B2	Victoria Rd B2
Library A1	Victoria Rd South B2
Library B2	Vincents Rd C1
Library C2	Waterloo La B2
Lionfield Terr . . . A1	Weight Rd B3
Lower Anchor St . C1	Westfield Ave . . . A1
Lynmouth Ave . . C2	Wharf Rd B3
Lynmouth Gdns . C2	Writtle Rd C1
Magistrates Court B2	YMCA A2
Maltese Rd A1	York Rd C1
Manor Rd C2	
Marconi Rd A2	

¼ mile
½ km

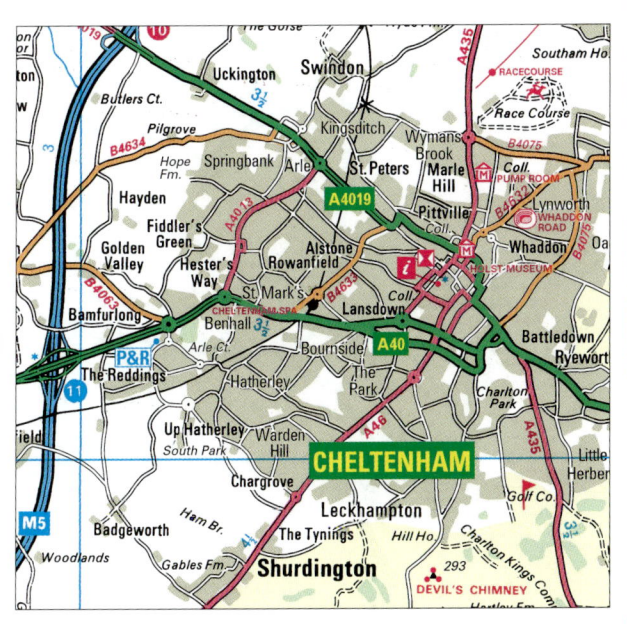

Cheltenham

An elegant town where medicinal waters were discovered in 1716, drawing King George III in 1788. A fashionable spa until 1840, attracting the likes of Byron, Jane Austen and Dickens, characterised by its wealth of Regency architecture; much of the centre is a Conservation Area. Notable buildings include the neo-Gothic Victorian Cheltenham College and Cheltenham Ladies' College, and the Holst Birthplace Museum. Additional attractions are the town's many parks and gardens, including the Promenade and Long Gardens, its upmarket shops, the nearby annual Badminton Horse Trials, and its proximity to the scenic Cotswolds. Add final sentence: Nearby attractions include Sudely Castle and Chedworth Roman Villa.

▲ The Promenade

★ Do not miss
- ★ **Cheltenham Art Gallery and Museum**, Clarence Street
- ★ **Cheltenham Racecourse**, Prestbury Park
- ★ **Pump Room**, Pittville Park

Cheltenham Tourism, 77 the Promenade, Cheltenham GL50 1PJ Tel 01242 522878

BBC Radio Gloucestershire
104.7 FM • Classic Gold 774 AM
Severn Sound 102.4 FM
Star 107.5 FM

www.visitcheltenham.gov.uk

Cheltenham

Street	Grid
Albert Rd	A3
Albion St	B3
All Saints Rd	B3
Andover Rd	C1
Art Gallery & Museum	B2
Axiom Centre	B2
Bath Pde	B2
Bath Rd	C2
Bays Hill Rd	B1
Beechwood Shopping Ctr	B3
Bennington St	B2
Berkeley St	B3
Brunswick St South	A2
Bus Station	B2
Carlton St	B3
Cheltenham & Gloucester College	A2
Cheltenham College	C2
Cheltenham F.C.	A3
Cheltenham General (A&E)	C3
Christchurch Rd	B1
Clarence Rd	A2
Clarence Sq	A2
Clarence St	B2
Cleeveland St	A1
Coach Park	A2
College Rd	C2
Colletts Dr	A1
Corpus St	C3
Devonshire St	A2
Douro Rd	B1
Duke St	B3
Dunalley Pde	A2
Dunalley St	A2
Everyman	B2
Evesham Rd	A3
Fairview Rd	B3
Fairview St	B3
Folly La	A2
Gloucester Rd	A1
Grosvenor St	B3
Grove St	B3
Gustav Holst	A3
Hanover St	A2
Hatherley St	C1
Henrietta St	A2
Hewlett Rd	B3
High St	B2/B3
Hudson St	A2
Imperial Gdns	C2
Imperial La	B2
Imperial Sq	C2
Information Ctr	B2
Keynsham Rd	C3
King St	A1
Knapp Rd	B2
Ladies College	B1
Lansdown Cr	C1
Lansdown Rd	C1
Leighton Rd	B3
London Rd	C3
Lypiatt Rd	C1
Malvern Rd	B1
Manser St	A2
Market St	A1
Marle Hill Pde	A2
Marle Hill Rd	A2
Millbrook St	A1
Milsom St	A2
Montpellier Gdns	C2
Montpellier Gr	C2
Montpellier Pde	C2
Montpellier Spa Rd	C2
Montpellier St	C1
Montpellier Terr	C1
Montpellier Walk	C2
New St	B2
North Pl	B2
Odeon	B3
Old Bath Rd	C3
Oriel Rd	B2
Overton Park Rd	B1
Overton Rd	B1
Oxford St	C3
Parabola Rd	B1
Park Pl	C1
Park St	A1
Pittville Circus	A3
Pittville Cr	A3
Pittville Lawn	A3
Pittville Pump Room & Racecourse	A3
Playhouse	B2
Police Station	B1/C1
Portland St	B3
Post Office	B2/C1/C2
Prestbury Rd	A3
Prince's Rd	C1
Priory St	B3
Promenade	B2
Queen St	A1
Recreation Grnd	A1
Regent Arcade	B2
Regent St	B2
Rodney Rd	B2
Royal Cr	B2
Royal Wells Rd	B2
Sandford Lido	C3
Sandford Park	C3
Sandford Rd	C2
Selkirk St	A3
Sherborne Pl	B3
Sherborne St	B3
St George's Pl	B2
St George's Rd	B1
St George's St	A1
St Gregory's	B2
St James St	B3
St John's Ave	B3
St Luke's Rd	C2
St Margaret's Rd	A2
St Mary's	B2
St Matthew's	B2
St Paul's La	A2
St Paul's Rd	A2
St Paul's St	A2
St Stephen's Rd	C1
Suffolk Pde	C1
Suffolk Rd	C1
Suffolk Sq	C1
Sun St	A1
Swindon Rd	B2
Sydenham Villas Rd	C3
Tewkesbury Rd	A1
The Courtyard	B1
Thirlstaine Rd	C2
Tivoli Rd	C1
Tivoli St	C1
Town Hall & Theatre	B2
Townsend St	A1
Trafalgar St	C2
Victoria Pl	B3
Victoria St	A2
Vittoria Walk	B2
Wellesley Rd	A2
Wellington Rd	A3
Wellington Sq	A3
Wellington St	A3
West Rd	A3
Western Rd	B1
Winchcombe St	B3

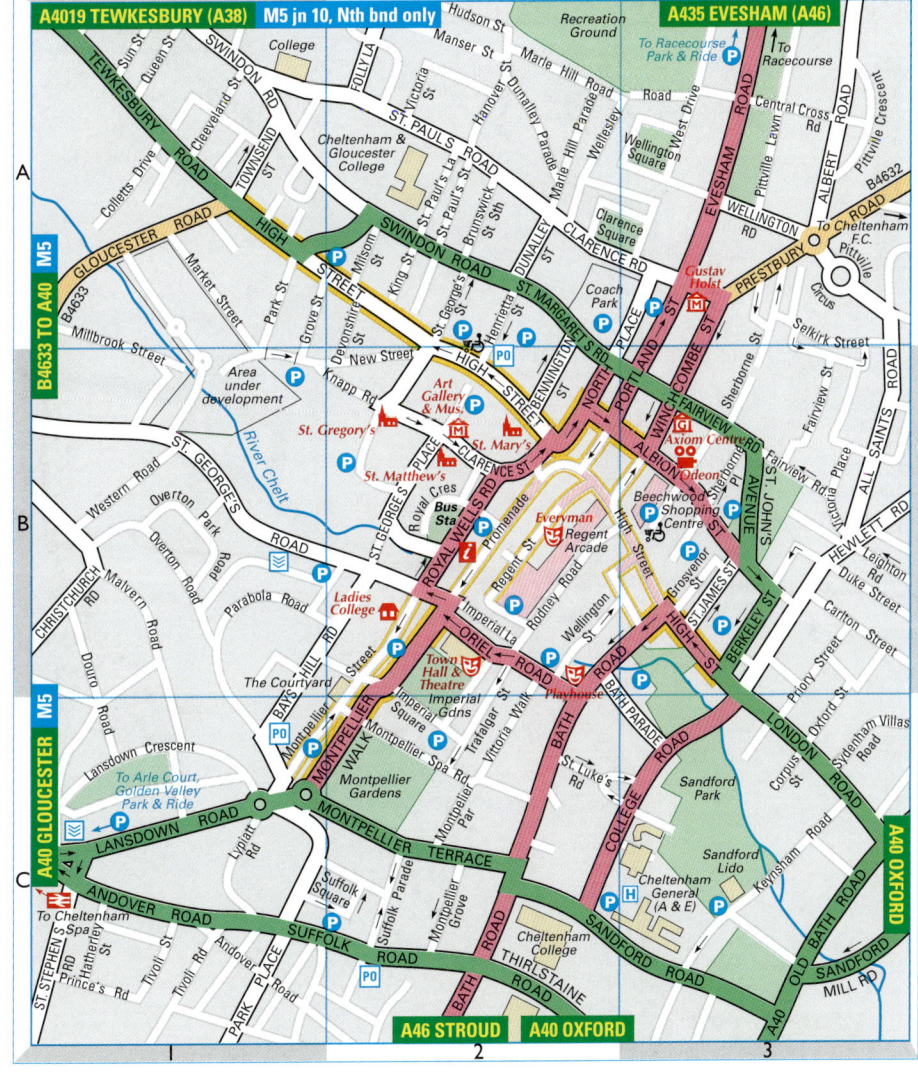

Chester

A town known to the Romans as Dewa, with an unparalleled range of Roman ruins, including a partially excavated amphitheatre (Britain's largest), and the country's most complete city walls, built in the 1st century AD and forming a 2-mile circular promenade with information plaques and views over the surrounding countryside. Among the countless sites of historical interest are the UK's oldest surviving mill dam, built by the Normans, the Roodee, Britain's oldest racecourse (constructed on the site of the Roman harbour), an 11th-century castle, a cathedral retaining parts of a Norman church (Handel rehearsed his Messiah here), the 1652 God's Providence House, the only one in the town spared the Plague, 17th-century Bishop Lloyd's House with its intricate carvings, the Rows, a set of unique half-timbered galleries forming a second row of shops above street level, and the Three Old Arches, the country's oldest shopfront. There is a wide variety of good shops.

▲ Half-timbered buildings in Chester

★ Do not miss
- ★ **Chester Zoo**, Upton-by-Chester
- ★ **Dewa Roman Experience**, Pierpoint Lane, Bridge Street
- ★ **Roman Amphitheatre**, Little St John Street

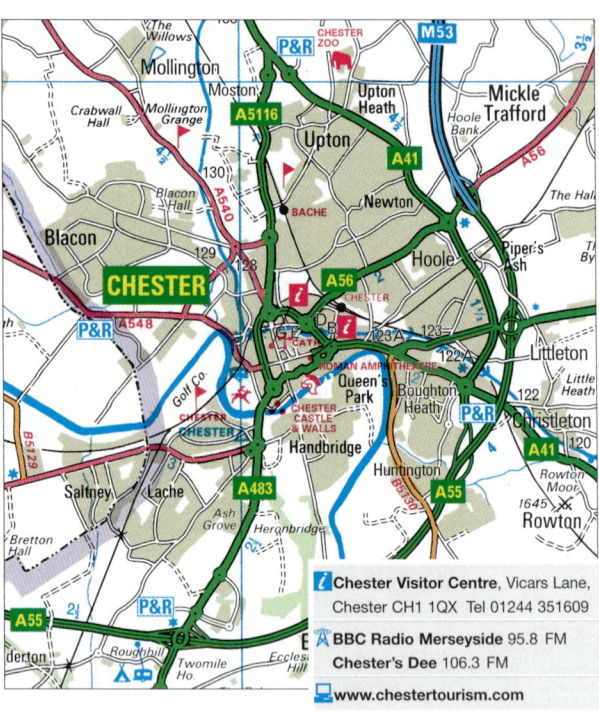

Chester Visitor Centre, Vicars Lane, Chester CH1 1QX Tel 01244 351609
BBC Radio Merseyside 95.8 FM
Chester's Dee 106.3 FM
www.chestertourism.com

Chester

Abbey Gateway	A2
Appleyards La	C3
Bedward Row	B1
Beeston View	C3
Bishop Lloyd's Palace	B2
Black Diamond St	A2
Bottoms La	C3
Boughton	B3
Bouverie St	A1
Bridge St	B2
Bridgegate	C2
British Heritage Centre	B2
Brook St	A3
Brown's La	C2
Bus Station	B2
Cambrian Rd	A1
Canal St	A2
Carrick Rd	C1
Castle	C2
Castle Dr	C2
Cathedral	B2
Catherine St	A1
Chester	A3
Cheyney Rd	A1
Chichester St	A1
City Rd	A3
City Walls	B1/B2
City Walls Rd	B1
Cornwall St	A2
County Hall	C2
Cross Hey	C3
Cuppin St	B2
Curzon Park N	C1
Curzon Park S	C1
Dee Basin	A1
Dee La	B3
Delamere St	A2
Dewa Roman Experience	B2
Duke St	B2
Eastgate	B2
Eastgate St	B2
Eaton Rd	C2
Egerton St	A3
Elizabeth Cr	B3
Fire Station	A2
Foregate St	B2
Frodsham St	A2
Gamul House	B2
Garden La	A1
Gateway	B2
George St	A2
Gladstone Ave	A1
God's Providence House	B2
Gorse Stacks	A2
Greenway St	C2
Grosvenor Bridge	C1
Grosvenor Mus	B2
Grosvenor Park	B3
Grosvenor Precinct	B2
Grosvenor Rd	C1
Grosvenor St	B2
Groves Rd	B3
Guildhall Mus	B1
Handbridge	C2
Hartington St	C3
Hoole Way	A2
Hunter St	B2
Information Ctr	B2
King Charles' Tower	A2
King St	A2
Library	A2
Lightfoot St	A3
Little Roodee	C2
Liverpool Rd	A1
Love St	B3
Lower Bridge St	B2
Lower Park Rd	B3
Lyon St	A2
Magistrates Court	C1
Meadows La	C3
Military Mus	C1
Milton St	A3
New Crane St	B1
Nicholas St	B2
Northgate	A2
Northgate Arena	A2
Northgate St	A2
Nun's Rd	B1
Old Dee Bridge	C2
Overleigh Rd	C1
Park St	B2
Police Station	B2
Post Office	A2/A3/B2/C2
Princess St	A2
Queen St	B2
Queen's Park Rd	C2
Queen's Rd	A3
Raymond St	A1
River La	C2
Roman Amphitheatre & Gardens	B2
Roodee, The (Chester Racecourse)	B1
Russell St	A3
St Anne St	A2
St George's Cr	C3
St Martin's Gate	A1
St Martin's Way	B1
St Oswalds Way	A2
Saughall Rd	A1
Sealand Rd	A1
South View Rd	A1
Stanley Palace	B1
Station Rd	A3
Steven St	A3
The Bars	B3
The Cross	B2
The Groves	B3
The Meadows	B3
Tower Rd	B1
Town Hall	B2
Union St	B3
Vicar's La	B2
Victoria Cr	C3
Victoria Rd	A2
Walpole St	A1
Water Tower St	A1
Watergate	B2
Watergate St	B2
Whipcord La	A1
White Friars	B2
York St	B3

Chichester Tourist Information Centre,
29a South Street, Chichester PO19 1AH
Tel 01243 775888

BBC Southern Counties 104.8 FM
Spirit 96.6, 102.3 FM

www.chichester.gov.uk

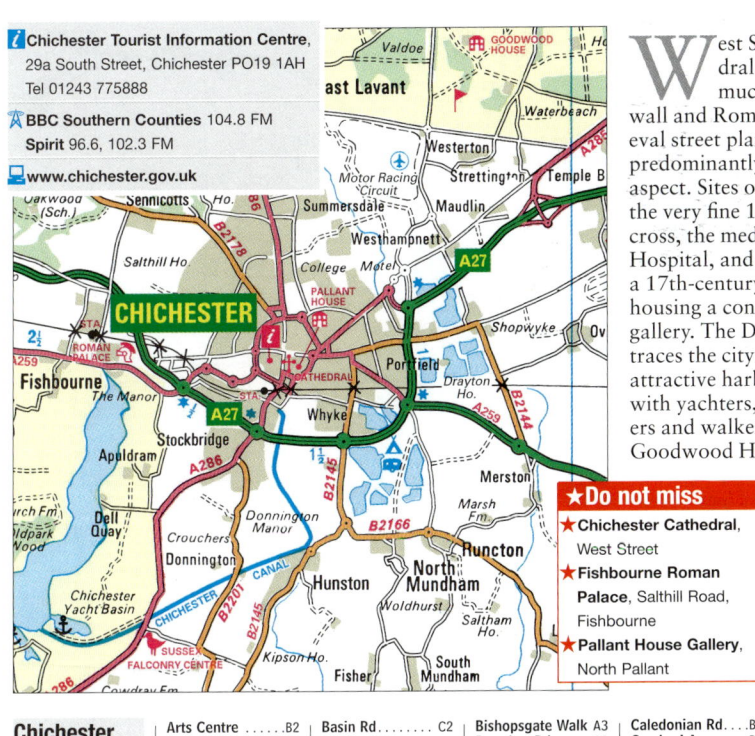

Chichester

West Sussex cathedral city retaining much of its Roman wall and Roman and medieval street plan, though it is predominantly Georgian in aspect. Sites of interest include the very fine 1501 market cross, the medieval St Mary's Hospital, and Pallant House, a 17th-century residence now housing a contemporary art gallery. The District Museum traces the city's history. The attractive harbour is popular with yachters, birdwatchers and walkers. Nearby are Goodwood House, an 18th-century mansion with a noteworthy art collection and outdoor sculpture exhibition, the Weald and Downland Open Air Museum of old buildings, West Dean Gardens and the Sussex Falconry Centre. The lovely South Downs are within easy reach.

▲ Chichester Cathedral

★ Do not miss
- ★ **Chichester Cathedral**, West Street
- ★ **Fishbourne Roman Palace**, Salthill Road, Fishbourne
- ★ **Pallant House Gallery**, North Pallant

Chichester

Adelaide Rd....A3	Arts Centre......B2	Basin Rd........C2
Alexandra Rd....A3	Ave de Chartres....B1/B2	Beech Ave......B1
	Barlow Rd......A1	Bishops Palace Gdns......B2

Bishopsgate Walk...A3
Bramber Rd......C3
Broyle Rd.......A2
Bus Station......B2

Caledonian Rd....B3
Cambrai Ave.....B3
Canal Wharf.....C2
Canon La........B2

Cathedral †......B2
Cavendish St......A1
Cawley Rd......B2
Cedar Dr........A1

Chapel St........A2
Cherry Orchard Rd...C3
Chichester By-Pass......C2/C3
Chichester Festival......A2
Chichester ⇌.....B2
Churchside......A2
Cinema B3/C1
City Walls........A2
Cleveland Rd....B3
College La......A2
College Of Science & Technology....B1
Cory Cl........C2
Council Offices....B2
County Hall.....B2
Courts........B2
District B2
Duncan Rd......A1
Durnford Cl......A1
East Pallant......B2
East Row........B2
East St.........B2
East Walls......B3
Eastland Rd......B2
Ettrick Cl......B3
Ettrick Rd......B3
Exton Rd........B3
Fire Station.....A2
Football Ground...A2
Franklin Pl......A2
Friary (Remains of)....B2
Garland Cl......C3
Green La........C3
Grove Rd........C3
Guilden Rd......B3
Guildhall B2
Hawthorn Cl.....A1
Hay Rd.........C3
Henty Gdns......B1
Herald Dr......C3
Information Ctr 🛈...B2
John's St........B2
Joys Croft......A3
Jubilee Pk......A3
Jubilee Rd......A3
Juxon Cl........B2
Kent Rd.........B2
King George Gdns...A2
King's Ave......C3
Kingsham Ave.....C3
Kingsham Rd......C2
Laburnum Gr......B2
Leigh Rd........C1
Lennox Rd......A3
Lewis Rd........A3
Library.........B2
Lion St.........B2
Litten Terr.....B3
Little London....B2
Lyndhurst Rd.....B3
Market..........B2
Market Ave......B2
Market Cross....B2
Market Rd.......B3
Martlet Cl......C2

Melbourne Rd....A3
Mount La........B1
New Park Rd.....A3
Newlands La.....A1
North Pallant....B2
North St........A2
North Walls.....A2
Northgate......A2
Oak Ave.........A1
Oak Cl..........A1
Oaklands Park....A1
Oaklands Way....A2
Orchard Ave.....A1
Orchard St......A1
Ormonde Ave.....B3
Pallant House 🏛...B2
Parchment St....A1
Parklands Rd....A1/B1
Peter Weston Pl...B3
Police Station 🚓...C2
Post Office......A1/B2/B3
Priory La........A2
Priory Park......A2
Priory Rd......A2
Queen's Ave.....C1
Riverside........A3
Roman Amphitheatre...B3
St Cyriacs......A2
St Pancras......A3
St Paul's Rd......A1
St Richard's Hospital (A&E) 🏥....A3
Shamrock Cl......A3
Sherbourne Rd....A1
Somerstown......A2
South Bank......C2
South Pallant....B2
South St........B2
Southgate......B2
Spitalfield La....A3
Stirling Rd......B3
Stockbridge Rd......C1/C2
Swanfield Dr.....A3
Terminus Industrial Estate........C1
Terminus Rd......C1
The Hornet......B3
The Litten......A3
Tower St........A2
Tozer Way......A3
Turnbull Rd......A3
Upton Rd........C1
Velyn Ave......B3
Via Ravenna......B1
Walnut Ave......A1
West St.........B2
Westgate........B2
Westgate Fields...B1
Westgate Leisure Centre.......B1
Weston Ave......C1
Whyke Cl.......C3
Whyke La......B3
Whyke Rd.......B3
Winden Ave......C3

¼ mile
½ km

59

Colchester

Colchester is Britain's oldest recorded town – documented since it was the Iron Age stronghold of Camulodunum. Archaeological evidence shows a settlement existed here 3,000 years ago. Today, most of Colchester town centre lies within the ancient boundaries of Camulodunum. Now home to the University of Essex, the town makes much of its heritage with places of interest such as Hollytrees Museum featuring local history, Colchester Castle Museum, and the Natural History Museum. The town centre offers a wide range of high street and a number of independent shops. Much of the main shopping can be found on the High Street and in the surrounding side streets as can the varied selection of pubs and restaurants. There are several activity centres to keep children amused whether it be bowling, karting or rollerskating.

▲ The Dutch Quarter

Visitor Information Centre,
1 Queen Street, Colchester CO1 2PG
Tel 01206 282 920

BBC Essex 103.5 FM
Essex FM 102.6 FM • SGR 96.1 FM
www.colchester.gov.uk

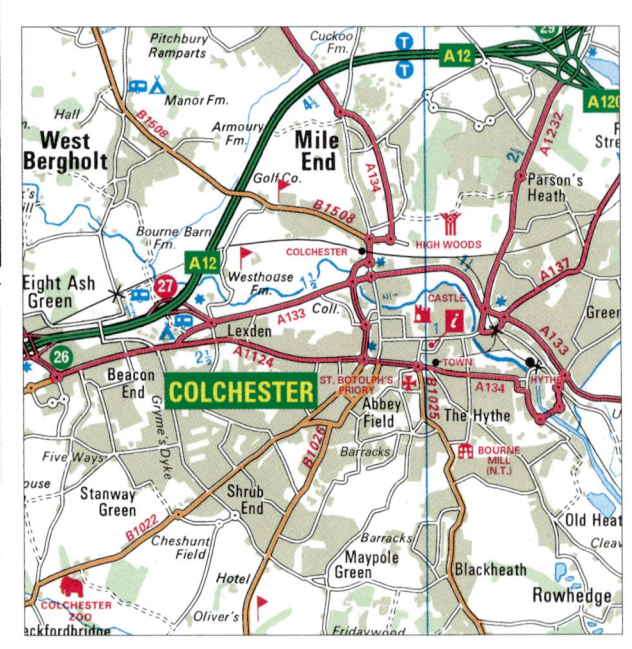

★ Do not miss
- ★ **Colchester Zoo**, Maldon Road
- ★ **Colchester Arts Centre**, Church Street – music, film, theatre

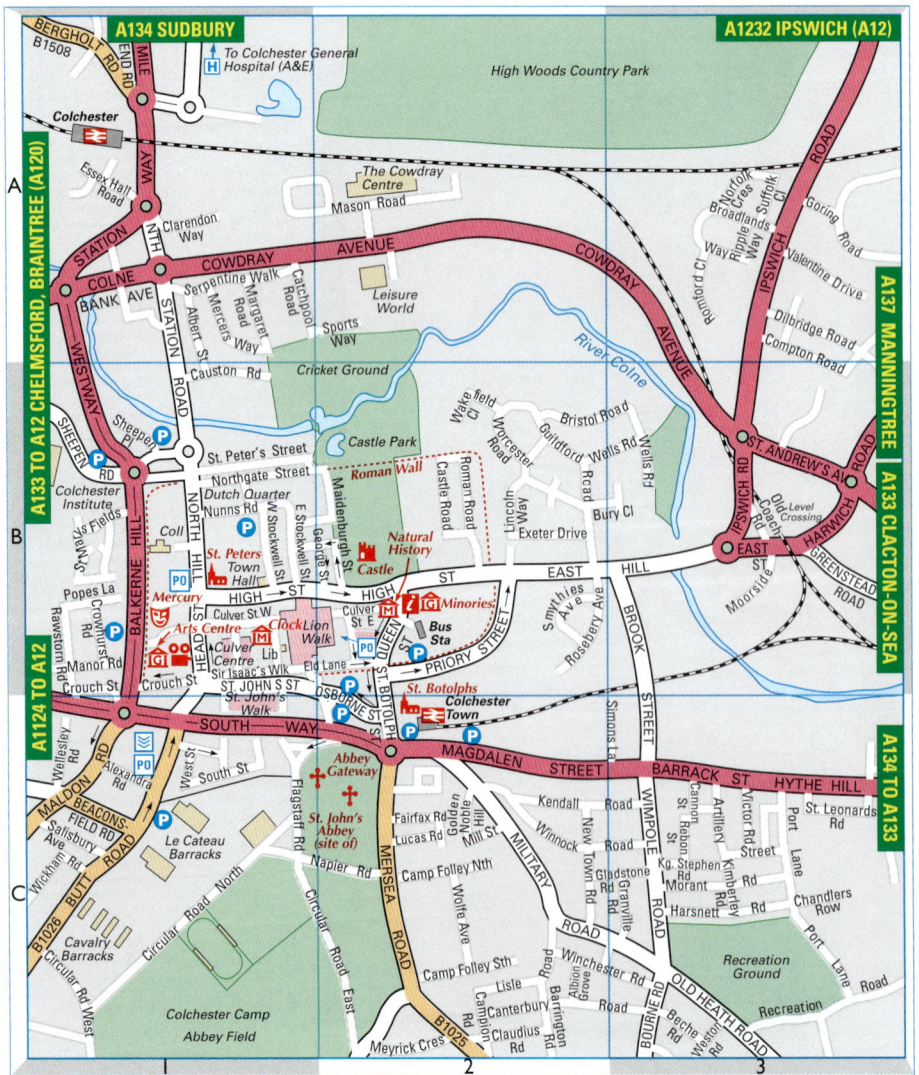

Colchester

Street	Grid
Abbey Gateway ✝	
Albert St.	A1
Albion Grove	C2
Alexandra Rd	C1
Artillery St	C3
Arts Centre	B1
Balkerne Hill	B1
Barrack St	C3
Barrington Rd	C2
Beaconsfield Rd	C1
Beche Rd	C3
Bergholt Rd	A1
Bourne Rd	C3
Bristol Rd	B2
Broadlands Way	A3
Brook St	B3
Bury Cl	B2
Bus Station	B2
Butt Rd	C1
Camp Folley North	C2
Camp Folley South	C2
Campion Rd	C2
Cannon St	C3
Canterbury Rd	C2
Castle	B2
Castle Rd	B2
Catchpool Rd	A1
Causton Rd	A1
Cavalry Barracks	C1
Chandlers Row	C3
Circular Rd East	C2
Circular Rd North	C1
Circular Rd West	C1
Clarendon Way	A1
Claudius Rd	C1
Clock	B1
Colchester Institute	B1
Colchester	A1
Colchester Town	C2
Colne Bank Ave	A1
Compton Rd	A3
Cowdray Ave	A1/A3
Cowdray Ctr, The	A2
Crouch St	B1
Crowhurst Rd	B1
Culver Centre	B1
Culver St East	B1
Culver St West	B1
Dilbridge Rd	A3
East Hill	B2
East St	B3
East Stockwell St	B1
Eld La	B1
Essex Hall Rd	A1
Exeter Dr	B2
Fairfax Rd	C2
Flagstaff Rd	C1
George St	B2
Gladstone Rd	C2
Golden Noble Hill	C2
Goring Rd	A3
Granville Rd	C3
Greenstead Rd	B3
Guildford Rd	B2
Harsnett Rd	C3
Harwich Rd	B3
Head St	B1
High St	B1
Hythe Hill	C3
Information Ctr	B2
Ipswich Rd	A3
Kendall Rd	C2
Kimberley Rd	C3
King Stephen Rd	C3
Le Cateau Barracks	C1
Leisure World	A2
Library	B1
Lincoln Way	B2
Lion Walk Shopping Centre	B1
Lisle Rd	C2
Lucas Rd	C2
Magdalen St	C2
Maidenburgh St	B2
Maldon Rd	C1
Manor Rd	B1
Margaret Rd	A1
Mason Rd	A2
Mercers Way	A1
Mercury	B1
Mersea Rd	C2
Meyrick Cr	C2
Mile End Rd	A1
Military Rd	C2
Mill St	C2
Minories	B2
Moorside	B3
Morant Rd	C2
Napier Rd	C1
Natural History	B2
New Town Rd	C2
Norfolk Cr	A3
North Hill	B1
North Station Rd	A1
Northgate St	B1
Nunns Rd	B1
Odeon	B1
Old Coach Rd	B3
Old Heath Rd	C3
Osborne St	C1
Police Station	C1
Popes La	B1
Port La	C3
Post Office	B1/B2/C1
Priory St	B2
Queen St	B1
Rawstorn Rd	B1
Rebon St	C2
Recreation Rd	C3
Ripple Way	A3
Roman Rd	B2
Roman Wall	B2
Romford Cl	A3
Rosebery Ave	B2
St Andrew's Ave	B3
St Botolph St	B2
St Botolphs	B1
St John's Abbey (Site of)	C2
St John's St	B1
St John's Walk Shopping Centre	B1
St Leonards Rd	C3
St Marys Fields	B1
St Peters	B1
St Peter's St	B1
Salisbury Ave	A1
Serpentine Walk	A1
Sheepen Pl	B1
Sheepen Rd	B1
Simons La	B1
Sir Isaac's Walk	B1
Smythies Ave	B2
South St	C1
Sports Way	A2
Station Way	A2
Suffolk Cl	A3
Town Hall	B1
Turner Rd	A1
Valentine Dr	A3
Victor Rd	C2
Wakefield Cl	B2
Wellesley Rd	C1
Wells Rd	B2
West St	C2
West Stockwell St	B1
Weston Rd	C1
Westway	A1
Wickham Rd	C1
Wimpole Rd	C3
Winchester Rd	C2
Winnock Rd	C2
Wolfe Ave	C2
Worcester Rd	B1

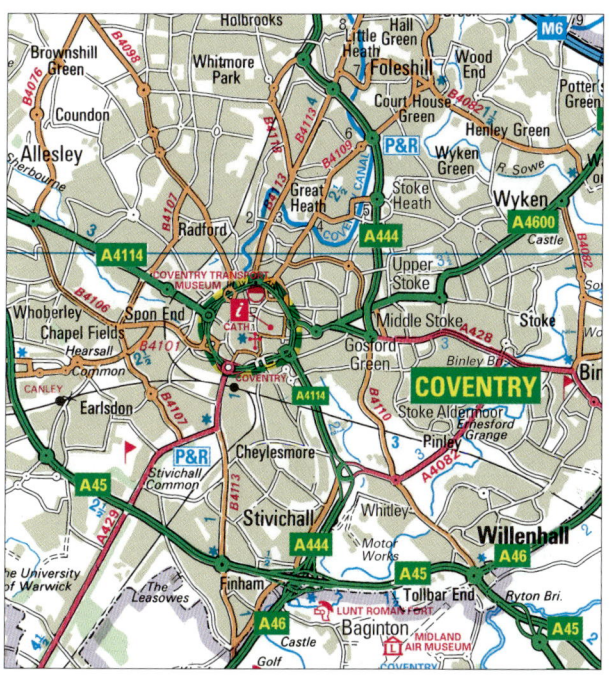

Coventry

Coventry is known for the legend of Lady Godiva who rode through the streets in protest at the high taxes imposed by her husband Earl Leofric. Attractions include the remains of Lady Godiva's church; the extensive collections of the Coventry Road Transport Museum; the medieval St Mary's Guildhall and the world-renowned cathedral that combines the foundations of part of the 12th-century priory cathedral, the ruins of the 14th-century building destroyed in 1940 and the present cathedral. The city centre is pedestrianised and has three shopping centres, Lower Precinct, West Orchards and Cathedral Lanes. Other shops can be found on Spon Street and City Arcade, there is also an indoor market by the name of Retail Market. Coventry also has a great choice of entertainment from bars and restaurants to theatres and cinemas.

▲ Coventry Cathedral

★ Do not miss:
- ★ **Coventry Cathedral**, Priory Row
- ★ **Coventry Transport Museum**, Millennium Place, Hales Street
- ★ **Herbert Art Gallery and Museum**, Jordan Well

Coventry Tourist Information Centre, 4 Priory Row, Coventry CV1 5EX Tel 024 7622 7264

BBC WM 94.8 FM
Classic Gold 1359 AM
Kix 96.2 FM • Mercia 97.0 FM

www.visitcoventry.co.uk

Coventry

Abbots La........A1	Lady Godiva Statue ◆......B2	Technology Park..C3	Tomson Ave......A1	Upper Hill St....A1	Waveley Rd....B1
Albany Rd........B1	Lamb St........A2	The Precinct....B2	Top Green......C1	Upper Well St....A2	Westminster Rd...C1
Alma St........B3	Leicester Row....A2	Theatre........B1	Toy Museum......B3	Victoria St......A3	White St........A3
Art Faculty......B3	Library........B2	Thomas Landsdail St....C2	Trinity St......B2	Vine St........A3	Windsor St......B1
Asthill Grove....C2	Little Park St....B2		University......B3	Warwick Rd......C2	
Bablake School...A1	London Rd......C3				
Barras La........A1	Lower Ford St....B3				
Barrs Hill School..A1	Magistrates & Crown Courts..B2				
Belgrade........B2	Manor House Drive........B2				
Bishop Burges St..A2	Manor Rd......B2				
Bond's Hospital..B1	Market........B2				
Broadgate......B2	Martyr's Mml ◆...C1				
Broadway......C1	Meadow St......B1				
Bus Station......A3	Meriden St......A1				
Butts Radial....B1	Michaelmas Rd...C2				
Canal Basin ◆....A2	Middleborough Rd..A1				
Canterbury St....A3	Mile La........C3				
Cathedral ✝......B3	Millennium Place..A2				
Chester St......A1	Much Park St....B3				
Cheylesmore Manor House....B2	Naul's Mill Park..A1				
Christ Church Spire ◆......B2	New Union......B2				
City Walls & Gates ◆......A2	Park Rd........A3				
Coach Park......A3	Parkside........C3				
Corporation St...B2	Police HQ......B3				
Council House...B2	Primrose Hill St..A3				
Coundon Rd.....A1	Priory Gardens & Visitor Centre..B2				
Coventry & Warwickshire Hospital (A&E)....A2	Priory St........B3				
Coventry C2	Puma Way......C3				
Coventry Transport Museum....A2	Quarryfield La....C3				
Cox St........A3	Queen's Rd......B1				
Croft Rd........B1	Quinton Rd......C2				
Deasy Rd......C3	Radford Rd......A2				
Earl St........B2	Raglan St........A2				
Eaton Rd........C2	Retail Park......C1				
Fairfax St......B2	Ringway (Hill Cross)....A2				
Foleshill Rd....A2	Ringway (Queens)..B1				
Ford's Hospital...B2	Ringway (Rudge)..B1				
Fowler Rd......A1	Ringway (St Johns)..B3				
Friars Rd........C2	Ringway (St Nicholas)..A2				
Gordon St......C1	Ringway (St Patricks)..C2				
Gosford St......B3	Ringway (Swanswell)..A3				
Greyfriars Green..B2	Ringway (Whitefriars)..B3				
Greyfriars Rd....B2	St John St......B2				
Gulson Rd......B3	St John The Baptist ◆....B2				
Hales St........A3	St Nicholas St...A2				
Harnall Lane East..A3	Skydome........B1				
Harnall Lane West..A2	Spencer Ave.....C1				
Herbert Art Gallery & Museum....B3	Spencer Park....C1				
Hertford St......B2	Spencer Rd......C1				
Hewitt Ave......A1	Spon St........B2				
High St........B2	Sports Centre....B3				
Hill St........B2	Stoney Rd......C2				
Holy Trinity ◆....B2	Stoney Stanton Rd..A3				
Holyhead Rd....A1	Swanswell Pool...A3				
Howard St......A3	Swanswell St....A3				
Huntingdon Rd...C1	Sydney Stringer School......A3				
Information Ctr...B2	Technical College..B1				
Jordan Well......B3					
King Henry VIII School........C1					

¼ mile / ½ km

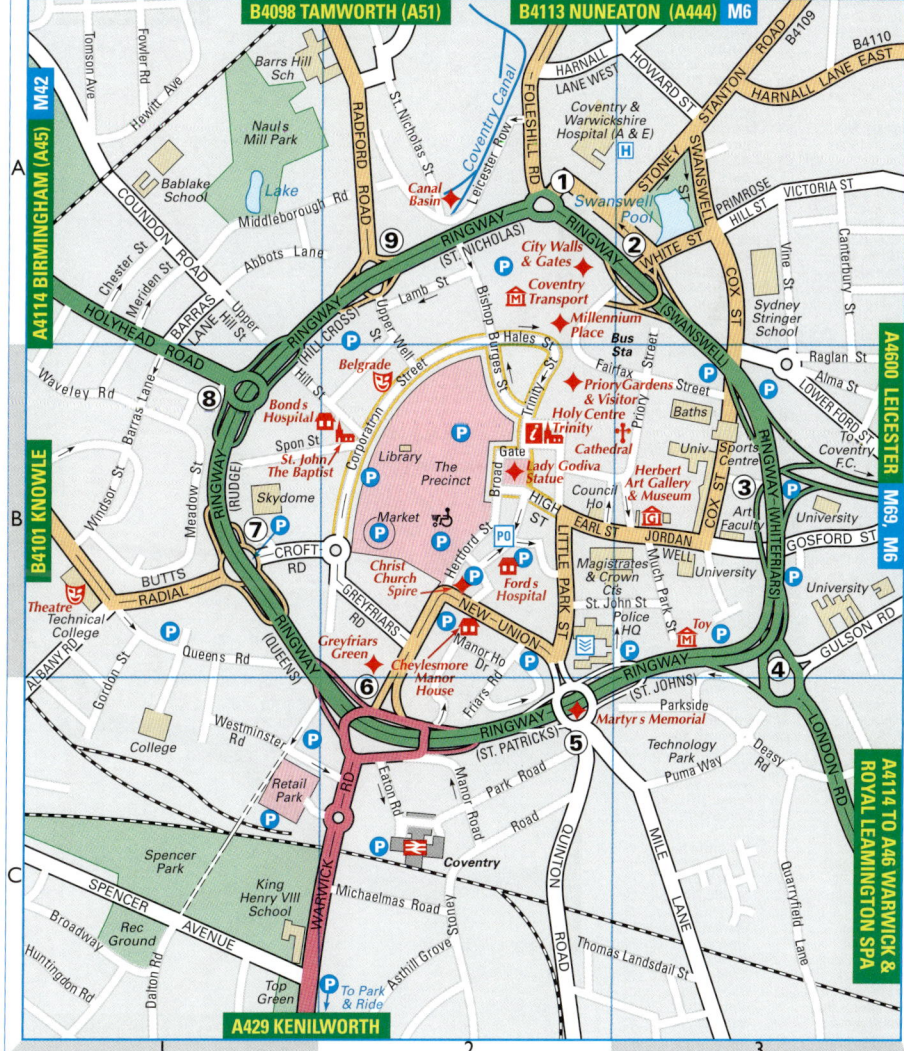

Croydon

▲ Croydon has an efficient tram network

Tourist Information Centre,
Croydon Clocktower, Katharine St,
Croydon CR9 1ET Tel 020 8253 1009

BBC London 94.9 FM • **Capital FM**
95.8 FM • **Capital Gold** 1548 AM
Heart 106.2 FM • **Kiss** 100.0 FM
LBC 97.3 FM • **Magic** 105.4 FM
Virgin 105.8 FM • **Xfm** 104.9 FM

www.croydononline.org

★ Do not miss
★ **Croydon Clocktower**, Katharine Street – multipurpose venue
★ **Croydon Palace**, Old Palace Road
★ **Croydon Parish Church of St John the Baptist**, Church Street

One of the largest towns in southern England and still a London borough, it is a focal point for an extensive residential and industrial area to the south of London. Places to visit include Croydon Clocktower, an arts centre featuring photographic exhibitions, sculpture, local history and arthouse cinema; Croydon Palace, 1,000-year-old former home of Archbishops of Canterbury; Croydon Parish Church of St John the Baptist, a 15th-century church. There are two shopping centres, the Whitgift and the Drummond with a pedestrianised area between the two. Surrey Street Market is open every day except Sunday. There are many pubs and restaurants centred on the High Street and South End.

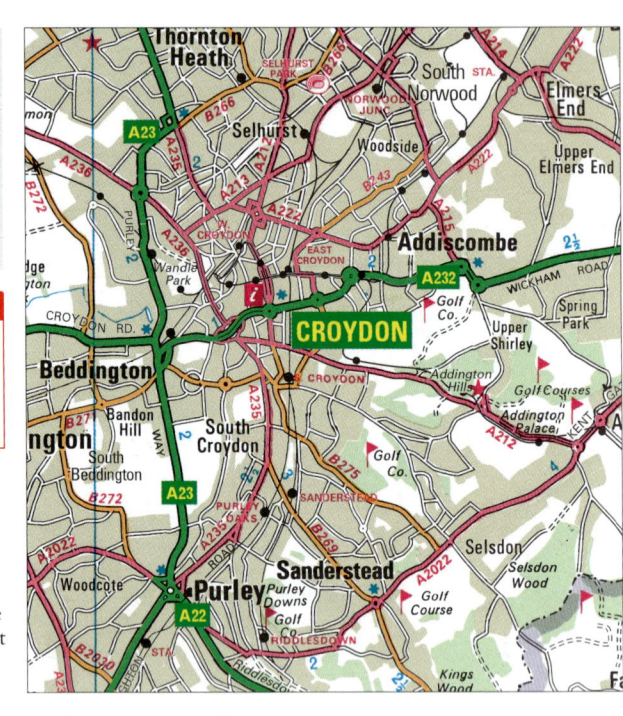

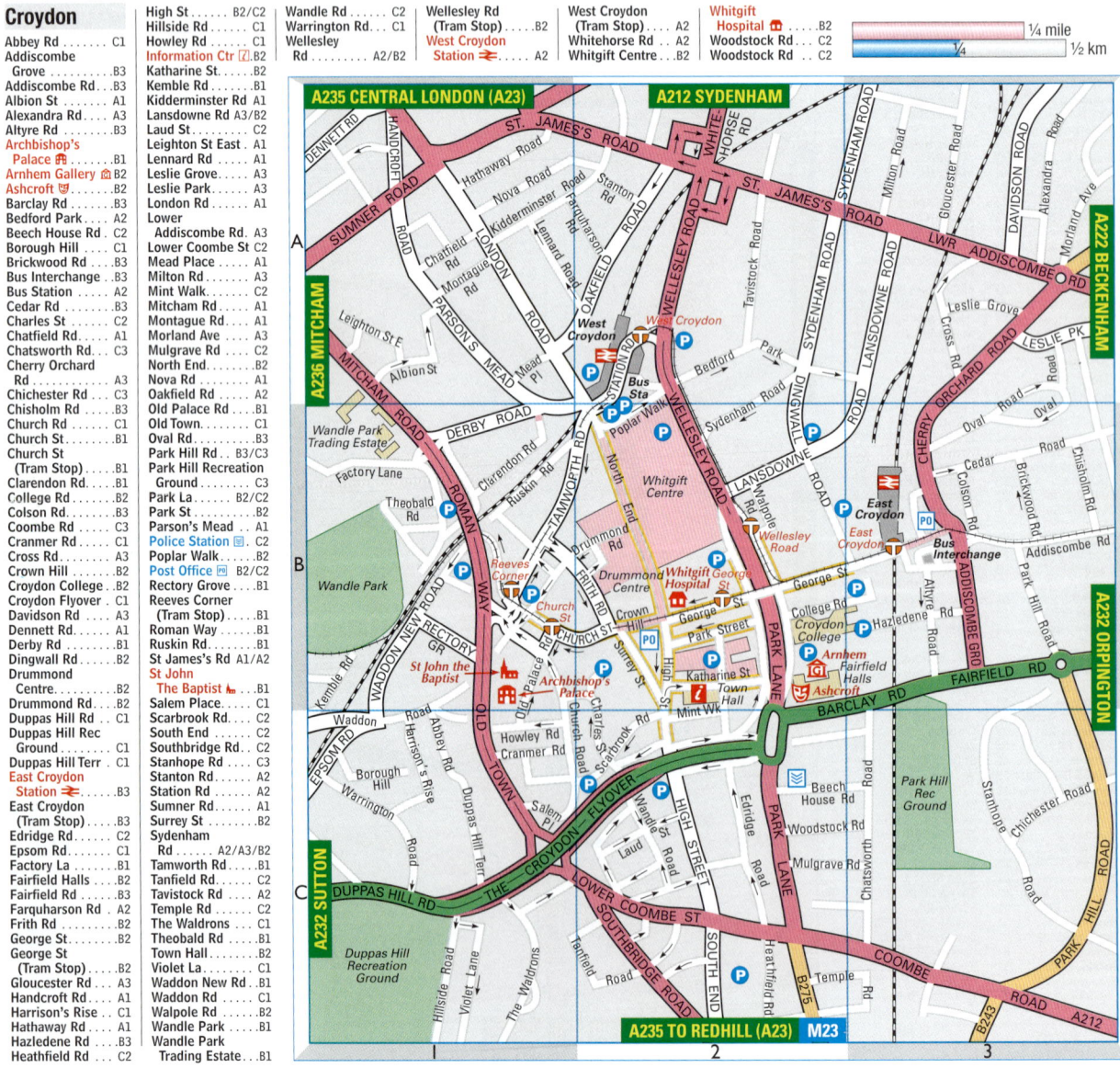

Croydon

Street	Grid
Abbey Rd	C1
Addiscombe Grove	B3
Addiscombe Rd	B3
Albion St	A1
Alexandra Rd	A3
Altyre Rd	B3
Archbishop's Palace	B1
Arnhem Gallery	B2
Ashcroft	B2
Barclay Rd	B3
Bedford Park	A2
Beech House Rd	C2
Borough Hill	C1
Brickwood Rd	B3
Bus Interchange	B3
Bus Station	A2
Cedar Rd	B3
Charles St	C2
Chatfield Rd	A1
Chatsworth Rd	C3
Cherry Orchard Rd	A3
Chichester Rd	C3
Chisholm Rd	C1
Church Rd	C1
Church St	B1
Church St (Tram Stop)	B1
Clarendon Rd	B1
College Rd	B2
Colson Rd	B3
Coombe Rd	C3
Cranmer Rd	C1
Cross Rd	A3
Crown Hill	B2
Croydon College	B2
Croydon Flyover	C1
Davidson Rd	A3
Dennett Rd	A1
Derby Rd	B1
Dingwall Rd	B2
Drummond Centre	B2
Drummond Rd	B2
Duppas Hill Rd	C1
Duppas Hill Rec Ground	C1
Duppas Hill Terr	C1
East Croydon Station	B3
East Croydon (Tram Stop)	B3
Edridge Rd	C2
Epsom Rd	B1
Factory La	B1
Fairfield Halls	B3
Fairfield Rd	B3
Farquharson Rd	A2
Frith Rd	B2
George St	B2
George St (Tram Stop)	B2
Gloucester Rd	A3
Handcroft Rd	A1
Harrison's Rise	C1
Hathaway Rd	A1
Hazledene Rd	B3
Heathfield Rd	C2
High St	B2/C2
Hillside Rd	C1
Howley Rd	C1
Information Ctr	B2
Katharine St	B2
Kemble Rd	B1
Kidderminster Rd	A1
Lansdowne Rd	A3/B2
Laud St	A1
Leighton St East	A1
Lennard Rd	A1
Leslie Grove	A3
Leslie Park	A3
London Rd	A1
Lower Addiscombe Rd	A3
Lower Coombe St	C3
Mead Place	A1
Milton Rd	A1
Mint Walk	C2
Mitcham Rd	A1
Montague Rd	A1
Morland Ave	A3
Mulgrave Rd	C3
North End	B2
Nova Rd	A1
Oakfield Rd	A2
Old Palace Rd	B1
Old Town	C1
Oval Rd	A3
Park Hill Rd	B3/C3
Park Hill Recreation Ground	C3
Park La	B2/C2
Park St	B2
Parson's Mead	A1
Police Station	C2
Poplar Walk	B2
Post Office	B2/C2
Rectory Grove	B1
Reeves Corner (Tram Stop)	B1
Roman Way	B1
Ruskin Rd	B1
St James's Rd	A1/A2
St John The Baptist	B1
Salem Place	C1
Scarbrook Rd	C2
South End	C2
Southbridge Rd	C2
Stanhope Rd	C3
Stanton Rd	A2
Station Rd	A2
Sumner Rd	A1
Surrey St	B2
Sydenham Rd	A2/A3/B2
Tamworth Rd	B1
Tanfield Rd	C2
Tavistock Rd	A3
Temple Rd	C2
The Waldrons	B2
Theobald Rd	B1
Town Hall	B2
Violet La	C1
Waddon New Rd	B1
Waddon Rd	C1
Walpole Rd	B2
Wandle Rd	B1
Wandle Park Trading Estate	B1
Wandle Rd	C2
Warrington Rd	C1
Wellesley Rd	A2/B2
Wellesley Rd (Tram Stop)	B2
West Croydon Station	A2
West Croydon (Tram Stop)	A2
Whitehorse Rd	A2
Whitgift Centre	B2
Whitgift Hospital	B2
Woodstock Rd	A2
Woodstock Rd	C2

¼ mile / ½ km

62

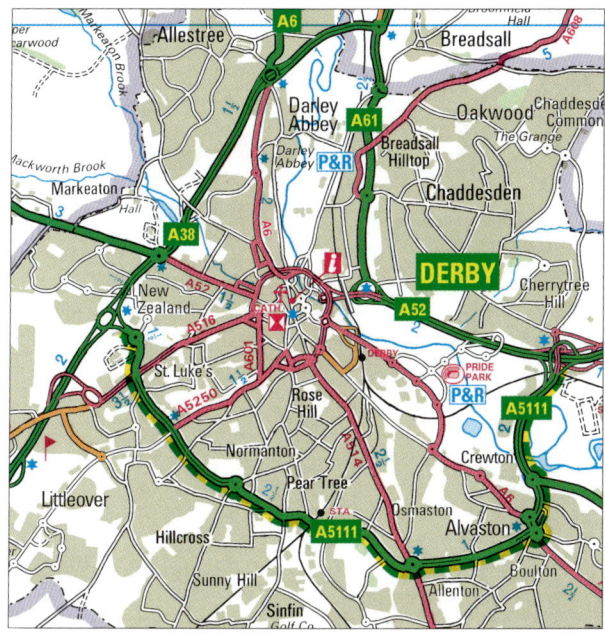

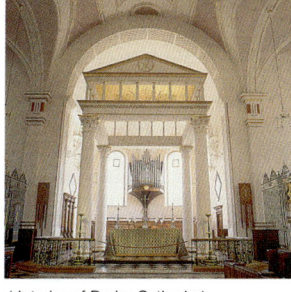

Derby

A small city with a cathedral boasting Britain's second-highest church tower, and a proud industrial heritage (notably in silk manufacture, later in the making of Rolls-Royce engines) that can be explored along the Derwent Valley Mills World Heritage Site stretching 15 miles to Matlock Bath. Other attractions include the Central Museum and Art Gallery, which includes displays on local regiments and local porcelain, Pickford's House Museum of Georgian life, and a 1756 jailhouse. Nearby are the National Trust properties of Kedleston Hall, Calke Abbey, and Sudbury Hall and Museum of Childhood, and the award-winning CONKERS National Forest Discovery Centre. Green spaces include the Derby Arboretum, Markeaton Park and Craft Village, and Alveston Park with its riverside cycletrack to Elvaston Castle Country Park, while to the northwest lies the stunning Peak District National Park.

▲ Interior of Derby Cathedral

★ Do not miss
- ★ **Derby Cathedral**, Iron Gate
- ★ **Royal Crown Derby Factory and Visitor Centre**, Osmaston Road
- ★ **Silk Mill Museum of Industry and History**, Full Street

Derby Tourist Information Centre, The Assembly Rooms, Market Place, DE1 3AH Tel 01332 255802

BBC Radio Derby 104.5 FM and 1116 AM (weekdays only)
Ram FM 102.8 FM • **Saga** 106.6 FM
96 Trent FM 96.0 FM

www.visitderby.com/tourism

Derby

Street	Ref
Abbey St	C1
Agard St	B1
Albert St	B2
Albion St	B2
Ambulance Station	B1
Arthur St	A1
Ashlyn Rd	B3
Assembly Rooms	B2
Babington La	C2
Becket St	C1
Belper Rd	A1
Bold La	B1
Bradshaw Way	C2
Bridge St	B1
Brook St	B1
Burrows Walk	C2
Burton Rd	C1
Bus Station	B2
Caesar St	A2
Canal St	C2
Carrington St	C3
Castle St	C2
Cathedral	B2
Cathedral Rd	B1
Charnwood St	C2
Chester Green Rd	A2
City Rd	A2
Clarke St	A3
Cock Pitt	C3
Council House	B2
Cranmer Rd	B3
Crompton St	C1
Crown & County Courts	
Crown Walk	C2
Curzon St	B1
Darley Grove	A1
Playhouse	C2
Derby	C3
Derbyshire County Cricket Ground	B3
Derbyshire Royal Infirmary (A&E)	C2
Derwent Business Centre	A2
Derwent St	B2
Devonshire Walk	C2
Drewry La	C1
Duffield Rd	A1
Duke St	A2
Dunton Cl	B3
Eagle Market	C2
Eastgate	B3
East St	C2
Exeter St	B2
Farm St	C1
Ford St	B1
Forester St	C1
Fox St	A2
Friar Gate	B1
Friary St	B1
Full St	B2
Gerard St	C1
Gower St	C2
Green La	C2
Grey St	C1
Guildhall	B2
Harcourt St	C1
Highfield Rd	A1
Hill La	C2
Industrial	B2
Information Ctr	B2
Iron Gate	B2
John St	C3
Kedleston Rd	A1
Key St	B2
King Alfred St	C1
King St	A1
Kingston St	A1
Leopold St	C2
Library	B1
Liversage St	C3
Lodge La	B1
London Rd	C2
Macklin St	C1
Main Centre	C2
Mansfield Rd	A2
Market	B2
Market Pl	B2
May St	C1
Meadow La	B3
Melbourne St	C2
Midland Rd	C3
Monk St	C1
Morledge	B2
Mount St	C1
Museum & Art Gallery	B1
Noble St	C3
North Parade	A1
North St	A1
Nottingham Rd	B3
Osmaston Rd	C2
Otter St	A1
Park St	C3
Parker St	A1
Pickfords House	B1
Police HQ	A2
Police Station	B1
Post Office	A1/A2/B1/B2/C2/C3
Pride Parkway	C3
Prime Parkway	A2
Queens Leisure Centre	B1
Racecourse	A3
Railway Terr	C3
Register Office	C2
Sacheverel St	C2
Sadler Gate	B1
St Alkmund's Way	B1/B2
St Helens House	A1
St Mary's	A1
St Mary's Bridge Chapel	A2
St Mary's Gate	B1
St Paul's Rd	A2
St Peter's	C2
St Peter's St	C2
Siddals Rd	C3
Sir Frank Whittle Rd	A3
Spa La	C1
Spring St	C1
Stafford St	B1
Station Approach	C3
Stockbrook St	C1
Stores Rd	A3
Traffic St	C2
Wardwick	B1
Werburgh St	C1
West Ave	A1
West Meadows Industrial Est	B3
Wharf Rd	A2
Wilmot St	C2
Wilson St	C1
Wood's La	C1

63

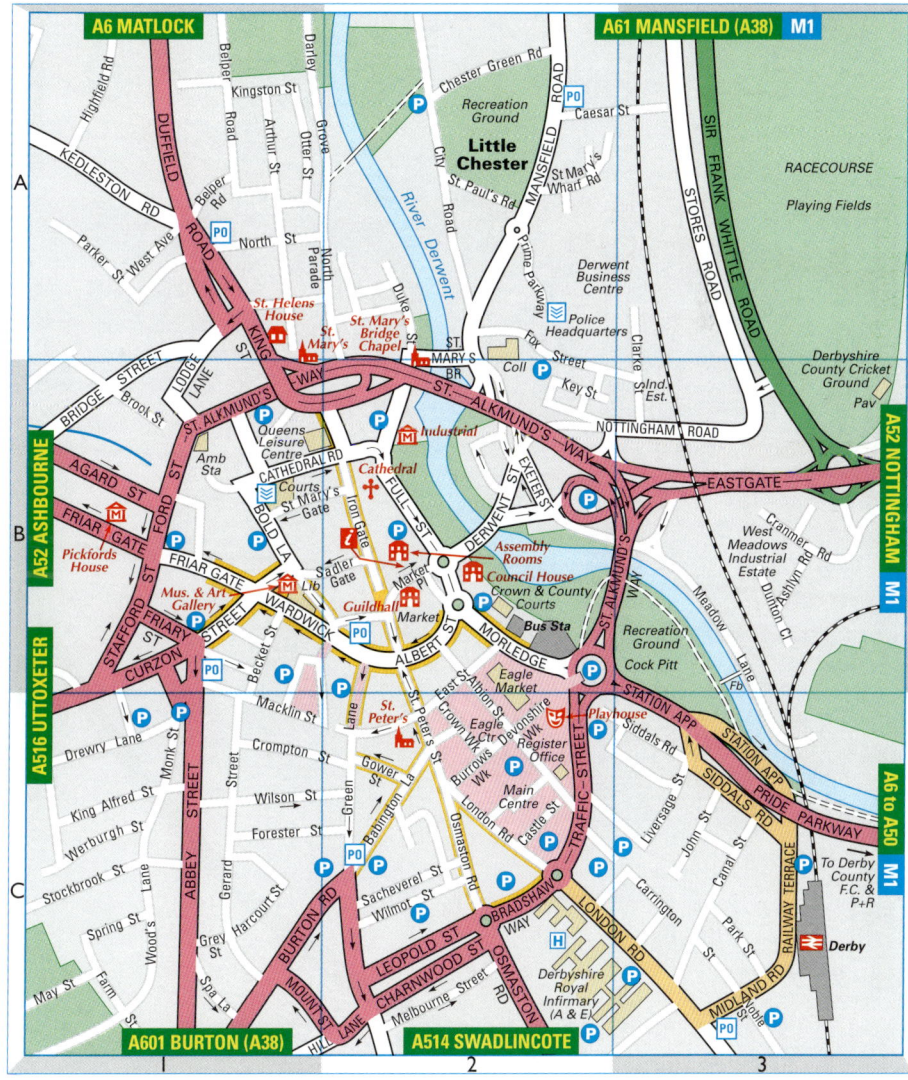

Dorchester

▲ Thomas Hardy's birthplace, Higher Bockhampton

Dorset's historic county town, most famous for its association with novelist Thomas Hardy (of whom there is a statue) but with Roman origins: among relics are Maiden Castle, England's biggest hillfort, built c.3000 BC on the site of a Neolithic longbarrow; and the Maumbury Rings, which began as a Neolithic henge and was converted into a large Roman amphitheatre, and later, in the 17th century, into an artillery fort. The Gallows Tour traces the history of Judge George Jeffreys, known as the Hanging Judge for his severe treatment of local rebels, who lodged in the town, while the Shire Hall was the venue for the trial of the Tolpuddle Martyrs. Other sights include the Dinosaur Museum, the Tutankhamun Museum and the Keep Military Museum. The town centre, which has many tree-lined walks along the line of the old Roman wall, has a good range of speciality shops, and there's a large, long-established Wednesday market. Nearby are T.E. Lawrence's home, Clouds Hill, and Chesil Beach.

Dorchester Tourist Information Centre, Antelope Walk, Dorchester DT1 1BE Tel 01305 267992

BBC Radio Solent 103.8 FM and 1359 AM • **Wessex FM** 97.2 FM

www.visit-dorchester.co.uk

★ Do not miss
- ★ **Dorset County Museum**, High West Street
- ★ **Hardy's Cottage**, Higher Bockhampton
- ★ **Roman Town House**, grounds of County Hall

Dorchester

Ackerman Rd	B3
Acland Rd	A2
Albert Rd	A1
Alexandra Rd	A1
Alfred Place	B3
Alfred Rd	B2
Alington Ave	B3
Alington Rd	B3
Ambulance Station	B3
Ashley Rd	B1
Balmoral Cres	C3
Barnes Way	B2/C2
Borough Gdns	A1
Bridport Rd	A1
Buckingham Way	C3
Caters Place	A1
Charles St	B1
Coburg Rd	B1
Colliton St	A1
Cornwall Rd	A1
Cromwell Rd	B1
Culliford Rd	B1
Culliford Rd North	B2
Dagmar Rd	B1
Damer's Rd	B1
Diggory Cres	B2
Dinosaur Museum	A2
Dorchester Bypass	C3
Dorchester South Station	B1
Dorchester West Station	B1
Dorset County Council Offices	A1
Dorset County Hospital	B1
Dorset County Museum	A1
Duchy Close	C3
Duke's Ave	B2
Durngate St	A2
Durnover Court	A2
Eddison Ave	B3
Edward Rd	A1
Egdon Rd	C2
Eldridge Pope Brewery ♦	B1
Elizabeth Frink Statue ♦	B2
Farfrae Cres	B2
Friary Hill	A2
Friary Lane	A2
Frome Terr	A2
Garland Cres	C3
Glyde Path Rd	A1
Gt. Western Rd	B1
Grosvenor Cres	C1
Grosvenor Rd	C1
HM Prison	A1
Herrington Rd	C1
High St East	A2
High Street Fordington	A2
High Street West	A1
Holloway Rd	A2
Icen Way	A2
Kings Rd	A3/B3
Kingsbere Cres	C2
Keep Military Museum, The	A1
Lancaster Rd	B2
Library	B1
Lime Cl	B1
Linden Ave	B2
London Cl	A3
London Rd	A3
Lubbecke Way	A3
Lucetta La	B2
Maiden Castle Rd	C1
Manor Rd	C2
Maumbury Rd	B1
Maumbury Rings	B1
Mellstock Ave	C1
Mill St	A3
Miller's Cl	B1
Mistover Cl	C1
Monmouth Rd	B1
North Sq	A2
Northernhay	A1
Old Crown Court & Cells	A1
Olga Rd	B1
Orchard St	A2
Police Station	B1
Post Office	A1/B1/B2
Pound Lane	A2
Poundbury Rd	A1
Prince of Wales Rd	B2
Prince's St	A1
Queen's Ave	B1
Roman Town House	A1
Roman Wall	A1
Rothesay Rd	C2
St George's Rd	B3
Salisbury Field	C2
Shaston Cres	C2
Smokey Hole La	B3
South Court Ave	A1
South St	B1
South Walks Rd	A1
Teddy Bear House	A1
Temple Cl	C1
The Grove	A1
Town Hall	A1
Town Pump ♦	A2
Trinity St	A1
Tutankhamun Exhibition	A1
Victoria Rd	B1
Weatherbury Way	C2
Wellbridge Cl	C1
West Mills Rd	A1
West Walks Rd	A1
Weymouth Ave	C1
Williams Ave	A1
Winterbourne Hospital	C1
Wollaston Rd	A2
York Rd	B2

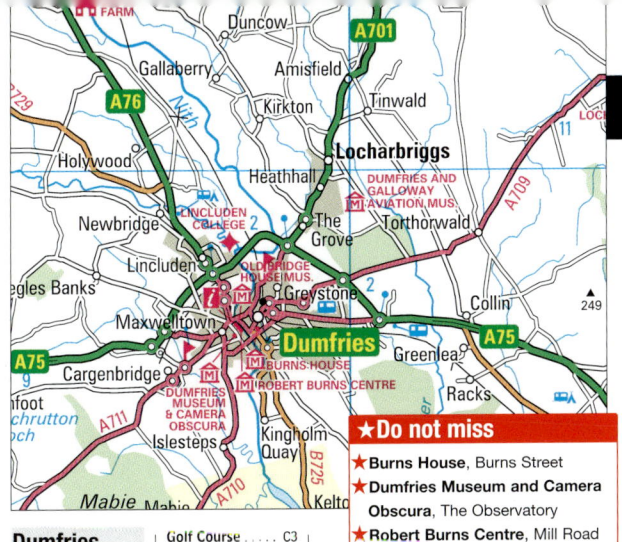

Dumfries

A former seaport, now southwest Scotland's largest town, best known for being the place where Robert Burns lived up until his death in 1796; visitors can view his house, containing some of his possessions, his mausoleum (St Michael's churchyard) and Ellisland Farm. Further sights of interest include the 15th-century Devorgilla Bridge across the Nith; Mid Steeple, an early-18th-century courthouse and prison; the remains of 15th-century Lincluden Collegiate Church; the Old Bridge House Museum of everyday life in the town and an award-winning aviation museum. Nearby attractions include Shambellie House Costume Museum, the ruined Sweetheart Abbey, the renovated New Abbey Corn Mill, Arbigland House and Gardens, the John Paul Jones Birthplace Museum about the father of the US navy and Mersehead RSPB Nature Reserve.

★ Do not miss

- ★ **Burns House**, Burns Street
- ★ **Dumfries Museum and Camera Obscura**, The Observatory
- ★ **Robert Burns Centre**, Mill Road

Dumfries Tourist Information Centre, Whitesands, Dumfries DG1 2RS Tel 01387 253862

BBC Radio Scotland 94.7 FM and 585 AM • South Westsound 97.0 FM

www.dumfriesandgalloway.co.uk

Dumfries

Street	Grid
Academy St	A2
Aldermanhill Rd	B3
Ambulance Station	C3
Annan Rd	A3
Ardwall Rd	C1
Ashfield Dr	A1
Atkinson Rd	C1
Averill Cres	C1
Balliol Ave	C1
Bank St	B2
Bankend Rd	C3
Barn Slaps	B3
Barrie Ave	C1
Beech Ave	A1
Bowling Green	B2
Brewery St	B2
Bridge House	B1
Brodie Ave	C3
Brooke St	C1
Broomlands Dr	C1
Brooms Rd	B3
Buccleuch St	A2
Burns House	B2
Burns Mausoleum	B3
Burns Statue ♦	B2
Bus Station	B1
Cardoness St	A3
Castle St	A2
Catherine St	A2
Cattle Market	A3
Cemetery	B3
Cemetery	C2
Church Cres	B2
Church St	B2
College Rd	A1
College St	A1
Corbelly Hill	B1
Corberry Park	B1
Cornwall Mt	A3
County Offices	A2
Court	A2
Craigs Rd	C3
Cresswell Ave	B3
Cresswell Hill	B3
Cumberland St	B3
David Keswick Athletic Centre	A3
David St	B1
Dock Park	C3
Dockhead	B2
Dumfries Academy	A2
Dumfries Museum & Camera Obscura	B2
Dumfries Royal Infirmary (A&E)	C3
Dumfries	A3
E. Riverside Dr	C3
Edinburgh Rd	A2
English St	B2
Fire Station	B3
Friar's Vennel	A2
Galloway St	B1
George Douglas Dr	C1
George St	C1
Gladstone Rd	C2
Glasgow St	A1
Glebe St	B3
Glencaple Rd	C3
Goldie Ave	A1
Goldie Cres	A1
Golf Course	C3
Greyfriars	A2
Grierson Ave	B3
HM Prison	B1
Hamilton Ave	C1
Hamilton Starke Park	C2
Hazelrigg Ave	C1
Henry St	B3
Hermitage Dr	C1
High Cemetery	C3
High St	A2
Hill Ave	C2
Hill St	B1
Holm Ave	C2
Hoods Loaning	A3
Howgate St	C1
Huntingdon Rd	A3
Information Ctr	B2
Irish St	B2
Irving St	A2
King St	A1
Kingholm Rd	C3
Kirkpatrick Ct	C2
Lauricknowe	B1
Leafield Rd	B3
Library	A2
Lochfield Rd	A1
Loreburn Pk	A3
Loreburn St	A2
Loreburne Shopping Centre	B2
Lover's Walk	A2
Martin Ave	C1
Maryholm Dr	A1
Mausoleum	B3
Maxwell St	B1
McKie Ave	C1
Mews La	A2
Mill Green	B2
Mill Rd	B1
Moat Rd	C2
Moffat Rd	A3
Mountainhall Pk	C3
Nelson St	C1
New Abbey Rd	B1/C1
New Bridge	B1
Newall Terr	A2
Nith Ave	A2
Nith Bank	C3
Nithbank Hospital	B3
Nithside Ave	A1
Odeon	B2
Old Bridge	B1
Palmerston Park (Queen of the South F.C.)	A1
Park Rd	C1
Pleasance Ave	C1
Police H.Q.	A3
Police Station	A2
Portland Dr	A1
Post Office	A2/B1/B2/B3/B3
Priestlands Dr	C1
Primrose St	B1
Queen St	B3
Queensberry St	A2
Rae St	A2
Richmond Ave	C1
Robert Burns Ctr	B2
Roberts Cres	C1
Robertson Ave	C3
Robinson Dr	C1
Rosefield Rd	C2
Rosemount St	B1
Rotchell Park	C1
Rotchell Rd	B1
Rugby Football Ground	C1
Ryedale Rd	C2
St Andrews	B2
St John the Evangelist	A2
St Josephs Coll	B3
St Mary's Industrial Estate	A3
St Mary's St	A3
St Michael St	B2
St Michael's Bridge Rd	B2
St Michael's Bridge	B2
St Michael's Cemetery	B3
St Michael's	B2
Shakespeare St	B2
Solway Dr	C2
Stakeford St	C1
Stark Cres	C2
Station Rd	A3
Steel Ave	A1
Sunderries Ave	A1
Sunderries Rd	A1
Suspension Brae	B2
Swimming Pool	A1
Terregles St	B1
Theatre Royal	B2
Troqueer Rd	C2
Union St	A1
West Riverside Dr	C3
Wallace St	B3
Welldale	B2
White Sands	B2

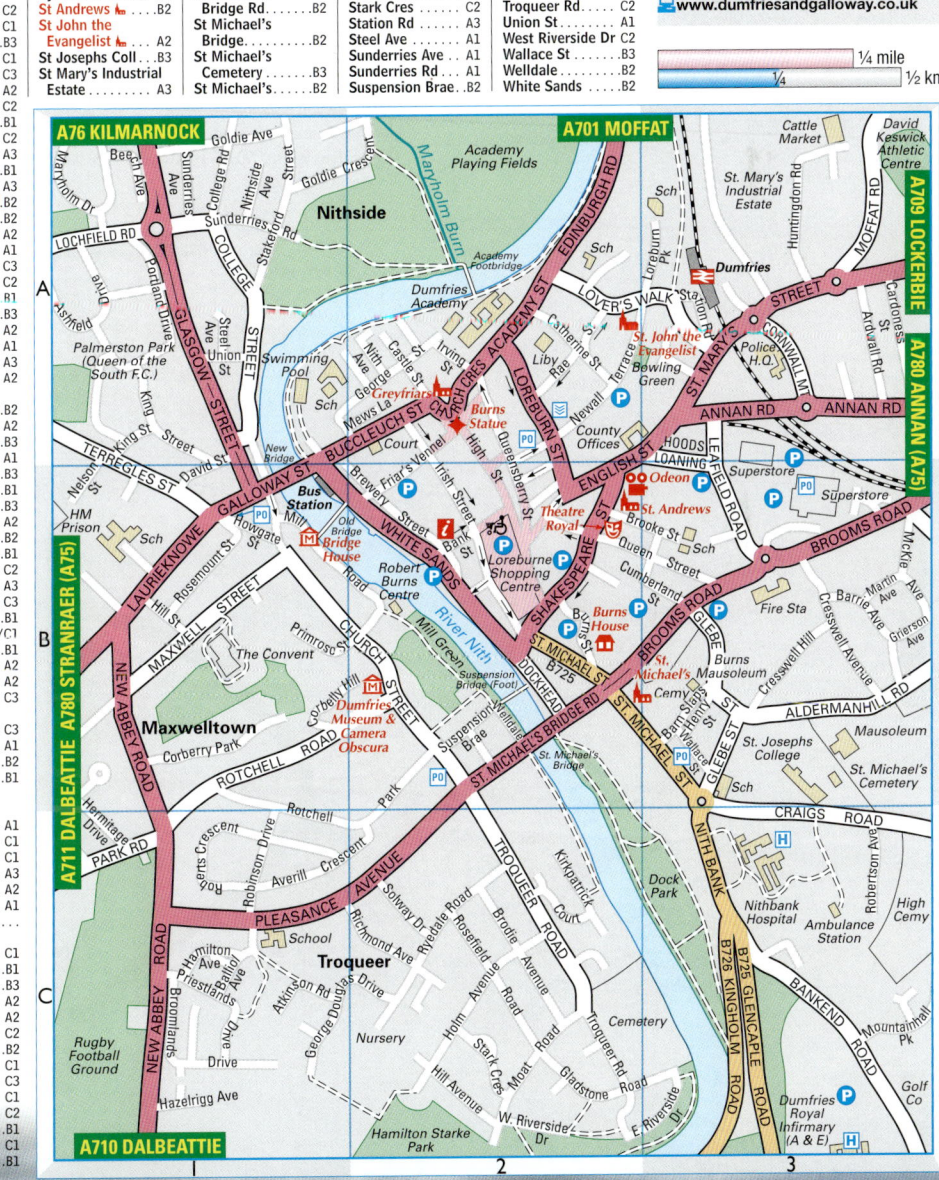

¼ mile / ½ km

Dundee

The fourth-largest city in Scotland, with a rich seafaring and industrial history, a thriving cultural quarter including the Dundee Contemporary Arts Centre, and a wide range of department stores and specialist and high-street shops. Attractions include the RRS (Royal Research Ship) *Discovery*, the ship used during Captain Scott's Antarctic expedition; the HMS Frigate *Unicorn*, a former warship; Broughty Castle, a coastal fort with panoramic views, used as a museum about local history and wildlife, including whaling in the area; and Mills Observatory, with a planetarium. Among the parks and gardens are Camperdown Country Park with its award-winning wildlife centre, Templeton Woods and the University Botanic Gardens.

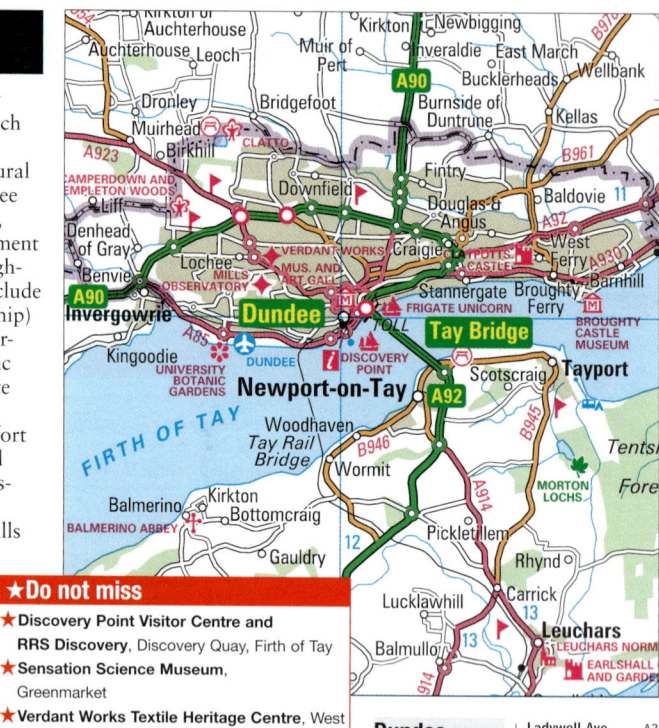

▲ RRS *Discovery*

Dundee Information Centre,
21 Castle Street, Dundee DD1 3AA
Tel 01832 527527

BBC Radio Scotland 94.3 FM and 810 AM • **Tay AM** 1161 AM
Tay FM 102.8 FM • **Wave 102** 102.0 FM

www.angusanddundee.co.uk

★ Do not miss
★ **Discovery Point Visitor Centre and RRS Discovery**, Discovery Quay, Firth of Tay
★ **Sensation Science Museum**, Greenmarket
★ **Verdant Works Textile Heritage Centre**, West Hendersons Wynd

Dundee

Adelaide Pl	A1
Airlie Pl	C1
Albany Terr	A1
Albert	B2
Albert St	A3
Alexander St	A2
Ann St	A2
Arthurstone Terr	A3
Bank St	B2
Barrack Rd	B2
Barrack St	B2
Bell St	B2
Blackscroft	A3
Blinshall St	B1
Brown St	B1
Bus Station	B3
Caird Hall	B2
Camperdown St	B3
Candle La	B3
Carmichael St	A1
Carnegie St	A2
City Churches	B2
City Quay	B3
City Sq	B2
Commercial St	B2
Constable St	A3
Constitution Ct	A1
Constitution Cres	A1
Constitution St	A1/B2
Contemporary Art Centre	C2
Cotton Rd	A3
Courthouse Sq	B1
Cowgate	A3
Crescent St	A3
Crichton St	B2
Dens Brae	A3
Dens Rd	A3
Discovery Point	C2
Douglas St	B1
Drummond St	A1
Dudhope Castle	A1
Dudhope St	A2
Dudhope Terr	A1
Dundee	C2
Dundee High School	B2
Dura St	A3
East Dock St	B3
East Whale La	B3
East Marketgait	B3
Erskine St	A3
Euclid Cr	B2
Forebank Rd	A2
Foundry La	B3
Gallagher Retail Park	B3
Gellatly St	B3
Government Offices	C2
Guthrie St	B1
Hawkhill	B1
Hilltown	A2
HMS Unicorn	B3
Howff Cem, The	B2
Information Ctr	B2
King St	A3
Kinghorne Rd	A1
Ladywell Ave	A3
Laurel Bank	A2
Law Hill, The	A1
Law Rd	A1
Law St	A1
Library	A2
Little Theatre	A2
Lochee Rd	B1
Lower Princes St	A3
Lyon St	A3
Meadow Side	B2
Meadowside St Pauls	B2
Mercat Cross	B2
Murraygate	B2
Nelson St	A2
Nethergate	B2/C1
North Marketgait	B2
North Lindsay St	B2
Old Hawkhill	B1
Olympia Swimming & Leisure Ctr	C3
Overgate Shopping Centre	B2
Park Pl	B1
Perth Rd	C1
Police Station	A2/B1
Post Office	A2/B2/C2
Princes St	A3
Prospect Pl	A2
Reform St	B2
Repertory	A2
Riverside Dr	C2
Roseangle	C1
Rosebank St	A2
RRS Discovery	C2
St Andrew's	C2
St Pauls Episcopal	B3
Science Centre	C2
Sea Captains House	B3
Sheriffs Court	B1
South Ward Rd	B2
South George St	A2
South Marketgait	B3
South Tay St	B2
Steps	A2
Tay Road Bridge	C3
Tayside House	B2
Trades La	B3
Union St	B2
Union Terr	A1
University Library	B2
Univ of Abertay	B2
Univ of Dundee	B1
Upper Constitution St	A1
Victoria Rd	A2
Victoria St	A3
West Marketgait	B1/B2
Ward Rd	B1
Wellgate	B2
West Bell St	B1
Westfield Pl	C1
William St	A3
Wishart Arch	A3

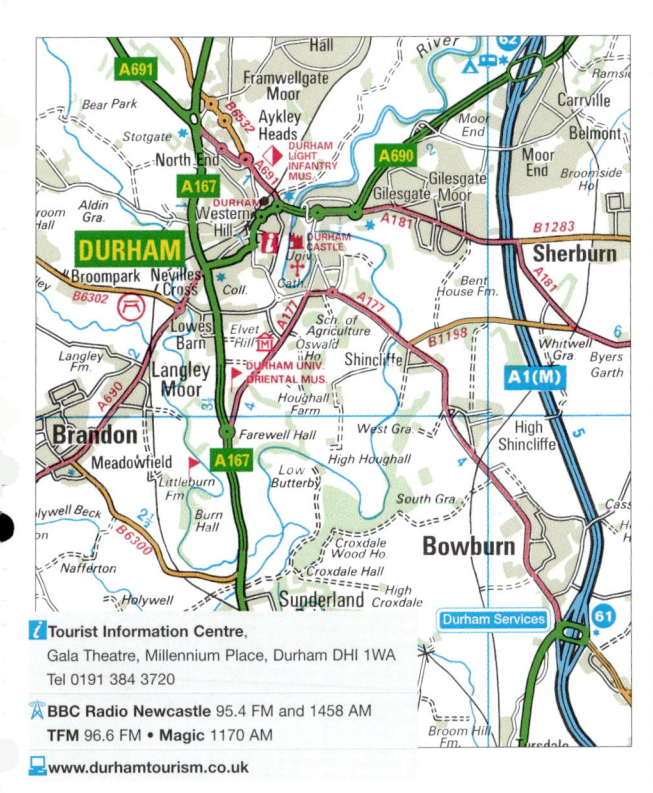

Durham

A compact city founded 1000 years ago with the arrival of a religious community seeking a resting place for St Cuthbert of Lindisfarne. Later it was the base from which King William defended Northumbria from the Scots and it was during this period that the magnificent Norman cathedral and castle were constructed; the two are now a UNESCO World Heritage Site. In the 19th century the castle became the first college of the city's famous university. Other historic structures include the 12th-century Elvet and Framwellgate bridges, the Guildhall (1356), and the 1777 Prebends Bridge, from which Turner painted. Among sights of interest are Durham Heritage Centre and Museum, the university's Museum of Archaeology and the Durham Light Industry Museum. The main outdoor attractions are the university's Botanic Garden and the 17th-century riverside Old Durham Gardens. Shopping amenities include a Victorian indoor market.

▲ Durham Castle

Tourist Information Centre,
Gala Theatre, Millennium Place, Durham DH1 1WA
Tel 0191 384 3720

BBC Radio Newcastle 95.4 FM and 1458 AM
TFM 96.6 FM • **Magic** 1170 AM

www.durhamtourism.co.uk

★ Do not miss
★ **Durham Cathedral and Castle,** Palace Green
★ **Crook Hall (14th-century manor) and Gardens,** Sidegate
★ **Oriental Museum,** Elvet Hill

Durham

Alexander Cr B2	Millburngate Bridge B2
Allergate B2	Millburngate Ctr . . . B2
Archery Rise C1	Millennium Bridge (foot/cycle) . . . A2
Assize Courts B3	Millennium Ctr B3
Back Western Hill . . A1	Museum of Archaeology B2
Bakehouse La . . . A3	Neville's Cross College C1
Baths Bridge B3	Nevilledale Terr . . . B1
Boat House B3	New Elvet B3
Boyd St C3	New Elvet Bridge . B3
Bus Station B2	North Bailey B3
Castle B2	North End A1
Castle Chare B2	North Rd A1/B2
Cathedral B2	Observatory C1
Church St B2	Old Elvet B3
Clay La C1	Oriental Mus C2
Claypath B2	Passport Office . . . A2
College of St Hild & St Bede B3	Percy Terr B1
County Hall A1	Pimlico C2
County Hospital . . . B1	Police Station B3
Crook Hall ♦ A3	Post Office A1/B2
Crossgate B2	Potters Bank C1/C2
Crossgate Peth . . . C1	Prebends Bridge . . C2
Darlington Rd C1	Prebends Walk . . . C2
Durham A2	Princes St A1
Durham Light Infantry Mus & Arts Centre A2	Providence Row . . A3
	Quarryheads La . . . C2
Durham School . . . C2	Redhills La B1
Ellam Ave C1	Redhills Terr B1
Elvet Bridge B3	Saddler St B3
Elvet Court B3	St Chad's College . C3
Farnley Hey B1	St Cuthbert's Society C2
Ferens Cl A3	St John's College . C2
Fieldhouse La A1	St Margaret's B2
Flass St B1	St Mary The Less C2
Framwelgate A2	St Mary's College . C2
Framwelgate Bridge B2	St Monica Grove . . B1
Framwelgate Peth . B2	St Nicholas B3
Framwelgate Waterside A2	St Oswald's C3
Frankland La A3	Sidegate A2
Freeman's Pl A3	Silver St B2
Gala & Sacred Journey B3	South Bailey C2
	South Rd C3
Geoffrey Ave C1	South St B2
Gilesgate B3	Springwell Ave . . . A1
Grey College B3	Stockton Rd B3
Grove St C2	Students' Rec Ctr . B3
Hallgarth St C3	Sutton St B2
Hatfield College . . B3	The Avenue B1
Hawthorn Terr . . . B1	The Crescent A1
Heritage Ctr B3	The Grove A1
HM Prison C3	The Sands A3
Information Ctr . . . B2	Town Hall B2
John St B1	Treasury Mus B2
Kingsgate Bridge . . B3	University ♦ B2
Laburnum Terr . . . B3	Univ Arts Block . . . B3
Lawson Terr C1	Univ Library C3
Leazes Rd B2/B3	Univ Science Labs . C3
Library B2	Wearside Dr A3
Margery La B2	Western Hill A1
Mavin St C3	Wharton Park A2
Millburngate B2	Whinney Hill C3

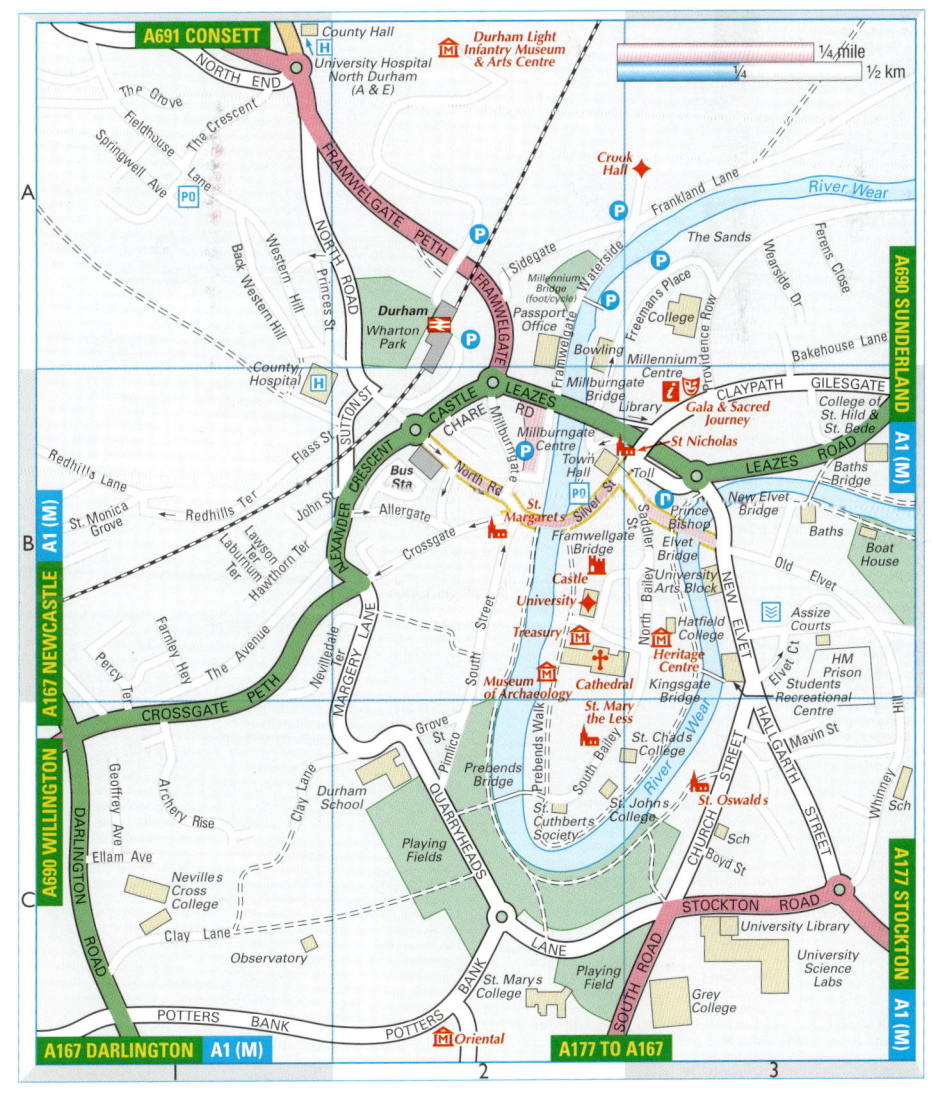

Edinburgh

Abbey Strand	B6
Abbeyhill	A6
Abbeyhill Cr	B6
Abbeymount	A6
Abercromby Pl	A3
Adam St	C5
Albany La	A4
Albany St	A4
Albert Memorial ✦	B2
Alva Pl	A6
Alva St	B1
Ann St	A1
Appleton Tower	C4
Archibald Pl	C3
Argyle House	C3
Assembly Rooms & Musical Hall	A3
Atholl Cr	B1
Atholl Crescent La	C1
BBC	A3
Bank St	B4
Barony St	A4
Beaumont Pl	C5
Belford Rd	B1
Belgrave Cr	A1
Belgrave Crescent La	A1
Bell's Brae	B1
Blackfriars St	B4
Blair St	B4
Bread St	C2
Bristo Pl	C4
Bristo St	C4
Brougham St	C2
Broughton St	A4
Brown St	C5
Brunton Terr	A6
Buckingham Terr	A1
Burial Ground	A6
Bus Station	A4
Caledonian Cr	C1
Caledonian Rd	C1
Calton Hill	A4
Calton Hill	A5
Calton Rd	B4
Camera Obscura & Outlook Tower ✦	B3
Candlemaker Row	C4
Canning St	B2
Canongate	B5
Canongate ⛪	B5
Carlton St	A1
Carlton Terr	A6
Carlton Terrace La	A6
Castle	B2
Castle Terr	B2
Castlehill	B3
Central Library	B4
Chalmers Hospital H	C3
Chalmers St	C3
Chambers St	C4
Chapel St	C4
Charles St	C4
Charlotte Sq	B2
Chester St	B1
Circus La	A2
Circus Pl	A2
City Art Centre	B4
City Chambers 🏛	B4
City Observatory	A5
Clarendon Cr	A1
Clerk St	C5
Coates Cr	B1
Cockburn St	B4
College of Art	C3
Comely Bank Ave	A1
Comely Bank Row	A1
Cornwall St	C2
Cowans Cl	C3
Cowgate	B4
Cranston St	B5
Crichton St	C4
Croft-An-Righ	A6
Cumberland St	A2
Dalry Cl	C1
Dalry Rd	C1
Danube St	A1
Darnawy St	B2
David Hume Tower	C4
Davie St	C5
Dean Bridge	A1
Dean Gdns	A1
Dean Park Cr	A1
Dean Park Mews	A1
Dean Park St	A1
Dean Path	B1
Dean St	A1
Dean Terr	A1
Dewar Pl	C1
Dewar Place La	C1
Doune Terr	A2
Drummond Pl	A3
Drummond St	C5
Drumsheugh Gdns	B1
Dublin Mews	A3
Dublin St	A4
Dublin Street La South	A4
Dumbiedykes Rd	B5
Dundas St	A3
Earl Grey St	C2
East Norton Pl	A6
East Crosscauseway	C5
East Market St	B4
East Princes St Gdns	B4
Easter Rd	A6
Edinburgh (Waverley) 🚂	B4
Edinburgh Castle 🏰	B3
Edinburgh Dungeon ✦	B4
Edinburgh Festival Theatre ⛪	C4
Edinburgh International Conference Ctr	C2
Elder St	A4
Esplanade	B3
Eton Terr	A1
Eye Hospital H	C3
Festival Office	B3
Filmhouse 🎬	C2
Fire Station	B2
Floral Clock ✦	B3
Forres St	A2
Forth St	A4
Fountainbridge	C2
Frederick St	A3
Freemasons' Hall	B3
Fruit Market 🏛	B4
Gardner's Cr	C2
George Heriot's School	C3
George IV Bridge	B4
George Sq	C4
George Sq La	C4
George St	B2
Georgian House ✦	B2
Gladstone's Land ✦	B4
Glen St	C3
Gloucester La	A2
Gloucester Pl	A2
Gloucester St	A2
Graham St	C3
Grassmarket	B3
Great King St	A3
Great Stuart	B1
Greenside La	A5
Greenside Row	A5
Greyfriars Kirk ⛪	C4
Grindlay St	C2
Grosvenor St	C1
Grove St	C1
Gullan's Cl	B5
Guthrie St	B4
Hanover St	A3
Hart St	A4
Haymarket Station 🚂	C1
Heriot Pl	C3
Heriot Row	A2
High School Yard	B5
High St	B4
Hill Pl	C5
Hill St	A2
Hillside Cr	A5
Holyrood Abbey (AD 1128) (Remains of)	A6
Holyrood Park	C6
Holyrood Rd	B5
Home St	C2
Hope St	B2
Horse Wynd	B6
Howden St	C5
Howe St	A2
India Pl	A2
India St	A2
Infirmary St	B4
Jamaica Mews	A2
Jeffrey St	B4
John Knox's House	B4
Johnston Terr	C3
Keir St	C3
Kerr St	A2
King's Stables Rd	B3
Lady Lawson St	C3
Lady Stair's House	B4
Laserquest ✦	C2
Lauriston Gdns	C3
Lauriston Park	C3
Lauriston Pl	C3
Lauriston St	C3
Lawnmarket	B3
Leith St	A4
Lennox St	A1
Lennox St La	A1
Leslie Pl	A2
London Rd	A5
Lothian Health Board	C5
Lothian Rd	B2
Lothian St	C4
Lower Menz Pl	A5
Lynedoch Pl	B1
Manor Pl	B1
Market St	B4
Marshall St	C4
Maryfield	A6
Maryfield Pl	A6
McEwan Hall	C4
Medical School	C4
Melville St	B1
Meuse La	B4
Middle Meadow Walk	C4
Milton St	A6
Montrose Terr	A6
Moray Circus	A2
Moray House (College)	B5
Morrison Link	C1
Morrison St	C1
Mound Pl	B3
Museum of Childhood	B5
Museum of Edinburgh	B5
National Gallery 🏛	B3
National Library of Scotland	B4
National Monument ✦	A5
National Portrait Gallery & Museum of Antiquities 🏛	A3
Nelson Monument ✦	A5
Nelson St	B5
New St	B5
Nicolson Sq	C4
Nicolson St	C4
Niddry St	B4
North Bridge	B4
North Meadow Walk	C3
North Bank St	B3
North Castle St	A2
North Charlotte St	A2
North St Andrew St	A3
North St David St	A3
North West Circus Pl	A2
Northumberland St	A3
Odeon 🎬	C2
Old Royal High School	A5
Old Tolbooth Wynd	B5
Our Dynamic Earth ✦	B6
Oxford Terr	A1
Palace of Holyrood House ✦	B6
Palmerston Pl	B1
Panmure Pl	C3
Parliament House 🏛	B4
Parliament Sq	B4
People's Story, The ✦	B5
Playhouse Theatre 🎭	A4
Pleasance	C5
Police Station 🚔	A4
Ponton St	C2
Post Office ✉	A2/A4/B2/B4/B5/C1/C2/C4/C5
Potterrow	C4
Princes Mall	B4
Princes St	B3
Queen St	B1
Queen Street Gdns	A3
Queen's Dr	B6/C6
Queensferry Rd	A1
Queensferry St	B1
Queensferry Street La	A1
Radical Rd	C6
Randolph Cr	B1
Regent Gdns	A5
Regent Rd	A5
Regent Rd Park	A6
Regent Terr	A5
Register House 🏛	A4
Richmond Pl	C5
Richmond St	C5
Rose St	B2
Rosemount Bldgs	C1
Ross Open Air Theatre 🎭	B3
Rothesay Pl	B1
Rothesay Terr	B1
Roxburgh Pl	C5
Roxburgh St	C5
Royal Bank of Scotland	A4
Royal Circus	A2
Royal Lyceum 🎭	C2
Royal Museum of Scotland	C4
Royal Scottish Academy 🏛	B3
Royal Terr	A5
Rutland Sq	B2
Rutland St	B2
St Andrew Sq	A3
St Andrew's House	A4
St Bernard's Cr	A1
St Cecilia's Hall	B4
St Cuthbert's ⛪	B2
St Giles' †	B4
St James Centre	A4
St John St	B5
St John's ⛪	B2
St John's Hill	B5
St Leonard's Hill	C5
St Leonard's La	C5
St Leonard's St	C5
St Mary's (R.C.) †	A4
St Mary's Scottish Episcopal †	B1
St Mary's St	B5
St Stephen St	A2
Salisbury Crags	C6
Saunders St	A2
Scott Monument ✦	B4
Scottish Arts Council Gallery	B2
Scottish Parliament	B6
Semple St	C2
Shandwick Pl	B2
South Bridge	C4
South Charlotte St	B2
South College St	C4
South Learmonth Gdns	A1
South St Andrew St	A4
South St David St	A4
Spittal St	C2
Stafford St	B1
Student Centre	C4
TA Centre	C4
Tattoo Office	B4
Teviot Pl	C4
The Mall	B5
The Mound	B3
The Royal Mile	B4
Thistle St	A3
Torphichen Pl	C1
Torphichen St	C1
Traverse Theatre 🎭	B2
Tron, The ✦	B4
Tron Sq	B4
Union St	A4
University	C4
University Library	C4
Upper Grove Pl	C1
Usher Hall 🎭	C2
Vennel	C3
Victoria St	B3
Viewcraig Gdns	B5
Viewcraig St	B5
Walker St	B1
Waterloo Pl	A4
Waverley Bridge	B4
Wemyss Pl	A2
West Crosscauseway	C5
West Maitland St	C1
West of Nicholson St	C5
West Port	C3
West Princes Street Gdns	B3
West Richmond St	C5
West Tollcross	C2
Western Approach Rd	C1
White Horse Cl	B5
William St	B1
Windsor St	A5
York La	A4
York Pl	A4
Young St	A2

68

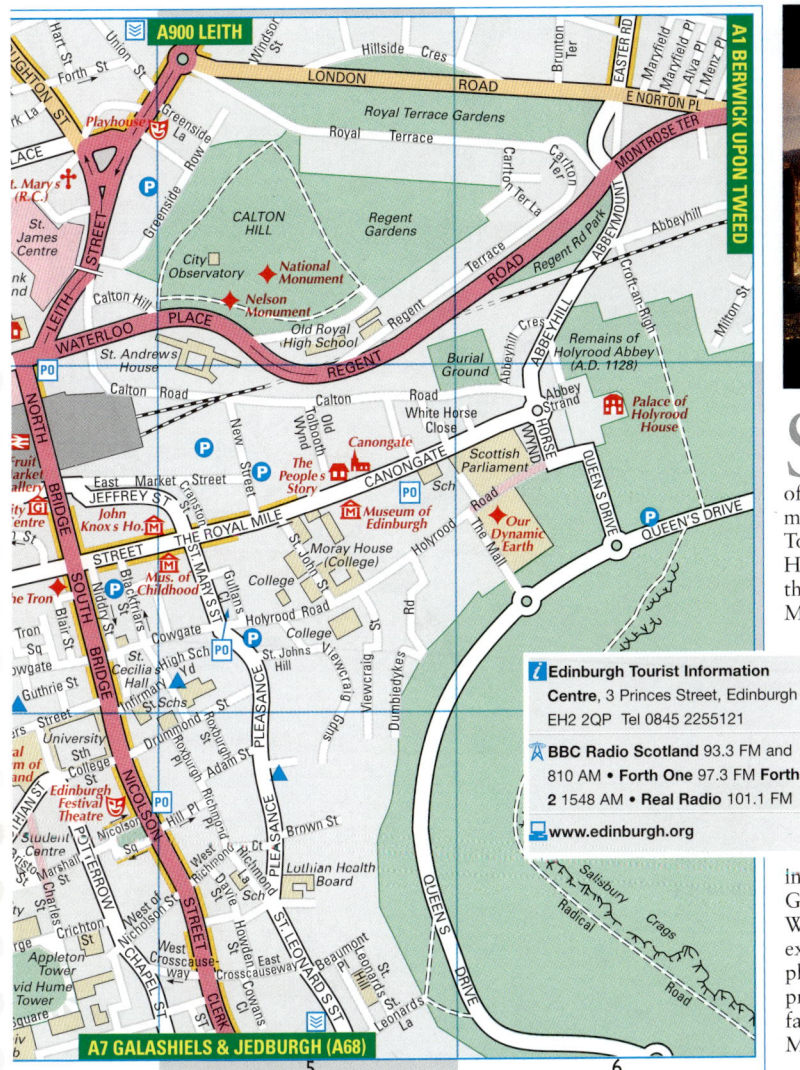

Edinburgh

Scotland's lively, eclectic capital is perhaps best known for its architecture, which ranges from the cramped medieval tenements of the Old Town (including Gladstone's Land museum) to the elegant townhouses of the New Town (including the National Trust's Georgian House), from the Gothic Scott Monument to the new Scottish Parliament building. The Royal Mile runs down from the city's castle, built on a rock inhabited by Celts as early as 800BC and home to the 12th-century St Margaret's Chapel, to the Palace of Holyroodhouse, official Scottish residence of the royal family and the site of Mary Queen of Scots' Chambers. The world-class array of art venues and museums includes the Scottish National Gallery of Modern Art, National Gallery of Scotland, Royal Museum, Writers' Museum and Royal Yacht *Britannia*. Of interest to nature lovers are the Royal Botanic Garden, Holyrood Park & Arthur's Seat, the Water of Leith, and Our Dynamic Earth. The excellent shops, hotels and restaurants include plenty of budget options, and the year-round programme of special events includes the world-famous International Festival of theatre, and the Military Tattoo.

▲ Princes Street

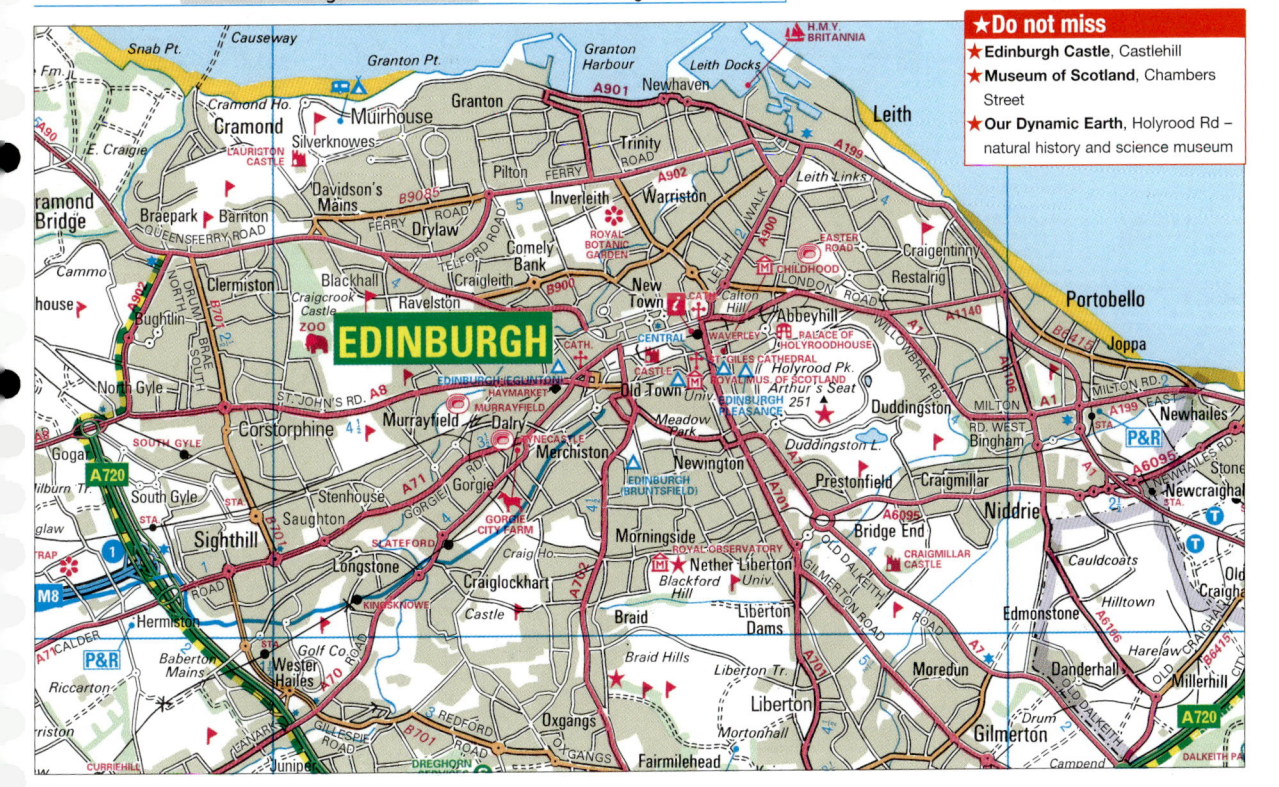

Edinburgh Tourist Information Centre, 3 Princes Street, Edinburgh EH2 2QP Tel 0845 2255121
BBC Radio Scotland 93.3 FM and 810 AM • **Forth One** 97.3 FM **Forth 2** 1548 AM • **Real Radio** 101.1 FM
www.edinburgh.org

★ Do not miss

★ **Edinburgh Castle**, Castlehill
★ **Museum of Scotland**, Chambers Street
★ **Our Dynamic Earth**, Holyrood Rd – natural history and science museum

Exeter

Exeter is an historic cathedral and university city and the county town of Devon. It has grown from Roman origins with the historic centre now designated as an Area of Archaeological Importance. Exeter's Quayside was once a Roman waterway and 16th century port and now functions as a city centre riverside resort with shops, restaurants and outdoor activities. The Guildhall, dating from 1330, is reputed to be the oldest municipal building still in full civic use in England. The city is well served for all forms of entertainment from cinemas to theatres, pubs and restaurants.

▲ The 17th-century Custom House on the Quayside

Exeter

Street	Grid
Alphington St	C1
Athelstan Rd	B3
Bampfylde St	B2
Barnardo Rd	B3
Barnfield Hill	B3
Barnfield Rd	B2/B3
Barnfield	B2
Bartholomew St East	B1
Bartholomew St West	B1
Bear St	B2
Beaufort Rd	C1
Bedford St	B2
Belgrave Rd	A3
Belmont Rd	A3
Blackall Rd	A2
Blackboy Rd	A3
Bonhay Rd	B1
Bull Meadow Rd	C2
Bus & Coach Sta	B3
Castle St	B2
Cecil Rd	C1
Cheeke St	A3
Church Rd	C1
Chute St	A3
City Industrial Est	C2
City Wall	B1/B2
Civic Centre	B2
Clifton Rd	B3
Clifton St	B3
Clock Tower	A1
College Rd	B3
Colleton Cr	C2
Commercial Rd	C1
Coombe St	B2
Cowick St	C1
Crown Courts	B2
Custom House	C2
Danes' Rd	A2
Denmark Rd	C3
Devon Cty Hall	C3
Devonshire Pl	A2
Dinham Rd	B1
East Grove Rd	C3
Edmund St	C1
Elmgrove Rd	A1
Exe St	B1
Exeter Central ≷	A1
Exeter City Football Ground	A3
Exeter College	A1
Exeter Picture House	B1
Fire Station	B1
Fore St	B1
Friars Walk	C2
Guildhall	B2
Guildhall Shopping Centre	B2
Harlequin's Shopping Centre	B1
Haven Rd	C2
Heavitree Rd	B3
Hele Rd	A1
High St	B2
HM Prison	A2
Holloway St	C2
Hoopern St	A2
Horseguards	A2
Howell Rd	A1
Information Ctr	B3
Iron Bridge	B1
Isca Rd	C1
Jesmond Rd	A3
King William St	A2
King St	B1
Larkbeare Rd	C2
Leisure Centre	C1
Library	B2
Longbrook St	A2
Longbrook Terr	A2
Lucky La	C2
Lower North St	B1
Lyndhurst Rd	C3
Magdalen Rd	B3
Magdalen St	B2
Magistrates & Crown Courts	A2
Market	B2
Market St	B2
Marlborough Rd	C3
Mary Arches St	B1
Matford Rd	C3
Matford Ave	C3
Matford La	C3
May St	A3
Mol's Coffee Ho	B2
New Bridge St	B1
New North Rd	A1/A2
North St	B1
Northernhay St	B1
Norwood Ave	C3
Odeon	A3
Okehampton St	C1
Old Mill Cl	C2
Old Tiverton Rd	A3
Oxford Rd	A3
Paris St	B2
Parr St	A3
Paul St	B1
Pennsylvania Rd	A2
Police H.Q.	B3
Portland Street	B3
Post Office	A3/B1/B3/C1
Powderham Cr	A3
Preston St	B1
Princesshay development (2007)	B2
Queen St	A1
Queen's Rd	C1
Queen's Terr	A1
Radford Rd	C2
Richmond Rd	A1
Roberts Rd	C2
Rougemont Castle	A2
Rougemont Ho	B2
Royal Albert Memorial Mus	B2
St David's Rd	A1
St James' Pk ≷	A3
St James' Rd	A3
St Leonard's Rd	C3
St Lukes College	B3
St Mary Steps	C1
St Nicholas Priory (AM)	B1
St Peter's Cathedral	B2
St Thomas	C1
Sandford Walk	B3
School for the Deaf	C2
School Rd	C1
Sidwell St	B1
Smythen St	B1
South St	B2
Southernhay East	B3
Southernhay West	B2
Spicer Rd	B3
Spacex Gallery	B1
Sports Centre	A3
Summerland St	A3
Swimming Pool	B3
Sydney Rd	C1
Tan La	C2
The Quay	C2
Thornton Hill	A2
Topsham Rd	C3
Tucker's Hall	B1
Tudor St	B1
Velwell Rd	A1
Verney St	A3
Water La	C1/C2
Weirfield Rd	C2
Well St	A3
West Ave	A2
Western Way	A3/B1/B2
West Grove Rd	C3
Wonford Rd	B3/C3
York Rd	A2

ℹ **Tourist Information Centre**, Civic Centre, Dix's Field, Exeter EX1 1RQ Tel 01392 265700

📻 **BBC Radio Devon** 95.8 FM and 990 AM • **Classic Gold** 666, 954 AM **Gemini** 97 FM

🌐 www.exeter.gov.uk

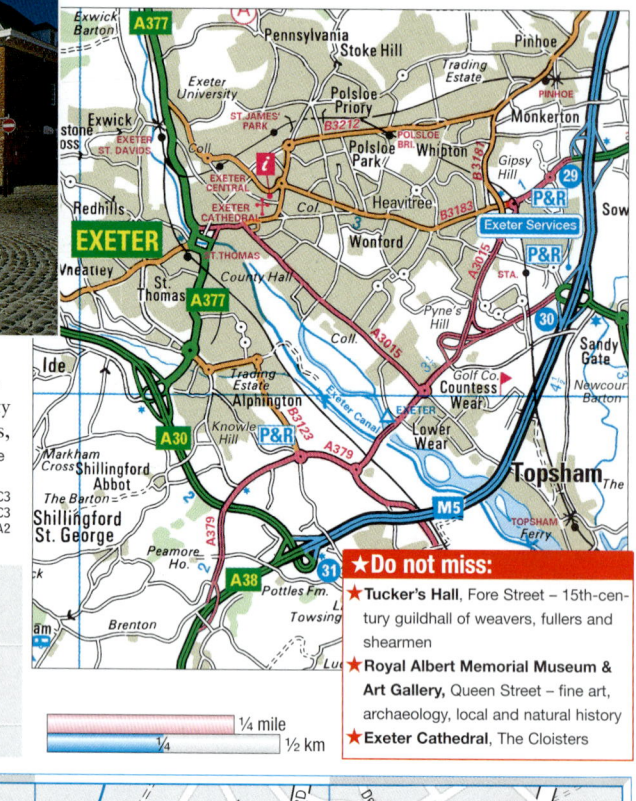

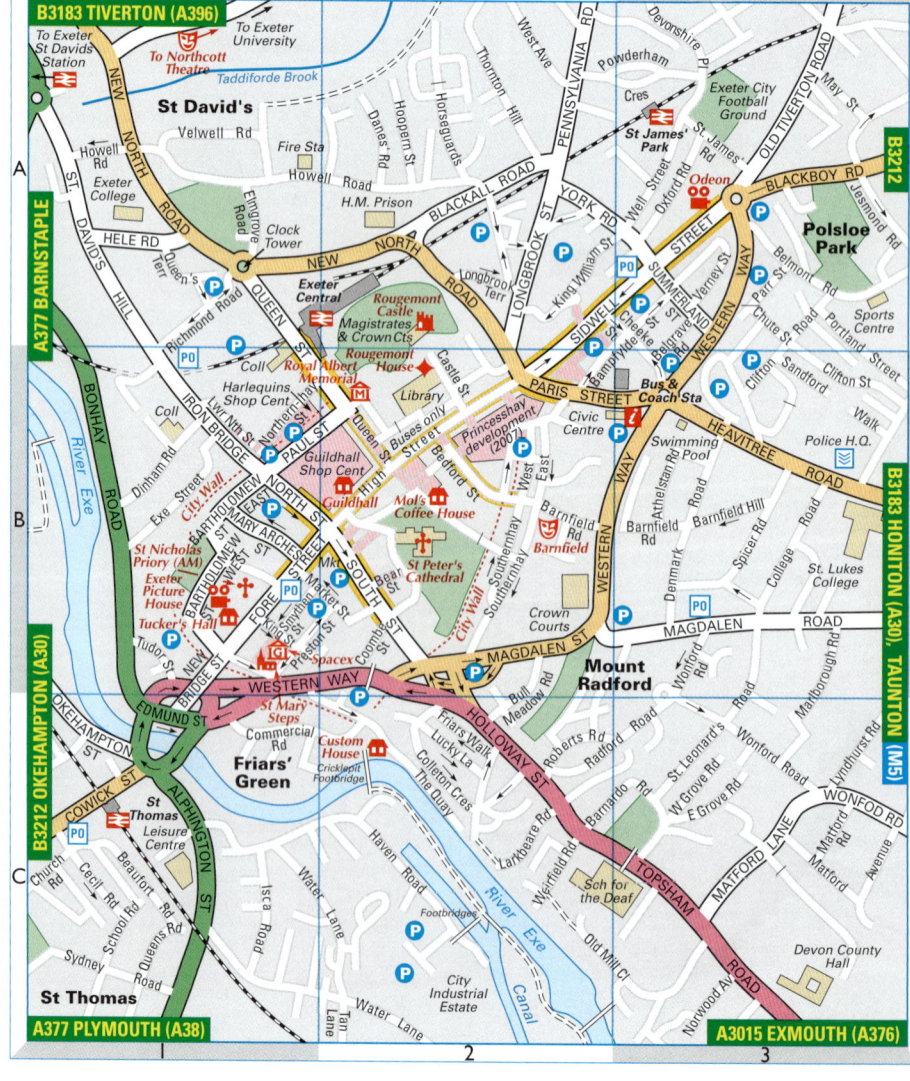

★ **Do not miss:**
- ★ **Tucker's Hall**, Fore Street – 15th-century guildhall of weavers, fullers and shearmen
- ★ **Royal Albert Memorial Museum & Art Gallery**, Queen Street – fine art, archaeology, local and natural history
- ★ **Exeter Cathedral**, The Cloisters

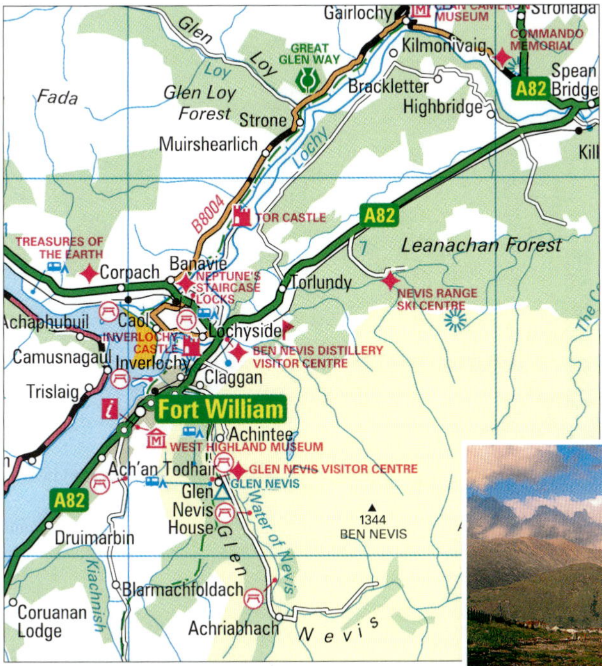

Fort William

A large town at the foot of Ben Nevis, Britain's highest mountain, in Scotland's scenic west Highlands, at the head of the Great Glen linking the Atlantic with the North Sea and accessible from London on a romantic sleeper train. Named after William of Orange's 18th-century military fort built for English Redcoat soldiers (of which the remains can be viewed), it is home to the West Highland Museum, Ben Nevis Distillery and two ruined castles, while nearby are Fort William Smelter & the Aluminium Story, the WWII Commando Memorial, the Clan Cameron Museum on the history of the Highlands and the Jacobite cause and Glen Roy National Nature Reserve, including the famous Parallel Roads glacial landform. There is reliable skiing and snowboarding in January, other outdoor sports year-round, and seal-spotting trips on Loch Linnhe.

71

▶ Ben Nevis from Corpach

i Fort William Tourist Information
Centre, Cameron Square, Fort William
PH33 6AJ Tel 01397 703781

BBC Radio Scotland 93.7 FM and 810 AM • **Nevis Radio** 96.6 FM

www.visit-fortwilliam.co.uk

★ **Do not miss**
★ **Mountain Gondola**, Nevis Range
★ **Treasures of the Earth**, Corpach
 – crystal, gemstone and fossil exhibition
★ **West Highland Way** – long-distance footpath to Milngavie

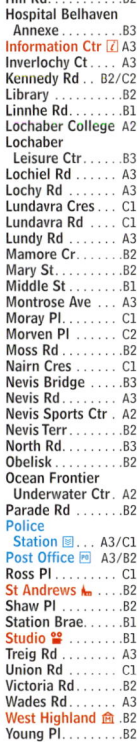

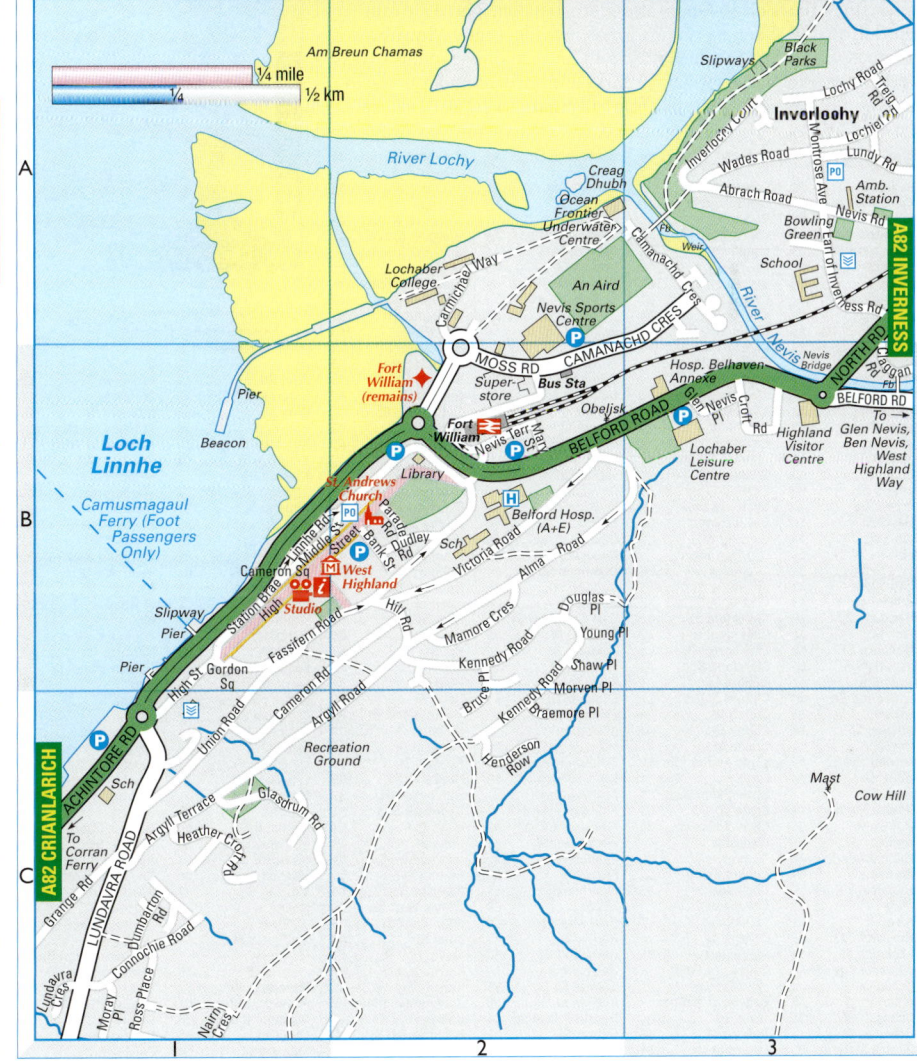

Fort William

Abrach Rd	A3
Achintore Rd	C1
Alma Rd	B2
Am Breun Chamas	A2
Ambulance Station	A3
An Aird	A2
Argyll Rd	C1
Argyll Terr	C1
Bank St	B2
Belford Hospital H	B2
Belford Rd	B2/B3
Black Parks	A3
Braemore Pl	C2
Bruce Pl	C2
Bus Station	B2
Camanachd Cr	A3/B2
Cameron Rd	C1
Cameron Sq	B1
Carmichael Way	A2
Claggan Rd	B3
Connochie Rd	C3
Cow Hill	C3
Creag Dhubh	A2
Croft Rd	B3
Douglas Pl	B2
Dudley Rd	B2
Dumbarton Rd	C1
Earl of Inverness Rd	A3
Fassifern Rd	B1
Fort William ⇌	B2
Fort William (Remains) ✠	B2
Glasdrum Rd	C1
Glen Nevis Pl	B3
Gordon Sq	B1
Grange Rd	C1
Heather Croft Rd	C1
Henderson Row	C2
High St	B1
Highland Visitor Ctr	B3
Hill Rd	B2
Hospital Belhaven Annexe	B3
Information Ctr i	A3
Inverlochy Ct	A3
Kennedy Rd	B2/C2
Library	B2
Linnhe Rd	B1
Lochaber College	A2
Lochaber Leisure Ctr	B3
Lochiel Rd	A3
Lochy Rd	A3
Lundavra Cres	C1
Lundavra Rd	C1
Lundy Rd	A3
Mamore Cr	B2
Mary St	B2
Middle St	B1
Montrose Ave	A3
Moray Pl	C1
Morven Pl	C2
Moss Rd	B2
Nairn Cres	C1
Nevis Bridge	B3
Nevis Rd	B3
Nevis Sports Ctr	A2
Nevis Terr	B2
North Rd	B3
Obelisk	B2
Ocean Frontier Underwater Ctr	A2
Parade Rd	C1
Police Station ⊠	A3/C1
Post Office	A3/C2
Ross Pl	C1
St Andrews ✠	B2
Shaw Pl	B2
Station Brae	B1
Studio 🎭	B1
Treig Rd	A3
Union Rd	C1
Victoria Rd	B2
Wades Rd	A3
West Highland 🏛	B2
Young Pl	B2

Glasgow

Scotland's largest city has a wealthy past and a great architectural and cultural heritage which is to be seen in the gold and red sandstone and the finest examples of Victorian architecture anywhere in the world. Glasgow is now a magnet for major investors, events, tourists and conference delegates worldwide. There is a wealth of choice for the visitor from museums and art galleries to great pubs and restaurants and a vibrant live music scene. The city is home to three universities, the Scottish Opera and Scottish Ballet. There are four centrally placed shopping centres Argyle Arcade, Princes Square, St Enoch Centre and Sauchiehall Street Centre and the famous Barras weekend market. Glasgow has 70 parks and gardens and is home to the two most successful Scottish football teams.

▲ The River Clyde

★ **Do not miss:**
- ★ **Burrell Collection**, Pollok Country Park (junction 1, M77 see approaches map) – art collection
- ★ **Transport Museum**, Bun House Road, Kelvin Hall
- ★ **Glasgow Gallery of Modern Art**, Royal Exchange Square
- ★ **St Mungo's Museum of Religious Life and Art**

Glasgow

Street	Grid
Admiral St	C2
Albert Bridge	C5
Albion St	B5
Anderston Centre	B3
Anderston Quay	B3
Anderston ≷	B3
Arches	B4
Argyle St	A1/A2/B3/B4/B5
Argyle Street ≷	A3
Argyll Arcade	B5
Arlington St	A3
Art Gallery & Mus	A1
Arts Centre	B3
Ashley St	A3
Bain St	C6
Baird St	A6
Baliol St	A3
Ballater St	C5
Barras, the (Market)	C6
Bath St	A3
Bell St	C6
Bell's Bridge	B1
Bentinck St	A2
Berkeley St	A3
Bishop La	B3
Black St	A6
Blackburn St	C2
Blackfriars St	B6
Blantyre St	A1
Blythswood Sq	A4
Blythswood St	B4
Bothwell St	B4
Brand St	C1
Breadalbane St	A2
Bridge St	C4
Bridge St (Metro Station)	C4
Bridgegate	C5
Briggait	C5
Broomfield Park	A6
Broomielaw	B4
Broomielaw Quay Gdns	B3
Brown St	B4
Brunswick St	B5
Buccleuch St	A3
Buchanan Bus Stn	A5
Buchanan Galleries	A5
Buchanan St	
Buchanan St (Metro Station)	B5
Cadogan St	B4
Caledonian Univ	A5
Calgary St	A5
Cambridge St	A4
Campbell St	B4
Canal St	A5
Candleriggs	B5
Carlton Pl	C4
Carnarvon St	A3
Carnoustie St	C3
Carrick St	B4
Castle St	B6
Cathedral Sq	B6
Cathedral St	B5
Centre for Contemporary Arts	A4
Centre St	C4
Cessnock (Metro Station)	C1
Cessnock St	C1
Charing Cross ≷	A3
Charlotte St	C6
Cheapside St	B3
Citizens'	C5
City Chambers Complex	B5
City Halls	B5
Clairmont Gdns	A2
Claremont St	A2
Claremont Terr	A2
Claythorne St	C6
Cleveland St	A3
Clifford La	C1
Clifford St	C1
Clifton Pl	A2
Clifton St	A2
Clutha St	C1
Clyde Auditorium	B2
Clyde Pl	C4
Clyde Place Quay	C4
Clyde St	C5
Clyde Walkway	C3
Clydeside Expressway	B2
Coburg St	C4
Cochrane St	B5
College of Building	C5
College of Commerce	B5
College of Food Technology	B5
College of Nautical Studies	C5
College St	B6
Collins St	B6
Commerce St	C4
Cook St	C4
Cornwall St	C2
Couper St	A5
Cowcaddens (Metro Station)	A4
Cowcaddens Rd	A4
Crimea St	B4
Custom House	C5
Custom House Quay Gdns	C5
Dalhousie St	A4
Dental Hospital	A4
Derby St	A2
Dobbie's Loan	A4/A5
Dobbie's Loan Pl	A5
Dorset St	A3
Douglas St	B4
Doulton Fountain	C6
Dover St	A2
Drury St	B4
Drygate	B6
Duke St	B6
Dunaskin St	A1
Dunblane St	A5
Dundas St	B5
Dunlop St	C5
East Campbell St	C6
Eastvale Pl	A1
Eglinton St	C4
Elderslie St	A3
Elliot St	B2
Elmbank St	A3
Esmond St	A1
Exhibition Centre ≷	B2
Exhibition Way	B2
Eye Infirmary	A3
Festival Park	C1
Finnieston Bridge	B2
Finnieston Quay	B2
Finnieston Sq	B2
Finnieston St	B2
Fitzroy Pl	A2
Florence St	C5
Fox St	C5
Gallowgate	C6
Garnet St	A3
Garnethill St	A4
Garscube Rd	A5
George Sq	B5
George St	B5
George V Bridge	C4
Gilbert St	A1
Glasgow Bridge	C4
Cathedral	B6
Glasgow Central ≷	B4
Glasgow Film Theatre	A4
Glasgow Green	C6
Glasgow Science Ctr	B1
Glasgow Science Ctr Footbridge	B1
Glassford St	B5
Glebe St	A6
Gloucester St	C3
Gorbals Cross	C5
Gorbals St	C5
Gordon St	B4
Govan Rd	B1/C1/C2
Grace St	B3
Grafton Pl	A5
Grant St	A3
Granville St	A3
Gray St	A2
Greendyke St	C6
Harley St	C1
Harvie St	C1
Haugh Rd	A1
Heliport	B1
Henry Wood Hall	A2
High St	B6
High Street ≷	B6
Hill St	A3
Holland St	A3
Holm St	B4
Hope St	A5
Houldsworth St	B2
Houston Pl	C3
Houston St	C3
Howard St	C5
Hunter St	B6
Hutcheson St	B5
Hydepark St	B3
IMAX	B1
India St	A3
Information Ctr	B5
Ingram St	B5
Jamaica St	B4
James Watt St	B4
John Knox St	B6
John St	B5
Kelvin Hall	A1
Kelvin Statue	A1
Kelvin Way	A2
Kelvingrove Park	A1
Kelvingrove St	A2
Kelvinhaugh St	A1
Kennedy St	A6
Kent Rd	A2
Killermont St	A5
King St	B5
King's	A4
Kingston Bridge	C3
Kingston St	C4
Kinning Park (Metro Station)	C2
Kinning St	C3
Kyle St	A5
Laidlaw St	C3
Lancefield Quay	B2
Lancefield St	B3
Langshot St	C1
Lendel Pl	C1
Lister St	A6
Little St	B3
London Rd	C6
Lorne St	C1
Lower Harbour	B1
Lumsden St	A1
Lymburn St	A1
Lyndoch Cr	A3
Lyndoch Pl	A3
Lyndoch St	A3
Maclellan St	C1
Mair St	C2
Maitland St	A4
Mavisbank Gdns	C2
Mcalpine St	B3
Mcaslin St	A6
McLean Sq	C2
McLellan Gallery	A4
McPhater St	A4
Merchants' House	B5
Middlesex St	C1
Middleton St	C1
Midland St	B4
Miller St	B5
Millroad St	C6
Milnpark St	C2
Milton St	A4
Minerva St	A1
Mitchell Library	A3
Mitchell St West	B4
Mitchell	C4
Modern Art Gallery	B5
Moir St	C6
Molendinar St	C6
Moncur St	C6
Montieth Row	C6
Montrose St	B5
Morrison St	C3
Mosque	C5
Museum of Religion	B6
Nairn St	A1
Nelson Mandela Sq	B5
Nelson St	C4
Nelson's Monument	C6
New City Rd	A4
Newton St	A3
Newton Pl	A2
Nicholson St	C4
Nile St	A5
Norfolk Court	C4
Norfolk St	C4
North Frederick St	B5
North Hanover St	B5
North Portland St	B5
North St	A3
North Wallace St	A5
Odeon	A5
Old Dumbarton Rd	A1
Osborne St	B5/C5
Oswald St	B4
Overnewton St	A1
Oxford St	C4
Pacific Dr	B1
Paisley Rd	C3
Paisley Rd West	C1
Park Circus	A2
Park Gdns	A2
Park St South	A2
Park Terr	A2
Parkgrove Terr	A1
Parnie St	C5
Parson St	A6
Partick Bridge	A1
Passport Office	A1
Paterson St	C3
Pavilion	A4
Pembroke St	A3
People's Palace	C6
Pinkston Rd	A6
Piping Ctr, The	A5
Pitt St	A4/B4
Plantation Park	C1
Plantation Quay	B1
Police Station	A4/A6/B5
Port Dundas Rd	A5
Port St	B2
Portman St	C2
Prince's Dock	B1
Princes Sq	B5
Provand's Lordship	B6
Queen St	B5
Queen Street ≷	B5
Regimental Mus	A3
Renfrew St	A3/A4
Renton St	A5
Richmond St	B5
Robertson St	B4
Rose St	A4
Rottenrow	B5
Royal Concert Hall	A5
Royal Cr	A2
Royal Exchange Sq	B5
Royal Hospital For Sick Children	A1
Royal Infirmary	B6
Royal Scottish Academy of Music & Drama	A4
Royal Terr	A2
Rutland Cr	C2
St Kent St	C6
St Andrew's (R.C.)	C5
St Andrew's	C6
St Andrew's St	C5
St Enoch (Metro Station)	B5
St Enoch Shopping Centre	B5
St Enoch Sq	B5
St George's Rd	A3
St James Rd	A6
St Mungo Ave	A5/A6
St Mungo Pl	A6
St Vincent Cr	A2
St Vincent Pl	B5
St Vincent St	B3/B4
St Vincent Street Church	B4
St Vincent Terr	B3
Saltmarket	C5
Sandyford Pl	A3
Sauchiehall St	A2/A4
School of Art	A4
Scotland St	C2/C3
Scott St	A4
Scottish Exhibition & Conference Ctr	B1
Scottish Television	A5
Seaward St	C2
Shaftesbury St	A3
Sheriff Court	C5
Shields Rd	C2
Shields Rd (Metro Station)	C2
Shuttle St	B6
Somerset Pl	A2
Springburn Rd	A6
Springfield Quay	C3
Stanley St	C2
Stevenson St	C6
Stewart St	A4

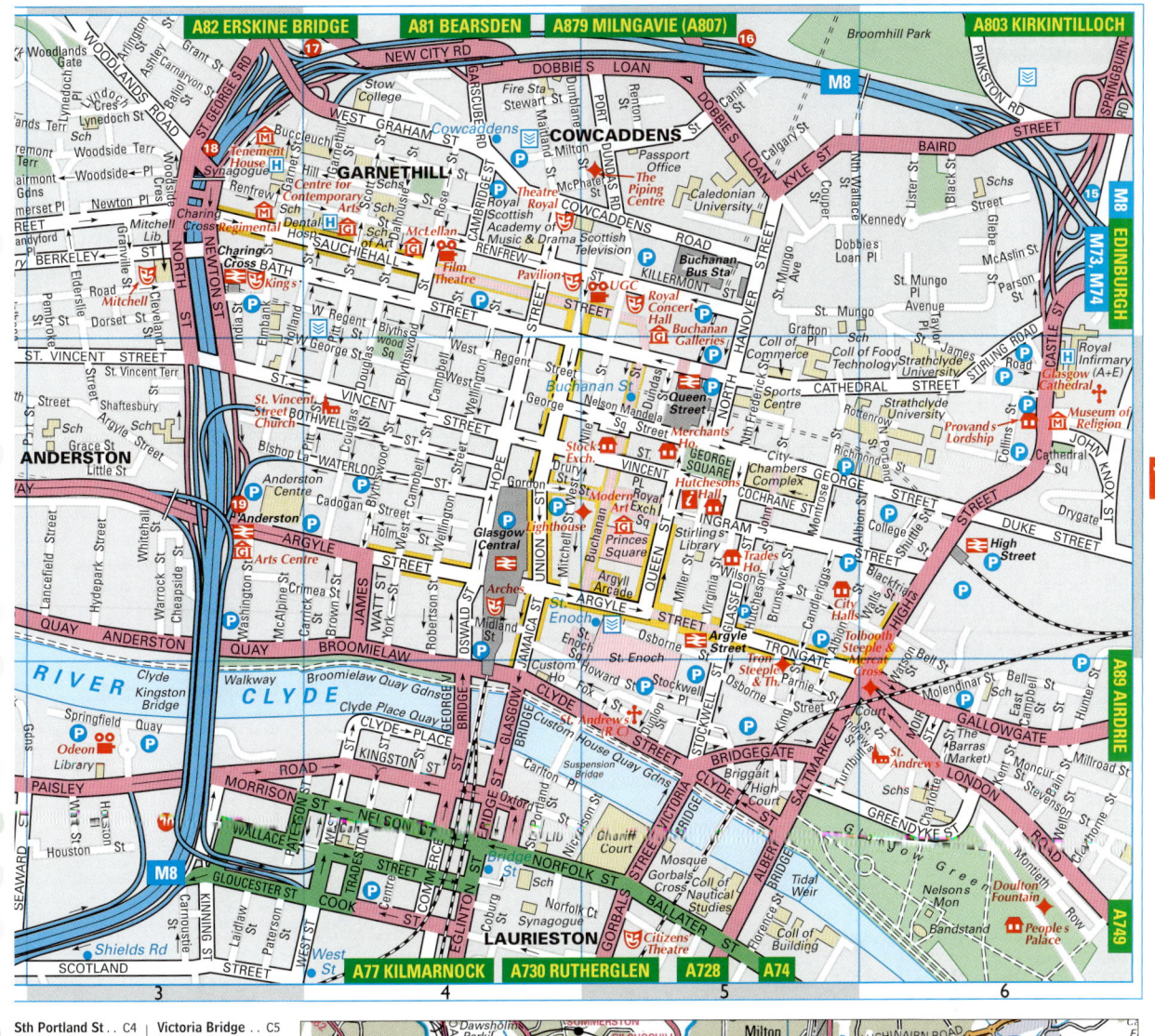

Sth Portland St . . C4	Victoria Bridge . . C5	
Stirling Rd B6	Virginia St B5	
Stirling's Library . . B5	West Greenhill Pl . . B2	
Stobcross Quay . . B1	West Regent St . . A4	
Stobcross Rd B1	Wallace St C3	
Stock	Walls St B6	
Exchange B5	Walmer Cr C1	
Stockwell Pl. C5	Warrock St B3	
Stockwell St. B5	Washington St. . . . B3	
Stow College A4	Waterloo St B4	
Strathclyde Univ . . B6	Watson St B6	
Sussex St C2	Watt St C3	
Synagogues . . A3/C4	Well St C6	
Tall Ship B1	Wellington St B4	
Taylor Pl A6	West George St . . . B4	
Tenement	West Graham St . . A4	
House A3	West Regent St . . . B4	
Teviot St A1	West St C4	
Theatre Royal . . . A3	West St	
Tolbooth Steeple &	(Metro Station) . . C4	
Mercat Cross . . C6	Westminster Terr. . . A2	
Tower St C2	Whitehall St B3	
Trades House B5	Wilson St B5	
Tradeston St C4	Woodlands Gate . . A3	
Transport Mus . . . A1	Woodlands Rd A3	
Tron Steeple &	Woodlands Terr. . . A2	
Theatre C5	Woodside Cr A3	
Trongate B5	Woodside Pl A3	
Tunnel St B2	Woodside Terr. . . . A3	
Turnbull St C5	York St West B4	
UGC A5	Yorkhill Pde A1	
Union St B4	Yorkhill St A1	

Greater Glasgow and Clyde Valley Tourist Board, 11 George Square, Glasgow G2 1DY Tel 0141 204 4400

BBC Radio Scotland 93.1 FM and 810 AM • **Beat** 106.1 FM
Clyde 1 102.5 FM • **Clyde 2** 1152 AM
Real Radio 100.3 FM

www.seeglasgow.com

Gloucester

A city that grew on the site of an important Roman fortress; Edward the Confessor and William the Conqueror held Christmas parliaments here, and Elizabeth I made it Britain's most inland port in 1580. The docks now house various attractions amidst the Victorian warehouses, including the Soldiers of Gloucestershire Museum, the ruins of the Augustinian Llanthony Secunda medieval priory, boat trips, a 5-floor antiques centre, and bars, cafés and restaurants. The city's history is charted in the City Museum & Art Gallery, while the splendid cathedral, founded as an abbey church 1,300 years ago, has a Norman nave the country's most complete medieval cloisters, and the tomb of Edward II. Child-friendly attractions include St James City Farm and the Barn Owl Centre, and nearby are Robinswood Hill Country Park & Rare Breeds Centre on the edge of the Cotswolds, the working Prinknash Abbey, with a pottery, farm and bird park, English Heritage's Great Witcombe Roman Villa, and the Nature in Art museum.

▲ Gloucester Cathedral

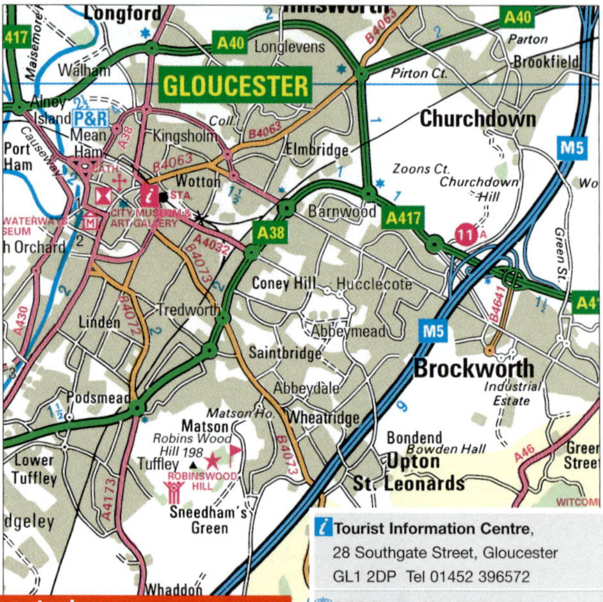

★ Do not miss
★ **Gloucester Folk Museum**, Westgate Street
★ **Historic Gloucester Docks & National Waterways Museum**, the Docks
★ **New Inn**, Northgate Street – Britain's finest surviving medieval galleried courtyard inn

Tourist Information Centre,
28 Southgate Street, Gloucester
GL1 2DP Tel 01452 396572

BBC Radio Gloucestershire
104.7 FM • Classic Gold 774 AM,
Severn Sound 102.4, 103.0 FM

www.glos-city.gov.uk

Gloucester

Street	Grid
Albion St	C1
Alexandra Rd	B3
Alfred St	C3
All Saints Rd	C2
Alvin St	B2
Arthur St	C3
Baker St	C1
Barton St	C2
Blackfriars ✝	B1
Blenheim Rd	C2
Bristol Rd	C1
Brunswick Rd	B2
Bruton Way	B2
Bus Station	B2
Cattle Market	A1
City Council Offices	B1
City Museum, Art Gallery & Library	B2
Clarence St	B2
College of Art	C2
Commercial Rd	B1
Cromwell St	C2
Deans Way	A2
Denmark Rd	A3
Derby Rd	C3
Docks ✝	C1
Eastgate Centre	C2
Eastgate St	B2
Edwy Pde	A2
Estcourt Cl	A3
Estcourt Rd	A3
Falkner St	C2
Folk Museum	B1
Cathedral ✝	B1
Gloucester	B2
Gloucestershire Royal Hospital (A&E)	B3
Goodyere St	C2
Gouda Way	A1
Great Western Rd	B3
Guildhall	B2
Heathville Rd	A3
Henry Rd	B3
Henry St	B2
High Orchard St	C1
Hinton Rd	A2
India Rd	C2
Information Ctr	B1
Jersey Rd	C3
King's Sq	B2
Kingsholm Rd	A2
Kingsholm Rugby Football Ground	A2
Lansdown Rd	A3
Leisure Centre	C2
Llanthony Rd	C1
London Rd	B3
Longsmith St	B1
Malvern Rd	A3
Market Pde	B2
Merchants Rd	C1
Mercia Rd	A1
Metz Way	C2
Midland Rd	C2
Millbrook St	C3
Market	B2
Montpellier	C1
Napier St	C3
National Waterways	C1
Nettleton Rd	C2
New Inn	B2
New Olympus	C3
North Rd	A3
Northgate St	B2
Oxford Rd	B2
Oxford St	B2
Park & Ride Gloucester	A1
Park Rd	C2
Park St	B2
Parliament St	C1
Pitt St	B1
Police Station	B1
Post Office	B1
Quay St	B1
Recreation Ground	A1/A2
Regent St	C2
Regimental	B1
Robert Opie	C1
Robert Raikes House	B1
Royal Oak Rd	B1
Russell St	B2
Ryecroft St	C2
St Aldate St	B2
St Ann Way	C1
St Catherine St	A2
St Mark St	A2
St Mary De Crypt	B1
St Mary De Lode	B1
St Nicholas's	B1
St Oswald's Rd	A1
St Oswald's Trading Estate	A1
St Peter's	B2
Seabroke Rd	A3
Sebert St	A2
Severn Rd	C1
Sherborne St	B2
Shire Hall	B2
Sidney St	C3
Southgate St	B1/C1
Spa Field	C1
Spa Rd	C1
Sports Ground	A2/B2
Station Rd	B3
Stratton Rd	C3
Stroud Rd	C1
Swan Rd	A2
Technical College	C1
The Park	C2
The Quay	B1
Transport	B1
Trier Way	C1/C2
Union St	A1
Vauxhall Rd	C3
Victoria St	C2
Wellington St	C1
Westgate St	B1
Widden St	C3
Worcester St	B2

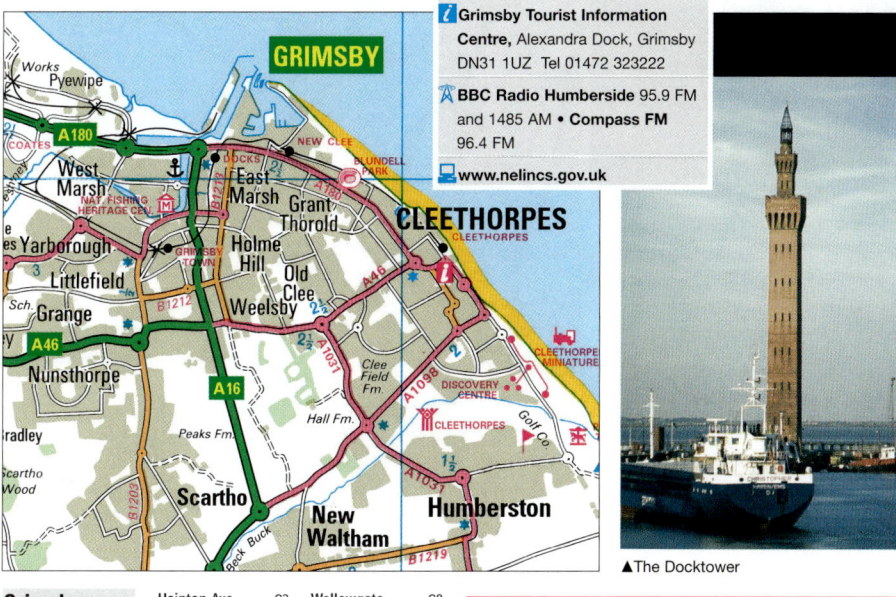

Grimsby

Grimsby Tourist Information Centre, Alexandra Dock, Grimsby DN31 1UZ Tel 01472 323222
BBC Radio Humberside 95.9 FM and 1485 AM • Compass FM 96.4 FM
www.nelincs.gov.uk

A North East Lincolnshire coastal town that was the world's largest port during the 1950s. The impressive 19th-century buildings include the 350ft landmark Dock Tower, and resort attractions include the Cleethorpes Coast Light Railway; Cleethorpes Boating Lake; Cleethorpes Country Park; Pleasure Island Theme Park, with both traditional and hi-tech rides; the Deep Sea Experience aquarium; and the Time Trap museum of local history in the old jail cells beneath the town hall. Trips can be taken around the Humber Estuary on a full working trawler, beginning at the fish docks and taking in Spurn Head lighthouse and the Humber forts. Within easy reach are the working 19th-century 6-sailed Waltham Windmill and the Lincolnshire Wolds Area of Outstanding Natural Beauty.

▲The Docktower

★ Do not miss
- ★ **National Fishing Heritage Centre**, Alexandra Dock
- ★ **Humber Estuary Discovery Centre**, Boating Lake, Kings Road, Cleethorpes
- ★ **The Jungle** Lakeside, Kings Road, Cleethorpes – exotic animal and plant centre and animal rescue unit

Grimsby

Street	Grid
Abbey Drive East	C2
Abbey Drive West	C2
Abbey Park Rd	C2
Abbey Rd	C2
Abbey Walk	C2
Abbotsway	C2
Adam Smith St	A1/A2
Ainslie St	C2
Albert St	A1
Alexandra Rd	A2/B2
Annesley St	A2
Armstrong St	A1
Arthur St	B1
Augusta St	C1
Bargate	C1
Beeson St	A1
Bethlehem St	C2
Bodiam Way	B3
Bradley St	C1
Brighowgate	C1/C2
Bus Station	
Canterbury Dr	C1
Cartergate	B1/C1
Catherine St	C3
Caxton	A3
Chantry La	B1
Charlton St	A1
Church La	C2
Church St	B1
Cleethorpe Rd	A3
College	A3
College St	C1
Compton Dr	C1
Corporation Bridge	
Corporation Rd	A1
Court	
Crescent St	B1
Deansgate	C1
Doughty Rd	C1
Dover St	B1
Duchess St	C2
Dudley St	B1
Duke of York Gdns	B1
Duncombe St	B3
Earl La	B1
East Marsh St	B3
East St	B2
Eastgate	B3
Eastside Rd	A3
Eaton Ct	C1
Eleanor St	B3
Ellis Way	B3
Fisherman's Chapel	A3
Fisherman's Wharf	B2
Fishing Heritage Centre	B2
Flour Sq	A3
Frederick St	B1
Frederick Ward Way	B2
Freeman St	A3/B3
Freshney Dr	B1
Freshney Pl	B2
Garden St	C2
Garibaldi St	A3
Garth La	B2
Grime St	B3
Grimsby Docks	A3
Grimsby Town	C2
Hainton Ave	C3
Har Way	B3
Hare St	C3
Harrison St	B1
Haven Ave	B1
Hay Croft Ave	B1
Hay Croft St	B1
Heneage Rd	B3/C3
Henry St	B1
Holme St	B3
Hume St	C1
James St	B1
Joseph St	B1
Kent St	A3
King Edward St	A3
Lambert Rd	C2
Library	B2
Lime St	B1
Lister St	B1
Littlefield La	C1
Lockhill	A3
Lord St	B1
Ludford St	B1
Macaulay St	B1
Mallard Mews	C3
Manor Ave	C2
Market	A3
Market Hall	B2
Market St	B3
Moss Rd	C2
Nelson St	A3
New St	B2
Osbourne St	B2
Pasture St	B3
Peaks Parkway	C3
Pelham Rd	C1
Police Station	A3/B2
Post Office	B1/B2/B3/C2/C3
PS Lincoln Castle	B2
Pyewipe Rd	A1
Railway Pl	A3
Railway St	A3
Rendel St	A2
Retail Park	A2
Retail Park	B3
Richard St	B1
Ripon St	B1
Robinson St East	B3
Royal St	A3
St Hilda's Ave	C1
St James	C2
Sheepfold St	B3/C3
Sixhills St	C3
South Park	B2
Spring St	A3
Superstore	B3
Tasburgh St	C3
Tennyson St	B2
The Close	C1
Thesiger St	A3
Time Trap	C2
Town Hall	B2
Veal St	B1
Victoria St North	B2
Victoria St South	B2
Victoria St West	B2
Watkin St	A1
Welholme Ave	C2
Welholme Museum & Gallery	C3
Welholme Rd	C3
Wellington St	B3
Wellowgate	C2
Werneth Rd	B3
West Coates Rd	A1
Westgate	A2
Westminster Dr	C1
Willingham St	C3
Wintringham Rd	C3
Wood St	B3
Yarborough Dr	B1
Yarborough Hotel	C2

¼ mile / ½ km

Hanley

Hanley is the city centre of Stoke-on-Trent, a city made up of six towns known collectively as The Potteries. The city is thus named as it is home to a host of world-renowned pottery manufacturers such as Aynsley, Portmeirion, Royal Doulton, Spode and Wedgwood. There are visitor centres, ceramic museums, and factory shops where you can buy direct from source. For your shopping requirements there is The Potteries Shopping Centre as well as two markets, one indoor and one outdoor. Hanley is very popular with the students of Staffordshire University who make good use of the theatres, pubs and restaurants in the Cultural Quarter, right in the centre of the town.

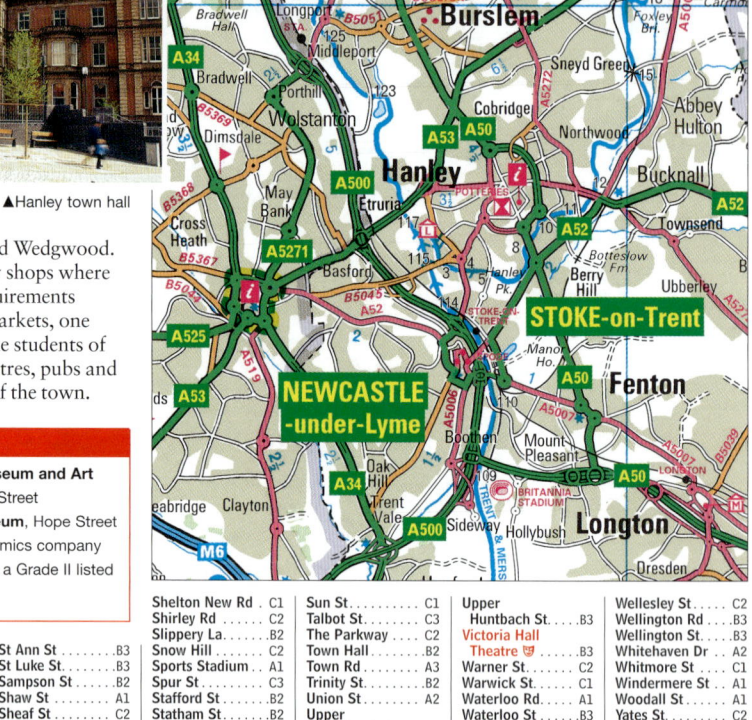

▲ Hanley town hall

Stoke-on-Trent Tourist Information Centre, Victoria Hall, Cultural Quarter, Stoke-on-Trent City Centre ST1 3AD
Tel 01782 236000

BBC Radio Stoke 94.6 FM • Signal 1 102.6 FM • Signal 2 1170 AM

www.visitstoke.co.uk

★ Do not miss
★ **The Potteries Museum and Art Gallery**, Bethesda Street
★ **The Dudson Museum**, Hope Street – 200 year old ceramics company museum housed in a Grade II listed bottle oven

Hanley

Street	Grid
Acton St	A3
Albion St	B2
Argyle St	C1
Ashbourne Gr	A2
Avoca St	A3
Baskerville Rd	B3
Bedford Rd	C1
Bedford St	C1
Bethesda St	B2
Bexley St	B3
Birches Head Rd	A3
Botteslow St	C3
Boundary St	A2
Broad St	C2
Broom St	A2
Bryan St	B3
Bucknall New Rd	B3
Bucknall Old Rd	B3
Bus Station	B3
Cannon St	C2
Castlefield St	C1
Cavendish St	B1
Central Forest Pk	A2
Charles St	B3
Cheapside	B3
Chell St	A3
Clarke St	C1
Cleveland Rd	C2
Clifford St	C3
Clough St	B2
Clyde St	C1
College Rd	C2
Cooper St	C2
Corbridge Rd	A1
Cutts St	C2
Davis St	C1
Denbigh St	B3
Derby St	C3
Dilke St	A3
Dundas St	A3
Dundee Rd	B1
Dyke St	B3
Eastwood Rd	C3
Eaton St	A3
Etruria Park	B1
Etruria Rd	B1
Etruria Vale Rd	C1
Festing St	B2
Fire Station	C2
Foundry St	B2
Franklyn St	C3
Garnet St	B1
Garth St	A3
George St	A3
Gilman St	B3
Glass St	B2
Goodson St	B3
Greyhound Way	A1
Grove Pl	C1
Hampton St	C2
Hanley Park	C2
Harding Rd	C2
Hassall St	B3
Havelock Pl	C1
Hazlehurst St	C1
Hinde St	C2
Hope St	B2
Houghton St	C2
Hulton St	A3
Hypermarket	A1/B2
Information Ctr	B3
Jasper St	C2
Jervis St	A3
John Bright St	A3
John St	B2
Keelings Rd	A3
Kimberley Rd	C1
Ladysmith Rd	C1
Lawrence St	C2
Leek Rd	C3
Library	C2
Lichfield St	C3
Linfield Rd	B3
Loftus St	A2
Lower Bedford St	C1
Lower Bryan St	A2
Lower Mayer St	A3
Lowther St	A1
Magistrates Court	C2
Malham St	A2
Marsh St	B2
Matlock St	C3
Mayer St	A3
Milton St	C1
Mitchell Memorial Theatre	B2
Morley St	B2
Moston St	C3
Mount Pleasant	C1
Mulgrave St	A1
Mynors St	B3
Nelson Pl	B3
New Century St	B1
New Forest Industrial Estate	A3
Octagon, The Shopping Park	B1
Ogden Rd	B3
Old Hall St	B3
Old Town Rd	A3
Pall Mall	B2
Palmerston St	C3
Park and Ride	C2
Parker St	B2
Pavilion Dr	A1
Pelham St	C3
Percy St	B2
Piccadilly	B2
Picton St	B3
Plough St	A3
Police Station	C2
Portland St	A1
Post Office	A3/B3/C3
Potteries Museum & Art Gallery	B2
Potteries Shopping Centre	B2
Potteries Way	C2
Powell St	A1
Pretoria Rd	C1
Quadrant Rd	B2
Ranelagh St	C2
Raymond St	C2
Rectory St	C1
Regent Rd	C2
Regent Theatre	B2
Richmond Terr	B3
Ridgehouse Dr	A1
Robson St	B3
St Ann St	B3
St Luke St	B3
Sampson St	B2
Shaw St	A1
Sheaf St	C2
Shearer St	C1
Shelton New Rd	C1
Shirley Rd	C2
Slippery La	B2
Snow Hill	C1
Sports Stadium	A1
Spur St	C2
Stafford St	B2
Statham St	C2
Stubbs La	C3
Sun St	C1
Talbot St	C3
The Parkway	C3
Town Hall	B2
Town Rd	B2
Trinity St	B2
Union St	A2
Upper Hillchurch St	A3
Upper Huntbach St	B3
Victoria Hall Theatre	B2
Warner St	C2
Warwick St	C1
Waterloo Rd	A1
Waterloo St	B3
Well St	B3
Wellesley St	C2
Wellington Rd	B3
Wellington St	B3
Whitehaven Dr	A2
Whitmore St	C1
Windermere St	A1
Woodall St	C1
Yates St	C2
York St	A2

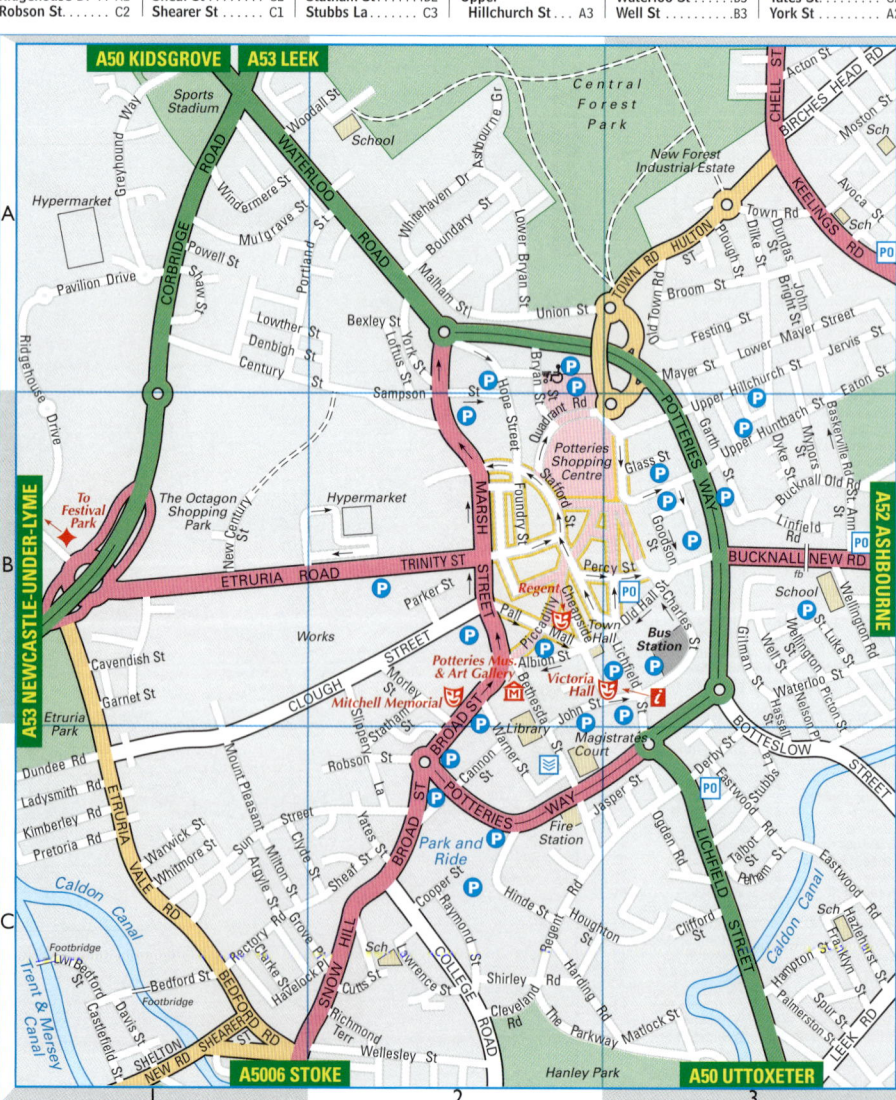

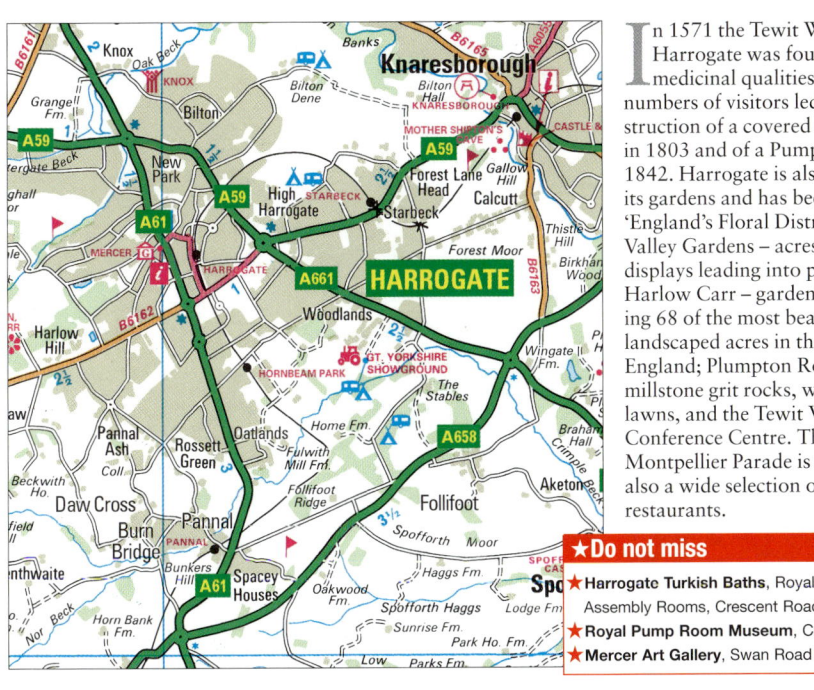

Harrogate

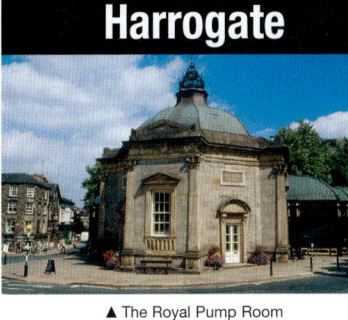

In 1571 the Tewit Well in High Harrogate was found to have medicinal qualities. Increasing numbers of visitors led to the construction of a covered well head in 1803 and of a Pump Room in 1842. Harrogate is also known for its gardens and has been coined 'England's Floral District' with Valley Gardens – acres of floral displays leading into pine woods; Harlow Carr – gardens including 68 of the most beautifully landscaped acres in the North of England; Plumpton Rocks – lake, millstone grit rocks, woods; The Stray – over 200 acres of resplendent lawns, and the Tewit Well. Also home to the Harrogate International Conference Centre. The town has a reputation for affluence and Montpellier Parade is one of its exclusive shopping streets, there is also a wide selection of pubs and restaurants.

▲ The Royal Pump Room

★ Do not miss
- ★ **Harrogate Turkish Baths**, Royal Baths Assembly Rooms, Crescent Road
- ★ **Royal Pump Room Museum**, Crown Place
- ★ **Mercer Art Gallery**, Swan Road

Tourist Information Centre, Royal Baths, Crescent Road, Harrogate HG1 2RR Tel 01423 537300
BBC Radio York 104.3 FM
Stray FM 97.2 FM
www.harrogate.gov.uk

Harrogate

Street	Grid
Albert St.	C2
Alexandra Rd	B2
Arthington Ave	B2
Ashfield Rd	A2
Back Cheltenham Mount	B2
Beech Grove	C1
Belmont Rd	C1
Bilton Dr	A2
Bower Rd	B2
Bower St	B2
Bus Station	B2
Cambridge Rd	B2
Cambridge St	B2
Chatsworth Pl	A2
Chatsworth Grove	A2
Chatsworth Rd	A2
Chelmsford Rd	B3
Cheltenham Cr	B2
Cheltenham Mt	B2
Cheltenham Pde	B2
Christ Church	B3
Christ Church Oval	B3
Chudleigh Rd	B3
Clarence Dr	B1
Claro Rd	A3
Claro Way	A3
Coach Park	B2
Coach Rd	B3
Cold Bath Rd	C1
Commercial St	B2
Coppice Ave	A1
Coppice Dr	A1
Coppice Gate	A1
Cornwall Rd	B1
Crescent Gdns	B1
Crescent Rd	B1
Dawson Terr	A2
Devonshire Pl	B3
Diamond Mews	C1
Dixon Rd	A2
Dixon Terr	A2
Dragon Ave	B3
Dragon Parade	B2
Dragon Rd	B2
Duchy Rd	C1
East Parade	B2
East Park Rd	C3
Esplanade	C1
Fire Station	B2
Franklin Mount	A2
Franklin Rd	B2
Franklin Square	A2
Glebe Rd	C1
Grove Park Ct	A3
Grove Park Terr	A3
Grove Rd	A2
Hampswaite Rd	A1
Harcourt Rd	B3
Harcourt Rd	B3
Harrogate International Ctr	B1
Harrogate Ladies College	B1
Harrogate ≷	B2
Harrogate	B2
Heywood Rd	C1
Hollins Cr	A1
Hollins Mews	A1
Hollins Rd	A1
Homestead Rd	C3
Hydro Leisure Centre, The	A1
Information Ctr	B1
James St	B2
Jenny Field Dr	A1
John St	B2
Kent Dr	A1
Kent Rd	A1
Kings Rd	A2
Kingsway	B3
Kingsway Dr	B3
Lancaster Rd	C1
Leeds Rd	C2
Library	C2
Lime Grove	B3
Lime St	A3
Mayfield Grove	B2
Mayfield Pl	A2
Mercer	B1
Montpellier Hill	B1
Mornington Cr	A3
Mornington Terr	B3
Mowbray Sq	B3
North Park Rd	B3
Nydd Vale Rd	B2
Oakdale Ave	A1
Oatlands Dr	C3
Odeon	B2
Osborne Rd	A2
Otley Rd	C2
Oxford St	B2
Park Chase	B3
Park Parade	B3
Park View	B2
Parliament St	B1
Police Station	B3
Post Office	A2/B2/B3/C1
Providence Terr	A2
Queen Parade	C3
Queen's Rd	C1
Raglan St	C2
Regent Ave	A3
Regent Grove	A3
Regent Parade	A3
Regent St	A3
Regent Terr	A3
Rippon Rd	A1
Robert St	C2
Royal Baths & Turkish Baths	B1
Royal Pump Room	B1
St Luke's Mount	A2
St Mary's Ave	C1
St Mary's Walk	C1
Scargill Rd	A1
Skipton Rd	A3
Skipton St	A2
Slingsby Walk	C1
South Park Rd	C2
Spring Grove	A1
Springfield Ave	B1
Station Ave	B2
Station Parade	B2
Strawberry Dale	B2
Stray Rein	C2
Studley Rd	A2
Swan Rd	B1
The Parade	B2
The Stray or Two Hundred Acre	C3
Tower St	C2
Trinity Rd	C2
Union St	B2
Valley Dr	C1
Valley Gdns	C1
Valley Mount	C1
Victoria Ave	C2
Victoria Rd	C1
Victoria Shopping Centre	B2
Waterloo St	A1
West Park	C2
West Park St	C2
Wood View	A1
Woodfield Ave	A3
Woodfield Dr	A3
Woodfield Grove	A3
Woodfield Rd	A3
Woodside	B3
York Pl	C3
York Rd	B1

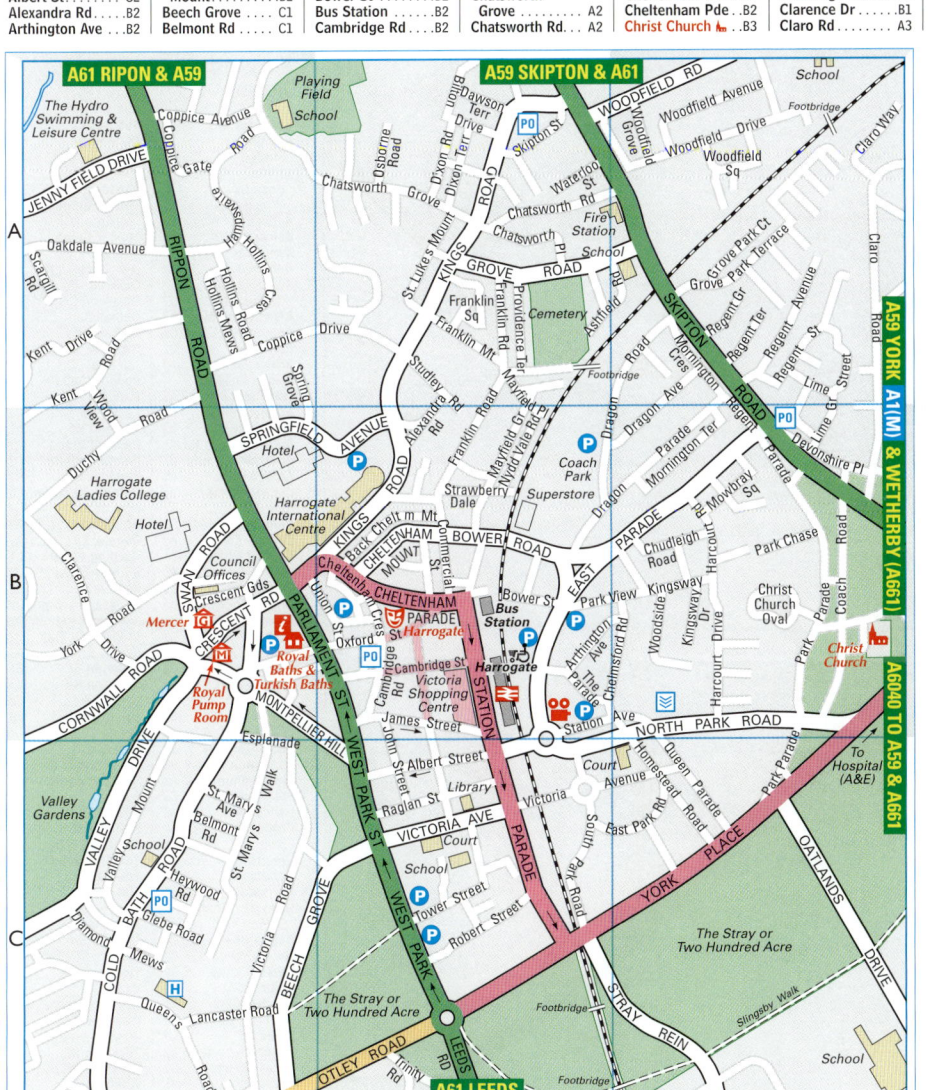

77

Haywards Heath

Mid Sussex's administrative centre, which flourished with the arrival of a railway link with London in 1841 and boasts nearly 50 listed buildings, including St Wilfrid's parish church. At its entrance is the Muster Green conservation area, consisting of a lovely green with a war memorial, surrounded by Victorian and Edwardian houses and the 16th-century Dolphin pub. Green spaces include Beech Hurst Gardens with its views of the South Downs, and nearby are Heaven Farm & Museum, Ditchling Common Country Park, Bookers Vineyard at Bolney, High Beeches Gardens and Nyman's Garden (National Trust) at Handcross, Leonardslee Gardens near Horsham and the wonderful Wakehurst Place Gardens, managed by the Royal Botanic Garden at Kew (in association with the National Trust).

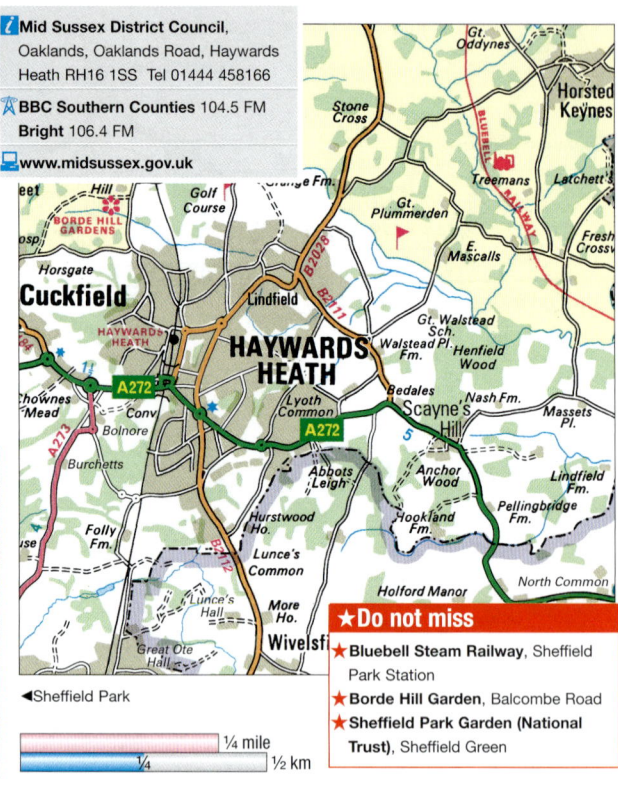

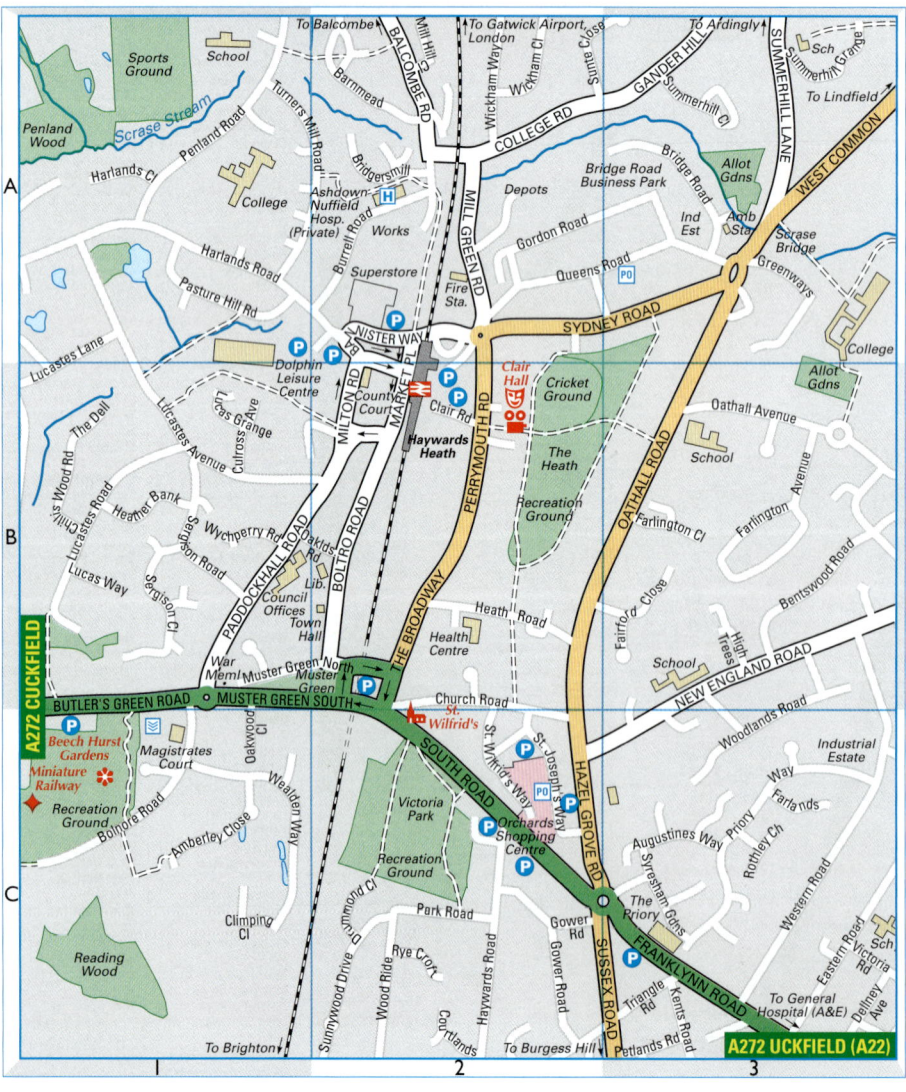

ℹ Mid Sussex District Council, Oaklands, Oaklands Road, Haywards Heath RH16 1SS Tel 01444 458166
📻 BBC Southern Counties 104.5 FM **Bright** 106.4 FM
🌐 www.midsussex.gov.uk

◀ Sheffield Park

★ Do not miss
- ★ **Bluebell Steam Railway**, Sheffield Park Station
- ★ **Borde Hill Garden**, Balcombe Road
- ★ **Sheffield Park Garden** (National Trust), Sheffield Green

Haywards Heath

Amberley Cl	C1
Ambulance Station	A3
Ashdown Nuffield Hospital (Private)	A2
Augustines Way	C3
Balcombe Rd	A2
Bannister Way	A2
Barnmead	A2
Beech Hurst Gardens	C1
Bentswood Rd	B3
Bolnore Rd	C1
Boltro Rd	B2
Bridge Rd	A3
Bridge Road Business Park	A3
Bridgersmill	A2
Burrell Rd	B2
Butler's Green Rd	B1
Chillis Wood Rd	B1
Church Rd	C2
Clair Hall	B2
Clair Rd	B2
Climping Cl	C1
College Rd	A2
Council Offices	B1
County Court	B2
Courtlands	C2
Cricket Ground	B2
Culross Ave	B1
Dellney Ave	C3
Dolphin Leisure Centre	A1
Drummond Cl	C2
Eastern Rd	C3
Fairford Cl	B3
Farlands	B3
Farlington Ave	B3
Farlington Cl	B3
Fire Station	A2
Franklynn Rd	C3
Gander Hill	A3
Gordon Rd	B2
Gower Rd	C2
Greenways	A3
Harlands Cl	A1
Harlands Rd	A1
Haywards Heath Station	B2
Haywards Rd	C2
Hazel Grove Rd	C2
Health Centre	B2
Heath Rd	B2
Heather Bank	B1
High Trees	B3
Kents Rd	C3
Library	B1
Lucas Grange	B1
Lucas Way	B1
Lucastes Ave	B1
Lucastes La	A1
Lucastes Rd	B1
Magistrates Court	C1
Market Pl	B2
Mill Green Rd	A2
Mill Hill Cl	A2
Milton Rd	B2
Miniature Railway ✦	C1
Muster Green	B2
Muster Green North	B1
Muster Green South	B1
New England Rd	B3
Oaklands Rd	B2
Oakwood Cl	C1
Oathall Ave	B3
Oathall Rd	B3
Orchards Shopping Centre	B2
Paddockhall Rd	B1
Park Rd	C2
Pasture Hill Rd	A1
Penland Rd	A1
Penland Wood	A1
Perrymouth Rd	B2
Petlands Rd	C3
Police Station	C1
Post Office	A3/C2
Priory Way	C3
Queens Rd	A2
Reading Wood	C1
Rothley Chase	C3
Rye Croft	C2
St Joseph's Way	C2
St Wilfrid's	C2
St Wilfrid's Way	C2
Scrase Bridge	A3
Sergison Cl	B1
Sergison Rd	B1
South Rd	C2
Summerhill Cl	A3
Summerhill Grange	A3
Summerhill La	A3
Sunnywood Dr	C2
Sunte Cl	A2
Sussex Rd	C3
Sydney Rd	A2/A3
Syresham Gdns	C3
The Broadway	B2
The Dell	B1
The Heath	B2
The Priory	C3
Town Hall	B2
Triangle Rd	C3
Turners Mill Rd	A1
Victoria Park	C2
Victoria Rd	C3
War Memorial	B1
Wealden Way	C1
West Common	A3
Wickham Cl	C3
Wickham Way	C3
Wood Ride	C2
Woodlands Rd	C3
Wychperry Rd	B1

Hull

Kingston-upon-Hull (known as Hull) is situated at the point where the River Hull flows into the River Humber and has long been an important port for the fish trade, though this has reduced significantly. Many places of interest dedicated to this heritage such as the Spurn Lightship and the Arctic Corsair – the last remaining side-fishing trawler of the Hull distant-water fishing fleet and now a tribute to the men of the Deep Sea Fisheries. There is also a fishing trail that takes you through the old town and an ale trail which takes you to various watering holes – from pubs to stylish bars – in the old town. The old docks are now home to the Marina, Princes Quay Shopping Centre and Queens Gardens. The centre offers the full range of shopping from high street names and department stores to boutiques and a covered market.

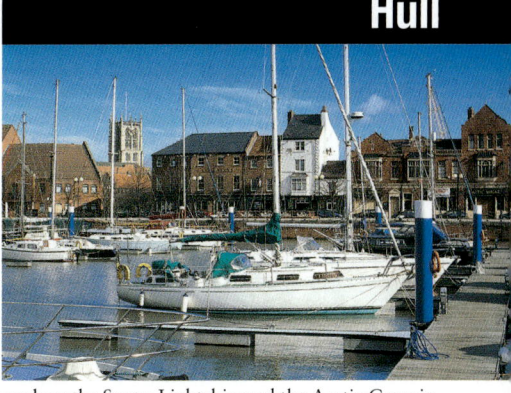

▲ Hull marina

i Tourist Information Centre, 1 Paragon Street, Hull HU1 3NA Tel 01482 223 559

BBC Radio Humberside 95.9 FM
Magic 1161 AM • **Viking** 96.9 FM
www.hullcc.gov.uk

★ Do not miss
★ **The Deep**, Old Harbour – the story of the world's oceans
★ **Ferens Art Gallery**, Queen Victoria Square – painting and sculpture
★ **Hull Maritime Museum**, Queen Victoria Square

Hull

Adelaide St C1	Jenning St A3	Wellington St C2	Wilberforce
Albion St B2	King Billy Statue ✦ C2	Wellington St W .. C2	Monument ✦ .. B3
Alfred Gelder St .. B2	King Edward St ... B2	West St B1	William St C1
Anlaby Rd B1	King St A2	Whitefriargate ... B2	Wincolmlee A3
Beverley Rd A1	Kingston Retail	Wilberforce Dr ... B2	Witham A3
Blanket Row C2	Park C1	Wilberforce Ho 🏛 B3	Wright St A1
Bond St B2	Kingston St C2		
Bridlington Ave .. A2	Library Theatre 🎭 B1		
Brook St B1	Liddell St A1		
Brunswick Ave ... A1	Lime St A3		
Bus Station B2	Lister St C1		
Camilla Cl C3	Lockwood St A1		
Canning St B1	Maister House 🏛 B3		
Cannon St C3	Maritime Mus 🏛 . B2		
Cannon's C1	Market B2		
Caroline St A2	Market Place B2		
Carr La	Minerva Pier C2		
Castle St	Mulgrave St A3		
Central Library . B1	Myton Bridge C3		
Charles St	Myton St B1		
Citadel Way B3	Nelson St C2		
City Hall B2	New Cleveland St A3		
Clarence St B3	New George St ... A2		
Cleveland St A3	New Theatre 🎭 .. A2		
Clifton St A1	Norfolk St A1		
Collier St	North Bridge A3		
Colonial St B1	North St B1		
Court	Odeon 🎬		
Deep, The ⚓ C3	Osborne St B1		
Dock Office Row . B3	Paragon St B2		
Dock St	Park St B1		
Drypool Bridge .. B3	Percy St A2		
Egton St A3	Pier St C2		
English St	Police Station 🛡 B2		
Ferens Gallery 🏛 B2	Post		
Ferensway B1	Office ✉ A3/B1/B2		
Francis St A2	Porter St C1		
Francis St West . A2	Portland St B1		
Freehold St A1	Postergate B2		
Freetown Way ... A2	Prince's Quay ... B2		
Garrison Rd B3	Prospect Centre . B1		
George St	Prospect St B1		
Gibson St A2	Queen's Gdns B2		
Great Union St .. A3	Railway Dock		
Green La A2	Marina C2		
Grey St A1	Railway St C2		
Grimston St	Reform St A2		
Grosvenor St A1	Riverside Quay .. C2		
Gt Thornton St .. B1	Roper St B2		
Guildhall 🏛 B2	St James St C1		
Guildhall Rd B2	St Luke's St		
Hands-on	St Mark St A3		
History 🏛 B2	St Mary the		
Harley St A1	Virgin ⛪ B3		
Hessle Rd C1	Scott St A2		
High St B3	South Bridge Rd . B3		
Holy Trinity ⛪ .. B2	Spring Bank A1		
Hull & East	Spring St B1		
Riding Mus 🏛 . B3	Spurn		
Hull Arena C1	Lightship ⚓ ... C2		
Hull College B3	Spyvee St A3		
Hull (Paragon) 🚂 B1	Streetlife Transport		
Hull Screen 🎬 .. C2	Mus 🏛 B3		
Hull Truck 🎭 B1	Sykes St A2		
Humber Dock	Tidal Surge		
Marina C2	Barrier ✦ C3		
Humber Dock St .. C2	Tower St B3		
Humber St C2	Trinity House ... B2		
Hyperion St A3	University B3		
Information Ctr i B2	Vane St A1		
Jameson St B1	Victoria Pier ... C2		
Jarratt St B2	Waterhouse La ... B2		
	Waterloo St A1		
	Waverley St C1		

Inverness

The Highlands capital, awarded city status in 2001, situated on the Caledonian Canal linking Loch Ness and the Moray Firth. Inverness Castle (1834), on the site of a 12th-century castle built by King David I and destroyed by Robert the Bruce, contains courthouses and the Castle Garrison Encounter re-creating the life of an 18th-century soldier. Other buildings of historic interest include Abertarff House (1590s), with one of the last surviving turnpike stairs, St Andrew's Cathedral (1860s), and the Old High Church, in the graveyard of which prisoners taken at Culloden were executed. The city's history is traced in the Museum & Art Gallery, while nature-based attractions include the awardwinning Bught Floral Hall, Dolphins & Seals of the Moray Firth, and Black Isle Wildlife & Country Park. On the outskirts of the city is the Clava Cairns Bronze Age burial ground, and on the shore of Loch Ness is the dramatic ruined Urquhart Castle (mostly 14th century), one of Scotland's biggest.

▶ Inverness from the air

Inverness Tourist Information Centre, Castle Wynd, Inverness IV2 3BJ Tel 01463 234353

BBC Radio Scotland 92.4–94.7 FM and 810 AM • **Moray Firth Radio** 97.4 FM and 1107 AM

www.inverness-scotland.com

★ Do not miss
★ **Culloden Battlefield & Visitor Centre (1745-6)**, east of city
★ **Loch Ness & Ness Islands**, south of city

Inverness

Street	Grid
Abban St	A1
Academy St	B2
Alexander Pl	B2
Anderson St	A2
Annfield Rd	C3
Ardconnel St	B3
Ardconnel Terr	B3
Ardross Pl	B2
Ardross St	B2
Argyle St	B3
Argyle Terr	B3
Attadale Rd	B1
Balliefary La	C2
Balliefary Rd	C1/C2
Balnacraig La	A1
Balnain St	B2
Bank St	B2
Bellfield Park	C2
Bellfield Terr	C3
Benula Rd	A1
Birnie Terr	A1
Bishop's Rd	C2
Bowling Green	A2
Bowling Green	A2
Bowling Green	C2
Bridge St	B2
Brown St	B2
Bruce Ave	C1
Bruce Gdns	C1
Bruce Pk	C1
Burial Ground	A2
Burnett Rd	A3
Bus Station	B3
Caledonian Rd	B1
Cameron Rd	A1
Cameron Sq	A1
Carse Rd	A1
Carsegate Rd S	A1
Castle (Courts)	B3
Castle Rd	B2
Castle St	B3
Celt St	A2
Chapel St	A2
Charles St	B3
Church St	B2
Clachnacuddin Football Ground	A1
College	A3
Columba Rd	B1/C1
Crown Ave	B3
Crown Circus	B3
Crown Dr	B3
Crown Rd	B3
Crown St	B3
Culduthel Rd	C3
Dalneigh Cres	B1
Dalneigh Rd	C1
Denny St	B3
Dochfour Dr	B1/C1
Douglas Row	B2
Duffy Dr	C2
Dunabran Rd	A1
Dunain Rd	B1
Duncraig St	B2
Eastgate Shopping Centre	B3
Eden Court	C2
Fairfield Rd	B1
Falcon Sq	B3
Fire Station	B3
Fraser St	B2
Fraser St	B3
Friars' Bridge	A2
Friars' La	B2
Friars' St	B2
George St	A2
Gilbert St	A2
Glebe St	A2
Glendoe Terr	A1
Glenurquhart Rd	C1
Gordon Terr	B3
Gordonville Rd	C2
Grant St	A2
Greig St	B2
HM Prison	B3
Harbour Rd	B3
Harrowden Rd	B1
Haugh Rd	C2
Heatherley Cres	C3
High St	B3
Highland Council H.Q.	C2
Hill Park	B3
Hill St	B3
Huntly Pl	A2
Huntly St	A2
India St	A2
Industrial Estate	A3
Information Ctr	B2
Innes St	A2
Inverness High School	B1
Inverness	B3
Jamaica St	A2
Kenneth St	B2
Kilmuir Rd	A1
King St	B2
Kingsmills Rd	B3
Laurel Ave	B1/C1
Library	A3
Lilac Gr	B1
Lindsay Ave	C1
Lochalsh Rd	A1/B1
Longman Rd	A3
Lotland St	A2
Lower Kessock St	A1
Madras St	A2
Market Hall	B3
Maxwell Dr	C1
Mayfield Rd	C3
Midmills College	B3
Millburn Rd	B3
Mitchell's La	C3
Montague Row	B2
Muirfield Rd	C3
Muirtown St	B1
Museum	B2
Nelson St	A2
Ness Bank	C2
Ness Bridge	B2
Ness Walk	B2/C2
Old Edinburgh Rd	C3
Old High	B2
Park Rd	C1
Paton St	C2
Perceval Rd	B1
Planefield Rd	B2
Police Station	B3
Porterfield Bank	C3
Porterfield Rd	C3
Portland Pl	A2
Post Office	A2/B1/B2/B3
Queen St	B2
Queensgate	B2
Railway Terr	A3
Rangemore Rd	B1
Reay St	B3
Riverside St	A2
Rose St	A2
Ross Ave	B1
Rowan Rd	B1
Royal Northern Infirmary	C1
St Andrew's	C2
St Columba	B2
St John's Ave	C1
St Mary's Ave	C1
Shore St	A2
Smith Ave	C1
Southside Pl	C3
Southside Rd	C3
Spectrum Centre	B2
Strothers La	B3
TA Centre	C2
Telford Gdns	B1
Telford Rd	A1
Telford St	A1
Tomnahurich Cem	C1
Tomnahurich St	B2
Town Hall	B3
Union Rd	B3
Union St	B3
Walker Pl	A2
Walker Rd	A2
War Memorial	C2
Waterloo Bridge	A2
Wells St	B1
Young St	B2

¼ mile
¼ ½ km

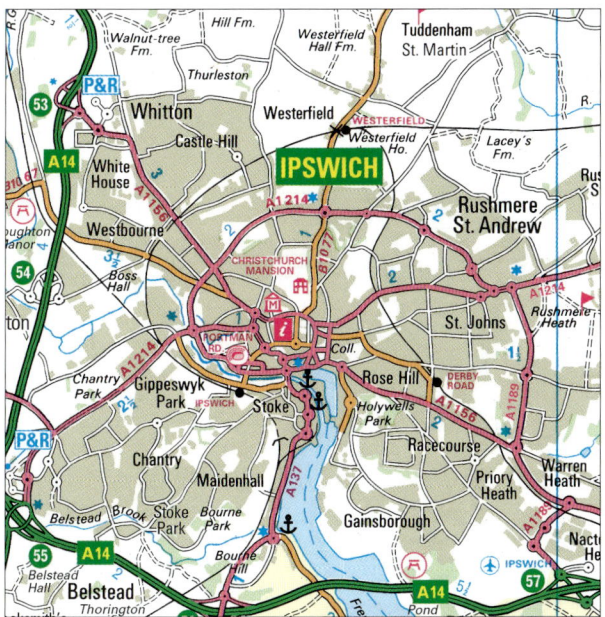

Ipswich

Ipswich was founded in the 6th/7th century as a port trading with continental Europe. It is now an important regional centre and county town. Places of interest include Christchurch Mansion a 16th-century house in historic park with a collection of paintings by Gainsborough and Constable; The Ancient House – an unusual timber-framed building (now a shop) with beautiful plasterwork 'pargeting' (a Suffolk speciality). There is a variety of trails taking you to some of the best churches, and the historic waterfront. There are three shopping centres featuring all the high street names and the centre is also well served with restaurants and pubs to suit all tastes. Nearby attractions include the royal Anglo-Saxon cemetery at Sutton Hoo near Woodbridge (National Trust).

★ Do not miss

- ★ **Christchurch Mansion**, Christchurch Park – Tudor house
- ★ **Unitarian Meeting House**, Friars St – 1699 grade I listed Meeting House
- ★ **Ipswich Transport Museum**, Old Trolleybus Depot, Cobham Road

Tourist Information Centre, St Stephen's Church, St Stephen's Lane, Ipswich IP1 1DP Tel 01473 258070

BBC Radio Suffolk 103.9 FM
Classic Gold Amber 1251 AM
SGR 97.1 FM • **Vibe FM** 106.4 FM

www.ipswich.gov.uk

Ipswich

Street	Grid
Alderman Rd	B2
All Saints' Rd	A1
Alpe St	B2
Ancaster Rd	C1
Ancient House	B3
Anglesea Rd	B2
Ann St	B2
Austin St	C2
Belstead Rd	B2
Berners St	B2
Bibb Way	B1
Birkfield Dr	C1
Black Horse La	B2
Bolton La	B3
Bond St	C3
Bowthorpe Cl	B1
Bramford La	A1
Bramford Rd	B1
Bridge St	C2
Brookfield Rd	A1
Brooks Hall Rd	A1
Broomhill Rd	A2
Broughton Rd	A2
Bulwer Rd	B1
Burrell Rd	C2
Bus Station	B2/C3
Butter Market	B2
Butter Market Ctr	B3
Carr St	B3
Cecil Rd	C3
Cecilia St	C2
Chancery Rd	C2
Charles St	B2
Chevallier St	A1
Christchurch Mans & Wolsey Art Gal	B3
Christchurch Park	A3
Christchurch St	B3
Civic Centre	B2
Civic Dr	B2
Clarkson St	B1
Cobbold St	B3
Commercial Rd	C2
Constable Rd	A3
Constantine Rd	C1
Constitution Hill	A2
Corder Rd	A3
Corn Exchange	B2
Cotswold Ave	A2
Council Offices	C2
County Hall	B3
Crown Court	C2
Crown St	C2
Cullingham Rd	B1
Cumberland St	B2
Curriers La	B2
Dale Hall La	A2
Dales View Rd	A1
Dalton Rd	B2
Dillwyn St	B1
Elliot St	B1
Elm St	B2
Elsmere Rd	A3
End Quay	C3
Falcon St	C3
Felaw St	C3
Flint Wharf	C3
Fonnereau Rd	B2
Fore St	C3
Foundation St	C3
Franciscan Way	C2
Friars St	C2
Gainsborough Rd	A3
Gatacre Rd	B1
Geneva Rd	B2
Gippeswyk Ave	C1
Gippeswyk Park	C1
Grafton Way	C2
Graham Rd	A1
Grimwade St	C3
Great Whip St	C3
Handford Cut	B1
Handford Rd	B1
Henley Rd	A2
Hervey St	B3
High St	B2
Holly Rd	A2
Information Ctr	B3
Ipswich	B2
Ipswich School	A2
Ipswich Town F.C. (Portman Road)	C2
Ivry St	A2
Kensington Rd	A1
Kesteven Rd	C1
Key St	C3
Kingsfield Ave	A3
Kitchener Rd	A1
Little's Cr	C2
London Rd	B1
Low Brook St	C3
Lower Orwell St	C3
Luther Rd	C3
Manor Rd	A3
Mornington Ave	A1
Mus & Art Gal	B2
Museum St	B2
Neale St	B3
New Cardinal St	C2
New Cut East	C3
New Cut West	C3
Newson St	B1
Norwich Rd	A1/B1
Oban St	B2
Old Customs House	C3
Old Foundry Rd	B3
Old Merchant's House	C3
Orford St	B2
Paget Rd	A2
Park Rd	A3
Park View Rd	A2
Peter's St	C2
Philip Rd	C2
Pine Ave	A2
Pine View Rd	A2
Police Station	B2
Portman Rd	B2
Portman Walk	C1
Post Office	B2/B3
Princes St	C2
Prospect St	B1
Queen St	B2
Ranelagh Rd	C1
Rectory Rd	C2
Regent Theatre	B3
Richmond Rd	A1
Rope Walk	C3
Rose La	C3
Russell Rd	C1
St Edmund's Rd	A2
St George's St	B2
St Helen's St	B3
Samuel St	B1
Sherrington Rd	A1
Silent St	C2
Sir Alf Ramsey Wy	C1
Sirdar Rd	B1
Soane St	B3
Springfield La	A1
Star La	C3
Stevenson Rd	B1
Suffolk College	C3
Suffolk Retail Pk	B1
Superstore	B1
Surrey Rd	B1
Swimming Pool	A1
Tacket St	C3
Tavern St	B3
The Avenue	A3
Tolly Cobbold Museum	C3
Tower Ramparts	B2
Tower St	B3
Town Hall	B2
Tuddenham Rd	A3
UGC	C2
Upper Brook St	B3
Upper Orwell St	B3
Valley Rd	A2
Vermont Cr	B3
Vermont Rd	B3
Vernon St	C3
Warrington Rd	A2
Waterloo Rd	A1
Waterworks St	C3
Wellington St	B1
West End Rd	B1
Westerfield Rd	A3
Westgate St	B2
Westholme Rd	A1
Westwood Ave	A1
Willoughby Rd	C2
Withipoll St	B3
Wolsey Theatre	B2
Woodbridge Rd	B3
Woodstone Ave	A3
Yarmouth Rd	B1

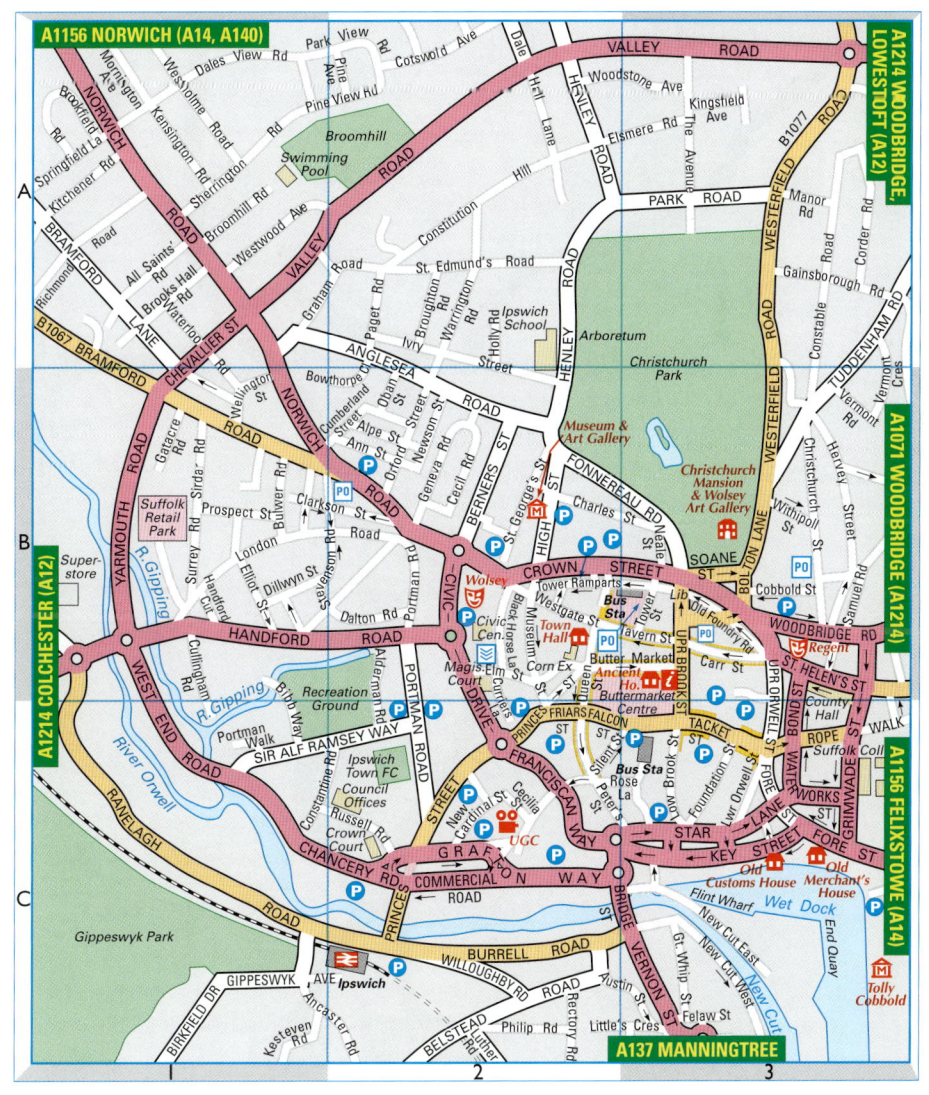

Kendal

The town of Kendal is just outside the Lake District National Park. The 12th-century stone ruins of Kendal Castle sit on a hill on the western edge of the town, offering views over the town and the surrounding hills. Holy Trinity is the largest parish church in Cumbria. Set beside the River Kent, Kendal has much in the way of historic buildings, galleries, museums, shopping and restaurants. The town's old cobbled lanes off the attractive main street feature many antique and speciality shops. There are also a number of high street shops in the main pedestrianised shopping area. The Brewery Arts Centre has a cinema, theatre, live music venue, bars and restaurant. The Westmorland Shopping Centre has both high-street shops and local independents. South of the town are Sizergh Castle and Gardens (National Trust) and Levens Hall with is spectacular topiary gardens.

Kendal Tourist Information Centre,
Town Hall, Highgate, Kendal LA9 4DL
Tel 01539 725758

BBC Radio Cumbria 95.2 FM
Lakeland Radio 100.8 FM
The Bay 96.9 FM, 103.2 FM

www.cumbria-the-lake-district.co.uk

▲ Branthwaite Brow, Kendal

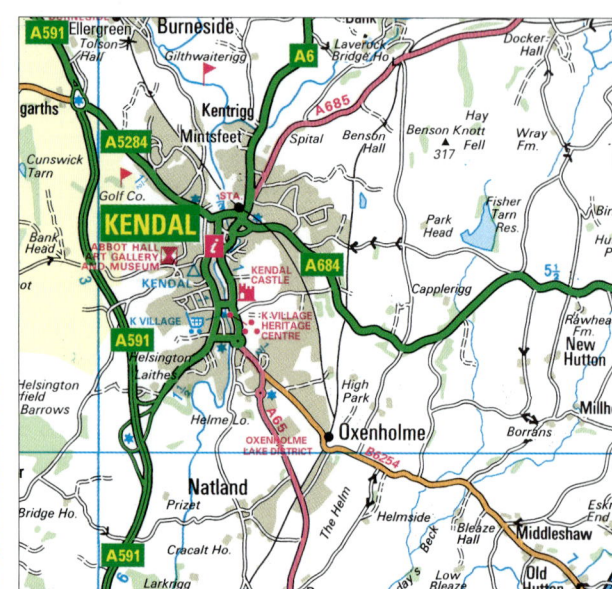

★ Do not miss
- ★ **Abbot Hall Art Gallery**, Kirkland
- ★ **Museum of Lakeland Life**, Kirkland
- ★ **The Quaker Tapestry**, Friends Meeting House, Stramongate

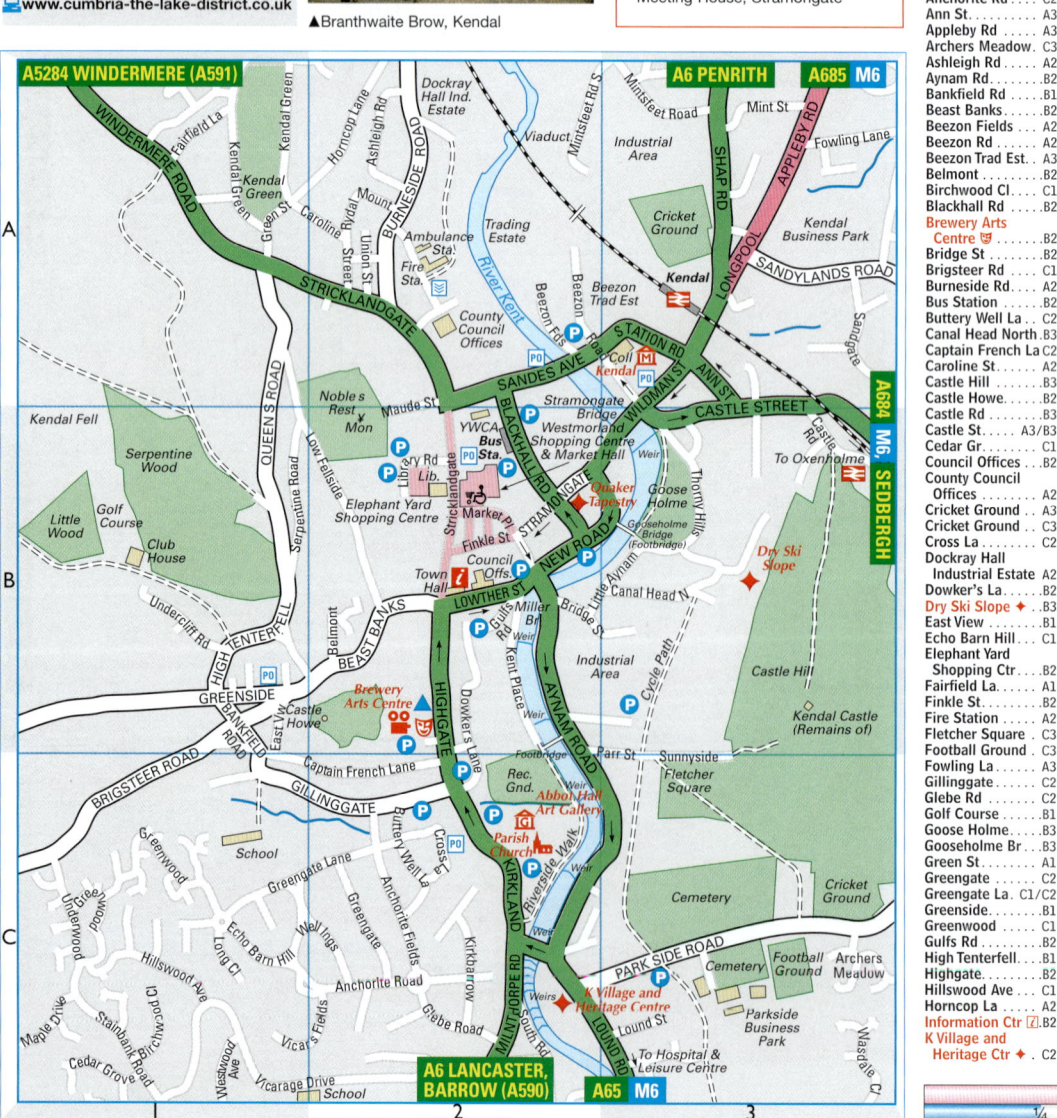

Kendal

Abbot Hall Art Gallery	C2
Ambulance Station	A2
Anchorite Fields	C2
Anchorite Rd	A3
Ann St.	A3
Appleby Rd	A3
Archers Meadow	C3
Ashleigh Rd	A2
Aynam Rd	B2
Bankfield Rd	B1
Beast Banks	B2
Beezon Fields	A2
Beezon Rd	A2
Beezon Trad Est.	A3
Belmont	B2
Birchwood Cl.	C1
Blackhall Rd	B2
Brewery Arts Centre	B2
Bridge St	B2
Brigsteer Rd	C1
Burneside Rd.	A2
Bus Station	B2
Buttery Well La	C2
Canal Head North	B3
Captain French La	C2
Caroline St.	A2
Castle Hill	B3
Castle Howe.	B2
Castle Rd	B3
Castle St.	A3/B3
Cedar Gr.	C1
Council Offices	B2
County Council Offices	A2
Cricket Ground	A3
Cricket Ground	C3
Cross La	C2
Dockray Hall Industrial Estate	A2
Dowker's La.	B2
Dry Ski Slope	B3
East View	B1
Echo Barn Hill	C1
Elephant Yard Shopping Ctr	B2
Fairfield La.	A1
Finkle St.	B2
Fire Station	A2
Fletcher Square	C3
Football Ground	C3
Fowling La	A3
Gillinggate	C2
Glebe Rd	C2
Golf Course	B1
Goose Holme	B3
Gooseholme Br	B3
Green St.	A1
Greengate	C2
Greengate La.	C1/C2
Greenside.	B1
Greenwood	C1
Gulfs Rd	B2
High Tenterfell.	B1
Highgate.	B2
Hillswood Ave	C1
Horncop La.	A1
Information Ctr	B2
K Village and Heritage Ctr	C2
Kendal Business Park	A3
Kendal Castle (Remains Of)	B3
Kendal Fell.	B1
Kendal Green.	A1
Kendal	A3
Kendal Station	A3
Kent Pl	B2
Kirkbarrow.	C2
Kirkland	C2
Library	B2
Library Rd	B2
Little Aynam	B3
Little Wood	B1
Long Cl	C1
Longpool	A3
Lound Rd	C3
Lound St.	C3
Low Fellside	B2
Lowther St	B2
Maple Dr	C1
Market Pl	B2
Maude St.	B2
Miller Bridge	B2
Milnthorpe Rd.	C2
Mint St.	A3
Mintsfeet Rd	A3
Mintsfeet Rd South	A2
New Rd.	B2
Noble's Rest	B2
Parish Church	B2
Park Side Rd	C3
Parkside Business Park	C3
Parr St	B3
Police Station	A2
Post Office	A2/A3/B1/B2/C2
Quaker Tapestry	B2
Queen's Rd	B1
Riverside Walk	C2
Rydal Mount	A2
Sandes Ave	A3
Sandgate	A3
Sandylands Rd.	A3
Serpentine Rd.	B1
Serpentine Wood	B1
Shap Rd	A3
South Rd	C2
Stainbank Rd.	C1
Station Rd	A3
Stramongate	B2
Stramongate Br.	B2
Stricklandgate	A2/B2
Sunnyside	C3
Thorny Hills	B3
Town Hall	B2
Undercliff Rd.	B1
Underwood	C1
Union St.	A2
Vicar's Fields	C2
Vicarage Dr	C1/C2
Wasdale Cl	C3
Well Ings	C2
Westmorland Shopping Ctr & Market Hall	B2
Westwood Ave.	C1
Wildman St	B2
Windermere Rd.	A1
YHA	B2
YWCA	B2

¼ mile / ½ km

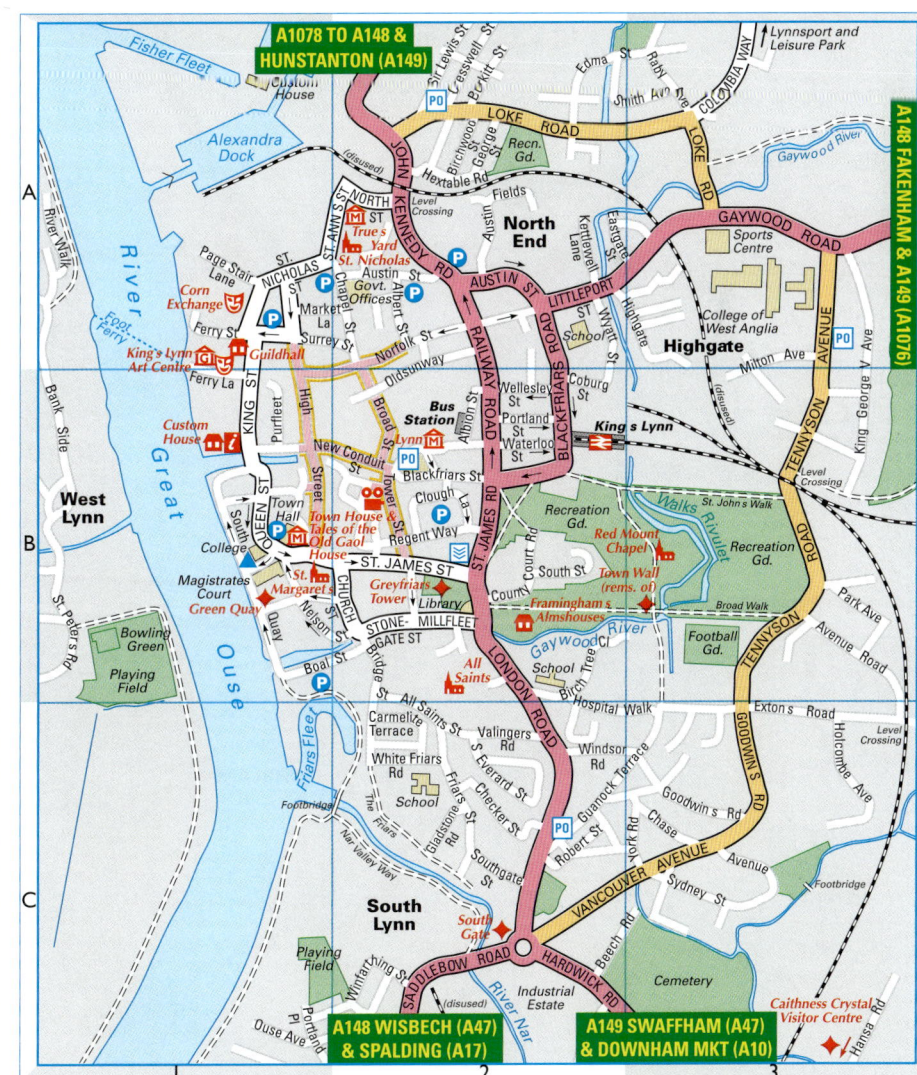

★ Do not miss
- ★ **Green Quay wildlife discovery centre**, Marriott's Warehouse
- ★ **St George's Guildhall (National Trust)**, King Street
- ★ **True's Yard Fishing Heritage Museum**, North Street

▲ The Custom House

King's Lynn Tourist Information Centre, The Custom House, Purfleet Quay, King's Lynn PE30 1HP
Tel 01553 763044

BBC Radio Norfolk 104.4 FM and 873 AM • KLFM 96.7 FM
North Norfolk Radio 96.2 FM

www.west-norfolk.gov.uk

King's Lynn

A West Norfolk market town and port dating back to the 12th century, with a rich maritime heritage. Attractions in the historic centre include Tales of the Old Gaol House, tracing the town's criminal past and housing its civic treasures, the Town House Museum charting local life from medieval times, the Lynn Museum of archaeology and history, and the country's largest surviving medieval guildhall, now housing an arts centre and Georgian theatre. Shopping amenities range from 3 weekly markets to specialist craft and antiques shops and high-street chains. Nearby sights include the ruined 12th-century Castle Rising Castle, Norfolk Lavender in Heacham, Castle Acre Priory, Sandringham House, Congham Hall Herb Garden and Peckover House and Garden (National Trust) in Wisbech.

Kings Lynn

Street	Grid
Albert St.	A2
Albion St.	B2
All Saints	B2
All Saints St.	B2
Austin Fields	A2
Austin St.	A2
Avenue Rd	B3
Bank Side	B1
Beech Rd	C2
Birch Tree Cl	B2
Birchwood St.	A2
Blackfriars Rd	B2
Blackfriars St.	B2
Boal St.	B1
Bridge St.	B2
Broad St.	B2
Broad Walk	B3
Burkitt St.	B2
Bus Station	B2
Carmelite Terr.	C2
Chapel St.	B2
Chase Ave	C2
Checker St.	C2
Church St.	B2
Clough La.	B2
Coburg St.	B2
College of West Anglia	A3
Columbia Way	A3
Corn Exchange	A1
County Court Rd	A2
Cresswell St.	A2
Custom House	A1
Eastgate St.	A2
Edma St.	A2
Exton's Rd	B3
Ferry La	A1
Ferry St	A1
Framingham's Almshouses	B2
Friars St.	C2
Gaywood Rd.	A3
George St.	B2
Gladstone Rd.	C2
Goodwin's Rd	C3
Green Quay	B1
Greyfriars' Tower	B2
Guanock Terr.	C2
Guildhall	A1
Hansa Rd	C3
Hardwick Rd	C2
Hextable Rd	A2
High St.	B1
Holcombe Ave.	C3
Hospital Walk	B2
Information Ctr	B1
John Kennedy Rd	A2
Kettlewell Lane	A2
King George V Ave.	B3
King's Lynn Art Centre	A1
King's Lynn Station	B2
King St.	B1
Library	B1
Littleport St.	A2
Loke Rd	A2
London Rd	B2
Lynn Museum	B2
Majestic	B2
Magistrates Court	B1
Market La.	A1
Millfleet	B2
Milton Ave	B2
Nar Valley Walk	C2
Nelson St	B1
New Conduit St.	B2
Norfolk St.	B2
North St	A2
Oldsunway	B2
Ouse Ave	B1
Page Stair Lane	A1
Park Ave.	B3
Police Station	B2
Portland Pl.	C1
Portland St.	B2
Post Office	A3/B2/C2
Purfleet	B1
Queen St	B1
Raby Ave	A3
Railway Rd.	A2
Red Mount Chapel	B3
Regent Way	B2
River Walk	A1
Robert St	C2
Saddlebow Rd	C2
St Ann's St	A1
St James' Rd	B2
St James St	B2
St John's Walk	B3
St Margaret's	B1
St Nicholas	B2
St Nicholas St	A1
St Peter's Rd	B1
S Everard St	C2
Sir Lewis St	A2
Smith Ave.	A3
South Gate	C2
Southgate St	C2
South Quay	B1
South St.	B2
Stonegate St.	B2
Surrey St	A1
Sydney St	C3
Tennyson Ave.	B3
Tennyson Rd	B3
The Friars	C2
Tower St.	B2
Town Hall	B1
Town House & Tales of The Old Gaol House	B1
Town Wall (Remains)	B3
True's Yard Museum	A2
Valingers Rd	C2
Vancouver Ave.	C2
Waterloo St	B2
Wellesley St	B2
White Friars Rd.	C2
Windsor Rd	C2
Winfarthing St.	C2
Wyatt St	A2
York Rd.	C3

83

Lancaster

The Romans established a settlement nearly 2,000 years ago and remains of one of their buildings are still visible on Castle Hill close to the Priory. The Norman castle is still a working court and prison. The town was an important maritime centre in the 19th century and many notable buildings still exist from this time, for example the former Town Hall in Market Square, now the City Museum, and the Custom House of 1764, which now serves as the Maritime Museum. Lancaster is now an important educational centre. As well as St Nicholas Arcades shopping centre and the Leisure Park and GB Antiques Centre, there is an indoor market, a twice-weekly outdoor charter market and twice-monthly farmers' market, while antiques, pop memorabilia and vintage, retro and alternative clothing can be found in the Assembly Rooms market.

▲ Lancaster Castle

★ **Do not miss**
- ★ Lancaster Castle
- ★ Ashton Memorial, Williamson Park – art gallery and park with butterfly house and exotic birds
- ★ Judge's Lodgings, Church Street – Gillow & Town House Museum; Museum of Childhood

i Lancaster Tourist Information Centre, 29 Castle Hill, Lancaster LA1 1YN Tel 01524 32878

BBC Radio Lancashire 104.5 FM • 105.4 Century 105.4 FM

www.lancaster.gov.uk

Lancaster

Aberdeen Rd....C3	Brook St....C1	City Museum....B2
Adult College, The....C3	Bulk Rd....A3	Clarence St....C3
Aldcliffe Rd....C2	Bulk St....B2	Common Gdn St....B2
Alfred St....B3	Bus Station....B2	Coniston Rd....A3
Ambleside Rd....A3	Cable St....B2	Cottage Mus....B2
Ambulance Sta....A3	Carlisle Bridge....A1	Council Offices....B2
Ashfield Ave....B1	Carr House La....C2	Court....B2
Ashton Rd....C2	Castle....B1	Cromwell Rd....C1
Assembly Rooms, The....B2	Castle Park....B1	Dale St....B3
Balmoral Rd....B3	Caton Rd....A3	Dallas Rd....B1/C1
Bath House....B2	China St....B2	Dalton Rd....B2
Bath Mill La....B3	Church St....B2	Dalton Sq....B2
Bath St....B3		Damside St....B2
Blades St....B1		De Vitre St....B3
Borrowdale Rd....B3		Dee Rd....A1
Bowerham Rd....C3		Denny Ave....A1
Brewery La....B2		Derby Rd....A2
Bridge La....B2		Dukes....B2
		Earl St....A2
		East Rd....B3
		Eastham St....C3
		Edward St....B3
		Fairfield Rd....B1
		Fenton St....B2
		Firbank Rd....B3
		Fire Station....B3
		Folly Gallery....B2
		Friend's Meeting House....B1
		Garnet St....B3
		George St....B2
		Giant Axe Field....B1
		Gov. Offices....B2
		Grand, The....B2
		Grasmere Rd....B3
		Greaves Rd....C2
		Green St....A3
		Gregson Ctr, The....B3
		Gregson Rd....C3
		Greyhound Br Rd....A2
		Greyhound Br....A2
		High St....B2
		Hill Side....B1
		Hope St....C3
		Hubert Pl....B1
		Information Ctr....B2
		Judges Lodgings....B2
		Kelsy St....B1
		Kentmere Rd....B3
		King St....B2
		Kingsway....A3
		Kirkes Rd....C3
		Lancaster & Lakeland....B2
		Lancaster City Football Club....B1
		Lancaster....B1
		Langdale Rd....A3
		Ley Ct....B1
		Library....B2
		Lincoln Rd....B1
		Lindow St....C2
		Lodge St....B2
		Long Marsh La....B1
		Lune Rd....A1
		Lune St....B1
		Lune Valley Ramble....A3
		Mainway....B2
		Maritime Mus....A1
		Market St....B2
		Marketgate Shopping Ctr....B2
		Meadowside....C2
		Meeting House La....B1
		Millennium Br....A2
		Moorgate....B3
		Moor La....B1
		Morecambe Rd....A1/A2
		Nelson St....B2
		North Rd....B2
		Orchard La....C1
		Owen Rd....A2
		Park Rd....B3
		Parliament St....B3
		Patterdale Rd....A3
		Penny St....B2
		Police Station....B2
		Portland St....C2
		Post Office....A2/A3/B1/B2/B3/C3
		Primrose St....C3
		Priory....B1
		Prospect St....C3
		Quarry Rd....B3
		Queen St....C2
		Regal....B2
		Regent St....C2
		Ridge La....A3
		Ridge St....A3
		Royal Lancaster Infirmary (A&E)....C2
		Rydal Rd....B3
		Ryelands Park....A1
		St John's....B2
		St Nicholas Arcades Shopping Ctr....B2
		St Peter's Rd....B3
		St Georges Quay....A1
		St Leonard's Gate....B2
		St Martin's Coll....C3
		St Martin's Rd....C3
		St Oswald St....C3
		St Peter's †....B3
		Salisbury Rd....B1
		Scotch Quarry Urban Park....C3
		Shire Hall/HM Prison....B1
		Sibsey St....B1
		Skerton Bridge....A2
		South Rd....C2
		Station Rd....B2
		Stirling Rd....C3
		Storey Ave....B1
		Storey Gallery....B2
		Sunnyside La....C1
		Sylvester St....C1
		Tarnsyke Rd....A1
		Thurnham St....B2
		Town Hall....B2
		Troutbeck Rd....B3
		Ullesater Rd....B3
		Vicarage Field....B1
		West Rd....B1
		Westbourne Dr....C1
		Westbourne Rd....B1
		Westham St....C3
		Wheatfield St....B1
		White Cross Education Ctr....C2
		Williamson Rd....B3
		Willow La....C3
		Windermere Rd....B3
		Wingate-Saul Rd....B1
		Wolseley St....B3
		Woodville St....B3
		Wyresdale Rd....C3

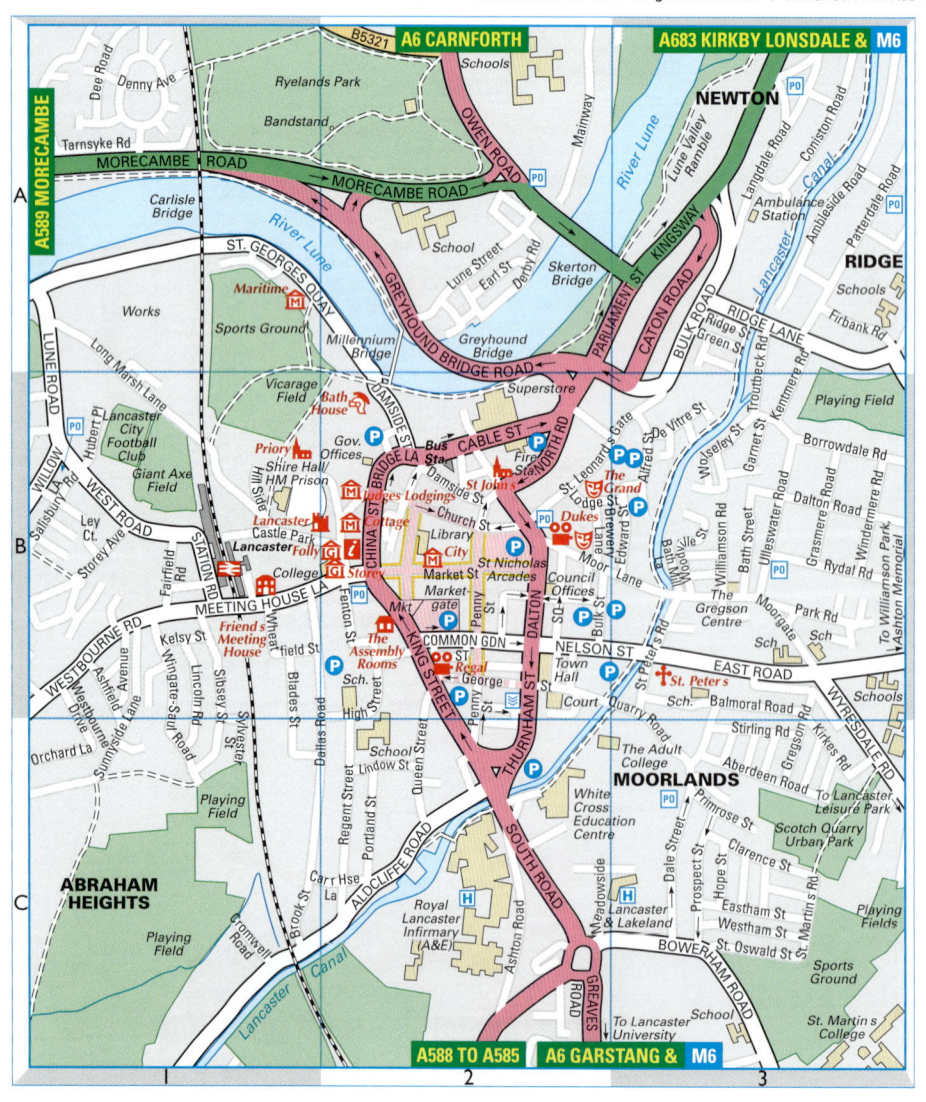

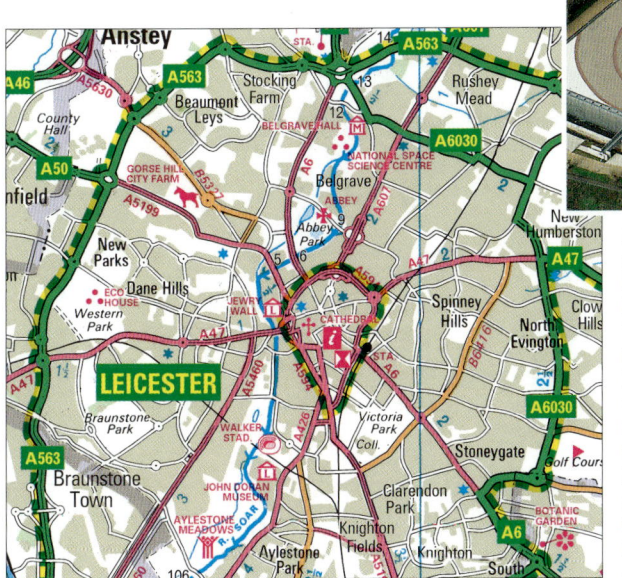

Leicester

A multi-ethnic city on the site of an important Roman settlement. Castle Park contains the timber-framed Guildhall, the Cathedral and St Mary de Castro church. The Newarke Houses Museum details the city's social history; the New Walk Museum & Art Gallery takes in Egyptology, natural history and German Expressionism; Belgrave Hall and Gardens has Georgian and Victorian period rooms and Wygston's House houses the museum of costume. Other sights include the Abbey Pumping Station science and technology museum; Ecohouse, an environmentally friendly showhouse and the National Gas Museum. Among green spaces are the award-winning Abbey Park, with the ruins of Leicester Abbey; the university's Botanic Garden; Gorse Hill City Farm; Stoughton Farm Park; and Aylestone Meadows and Water-mead country parks. There is a wide range of shops, and a 700-year-old produce market. Outside the city centre, the 'Golden Mile' on Belgrave Road is the place to go for Indian food and jewellery.

▲ National Space Centre

★ Do not miss
- ★ Guru Nanak Sikh Museum, 9 Holy Bones
- ★ Jewry Wall History Museum, St Nicholas Circle
- ★ National Space Centre, Exploration Drive

Leicester Tourist Information Centre, 7-9 Every Street, Town Hall Square, Leicester LE1 6AG, Tel 0906 294 1113 (25p per minute)

BBC Radio Leicester 104.9 FM
Leicester Sound 105.4 FM
Sabras Radio 1260 AM

www.leicester.gov.uk

Leicester

Street	Grid
Abbey St	A2
All Saints'	A1
Aylestone Rd	C2
Bath La	A1
Bede Park	C1
Bedford St	A3
Bedford St South	A3
Belgrave Gate	A2
Belle Vue	A2
Belvoir St	B2
Braunstone Gate	B1
Burleys Way	A2
Burnmoor St	C2
Bus Station	A2
Canning St	A2
Castle	B1
Castle Gardens	B1
Cathedral	B2
Causeway La	B2
Charles St	B3
Chatham St	B2
Christow St	A3
Church Gate	A2
City Gallery	B3
Civic Centre	B2
Clock Tower	B2
Clyde St	A3
Colton St	B3
Conduit St	B3
Corn Exchange	B2
Crafton St	A3
Craven St	A1
Crown Courts	B3
Deacon St	C2
De Montfort Hall	C3
De Montfort St	C3
De Montfort Univ	C1
Dover St	B3
Duns La	B1
Dunton St	A1
East St	B3
Eastern Boulevard	C1
Edmonton Rd	A3
Erskine St	A3
Filbert St	C1
Filbert St East	C1
Fire Station	C3
Fleet St	A3
Friar La	B2
Friday St	A2
Gateway St	C1
Glebe St	B3
Granby St	B3
Grange La	C2
Grasmere St	C1
Great Central St	A1
Guildhall	B2
Guru Nanak Sikh Museum	B1
Halford St	B3
Havelock St	C2
Haymarket	A2
Haymarket Shopping Ctr	A2
High St	B2
Highcross St	A1
HM Prison	C2
Horsefair St	B2
Humberstone Gate	B2
Humberstone Rd	A3
Information Ctr	B2
Jarrom St	C2
Jewry Wall	B1
Kamloops Cr	A3
King Richards Rd	B1
King St	B2
Lancaster Rd	C3
Lee St	A3
Leicester ≠	B3
Leicester R.F.C.	C2
Leicester Royal Infirmary (A&E)	C2
Library	B2
Little Theatre	B3
London Rd	B3
Lower Brown St	B2
Magistrates Court	B2
Manitoba Rd	A3
Mansfield St	A2
Market	B2
Market St	B2
Mill La	C2
Montreal Rd	A3
Museum & Art Gallery	C3
Narborough Rd N	B1
Nelson Mandela Park	C2
New St	B2
New Walk	C3
New Park St	B1
Newarke Houses	B2
Newarke St	B2
Northgate St	A1
Orchard St	A2
Ottawa Rd	A3
Oxford St	C2
Phoenix	B2
Police Station	B3
Post Office	A1/B2/C2/C3
Prebend St	C3
Princess Rd East	C3
Princess Rd West	C3
Queen St	B3
Rally Community Park, The	A2
Regent College	C3
Regent Rd	C2/C3
Repton St	A1
Rutland St	B3
St George St	B3
St Georges Way	A3
St John St	A2
St Margaret's	A2
St Margaret's Way	A2
St Martins	B2
St Mary de Castro	B1
St Matthew's Way	A3
St Nicholas	B1
St Nicholas Circle	B1
St Peter's La	A2
Sanvey Gate	A2
Shires Shopping Centre	A2
Silver St	B2
Slater St	A1
Soar La	A1
South Albion St	B3
Southampton St	B3
Swain St	B3
Swan St	A1
The Gateway	C2
The Newarke	B1
Tigers Way	C2
Tower St	C3
Town Hall	B2
Tudor Rd	A1
Univ of Leicester	C3
University Rd	C3
Upperton Rd	C1
Vaughan Way	A1
Walnut St	C2
Watling St	A2
Welford Rd	B2
Wellington St	B2
West Bridge	B1
West St	C2
West Walk	C3
Western Blvd	C1
Western Rd	C1
Wharf St North	A3
Wharf St South	A3
'Y' Theatre	B3
Yeoman St	A3
York Rd	B2

Leeds

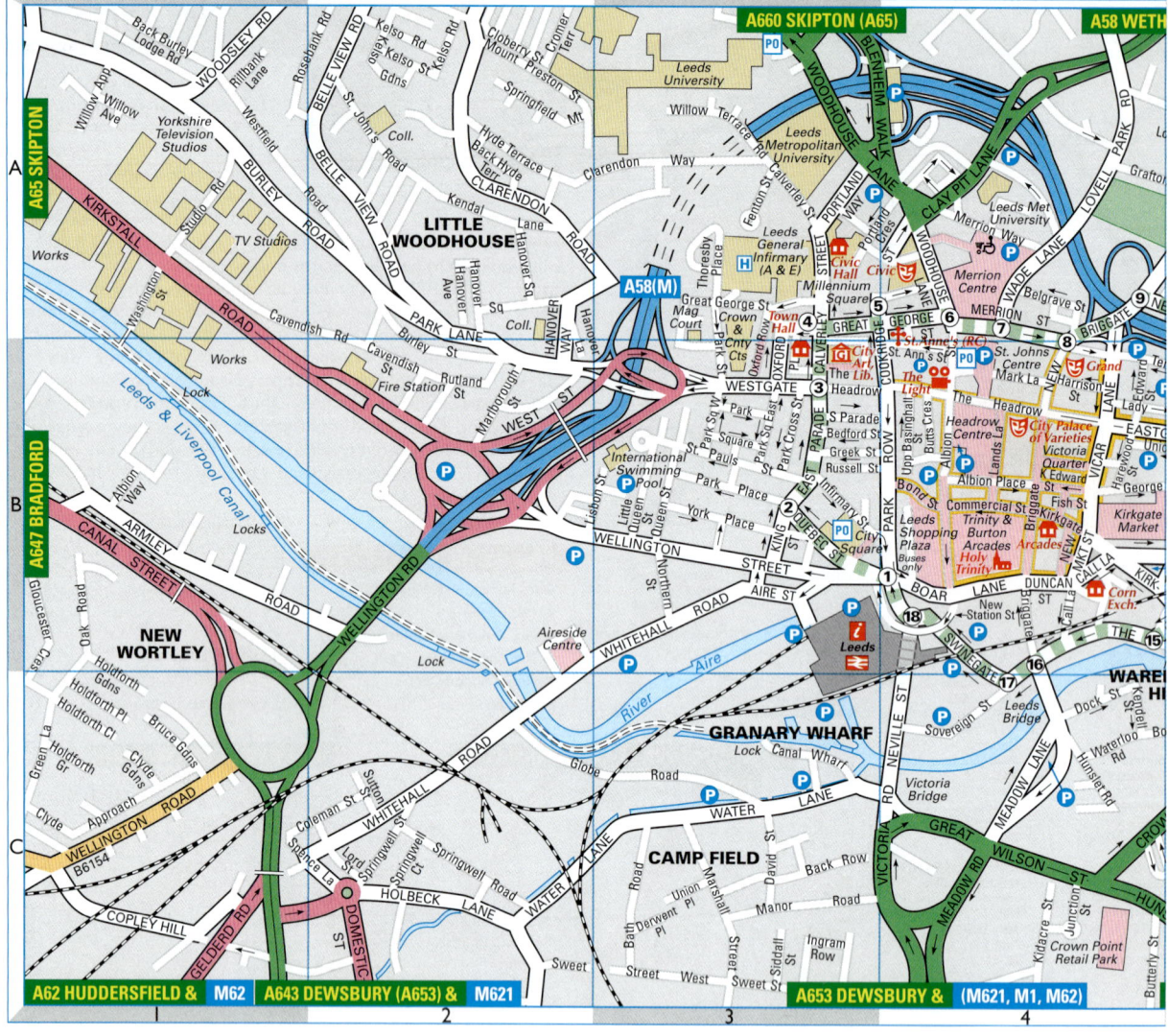

Street	Grid
Aire St.	B3
Aireside Centre	B2
Albion Pl	B4
Albion St	A4
Albion Way	B1
Alma St	A6
Arcades	B4
Armley Rd	B1
Back Burley Lodge Rd	A1
Back Hyde Terr	A2
Back Row	C3
Bath Rd	C3
Beckett St	A6
Bedford St	B3
Belgrave St	A4
Belle View Rd	A2
Benson St	A5
Black Bull St	C5
Blenheim Walk	A3
Boar La	B4
Bond St	B4
Bow St	C5
Bowman La	C4
Bridge St	A5/B5
Briggate	B4
Bruce Gdns	C1
Burley Rd	A1
Burley St	B1
Burmantofts St	B6
Bus & Coach Station	B5
Butterly St	C4
Butts Cr	B4
Byron St	A5
Call La	C4
Calverley St	A3/B3
Canal St	B1
Canal Wharf	C3
Carlisle Rd	C5
Cavendish Rd	A1
Cavendish St	A2
Chadwick St	C5
Cherry Pl	A6
Cherry Row	A5
City Art Gallery & Library	B3
City Palace of Varieties	B4
Cinemas	B4
City Sq	B3
Civic Theatre	A4
Civic Hall	A3
Clarendon Rd	A3
Clarendon Way	A3
Clark La	C6
Clay Pit La	A4
Cloberry St	A3
Clyde Approach	C1
Clyde Gdns	C1
Coleman St	C2
Commercial St	B4
Concord St	A5
Cookridge St	A4
Copley Hill	C1
Corn Exchange	B4
Cromer Terr	A2
Cromwell St	A5
Cross Catherine St	B6
Cross Green La	C6
Cross Stamford St	A5
Crown & County Courts	A3
Crown Point Bridge	C5
Crown Point Retail Park	C4
Crown Point Rd	C4
David St	C3
Dent St	C6
Derwent Pl	C3
Dial St	C6
Dock St	C4
Dolly La	A6
Domestic St	C2
Duke St	B5
Duncan St	B4
Dyer St	B5
East Field St	B6
East Pde	B3
East St	C5
Eastgate	B5
Easy Rd	C6
Edward St	B4
Ellerby La	C6
Ellerby Rd	C6
Fenton St	A3
Fire Station	B2
Fish St	B4
Flax Pl	B5
Gelderd Rd	C1
George St	B4
Globe Rd	C2
Gloucester Cr	B1
Gower St	A5
Grafton St	A5
Granville Rd	A5
Great George St	A3
Great Wilson St	C4
Greek St	B4
Green La	C1
Hanover Ave	A2
Hanover La	A2
Hanover Sq	A2
Hanover Way	A2
Harewood St	B4
Harrison St	B4
Haslewood Cl	B6
Haslewood Drive	B6
Headrow Centre	B4
High Court	B5
Hill St	A6
Holbeck La	C2
Holdforth Cl	C1
Holdforth Gdns	B1
Holdforth Gr	C1
Holdforth Pl	C1
Holy Trinity	B4
Hope Rd	A5
Hunslet La	C4
Hunslet Rd	C4
Hyde Terr	A2
Infirmary St	B4
Information Ctr	B3
Ingram Row	C3
International Swimming Pool	B3
Junction St	C4
King Edward St	B4
Kelso Gdns	A2
Kelso Rd	A2
Kelso St	A2
Kendal La	A2
Kendell St	C4
Kidacre St	C4
King St	B3
Kippax Pl	C6
Kirkgate	B4
Kirkgate Market	B4
Kirkstall Rd	A1
Kitson St	C6
Lady La	A5
Lands La	B4
Lavender Walk	B6
Leeds Bridge	C4
Leeds General Infirmary (A&E)	A3
Leeds Metropolitan University	A3/A4
Leeds Shopping Plaza	B4
Leeds Station	B3
Leeds University	A3
Light, The	B4
Lincoln Green Rd	A6
Lincoln Rd	A6
Lindsey Gdns	A6
Lindsey Rd	A6
Lisbon St	B3
Little Queen St	B3
Long Close La	C6
Lord St	C2
Lovell Park Rd	A4
Lovell Rd	A5
Lower Brunswick St	A5
Mabgate	A5
Macauly St	A5
Magistrates Court	A3
Manor Rd	C3
Mark La	B4
Marlborough St	B1
Marsh La	B6
Marshall St	C3
Meadow La	C4
Meadow Rd	C4
Melbourne St	A5
Merrion Centre	A4
Merrion St	A4
Merrion Way	A4
Mill St	B5
Millennium Sq.	A3
Mount Preston St	A2
Mushroom St	A5
Neville St	C4
New Briggate	A4/B4
New Market St	B4
New Station St	B4
New Wade La	A4
New York Rd	A5
New York St	B5
Nile St	A5
Nippet La	A6
North St	A5
Northern St	B3
Oak Rd	B1
Oxford Pl	A3
Oxford Row	A3
Park Cross St	B3
Park La	A2
Park Pl	B3
Park Row	B4
Park Sq	B3
Park Sq East	B3
Park Sq West	B3
Park St	B3
Police Station	B5
Pontefract La	B6
Portland Cr	A3
Portland Way	A3
Post Office	A3/B3/B5
Quarry House (NHS/DSS) Headquarters	B5
Quebec St	B3
Queen St	B3
Railway St	C5
Rectory St	A6
Regent St	A5
Richmond St	C5
Rigton Approach	B6
Rigton Dr	B6
Rillbank La	A1
Rosebank Rd	A1
Royal Armouries	C5
Russell St	B3
Rutland St	A1
St Ann's St	B4
St Anne's Cathedral (RC)	A4
St James' Hospital	A6
St Johns Centre	B4
St John's Rd	A2
St Mary's St	B5
St Pauls St	B3
St Peter's	B4
Saxton La	B5
Sayner La	C5
Shakespeare Ave	A6
Shannon St	B6
Sheepscar St South	A5
Siddall St	C3
Skinner La	A5
South Pde	B3
Sovereign St	C3
Spence La	C2
Springfield Mt	A2
Springwell Ct	C2
Springwell Rd	C2
Stoney Rock La	A6
Studio Rd	A1
Sutton St	C2
Sweet St	C3
Sweet St West	C3
Swinegate	B4
Templar St	B5
The Calls	B5
The Close	B6
The Drive	B6
The Garth	B5
The Headrow	B3/B4
The Lane	B5
The Parade	B6
Thoresby Pl	A3
Torre Rd	A6
Town Hall	A3
Trinity & Burton Arcades	B4
Union Pl	C3
Union St	B5
Upper Basinghall St	B4
Upper Accomodation Rd	B6
Vicar La	B4
Victoria Bridge	C4
Victoria Quarter	B4
Victoria Rd	C4
Washington St	A1
Water La	C3
Waterloo Rd	C3
Wellington Rd	B2/C1
Wellington St	B3
West St	B1
West Yorkshire Playhouse	B5
Westfield Rd	A1
Westgate	B3
Whitehall Rd	B3/C2
Whitelock St	A5
Willis St	B5
Willow Approach	A1
Willow Ave	A1
Willow Terrace Rd	A1
Wintoun St	A5
Woodhouse La	A3/A4
Woodsley Rd	A1
York Pl	B3
York Rd	B6
Yorkshire Television Studios	A1

Gateway Yorkshire, Regional Travel & Tourism Centre, The Arcade, Leeds City Station, Leeds LS1 1PL Tel 0113 242 5242

BBC Radio Leeds 92.4 FM and 774 AM • **Radio Aire** 96.3 FM **Galaxy 105** 105 FM

www.leeds.gov.uk

Leeds

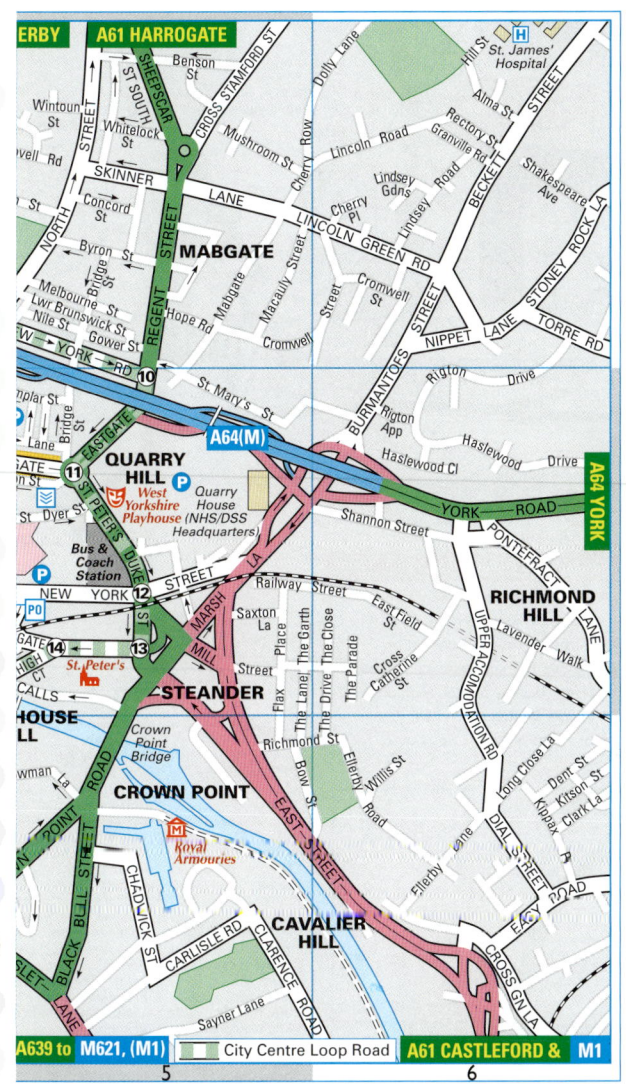

The history of Leeds is in the engineering and textiles industries, in the manufacture of machinery for spinning, machine tools, steam engines and gears as well as other industries based on textiles, chemicals and leather and pottery. In recent years Leeds has been rejuvenated and has become a major shopping centre for northern England, attracting names such as Harvey Nichols, Vivienne Westwood and Joseph in the Victoria Quarter, whilst Briggate boasts a selection of independents, Corngate Exchange and surrounds features all manner of styles. There is also Granary Wharf featuring more alternative style, and gift shops. Kirkgate Market is the largest of its kind in Europe and sells everything from groceries to underwear. Several important theatres have made their home in Leeds and there's no shortage of clubs, bars and restaurants.

▲ Leeds Town Hall

★ Do not miss
- ★ Leeds Art Gallery, The Headrow
- ★ Henry Moore Institute, The Headrow
- ★ Royal Armouries Museum, Armouries Drive

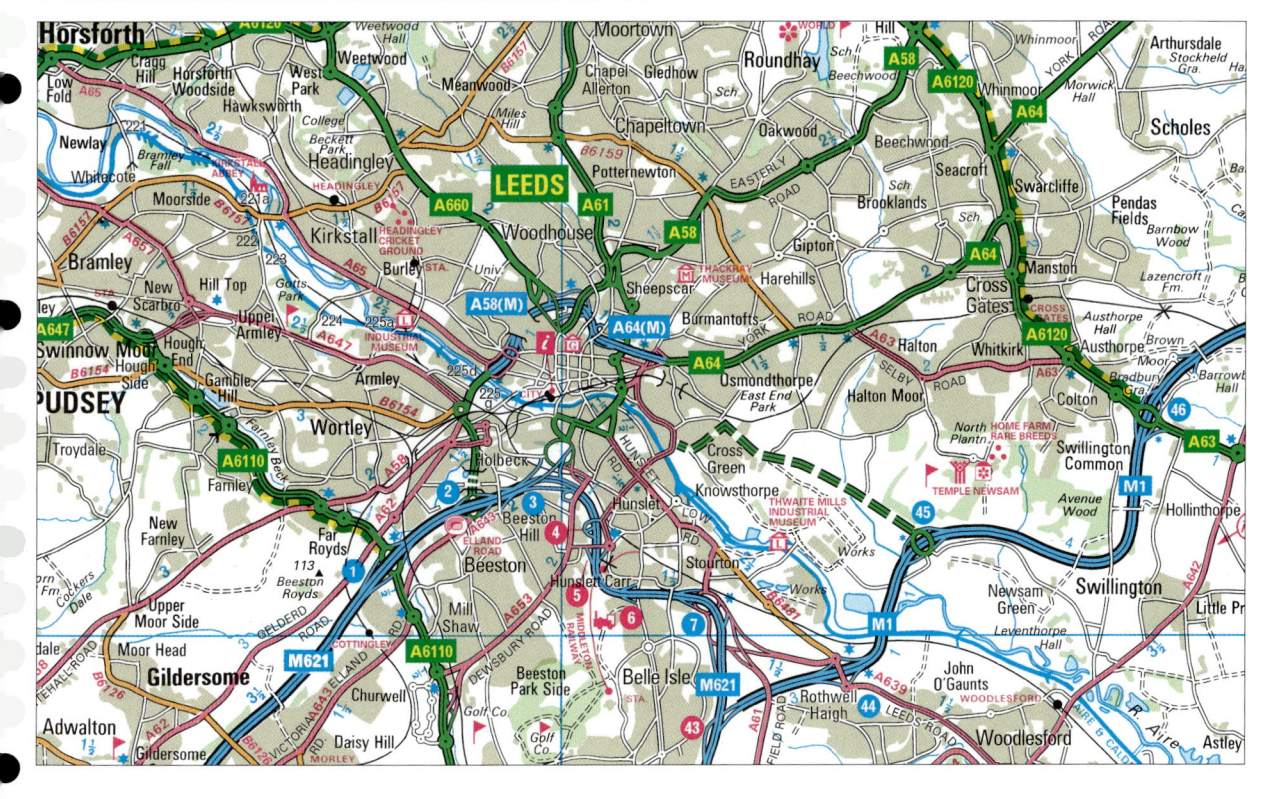

Lewes

A Saxon-origin county town on the edge of the rolling South Downs, where William de Warenne, a favourite of William the Conqueror, built an impressive castle and priory (now ruined). Characterised by its narrow medieval 'twittens' (twisting lanes), it also has some impressive Georgian townhouses. Other buildings of interest are the Victorian-Gothic Harvey's Brewery, the restored late-16th-century Southover Grange, the town hall with its Renaissance staircase and mayor's parlour displaying local treasures. The many speciality and antiques shops include the The Old Needlemakers' Factory crafts centre. Nearby attractions include the South Downs; Firle Place and Glynde Place country houses and parks; Charleston Farmhouse and Monks House, both owned by members of the Bloomsbury set; Berwick Church, which has murals they painted; Michelham Priory; Glyndebourne Opera House; the Long Man of Wilmington and Bentley Wildfowl & Motor Museum.

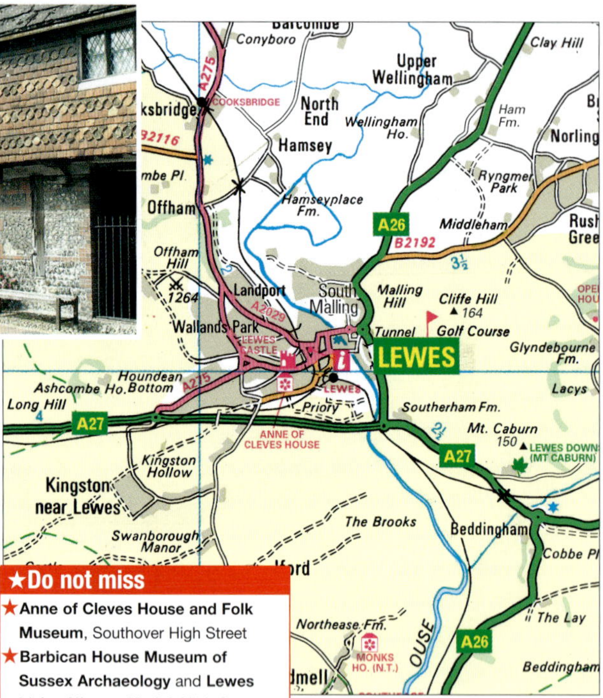

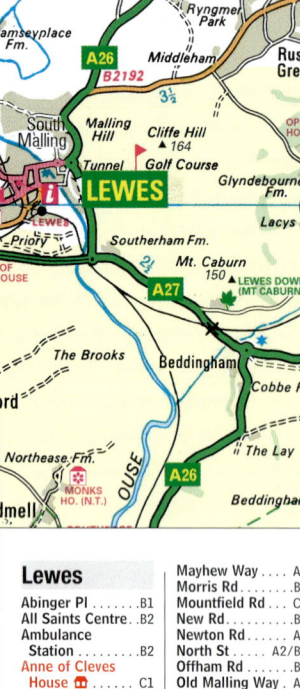

▲ Anne of Cleves House

Lewes Tourist Information Centre, 187 High Street, Lewes BN7 2DE
Tel 01273 483448

BBC Southern Counties 104.5 FM and 1161 AM • **Southern FM** 103.5 FM

www.lewes.gov.uk

★ Do not miss
- ★ **Anne of Cleves House and Folk Museum**, Southover High Street
- ★ **Barbican House Museum of Sussex Archaeology** and **Lewes Living History Model**, High Street
- ★ **Lewes Castle**, Castle Hill
- ★ **St Pancras Priory**, Southover

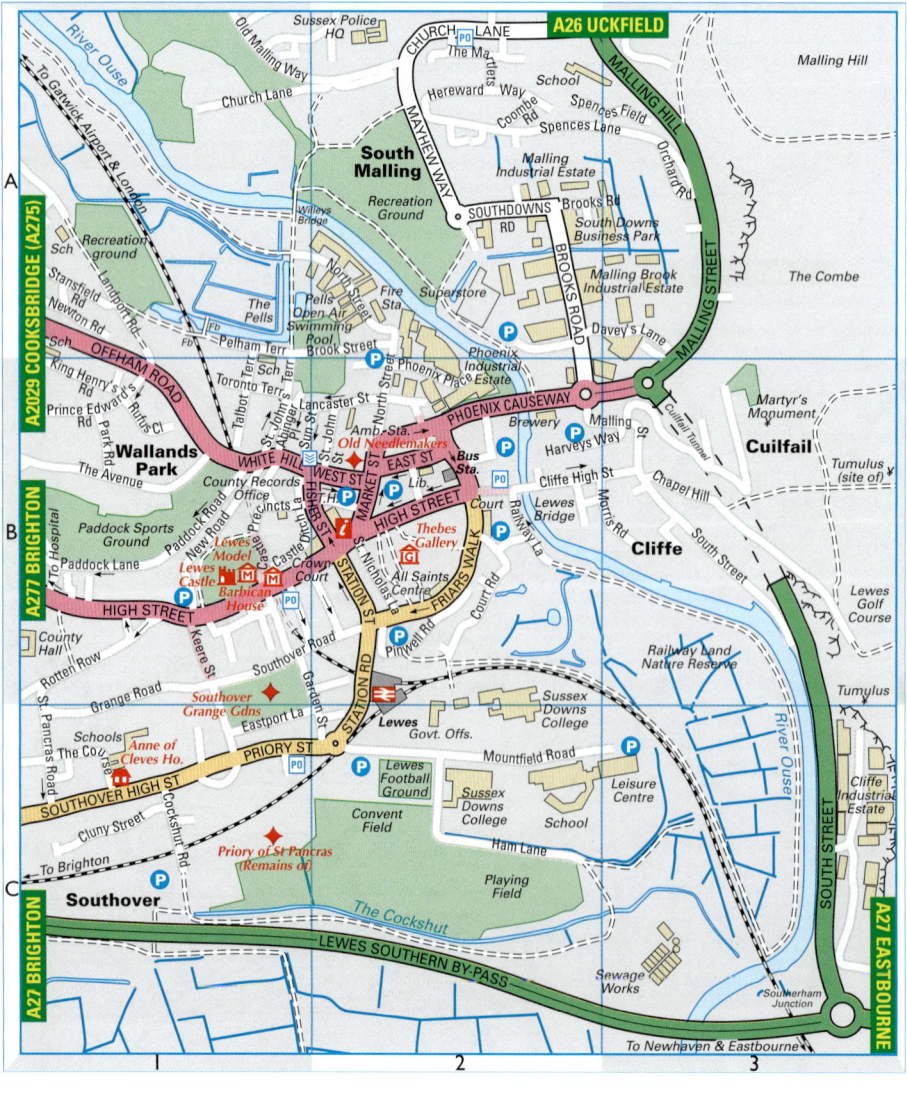

Lewes

Abinger Pl	B1
All Saints Centre	B2
Ambulance Station	B2
Anne of Cleves House	C1
Barbican House Museum	B1
Brewery	B2
Brook St	A2
Brooks Rd	A2
Bus Station	B2
Castle Ditch La	B1
Castle Precincts	B1
Chapel Hill	B3
Church La	A1/A2
Cliffe High St	B2
Cliffe Industrial Estate	C3
Cluny St	C1
Cockshut Rd	C1
Convent Field	C1
Coombe Rd	A2
County Hall	B1
County Records Office	B1
Court	B2
Court Rd	B2
Crown Court	B2
Cuilfail Tunnel	B3
Davey's La	A3
East St	C2
Eastport La	C1
Fire Station	A2
Fisher St	B1
Friars Walk	B2
Garden St	B1
Government Offices	C2
Grange Rd	B1
Ham La	C2
Harveys Way	B2
Hereward Way	A2
High St	B1/B2
Information Ctr	B2
Keere St	B1
King Henry's Rd	B1
Lancaster St	B2
Landport Rd	A1
Leisure Centre	C3
Lewes Bridge	B2
Lewes Castle	B1
Lewes Football Ground	C2
Lewes Golf Course	B3
Lewes Living History Model	B2
Lewes Southern By-Pass	C2
Lewes Station	B2
Library	B2
Malling Ind Est	A2
Malling Brook Ind Est	A3
Malling Hill	A3
Malling St	A3/B3
Market St	B2
Martyr's Monument	B3
Mayhew Way	A2
Morris Rd	B3
Mountfield Rd	C2
New Rd	B1
Newton Rd	A1
North St	A2/B2
Offham Rd	B1
Old Malling Way	A1
Old Needlemakers Craft Centre	B2
Orchard Rd	A3
Paddock La	B1
Paddock Rd	B1
Paddock Sports Ground	B1
Park Rd	B1
Pelham Terr	A1
Pells Open Air Swimming Pool	A1
Phoenix Causeway	B2
Phoenix Ind Est	B2
Phoenix Pl	B2
Pinwell Rd	B2
Police Station	B1
Post Office	A2/B1/B2/C1
Prince Edward's Rd	B1
Priory St	C1
Priory of St Pancras (remains of)	C1
Railway La	B2
Railway Land Nature Reserve	B3
Rotten Row	B1
Rufus Cl	B1
St Pancras Rd	C1
St John St	B2
St John's Terr	B1
St Nicholas La	B2
Sewage Works	C3
South Downs Business Park	A3
South St	B3/C3
Southdowns Rd	A2
Southerham Junction	C3
Southover Grange Gdns	B1
Southover High St	C1
Southover Rd	B1
Spences Field	A3
Spences La	A2
Stansfield Rd	A1
Station Rd	B2
Station St	B2
Sun St	B2
Sussex Downs College	C2
Sussex Police HQ	A2
Talbot Terr	B1
The Avenue	B1
The Course	C1
The Martlets	A2
The Pells	A1
Thebes Gallery	B2
Toronto Terr	B1
Town Hall	B1
West St	C1
White Hill	B1
Willeys Bridge	A1

Lincoln

Lincoln Tourist Information Centre, 21 The Cornhill, Lincoln LN5 7NH Tel 01522 873256

BBC Radio Lincolnshire 94.9 FM • **Lincs FM** 102.2 FM

www.visitlincolnshire.com

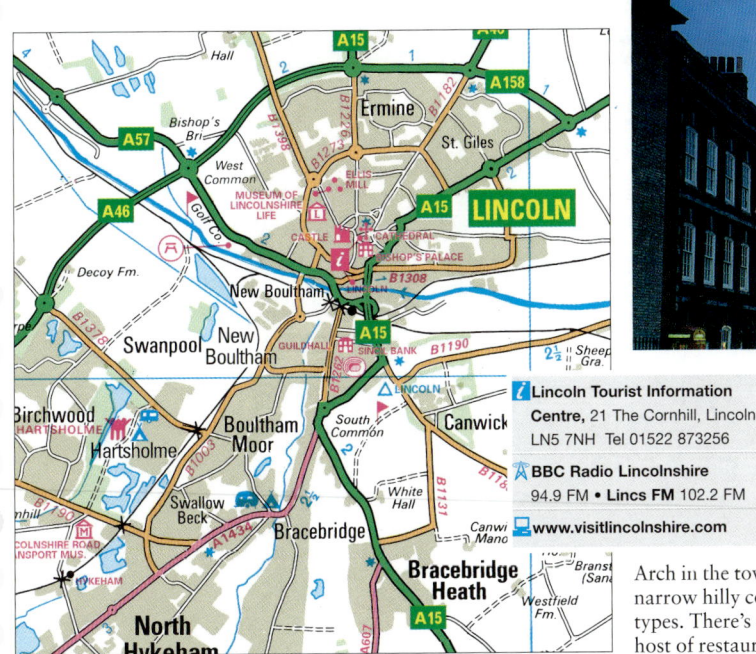

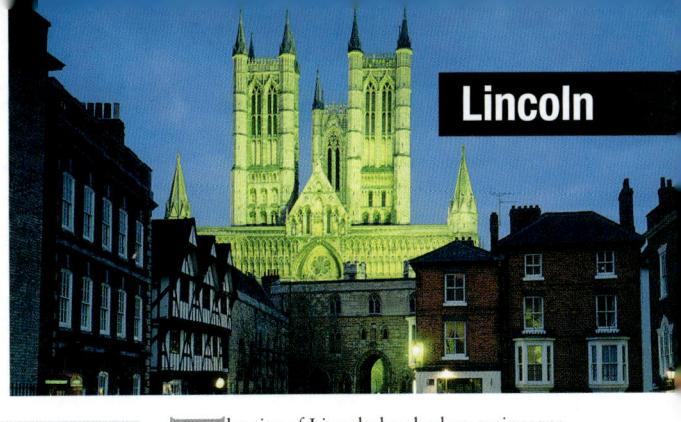

The city of Lincoln has had many incarnations – a prehistoric fort, a Roman settlement, captured by the Angles, then the Danes, and one of the largest cities in the country. William the Conqueror commissioned the magnificent castle in 1068 and the Cathedral in 1072. One of only four copies of the Magna Carta, sealed by King John, is to be found at the castle. Newport Arch in the town is the only Roman arch still used by traffic. The narrow hilly cobbled streets are lined with interesting shops of all types. There's a regular Farmer's Market and a host of restaurants and pubs for every taste.

▲Lincoln Cathedral

★ Do not miss
- ★ Lincoln Cathedral
- ★ Lincoln Castle
- ★ Bishop's Palace, Minster Yard

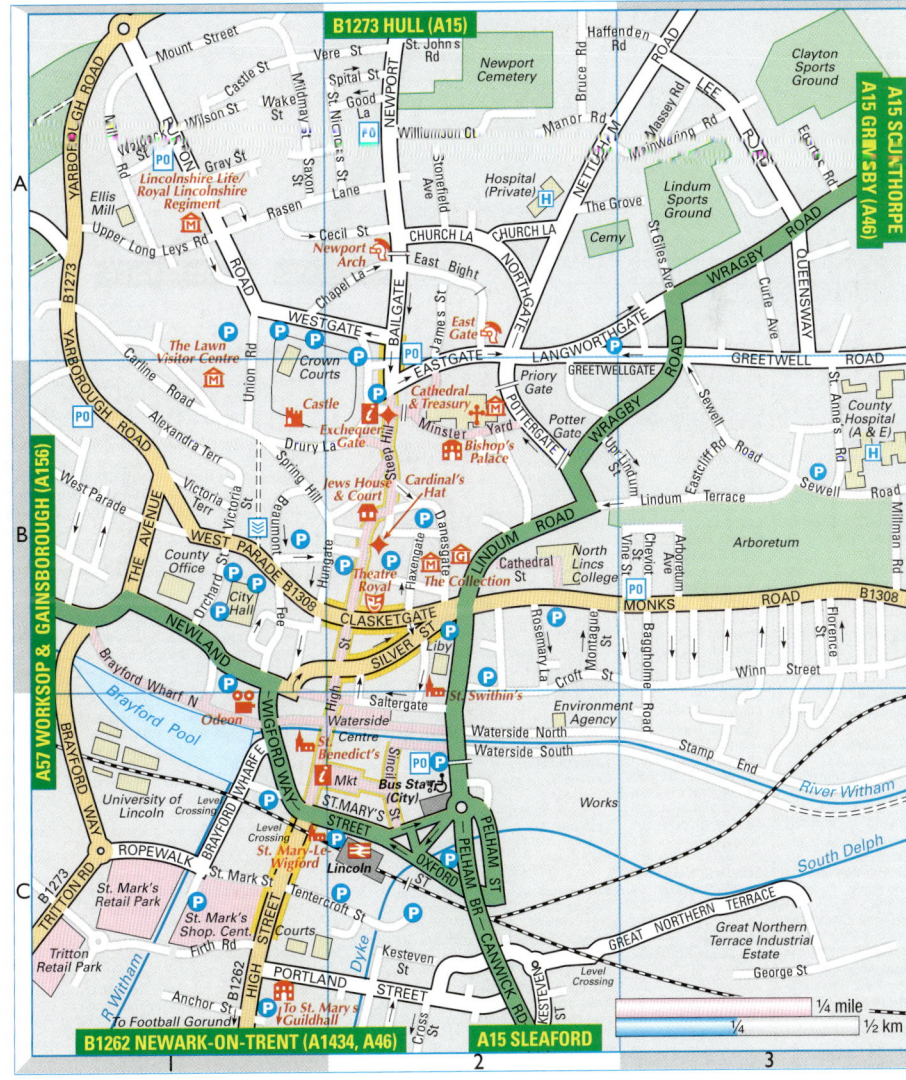

Lincoln

Street	Grid
Alexandra Terr	B1
Anchor St	C1
Arboretum	B3
Arboretum Ave	B3
Baggholme Rd	B3
Bailgate	B1
Beaumont Fee	B1
Bishop's Palace	B2
Brayford Way	C1
Brayford Wharf East	C1
Brayford Wharf North	B1
Bruce Rd	A2
Burton Rd	A1
Bus Station (City)	C2
Canwick Rd	C2
Cardinal's Hat	B2
Carline Rd	B1
Castle	B1
Castle St	A1
Cathedral & Treasury	B2
Cathedral St	B2
Cecil St	A2
Chapel La	A2
Cheviot St	B3
Church La	A2
City Hall	B1
Clasketgate	B2
Clayton Sports Ground	A3
Collection, The	B2
County Hospital (A&E)	B3
County Office	B1
Courts	B1
Croft St	B2
Cross St	B1
Crown Courts	B1
Curle Ave	A3
Danesgate	B2
Drury La	B1
East Bight	A2
East Gate	A2
Eastcliff Rd	B3
Eastgate	A2
Egerton Rd	A3
Ellis Mill	A1
Environment Agency	C2
Exchequer Gate	B2
Firth Rd	C1
Flaxengate	B2
Florence St	B3
George St	C3
Good La	A2
Gray St	A1
Great Northern Terr	C3
Great Northern Terrace Industrial Estate	C3
Greetwell Rd	B3
Greetwellgate	B3
Haffenden Rd	A2
High St	B2/B1
Hospital (Private)	A2
Hungate	B2
Information Ctr	B2
James St	A2
Jews House & Court	B2
Kesteven St	C2
Langworthgate	A2
Lawn Visitor Centre, The	B1
Lee Rd	A3
Library	B2
Lincoln	C2
Lincolnshire Life/Royal Lincolnshire Regiment Mus	A1
Lindum Rd	B2
Lindum Sports Ground	A3
Lindum Terr	B3
Mainwaring Rd	A3
Manor Rd	A2
Massey Rd	A3
Mildmay St	A1
Mill Rd	A1
Millman Rd	B3
Minster Yard	B2
Market	C2
Monks Rd	B3
Montague St	B3
Mount St	A1
Nettleham Rd	A2
Newland	B1
Newport	A2
Newport Arch	A2
Newport Cemetery	A2
North Lincs College	B2
Northgate	A2
Odeon	C1
Orchard St	B1
Oxford St	C2
Pelham Bridge	C1
Pelham St	C2
Police Station	B1
Portland St	C2
Post Office	A1/A2/B1/B3/C2
Potter Gate	B2
Priory Gate	B2
Queensway	A3
Rasen La	A1
Ropewalk	C1
Rosemary La	B2
St Anne's Rd	A3
St Benedict's	C1
St Giles Ave	A3
St John's Rd	A2
St Mark St	C1
St Mark's Retail Park	C1
St Mark's Shopping Centre	C1
St Mary-Le-Wigford	C1
St Mary's St	C1
St Nicholas St	A2
St Swithin's	B2
Saltergate	C1
Saxon St	A1
Sewell Rd	B3
Silver St	B2
Sincil St	C2
Spital St	A2
Spring Hill	B1
Stamp End	C3
Steep Hill	B2
Stonefield Ave	A3
Tentercroft St	C1
The Avenue	B1
The Grove	A3
Theatre Royal	B2
Tritton Retail Pk	C1
Tritton Rd	C1
Union Rd	B1
Univ of Lincoln	C1
Upper Lindum St	B3
Upper Long Leys Rd	A1
Vere St	A2
Victoria St	B1
Victoria Terr	B1
Vine St	B3
Wake St	A1
Waldeck St	A1
Waterside Ctr	C2
Waterside North	C2
Waterside South	C2
West Pde	B1
Westgate	A2
Wigford Way	C1
Williamson St	A2
Wilson St	A1
Winn St	B3
Wragby Rd	A3
Yarborough Rd	A1

Liverpool

Name	Grid
Abercromby Sq.	C5
Addison St	A3
Adelaide Rd	B6
Ainsworth St	B4
Albany Rd	B6
Albert Dock	C2
Albert Edward Rd	B6
Angela St	C6
Anson St	B4
Archbishop Blanche High School	B6
Argyle St	C2
Arrad St	C4
Ashton St	B5
Audley St	A4
Back Leeds St	A2
Basnett St	B3
Bath St	A1
Battle of the Atlantic	B2
BBC Radio Merseyside	C2
Beatles Story	C2
Beckwith St	C3
Bedford Close	C5
Bedford St North	C5
Bedford St South	C5
Benson St	C4
Berry St	C4
Birkett St	A4
Bixteth St	B2
Blackburne Place	C4
Bold Place	C4
Bold St	C4
Bolton St	B3
Bridport St	B4
Bronte St	B4
Brook St	A1
Brownlow Hill	B4/B5
Brownlow St	B5
Brunswick Rd	A5
Brunswick St	B1
Butler Cr	A6
Byrom St	A3
Cable St	B2
Caledonia St	C4
Cambridge St	C5
Camden St	A4
Canada Blvd	B1
Canning Dock	C2
Canning Place	C2
Canterbury St	A4
Cardwell St	C6
Carver St	A4
Cases St	B3
Castle St	B2
Cavern Walks	B3
Central Library	A3
Central Station	B3
Chapel St	B2
Charlotte St	B3
Chatham Place	C6
Chatham St	C5
Cheapside	B2
Chestnut St	C5
Christian St	A3
Church St	B3
Churchill Way North	A3
Churchill Way South	B3
Clarence St	B4
Coach Station	A4
Cobden St	C5
Cockspur St	A2
College La	C3
College St North	A5
College St South	A5
Colquitt St	C4
Comus St	A3
Concert St	C3
Connaught Rd	B6
Conservation Centre	B2
Cook St	B2
Copperas Hill	B3
Cornwallis St	C3
Covent Garden	B2
Craven St	A4
Cropper St	B3
Crown St	B5/C6
Cumberland St	B2
Cunard Building	B1
Dale St	B2
Dansie St	B4
Daulby St	B5
Dawson St	B3
Dental Hospital Museum	B5
Derby Sq	B2
Drury La	B2
Duckinfield St	B4
Duke St	C3
Earle St	A2
East St	A2
Eaton St	A2
Edgar St	A3
Edge La	B6
Edinburgh Rd	B6
Edmund St	B2
Elizabeth St	B5
Elliot St	B3
Empire Theatre	B4
Empress Rd	B6
Epworth St	A5
Erskine St	A5
Everyman Theatre	C5
Exchange St East	B2
Fact Centre, The	C4
Falkland St	A5
Falkner St	C5/C6
Farnworth St	B6
Fielding St	A6
Fingerprints of Elvis	C2
Fleet St	C3
Fraser St	A4
Freemasons Row	A2
Gardner Row	A3
Gascoyne St	A2
George St	B2
Gibraltar Row	A1
Gilbert St	C3
Gildart St	A4
Gill St	B4
Goree	B2
Gower St	C2
Gradwell St	C3
Granada TV Studios	C2
Great Crosshall St	A3
Great George St	C4
Great Howard St	A1
Great Newton St	B4
Greek St	B4
Green La	B4
Greenside	A5
Greetham St	C3
Gregson St	A5
Grenville St	C3
Grinfield St	C6
Grove St	C5
Guelph St	A6
Hackins Hey	B2
Haigh St	A4
Hall La	B6
Hanover St	B3
Harbord St	A5
Hardman St	C4
Harker St	A4
Hart St	A4
Hatton Garden	A2
Hawke St	B4
Helsby St	C6
Henry St	C3
Highfield St	A2
Highgate St	B6
Hilbre St	B4
HM Customs & Excise National Museum	C2
Hope Place	C4
Hope St	C4
Houghton St	B3
Hunter St	A3
Hutchinson St	A6
Information Ctr	B3/C2
Institute For The Performing Arts	C4
Irvine St	B6
Irwell St	B2
Islington	A4
James St	B2
James St Station	B2
Jenkinson St	A4
Johnson St	A3
Jubilee Drive	B6
Kempston St	A4
Kensington	A6
Kensington Gdns	A6
Kensington St	A6
Kent St	C3
King Edward St	A1
Kinglake St	B6
Knight St	C4
Lace St	A3
Langsdale St	A4
Law Courts	C2
Leece St	C4
Leeds St	A2
Leopold Rd	B6
Lime St	B3
Lime St Station	B4
Little Woolton St	B5
Liver St	C2
Liverpool John Moores University	A3/B4/C4
Liverpool Landing Stage	B1
London Rd	A4/B4
Lord Nelson St	B4
Lord St	B2
Lovat St	C6
Low Hill	A5
Low Wood St	A6
Lydia Ann St	C3
Manesty La	B3
Mann Island	B2
Mansfield St	A4
Marmaduke St	B6
Marsden St	A6
Martensen St	C4
Marybone	A3
Maryland St	C4
Mason St	B6
Mathew St	B3
May St	B4
Melville Place	C6
Merseyside Maritime Museum	C2
Metropolitan Cathedral (RC)	B5
Midghall St	A2
Molyneux Rd	A6
Moor Place	B4
Moorfields	B2
Moorfields Station	B2
Moss St	A5
Mount Pleasant	B4/B5
Mount St	C4
Mount Vernon View	B6
Mulberry St	C5
Municipal Buildings	B2
Museum of Liverpool Life	C2
Myrtle Gdns	C5
Myrtle St	C5
Naylor St	A2
Nelson St	C4
Neptune Theatre	B3
New Islington	A4
New Quay	B1
Newington St	C4
North John St	B2
North St	A3
North View	B6
Norton St	A4
Oakes St	B5
Odeon	B4
Old Hall St	A1
Old Leeds St	A2
Oldham Place	C4
Oldham St	C4
Olive St	C4
Open Eye Gallery	C3
Oriel St	A2
Ormond St	B2
Orphan St	C6
Overbury St	C6
Overton St	B6
Oxford St	C5
Paisley St	A1
Pall Mall	A2
Paradise St	C3
Paradise St Bus Station	B2
Park La	C3
Parker St	B3
Parr St	C3
Peach St	B5
Pembroke Place	B4
Pembroke St	B5
Peter's La	C3
Philharmonic Hall	C4
Pickop St	A2
Pilgrim St	C4
Pitt St	C3
Playhouse Theatre	B3
Pleasant St	B4
Police Headquarters	C2
Police Station	A4/B4
Pomona St	B4
Port of Liverpool Building	B2
Post Office	A2/A4
Pownall St	C2
Prescot St	A5
Preston St	B3
Princes Dock	A1
Princes Gdns	A2
Princes Jetty	A1
Princes Pde	B1
Princes St	B2
Pythian St	A6
Queen Square Bus Station	B3
Queensland St	C6
Queensway Tunnel (Docks exit)	B1
Queensway Tunnel (Entrance)	B3
Radio City	B2
Ranelagh St	B3
Redcross St	B2
Renfrew St	B6
Renshaw St	B4
Richmond Row	A4
Richmond St	B3
Rigby St	A2
Roberts St	A1
Rock St	B4
Rodney St	C4
Rokeby St	A4
Romilly St	A6
Roney St	C4
Roscoe La	C4
Roscoe St	C4
Rose Hill	A3
Royal Court Theatre	B3
Royal Liver Building	B1
Royal Liverpool Hospital (A&E)	B5
Royal Mail St	B4
Rumford Place	B2

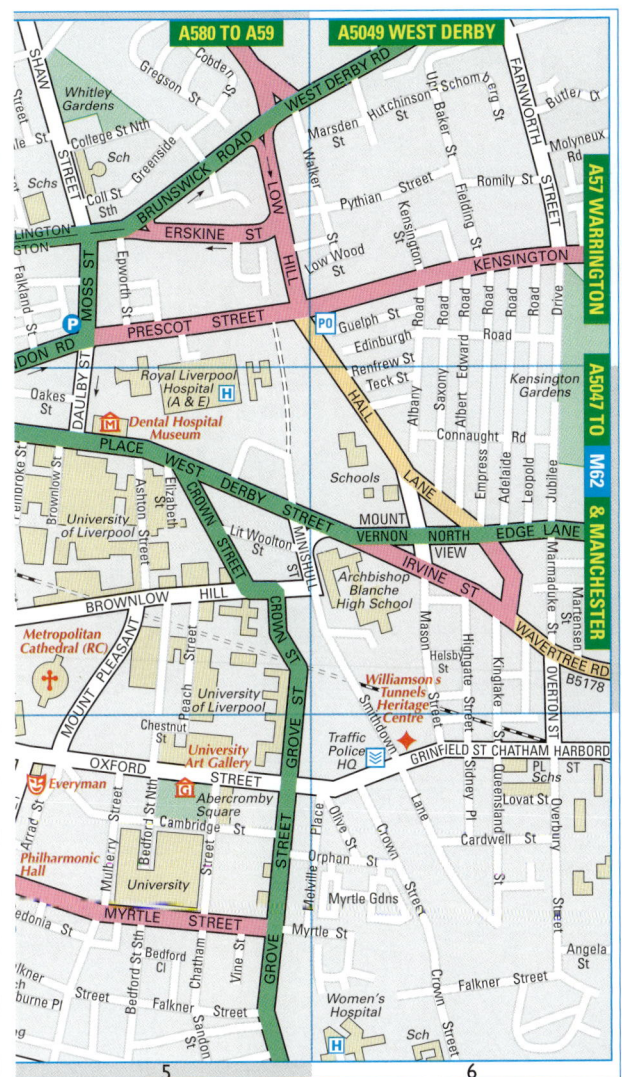

Liverpool

A city on the site of a port founded by King John in 1207 and focused around the 1846 Albert Dock, now a heritage attraction including the Merseyside Maritime Museum, the Pier Master's House & Offices; and the HM Customs & Excise National Museum. Other historic houses and buildings include Croxteth Hall & Country Park (Edwardian); the half-timbered Speke Hall; Sudley House, home to a Victorian shipping magnate and art collector; the Royal Liver Building; and Liverpool Cathedral, off Upper Duke Street, the UK's largest Anglican cathedral, designed in 1901 by Giles Gilbert Scott (there's also a Roman Catholic Metropolitan Cathedral, built 1967). Important art venues include the Walker Art Gallery, The Lady Lever Art Gallery at Port Sunlight and the University of Liverpool Art Gallery. There are many Beatles-related attractions. For sports fans there are tours of Everton Football Club and the Liverpool Football Club Museum, and tours of the Aintree racecourse.

▲The waterfront

★ Do not miss
- ★ **The Beatles Story**, Britannia Vaults, Albert Dock
- ★ **Mersey Ferries**, Pier Head
- ★ **Tate Liverpool**, Albert Dock – modern art gallery

Tourist Information Centre, Queens Square, Liverpool L1 1RG Tel 0906 680 6886 (calls cost 25p per minute)

BBC Radio Merseyside 95.8 FM and 1485 AM • **Radio City** 96.7 FM **Juice** 107.6 FM • **Magic** 1548 AM

www.visitliverpool.com

Rumford St B2	Traffic Police
Russell St B4	Headquarters . . C6
St Andrew St B4	Trowbridge St . . . B4
St Anne St A4	Trueman St A3
St Georges	Union St B1
Hall B3	Unity Theatre . . C4
St John's Centre . . B3	University Art
St John's Gdns . . . B3	Gallery C5
St John's La. B3	University C5
St Joseph's Cr . . . B4	University of
St Minishull St. . . . B5	Liverpool B5
St Nicholas Place .B1	Upper Duke St. . . C4
St Paul's Sq A2	Upper Frederick
St Vincent Way . . . B4	St. C3
Salisbury St A4	Upper Baker St . . A6
Salthouse Dock. . . C2	Vauxhall Rd A2
Salthouse Quay. . . C2	Vernon St B2
Sandon St C5	Victoria St B2
Saxony Rd B6	Vine St C5
Schomberg St . . . A6	Wakefield St A4
School La B5	Walker Art
Seel St C3	Gallery A3
Seymour St B4	Walker St A6
Shaw St A4	Wapping C2
Sidney Place C6	Water St B1/B2
Sir Thomas St . . . B3	Waterloo Rd A1
Skelhorne St B4	Wavertree Rd. . . . B6
Slater St C3	West Derby Rd . . A6
Smithdown La . . . B5	West Derby St . . . B5
Soho Sq A4	Whitechapel B3
Soho St. A4	Whitley Gdns A5
Springfield A4	Williamson Sq . . . B3
Stafford St A4	Williamson St . . . B3
Standish St A3	**Williamson's**
Stanley St B3	Tunnels Heritage
South John St . . . B2	Centre ✦ C6
Strand St C2	William Brown St .B3
Suffolk St C3	William Henry St . A4
Tabley St C2	Women's
Tarleton St B3	Hospital C6
Tate Liverpool . . C2	Wood St B3
Teck St B6	World Museum,
Temple St B2	Liverpool A3
The Strand C2	York St C3
Tithebarn St. B2	
Town Hall B2	

Llandudno

A North Wales Victorian seaside resort with a promenade; a 120-year-old Indian-Gothic-style pier (Wales' longest); two beaches; a cablecar and tramway to the summit of the Great Orme headland, where there is a country park with a Bronze Age copper mine and a visitor centre offering a live video link to a seabird colony; Happy Valley Park with its restored 1890 camera obscura, toboggan run and more; and St Tudno's 12th-century church on the site of the cave-cell of a 6th-century Celtic monk. Llandudno Museum shows the town's history from prehistoric times, The Llandudno Story charts how the town developed as a resort and the Oriel Mostyn contemporary art gallery has a programme of exhibitions. Nature/animal attractions include Bodafon Farm Park and RSPB Conwy Nature Reserve, and nearby are Bodnant Gardens with their views across to Snowdonia.

▲ Great Orme Tramway

★ Do not miss
- ★ **Alice in Wonderland Centre**, Trinity Square
- ★ **Great Orme Country Park**, Great Orme headland
- ★ **Conwy Castle**, Conwy

Llandudno Tourist Information Centre, 1-2 Chapel Street, Llandudno LL30 2SY Tel 01492 876413

BBC Radio Wales 94.8 FM
Champion 103.0 FM • Coast 96.3 FM
www.llandudno-tourism.co.uk

Llandudno

Street	Grid
Abbey Pl.	B1
Abbey Rd.	B1
Adelphi St.	B3
Alexandra Rd.	C2
Alice in Wonderland Centre ◆	B3
Anglesey Rd.	A1
Argyll Rd.	B3
Arvon Ave.	A2
Atlee Cl.	B3
Augusta St.	B3
Back Madoc St.	B2
Bodafon St.	B3
Bodhyfryd Rd.	A2
Bodnant Cr.	B3
Bodnant Rd.	C3
Bridge Rd.	C1
Bryniau Rd.	C1
Builder St.	C2
Builder St West.	C2
Cabin Lift.	A2
Camera Obscura ◆	A3
Caroline Rd.	B2
Chapel St.	A2
Charlton St.	B3
Church Cr.	B2
Church Walks.	A2
Claremont Rd.	B2
Clement Ave.	A2
Clifton Rd.	B2
Clonmel St.	B3
Conway Rd.	B3
Council St West.	C3
Cricket and Recreation Grnd.	B2
Cwlach Rd.	A2
Cwlach St.	A1
Cwm Howard La.	C3
Cwm Pl.	C3
Cwm Rd.	C3
Dale Rd.	C1
Deganwy Ave.	B2
Denness Pl.	C2
Dinas Rd.	C2
Dolydd.	B1
Erol Pl.	B2
Ewloe Dr.	C3
Fairways.	C1
Ffordd Dewi.	C3
Ffordd Dulyn.	C2
Ffordd Dwyfor.	C2
Ffordd Elisabeth.	C3
Ffordd Gwynedd.	C3
Ffordd Las.	C3
Ffordd Morfa.	C3
Ffordd Penrhyn.	C3
Ffordd Tudno.	C3
Ffordd yr Orsedd.	C3
Ffordd Ysbyty.	C2
Garage St.	B3
George St.	B2
Gloddaeth Ave.	B1
Gloddaeth St.	B2
Gogarth Rd.	B1
Great Orme Mines ◆	A1
Great Ormes Rd.	B1
Happy Valley.	A2
Happy Valley Rd.	A3
Haulfre Gdns ❀.	A1
Herkomer Cr.	C1
Hill Terr.	A2
Hospice.	B1
Howard Rd.	B1
Information Ctr.	B2
Invalids' Walk.	B1
James St.	B2
Jubilee St.	B3
King's Ave.	C2
King's Rd.	C2
Knowles Rd.	C2
Lees Rd.	C2
Library.	B2
Lifeboat Station.	B2
Llandudno 🚉.	A2
Llandudno (A&E) 🏥.	C2
Llandudno 🚉.	B3
Llandudno Story ◆	B2
Llandudno Town Football Ground.	C2
Llewelyn Ave.	A2
Lloyd St West.	B1
Lloyd St.	B2
Llwynon Rd.	A1
Llys Maelgwn.	B1
Madoc St.	B2
Maelgwn Rd.	B2
Maesdu Bridge.	C2
Maesdu Rd.	C2/C3
Maes-y-Cwm.	C3
Maes-y-Orsedd.	C3
Marian Pl.	C2
Marian Rd.	C2
Marine Dr (Toll).	A3
Market Hall.	A2
Market St.	A2
Miniature Golf Course.	A1
Morfa Rd.	B1
Mostyn 🏛.	B3
Mostyn Broadway.	B3
Mostyn St.	B3
Mowbray Rd.	C2
New St.	A2
Norman Rd.	C3
North Parade.	A2
North Wales Golf Links.	C1
North Wales 🏛.	A3
Old Rd.	A2
Oxford Rd.	B3
Pier ◆.	A2
Plas Rd.	A2
Police Station.	B2
Post Office.	B3/C2
Promenade.	A3
Pyllau Rd.	A1
Rectory La.	A2
Retail Park.	C3
Rhuddlan Ave.	C3
St Andrew's Ave.	B2
St Andrew's Pl.	B2
St Beuno's Rd.	A1
St David's Pl.	B2
St David's Rd.	B2
St George's Pl.	A3
St Mary's Rd.	B2
St Seriol's Rd.	C2
Salisbury Pass.	B1
Salisbury Rd.	B1
Somerset St.	B3
South Parade.	A2
Stephen St.	B3
TA Centre.	B3
Tabor Hill.	A2
The Oval.	B1
The Parade.	A3
Town Hall.	B2
Trinity Ave.	B1
Trinity Cres.	C1
Trinity Sq.	B3
Tudno St.	A2
Ty-Coch Rd.	A2
Ty-Gwyn Rd.	A1
Ty-Gwyn Rd.	B1
Ty'n-y-coed Rd.	A1
Vaughan St.	B3
Victoria Shopping Centre.	B3
Victoria Tram Station.	A2
War Memorial ◆.	A2
Werny Wylan.	C3
West Parade.	B1
Whiston Pass.	A2
Winllan Ave.	C2
Wyddfyd Rd.	A1
York Rd.	A2

★ Do not miss
- ★ **Millennium Coastal Park**, North Dock
- ★ **National Wetlands Centre**, Penclacwydd, Llwynhendy
- ★ **Park Howard Museum and Art Gallery**, Felinfoel Road

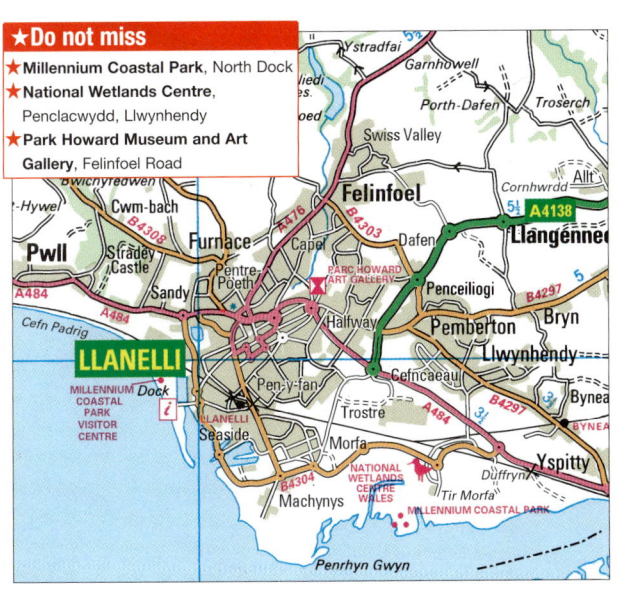

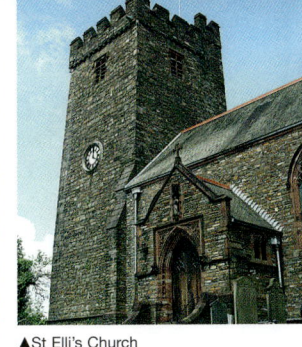

▲ St Elli's Church

Llanelli

A Carmarthenshire town that grew prosperous in the late 18th century through its metal manufacture and role as a coal port, now a popular venue for watersports, with a 12-mile coastal park with a promenade, a cyclepath (part of the Celtic Trail or Lon Geltaidd), 250 acres of wetland habitat, a golf course, and views over the Gower Peninsula. Nearby are Kidwelly with its well-preserved half-moon-shaped castle, Industrial Museum and award-winning 7-mile sandy beach; Pembrey Country Park with its outstanding beach, children's attractions and picnic sites; and the mainly 13th-century remains of Loughor Castle across the River Loughor.

Llanelli Tourist Information Centre, Public Library, Vaughan Street, Llanelli SA15 3AS Tel 01554 772020

BBC Radio Wales 93.9 FM • Real Radio 106 FM • The Wave 96.4 FM
Swansea Sound 1170 AM

www.carmarthenshire.gov.uk

Llanelli

Alban Rd...B3	Goring Rd...A2	Park St...B2	Prospect Pl...A2	Richard St...B2	Stepney St...B2	Thomas St...A2	Upper Robinson St B2

(Street index — see map)

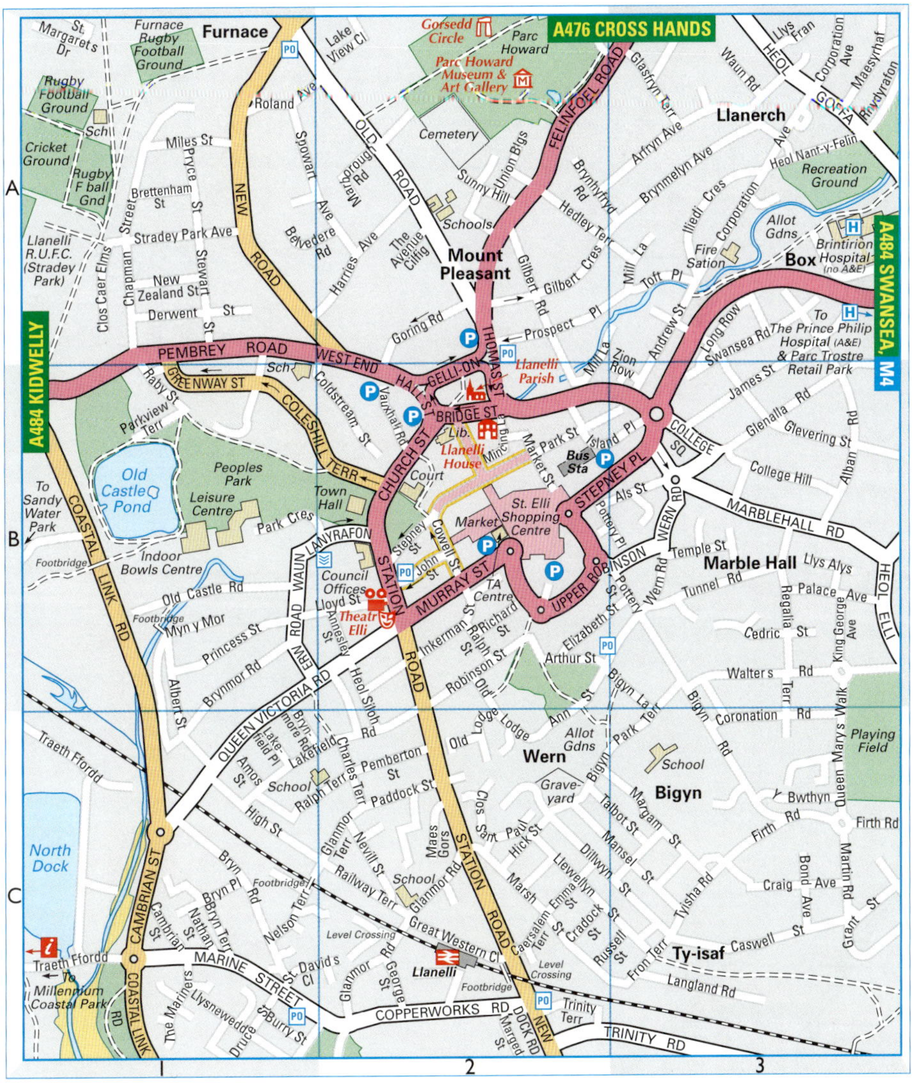

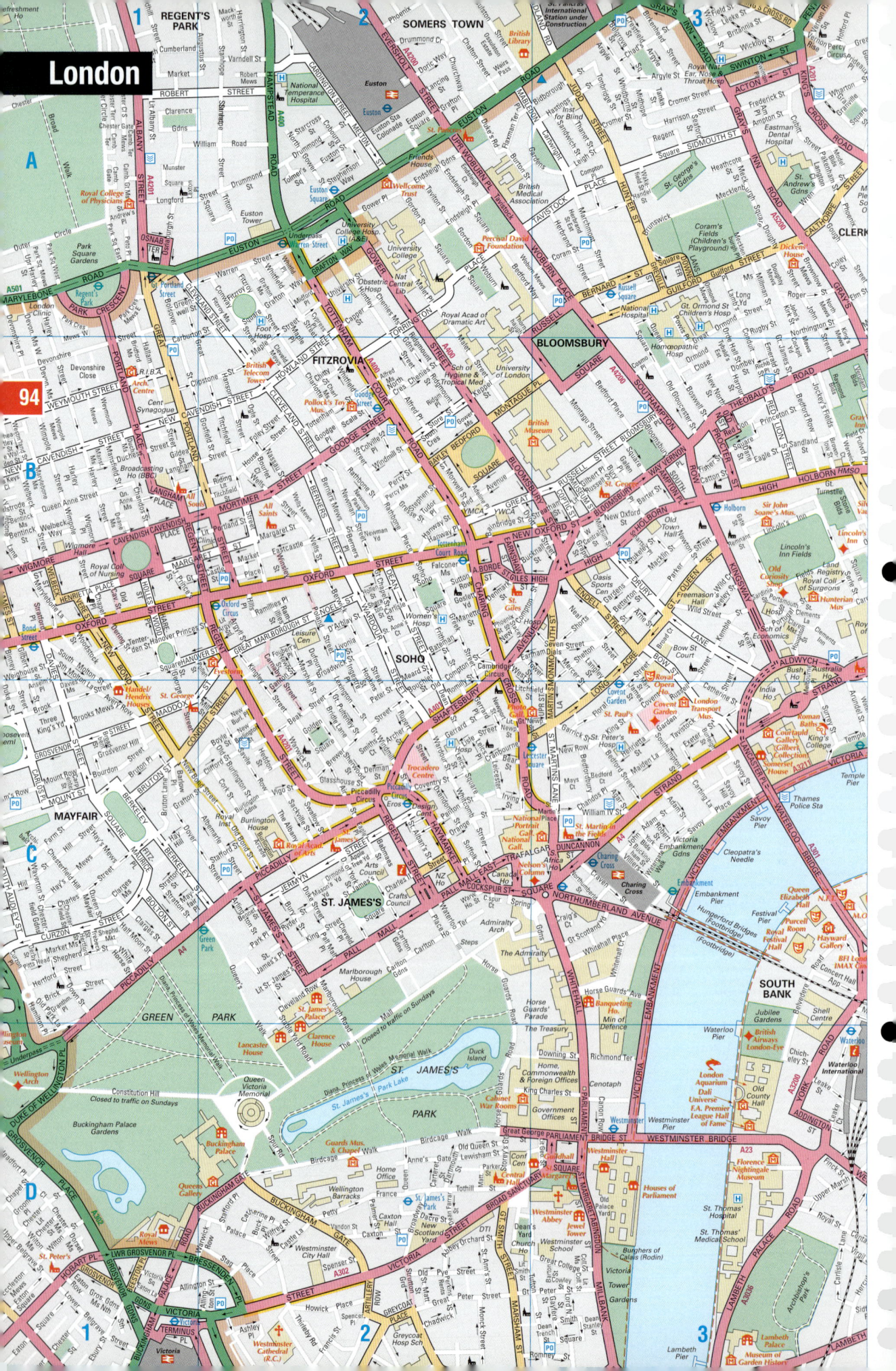

London

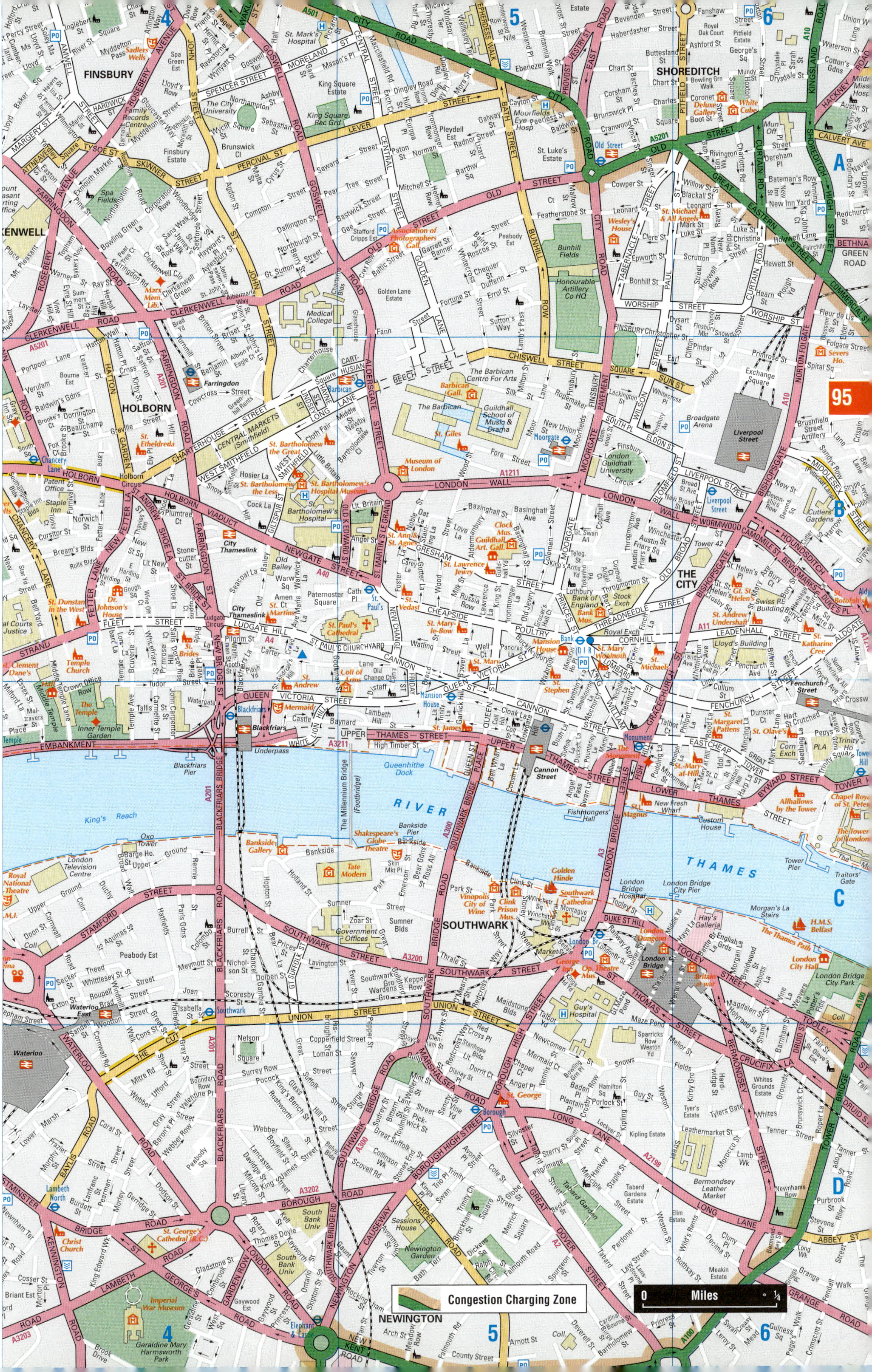
FINSBURY
SHOREDITCH
HOLBORN
THE CITY
SOUTHWARK
NEWINGTON
CLERKENWELL
RIVER THAMES
The Barbican
Barbican Centre For Arts
Museum of London
St. Paul's Cathedral
St. Bartholomew's Hospital
Guildhall
Bank of England
Liverpool Street
Cannon Street
London Bridge
Blackfriars
Waterloo
Tate Modern
Southwark Cathedral
Guy's Hospital
Imperial War Museum
Bunhill Fields
Honourable Artillery Co HQ
Inner Temple Garden
Fenchurch Street
Congestion Charging Zone
Miles
95
4
5
6
A
B
C
D

London

▲ Shaftesbury Avenue

A vibrant modern capital that grew from the nucleus of the one-square-mile Roman city, which is now an international finance centre but retains, among the office blocks, some of the old Roman wall, much of its medieval street plan, many of the churches constructed after the Great Fire of 1666 and a variety of ceremonial buildings. Areas range from 'villagey' Marylebone to the regenerated riverside South Bank area, home to some of the city's foremost art venues and theatres (many in the vast complex of the South Bank Centre), as well as historic inns and fashionable restaurants.

London's heritage comes to life in historic buildings and attractions such as the Monument, commemorating the Great Fire; the Mansion House, the Lord Mayor's official residence; the Guildhall, seat of the Corporation of London; the Museum of London, which is particularly informative on London's Roman heritage; the Jewish Museum; the National Maritime Museum and the Museum of Docklands, which charts the history of London's river and historic port. In addition, there are many past and present royal residences that can be visited: Buckingham Palace and the Royal Mews, Hampton Court Palace, Kensington Palace, Kew Palace and the Queen's House at Greenwich. Religious buildings of particular note are Hawksmoor's Christ Church Spitalfields, London Central Mosque, the Brompton Oratory, Wren's St Stephen Walbrook, Southwark Cathedral, St Bartholomew the Great and the Shri Swaminarayan Mandir Hindu temple in Neasden.

Among the historic houses and buildings owned or administered by the conservation-oriented National Trust and English Heritage are the George Inn, Chiswick House, Osterley, Eltham Palace, Ham House and the landmark Wellington Arch (1925). Modern structures of note include City Hall, headquarters of the Mayor of London; the stations of the Jubilee Line underground extension; Lloyd's of London; the Millennium Bridge; the Swiss-Re building (the Gherkin); and 1 Canada Square (Canary Wharf tower), London's tallest building.

The array of world-class art venues includes the National Portrait Gallery, the Royal Academy of Arts, Somerset House (comprising the Courtauld Institute Galleries, the Gilbert Collection of Decorative Arts and the Hermitage Rooms) and Tate Britain. For modern and contemporary art, there is the Dali Universe, the Estorick Collection of Modern Italian Art, the Photographers' Gallery and the Saatchi Collection. Exhibitions are also held at the Serpentine and Hayward Galleries and the ICA. Smaller-scale art galleries/museums include Sir John Soane's Museum, Dulwich Picture Gallery, the Museum of Garden History and the Wallace Collection, while the Design Museum traces the evolution of everyday objects and the Geffrye Museum deals with interior design from Tudor times on. Much cutting-edge artistic activity can be found in the rapidly gentrifying areas of the East End (Hoxton, Shoreditch, Spitalfields and Whitechapel) with their artists' studios and small commercial galleries.

The city's rich literary history can be explored in, for example, the former houses of Dickens, Dr Johnson, Keats, Freud and Carlyle, as well as the British Library Exhibition Galleries while those interested in legal London should visit the Inns of Court, the Old Bailey and the Royal Courts of Justice. Various aspects of medical history can be traced at the Florence Nightingale Museum; the Old Operating Theatre, Museum & Herb Garret, the Welcome Trust Gallery; the Royal London Hospital Museum and the Hunterian Museum (Royal College of Surgeons). Military museums include the Imperial War Museum, the Cabinet War Rooms, the RAF Museum at Hendon and HMS *Belfast*.

Venues that will appeal to children include Madame Tussaud's, the London Aquarium, the Diana Princess of Wales Memorial Playground and Fountain, the London Transport Museum, the Thames Barrier Visitor Centre, Pollock's Toy Museum and the Tower Bridge exhibition.

Green spaces amidst the urban sprawl include Hyde Park and Kensington Gardens, Regent's Park, Green Park, St James' Park, Holland Park, Greenwich Park, Richmond Park, Wimbledon Common, Chelsea Physic Garden, Highgate Wood, the London Wetland Centre, many squares and the Victorian cemetaries including Highgate and Kensal Green.

The unparalleled range of shopping facilities takes in everything from the high-street chains of Oxford Street to the boutiques of Covent Garden; the designer shops of Regent Street, Bond Street and Knightsbridge and landmark stores such as Liberty, Fortnum & Mason and Harrods. Charing Cross Road is home to secondhand bookshops and Tottenham Court Road to computer stores. There is a wide range of markets, which tend to have their own specialities: Portobello Road for jewellery and clothes; Columbia Road for flowers; Petticoat Lane for bargain clothing and bags; and Brick Lane and Whitechapel for food, clothing and bric-a-brac. The six markets in Camden sell just about anything, but specialise in second-hand clothing and music. There is a growing number of weekly farmers' markets, the best known of which, if by far most expensive, is Borough Market.

Seasonal attractions include events such as Wimbledon Lawn Tennis Championships; the Chelsea Flower Show; Shakespeare's Globe Theatre Season, the Regents Park Open-Air season and the Proms season of classical concerts at the Royal Albert Hall. More frequent events include the Ceremony of the Keys at the Tower of London (daily) and the Changing of the Guard at Buckingham Palace (daily or every other day).

Popular entertainment is clustered around Leicester Square and Shaftsbury Avenue, but there is a vast choice of superb venues elsewhere, including the National Theatre, the National Film Theatre and the Barbican.

The eclectic range of restaurants, bars and clubs has something to suit everyone's taste and wallet. Many of the best are to be found in Soho, Covent Garden or Mayfair, while Chinatown is great for far-eastern food and Brick Lane is the place to head for a curry.

Tourist Information Centre, 1 Regent Street, SW1Y 4XT (personal callers only)
BBC London 94.9 FM **Capital FM** 94.8 FM
www.london.gov.uk

★ Do not miss

- ★ **British Museum**, Great Russell St, WC1
- ★ **Hampstead Heath & Kenwood House**, NW3
- ★ **Houses of Parliament**, St Margaret St, SW1
- ★ **Royal Botanic Gardens, Kew**, Kew Rd, TW9
- ★ **London Eye**, Jubilee Gardens, SE1
- ★ **London Zoo**, Regent's Park, NW1
- ★ **National Gallery**, Trafalgar Square, WC2
- ★ **Natural History Museum**, Cromwell Rd, SW7
- ★ **St Paul's Cathedral**, EC4
- ★ **Science Museum**, Exhibition Rd, SW7
- ★ **Tate Modern**, Queen's Walk, SE1
- ★ **Tower of London**, Tower Hill, EC3
- ★ **Victoria & Albert Museum**, Cromwell Rd, SW7
- ★ **Westminster Abbey**, SW1

London

Street	Grid
Abingdon St	D3
Acton St	A3
Addington St	D3
Air St	C1
Albany St	A1
Albemarle St	C2
Aldersgate St	B5
Aldgate	B6
Aldgate ⊖	B6
Aldwych	B3
Amwell St	A4
Andrew Borde St	B2
Appold St	B6
Argyle Sq	A3
Argyle St	A3
Argyll St	B2
Arnold Circus	A6
Artillery La	B6
Artillery Row	D2
Association of Photographers Gallery	A5
Baldwin's Gdns	B4
Baltic St	A5
Bank ⊖	B5
Bank Museum	B5
Bank of England	B5
Bankside	C4
Bankside Gallery	C4
Banner St	A5
Barbican ⊖ ≷	B5
Barbican Gallery	B5
Basinghall St	B5
Bastwick St	A5
Bateman's Row	A6
Bath St	A5
Bath Terr	D5
Bayley St	B2
Baylis Rd	D4
Beak St	C2
Becket St	D5
Bedford Row	B3
Bedford St	C3
Bedford Way	A2
Beech St	B5
Bell La	B6
Belvedere Rd	D3
Berkeley Sq	C1
Bermondsey St	D6
Bernard St	A3
Berners Pl	B2
Berners St	B2
Berwick St	B2
Bethnal Green Rd	A6
Bevenden St	A6
Bevis Marks	B6
BFI London IMAX Cinema	C4
Bidborough St	A3
Binney St	B1
Birdcage Walk	D2
Bishopsgate	B6
Blackfriars Bridge	C4
Blackfriars ⊖ ≷	C4
Blackfriars Rd	C4
Blomfield St	B5
Bloomsbury St	B2
Bloomsbury Way	B3
Bolton St	C1
Bond St ⊖	B1
Borough ⊖	D5
Borough High St	D5
Borough Rd	D4
Boswell St	B3
Bowling Green La	A4
Bow St	B3
Brad St	C4
Bressenden Pl	D2
Brewer St	C2
Brick St	C1
Bridge St	D3
Britain at War	C6
Britannia Walk	A5
London-Eye ⊖	D3
British Library	A3
British Museum	B3
Britton St	A4
Broad Sanctuary	D2
Broadway	D2
Brook St	C1
Brunswick Pl	A5
Brunswick Sq	A3
Brushfield St	B6
Bruton St	C1
Buckingham Gate	D2
Buckingham Palace	D2
Buckingham Palace Rd	D1
Bunhill Row	A5
Byward St	C6
Cabinet War Rooms	D2
Calthorpe St	A4
Calvert Ave	A6
Cambridge Circus	B3
Camomile St	B6
Cannon St ⊖ ≷	C5
Carey St	B3
Carlisle La	D3
Carlton House Terr	D2
Carmelite St	C4
Carnaby St	B2
Carter La	B4
Carthusian St	A5
Cartwright Gdns	A3
Castle Baynard St	C4
Cavendish Pl	B1
Cavendish Sq	B1
Caxton Hall	D2
Caxton St	D2
Central St	A5
Chalton St	A2
Chancery Lane ⊖	B4
Chapel St	D1
Charing Cross ⊖ ≷	C3
Charing Cross Rd	B2
Charles II St	C2
Charles Sq	A5
Charles St	C1
Charlotte Rd	A6
Charlotte St	B2
Charterhouse Sq	B4
Charterhouse St	B4
Chart St	A5
Cheapside	B5
Chenies St	B2
Chesterfield Hill	C1
Chiltern St	B1
Chiswell St	B5
City Rd	A5
City Thameslink	B4
Clarges St	C1
Clerkenwell Cl	A4
Clerkenwell Green	A4
Clerkenwell Rd	A4
Cleveland St	B2
Clifford St	C2
Clink Prison Museum	C5
Clock Museum	B5
Cockspur St	C2
Coleman St	B5
Commercial St	A6
Compton St	A4
Conduit St	C1
Constitution Hill	D1
Copperfield St	D4
Coptic St	B3
Cornhill	B5
Cornwall Rd	C4
Coronet St	A6
Courtauld Gallery	C3
Covent Garden ✦	C3
Covent Garden ⊖	C3
Cowcross St	B4
Cowper St	A5
Cranbourne St	C2
Craven St	C3
Creechurch La	B6
Cromer St	A3
Crucifix La	D6
Curtain Rd	A6
Curzon St	C1
Dali Universe	D3
Davies St	B1
Dean St	B2
Deluxe Gallery	A6
Denmark St	B2
Dering St	B1
Devonshire St	A1
Diana, Princess of Wales Memorial Walk	D2
Dingley Rd	A5
D'arblay St	B2
Doughty St	A3
Dover St	C1
Downing St	D3
Druid St	D6
Drummond St	A2
Drury La	B3
Drysdale St	A6
Duchess St	B1
Dufferin St	A5
Duke of Wellington Pl	D1
Duke's Pl	B6
Duke St	C2
Duke St Hill	C5
Duncannon St	C3
Eastcastle St	B2
Eastcheap	C6
Eastman Dental Hospital	A3
East Rd	A5
Eaton Sq	D1
Ebury St	D1
Eldon St	B5
Elephant and Castle ⊖ ≷	D4
Elizabeth Garret Anderson Hospital	A3
Embankment ⊖	C3
Endell St	B3
Endsleigh Pl	A2
Euston ⊖ ≷	A2
Euston Rd	A2
Euston Square ⊖	A2
Eversholt St	A2
Exmouth Market	A4
Eyestorm	B1
Fair St	D6
Falmouth Rd	D5
Fann St	A5
Farringdon ⊖ ≷	B4
Farringdon Rd	B4
Farringdon St	B4
Featherstone St	A5
Fenchurch St	C6
Fenchurch St ≷	C6
Fetter La	B4
Finsbury Circus	B5
Finsbury Pavement	B5
Finsbury Sq	A5
Fitzmaurice Pl	C1
Fleet St	B4
Floral St	C3
Florence Nightingale Museum	D3
Folgate St	B6
Foot Hospital	A3
Fore St	B5
Foster La	B5
Frazier St	D4
Freemason's Hall	B3
Friday St	B5
Garden Row	D4
Gee St	A5
Gerrard St	C2
Giltspur St	B4
Glasshouse St	C2
Golden Hinde	C5
Golden La	A5
Golden Sq	C2
Goodge St ⊖	B2
Goodge Street	B2
Gordon Sq	A2
Goswell Rd	A4
Gough St	A3
Gower St	A2
Gracechurch St	C5
Grafton Way	A2
Grange Rd	D6
Grange Walk	D6
Gray's Inn Rd	A3
Great College St	D3
Great Dover St	D5
Great Eastern St	A6
Great Guildford St	C5
Great Marlborough St	B2
Great Ormond St	B3
Great Ormond St Children's Hospital	A3
Great Percy St	A3
Great Peter St	D3
Great Portland St	B1
Great Portland Street ⊖	A1
Great Queen St	B3
Great Russell St	B2
Great Scotland Yd	C3
Great Smith St	D3
Great Suffolk St	D4
Great Titchfield St	B2
Great Tower St	C6
Great Windmill St	B2
Greek St	B2
Green Park ⊖	C2
Gresham St	B5
Greville St	B4
Greycoat Hospital School	D2
Greycoat Pl	D2
Grosvenor Gdns	D1
Grosvenor Pl	D1
Grosvenor St	C1
Guards Museum & Chapel	D2
Guildhall Art Gallery	B5
Guilford St	A3
Guy's Hospital	C5
Haberdasher St	A5
Hackney Rd	A6
Half Moon St	C1
Hallam St	B1
Hall St	A4
Hampstead Rd	A2
Hanover Sq	B1
Hanway St	B2
Hardwick St	A4
Harley St	B1
Harper Rd	D5
Harrison St	A3
Hastings St	A3
Hatfields	C4
Haymarket	C2
Hayne St	B4
Hay's Galleria	C6
Hay's Mews	C1
Hayward Gallery	C3
Helmet Row	A5
Herbrand St	A3
Hercules Rd	D3
Hertford St	C1
High Holborn	B3
Hill St	C1
HMS Belfast	C6
Hobart Pl	D1
Holborn ⊖	B3
Holborn	B4
Holborn Viaduct	B4
Holland St	C4
Holywell La	A6
Horse Guards' Rd	C2
Houndsditch	B6
Houses of Parliament	D3
Howland St	B2
Hoxton Sq	A6
Hoxton St	A6
Hunter St	A3
Hunterian Museum	B3
Hyde Park Corner ⊖	D1
Imperial War Museum	D4
Ironmonger Row	A5
James St	B1/C3
Jermyn St	C2
Jockey's Fields	B3
John Carpenter St	C4
John St	A3
Judd St	A3
Kennington Rd	D4
Keyworth St	D4
King Charles St	D3
King James St	D4
Kingley St	B2
King's Cross Rd	A3
King's Cross Thameslink ≷	A3
Kingsland Rd	A6
King St	C2/C3
Kingsway	B3
King William St	C5
Kipling St	D5
Lambeth North ⊖	D4
Lambeth Palace	D3
Lambeth Palace Rd	D3
Lambeth Rd	D3/D4
Lamb's Conduit St	B3
Lancaster Pl	C3
Lancaster St	D4
Langham Pl	B1
Lant St	D5
Leadenhall St	B6
Leake St	D3
Leather La	B4
Leathermarket St	D6
Leicester Sq ⊖	C2
Leicester St	C2
Leonard St	A5
Lever St	A5
Lexington St	B2
Lime St	C6
Lincoln's Inn Fields	B3
Lindsey St	B4
Lisle St	C2
Liverpool St	B6
Liverpool St ⊖ ≷	B6
Lloyd Baker St	A4
Lloyd Sq	A4
Lombard St	B5
London Aquarium ✦	D3
London Bridge	C5
London Bridge Hospital	C5
London Bridge ⊖ ≷	C5
London City Hall	C6
London Dungeon ✦	C5
London Guildhall University	B5
London Rd	D4
London Transport Museum	C3
London Wall	B5
Long Acre	C3
Longford St	A1
Long La	B4/D5
Lower Belgrave St	D1
Lower Grosvenor Pl	D1
Lower Marsh	D4
Lower Thames St	C5
Ludgate Circus	B4
Ludgate Hill	B4
Macclesfield Rd	A5
Maddox St	C1
Malet St	B2
Manciple St	D5
Mansion House ⊖	C5
Mansion House	B5/C5
Maple St	B2
Marchmont St	A3
Margaret St	B2
Margery St	A4
Mark La	C6
Marlborough Rd	D2
Marshall St	B2
Marshalsea Rd	D5
Marsham St	D2
Martin's La	C3
Marylebone La	B1
Marylebone Rd	A1
Marylebone St	B1
Mecklenburgh Sq	A3
Middlesex St (Petticoat La)	B6
Middle Temple La	B4
Midland Rd	A2/A3
Mildmay Mission Hospital	A6
Millbank	D3
Monck St	D2
Monmouth St	B3
Montague Pl	B2
Montagu St	B2
Monument ⊖	C5
Monument St	C5
Moorfields	B5
Moorfields Eye Hospital	A5
Moorgate	B5
Moorgate ⊖ ≷	B5
Moor La	B5
Moreland St	A4
Morley St	D4
Mortimer St	B2
Mount Pleasant	A4
Museum of Garden History	D3
Museum of London	B5
Myddelton Sq	A4
Myddelton St	A4
National Film Theatre	C3
National Gallery	C2
National Hospital	B3
National Portrait Gallery	C2
Neal St	B3
Nelson's Column ✦	C3
New Bond St	B1/C1
New Bridge St	C4
New Cavendish St	B1
New Change	B5
Newcomen St	D5
New Fetter La	B4
Newgate St	B4
Newington Causeway	D5
New Inn Yard	A6
New Kent Rd	D5
New Oxford St	B3
New Scotland Yd	D2
New Sq	B3
Newton St	B3
Nile St	A5
Noble St	B5
Noel St	B2
Northampton Sq	A4
North Cr	A3
Northington St	A3
Northumberland Ave	C3
Norton Folgate	B6
Old Bailey	B4
Old Broad St	B5
Old Compton St	B2
Old County Hall	D3
Old Gloucester St	B3
Old King Edward St	B5
Old Street ⊖ ≷	A5
Old St	A5
Old Town Hall	B3
Ontario St	D4
Operating Theatre Museum	C5
Orange St	C2
Outer Circle	A1
Oxford Circus ⊖	B2
Oxford St	B1/B2
Palace St	D2
Pall Mall	C2
Pall Mall East	C2
Panton St	C2
Paris Gdns	C4
Park Cr	A1
Parker St	B3
Park St	C5
Parliament Sq	D3
Parliament St	D3
Paternoster Sq	B4
Paul St	A5
Pear Tree St	A4
Penton Rise	A4
Percival St	A4
Petticoat La (Middlesex St)	B6
Petty France	D2
Phoenix Pl	A4
Photo Gallery	C2
Piccadilly	C1/C2
Piccadilly Circus ⊖	C2
Pilgrimage St	D5
Pitfield St	A6
Pocock St	D4
Pollock's Toy Museum	B2
Portland Pl	B1
Portugal St	B3
Poultry	B5
Primrose St	B6
Princes St	B5
Procter St	B3
Provost St	A5
Queen Anne St	B1
Queen Elizabeth Hall	C3
Queens Gallery	D2
Queen Sq	A3
Queen St	C5
Queen St Pl	C5
Queen Victoria St	C5
Radnor St	A5
Rathbone Pl	B2
Rawstorne St	A4
Redchurch St	A6
Redcross Way	C5
Red Lion Sq	B3
Red Lion St	B3
Regent's Park ⊖	A1
Regent Sq	A3
Regent St	B2
Richmond Terr	C3
Ridgmount St	B2
Riley Rd	D6
Rivington St	A6
Robert St	A1
Rockingham St	D5
Ropemaker St	B5
Rosebery Ave	A4
Rothsay St	D6
Roupell St	C4
Royal Academy of Arts	C2
Royal Academy of Dramatic Art	A2
Royal College of Nursing	A1
Royal College of Surgeons	B3
Royal Festival Hall	C3
Royal National Theatre	C4
Royal National Throat, Nose & Ear Hospital	B3
Royal Opera House	C3
Rushworth St	D4
Russell Sq ⊖	A3
Russell Sq	A2/A3
Sackville St	C2
Sadlers Wells	A4
Saffron Hill	B4
St Alban's St	C2
St Andrew St	B4
St Bartholomew's Hospital	B4
St Bride St	B4
St George's Rd	D4
St Giles High St	B2
St James's Palace	C2
St James's Park ⊖	D2
St James's St	C2
St John St	A4
St Margaret St	D3
St Mark's Hosp	A4
St Martin's le Grand	B5
St Mary Axe	B6
St Paul's ⊖	B5
St Paul's Cathedral †	B5
St Paul's Churchyard	B4
St Peter's Hospital	C3
St Thomas' Hospital	D3
St Thomas St	C5
Savile Row	C2
Savoy Pl	C3
Savoy St	C3
School of Hygiene & Tropical Medicine	B2
Scrutton St	A6
Sekforde St	A4
Seven Dials	B3
Seward St	A4
Shaftesbury Ave	C2
Shakespeare's Globe Theatre	C5
Shepherdess Walk	A5
Shepherd Market	C1
Sherwood St	C2
Shoe La	B4
Shoreditch High St	A6
Shorts Gardens	B3
Sidmouth St	A3
Silk St	A5
Sir John Soane's Museum	B3
Skinner St	A4
Snow Hill	B4
Snows Fields	D5
Soho Sq	B2
Somerset House	C3
Southampton Row	B3
Southampton St	C3
South Audley St	C1
South Bank Univ	D4
South Molton St	B1
South Pl	B5
Southwark Bridge	C5
Southwark Bridge Rd	C5
Southwark ⊖	C4
Southwark Cathedral †	C5
Southwark St	C5
Spencer St	A4
Spital Sq	B6
Stamford St	C4
Stanhope St	A2
Stephenson Way	A2
Stoney St	C5
Strand	B4/C3
Stratton St	C1
Sumner St	C5
Swan St	D5
Swinton St	A3
Tabard St	D5
Tabernacle St	A6
Tanner St	D6
Tate Modern	C5
Tavistock Pl	A3
Tavistock Sq	A2
Temple ⊖	C4
Temple Ave	C4
Temple Pl	C3
Terminus Pl	D1
The Barbican Centre for Arts	B5
The City Univ	A4
The Cut	D4
The Grange	D6
The Mall	C2
The Monument ✦	C5
Theobald's Rd	B3
The Tower of London	C6
Threadneedle St	B5
Throgmorton St	B5
Tonbridge St	A3
Tooley St	C5/C6
Torrington Pl	A2
Tothill St	D2
Tottenham Court Rd ⊖	B2
Tottenham Court Rd	A2/B2
Tottenham St	B2
Tower Bridge Rd	D6
Tower Hill	C6
Tower Hill ⊖	C6
Trafalgar Sq	C3
Trinity Sq	C6
Trinity St	D5
Trocadero Centre	C2
Tudor St	C4
Turnmill St	B4
Ufford St	D4
Union St	C5
Univ College A2	A2
Univ College Hospital (A&E)	B2
Univ of London	A2
University St	A2
Upper Belgrave St	D1
Upper Ground	C4
Upper St Martin's La	C3
Upper Thames St	C5
Upper Wimpole St	B1
Upper Woburn Pl	A2
Vere St	B1
Vernon Pl	B3
Vestry St	A5
Victoria ⊖ ≷	D1
Victoria Embankment	D3
Victoria St	D2
Villiers St	C3
Vinopolis City of Wine	C5
Virginia Rd	A6
Wakley St	A4
Walbrook	C5
Wardour St	B2/C2
Warner St	A4
Warren St	A2
Warren Street ⊖	A2
Waterloo Bridge	C3
Waterloo ⊖ ≷	D3
Waterloo East ≷	C4
Waterloo International ≷	D3
Waterloo Rd	D4
Watling St	B5
Webber St	D4
Welbeck St	B1
Wellington Arch ✦	D1
Wellington Museum	D1
Wells St	B2
Westminster Abbey †	D3
Westminster Bridge	D3
Westminster Bridge Rd	D4
Westminster Cathedral (RC) †	D2
Westminster City Hall	D2
Westminster ⊖	D3
Westminster Hall	D3
Weston St	D5
West Smithfield	B4
Weymouth St	B1
Wharf Rd	A5
Wharton St	A3
Whitcomb St	C2
Whitecross St	A5
Whitefriars St	B4
Whitehall	C3
Whitehall Pl	C3
White Lion Hill	C4
Whites Grounds	D6
Wigmore Hall	B1
Wigmore St	B1
William IV St	C3
Wilmington Sq	A4
Wilson St	B5
Wimpole St	B1
Windmill Walk	C4
Woburn Pl	A3
Woburn Sq	A2
Women's Hospital	B2
Woodbridge St	A4
Wood St	B5
Wootton St	C4
Wormwood St	B6
Worship St	A5
Wren St	A3
Wynyatt St	A4
York Rd	D3

▲ The Queen Elizabeth II Great Court at the British Museum.

97

98

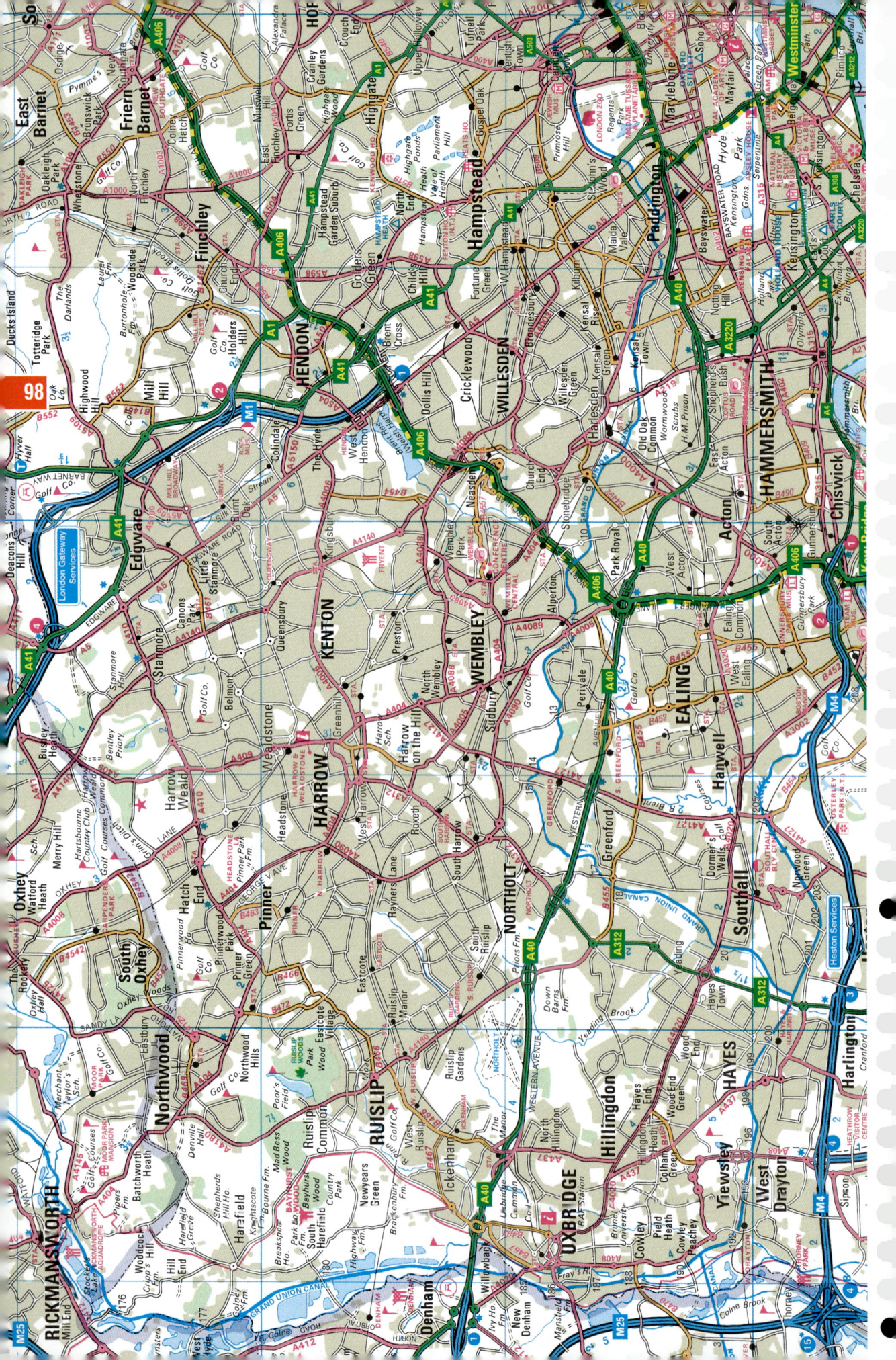

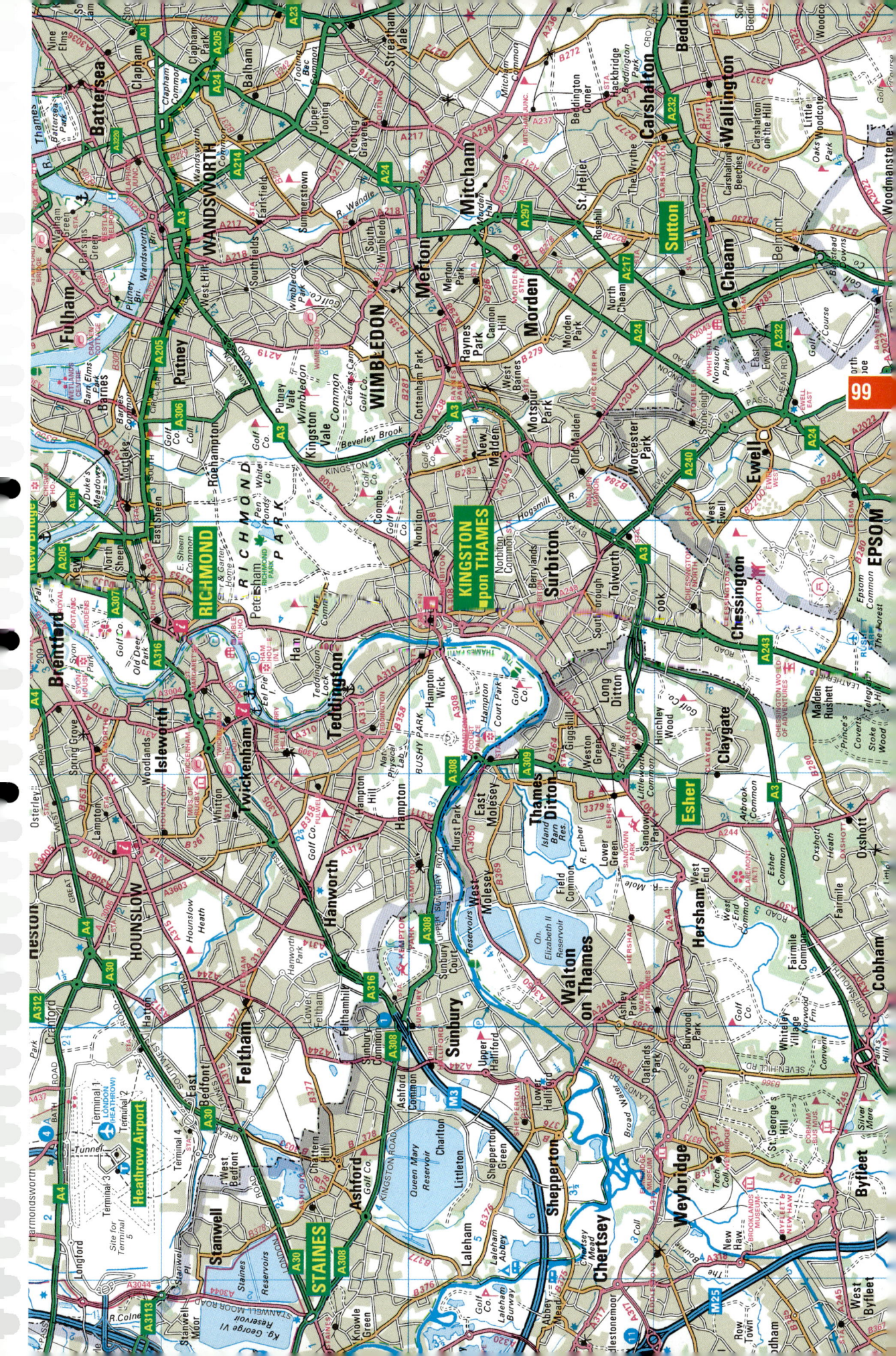

100
ENFIELD
Southgate
Edmonton
Tottenham
Wood Green
HORNSEY
Islington
Hackney
Stoke Newington
Walthamstow
Chingford
Woodford
Loughton
Chigwell
Hainault
Wanstead
Leyton
Leytonstone
Stratford
West Ham
East Ham
ILFORD
BARKING
Dagenham
ROMFORD
Hornchurch
Rainham
Harold Hill
Stapleford Abbots
Poplar
City
Blackwall Tunnel
Thamesmead
Becontree
Goodmayes
Seven Kings
Chadwell Heath
Redbridge
Canning Town
Plaistow
Upton
Bow
Mile End
Stepney
Whitechapel
Holborn
Finsbury
Abridge
South Hornchurch
A406
A12
A13
A10
M11
M25
A1400
A1020
A127

101

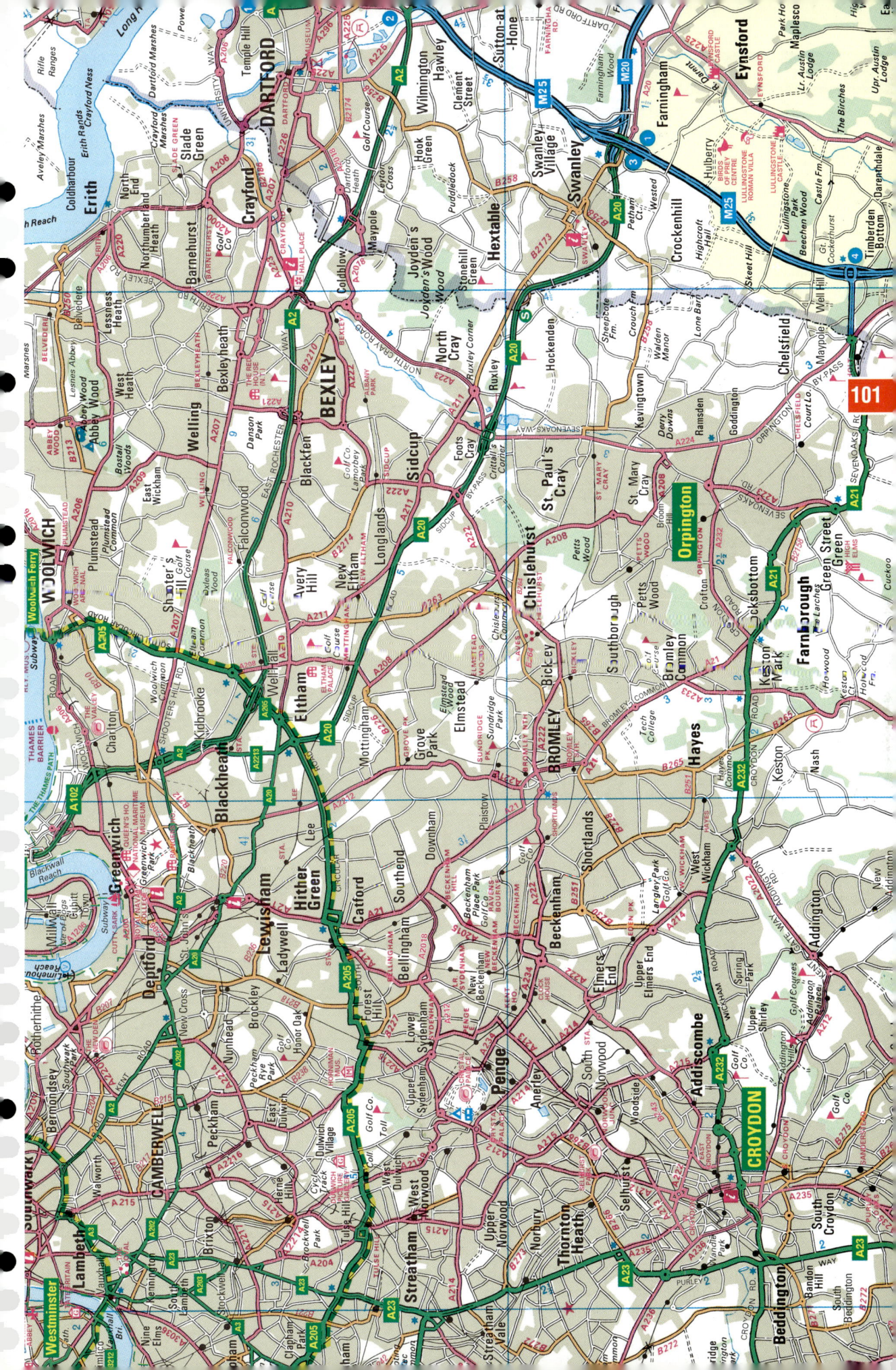

Luton

Luton lies at the northern end of a river gap in the Chiltern Hills and spans about 12 square miles. Early in the 19th century, the straw hat industry changed Luton into a factory town. The 20th century decline of the hat industry brought new industries, primarily in the engineering fields. The Luton Arndale Centre is a focal point for shopping in the town and the recently opened Hat Factory is now a major centre for art exhibitions, theatre, cinema and music. There are also many pubs, restaurants and clubs. Attractions nearby include Dunstable Downs and Shaw's Corner (both National Trust) and Whipsnade Wild Animal Park.

▲ The Hat Factory in 1930

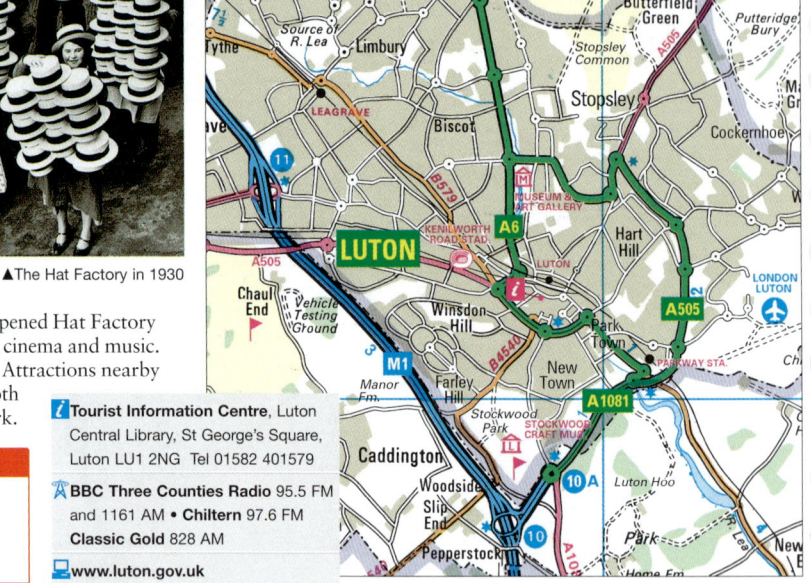

★ Do not miss
- ★ **The Hat Factory**, Bute Street – Arts centre
- ★ **Luton Museum and Art Gallery**, Wardown Park, Old Bedford Road – local history
- ★ **Stockwood Craft Museum and Gardens**, Farley Hill

Tourist Information Centre, Luton Central Library, St George's Square, Luton LU1 2NG Tel 01582 401579

BBC Three Counties Radio 95.5 FM and 1161 AM • **Chiltern** 97.6 FM
Classic Gold 828 AM

www.luton.gov.uk

Luton

Street	Grid
Adelaide St	B1
Albert Rd	C2
Alma St	B2
Alton Rd	C3
Anthony Gdns	C1
Arndale Centre	B2
Arthur St	C2
Ashburnham Rd	B1
Ashton Rd	C2
Avondale Rd	A1
Back St	A2
Bailey St	C3
Baker St	C2
Biscot Rd	A1
Bolton Rd	B3
Boyle Cl	A2
Brantwood Rd	B1
Bretts Mead	C1
Bridge St	B2
Brook St	A1
Brunswick St	A3
Burr St	A3
Bury Park Rd	A1
Bus Station	B2
Bute St	B2
Buxton Rd	C1
Cambridge St	C3
Cardiff Grove	B1
Cardiff Rd	B1
Cardigan St	B1
Castle St	B2/C2
Chapel St	C2
Charles St	A3
Chase St	C2
Cheapside	B2
Chequer St	C3
Church St	B2/B3
Cinema	A2
Cobden St	A3
Collingdon St	A2
Concorde Ave	A3
Corncastle Rd	C1
Cowper St	C2
Crawley Green Rd	B3
Crawley Rd	A1
Crescent Rise	A3
Crescent Rd	A3
Cromwell Rd	A1
Cross St	A2
Crown Court	B2
Cumberland St	B2
Cutenhoe Rd	C3
Dallow Rd	B1
Downs Rd	B1
Dudley St	A2
Duke St	A2
Dumfries St	B1
Dunstable Place	B2
Dunstable Rd	A1/B1
Edward St	A3
Elizabeth St	C1
Essex Cl	C3
Farley Hill	C1
Flowers Way	B2
Francis St	A1
Frederick St	A2
Galaxy Leisure Complex	A2
George St West	D2
George St	
Gillam St	A3
Gordon St	B1
Grove Rd	B1
Guildford St	A2
Haddon Rd	A3
Harcourt St	C2
Hart Hill Drive	A3
Hart Hill Lane	A3
Hartley Rd	A3
Hastings St	B2
Hat Factory, The	B2
Hatters Way	A1
Havelock Rd	A3
Hibbert St	C2
High Town Rd	A3
Highbury Rd	A1
Hillary Cres	A1
Hillborough Rd	C1
Hitchin Rd	A3
Holly St	C2
Holm	C1
Hucklesby Way	A2
Hunts Cl	C1
Information Ctr	B2
Inkerman St	A2
John St	B2
Jubilee St	A3
Kelvin Cl	C2
King St	B2
Kingsland Rd	C3
Latimer Rd	C3
Lawn Gdns	C2
Lea Rd	B3
Library	B2
Library Rd	B2
Liverpool Rd	B1
London Rd	C2
Luton Station	A2
Lyndhurst Rd	B1
Magistrates Court	B2
Manchester St	B2
Manor Rd	B3
May St	C3
Meyrick Ave	C1
Midland Rd	A2
Mill St	A2
Milton Rd	B1
Moor, The	A1
Moor St	A1
Moorland Gdns	A2
Moulton Rise	A3
Museum & Art Gallery	A2
Napier Rd	B1
New Bedford Rd	A1
New Town St	C2
North St	A3
Old Bedford Rd	A2
Old Orchard	C2
Osbourne Rd	C3
Oxen Rd	A3
Park Sq	B2
Park St	B3/C3
Park St West	B2
Park Viaduct	B3
Parkland Dr	C1
Police Station	B2
Pomfret Ave	A3
Pondwicks Rd	B3
Post Office	A1/A2/B2/C3
Power Court	B3
Princess St	B1
Red Rails	C1
Regent St	B2
Reginald St	A2
Rothesay Rd	B1
Russell Rise	C1
Russell St	C1
Ruthin Cl	C1
St Ann's Rd	B3
St George's	B2
St Mary's	B3
St Mary's Rd	B3
St Paul's Rd	C2
St Saviour's Cres	C1
Salisbury Rd	B1
Seymour Ave	C3
Seymour St	C3
Silver St	B2
South Rd	C2
Stanley St	B1
Station Rd	A2
Stockwood Cres	C2
Stockwood Park	C1
Strathmore Ave	C1
Stuart St	B2
Studley Rd	A1
Surrey St	C3
Sutherland Place	C1
Tavistock St	C2
Taylor St	A3
Telford Way	A1
Tennyson Rd	C2
Tenzing Grove	C1
The Cross Way	C1
The Larches	A2
Thistle Rd	B3
Town Hall	B2
Townsley Cl	C2
Union St	B2
University of Luton	B3
Upper George St	B2
Vicarage St	B3
Villa Rd	A1
Waldeck Rd	A1
Wellington St	B1/B2
Wenlock St	A2
Whitby Rd	A1
Whitehill Ave	C1
William St	A2
Wilsden Ave	C1
Windmill Rd	B3
Windsor St	C2
Winsdon Rd	B1
York St	A3

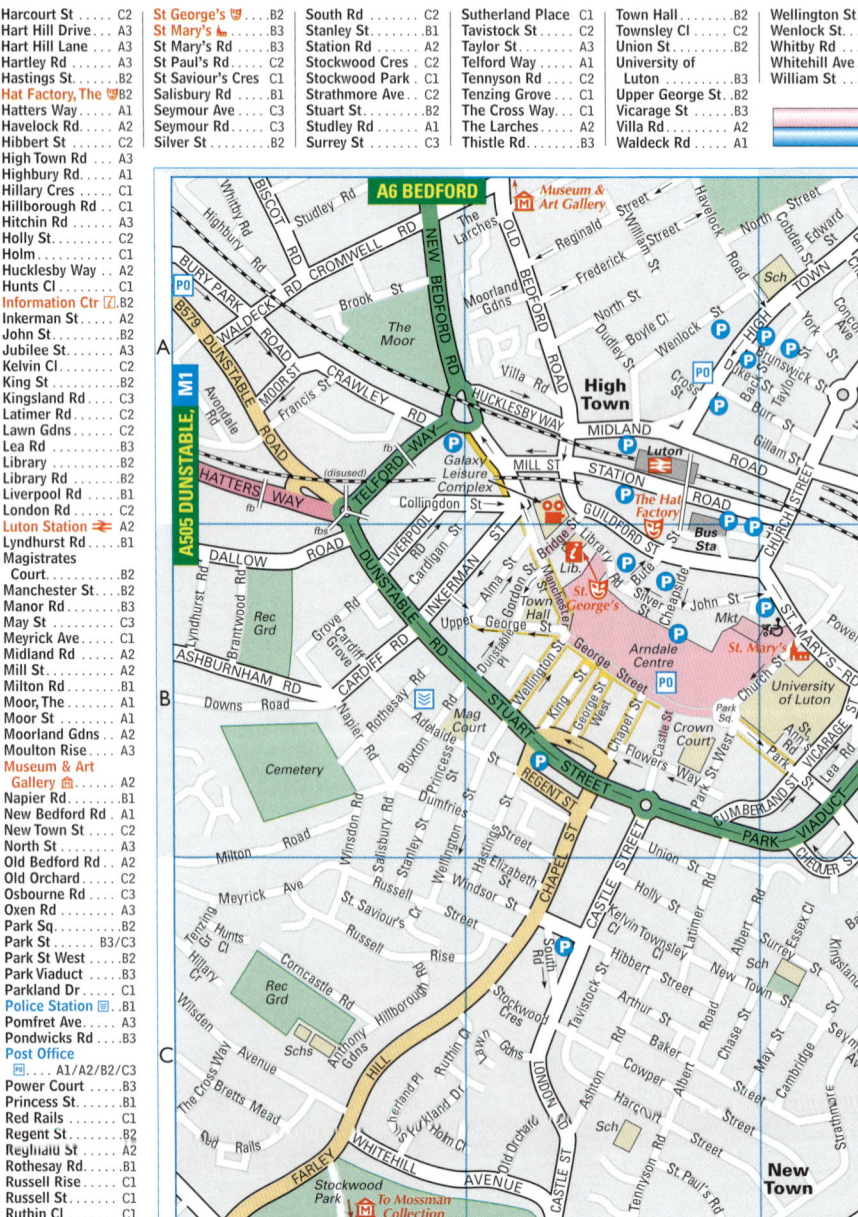

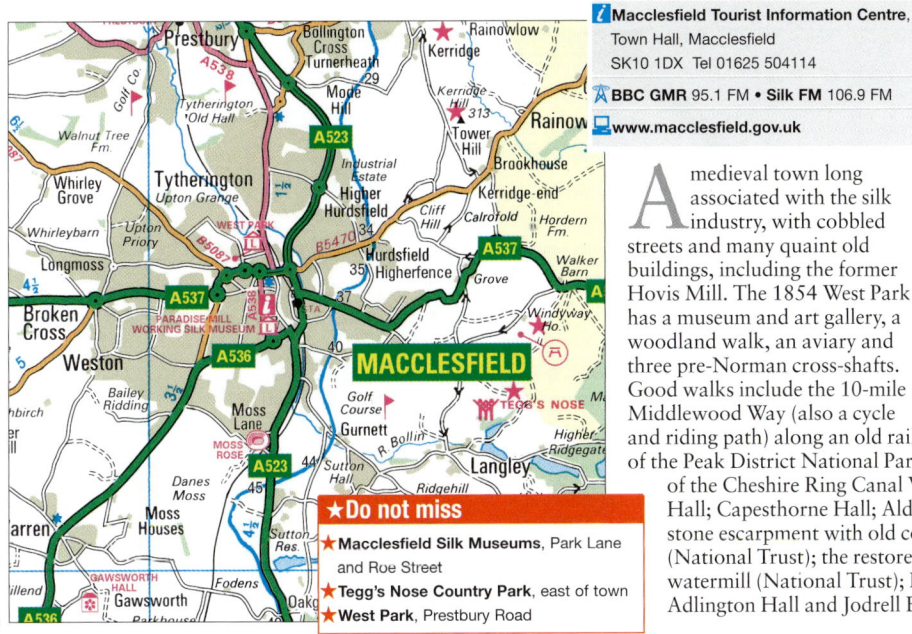

Macclesfield

Macclesfield Tourist Information Centre,
Town Hall, Macclesfield
SK10 1DX Tel 01625 504114
BBC GMR 95.1 FM • Silk FM 106.9 FM
www.macclesfield.gov.uk

A medieval town long associated with the silk industry, with cobbled streets and many quaint old buildings, including the former Hovis Mill. The 1854 West Park has a museum and art gallery, a woodland walk, an aviary and three pre-Norman cross-shafts. Good walks include the 10-mile Middlewood Way (also a cycle and riding path) along an old railway line to Marple near the border of the Peak District National Park, and the Macclesfield Canal (part of the Cheshire Ring Canal Walk). Close by are Gawsworth Hall; Capesthorne Hall; Alderley Edge, a dramatic red sandstone escarpment with old copper mines and a historic beacon (National Trust); the restored 15th-century Nether Alderley watermill (National Trust); Hare Hill Garden (National Trust), Adlington Hall and Jodrell Bank Visitor Centre.

▲ Outdoor market and Town Hall

★ Do not miss
- ★ **Macclesfield Silk Museums**, Park Lane and Roe Street
- ★ **Tegg's Nose Country Park**, east of town
- ★ **West Park**, Prestbury Road

Macclesfield

108 Steps B2	Half St. C2	Richmond Hill C3	St George's St C2	Statham St C2	Town Hall B2	West Bond St B1	Whalley Hayes B1
Abbey Rd A1	Hallefield Rd B3	Riseley St B1	Samuel St B2	Station St A2	Townley St B2	West Park A1	Windmill St C3
Alton Dr A3	Hatton St C1	Roan Ct B3	Saville St C3	Steeple St A3	Turnock St C3	Westbrook Dr A1	Withyfold Dr A2
Armett St C2	Hawthorn Way . . . A3	Roe St B2	Shaw St B1	Sunderland St B2	Union Rd B3	Westminster Rd . . . A1	York St B3
Athey St B1	Heapy St. B2	Rowan Way A3	Slater St C1	Swettenham St . . . B3	Union St B2		
Bank St C3	Henderson St B1	Ryle St C2	Snow Hill C3	The Silk Rd A2/B2	Victoria Park B3		
Barber St C1	Heritage Centre &	Ryle's Park Rd C1	South Park C3	Thistleton Cl C2	Vincent St C2		
Barton St C1	Silk Museum . . B2	St Michael's B2	Spring Gdns A2	Thorp St B2	Waterside C2		
Beech La B3	Hibel Rd A2						
Beswick St B1	High St C2						
Black La A2	Hobson St C2						
Black Rd C3	Hollins Rd C3						
Blakclow Gdns . . . C3	Hope St West. B1						
Blakelow Rd C3	Horseshoe Dr B1						
Boden St B2	Hurdsfield Rd A3						
Bond St B1/C1	Information Ctr . . B2						
Bread St C2	James St C2						
Bridge St B1	Jodrell St B3						
Brock St A2	John St C2						
Brocklehurst Ave . . A3	Jordangate B2						
Brook St B3	King Edward St . . . B2						
Brookfield La B3	King George's						
Brough St West . . . C1	Field C3						
Brown St C1	King St B2						
Brynton Rd A3	King's School A1						
Buckley St C2	Knight St C3						
Bus Station B2	Lansdowne St A3						
Buxton Rd B3	Library B2						
Byrons St C2	Lime Gr B3						
Canal St B3	Little Theatre C2						
Carlsbrook Ave . . . A3	Loney St B1						
Castle St. C2	Longacre St B1						
Catherine St B1	Lord St C2						
Chadwick Terr A1	Lowe St C2						
Chapel St C2	Lowerfield Rd A3						
Charlotte St B2	Lyon St B1						
Chester Rd B1	Macclesfield B2						
Chestergate B1	Marina B3						
Churchill Way B2	Market B2						
Coare St A1	Market Pl B2						
Commercial Rd . . . B2	Masons La A3						
Conway Cres A3	Mill La. C2						
Copper St. C3	Mill Rd C2						
Cottage St C1	Mill St B2						
Court. A2	Moran Rd C1						
Court. B2	New Hall St A2						
Crematorium A1	Newton St C1						
Crew Ave A1	Nicholson Ave . . . A3						
Crompton Rd . . B1/B2	Nicholson Cl A3						
Cross St C2	Northgate Ave A1						
Crossall St C2	Old Mill La C2						
Cumberland St . A1/B1	Paradise Mill C2						
Dale St B3	Paradise St B1						
Duke St. B2	Park Green B2						
Eastgate B3	Park La C1						
Exchange St. B2	Park Rd C1						
Fence Ave B3	Park St C2						
Fence Avenue	Park Vale Rd C1						
Industrial Estate A3	Parr St B1						
Flint St B2	Peel St C2						
Foden St A2	Percyvale St A3						
Fountain St B3	Peter St C1						
Garden St B3	Pickford St B2						
Gas Rd B2	Pierce St B1						
George St B2	Pinfold St B1						
Glegg St B3	Pitt St C2						
Golf Course C3	Police Station B2						
Goodall St B3	Pool St B2						
Grange Rd C1	Poplar Rd C2						
Great King St. B1	Post						
Green St B3	Office . . . B1/B2/B3						
Grosvenor	Pownall St A2						
Shopping Centre. B2	Prestbury Rd . . . A1/B1						
Gunco La C3	Queen Victoria St . . C1						
	Queen's Ave A3						
	Registrar B2						

103

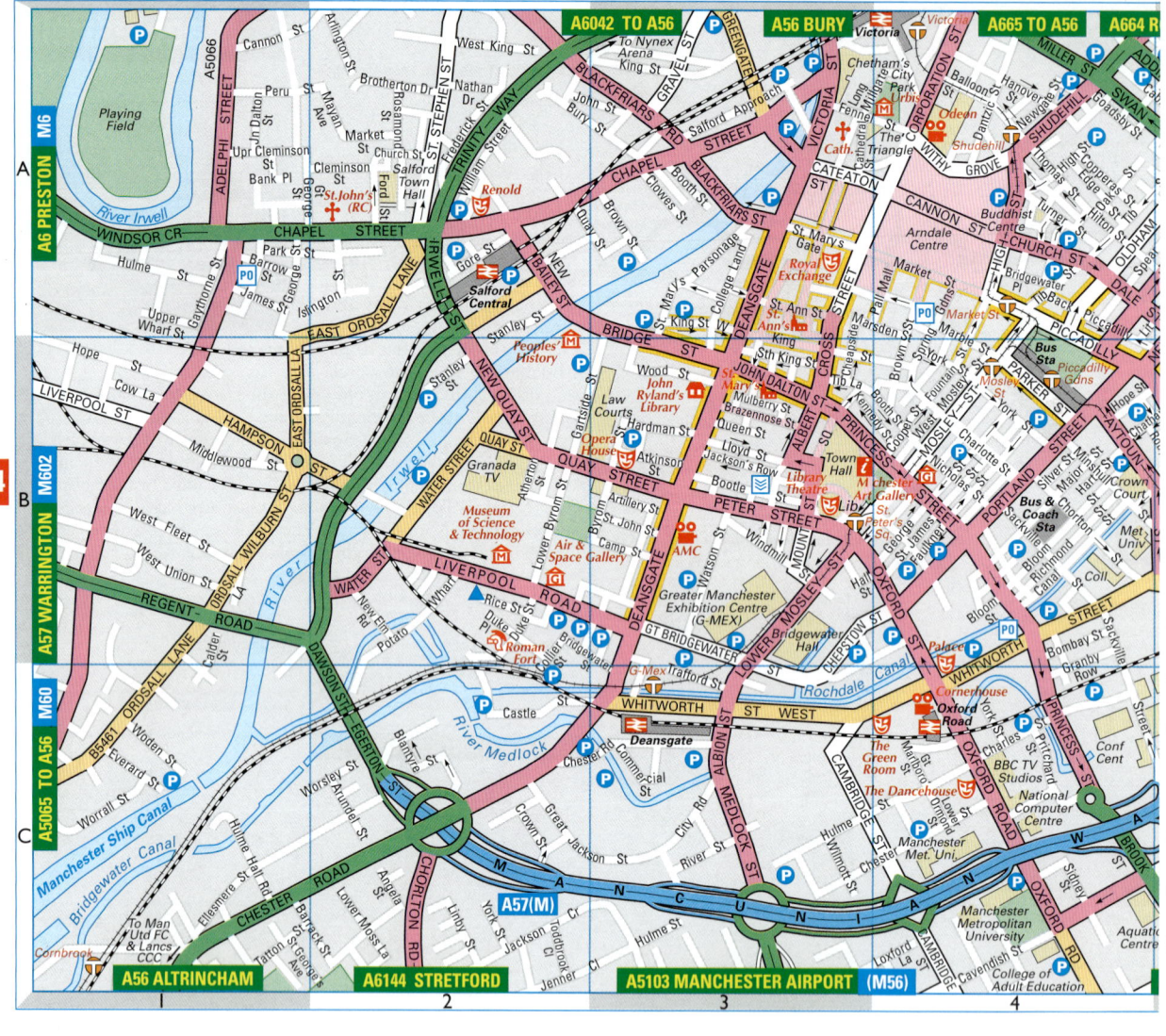

Manchester

Street	Grid
Adair St	B6
Addington St	A5
Adelphi St	A1
Air & Space Gallery	B2
Albert Sq	B3
Albion St	C3
AMC Great Northern 16	B3
Ancoats Gr	B6
Ancoats Gr North	B6
Angela St	C2
Aquatic Centre	C4
Ardwick Green	C5
Ardwick Green North	C5
Ardwick Green South	C5
Arlington St	A2
Arndale Centre	A4
Artillery St	B3
Arundel St	C2
Atherton St	B2
Atkinson St	B3
Aytoun St	B4
Back Piccadilly	A5
Baird St	B5
Balloon St	A4
Bank Pl	A1
Baring St	B5
Barrack St	C1
Barrow St	A1
BBC TV Studios	C4
Bendix St	A5
Bengal St	A5
Berry St	C5
Blackfriars Rd	A3
Blackfriars St	A3
Blantyre St	C2
Bloom St	B4
Blossom St	A5
Boad St	B5
Bombay St	B4
Booth St	A3
Booth St	B4
Bootle St	B3
Brazennose St	B3
Brewer St	A5
Bridge St	B3
Bridgewater Hall	B3
Bridgewater Pl	A4
Bridgewater St	B2
Brook St	C4
Brotherton Dr	A2
Brown St	A3
Brown St	B4
Brunswick St	C6
Brydon Ave	C6
Buddhist Centre	A4
Bury St	A2
Bus & Coach Station	B4
Bus Station	B4
Butler St	A6
Buxton St	C5
Byrom St	B3
Cable St	A4
Calder St	B1
Cambridge St	C3/C4
Camp St	B3
Canal St	B4
Cannon St	A1
Cannon St	A4
Cardroom Rd	A6
Carruthers St	A6
Castle St	C2
Cateaton St	A3
Cathedral	A3
Cathedral St	A3
Cavendish St	C4
Chapel St	A1/A3
Chapeltown St	B5
Charles St	C4
Charlotte St	B4
Chatham St	B4
Cheapside	A3
Chepstow St	B3
Chester Rd	C1/C2
Chester St	C4
Chetham's (Dept Store)	A3
China La	B5
Chippenham Rd	A6
Chorlton Rd	C2
Chorlton St	B4
Church St	A2
Church St	A4
City Park	A4
City Rd	C3
Cleminson St	A2
Clowes St	A3
College Land	A3
College of Adult Education	C4
Collier St	B2
Commercial St	C3
Conference Centre	C4
Cooper St	B4
Copperas St	A4
Cornbrook (Metro Station)	C1
Cornell St	A5
Cornerhouse	C4
Corporation St	A4
Cotter St	C6
Cotton St	A5
Cow La	B1
Cross St	B3
Crown Court	A4
Crown St	C2
Dalberg St	C6
Dale St	A4/B5
Dancehouse Theatre	C4
Dantzic St	A4
Dark La	C6
Dawson St	C2
Dean St	A4
Deansgate	A3/B3
Deansgate	C3
Dolphin St	C6
Downing St	C5
Ducie St	B5
Duke Pl	B2
Duke St	B2
Durling St	C6
East Ordsall La	A2/B1
Edge St	A4
Egerton St	C2
Ellesmere St	C1
Every St	B6
Fairfield St	B5
Faulkner St	B4
Fennel St	A3
Ford St	A2
Ford St	C6
Fountain St	B4
Frederick St	A2
Gartside St	B2
Gaythorne St	A1
George St	A4
George Leigh St	A5
George St	B4
G-Mex (Metro Station)	C3
Goadsby St	A4
Gore St	A3
Goulden St	A4
Granada TV Studios	B2
Granby Row	B4
Gravel St	A3
Great Ancoats St	A5
Great Bridgewater St	B3
Great George St	A1
Great Jackson St	C3
Great Marlborough St	C4
Greater Manchester Exhibition Centre (G-Mex)	B3
Green Room, The	C4
Greengate	A3
Grosvenor St	C5
Gun St	A5
Hadrian Ave	B6
Hall St	B3
Hampson St	A1
Hanover St	A4
Hanworth Cl	C6
Hardman St	B3
Harkness St	C6
Harrison St	B6
Hart St	A4
Helmet St	B6
Henry St	A5
Heyrod St	B6
High St	A4
Higher Ardwick	C6
Hilton St	A4/A5
Holland St	A6
Hood St	A5
Hope St	B1
Hope St	B4
Houldsworth St	A5
Hoyle St	C6
Hulme	C1
Hulme	A1
Hulme St	C3
Hyde Rd	C6
Information Ctr	B3
Irwell St	A2
Islington St	A1
Jackson Cr	C2
Jackson's Row	B3
James St	A1
Jenner Cl	C2
Jersey St	A5
John Dalton St	A3
John Dalton St	B3
John Ryland's Library	B3
John St	A3
Kennedy St	B3
Kincardine Rd	C4
King St	A3
King St West	A3
Law Courts	B3
Laystall St	B5
Lever St	A5
Library	B3
Library Theatre	B3
Linby St	C2
Little Lever St	A4
Liverpool Rd	B1
Liverpool St	B1
Lloyd St	B3
Lockton Cl	C5
London Rd	B5
Long Millgate	A3
Longacre St	B6
Loom St	A5
Lower Byrom St	B2
Lower Mosley St	B3
Lower Moss La	C2
Lower Ormond St	C4
Loxford La	C4
Luna St	A5
Major St	B4
Manchester Art Gallery	B4
Manchester Metropolitan University	B4/C4
Mancunian Way	C3
Manor St	C5
Marble St	A4
Market St	A3
Market St	A4
Market St (Metro Station)	A4
Marsden St	A3
Marshall St	A5
Mayan Ave	A2
Medlock St	C3
Middlewood St	B1
Miller St	A4
Minshull St	B5
Mosley St	A4
Mosley St (Metro Station)	B4
Mount St	A3
Mulberry St	B3
Murray St	A5
Museum of Science & Technology	B2
Nathan Dr	A2
National Computer Centre	C4
Naval St	A5
New Bailey St	A2
New Elm Rd	B2
New Islington	A6
New Quay St	B2
New Union St	A6
Newgate St	A4
Newton St	A5
Nicholas St	B4
North George St	A1
North Western St	C6
Oak St	A4
Odeon	A4
Old Mill St	A6
Oldfield Rd	A1/C1
Oldham St	A4
Oldham St	A4
Opera House	B3
Ordsall La	C1
Oxford Rd	C4
Oxford St	B4
Paddock St	C6
Palace Theatre	B4
Pall Mall	A3
Palmerston St	B6
Park St	A1
Parker St	B4
Peak St	B5
Penfield Cl	C5
Peoples' History Museum	B2
Peru St	A1
Peter St	B3
Piccadilly	B5
Piccadilly (Metro Station)	B5
Piccadilly Gdns (Metro Station)	B4
Piccadilly	B5
Piercy St	A6
Poland St	A5
Police Station	B3/B5
Pollard St	B6
Port St	A5
Portland St	B4
Portugal St East	B5
Post Office	A1/A4/A5/B4/B6
Potato Wharf	B2
Princess St	B3/C4
Pritchard St	C5
Quay St	A2
Quay St	B3
Queen St	B3
Radium St	A5
Redhill St	A5
Regent Rd	B1
Renold Theatre	A5
Retail Park	A5
Rice St	C3
Richmond St	B4
River St	C3
Roby St	B5
Rodney St	A6
Roman Fort	B2
Rosamond St	A2
Royal Exchange	A3
Sackville St	B4
St Andrew's St	B6
St Ann's	A3
St Ann's St	A3
St George's Ave	C6
St James St	B4
St John St	B2
St John's Cathedral (RC)	A2

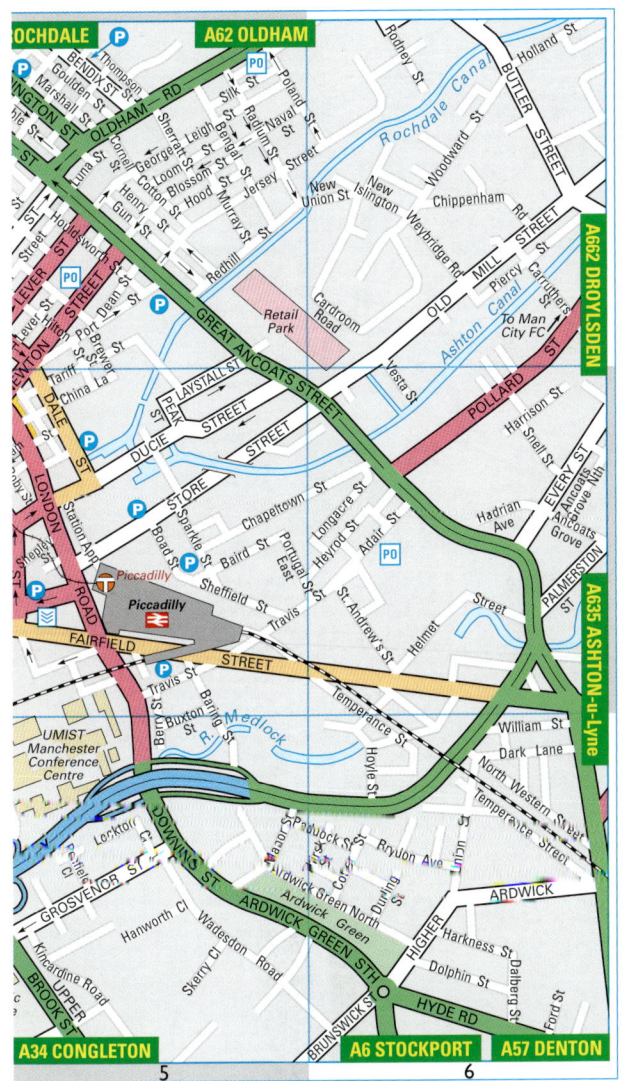

Manchester

A city founded on a Roman settlement of AD79 (with a re-created fort on the original Castlefields site) and a main player in the Industrial Revolution. Historic buildings include the Victorian Gothic Town Hall, the Royal Exchange, the Cathedral and local artist JS Lowry's House in Salford. Much activity is focused around the revitalised Salford Quays at the head of the Manchester Ship Canal, linked to the centre by the flamboyant curving Calatrava Bridge (1995) and also crossed by the £5 million Lowry Footbridge. Among museums and art venues are the Manchester Jewish Museum; the Pankhurst Centre, where the suffragette movement was formed; the Pumphouse People's History Museum; the Museum of Science and Technology; the Museum of Transport; the Imperial War Museum North; the Chinese Arts Centre; Manchester Art Gallery; and the outstanding Whitworth Art Gallery. Manchester has been regenerated with a wealth of smart new shops, restaurants and hotels from the high street chains in the Arndale Centre to the more bohemian individual shops and markets of the Northern Quarter. It is also home to a large gay community and this is reflected in the some of the more flamboyant bars and restaurants in the centre of town.

▲ Canal Street

★ Do not miss

- ★ The Lowry art museum, Pier 8, The Quays, Salford
- ★ Steam, Coal and Canal: the Bridgewater Canal Linear Industrial Heritage Park, Salford
- ★ Urbis – Museum of the Modern City, Cathedral Gardens

Tourist Information Centre, Town Hall Extension (off St Peter's Square), Lloyd Street, Manchester M60 2LA
Tel 0161 222 8223

BBC GMR 95.1 FM • **Capital Gold** 1458 AM • **Century** 105.4 FM
Galaxy 102 FM • **Key** 103 FM
Magic 1152 AM

www.manchester.gov.uk

St Mary's	B3	Travis St	B5
St Mary's Gate	A3	Trinity Way	A2
St Mary's Parsonage	A3	Turner St	A4
St Peter's Sq (Metro Station)	B3	UMIST Manchester Conference Centre	C5
St Stephen St	A2	Union St	C6
Salford Approach	A3	Upper Brook St	C5
Salford Central ≷	A2	Upper Cleminson St	A1
Sheffield St	B5	Upper Wharf St	A1
Shepley St	B5	Urbis Museum	A4
Sherratt St	A5	Vesta St	B6
Shudehill	A4	Victoria (Metro Station)	A4
Shudehill (Metro Station)	A4	Victoria Station ≷	A4
Sidney St	C4	Victoria St	A3
Silk St	B4	Wadesdon Rd	C5
Silver St	B4	Water St	B2
Skerry Cl	C5	Watson St	B3
Snell St	B6	Wellington St	A2
South King St	B3	West Fleet St	B1
Sparkle St	B5	West King St	A2
Spear St	A4	West Mosley St	B4
Spring Gdns	B4	West Union St	B1
Stanley St	A2/B2	Weybridge Rd	A6
Station Approach	B5	Whitworth St	B4
Store St	B5	Whitworth St West	C3
Swan St	A4	Wilburn St	B1
Tariff St	B5	William St	A2
Tatton St	C1	William St	C6
Temperance St	B6/C6	Wilmott St	C3
The Triangle	A4	Windmill St	B3
Thirsk St	C6	Windsor Cr	A1
Thomas St	A4	Withy Gr	A4
Thompson St	A5	Woden St	C1
Tib La	B3	Wood St	B3
Tib St	A4	Woodward St	A6
Toddbrook Cl	C2	Worrall St	C1
Town Hall (Manchester)	B3	Worsley St	C2
Town Hall (Salford)	A2	York St	B4
Trafford St	C3	York St	C2
		York St	C4

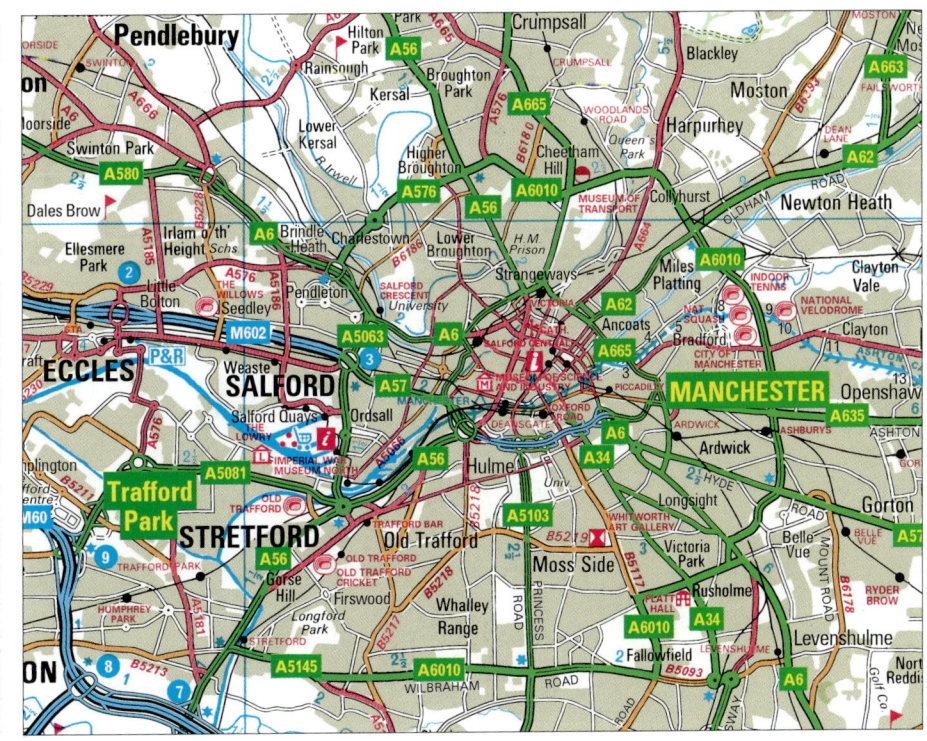

Maidstone

A town of Roman origins that lay on the pilgrimage route between London and Dover, became a medieval market centre and was awarded a royal charter in 1549. Buildings of interest include the 14th-century visitors lodgings of the Archbishop's Palace (containing the Tyrwhitt-Drake Carriage Museum) and All Saints parish church (1395). The Maidstone Museum and Bentlif Art Gallery includes an Earth Heritage gallery. After the decline of the papermaking and brewing industries in the 20th century, tourism and retail expanded. Close by are the prehistoric burial chambers of Kits Coty House; The Friars, a working medieval priory; Yalding Organic Gardens; the ruins of 12th-century Boxley Abbey; Stoneacre (National Trust), and Boughton Monchelsea Place, a 16th-century manor.

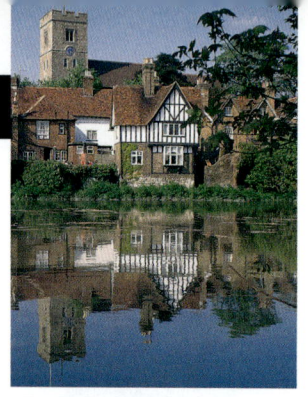

▲ The River Medway at Aylesford

The Town Hall Information Centre,
Town Hall, High Street, Maidstone,
Kent ME14 1TF Tel 01622 602169

BBC Radio Kent 69.7 FM and 1602 AM • **Capital Gold** 1242 AM
CTR 105.6 FM • **Invicta** 102.8 FM

www.maidstone.gov.uk

★ Do not miss
- ★ **Leeds Castle**, Hollingbourne
- ★ **Maidstone Millennium River Park** and **Whatman Recreational Park**, banks of the Medway
- ★ **Amphitheatre**
- ★ **Museum of Kent Life**, Lock Lane, Sandling

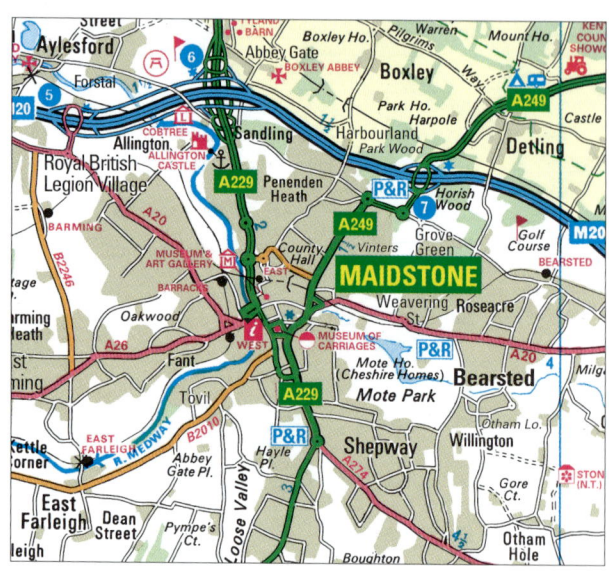

Maidstone

Albion Pl	B3
All Saints	B2
Allen St	A3
Amphitheatre	C2
Archbishop's Palace	B2
Bank St	B2
Barker Rd	C2
Barton Rd	C3
Beaconsfield Rd	C1
Bedford Pl	B1
Bishops Way	B2
Bluett St	A3
Bower La	C1
Bower Mount Rd	B1
Bower Pl	C1
Bower St	B1
Bowling Alley	A3
Boxley Rd	A3
Brenchley Gdns	A2
Brewer St	A3
Broadway	B2
Brunswick St	C3
Buckland Hill	A1
Buckland Rd	B1
Bus Station	B3
Campbell Rd	C3
Carriage Mus	B2
Chequers Shopping Ctr	B3
Church Rd	C3
Church St	B3
Cinema	B2
College Ave	C2
College Rd	C2
Collis Memorial Gdn	C3
Cornwallis Rd	B1
Corpus Christi Hall	B2
County Rd	A3
Crompton Gdns	C3
Crown & County Courts	B2
Curzon Rd	C1
Dixon Cl	C2
Douglas Rd	C1
Earl St	B2
Eccleston Rd	C2
Fairmeadow	B2
Fisher St	A2
Florence Rd	C1
Foley St	A3
Foster St	C3
Fremlin Walk Shopping Ctr	B2
Gabriel's Hill	B3
George St	C3
Grecian St	A3
Hardy St	A3
Hart St	C1
Hastings Rd	C3
Hayle Rd	C3
Hazlitt Theatre	B2
Heathorn St	A3
Hedley St	A3
High St	B2
HM Prison	A3
Holland Rd	A3
Hope St	A3
Information Ctr	B2
James St	A3
James Whatman Way	A2
Jeffrey St	A3
Kent County Council Offices	A2
King Edward Rd	C2
King St	B3
Kingsley Rd	C3
Knightrider St	B3
Launder Way	C1
Lesley Pl	A1
Library	B2
Little Buckland Ave	A1
Lockmeadow Leisure Complex	C2
London Rd	B1
Lower Boxley Rd	A2
Lower Fant Rd	C1
Magistrates Court	B3
Maidstone Barracks Station	A1
Maidstone Borough Council Offices	B2
Maidstone East Station	A2
Maidstone West Station	B2
Market	C2
Market Buildings	B2
Marsham St	B3
Medway St	B2
Medway Trading Estate	C2
Melville Rd	C3
Mill St	B2
Millennium Br	C2
Mote Rd	B3
Muir Rd	C3
Old Tovil Rd	C2
Palace Ave	B3
Perryfield St	A2
Police Station	B2
Post Office	A2/A3/B2/B3/C1
Priory Rd	C3
Prospect Pl	C1
Pudding La	B2
Queen Anne Rd	B3
Queens Rd	A1
Randall St	A2
Rawdon Rd	C3
Reginald Rd	C1
Rock Pl	B1
Rocky Hill	B1
Romney Pl	B3
Rose Yard	B2
Rowland Cl	C1
Royal Engineers' Rd	A2
Royal Star Arcade	B2
St Annes Ct	B1
St Faith's St	B2
St Luke's Rd	A3
St Peter's Br	C1
St Peter St	B2
St Philip's Ave	C1
Salisbury Rd	A3
Sandling Rd	A2
Scott St	A2
Scrubs La	B1
Sheal's Cres	C3
Somerfield, The	A1
Somerfield La	B1
Somerfield Rd	B1
Staceys St	A2
Station Rd	A2
Terrace Rd	B1
Tonbridge Rd	C1
Tovil Rd	C2
Town Hall	B2
Trinity Park	B3
Tufton St	B3
Union St	B3
Upper Fant Rd	C1
Upper Stone St	C3
Victoria St	B1
Visitor Centre	A1
Warwick Pl	B1
Wat Tyler Way	B3
Waterloo St	C3
Waterlow Rd	A3
Week St	B2
Well Rd	A3
Westree Rd	C1
Wharf Rd	C1
Wheeler St	A3
Whitchurch Cl	B1
Woodville Rd	C1
Wyatt St	B3
Wyke Manor Rd	B3

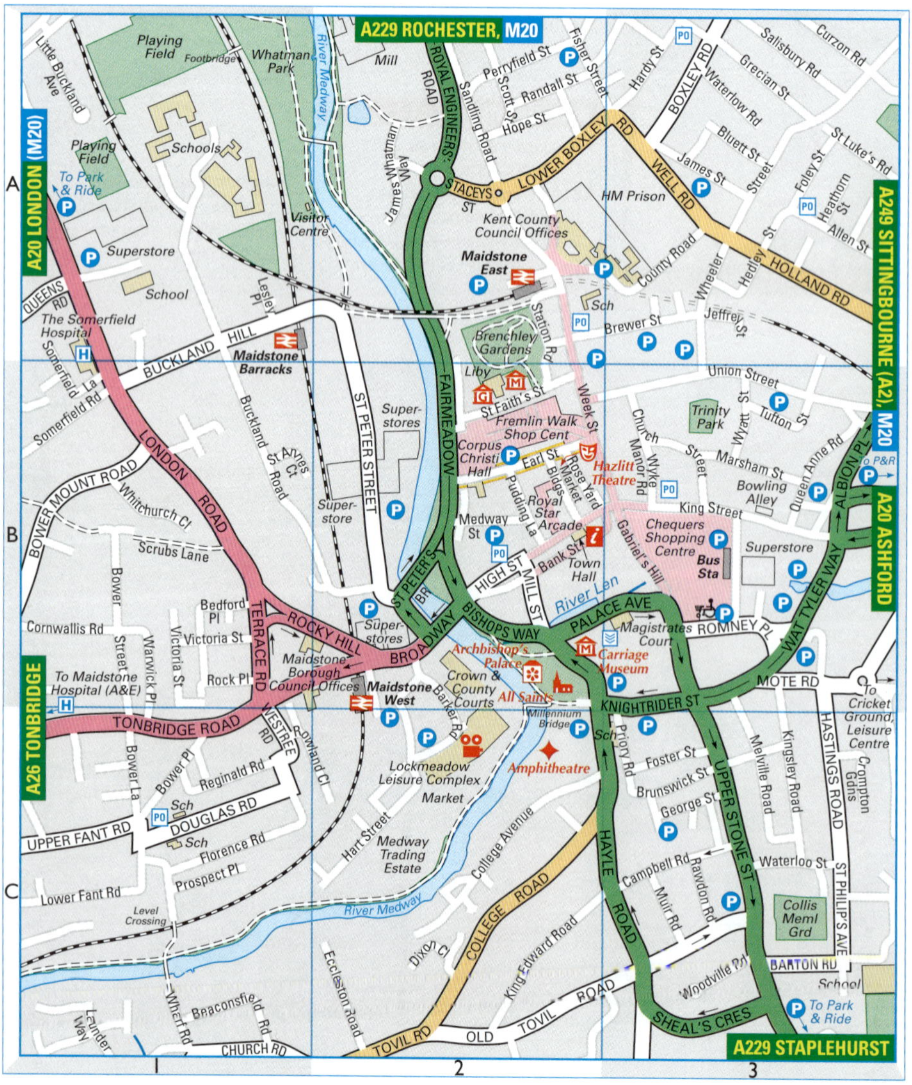

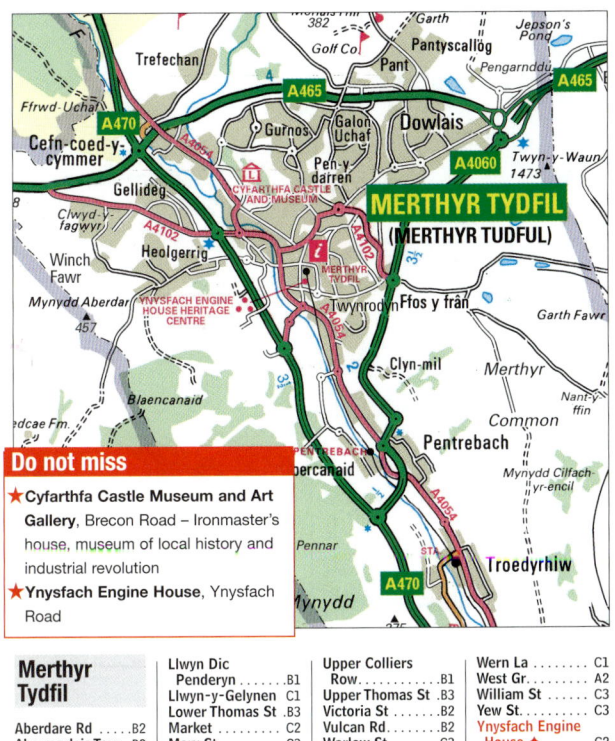

Merthyr Tydfil

Merthyr Tydfil was the largest iron-making town in the world in the early to mid-nineteenth century and the most significant Welsh town of the Industrial Revolution. The primarily late-eighteenth to nineteenth centuries landscape is still evident. Dr Joseph Parry's house, built by the Cyfarthfa Iron Company is a restored example of a period ironworker's cottage in Chapel Row and also the birthplace of the renowned composer. Adjoining the Cyfarthfa Ironworks lies the Pontycafnau bridge, built in 1793, the first ever iron railway bridge to be built. Other local sites of interest include St Tydfil's Church and the Robert and Lucy Thomas Cast Iron Fountain Canopy, situated adjacent to each other at the lower end of the town centre. The town is the commercial and shopping destination for the Heads of the Valleys region, in addition to which there are several night clubs and many restaurants and pubs.

▲ Cyfarthfa Castle

Tourist Information Centre, 14a Glebeland Street, Merthyr Tydfil CF47 8AU Tel 01685 379884

BBC Radio Wales 103.7 FM
Real Radio 105-106 FM
Valleys 999, 1116 AM

www.merthyr.gov.uk

Do not miss
★ **Cyfarthfa Castle Museum and Art Gallery**, Brecon Road – Ironmaster's house, museum of local history and industrial revolution
★ **Ynysfach Engine House**, Ynysfach Road

Merthyr Tydfil

Street	Grid
Aberdare Rd	B2
Abermorlais Terr	B2
Alexandra Rd	A3
Alma St	C3
Arfryn Pl	C3
Argyle St	C3
Avenue De Clichy	C2
Bethesda St	B2
Bishops Gr	A3
Brecon Rd	A1/B2
Briarmead	A3
Bryn St	C3
Bryntirion Rd	B2/C3
Bus Station	B2
Cae Mari Dwn	B3
Caedraw Rd	C2
Castle Sq	A1
Castle St	C2
Chapel	B2
Chapel Bank	B1
Church St	B2
Civic Centre	B2
Coedcae'r Ct	C3
Court	B3
Court St	B3
Courts	B2
Cromwell St	B2
Cyfarthfa Castle School and Museum	A1
Cyfarthfa Ind Est	A1
Cyfarthfa Park	A1
Cyfarthfa Rd	A1
Dane St	A2
Dane Terr	A2
Danyparc	B3
Darren View	A1
Dixon St	B2
Dyke St	C3
Dynevor St	B2
Elwyn Dr	C3
Fire Station	B2
Fothergill St	B3
Galonuchaf Rd	A3
Garth St	B2
Georgetown	B2
Grawen Terr	A2
Grove Pk	A2
Gurnos Rd	A2
Gwaelodygarth Rd	A2/A3
Gwaunfarren Gr	A3
Gwaunfarren Rd	A3
Gwendoline St	A3
Hampton St	C3
Hanover St	A2
Heol S O Davies	A3
Heol-Gerrig	B1
High St	A3/B2/B3/C2
Highland View	C3
Howell Cl	B1
Information Ctr	B2
Jackson's Bridge	B2
James St	C3
John St	B3
Joseph Parry's Cottage	B2
Lancaster St	A2
Llewellyn St	B2
Llwyfen St	B2
Llwyn Berry	B1
Llwyn Dic Penderyn	B1
Llwyn-y-Gelynen	C1
Lower Thomas St	B3
Market	C2
Mary St	C3
Masonic St	C2
Merthyr College	B2
Merthyr Tydfil FC	B2
Merthyr Tydfil R.U.F.C.	C2
Merthyr Tydfil ≋	C3
Meyrick Villas	A2
Miniature Railway ◆	A1
Mount St	A2
Nantygwenith St	B1
Norman Terr	B2
Oak Rd	A2
Old Cemetery	B3
Pandy Cl	A1
Pantycelynen	B1
Park Terr	B2
Penlan View	C2
Penry St	B2
Pentwyn Villas	A2
Penyard Rd	B3
Penydarren Park	A3
Penydarren St	A2
Plymouth St	C3
Police Station	C2
Pont Marlais West	B2
Post Office	A3/B2/C3
Quarry Row	B2
Queen's Rd	A3
Rees St	C3
Rhydycar Leisure Centre	C3
Rhydycar Link	C2
Riverside Park	A1
St David's	B3
St Tydfil's	C3
St Tydfil's Ave	C3
St Tydfil's Hospital (No A&E)	B3
St Tydfil's Square Shopping Centre	C2
Saxon St	A2
School of Nursing	A2
Seward St	A3
Shiloh La	B3
Stone Circles	B3
Stuart St	A2
Summerhill Pl	A3
Superstore	B3
Swan St	C2
Swansea Rd	B1
Taff Glen View	C3
Taff Vale Ct	B3
The Grove	A2
The Parade	C3
The Walk	B3
Thomastown Park	B3
Tramroad La	A3
Tramroad Side	B2
Tramroad Side North	B3
Tramroad Side South	C3
Trevithick Gdns	B3
Trevithick St	A3
Tudor Terr	B2
Twynyrodyn Rd	C3
Union St	B3
Upper Colliers Row	B1
Upper Thomas St	B3
Victoria St	B2
Vulcan Rd	B2
Warlow St	A2
Well St	A2
Wern La	C1
West Gr	A2
William St	C3
Yew St	C3
Ynysfach Engine House ◆	C2
Ynysfach Rd	C2

Middlesbrough

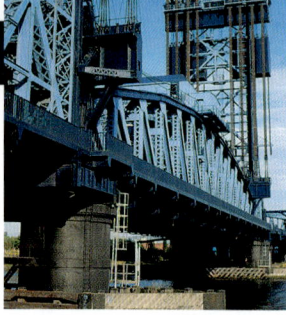

An agricultural hamlet until 1829, when Quaker businessmen founded the town to supply labour to a nearby coal port. The 18th-century maritime explorer was baptised in St Cuthbert's church, Marton, and educated at what is now the Captain Cook Schoolroom Museum. Notable structures in the town include the Victorian Gothic town hall, the Transporter Bridge and Visitor Centre, and Newport Bridge, Britain's first vertical-lift bridge. Outdoor attractions include Stewart Park; Newham Grange Farm and Rare Breeds Centre; and Nature's World explores sustainable technologies. There are four shopping centres. A new contemporary arts gallery – MIMA – opens in summer 2006.

▲ Newport Bridge

★ Do not miss
- ★ **Captain Cook Birthplace Museum**, Stewart Park
- ★ **Dorman Museum** of local history and Linthorpe pottery, Linthorpe Rd
- ★ **Ormesby Hall**, Church Lane

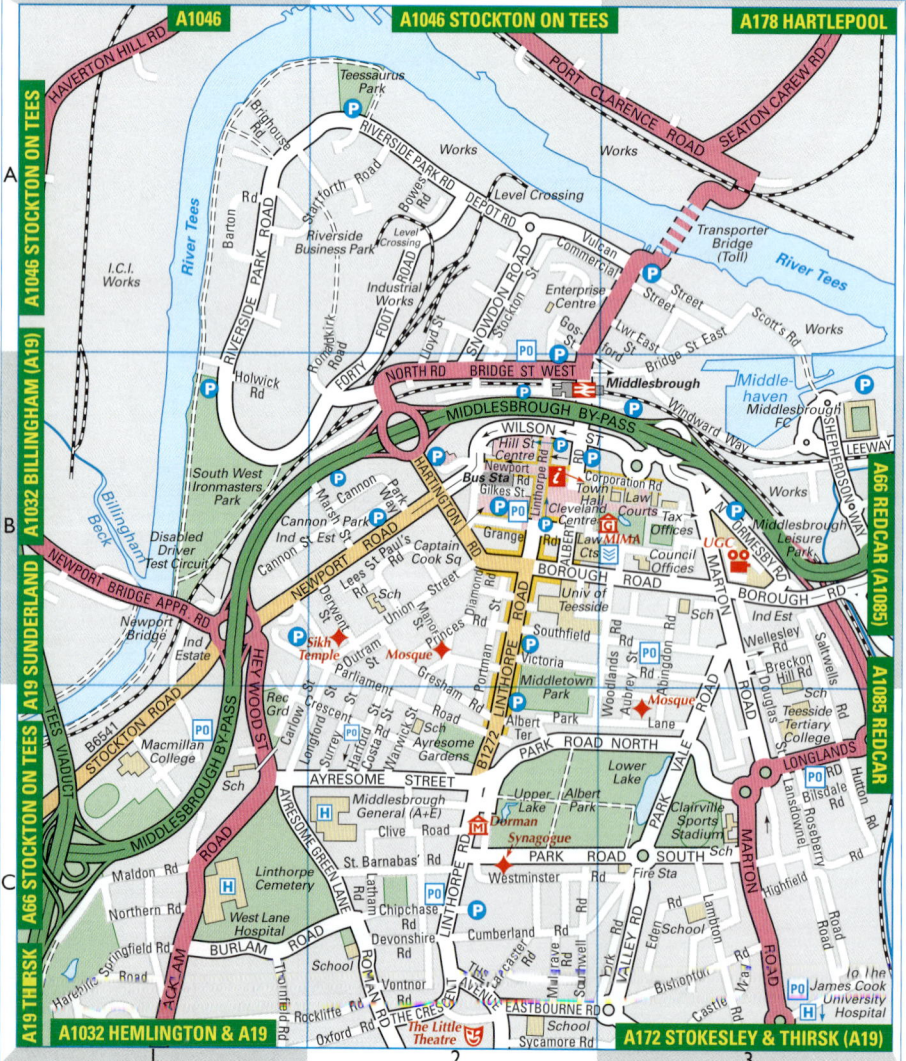

Tourist Information Centre, The Town Hall, Albert Rd, Middlesbrough TS1 2PA Tel 01642 729700

BBC Radio Cleveland 95 FM
Magic 1170 AM • **96.6TFM** 96.6 FM

www.middlesbrough.gov.uk

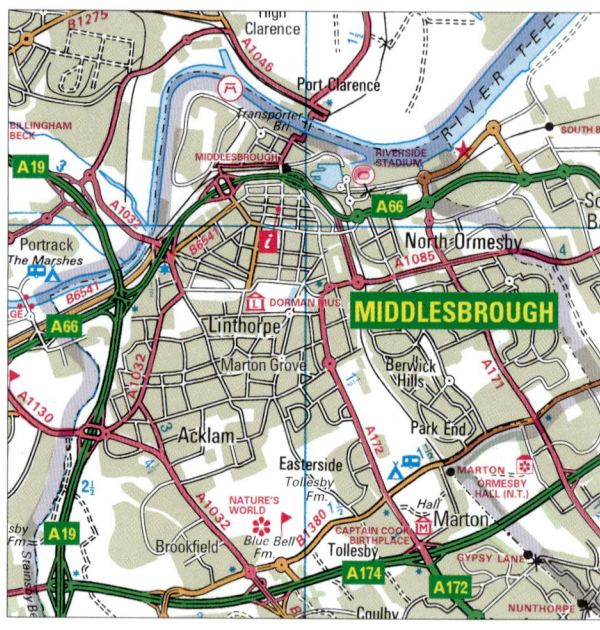

Middlesbrough

Abingdon Rd C3	Ayresome Gdns . . . C2	Bowes Rd A2	Cannon Park Way . B2	Cleveland Centre . B2	Newport Bridge. . . B1
Acklam Rd C1	Ayresome Green	Breckon Hill Rd . . . B3	Cannon St B1	Clive Rd C2	Newport Bridge
Albert Park B2	La C1	Bridge St East B3	Captain Cook Sq . . B2	Commercial St . . A2	Approach Rd . . . B1
Albert Rd B2	Ayresome St C2	Bridge St West B2	Carlow St B1	Corporation Rd . . B2	Newport Rd B2
Albert Terr C3	Barton Rd A1	Brighouse Rd A1	Castle Way C3	Costa St C2	North Rd B2
Aubrey St C3	Bilsdale Rd C3	Burlam Rd C1	Chipchase Rd C2	Council Offices . . B3	Northern Rd C1
	Bishopton Rd . . . C2	Bus Station B2	Clairville Sports	Crescent Rd B2	Outram St B2
	Borough Rd . . . B2/B3	Cannon Park B1	Stadium C3	Cumberland Rd . . C2	Oxford Rd C2
				Depot Rd A2	Park La C1
				Derwent St B1	Park Rd North . . . C2
				Devonshire Rd . . C2	Park Rd South . . . C2
				Diamond Rd B2	Park Vale Rd C3
				Disabled Driver	Parliament Rd . . . B1
				Test Circuit B1	Police Station . . B3
				Dorman Mus C2	Port Clarence Rd . A3
				Douglas St B3	Portman St C2
				Eastbourne Rd . . . C2	Post Office
				Eden Rd C2	. . . B2/B3/C1/C2/C3
				Enterprise Centre . A2	Princes Rd B2
				Forty Foot Rd . . . A2	Riverside
				Gilkes St B2	Business Park . . A2
				Gosford St A2	Riverside Park Rd . A1
				Grange Rd B2	Rockliffe Rd C1
				Gresham Rd B2	Romaldkirk Rd . . . B1
				Harehills Rd C1	Roman Rd C2
				Harford St B2	Roseberry Rd . . . C3
				Hartington Rd . . . B2	St Paul's Rd B2
				Haverton Hill Rd . . A1	St Barnabas' Rd . . C2
				Hey Wood St B1	Saltwells Rd B3
				Highfield Rd C3	Scott's Rd A3
				Hill St Centre B2	Seaton Carew Rd . A3
				Holwick Rd B1	Shepherdson Way. B3
				Hutton Rd C3	Sikh Temple ✦ . . . B2
				I.C.I. Works A1	Snowdon Rd B1
				Information Ctr . . B2	South West
				Lambton Rd C3	Ironmasters Pk . . B1
				Lancaster Rd C2	Southfield Rd . . . C2
				Lansdowne Rd . . . C3	Southwell Rd . . . C2
				Latham Rd C2	Springfield Rd . . . C1
				Law Courts B2/B3	Startforth Rd . . . A2
				Lees Rd B2	Stockton Rd C1
				Leeway B2	Stockton St A2
				Linthorpe Cem . . . C1	Surrey St C2
				Linthorpe Rd B2	Sycamore Rd . . . C2
				Little Theatre,	Synagogue ✦ . . . B2
				The ☺ C2	Tax Offices B3
				Longford St C2	Tees Viaduct C1
				Longlands Rd C3	Teessaurus Park . . A2
				Lower East St . . . A3	Teesside Tertiary
				Lower Lake C3	Coll C3
				Macmillan Coll . . . C1	The Avenue C3
				Maldon Rd C1	The Crescent . . . C2
				Manor St C2	Thornfield Rd . . . C1
				Marsh St. B1	Town Hall B2
				Marton Rd B3	Transporter
				Middlehaven B3	Bridge (Toll) . . . A3
				Middlesbrough	UGC ☺ B3
				By-Pass B2/C1	Union St B2
				Middlesbrough	Univ of Teesside . . B2
				F.C. B3	Upper Lake C2
				Middlesbrough	Valley Rd C3
				General (A&E) H . C2	Ventnor Rd C2
				Middlesbrough	Victoria Rd B2
				Leisure Park . . . B3	Vulcan St A2
				Middlesbrough	Warwick St C2
				Station ☒ B2	Wellesley Rd B3
				Middletown Park . . B3	West Lane H . . . C1
				MIMA B3	Westminster Rd . . C2
				Mosque ✦ B2	Wilson St B2
				Mosque ✦ C3	Windward Way . . B3
				Mulgrave Rd C2	Woodlands Rd . . . B2
				North Ormesby Rd B3	York Rd B3

Milton Keynes

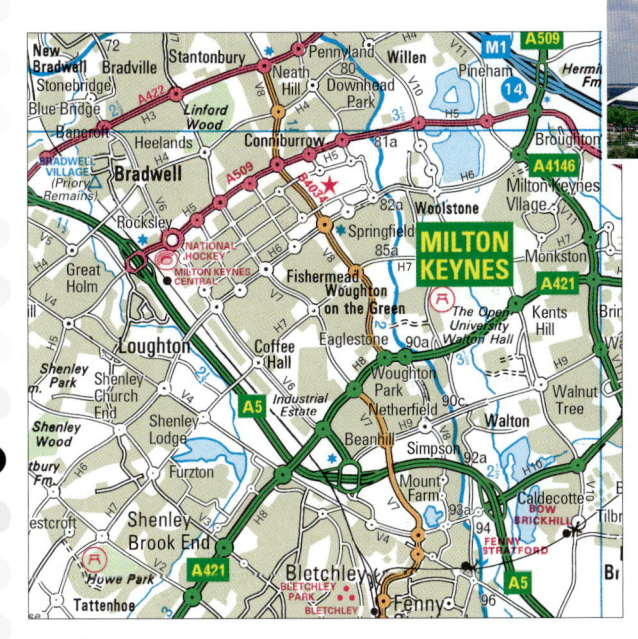

▲ Xscape

The famous Buckinghamshire 'new town', built in the 1970s on a site that had been settled as early as 2000BC. A major Roman villa with mosaic floors was uncovered at Bancroft and the remains can still be seen. The city boasts the country's biggest collection of publicly sited artworks (more than 200, including Elisabeth Frink's Black Horse). It is also home to the vast National Bowl concert venue and the more intimate Stables live music venue. Trips can be taken on the Grand Union Canal through the city, along which there are a number of traditional pubs, and Linford Manor Park is a good place for walks. Family entertainment is provided at Xscape, with an indoor ski slope, rock-climbing wall and more, Gulliver's Land, and Willen Lakeside Park. There is a very wide selection of shops centred on The Centre: MK and Midsummer Place shopping centres, plus plenty of bars and restaurants for the evening's entertainment.

★ Do not miss
- ★ 'Artwalks', various locations
- ★ Bletchley Park (home to WWII codebreakers), off Wilton Avenue, Bletchley
- ★ Milton Keynes Gallery, Midsummer Boulevard – contemporary art

Milton Keynes Visitor Information Centre, 890 Midsummer Boulevard, Milton Keynes MK9 3QA
Tel 01908 558300

BBC Three Counties Radio
104.5 FM • Horizon 103.3 FM
Classic Gold AM 828, 792 AM

www.mkweb.co.uk

Milton Keynes

Abbey Way	A1
Arbrook Ave	B1
Armourer Dr	A3
Arncliffe Dr	A1
Avebury (r'about)	C2
Avebury Blvd	C2
Bankfield (r'about)	B3
Bayard Ave	A2
Belvedere (r'about)	A2
Bishopstone	A1
Blundells Rd	A1
Boycott Ave	C2
Bradwell Common Blvd	B1
Bradwell Rd	C1
Bramble Ave	A2
Brearley Ave	C2
Breckland	A1
Brill Place	B1
Burnham Dr	B1
Bus Station	C1
Campbell Park (r'about)	B3
Cantle Ave	A3
Central Milton Keynes Shopping Area	B2
Century Ave	C2
Chaffron Way	C3
Childs Way	C1
Christ the Cornerstone	B2
Cineworld	B3
Civic Offices	B2
Cleavers Ave	B2
Colesbourne Dr	A3
Conniburrow Blvd	B2
County Court	B2
Currier Dr	A2
Dansteed Way	A2/A3/B1
Deltic Ave	B1
Downs Barn (r'about)	A2
Downs Barn Blvd	A3
Eaglestone (r'about)	C3
EasyCinema	B2
Eelbrook Ave	B1
Elder Gate	B1
Evans Gate	C2
Fairford Cr	A3
Falcon Ave	B3
Fennel Dr	A2
Fishermead Blvd	C3
Food Centre	B3
Fulwoods Dr	C3
Glazier Dr	A2
Glovers La	C1
Grafton Gate	C1
Grafton St	A1/C2
Gurnards Ave	B3
Harrier Dr	C3
Ibstone Ave	B1
Langcliffe Dr	A1
Leisure Plaza	C1
Leys Rd	C1
Library	B2
Linford Wood	A2
Marlborough Gate	B3
Marlborough St	A2/B3
Mercers Dr	A1
Midsummer (r'about)	C2
Midsummer Blvd	B2
Milton Keynes Central	C1
Monks Way	A1
Mullen Ave	A3
Mullion Pl	C3
National Hockey Stadium	B1
Neath Hill (r'about)	A3
North Elder (r'about)	C1
North Grafton (r'about)	B1
North Overgate (r'about)	A3
North Row	B2
North Saxon (r'about)	B2
North Secklow (r'about)	B2
North Skeldon (r'about)	A3
North Witan (r'about)	B2
Oakley Gdns	A3
Oldbrook Blvd	C2
Open-Air Theatre	B3
Overgate	A3
Overstreet	A3
Patriot Dr	B1
Pencarrow Pl	B3
Penryn Ave	B3
Perran Ave	C3
Pitcher La	C1
Place Retail Park, The	C1
Point Centre, The	B3
Police Station	B2
Portway (r'about)	B2
Post Office	A2/B2/C3
Precedent Dr	B1
Quinton Dr	B1
Ramsons Ave	B2
Rockingham Dr	A1
Rooksley (r'about)	B1
Rooksley Retail Park	C1
Saxon Gate	B2
Saxon St	A1/C3
Secklow Gate	B2
Shackleton Pl	C3
Silbury (r'about)	C1
Silbury Blvd	C2
Skeldon (r'about)	A3
South Grafton (r'about)	C2
South Row (r'about)	C2
South Saxon (r'about)	C2
South Secklow (r'about)	B3
South Witan (r'about)	C2
Springfield (r'about)	B3
Stanton Wood	A1
Stantonbury (r'about)	A1
Stantonbury Leisure Ctr	A1
Strudwick Dr	C2
Sunrise Parkway	A2
Telephone Exchange	C3
Theatre & Art Gallery	B3
Tolcarne Ave	C3
Towan Ave	C3
Trueman Pl	C2
Vauxhall	A1
Winterhill Retail Park	C2
Witan Gate	B2
Xscape	B3

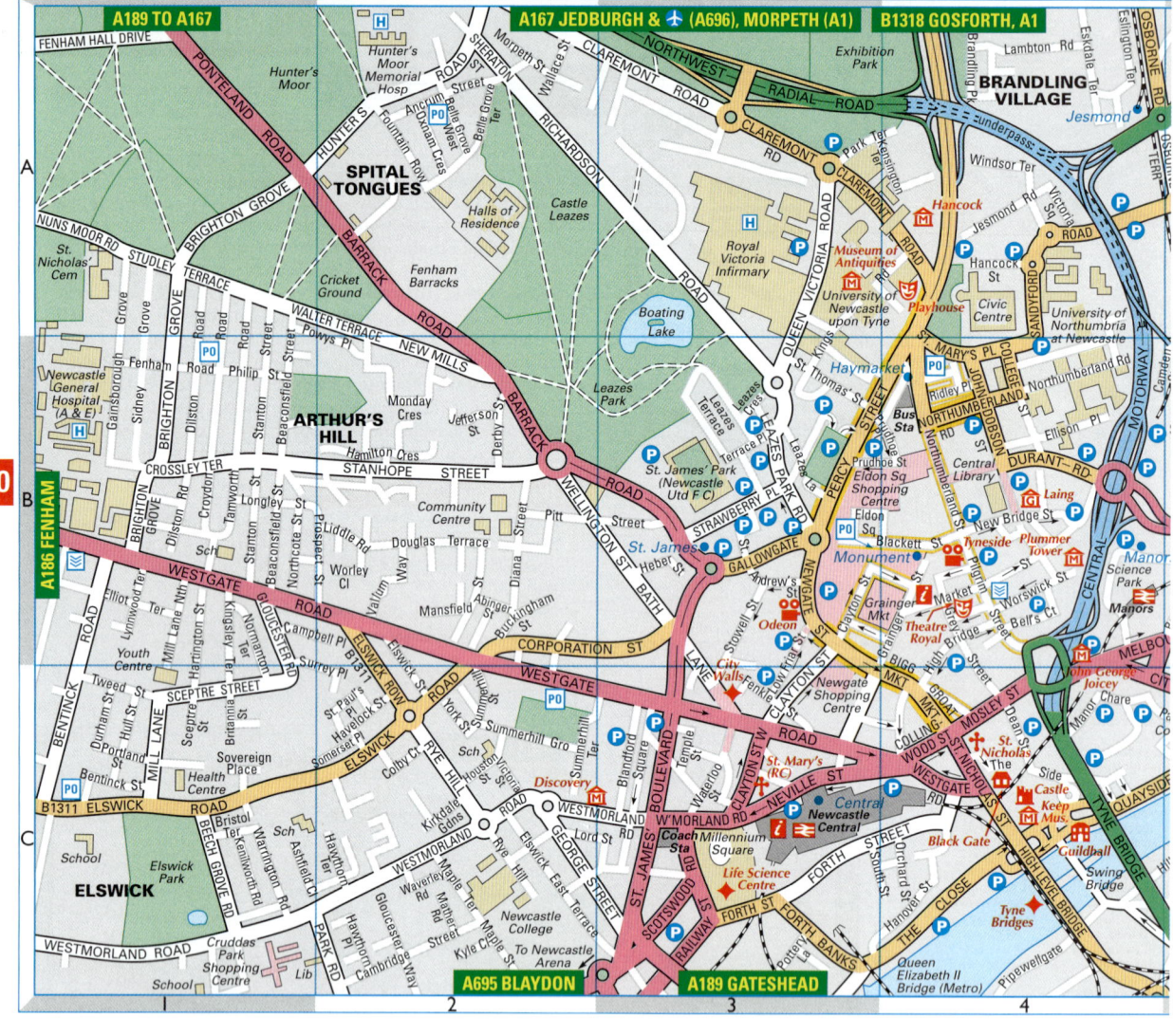

Newcastle upon Tyne

Street	Grid
Abinger St	B2
Albany Rd	C6
Albert St	B5
Albion Row	B6
Ancrum St	A2
Argyle St	B5
Arthur's Hill	B1
Ashfield Cl	C1
Athletics Stadium	C6
Back New Bridge St	B5
Ballast Hills Park	B6
BALTIC The Centre for Contemporary Art	C5
Bank Rd	C5
Barker St	B1
Barrack Rd	A2/B2
Bath La	B3
Beaconsfield St	B1
Beckett St	C6
Beech Grove Rd	A2
Belle Grove Terr	A2
Belle Grove West	A2
Bell's Court	B4
Bentinck Rd	C1
Bentinck St	C1
Bigg Market	B4
Biscuit Factory	B5
Black Gate	C4
Blackett St	B4
Blandford Sq	C3
Boating Lake	A3
Bolingbroke St	A6
Boyd St	B5
Brandling Park	A4
Breamish St	B5
Brighton Gr	A1/B1
Bristol Terr	C1
Britannia St	C1
Buckingham St	B2
Bus Station	B4
Buxton St	B5
Byker Bank	B6
Byker Bridge	B6
Byron St	A5
Cambridge St	C2
Camden St	B4
Campbell Pl	B1
Cardigan Terr	A6
Castle	C4
Castle Leazes	A2
Central (Metro Station)	C3
Central Library	A3
Central Motorway	B4
Chelmsford Gr	A5
Chester St	A5
City Rd	B5/C5
City Walls	C3
Civic Centre	A4
Claremont Rd	A3
Clarence St	B5
Clarence Walk	B5
Clayton St	B3
Clayton St West	C3
Coach Station	C3
Colby Court	C2
College St	B4
Collingwood St	C4
Community Ctr	B2
Copland Terr	B5
Coppice Way	B5
Coquet St	B5
Corporation St	B2
Coulthards La	C5
Coulthards Pl	C6
Courts	B4
Crawhall Rd	B5
Cricket Ground	A2
Criddle St	C6
Crossley Terr	B1
Croydon Rd	C1
Cruddas Park Shopping Ctr	C1
Cut Bank	B6
Dean St	C4
Deptford Rd	C6
Derby St	B2
Diana St	B2
Dilston Rd	B1
Dinsdale Pl	A5
Dinsdale Rd	A5
Discovery Mus	C2
Doncaster Rd	A5
Dorset Rd	C6
Douglas Terr	B2
Durant Rd	B4
Durham St	C1
Eldon Sq	B4
Eldon Sq Shopping Ctr	B3
Elizabeth St	B6
Elliot Terr	B1
Ellison Pl	B4
Elswick East Terr	C2
Elswick Park	C1
Elswick Rd	C1/C2
Elswick Row	B2
Elswick St	B2
Eskdale Terr	A4
Eslington Terr	A4
Exhibition Park	A3
Falconar St	B5
Falmouth Rd	A5
Fenham Barracks	A2
Fenham Hall Dr	A1
Fenham Rd	B1
Fenkle St	B4
Ford St	B6
Forth Banks	C3
Forth St	C3
Foundry La	B6
Fountain Row	A2
Gainsborough Gr	B1
Gallowgate	B3
Gateshead Millennium Bridge	C5
George St	C2
Gibson St	B5
Gloucester Rd	B1
Gloucester Way	C1
Goldspink La	A5
Grainger Market	B4
Grainger St	B4
Grantham Rd	A5
Granville Rd	A5
Grey St	B4
Greystoke Ave	A5
Groat Market	C4
Guildhall	C4
Halls of Residence	A2
Hamilton Cr	B2
Hancock Mus	A4
Hanover St	C4
Hartington St	A1
Havelock St	C2
Hawks Rd	C5
Hawthorn Pl	C2
Hawthorn Terr	C2
Haymarket (Metro Station)	B4
Health Centre	C1
Heaton Park	A6
Heaton Park Rd	A6
Heaton Park View	A6
Heaton Rd	A6
Heaton Terr	B6
Heber St	B3
Helmsley Rd	A5
High Bridge	B4
High Level Bridge	C4
Hillgate	C5
Horatio St	B6
Hotspur St	A6
Houston St	C2
Howard St	B5
Hull St	C1
Hunter's Moor	A1
Hunter's Moor Memorial Hospital	A2
Hunter's Rd	A2
Hutton Terr	A5
Information Ctr	B3/B4/C3
Jefferson St	B2
Jesmond (Metro Station)	A4
Jesmond Rd	A4/A5
John Dobson St	B4
John George Joicey Mus	C4
Jubilee Rd	A5
Keep Mus	C4
Kelvin Gr	A5
Kenilworth Rd	C1
Kensington Terr	A4
Kings Rd	A5
Kingsley Terr	B1
Kirkdale Gdns	C2
Kyle Cl	C2
Laing Gallery	B4
Lambton Rd	A4
Leazes Cr	B3
Leazes La	B3
Leazes Park	B3
Leazes Park Rd	B3
Leazes Terr	B3
Library	A6/C1
Liddle Rd	B2
Life Science Centre	C3
Lime St	B6
Longley St	B1
Lord St	C2
Low Friar St	B4
Lynnwood Terr	B1
Malcolm St	A6
Manor Chare	C4
Manors (Metro Station)	B4
Mansfield St	B2
Maple St	C2
Maple Terr	B2
Market St	B4
Mather Rd	B4
Melbourne St	B4
Mill La	C1
Mill La North	B1
Mill Rd	C5
Millennium Sq	C5
Monday Cr	B2
Monument (Metro Station)	B4
Morpeth St	A2
Mosley St	C4
Mowbray St	A6
Museum of Antiquities	A3
Napier St	A5
Nazareth House	A5
Neville St	C3
New Bridge St	B4/B5
New Mills	B2
Newcastle Central Station	C3
Newcastle College	C2
Newcastle General Hospital (A&E)	B1
Newgate Shopping Centre	C3
Newgate St	B3
Newington Rd	A5/A6
Nixon St	C6
Norfolk Rd	C6
Normanton Terr	B1
North View	A6
Northcote St	C3
Northumberland Rd	B4
Northumberland St	B4
Northwest Radial Rd	A3
Nuns Moor Rd	A1
Oakwellgate	C5
Odeon	B3
Orchard St	C4
Osborne Rd	A4
Osborne Terr	A5
Ouse Burn	A6
Ouse St	B6
Ouseburn Rd	A6
Oxnam Cr	A2
Pandon Bank	C5
Pandon	C5
Park Rd	C2
Park Terr	A3
Percy St	B3
Philip St	B1
Pilgrim St	B4
Pipewellgate	C4
Pitt St	B2
Playhouse Theatre	A4
Plummer Tower	B4
Police Station	B1/B4/C3
Ponteland Rd	A1
Portland Rd	A5/B5
Portland St	C1
Portland Terr	A5
Post Office	A2/A5/A6/B1/B3/B4/B5/C1/C2
Pottery La	C3
Powys Pl	A1
Prospect St	C1
Prudhoe Pl	B3
Prudhoe St	B3
Quality Row	A6
Quayside	C4/C6
Queen Elizabeth II Bridge	C4
Queen Victoria Rd	A3
Railway St	C3
Richardson Rd	A3
Ridley Pl	B4
Rock Terr	B4
Roger St	B6
Rosedale Terr	A5
Royal Victoria Infirmary	A3
Rye Hill	C2
St Andrew's St	B3
St James (Metro Station)	B3
St James' Blvd	C3
St James' Park (Newcastle Utd F.C.)	B3
St Lawrence Rd	C6
St Mary's (RC)	C3
St Mary's Place	B4
St Nicholas	C4
St Nicholas' Cem	A1
St Nicholas St	C4
St Paul's Pl	C2
St Thomas' St	B3
Saltmeadows Rd	C6
Sandyford Rd	A4/A5
Sceptre St	C1
Science Park	B5
Scotswood Rd	C3
Sheraton St	A2
Shield St	B5
Shieldfield	B5
Shields Rd	B6
Shields Rd By-Pass	B6
Sidney Gr	B1
Simpson Terr	B5
Somerset Pl	C2
South Shore Rd	C5
South St	C3
South View West	B6
Sovereign Pl	C1
Springbank Rd	A6
Stanhope St	B2
Stanton St	B1
Starbeck Ave	A5
Stepney Bank	B5
Stepney Rd	B5
Stoddart St	B5
Stowell St	B3
Stratford Gr West	A6
Stratford Rd	A6
Strawberry Pl	B3
Studley Terr	A1
Suffolk Pl	C6
Summerhill Gr	C2

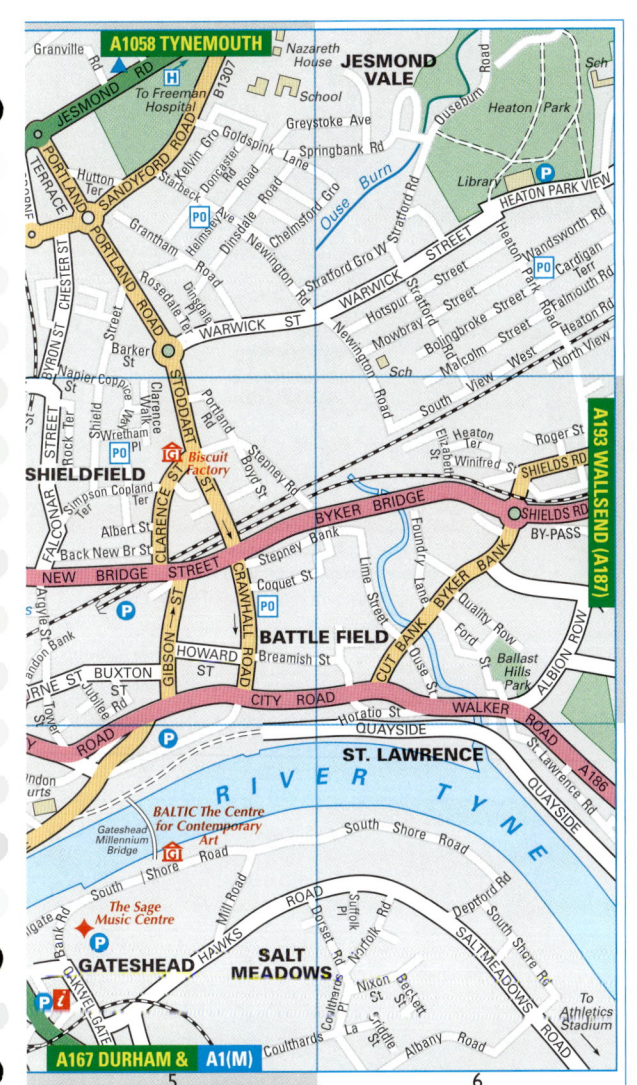

Newcastle-upon-Tyne

A large city that grew from a Roman fort, over which a castle was built in 1080 by William the Conqueror's son; the fine keep added by Henry II now houses a museum of local history. A key player in the Industrial Revolution (chiefly as a coal supplier), Newcastle is now undergoing large-scale regeneration, especially around its Quayside area with its public artworks, new hotels and restaurants, and the dramatic Millennium Bridge across to Gateshead. Other attractions include the 12th-century cathedral, Hancock Museum of Natural History, Life Science interactive centre with its motion rides, John George Joicey Museum of Natural History, and Military Vehicle Museum. The best green space is the Tyne Riverside Country Park, while the story of the railways is traced at the nearby George Stephenson's Birthplace (National Trust) and Stephenson Railway Museum and Steam Railway. Newcastle is the main city in the northeast with the centre made up of seven distinct quarters between them offering a wealth of choice in shopping, drinking and eating, plus theatre, cinema, music venues and St James's Park for Newcastle Football Club.

▲The Baltic Centre

i **Tourist Information Centre,**
132 Grainger Street, Newcastle-upon-Tyne NE1 5AF Tel 0191 2778000

BBC Radio Newcastle 95.4 FM and 1458 AM • **Century** 101.8 FM
Galaxy 105.3 FM • **Magic** 1152 AM
Metro Radio 97.1 FM

www.newcastle.gov.uk

★ Do not miss
★ **Baltic Centre for Contemporary Art,** Gateshead
★ **Castle Keep Museum,** Castle Garth
★ **Discovery Museum,** Blandford Square – history of the Tyne

Street	Grid
Summerhill St	C2
Summerhill Terr	C2
Surrey Pl	B1
Swing Bridge	C4
Tamworth Rd	B1
Temple St	C3
Terrace Pl	B3
The Close	C4
The Sage Music Centre ✦	C5
The Side	C4
Theatre Royal	B4
Tower St	B5
Tweed St	C1
Tyne Bridge	C4
Tyne Bridges ✦	C4
Tyneside	B4
University of Newcastle upon Tyne	A3
University of Northumbria at Newcastle	A4
Vallum Way	B2
Victoria Sq	A4
Victoria St	C2
Walker Rd	B6
Wallace St	A2
Walter Terr	A1
Wandsworth Rd	A6
Warrington Rd	C1
Warwick St	A5/A6
Waterloo St	C3
Waverley Rd	C2
Wellington St	B2
Westgate Rd	B1/C2/C4
Westmorland Rd	C1/C2/C3
Windsor Terr	A4
Winifred St	B6
Worley Cl	B2
Worswick St	B4
Wretham Pl	B5
York St	C2
Youth Centre	C1

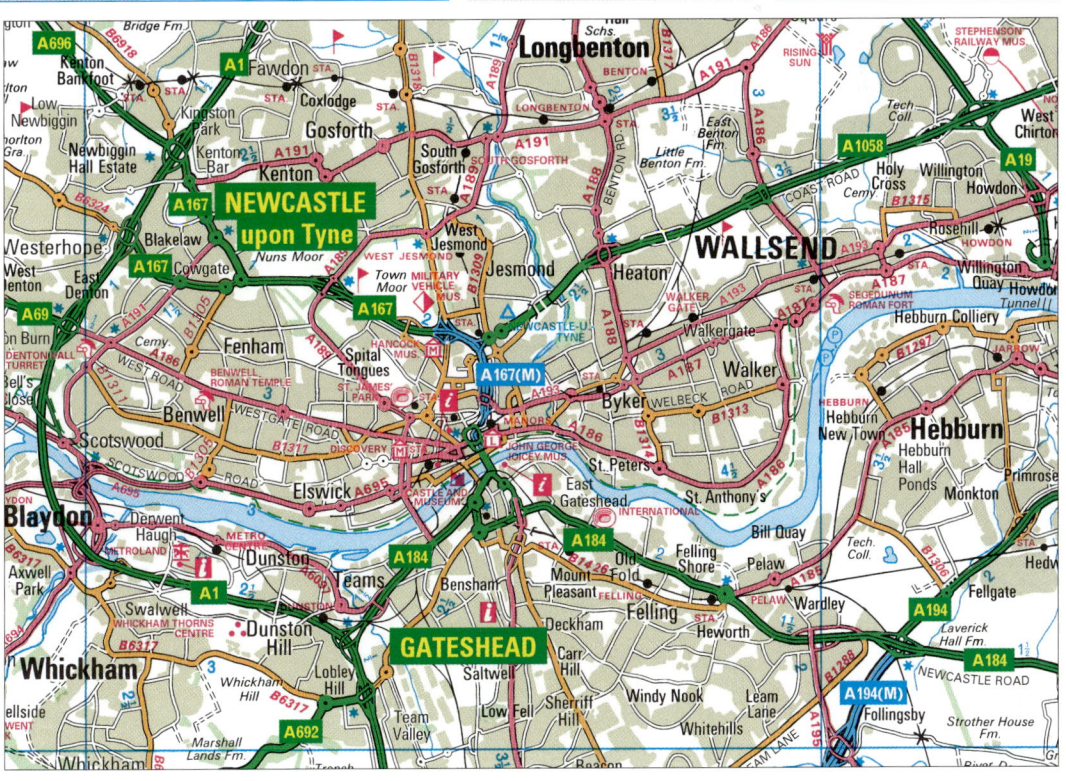

Newport

A South Wales cathedral and university city on the western bank of the Severn Estuary, with a rich Roman heritage concentrated in Caerleon, with its excellent museum and the remains of a fortress baths, amphitheatre and barracks. Other attractions include the remains of an early 14th-century castle; the 12th-century St Woolos Cathedral; the 17th-century Tredegar House; and Newport Museum and Art Gallery. The Riverfront Arts Centre will eventually display the remains of the Newport Medieval Ship, and Newport is home to the Newport International Sports Village. The Newport Wetlands nature reserve is near Uskmouth. Nearby Penhow Castle is the oldest inhabited castle in Wales, and there's a 30-mile walk along the Brecon and Monmouthshire Canal through the Brecon Beacons National Park to Brecon.

▲ Newport Transporter Bridge

Tourist Information Centre, John Frost Square, Newport NP20 1PA
Tel 01633 842962

BBC Radio Wales 95.9 FM • Capital Gold 1305 AM • Real Radio Wales 105.9 FM • Red Dragon FM 97.4 FM

www.newport.gov.uk

★ Do not miss
★ Fourteen Locks Canal Centre, High Cross
★ Newport Transporter Bridge and Visitor Centre, Usk Way
★ Roman Legionary Museum, High Street, Caerleon

Newport/Casnewydd

Street	Grid
Albert Terr	B1
Allt-yr-Yn Ave	A1
Alma St	C2
Ambulance Station	C3
Bailey St	B1
Barrack Hill	A2
Bath St	B1
Bedford Rd	B3
Belle Vue La	C1
Belle Vue Park	C1
Bishop St	A3
Blewitt St	B1
Bolt Cl	C3
Bolt St	C3
Bond St	A2
Bosworth Dr	A1
Bridge St	B2
Bristol St	A3
Bryngwyn Rd	B1
Brynhyfryd Ave	C1
Brynhyfryd Rd	C1
Bus Station	B2
Caerau Cres	C1
Caerau Rd	B1
Caerleon Rd	A3
Cambrian Retail Centre	B2
Capel Cres	C1
Cardiff Rd	C2
Caroline St	B3
Castle (Remains)	A2
Cattle Market and Saturday General Market	C3
Cedar Rd	A3
Charles St	B2
Charlotte Dr	C2
Chepstow Rd	A3
Church Rd	A3
City Cinema	B1
Civic Centre	B1
Clarence Pl	B1
Clifton Pl	B1
Clifton Rd	C1
Clyffard Cres	B1
Clytha Park Rd	B1
Clytha Sq	C2
Coldra Rd	C1
Collier St	B3
Colne St	B3
Comfrey Cl	A1
Commercial Rd	C3
Commercial St	B2
Corelli St	B3
Corn St	B2
Corporation Rd	B3
Coulson Cl	C2
County Court	A1
Courts	A1
Courts	B1
Crawford St	B1
Cyril St	B3
Dean St	C1
Devon Pl	B2
Dewsland Park Rd	C2
Dolman	B2
Dolphin St	C3
East Dock Rd	C3
East St	B1
East Usk Rd	A3
Ebbw Vale Wharf	B3
Emlyn St	A1
Enterprise Way	C3
Eton Rd	B3
Evans St	A2
Factory Rd	A2
Fields Rd	B1
Francis Dr	C2
Frederick St	C3
Friars Rd	C1
Gaer La	C1
George St	C3
George Street Bridge	C3
Godfrey Rd	B1
Gold Tops	B1
Gore St	A3
Gorsedd Circle	C1
Grafton Rd	A3
Graham St	B1
Granville St	C3
Harlequin Dr	A1
Harrow Rd	B3
Herbert Rd	A3
Herbert Walk	C2
Hereford St	C3
High St	B2
Hill St	B2
Hoskins St	A2
Information Ctr	B2
Ivor Sq	A3
John Frost Sq	B2
Jones St	B1
Junction Rd	A3
Keynshaw Ave	C1
King St	C2
Kingsway	B2
Kingsway Shopping Centre	B2
Ledbury Dr	A1
Library	A3
Library, Museum & Art Gallery	B2
Liverpool Wharf	B3
Llanthewy Rd	B1
Llanvair Rd	A3
Locke St	A2
Lower Dock St	C3
Lucas St	A2
Manchester St	A3
Market	A2
Marlborough Rd	B3
Mellon St	C3
Mill St	A2
Morgan St	A3
Mountjoy Rd	C2
Newport Athletic Club Grounds	B3
Newport Bridge	A2
Newport Leisure & Conference Ctr	B2
Newport	B2
North St	B2
Oakfield Rd	B1
Park Sq	C2
Police Station	A3/C3
Post Office	B1/B2/C1/C3
Power St	A1
Prince St	A3
Pugsley St	A2
Queen St	C2
Queen's Cl	B1
Queen's Hill	A1
Queen's Hill Cres	A1
Queensway	B2
Railway St	B1
Riverfront Arts Centre	B2
Riverside	A3
Rodney Rd	B2
Royal Gwent (A&E)	C2
Rudry St	A3
Rugby Rd	B3
Ruperra La	C3
Ruperra St	C3
St Edmund St	B1
St Mark's Cres	A1
St Mary St	B1
St Vincent Rd	A3
St Woolos †	C2
St Woolos General (no A&E)	C1
St Woolos Rd	B1
School La	C1
Serpentine Rd	B1
Shaftesbury Park	A2
Sheaf La	A3
Skinner St	B2
Sorrel Dr	A1
South Market St	C3
Spencer Rd	B1
Stow Hill	B2/C1/C2
Stow Park Ave	C1
Stow Park Dr	C1
TA Centre	A1
Talbot St	B2
Tennis Club	A1
Tregare St	A3
Trostrey St	A3
Tunnel Terr	B1
Turner St	A3
Usk St	A3
Usk Way	B3/C3
Victoria Cr	B1
War Memorial	A3
Waterloo Rd	C1
West St	B1
Wharves	B2
Wheeler St	A2
Whitby Pl	A3
Windsor Terr	B1
York Pl	C1

Newquay

A popular 11-beach resort that began life as a fortified Iron Age cliff settlement (the history of which is explored in Tunnels Through Time), and became an important fishing port; the whitewashed Huer's Hut is one of few surviving buildings recalling its pilchard fishing industry. The best family beach is sheltered Lusty Glaze with its creche, bar and restaurant. Attractions include the Blue Reef Aquarium, Trenance Leisure Park and Gardens with its waterworld, and nearby Holywell Bay Fun Park, World in Miniature Theme Park, Dairyland Farm World and Lappa Valley Steam Railway. To the south, Perranporth is the site of an early Celtic monastery and pilgrimage site excavated in the 19th century but reburied for preservation purposes in 1981; the location is marked by a memorial stone. Some nearby Norman walls remain from the parish church of St Piran's, also abandoned to the sand, and beside them is the Perran Cross, possibly an ancient boundary point. Just to the north, Carnewas and the Bedruthan Steps is a dramatic National Trust owned stretch of coastline with spectacular clifftop views over rock stacks.

▲ Gig racing

★ Do not miss
- **Fistral Beach** (famous for its surfing), west of Towan Head
- **Newquay Zoo and Conservation Centre**, Trenance Gardens
- **Trerice** (Elizabethan manor; National Trust), Kestle Mill

Tourist Information Centre, Marcus Hill, Newquay TR7 1BD
Tel 01637 854020

BBC Radio Cornwall 103.9 FM
Pirate FM 102.8 FM

www.newquay.co.uk

Newquay

Agar Rd	B2
Alma Pl	B1
Ambulance Station	B2
Anthony Rd	C1
Atlantic Hotel	A1
Bank St	B1
Barrowfields	A3
Bay View Terr	B2
Beach St	B1
Beachfield Ave	B1
Beacon Rd	A1
Belmont Pl	A1
Berry Rd	B2
Blue Reef Aquarium	B1
Boating Lake	C2
Bus Station	B2
Chapel Hill	B1
Chester Rd	A3
Cheviot Rd	C1/C2
Chichester Cres	C2
Chynance Drive Rd	C1
Chyverton Cl	C1
Cliff Rd	B2
Colvreath Rd	A3
Crantock St	B1
Criggar Rocks	A3
Dale Cl	C3
Dale Rd	C3
Dane Rd	A1
East St	B2
Edgcumbe Ave	B3
Edgcumbe Gdns	B3
Eliot Gdns	B3
Elm Cl	B3
Ennor's Rd	B1
Fernhill Rd	B1
Fire Station	B1
Fore St	B1
Gannel Rd	C2
Golf Driving Range	B3
Gover La	B1
Great Western Beach	A2
Grosvenor Ave	B2
Harbour	A1
Hawkins Rd	C2
Headleigh Rd	B2
Hillgrove Rd	A3/B3
Holywell Rd	B2
Hope Terr	B1
Huer's House, The	A1
Information Ctr	A2
Island Cres	B2
Jubilee St	B1
Kew Cl	B2
Killacourt Cove	A2
King Edward Cres	A1
Lanhenvor Ave	B2
Library	B1
Lifeboat Station	A1
Linden Ave	C2
Listry Rd	C2
Lusty Glaze Beach	A3
Lusty Glaze Rd	A3
Manor Rd	B1
Marcus Hill	B1
Mayfield Rd	B2
Meadowside	C3
Mellanvrane La	C2
Michell Ave	B2
Miniature Golf Course	C3
Miniature Railway	B3
Mount Wise	B1
Mowhay Cl	C3
Narrowcliff	A3
Newquay	B2
Newquay & District Hospital (No A&E)	C1
Newquay Town Football Ground	B1
Newquay Zoo	B3
North Pier	A1
Northquay Hill	A1
Oakleigh Terr	B2
Pargolla Rd	B2
Pendragon Cres	C3
Pengannel Cl	C1
Penina Ave	C3
Police Station	B2
Post Office	B1/B2
Quarry Park Rd	B3
Rawley La	C2
Reeds Way	B1
Robartes Rd	B2
St Anne's Rd	A3
St Aubyn Cres	B3
St George's Rd	B1
St John's Rd	B1
St Mary's Rd	B1
St Michael's	B1
St Michael's Rd	B1
St Thomas' Rd	B2
Seymour Ave	B2
South Pier	A1
Southquay Hill	A1
Sweet Briar Cres	C3
Sydney Rd	A1
The Crescent	B1
Tolcarne Beach	A2
Tolcarne Point	A2
Tolcarne Rd	B2
Tor Rd	B2
Towan Beach	A1
Towan Blystra Rd	B3
Tower Rd	A1
Trebarwith Cres	B2
Tredour Rd	C2
Treforda Rd	C3
Tregoss Rd	B3
Tregunnel Hill	B1/C1
Tregunnel Saltings	C1
Trelawney Rd	B2
Treloggan La	C3
Treloggan Rd	C3
Trembath Cres	C1
Trenance Ave	B2
Trenance Gardens	C2
Trenance La	C2
Trenance Leisure Park	B3
Trenance Rd	B2
Trenarth Rd	B2
Treninnick Hill	C3
Tretherras Rd	B3
Tretheway Way	C1
Trevemper Rd	C2
Tunnels Through Time	B1
Ulalia Rd	B3
Vivian Cl	B3
Waterworld	B3
Whitegate Rd	B3
Wych Hazel Way	C3

113

Northampton

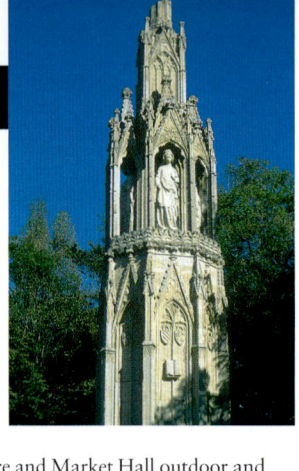

Northampton is a town with its origins before the Domesday book of 1086, which has built itself into an important town at the centre of the shoe manufacturing industry. The town is fortunate to retain several buildings of historic interest such as the Church of the Holy Sepulchre, which was built in 1100 to commemorate the return of the 1st Earl of Northampton from the Crusades. Shopping opportunities include Market Square and Market Hall outdoor and indoor markets, and the Grosvenor shopping centre. The River Nene, parks and gardens are all pleasant characteristics of the town. The railway station now occupies the site of the old castle. Both the cathedral and the Guildhall date from 1864.

▲ Queen Eleanor's Cross

Visitor Information Centre,
The Guildhall, St Giles Square,
Northampton NN1 1DE
Tel 01604 838800

BBC Radio Northampton 104.2 FM
Classic Gold 1557AM
Northants 96.6 FM

www.northampton.gov.uk

★ Do not miss:
- **Northampton Museum and Art Gallery**, Guildhall Road – includes world's largest collection of footwear
- **Abington Museum**, Abington Park – local history
- **Church of the Holy Sepulchre**, Sheep Street

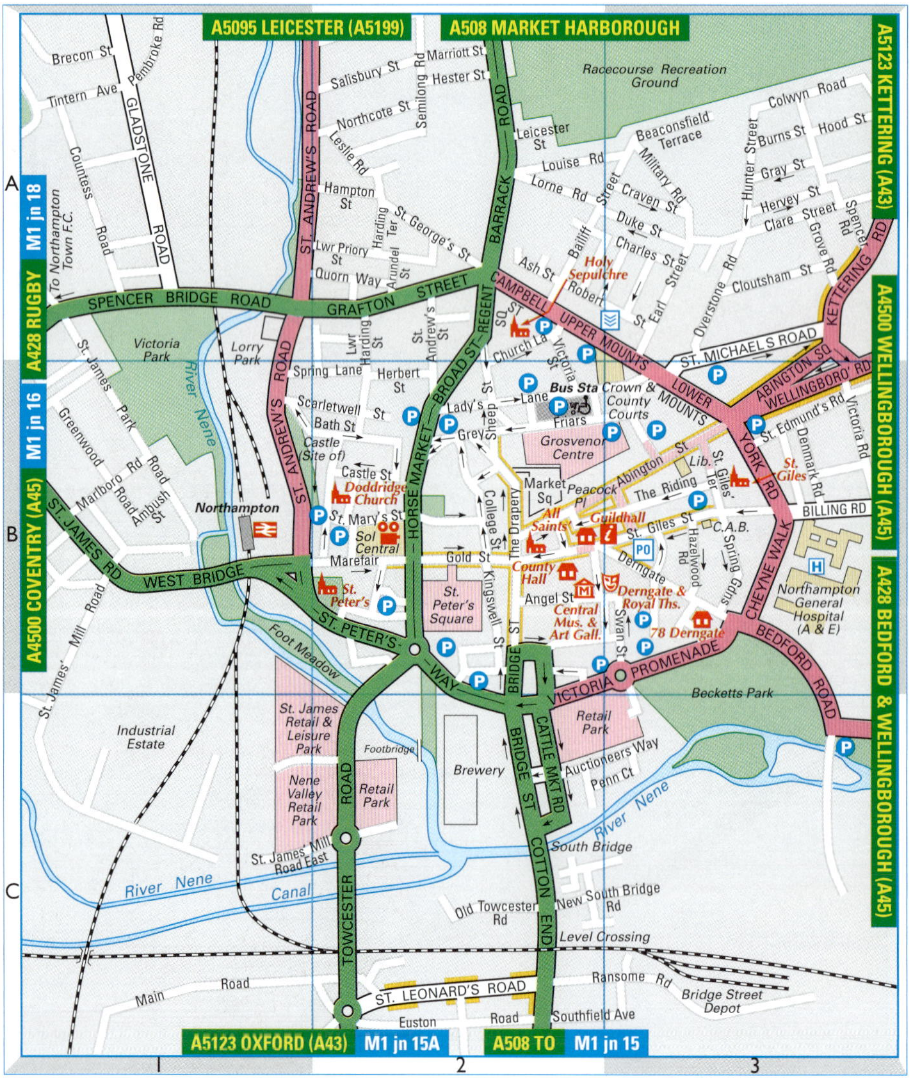

Northampton

78 Derngate	B3
Abington Sq	B3
Abington St	B3
All Saints'	B2
Ambush St	B1
Angel St	B2
Arundel St	A2
Ash St	A2
Auctioneers Way	C2
Bailiff St	A2
Barrack Rd	A2
Bath St	B3
Beaconsfield Terr	A3
Becketts Park	C3
Bedford Rd	B3
Billing Rd	B3
Brecon St	A1
Brewery	C2
Bridge St	C2
Bridge St Depot	C3
Broad St	B2
Burns St	A3
Bus Station	B2
Campbell St	A2
Castle (Site of)	B2
Castle St	B2
Cattle Market Rd	C2
Central Museum & Art Gallery	B2
Charles St	A3
Cheyne Walk	B3
Church La	A2
Clare St	A3
Cloutsham St	A3
College St	B2
Colwyn Rd	A3
Cotton End	C2
Countess Rd	A1
County Hall	B2
Craven St	A3
Crown & County Courts	B3
Denmark Rd	B3
Derngate	B3
Derngate & Royal Theatres	B2
Doddridge	B2
Duke St	A3
Earl St	A3
Euston Rd	C2
Foot Meadow	A2
Gladstone Rd	A1
Gold St	B2
Grafton St	A2
Gray St	A3
Greenwood Rd	B1
Grey Friars	B2
Grosvenor Centre	B2
Grove Rd	A3
Guildhall	B2
Hampton St	A2
Harding Terr	A2
Hazelwood Rd	B3
Herbert St	B2
Hervey St	A3
Hester St	A2
Holy Sepulchre	B2
Hood St	A3
Horse Market	B2
Hunter St	A3
Industrial Estate	C1
Information Ctr	B2
Kettering Rd	A3
Kingswell St	B2
Lady's La	B2
Leicester St	A2
Leslie Rd	A2
Library	B3
Lorne Rd	A2
Lorry Park	A1
Louise Rd	A2
Lower Harding St	A2
Lower Mounts	B3
Lower Priory St	A2
Main Rd	C1
Marefair	B2
Market Sq	B2
Marlboro Rd	B1
Marriott St	A2
Military Rd	A3
Nene Valley Retail Park	C1
New South Bridge Rd	C2
Northampton General Hospital (A&E)	B3
Northampton Station	B1
Northcote St	A2
Old Towcester Rd	C2
Overstone Rd	A3
Peacock Pl	B2
Pembroke Rd	A1
Penn Court	C2
Police Station	B3
Post Office	B3
Quorn Way	A2
Ransome Rd	C3
Regent Sq	A2
Retail Park	C2
Robert St	A2
St Andrew's Rd	B1
St Andrew's St	A2
St Edmund's Rd	B3
St George's St	A2
St Giles	B3
St Giles St	B3
St Giles' Terr	B3
St James' Mill Rd	B1
St James' Mill Rd East	C1
St James Park Rd	B1
St James Retail & Leisure Park	C1
St James Rd	B1
St Leonard's Rd	C2
St Mary's St	B2
St Michael's Rd	A3
St Peter's	B2
St Peter's Square Shopping Precinct	B2
St Peter's Way	B2
Salisbury St	A2
Scarletwell St	B2
Semilong Rd	A2
Sheep St	B2
Sol Central (Leisure Centre)	B2
South Bridge	C2
Southfield Ave	C3
Spencer Bridge Rd	A1
Spencer Rd	A3
Spring Gdns	B2
Spring La	B2
Swan St	B2
The Drapery	B2
The Riding	B3
Tintern Ave	A1
Towcester Rd	C2
Upper Mounts	A2
Victoria Park	A1
Victoria Promenade	B2
Victoria Rd	B3
Victoria St	A3
Wellingborough Rd	B3
West Bridge	B1
York Rd	A3

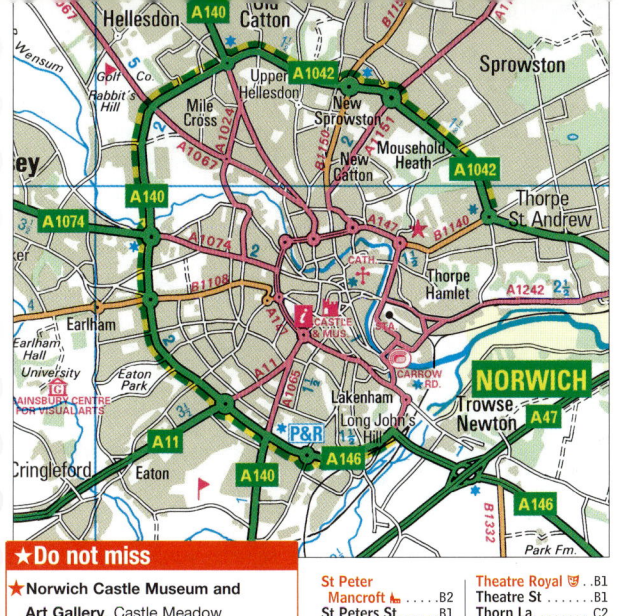

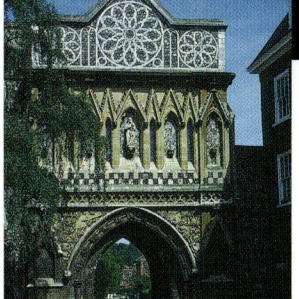

Norwich

A bustling, prosperous East Anglian city, originally an Anglo-Saxon settlement, with more than 1,500 historic buildings, including a magnificent Norman cathedral, a Catholic cathedral, more than 30 pre-Reformation churches (more than any other Western European city), a fine medieval guildhall, a Norman castle, England's most complete medieval street plan, and remnants of the ancient city walls. Outdoor attractions include riverside walks and the 4-acre Castle Green Park on top of Castle Mall. The city centre with its cobbled lanes and alleys has both familiar high-street outlets and a good range of traditional independent shops, and a local speciality can be sampled at Colman's Mustard Shop. The nearby University of East Anglia is home to the Sainsbury Centre for Visual Arts and between Norwich and the east coast lie the Norfolk Broads, popular for boating, walking, birdwatching and cycling.

▲ St Ethelbert's Gate

Norwich Tourist Information Centre,
The Forum, Norwich NR2 1TF
Tel 01603 727927

BBC Radio Norfolk 95.1, 104.4FM
Broadland 102.4 FM • **Classic Gold** 1152 AM • **Vibe FM** 106.1 FM

www.norwich.gov.uk

★ Do not miss

- ★ **Norwich Castle Museum and Art Gallery**, Castle Meadow
- ★ **Norwich Cathedral** (1096-1278), Cathedral Close
- ★ **Origins**, The Forum – history discovery centre

Norwich

Street	Grid
Albion Way	C3
All Saints Green	C2
Anchor Cl	A3
Anchor St	A3
Anglia Sq	B2
Argyle St	C3
Ashby St	C2
Assembly House	B1
Bank Plain	B2
Barker St	A1
Barn Rd	A1
Barrack St	A3
Ber St	C2
Bethel St	B1
Bishop Bridge	A3
Bishopbridge Rd	A3
Bishopgate	A3
Blackfriars St	A2
Botolph St	A2
Bracondale	C3
Brazen Gate	C1
Bridewell	B2
Brunswick Rd	C1
Bull Close Rd	A3
Bus Station	C2
Calvert St	A2
Cannell Green	A3
Carrow Rd	C3
Castle Mall	B2
Castle Meadow	B2
Castle & Mus	B2
Cathedral	B2
Cattlemarket St	B2
Chantry Rd	B1
Chapel Loke	C2
Chapelfield East	B1
Chapelfield Gdns	B1
Chapelfield North	B1
Chapelfield Rd	B1
Chapelfield Shopping Ctr	C1
City Hall	B1
City Rd	C2
City Wall	C1/C3
Colegate	B1
Coslany St	B1
Cow Hill	B1
Cow Tower	A3
Cowgate	A2
Crown & Magistrates Courts	B2
Dragon Hall Heritage Ctr	C3
Duke St	A1
Edward St	A2
Elm Hill	B2
Erpingham Gate	B2
Fire Station	B1
Fishergate	A2
Foundry Bridge	B3
Fye Bridge	A2
Garden St	C1
Gas Hill	B3
Grapes Hill	B1
Great Hospital Halls, The	A3
Grove Ave	C1
Grove Rd	C1
Guildhall	B1
Gurney Rd	A3
Hall Rd	C2
Heathgate	A3
Heigham St	A1
Horn's La	C2
Information Ctr	B1
Inspire (Science Centre)	A1
Ipswich Rd	C1
James Stewart Gdns	B3
King Edward VI School	B2
King St	B2
King St	B2
Koblenz Ave	C3
Library	B1
London St	B2
Lower Clarence Rd	B3
Lower Cl	B3
Maddermarket	B1
Magdalen St	A2
Mariners La	C2
Market	B2
Market Ave	B2
Mountergate	B3
Mousehold St	A3
Newmarket Rd	C1
Norfolk Gallery	B2
Norfolk St	C1
Norwich City FC	C1
Norwich	B3
Oak St	A1
Palace St	A2
Pitt St	A1
Police Station	B1
Post Office	A2/B1/B2/C2
Pottergate	B1
Prince of Wales Rd	B2
Princes St	B2
Pull's Ferry	B3
Puppet Theatre	A2
Quebec Rd	B3
Queen St	B2
Queens Rd	C2
Recorder Rd	B3
Retail Park	C3
Riverside Leisure Complex	C3
Riverside Rd	B3
Rosary Rd	B3
Rose La	B2
Rouen Rd	C2
Royal Norfolk Regiment Mus	B2
St Andrew's & Blackfriars Hall	B2
St Andrews St	B1
St Augustines St	A1
St Benedicts St	B1
St Crispins Rd	A1
St Ethelbert's Gate	B2
St Faiths La	B3
St Georges St	B2
St Giles St	B1
St James Cl	A3
St Julians	B2
St Martin's La	A1
St Peter Mancroft	B2
St Peters St	B1
St Stephens Rd	C1
St Stephens St	B1
Silver Rd	A2
Silver St	A2
Southwell Rd	C2
Strangers Hall	B1
Superstore	C2
Surrey St	C2
Sussex St	A1
Swimming Pool	B3
The Close	B3
The Forum	B1
The Walk	B2
Theatre Royal	B1
Theatre St	B1
Thorn La	C2
Thorpe Rd	B3
Tombland	B2
Union St	C1
Vauxhall St	B1
Victoria St	C1
Walpole St	B1
Wensum St	A2
Wessex St	C1
Westwick St	A1
Wherry Rd	C3
Whitefriars	A2
Willow La	B1
Yacht Station	B3

Nottingham

▲ Robin Hood Statue

A vibrant Midlands city with a host of new bars, restaurants, hotels and designer shops, many around the cobbled Lace Market area, once the focus of the local lace-making industry. The city is considered one of the top three centres for shopping in the country. Henry II replaced William the Conqueror's original castle with a stone structure in the 12th century. Other sights include the Brewhouse Yard Museum of local history; Green's Mill, a functioning windmill with a science centre; Britain's biggest market square; medieval St Mary's Church; Ye Olde Trip to Jerusalem, said to be Britain's oldest pub; Tales of Robin Hood recounting exploits of the famous outlaw; and the Tudor Wollaton Hall with its industrial and natural history museums. Contemporary art is strong at the Angel Row Gallery and the university's Bonington Gallery, and sports amenities include the new National Ice Centre and the National Watersports Centre. The annual Goose Fair is the country's biggest, oldest travelling fair.

★ Do not miss

- ★ **City of Caves**, Broadmarsh Centre – 13th century man-made dwellings
- ★ **Galleries of Justice**, Old Gaol, Shire Hall, High Pavement – museum of law, crime and punishment
- ★ **Nottingham Castle**, Museum and Art Gallery, off Friar Lane

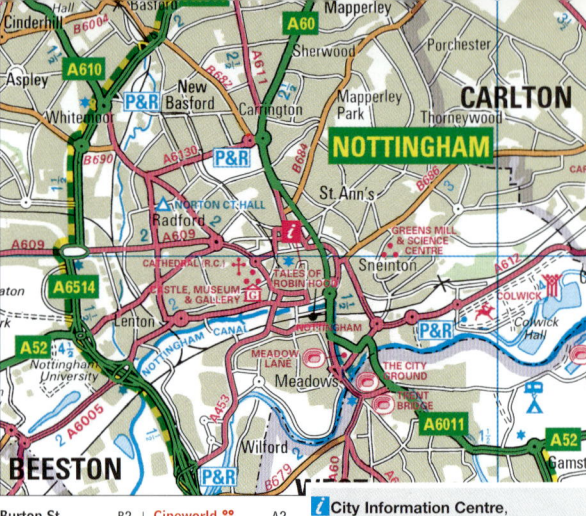

Nottingham

Abbotsford Dr ... A3	Balmoral Rd. ... A1	Burton St ... B2	Cineworld ... A2	
Addison St ... A1	Barker Gate ... B3	Bus Station ... A2	City Link ... C3	
Albert Hall ✦ ... B1	Bath St ... B3	Canal St ... C2	**City of Caves ✦** ... C3	
Alfred St South ... A3	Belgrave Centre ... B1	Carlton St ... B3	Clarendon St ... B1	
Alfreton Rd ... B1	Bellar Gate ... B3	Carrington St. ... C2	Cliff Rd ... C2	
All Saints Rd ... B1	Belward St ... B3	Castle Blvd. ... C1	Clumber Rd East. ... C1	
Annesley Gr ... A2	Blue Bell Hill Rd ... B3	**Castle ✦** ... C2	Clumber St. ... B2	
Arboretum ✦ ... A1	**Brewhouse Yd ✦** ... C2	Castle Gate ... C2	College St ... B1	
Arboretum St ... A1	Broad Marsh Bus Station ... C2	Castle Meadow Retail Park. ... C1	Collin St ... C2	
Arthur St ... A1	Broadmarsh Ctr. ... C2	Castle Meadow Rd ... C2	Conway Cl ... A2	
Arts Theatre ✦ ... B3	Broad St ... B3	Castle Wharf ... C2	**Council House ✦** ... B2	
Ashforth St. ... A3	Brook St ... B3	Cavendish Rd East ... C1	Court. ... C2	
	Burns St ... A1	Cemetery ... B1	Cranbrook St. ... B3	
		Chaucer St. ... B1	Cranmer St. ... A2	
		Cheapside ... B2	Cromwell St. ... B1	
		Church Rd ... A3	Curzon St. ... B3	
			Derby Rd ... B1	
			Dryden St. ... B1	
			Fishpond Dr. ... C1	
			Fletcher Gate. ... B3	

Forest Rd East ... A1	Post Office ... B2/C1
Forest Rd West ... A1	Queen's Rd ... C3
Friar La. ... C2	Raleigh St ... A1
Galleries of Justice ✦ ... C3	Regent St. ... B1
Gedling Gr ... A1	Rick St ... B3
Gedling St. ... B3	**Robin Hood Statue ✦** ... C2
George St. ... B3	Robin Hood St. ... B3
Gill St ... A2	Royal Centre (Tram stop) ... B2
Glasshouse St ... B2	**Royal Children Inn ✦** ... C2
Goldsmith St ... B2	**Royal Concert Hall ✦** ... B2
Goose Gate ... B3	St Ann's Hill Rd. ... A2
Great Freeman St ... A2	St Ann's Way ... A2
Guildhall ✦ ... B2	St Ann's Well Rd ... A3
Hamilton Dr ... C1	**St Barnabas ✝** ... B1
Hampden St. ... A1	St James' St. ... B2
Heathcote St ... B3	St Mark's St. ... B3
High Pavement ... C3	St Mary's Garden of Rest ... B3
High School (Tram stop) ... A1	St Mary's Gate. ... B3
Holles Cr ... B3	**St Nicholas ✝** ... C2
Hope Dr ... C2	**St Peter's ✝** ... C2
Hungerhill Rd ... A3	St Peter's Gate ... B2
Huntingdon Dr ... C1	**Salutation Inn ✦** ... C2
Huntingdon St. ... A2	Shakespeare St. ... B2
Ice Centre ... C3	Shelton St ... A2
Information Ctr [i] ... B2	South Pde ... B2
Instow Rise ... A3	South Rd ... C1
Int Community Ctr ... A2	South Sherwood St ... B2
Kent St ... B3	Station St. ... C3
King St ... B2	Station Street (Tram stop) ... C3
Lace Market (Tram stop) ... B3	Stoney St. ... B3
Lamartine St. ... B3	Talbot St. ... B1
Lenton Rd ... C1	**Tales of Robin Hood ✦** ... C1
Lewis Cl ... A3	Tattershall Dr. ... C1
Lincoln St. ... B2	Tennis Dr ... B1
London Rd ... C3	Tennyson St. ... A1
Long Row ... B2	The Park. ... C1
Low Pavement ... C2	The Ropewalk ... B1
Lower Parliament St. ... B3	**Theatre Royal ✦** ... B2
Magistrates Court ... C2	Trent St. ... C2
Maid Marian Way ... B2	Trent Univ ... A2/B2
Mansfield Rd. ... A2/B2	Trent University (Tram stop) ... B2
Middle Hill ... C2	**Trip To Jerusalem Inn ✦** ... C2
Milton St ... B2	Union Rd ... B3
Mount St ... B2	Upper Parliament St. ... B2
Newcastle Dr ... B1	Victoria Centre ... B2
Newdigate House ✦ ... C2	Victoria Leisure Centre. ... B3
Newstead Gr ... A2	Victoria Park ... B3
North Sherwood St. ... A2	Victoria St. ... B2
Nottingham 🚉 ... C3	Walter St ... A1
Old Market Square (Tram stop) ... B2	Warser Gate. ... B3
Oliver St. ... A1	Watkin St. ... A2
Park Dr. ... C1	Waverley St. ... A1
Park Row ... B1	Wheeler Gate. ... B2
Park Terr. ... B1	Wilford Rd ... C2
Park Valley ... C1	Wilford St. ... C2
Peas Hill Rd. ... A3	**Willoughby House ✦** ... C2
Peel St ... B1	Wollaton St. ... B2
Pelham St ... B2	Woodborough Rd ... A2
Peveril Dr. ... C1	Woolpack La ... B3
Plantagenet St ... A3	York St ... B2
Playhouse ✦ ... B1	
Plumptre St ... C3	
Police Station 🛡 ... B2	
Poplar St ... C3	
Portland Rd ... B1	

ℹ City Information Centre,
1-4 Smithy Row, Nottingham
NG1 2BS Tel 0115 915 5330

📻 **BBC Radio Nottingham** 103.8 FM
Classic Gold GEM 999 AM
Saga 106.6 FM • **Trent** 96.2 FM

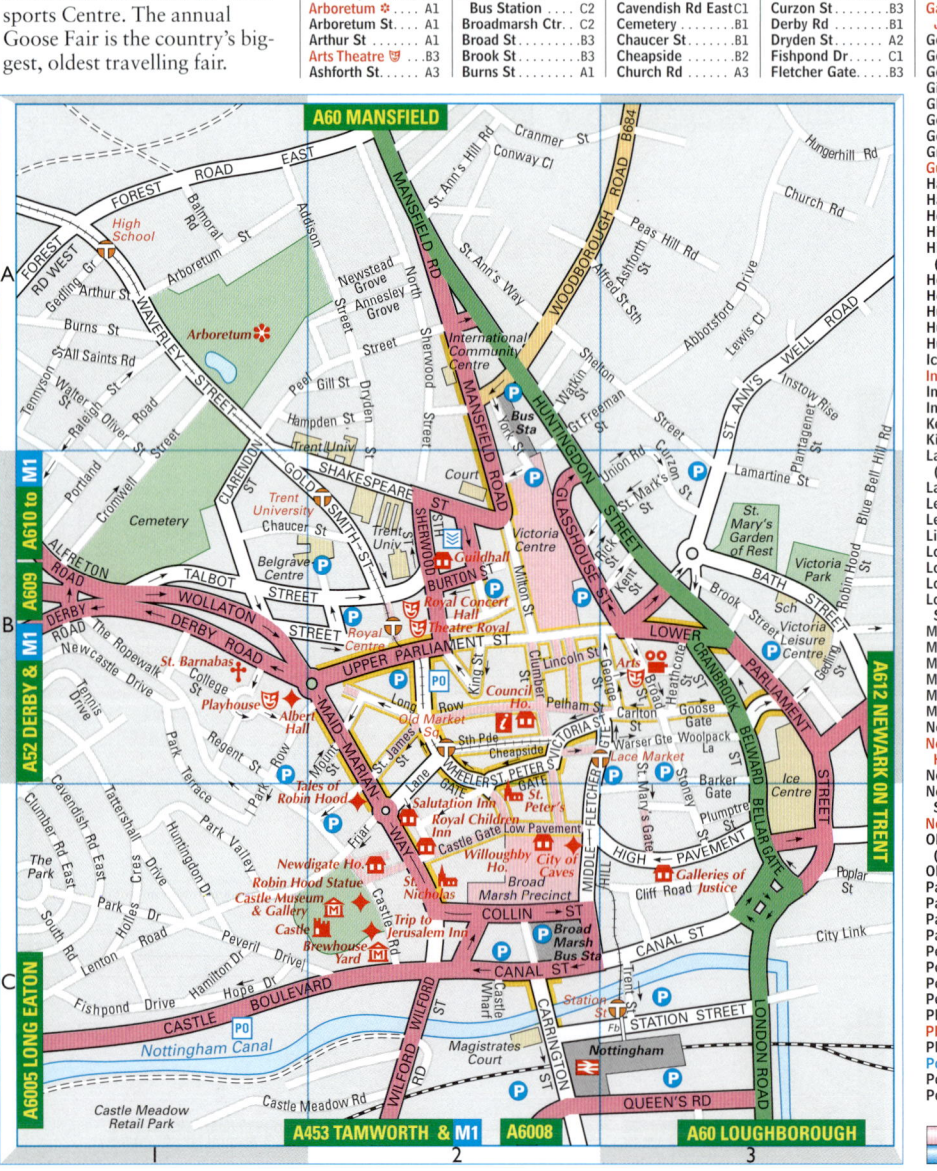

💻 www.nottinghamcity.gov.uk

116

Oban

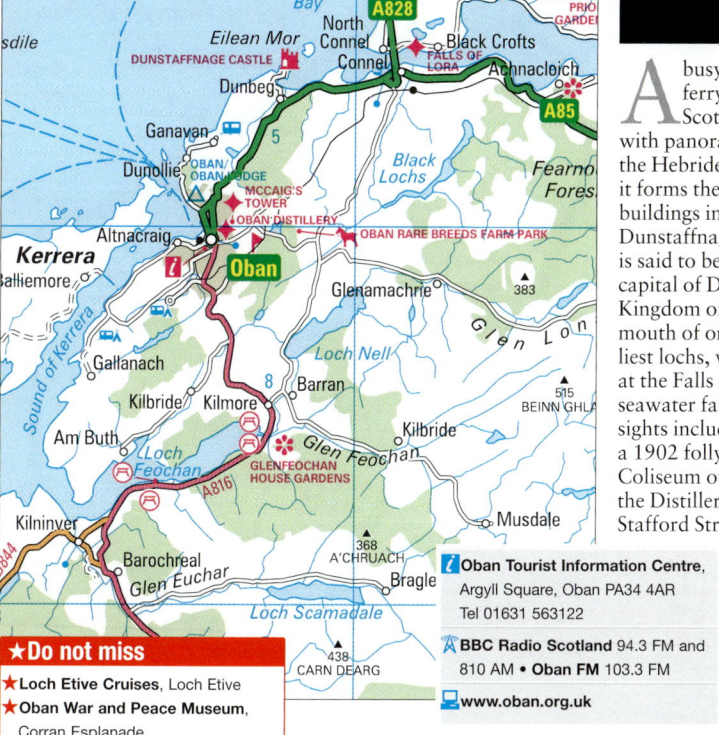

A busy port, resort and ferry terminal on Scotland's west coast, with panoramic views towards the Hebrides islands to which it forms the gateway. Historic buildings include 13th-century Dunstaffnage Castle, on what is said to be the site of the capital of Dalriada (the original Kingdom of the Scots) at the mouth of one of Scotland's loveliest lochs, which forms rapids at the Falls of Lora, the only seawater falls in Europe. Other sights include McCaig's Tower, a 1902 folly in the form of the Coliseum overlooking the town, the Distillery Visitor Centre on Stafford Street, the Rare Breeds Farm Park, and the Zoological World. The surrounding waters attract watersports enthusiasts, and there are several local marinas from which boat trips are run. Nearby attractions include the gardens of Barguillean, Achnacloich and Ardchattan Priory.

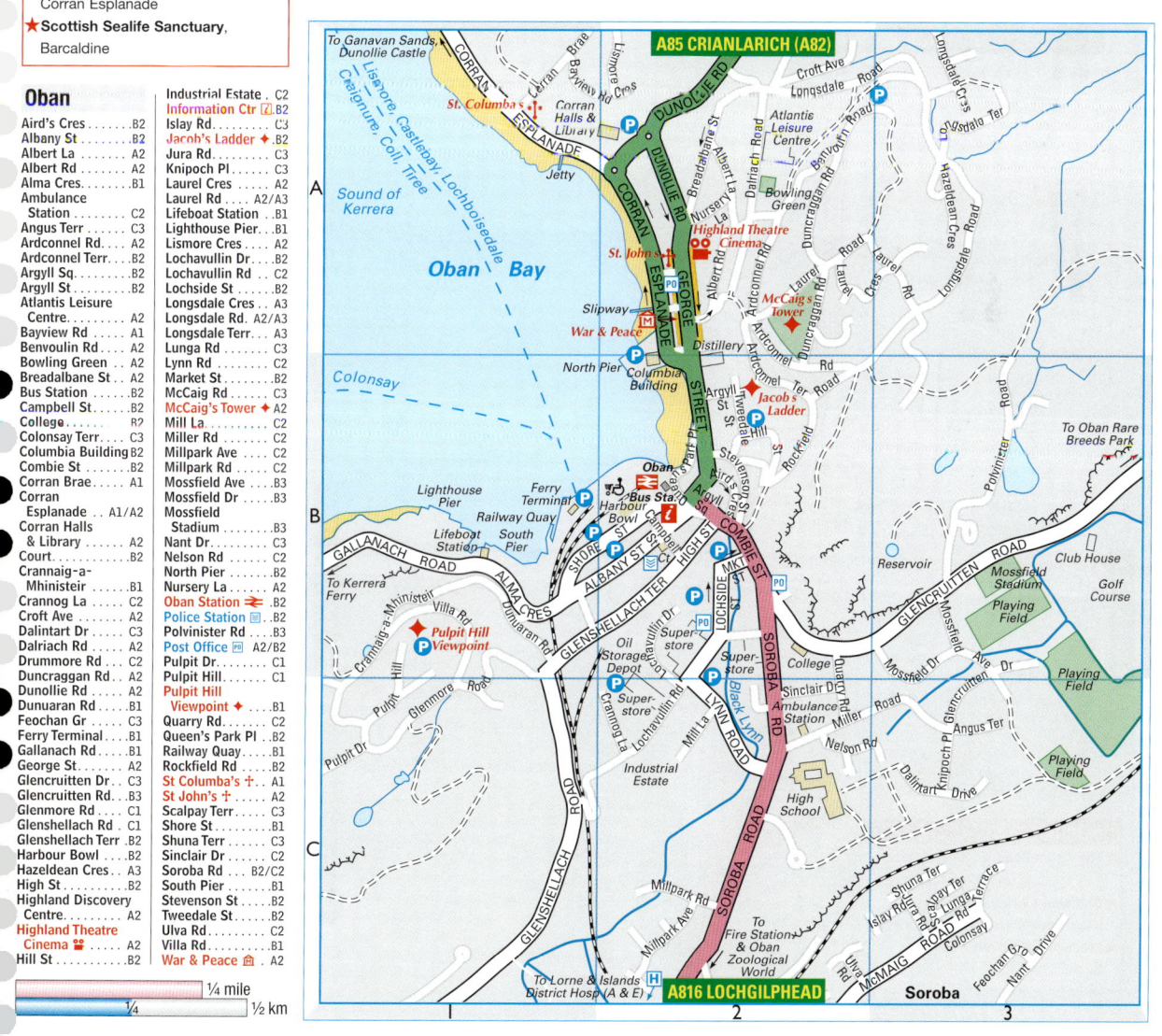

▲Oban, looking towards Lismore

Oban Tourist Information Centre,
Argyll Square, Oban PA34 4AR
Tel 01631 563122

BBC Radio Scotland 94.3 FM and 810 AM • **Oban FM** 103.3 FM

www.oban.org.uk

★ Do not miss
- ★ **Loch Etive Cruises**, Loch Etive
- ★ **Oban War and Peace Museum**, Corran Esplanade
- ★ **Scottish Sealife Sanctuary**, Barcaldine

Oban

Street	Grid
Aird's Cres	B2
Albany St	B2
Albert La	A2
Albert Rd	A2
Alma Cres	B1
Ambulance Station	C2
Angus Terr	C3
Ardconnel Rd	A2
Ardconnel Terr	B2
Argyll Sq	B2
Argyll St	B2
Atlantis Leisure Centre	A2
Bayview Rd	A1
Benvoulin Rd	A2
Bowling Green	A2
Breadalbane St	A2
Bus Station	B2
Campbell St	B2
College	B2
Colonsay Terr	A2
Columbia Building	B2
Combie St	B2
Corran Brae	A1
Corran Esplanade	A1/A2
Corran Halls & Library	A2
Court	B2
Crannaig-a-Mhinisteir	B1
Crannog La	C2
Croft Ave	A2
Dalintart Dr	C3
Dalriach Rd	A2
Drummore Rd	C2
Duncraggan Rd	A2
Dunollie Rd	A2
Dunuaran Rd	B1
Feochan Gr	C3
Ferry Terminal	B1
Gallanach Rd	B1
George St	A2
Glencruitten Dr	C3
Glencruitten Rd	B3
Glenmore Rd	C1
Glenshellach Rd	C1
Glenshellach Terr	B2
Harbour Bowl	B2
Hazeldean Cres	A3
High St	B2
Highland Discovery Centre	A2
Highland Theatre Cinema	A2
Hill St	B2
Industrial Estate	C2
Information Ctr	B2
Islay Rd	C3
Jacob's Ladder	B2
Jura Rd	C3
Knipoch Pl	C1
Laurel Cres	A2
Laurel Rd	A2/A3
Lifeboat Station	B1
Lighthouse Pier	B1
Lismore Cres	A2
Lochavullin Dr	B2
Lochavullin Rd	C2
Lochside St	B2
Longsdale Cres	A3
Longsdale Rd	A2/A3
Longsdale Terr	A3
Lunga Rd	C3
Lynn Rd	C2
Market St	B2
McCaig Rd	C3
McCaig's Tower	A2
Mill La	B2
Miller Rd	C2
Millpark Ave	C2
Millpark Rd	C2
Mossfield Ave	B3
Mossfield Dr	B3
Mossfield Stadium	B3
Nant Dr	C3
Nelson Rd	C2
North Pier	B2
Nursery La	A2
Oban Station	B2
Police Station	B2
Polvinister Rd	B3
Post Office	A2/B2
Pulpit Dr	C1
Pulpit Hill	C1
Pulpit Hill Viewpoint	B1
Quarry Rd	C2
Queen's Park Pl	B2
Railway Quay	B1
Rockfield Rd	B2
St Columba's †	A1
St John's †	A2
Scalpay Terr	C3
Shore St	B1
Shuna Terr	C3
Sinclair Dr	C2
Soroba Rd	B2/C2
South Pier	B1
Stevenson St	B2
Tweedale St	B2
Ulva Rd	C2
Villa Rd	B1
War & Peace	A2

¼ mile / ½ km

Oxford

A world-famous university city, founded by Alfred the Great and centre of learning since the 12th century. Christ Church Cathedral is among the city's oldest buildings. Museums and galleries include the Museum of Oxford, about the city and University; The Oxford Story, about the University; Handson, an interactive science exhibition; the Pitt Rivers Museum of anthropology and world archaeology; and Christ Church Gallery. The University also owns the lovely Botanic Garden and Harcourt Arboretum. Oxford has a wide selection of shops, with the Covered Market offering an eclectic range from butchers to boot shops via cakes and candles. There are countless alehouses, and restaurants of all nations.

▲ Radcliffe Camera

The Oxford Information Centre, 15-16 Broad Street, Oxford OX1 3AS
Tel 01865 726811

BBC Radio Oxford 95.2 FM
Fox 102.6 FM • Passion 107.9 FM

www.oxford.gov.uk

Oxford

Adelaide St A1
All Souls (Coll) . . . B2
Ashmolean Mus B2
Balliol (Coll) B2
Banbury Rd A2
Beaumont St B1
Becket St B1
Blackhall Rd A2
Blue Boar St B2
Bodleian Library B2
Botanic Garden . . B3
Brasenose (Coll) . . B2
Brewer St C2
Broad St B2
Burton-Taylor Theatre B2
Bus Station B1
Cardigan St A1
Carfax Tower . . . B2
Castle B1
Castle St B1
Catte St B2
Cemetery C1
Christ Church (Coll) B2
Christ Church . . . C2
Christ Church Meadow C2
Clarendon Centre . B2
Coach & Lorry Park C1
College of Further Education C1
Cornmarket St B2
Corpus Christi (Coll) B2
County Hall B1
Covered Market . . B2
Cowley Pl C3
Cranham St A1
Cranham Terr A1
Cricket Ground . . . B1
Crown & County Courts C2
Deer Park B3
Exeter (Coll) B2
Folly Bridge C2
George St B1
Great Clarendon St. A1
Hart St A1
Hertford (Coll) . . . B2
High St B2
HM Prison B1
Hollybush Row . . . B1
Holywell St B2
Hythe Bridge St . . B1
Ice Rink C1
Information Ctr . . B2
Jericho St A1
Jesus (Coll) B2
Jowett Walk B3
Juxon St A1
Keble (Coll) A2
Keble Rd A2
Library B2
Linacre (Coll) A3
Lincoln (Coll) B2
Little Clarendon St. A1
Longwall St B3
Magdalen (Coll) . . B3
Magdalen Bridge . B2
Magdalen St B2
Magistrate's Court C2
Manchester(Coll) . B2
Manor Rd B3
Mansfield(Coll) . . . A2
Mansfield Rd A3
Market B1
Marlborough Rd . . C2
Martyrs' Memorial B2
Merton Field B3
Merton (Coll). . . . B3
Merton St B3
Museum of Modern Art . . . B2
Museum of Oxford B2
Museum Rd A2
New College (Coll) B3
New Rd B1
New Theatre . . . B2
Norfolk St C1
Nuffield (Coll) . . . B1
Observatory A1
Observatory St. . . A1
Odeon B1/B2
Old Fire Station . . B1
Old Greyfriars St . . C2
Oriel (Coll) B2
Oxford Station . . B1
Oxpens Rd C1
Oxford Story, The ✦ B2
Paradise Sq C1
Paradise St B1
Park End St B1
Parks Rd A2/B2
Pembroke (Coll) . . C2
Phoenix A1
Picture Gallery . . C2
Plantation Rd A1
Playhouse B2
Police Station . . . C2
Post Office B2
Pusey St B1
Queen's La B3
Queen's (Coll) . . . B3
Radcliffe Camera B2
Radcliffe Infirmary A1
Rewley Rd B1
Richmond Rd A1
Rose La B3
Ruskin (Coll) B1
Said Business School A2
St Aldates C2
St Anne's (Coll) . . A1
St Antony's (Coll) . A1
St Bernard's Rd . . A1
St Catherine's (Coll) B3
St Cross Rd A3
St Edmund Hall (Coll) B3
St Giles St A2
St Hilda's (Coll) . . . C3
St John St B2
St John's (Coll) . . . B2
St Mary the Virgin B2
St Michael at the Northgate B2
St Peter's (Coll) . . . B1
St Thomas St B1
Science Area A2
Science Mus B2
Sheldonian Theatre B2
Somerville (Coll) . . A1
South Parks Rd . . A2
Speedwell St C2
Sports Ground . . . C3
Thames St C2
Town Hall B2
Trinity (Coll) B2
Turl St B2
University College (Coll) B3
University Mus & Pitt Rivers Mus . . . A2
University Parks . . A2
Wadham (Coll) . . . B2
Walton Cr A1
Walton St A1
Western Rd C1
Westgate Shopping Centre B2
Woodstock Rd . . . A1
Worcester (Coll) . . B1

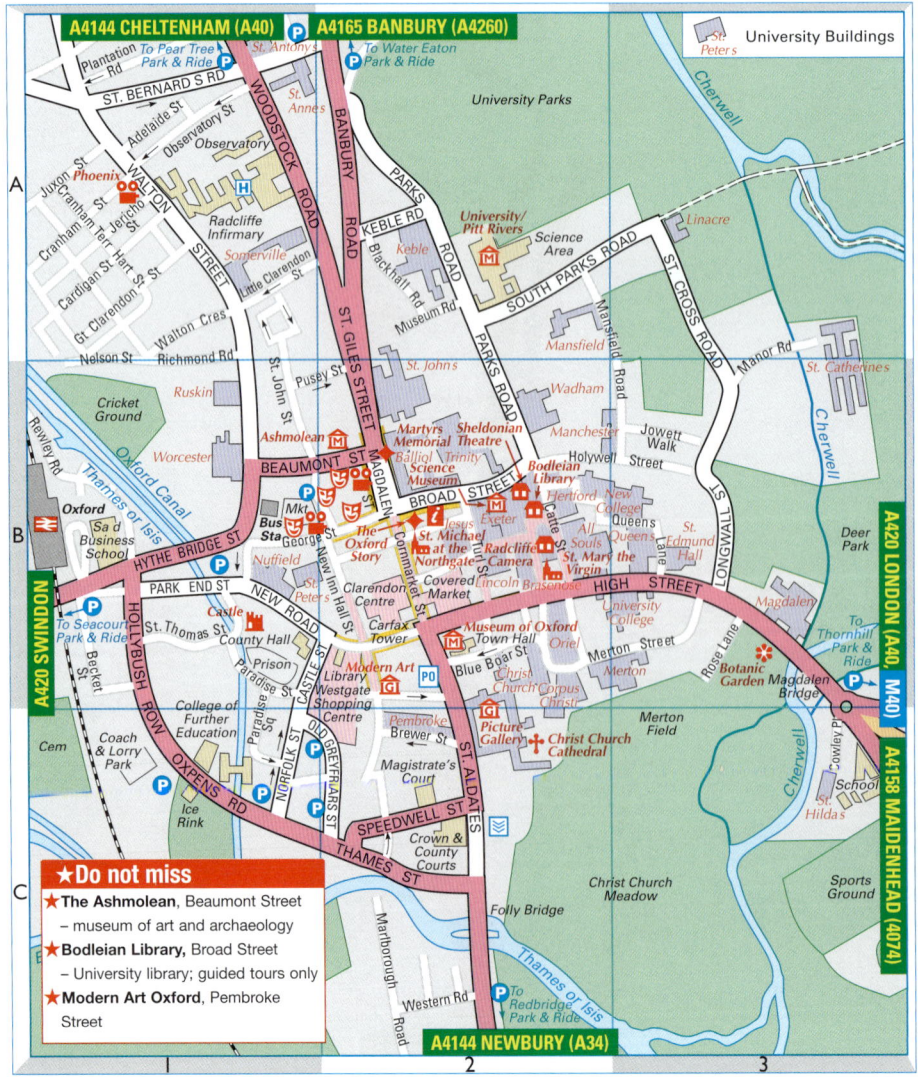

★ Do not miss

★ **The Ashmolean**, Beaumont Street – museum of art and archaeology
★ **Bodleian Library**, Broad Street – University library; guided tours only
★ **Modern Art Oxford**, Pembroke Street

Perth

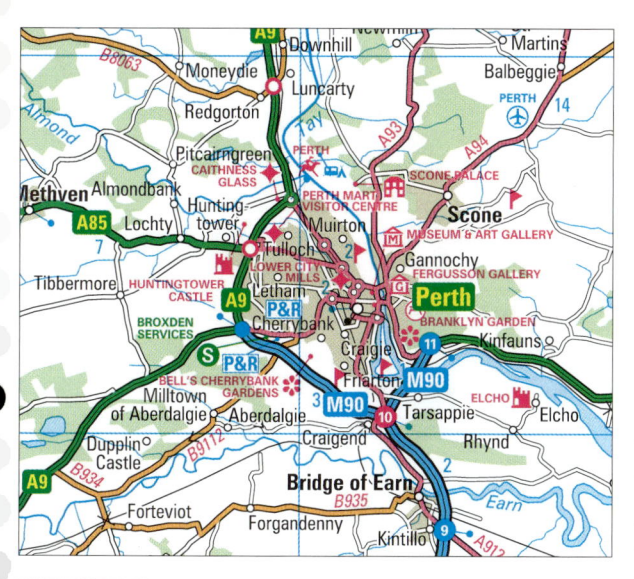

A market town known to the Romans as Bertha and dubbed 'the ancient capital of Scotland' for its role as a medieval royal residence; nearby Scone was the coronation site of all 42 Scottish kings until union with Britain. In the town centre visitors can explore the striking medieval St John's Kirk, the Perth Mart Visitor Centre tracing the area's agricultural history, the Museum and Art Gallery, the JD Fergusson Collection of art in the historic Round House, and the Caithness Glass Visitor Centre, and relax in Branklyn Gardens and the public parks of the North and South Inches. Houses to visit within easy reach include Elcho, Huntingtower Castle and Megginch Castle, while at nearby Abernethy is an 11th-century Round Tower and local-history museum. Perth Racecourse is just on the outskirts of the town, and just to the east is the Fairways Heavy Horse Centre with its Clydesdale horses.

▲ Scone Place

Perth Tourist Information Centre, Lower City Mills, West Mill Street, Perth PH1 5QP Tel 01738 450600

BBC Radio Scotland 93.5 FM and 810 AM • **Tay FM** 96.4
Tay AM 1584 AM • **Wave** 102.0 FM

www.perthshire.co.uk

★ Do not miss
★ **Balhousie Castle and Black Watch Regimental Museum**, Hay Street
★ **Cherrybank Gardens and Bells National Heather Collection**, Cherrybank
★ **Scone Place (early 1800s)**, Scone

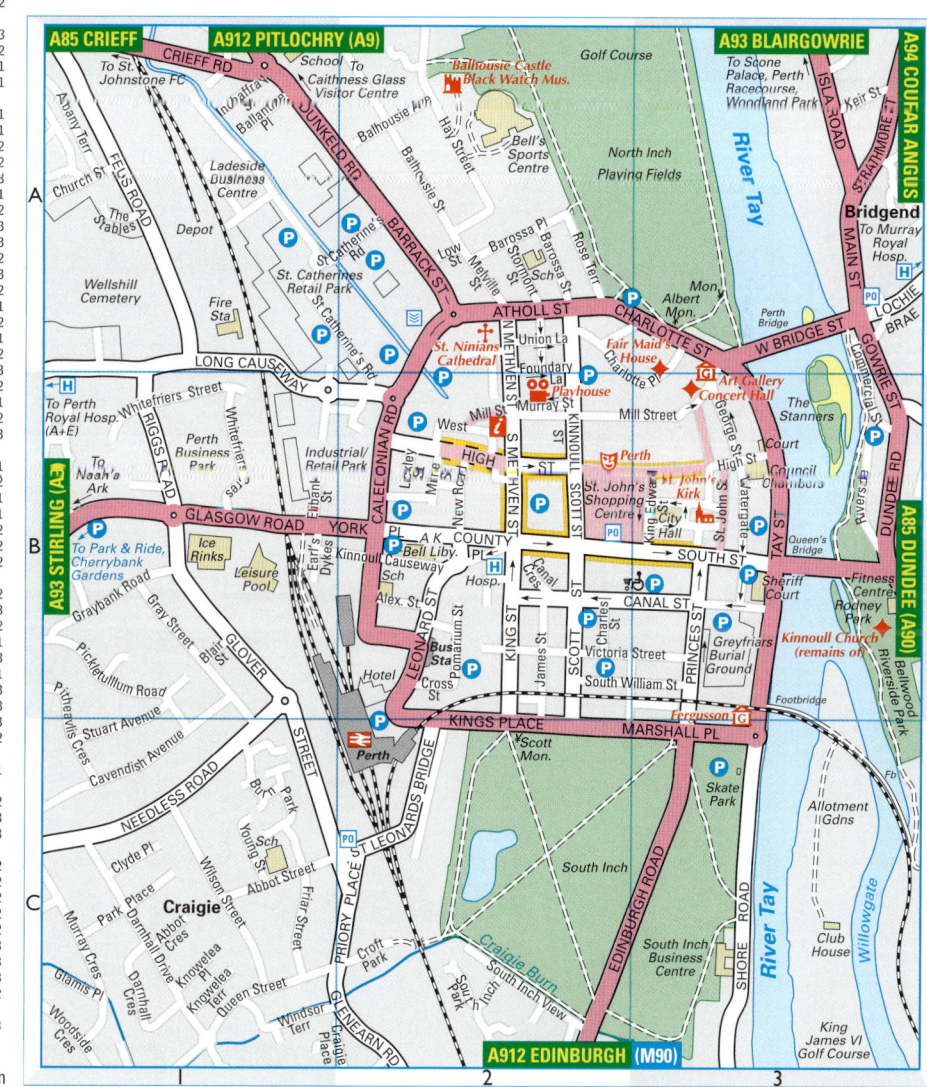

Perth

Name	Grid
A K Bell Library	B2
Abbot Cres	C1
Abbot St	C1
Albany Terr	A1
Albert Monument	A3
Alexandra St	B2
Art Gallery	B3
Atholl St	B2
Balhousie Ave	A2
Balhousie Castle Black Watch Museum	A2
Balhousie St	A2
Ballantine Pl	A1
Barossa Pl	A2
Barossa St	A2
Barrack St	A2
Bell's Sports Ctr	A2
Bellwood	B3
Blair St	B1
Burn Park	C1
Bus Station	B2
Caledonian Rd	B2
Canal Cres	B3
Canal St	B3
Cavendish Ave	C1
Charles St	B2
Charlotte Pl	A2
Charlotte St	A3
Church St	A1
City Hall	B3
Club House	C3
Clyde Pl	C1
Commercial St	A3
Concert Hall	B3
Council Chambers	B3
County Pl	B2
Court	B3
Craigie Pl	C2
Crieff Rd	A1
Croft Park	C2
Cross St	B2
Darnhall Cres	C1
Darnhall Dr	C1
Dundee Rd	B3
Dunkeld Rd	A1
Earl's Dykes	B1
Edinburgh Rd	C3
Elibank St	B1
Fair Maid's House	A3
Fergusson	B3
Feus Rd	A1
Fire Station	A1
Fitness Centre	B3
Foundary La	C1
Friar St	C1
George St	B3
Glamis Pl	C1
Glasgow Rd	B1
Glenearn Rd	C2
Glover St	B1/C1
Golf Course	A1
Gowrie St	A3
Gray St	B1
Graybank Rd	B1
Greyfriars Burial Ground	B3
Hay St	A2
High St	B2/B3
Hospital	B2
Hotel	B2
Ice Rinks	B1
Inchaffray St	A1
Industrial/Retail Park	B1
Information Ctr	B2
Isla Rd	A3
James St	B2
Keir St	A2
King Edward St	B3
King James VI Golf Course	C3
King St	B2
Kings Pl	B2
Kinnoull Causeway	B2
Kinnoull Church (Remains of)	B3
Kinnoull St	B2
Knowelea Pl	C1
Knowelea Terr	C1
Ladeside Business Centre	A1
Leisure Pool	B1
Leonard St	B2
Lickley St	B2
Lochie Brae	A3
Long Causeway	A1
Low St	A2
Main St	A3
Marshall Pl	C3
Melville St	A2
Mill St	B3
Milne St	B2
Murray Cres	C1
Murray St	B2
Needless Rd	C1
New Rd	B2
North Inch	A3
North Methven St	A2
Park Pl	C1
Perth	B2
Perth Bridge	A3
Perth Business Park	D1
Perth Station	C2
Pickletulllum Rd	B1
Pitheavlis Cres	C1
Playhouse	B2
Police Station	B2
Pomarium Rd	B2
Post Office	
Princes St	A3/B2/C2
Priory Pl	C2
Queen St	C1
Queen's Bridge	B3
Riggs Rd	B1
Riverside	B3
Riverside Park	B3
Rodney Park	B3
Rose Terr	A2
St Catherines Retail Park	A1
St Catherine's Rd	A1/A2
St John St	B3
St John's Kirk	B3
St John's Shopping Ctr	B2
St Leonards Br	C2
St Ninians	A2
Scott Monument	C2
Scott St	B2
Sheriff Court	B3
Shore Rd	C3
Skate Park	C3
South Inch	C2
South Inch Business Centre	C3
South Inch Park	C2
South Inch View	C2
South Methven St	B2
South St	B3
South William St	B2
Stormont St	A2
Strathmore St	A3
Stuart Ave	C1
Tay St	B3
The Stables	A1
The Stanners	B3
Union La	A2
Victoria St	B2
Watergate	B3
Wellshill Cem	A1
West Bridge St	A3
West Mill St	B2
Whitefriars Cres	B1
Whitefriars St	B1
Wilson St	C1
Windsor Terr	C1
Woodside Cres	A1
York Pl	B2
Young St	C1

Peterborough

★ Do not miss
- ★ **Flag Fen Excavations and Museum**, East of city
- ★ **Nene Valley Railway**, half a mile from Peterborough station
- ★ **Peterborough Cathedral and Tomb of Katherine of Aragon**, Cathedral Square

An ancient cathedral city and thriving modern business centre on the site of a Roman fortified town established c.AD 43, with an important Bronze Age archaeological site at nearby Flag Fen. Later a major pottery production centre, it was also the site of a Saxon monastery built by Paeda, King of Mercia, in AD 654, over which the splendid Norman cathedral was constructed. Other buildings of historical interest include Longthorpe Tower (1300) with its medieval wall paintings, and Thorpe Hall, a mansion built under Cromwell with gardens open to the public, and there's a Museum and Art Gallery. The best green space is Ferry Meadows, focal point of Nene Park, with 50 acres of riverside meadows, woods and lakes and a host of sports activities.

▲ Peterborough Cathedral

i Peterborough Tourist Information Centre, 3-5 Minster Precincts, Peterborough PE11XS
Tel 01733 452336

BBC Radio Cambridgeshire
95.7 FM • Classic Gold 1332 AM
Hereward 102.7 FM • Lite 106.8 FM

🌐 www.peterborough.gov.uk

Peterborough

Bishop's Palace	B2
Bishop's Rd	B2/B3
Boongate	A3
Bourges Blvd	A1
Bread St	C1
Bourges Retail Park	B1/B2
Bridge House (Council Offices)	C2
Bridge St	B2
Bright St	A1
Broadway	A2
Broadway	A2
Brook St	A2
Burghley Rd	A2
Bus Station	B2
Cavendish St	A3
Charles St	A3
Church St	B2
Church Walk	A2
Cobden Ave	A1
Cobden St	A1
Cowgate	B2
Craig St	A2
Crawthorne Rd	A2
Cripple Sidings La	C2
Cromwell Rd	A1
Dickens St	A3
Eastfield Rd	A3
Eastgate	B3
Fire Station	A1
Fletton Ave	C2
Frank Perkins Parkway	C3
Geneva St	A2
George St	C1
Gladstone St	A1
Glebe Rd	C2
Gloucester Rd	C3
Granby St	B3
Grove St	C1
Guildhall	B2
Hadrians Ct	C3
Henry St	A2
Hereward Rd	B3
Information Ctr	B2
Jubilee St	C1
Key Theatre	B2
Kent Rd	B1
Kirkwood Cl	B1
Lea Gdns	B1
Library	A2
Lincoln Rd	A1
London Rd	C2
Long Causeway	B2
Lower Bridge St	C2
Magistrates Court	B2
Manor House St	A2
Mayor's Walk	A1
Midland Rd	A1
Monument St	A2
Museum & Art Gallery	B2
Nene Valley Railway	C1
New Rd	A2
New Rd	C1
North Minster	A2
Old Customs House	C2
Oundle Rd	C1
Padholme Rd	A3
Palmerston Rd	C1
Park Rd	A2
Passport Office	B2
Peterborough District Hospital (A&E)	B1
Peterborough ⇌	B1
Peterborough Nene Valley Station	A1
Peterborough United FC	C2
Police Station	B2
Post Office	A3/B1/B2/B3/C1
Priestgate	B2
Queen's Walk	C2
Queensgate Ctr	B2
Railworld	C1
River La	B1
Rivergate Shopping Centre	B2
Riverside Mead	C3
Russell St	A1
St John's	B2
St John's St	A3
St Mark's St	A2
St Peter's †	B2
St Peter's Rd	B2
Saxon Rd	A3
Spital Bridge	A1
Stagshaw Dr	C3
Star Rd	A3
Thorpe Lea Rd	B1
Thorpe Rd	B1
Thorpe's Lea Rd	B1
Town Hall	B2
Viersen Platz	B2
Vineyard Rd	B3
Wake Rd	B3
Wellington St	A3
Wentworth St	B2
Westgate	B2
Whalley St	A3
Wharf Rd	C1
Whitsed St	A3
YMCA	A3

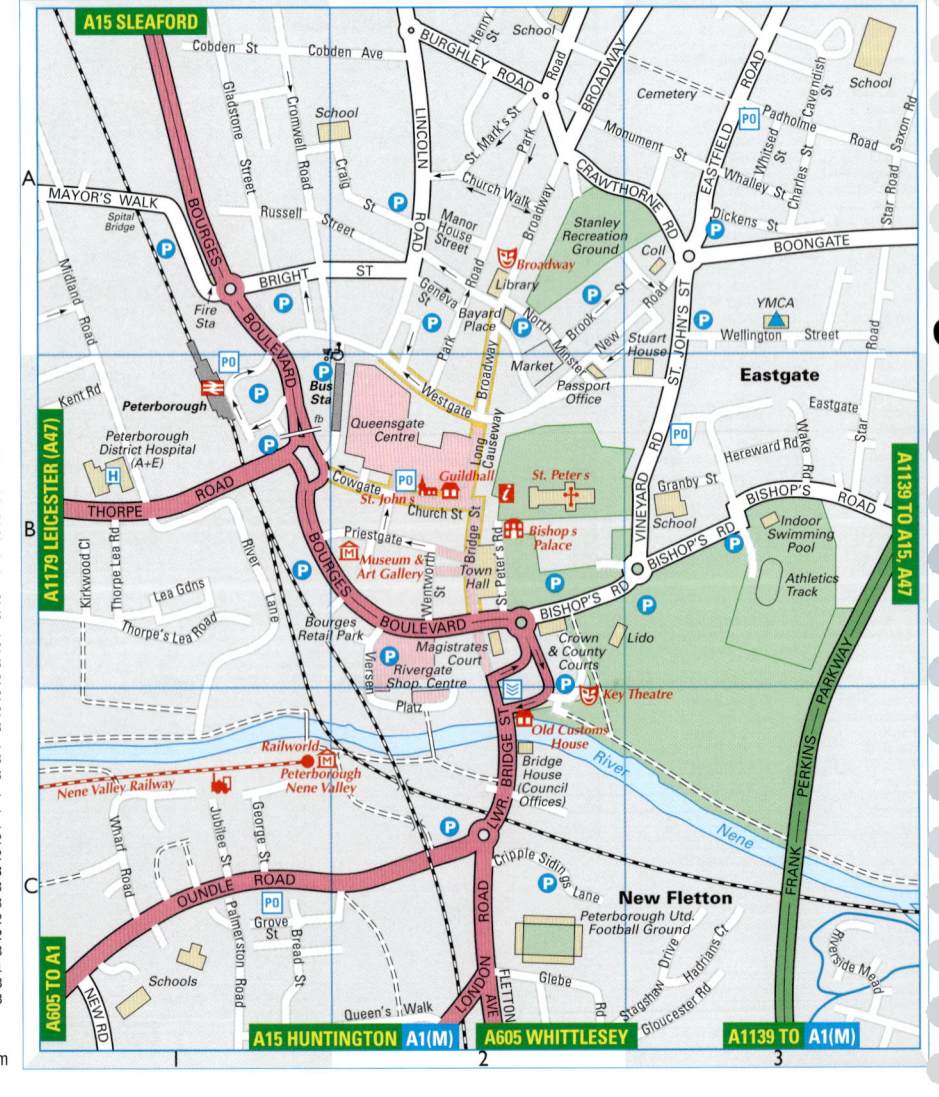

¼ mile / ½ km

Plymouth

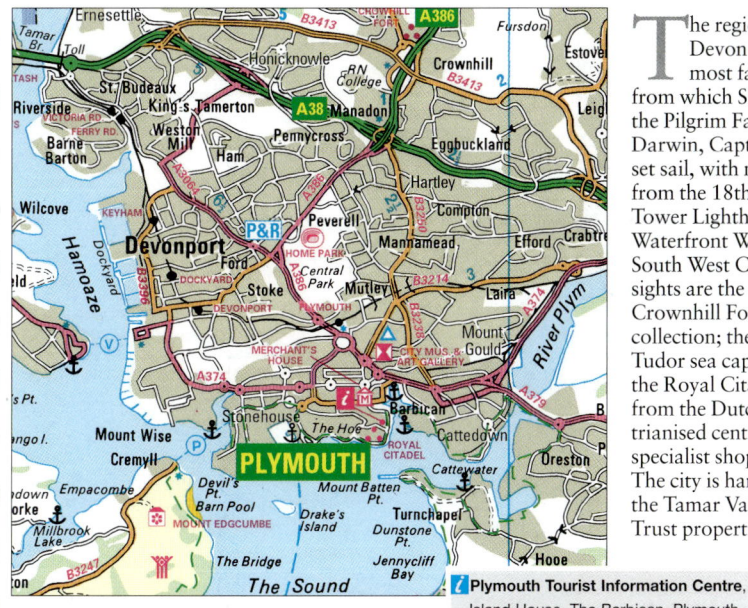

The regional capital of Devon and Cornwall, most famous as the city from which Sir Francis Drake, the Pilgrim Fathers, Charles Darwin, Captain Cook and others set sail, with magnificent views from the 18th-century Smeaton's Tower Lighthouse and from the Waterfront Walkway (part of the South West Coast Path). Other sights are the mid-18th-century Crownhill Fort with its artillery collection; the Black Friars gin distillery; the Elizabethan House, a Tudor sea captain's home; the City Museum and Art Gallery; and the Royal Citadel, built in the 17th century to defend the coastline from the Dutch. There are excellent shopping facilities in the pedestrianised centre and the narrow streets of The Barbican, with its specialist shops, craft workshops, art galleries, restaurants and cafes. The city is handy for Dartmoor National Park and Wildlife Park, the Tamar Valley Area of Outstanding Natural Beauty, the National Trust properties Saltram House and Antony House, Mount Edgcumbe House and Country Park and Mary Newman's Cottage, the family home of Drake's first wife.

▲ Smeaton's Tower and The Hoe

Plymouth Tourist Information Centre, Island House, The Barbican, Plymouth PL1 2LS Tel 01752 304849

BBC Radio Devon 103.4 FM and 855 AM • Classic Gold 1152 AM
Plymouth Sound 97 FM

www.visitplymouth.co.uk

★ Do not miss

★ **The Merchants House**, St Andrew's Street – features reconstructed Elizabethan chemist's shop
★ **National Marine Aquarium**, The Barbican
★ **Plymouth Dome**, The Hoe – local-history visitor centre

Plymouth

Name	Grid
ABC	B2
Alma Rd	A1
Anstis St	B1
Armada Centre	B2
Armada St	A3
Armada Way	B2
Art College	B2
Athenaeum St	C1
Athenaeum	B1
Barbican	C3
Barbican	C3
Baring St	B1
Bath St	B1
Beaumont Park	B3
Beaumont Rd	B3
Black Friars Gin Distillery	C2
Breton Side	B3
Bus Station	B3
Castle St	C3
Cathedral (RC)	B1
Cecil St	B1
Central Park	A1
Central Park Ave	A2
Charles Church	B3
Charles Cross (r'about)	B3
Charles St	B2
Citadel Rd	C2
Citadel Rd East	C2
Civic Centre	B2
Cliff Rd	C1
Clifton Pl	A3
Cobourg St	A2
Continental Ferry Port	B1
Cornwall St	B2
Dale Rd	A2
Deptford Pl	A3
Derry Ave	A2
Derry's Cross (r'about)	B1
Drake Circus	B2
Drake's Memorial	C2
Eastlake St	B2
Ebrington St	B3
Elizabethan House	C3
Elliot St	C1
Endsleigh Pl	A2
Exeter St	B3
Fire Station	A3
Fish Quay	C3
Gibbons St	A3
Glen Park Ave	A2
Grand Pde	C1
Great Western Rd	C1
Greenbank Rd	A3
Greenbank Terr	A3
Guildhall	B2
Hampton St	B3
Harwell St	B1
Hill Park Cr	A3
Hoe Approach	B2
Hoe Rd	C2
Hoegate St	C2
Houndiscombe Rd	A2
Information Ctr	C3
James St	A2
Kensington Rd	A3
King St	B1
Lambhay Hill	C3
Leigham St	C1
Library	B2
Lipson Rd	A3/B3
Lockyer St	C2
Lockyers Quay	C3
Madeira Rd	C2
Marina	B3
Market	B1
Market Ave	B2
Martin St	B1
Mayflower St	B2
Mayflower Stone & Steps	C3
Mayflower Visitor Ctr	C3
Merchants House	B2
Millbay Rd	B1
Museum & Art Gallery	B2
National Marine Aquarium	C3
Neswick St	B1
New George St	B2
New St	C3
North Cross (r'about)	A2
North Hill	A3
North Quay	B2
North Rd East	A2
North Rd West	A1
North St	B3
Notte St	B2
Octagon St	B1
Pennycomequick (r'about)	A1
Pier St	C1
Plymouth Dome	C2
Plymouth Pavilions	B1
Plymouth (station)	A2
Police Station	B3
Portland Sq	A2
Post Office	A1/A2/B2/C1
Princess St	B2
Prysten House	B2
Queen Anne's Battery Seasports Centre	C3
Radford Rd	C1
Regent St	B3
Rope Walk	C3
Royal Citadel	C2
Royal Pde	B2
St Andrew's	B2
St Andrew's Cross (r'about)	B2
St Andrew's St	B2
St Lawrence Rd	A2
Saltash Rd	A2
Smeaton's Tower	C2
Southern Terr	A3
Southside St	C2
Stuart Rd	A1
Sutherland Rd	A2
Sutton Rd	B3
Sydney St	A1
Teats Hill Rd	C3
The Crescent	B1
The Hoe	C2
The Octagon (r'about)	B1
The Promenade	C1
Theatre Royal	B2
Tothill Ave	B3
Union St	B1
Univ of Plymouth	A2
Vauxhall St	B2/3
Victoria Park	A1
West Hoe Rd	C1
Western Approach	B1
Whittington St	A1
Wyndham St	B1
YMCA	B2
YWCA	C2

Poole

An important Middle Ages port and modern Channel ferry terminus on Europe's largest natural harbour, in the middle of which lies the National Trust's wildlife-rich Brownsea Island, visitable by boat trip. The lively Quayside area with its cobbled streets and 18th-century architecture is home to the Poole Pottery factory shop and a wide range of shops, pubs, cafes and restaurants. Scalpens Court Museum, in Poole's most complete medieval domestic building, is open to the general public in August, and there's a small lifeboat museum. There are also 3 miles of sandy beaches popular with watersports enthusiasts, including the award-winning Sandbanks, the 100-acre Upton Country Park, and Compton Acres Gardens, and within close proximity are the National Trust's Corfe Castle and Kingston Lacy Italian Renaissance palazzo, Farmer Palmer's Farm Park, and some outstanding areas of natural beauty, including the New Forest and the Isle of Purbeck. Poole and adjoining Bournemouth are also home to the famous Chines (dry wooded ravines).

▲ Poole Harbour

★ Do not miss
- **Cockle Trail** – around the Quayside and Old Town
- **Upton Country Park**, A35
- **Waterfront Museum**, Lower High Street – Poole's social, domestic and maritime history

Poole Tourist Information Centre, Waterfront Museum, Lower High St, Poole BH15 1BW Tel 01202 253253

BBC Radio Solent 103.8 FM 1359 AM
Fire 107.6 FM • **Classic Gold** 828 AM

www.pooletourism.com

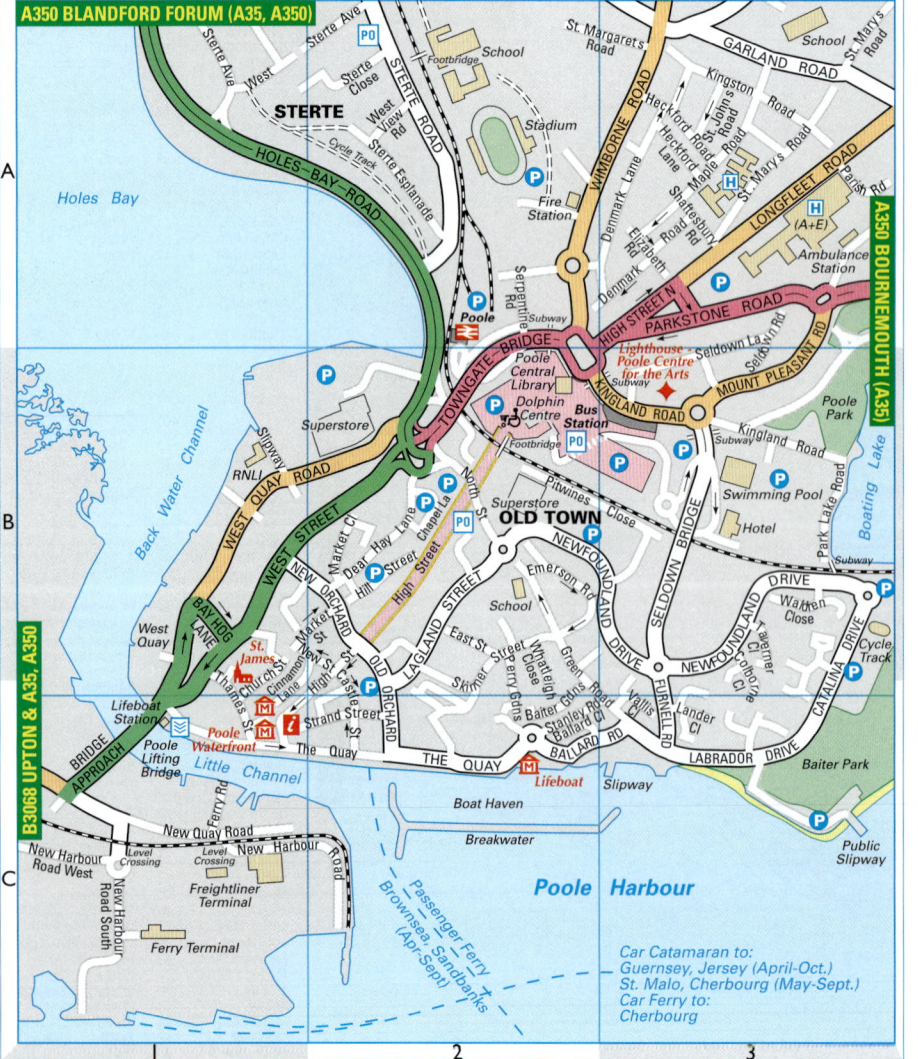

Poole

Ambulance Station	A3
Baiter Gdns	C2
Baiter Park	C3
Ballard Cl	C2
Ballard Rd	C2
Bay Hog La	B1
Bridge Approach	C1
Bus Station	B2
Castle St	B2
Catalina Dr	B3
Chapel La	B2
Church St	B1
Cinnamon La	B1
Colborne Cl	B3
Dear Hay La	B2
Denmark La	A3
Denmark Rd	A3
East St	B2
Elizabeth Rd	C1
Emerson Rd	B2
Ferry Rd	C1
Ferry Terminal	C1
Fire Station	A2
Freightliner Terminal	C1
Furnell Rd	B3
Garland Rd	A3
Green Rd	B2
Heckford La	A3
Heckford Rd	A3
High St	B2
High St North	A3
Hill St	B2
Holes Bay Rd	A1
Hospital (A&E)	A3
Information Ctr	C1
Kingland Rd	B3
Kingston Rd	A3
Labrador Dr	C3
Lagland St	B2
Lander Cl	C3
Lifeboat	C2
Lighthouse – Poole Centre for the Arts	B2
Longfleet Rd	A3
Maple Rd	A3
Market Cl	B2
Market St	B2
Mount Pleasant Rd	B3
New Harbour Rd	C1
New Harbour Rd South	C1
New Harbour Rd West	C1
New Orchard	B1
New Quay Rd	C1
New St	B2
Newfoundland Dr	B2
North St	B2
Old Orchard	B2
Parish Rd	A3
Park Lake Rd	B3
Parkstone Rd	A3
Perry Gdns	B2
Pitwines Cl	B2
Police Station	C1
Poole Lifting Br	C1
Poole Central Library	B2
Poole Park	B2
Poole Station	A2
Poole Waterfront Museum	B2
Post Office	A2/B2
RNLI	B2
St John's Rd	A3
St Margaret's Rd	A3
St Mary's Rd	A3
Seldown Bridge	B3
Seldown La	B3
Seldown Rd	B3
Serpentine Rd	C2
Shaftesbury Rd	A3
Skinner St	B2
Slipway	B1
Stanley Rd	C2
Sterte Ave	A2
Sterte Ave West	A1
Sterte Cl	A2
Sterte Esplanade	A2
Sterte Rd	A2
Strand St	C2
Swimming Pool	B3
Taverner Cl	B3
Thames St	B1
The Quay	B2
Towngate Bridge	B2
Vallis Cl	C3
Waldren Cl	B3
West Quay	B1
West Quay Rd	B1
West St	B1
West View Rd	A1
Whatleigh Cl	B2
Wimborne Rd	A3

Car Catamaran to:
Guernsey, Jersey (April–Oct.)
St. Malo, Cherbourg (May–Sept.)
Car Ferry to:
Cherbourg

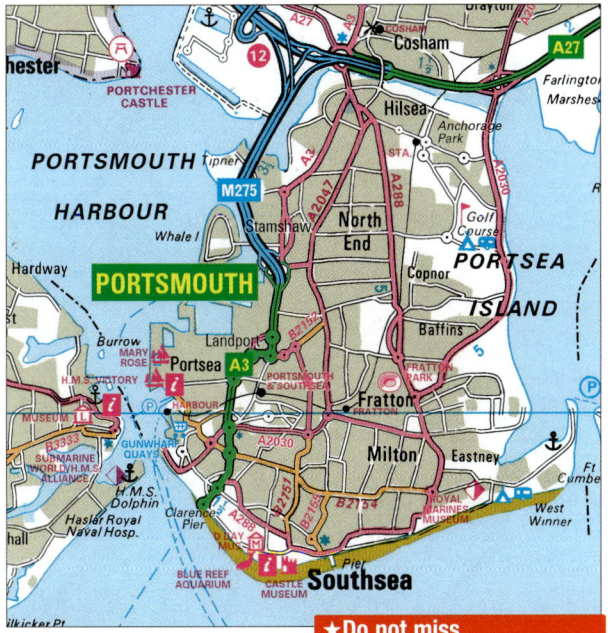

Portsmouth

The city of Portsmouth dates back to medieval times and has been home to the British Royal Navy for more than 500 years. The historic dockyard houses Nelson's flagship HMS *Victory*, HMS *Warrior*, 1860, Britain's first iron-clad battleship, the Royal Naval Museum and the remains of Henry VIII's 16th century warship, the *Mary Rose*. There is also a new interactive naval attraction – Action Stations. Other attractions include Charles Dickens' Birthplace Museum, the City Museum and the D-Day Museum. The Continental Ferry Port links the city with north-west France, northern Spain and the Channel Islands. St Thomas' Cathedral has maritime links as does the Garrison Church. Two major shopping centres serve the city – Cascades and Gunwharf Quays. The 170-m Spinnaker Tower's three viewing platforms allow views of up to 23 miles.

▲ HMS *Warrior*

Tourist Information Centre, The Hard, Portsmouth PO1 3QJ
Tel 023 9282 6722

BBC Radio Solent 96.1 FM, 999 AM
- **The Quay** 107.4 FM • **Capital Gold** 1170 AM • **Ocean** 97.5 FM
Power 103.2 FM • **Wave** 105.2 FM

www.visitportsmouth.co.uk

★ Do not miss

- ★ **HMS Victory**, HM Naval Base
- ★ **Royal Naval Museum**, HM Naval Base
- ★ **The Mary Rose**, HM Naval Base

Portsmouth

Action Stations ✦	A1
Admiralty Rd	A1
Alfred Rd	A2
Anglesea Rd	B2
Arundel St	B3
Bishop St	B1
Broad St	C1
Buckingham House	C2
Burnaby Rd	B2
Bus Station	B1
Camber Dock	C1
Cambridge Rd	B2
Car Ferry to Isle of Wight	A1
Cascades Shopping Centre	A3
Castle Rd	C3
Cathedral †	C1
Cathedral (RC) †	A3
City Museum & Art Gallery	B3
Civic Offices	B3
Clarence Pier	C2
College of Art	B3
College St	B1
Commercial Rd	A3
Cottage Gr	B3
Cross St	A1
Cumberland St	A2
Duisburg Way	C2
Durham St	B3
East St	B1
Edinburgh Rd	A2
Elm Gr	B3
Great Southsea St	C3
Green Rd	B3
Greetham St	B3
Grosvenor St	B3
Grove Rd North	B3
Grove Rd South	B3
Guildhall	B3
Guildhall Walk	B3
Gunwharf Quays Retail Park	B1
Gunwharf Rd	B1
Hambrook St	C2
Hampshire Terr	B2
Hanover St	A1
High St	C1
HM Naval Base	A1
HMS Nelson (Royal Naval Barracks)	A2
HMS Victory ⚓	A1
HMS Warrior ⚓	A1
Hovercraft Terminal	C2
Hyde Park Rd	B3
Information Ctr	A1/B3
Isambard Brunel Rd	B3
Isle of Wight Car Ferry Terminal	B1
Kent Rd	C3
Kent St	A2
King St	C2
King's Rd	C3
King's Terr	C2
Lake Rd	A3
Law Courts	B3
Library	B3
Long Curtain Rd	C2
Market Way	A3
Marmion Rd	C3
Mary Rose Exhibition	A1
Mary Rose Ship Hall	A1
Middle St	B3
Millennium Blvd	B2
Millennium Promenade	A1/C1
Museum Rd	B2
Naval Recreation Ground	C2
Nightingale Rd	C3
Norfolk St	B3
North St	A2
Osborne Rd	C3
Park Rd	B2
Passenger Catamaran to Isle of Wight	B1
Passenger Ferry to Gosport	B1
Pelham Rd	C3
Pembroke Gdns	C2
Pembroke Rd	C2
Pier Rd	C2
Point Battery	C1
Police Station	B3
Portsmouth & Southsea ⟷	A3
Portsmouth Harbour ⟷	B1
Post Office	A1/A3/B3/C3
Queen St	A1
Queen's Cr	C3
Round Tower ✦	C1
Royal Garrison Church	C1
Royal Naval Museum	A1
St Edward's Rd	C3
St George's Rd	B2
St George's Sq	B1
St George's Way	B2
St James's Rd	B3
St James's St	A2
St Thomas's St	B2
Somers Rd	B3
Southsea Com	C2
Southsea Terr	C2
Station St	B3
Spinnaker Tower ✦	B1
Square Tower ✦	C1
Swimming Pool	A2
The Hard	B1
Town Fortifications ✦	C1
Unicorn Rd	A2
United Services Recreation Ground	B2
University of Portsmouth	A2/B2
Upper Arundel St	A3
Victoria Park	A2
Victory Gate	A1
Vue	B1
Warblington St	B1
Western Pde	C2
White Hart Rd	C1
Winston Churchill Ave	B3

123

Preston

One of England's oldest boroughs, dating back to 670 AD, Preston was a wealthy market town by the 17th century and became an important cotton and textile finishing centre in the 19th century. It boasts the largest single dock basin in Europe, Riversway, containing a marina, leisure complex and shops. Interesting structures are Giles Gilbert Scott's classical Cenotaph; the 1903 neo-Baroque Sessions house; the Harris Museum and Art Gallery; Winckley Square, a Georgian development. Outdoor attractions include Avenham Park with its Japanese rock gardens. The Forest of Bowland Area of Outstanding Natural Beauty, home to a Wild Boar Park and the Beacon Fell moorland with its sculptures and visitor centre, is within easy reach. Nearby is Samlesbury Hall Tudor manor and Hoghton Tower, a 16th-century Renaissance house and the Ribble Steam Railway.

▲ Preston marina

Tourist Information Centre, Guild Hall, Lancaster Road, Preston PR1 1HT Tel 01772 253731

BBC Radio Lancashire 103.9 FM
Magic 999 AM • **Rock** 97.4 FM

www.visitpreston.com

★ Do not miss
- ★ **Museum of Lancashire and Museum of the Queen's Lancashire Regiment**, Stanley Street
- ★ **National Football Museum**, Sir Tom Finney Way, Deepdale
- ★ **Ribble Way** – footpath from Preston estuary to Ribblehead

Street	Grid
Adelphi St	A2
Anchor Ct	B3
Aqueduct St	A1
Ardee Rd	C1
Arthur St	B2
Ashton St	A1
Avenham La	B3
Avenham Park	C3
Avenham Rd	B3
Avenham St	B3
Bairstow St	B3
Balderstone Rd	C1
Beamont Dr	A1
Beech St South	C2
Bird St	C1
Bow La	B2
Brieryfield Rd	A1
Broadgate	C1
Brook St	A2
Bus Station	A3
Butler St	B2
Cannon St	B3
Carlton St	A1
Chaddock St	B3
Channel Way	B1
Chapel St	B3
Christ Church St	B2
Christian Rd	B2
Cold Bath St	A2
Coleman Ct	C1
Connaught Rd	C2
Corn Exchange	B3
Corporation St	A2/B2
County Hall	B3
County Records Office	A3
Court	A3
Court	B3
Cricket Ground	C2
Croft St	A1
Cross St	B3
Crown Court	B3
Crown St	A3
East Cliff	C3
East Cliff Rd	B3
Edward St	B3
Elizabeth St	A3
Euston St	B1
Fishergate	B2/B3
Fishergate Hill	B2
Fishergate Shopping Ctr	B2
Fitzroy St	B3
Fleetwood St	A1
Friargate	A3
Fylde Rd	A1/A2
Gerrard St	B2
Glover's Ct	B3
Good St	B2
Grafton St	B3
Great George St	A3
Great Shaw St	A3
Greenbank St	A3
Guild Way	B1
Guildhall & Charter	B3
Guildhall St	B3
Harrington St	A2
Harris Mus	B3
Hartington Rd	B1
Hasset Cl	C2
Heatley St	B2
Hind St	C2
Information Ctr	B3
Kilruddery Rd	C1
Lancaster Rd	A3/B3
Latham St	B3
Lauderdale St	C2
Lawson St	A3
Leighton St	A2
Leyland Rd	C1
Library	A1
Library	B3
Liverpool Rd	C1
Lodge St	B2
Lune St	B3
Main Street West	B3
Maresfield Rd	C1
Market St West	A3
Marsh La	B1/B2
Maudland Bank	A2
Maudland Rd	A2
Meadow Ct	C2
Meath Rd	C1
Mill Hill	C2
Miller Arcade	B3
Miller Park	C3
Moor La	A3
Mount St	B3
North Rd	A3
North St	A3
Northcote Rd	B1
Old Milestones	B1
Old Tram Rd	C3
Pedder St	A1/A2
Peel St	A2
Penwortham Br	C2
Penwortham New Br	C1
Pitt St	B2
Playhouse	B3
Police Station	A3
Port Way	B1
Post Office	A1/B3//C1
Preston	B3
Ribble Bank St	B2
Ribble Viaduct	C3
Ribblesdale Pl	B3
Ringway	B3
River Parade	C1
Riverside	C2
St Georges	B3
St Georges Shopping Ctr	B3
St Johns	B3
St Johns Shopping Ctr	A3
St Mark's Rd	A1
St Walburges	A1
Salisbury Rd	B1
Sessions House	B3
Snow Hill	A3
South End	C2
South Meadow La	C2
Spa Rd	B1
Sports Ground	C2
Strand Rd	B1
Syke St	B3
Talbot Rd	B1
Taylor St	C1
Tithebarn St	A3
Town Hall	B3
Tulketh Brow	A1
Univ of Central Lancashire	A2
Valley Rd	C1
Victoria St	A2
Walker St	A3
Walton's Parade	A3
Warwick St	A3
Wellfield Business Park	A1
Wellfield Rd	A1
Wellington St	A1
West Cliff	C2
West Strand	C1
Winckley Rd	C1
Winckley Square	B3
Wolseley Rd	

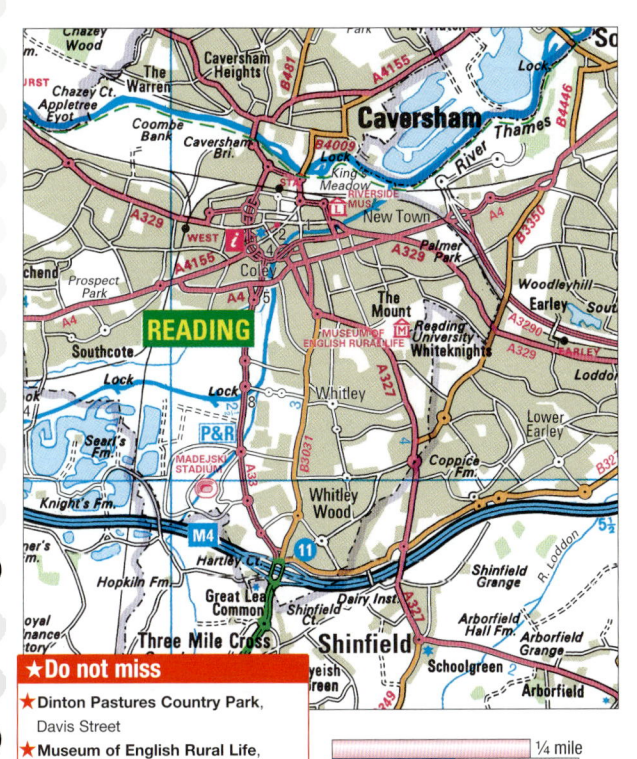

Reading

The Saxon-origin county town of Royal Berkshire, burial place of Henry I, has a wealth of medieval churches, old coaching inns and red-brick Victorian buildings, though today it's best known as a retail centre, transport hub and focus of hi-tech industry. Landmarks in its historic centre include the Gothic town hall, also home to the Museum and Art Gallery (including Roman items and a copy of the Bayeux Tapestry); Forbury Gardens, once part of Reading Abbey, the ruins of which can still be seen; and Reading Gaol, the most famous inmate of which was Oscar Wilde. The University has a museum of Greek archaeology and a museum of zoology. The nearby Herb Farm at Sonning has one of the UK's biggest collections of herbal plants and a Saxon maze, Stratfield Saye has memorabilia of the Duke of Wellington, and Mapledurham House is an Elizabethan mansion with one of the country's last working watermills.

▲ Kennet and Avon canal and River Thames

Reading Visitor Centre and Travel Shop, Church House, Chain Street, Reading RG2 7HD Tel 0118 956 6226

BBC Radio Berkshire 104.4 FM
Classic Gold 1431 AM
Reading 107 FM • 2-Ten 97.0 FM

www.readingtourism.org.uk

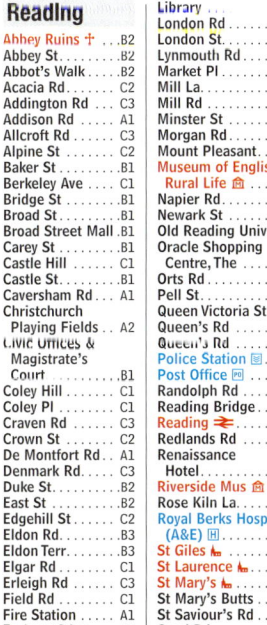

★ Do not miss

★ **Dinton Pastures Country Park**, Davis Street
★ **Museum of English Rural Life**, University of Reading, Shinfield Road
★ **Riverside Museum at Blake's Lock**, New Town – about the Kennet and Thames rivers

Reading

Abbey Ruins † B2	Library ....B?	
Abbey St. B2	London Rd C3	
Abbot's Walk B2	London St............B1	
Acacia Rd. C2	Lynmouth Rd A1	
Addington Rd C3	Market Pl B2	
Addison Rd A1	Mill La................B1	
Allcroft Rd C3	Mill Rd A2	
Alpine St C2	Minster St B1	
Baker St B1	Morgan Rd C3	
Berkeley Ave C1	Mount Pleasant....C2	
Bridge St B1	Museum of English	
Broad St B1	Rural Life C3	
Broad Street Mall ...B1	Napier Rd A2	
Carey St B1	Newark St C2	
Castle Hill C1	Old Reading Univ..C3	
Castle St..............B1	Oracle Shopping	
Caversham Rd......A1	Centre, The B1	
Christchurch	Orts Rd B3	
Playing Fields A2	Pell St C1	
Civic Offices &	Queen Victoria St..B1	
Magistrate's	Queen's Rd A2	
Court	Queen's Rd B1	
Coley Hill C1	Police Station B1	
Coley Pl C1	Post Office B2	
Craven Rd C1	Randolph Rd A1	
Crown St C1	Reading ≠..........A2	
De Montfort Rd A1	Redlands Rd C3	
Denmark Rd.........C3	Renaissance	
Duke St B2	Hotel.................B1	
East St B2	Riverside Mus.....B3	
Edgehill St C2	Rose Kiln La.........C1	
Eldon Rd.............B3	Royal Berks Hospital	
Eldon Terr...........B3	(A&E) C3	
Elgar Rd C3	St Giles C2	
Erleigh Rd C3	St Laurence B1	
Field Rd C1	St Mary's B1	
Fire Station A1	St Mary's Butts B1	
Forbury Gdns B2	St Saviour's Rd C1	
Forbury Retail Pk ..B2	Send Rd A3	
Forbury Rd..........B2	Sherman Rd C2	
Francis St............B1	Sidmouth St B2	
Friar St B1	Silver St C2	
Gas Works Rd B2	South St B2	
George St A2	Southampton St ...C2	
Greyfriars B1	Station Hill..........A1	
Gun St B1	Station Rd A1	
Hexagon, The B1	Superstore A3	
Hill's Meadow A2	Swansea Rd A1	
HM Prison B2	Technical College..B3	
Howard St B1	The Causeway A3	
Information Ctr B1	The Grove...........B2	
Inner Distribution	Valpy St B2	
Rd B1	Vastern Rd A1	
Katesgrove La C1	Vue...................B2	
Kenavon Dr B2	Waldeck St..........C2	
Kendrick Rd C2	Watlington St B2	
King's Meadow	West St B1	
Rec Ground A2	Wolseley St C1	
King's Rd B2	York Rd..............B1	
	Zinzan St B1	

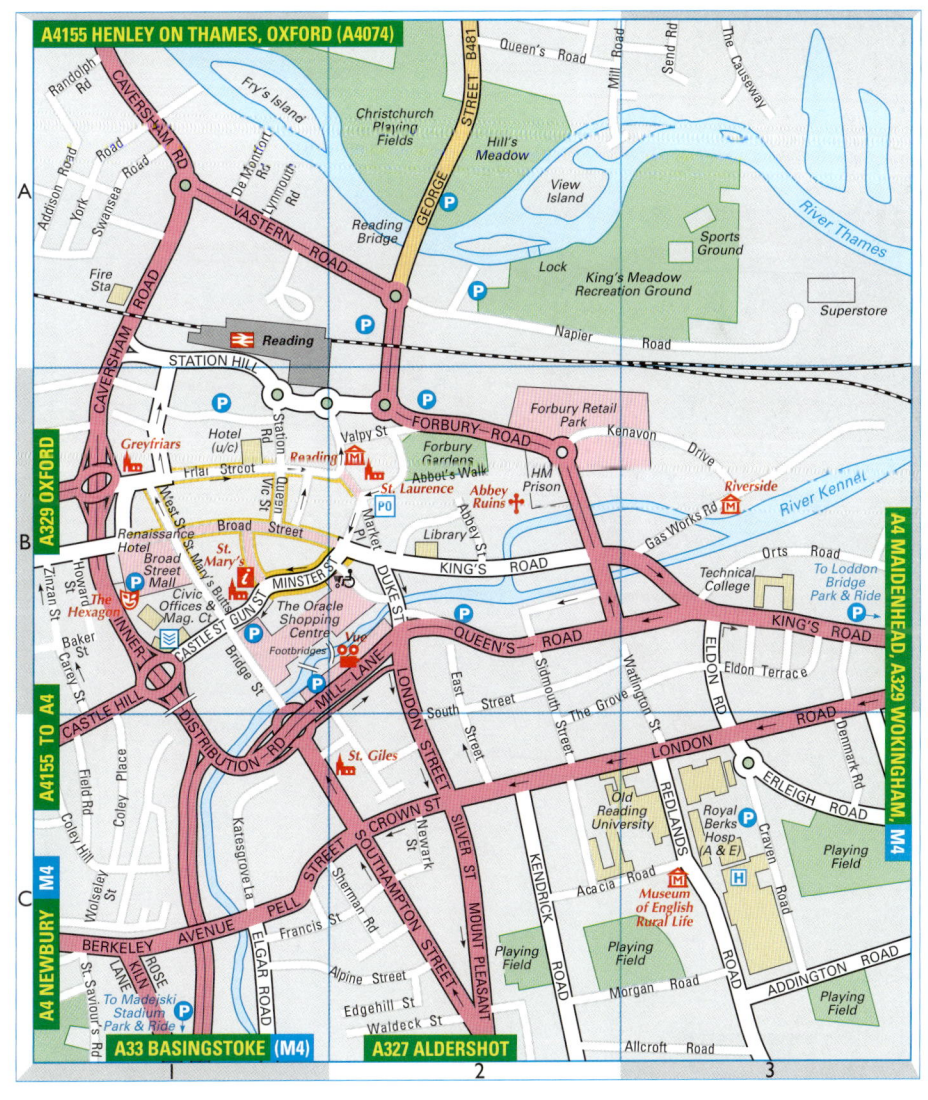

St Andrews

A picturesque royal burgh best known as the home of golf (it is the seat of the sport's main authority and home to the famous Old Course) but also the site of Scotland's oldest university, dating back to 1412. Especially noteworthy are the ruined Middle Ages archbishops' castle, and the remains of what was Scotland's largest cathedral, with a collection of Celtic and medieval carved stones and wonderful views over the town from its St Rule's tower. For nature lovers there's a Botanic Garden and Craigtoun Country Park, and local history is explored at St Andrews Museum and St Andrews Preservation Trust Museum and Garden. The wealth of attractions around the Fife coast south of St Andrews include Scotland's Secret Bunker, a remnant of the Cold War, while to the north at Guardbridge is the Eden Centre birdwatching observatory.

▲ St Andrews Cathedral ruins

Kingdom of Fife Tourist Information Centre, 70 Market Street, St Andrews KY16 9NU
Tel 01334 472021

BBC Radio Scotland 94.3 FM and 810 AM • **Tay FM** 96.4, 102.8 FM
Tay AM 1161, 1584 AM

www.standrews.co.uk

★ Do not miss
- ★ **British Golf Museum**, Bruce Embankment
- ★ **St Andrews Aquarium**, The Scores
- ★ **St Andrews Castle and Visitor Centre**, The Scores

St Andrews

Abbey St	B2
Abbey Walk	B3
Abbotsford Cres	A1
Albany Pk	C3
Allan Robertson Dr	C2
Ambulance Station	C1
Anstruther Rd	C3
Argyle St	B1
Argyll Business Park	C1
Auld Burn Rd	B2
Bassaguard Industrial Estate	B1
Bell St	B2
Blackfriars Chapel (Ruins)	B2
Boase Ave	B2
Braid Cres	C3
Brewster Pl	C3
Bridge St	B1
British Golf Museum	A1
Broomfaulds Ave	C1
Bruce Embankment	A1
Bruce St	C2
Bus Station	B1
Byre	B2
Canongate	C1
Cathedral and Priory (Ruins)	B3
Cemetery	B3
Chamberlain St	C1
Church St	B2
Churchill Cres	C2
City Rd	A1
Claybraes	C1
Cockshaugh Public Park	B1
Cosmos Community Ctr	B3
Council Office	A2
Crawford Arts Ctr	A2
Crawford Gdns	C1
Doubledykes Rd	B1
Drumcarrow Rd	C1
East Sands	B3
East Scores	A3
Fire Station	C1
Forrest St	C1
Fraser Ave	C1
Freddie Tait St	C1
Gateway Centre	A1
Glebe Rd	B2
Golf Pl	A1
Grange Rd	C3
Greenside Pl	B2
Greyfriars Gdns	A2
Hamilton Ave	C2
Hepburn Gdns	B1
Horseleys Park	C1
Information Ctr	B2
Irvine Cres	C3
James Robb Ave	C1
James St	B1
John Knox Rd	C1
Kennedy Gdns	B1
Kilrymont Cres	C3
Kilrymont Pl	C3
Kilrymont Rd	C3
Kinburn Park	B1
Kinkell Terr	C3
Kinnesburn Rd	B2
Ladebraes Walk	B2
Lady Buchan's Cave	A3
Lamberton Pl	C1
Lamond Dr	C2
Langlands Rd	C1
Largo Rd	C1
Learmonth Pl	C1
Library	B2
Links Clubhouse	A1
Livingstone Cres	B2
Long Rocks	A2
Madras College	B2
Market St	A2
Martyr's Monument	A1
Memorial Hospital (No A&E)	B3
Murray Pk	A2
Murray Pl	A2
Nelson St	B2
New Picture House	A2
North Castle St	A3
North St	A2
Old Station Rd	A1
Park & Ride	A1
Pilmour Links	A1
Pipeland Rd	B2/C2
Police Station	A2
Post Office	B2
Preservation	B3
Priestden Pk	C3
Priestden Pl	C3
Priestden Rd	C3
Queen's Gdns	B2
Queen's Terr	B2
Roundhill Rd	C2
Royal & Ancient Golf Club	A1
St Andrews	B1
St Andrews Aquarium	A2
St Andrews Botanic Gardens	B1
St Andrews Castle (Ruins) & Visitor Centre	A2
St Mary St	B3
St Mary's College	B2
St Nicholas St	C3
St Rules Tower	B3
St Salvator's Coll	A2
Sandyhill Cres	C2
Sandyhill Rd	C2
Scooniehill Rd	C2
Shields Ave	C3
Shoolbraids	C2
Sloan St	B1
South St	B2
Spottiswoode Gdns	C1
Station Rd	A1
Swilken Bridge	A1
The Links	A1
The New Course	A1
The Old Course	A1
The Pends	B3
The Scores	A2
The Shore	B3
Tom Morris Dr	C2
Tom Stewart La	C1
Town Church	B2
Town Hall	B2
Union St	A2
University Chapel	A2
University of St Andrews	A1
University Library	A2
Viaduct Walk	B1
War Memorial	A3
Wardlaw St	B1
Warrack St	C3
Watson Ave	B2
West Port	B2
West Sands	A1
Westview	B2
Windmill Rd	A1
Winram Pl	C1
Wishart Gdns	C2
Woodburn Pk	B3
Woodburn Pl	B3
Woodburn Terr	B3
Younger Hall	A2

Salisbury

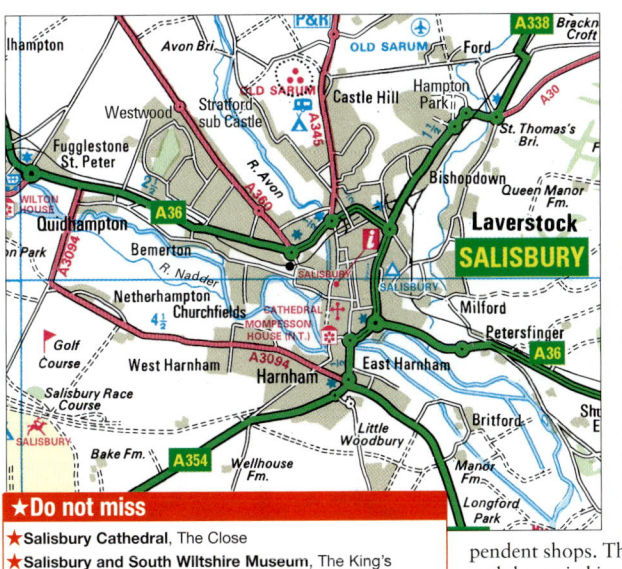

A market town, Salisbury was founded in 1220 when the bishopric was moved there from Old Sarum. The cathedral has the tallest spire in England: at 404 feet it dominates the city. The cathedral clock's mechanism dates from 1386 and is said to be the oldest piece of machinery still at work in Britain. The city boasts many diverse places of interest such as Salisbury Arts Centre featuring music, dance, theatre and exhibitions; Mompesson House, an 18th-century period house; and The Wardrobe, the museum of the local regiment. For shopping there is the Maltings Shopping Centre, Wilton Shopping Village and Salisbury Charter Market (outdoor), plus many small independent shops. There are many pubs and bars, and the varied international cuisine on offer in the city's restaurants reflects its popularity as a tourist destination. Nearby attractions include the Wilton Carpet Factory and Wilton House.

▲ Salisbury Cathedral

Tourist Information Centre,
Fish Row, Salisbury SP1 1EJ
Tel 01722 334956

BBC Radio Wiltshire 103.5 FM
Spire 102 FM

www.visitsalisburyuk.com

★ Do not miss
- ★ **Salisbury Cathedral**, The Close
- ★ **Salisbury and South Wiltshire Museum**, The King's House, The Close – archaeology, costume, art
- ★ **The Medieval Hall, Cathedral Close** – 13th-century banqueting hall including Discover Salisbury

Salisbury

Street	Grid
Albany Rd.	A2
Arts Centre	A3
Ashley Rd.	A1
Avon Approach	A1
Ayleswade Rd.	C2
Bedwin St.	A2
Belle Vue	A2
Bishop's Palace	C2
Bishops Walk	B2
Blue Boar Row	B2
Bourne Ave	A3
Bourne Hill	A3
Britford La	C2
Broad Walk	C2
Brown St	B2
Bus Station	B2
Castle St.	B2
Catherine St	B2
Chapter House	B2
Church House	B2
Churchfields Rd	B1
Churchill Way East	B3
Churchill Way North	A3
Churchill Way South	C2
Churchill Way West	A1
City Hall	B1
Close Wall	B2
Coldharbour La	A1
College of Further Education	B3
College St	A3
Council House	A3
Court	A1
Crane Bridge Rd	B2
Crane St	B2
Cricket Ground	C1
Culver St South	B3
De Vaux Pl	C2
Devizes Rd	A1
Dews Rd	B1
Elm Grove	A3
Elm Grove Rd	A3
Endless St	A2
Estcourt Rd	A3
Exeter St	C2
Fairview Rd	A3
Fire Station	A2
Fisherton St.	A1
Folkestone Rd	C1
Fowlers Hill	B3
Fowlers Rd	B3
Friary Estate	C3
Friary La	B2
Gas La	B2
Gigant St	B3
Greencroft	B3
Greencroft St	B3
Guildhall	B2
Hall of John Halle	B2
Hamilton Rd	A2
Harnham Mill	B1
Harnham Rd	C1/C2
High St	B2
House of John A'Port	B2
Information Ctr	B2
Kelsey Rd	A3
King's Rd	A2
Laverstock Rd	B3
Library	B2
London Rd	A3
Lower St	C1
Manor Rd	A3
Marsh La	A1
Medieval Hall & Discover Salisbury	B2
Milford Hill	B3
Milford St	B3
Mill Rd	B1
Millstream Approach	A2
Mompesson House (N.T.)	B2
New Bridge Rd	C2
New Canal	B2
New Harnham Rd	C2
New St	B2
North Canonry	B2
North Gate	B2
North Walk	B2
Old Blandford Rd	C1
Old Deanery	B2
Hospital	A1
Park St	A3
Parsonage Green	C1
Playhouse Theatre	A2
Post Office	A2/B2/C2
Poultry Cross	B2
Precinct	B2
Queen Elizabeth Gdns	B1
Queen's Rd	A3
Rampart Rd	B3
St Ann's Gate	B2
St Ann St	B2
St Marks Rd	A3
St Martins	B3
St Mary's Cathedral	B2
St Nicholas Hospital	C2
St Paul's	A1
St Thomas	B2
Salisbury & South Wiltshire Museum	B2
Salisbury General Hospital (A&E)	C2
Salisbury Station	A1
Salt La	A3
Saxon Rd	C1
Scots La	A2
Shady Bower	B3
South Canonry	C2
South Gate	C2
Southampton Rd	B3
Sports Ground	C3
The Friary	B3
The Maltings	B2
Tollgate Rd	B3
Town Path	B1
Wain-a-Long Rd	A3
Wardrobe, The	B2
Wessex Rd	A3
West Walk	C2
Wilton Rd	A1
Winchester St	B3
Windsor Rd	A1
Winston Churchill Gdns	C3
Wyndham Rd	A2
YHA	B3
York Rd	A1

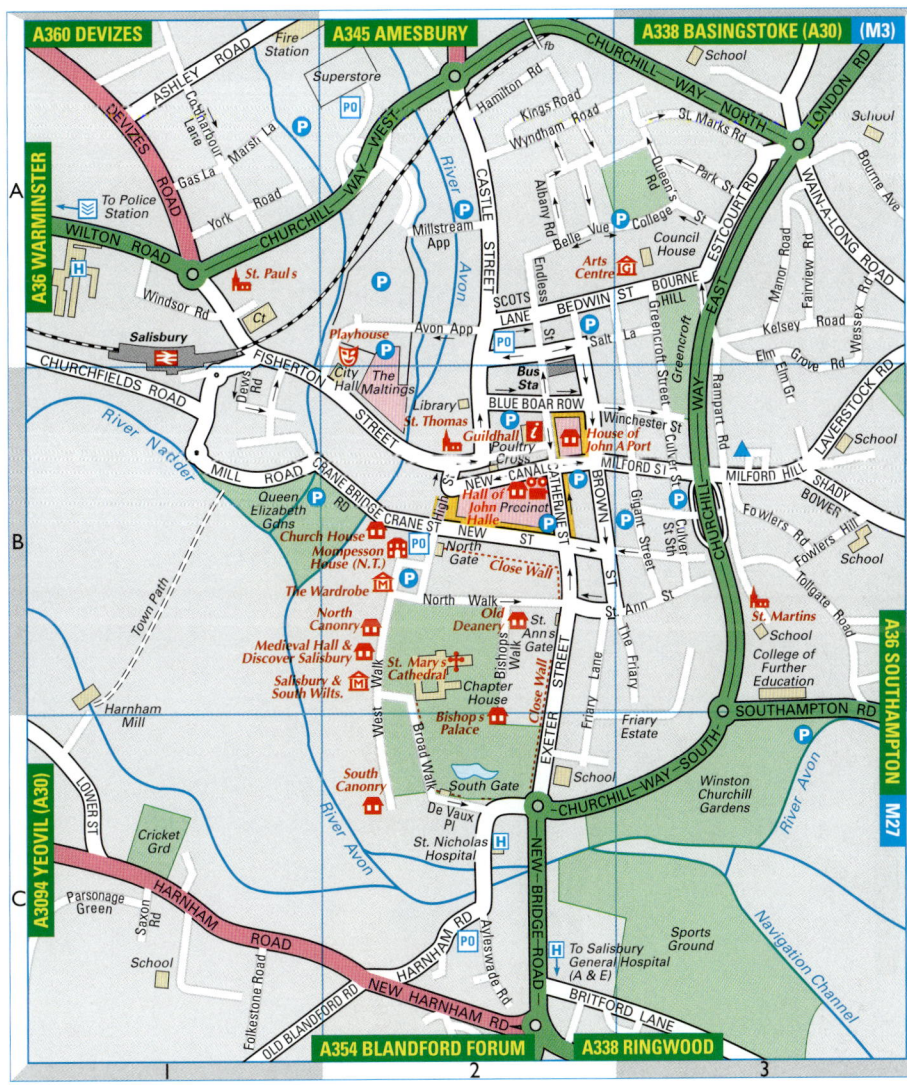

127

Scarborough

▲ Scarborough Harbour

A busy Victorian family resort with a still-active harbour, safe, sandy beaches accessed by famous cliff-lifts, a fine esplanade, some elegant parks and gardens (including Northstead Manor Gardens with its miniature railway), a spa complex and a popular shopping centre. It is overlooked by the ruins of its 12th-century Norman castle, now the setting for mock battles, and has a magnificent church in the form of St-Martin-on-the-Hill, with superb pre-Raphaelite stained glass. Museums include the Wood End Museum of natural history (in the house where Edith Sitwell was born), the Rotunda Museum and Art Gallery, and a contemporary toy museum in the Windmill Hotel. Typical seaside attractions include Watersplash World, with 2 of the world's longest waterslides, while nearby are the Betton Visitor Centre and Animal Farm (including a honey farm and bird of prey centre) and the North York Moors National Park with its moorland, dales, woodland and spectacular coastline.

Scarborough Tourist Information Centre, Brunswick Shopping Centre, Westborough, Scarborough YO11 1UE Tel 01723 383636

BBC Radio York 95.5 FM and 1260 AM • **Yorkshire Coast Radio** 96.2, 103.1 FM • **Galaxy** 105.0 FM

www.discoveryorkshirecoast.com

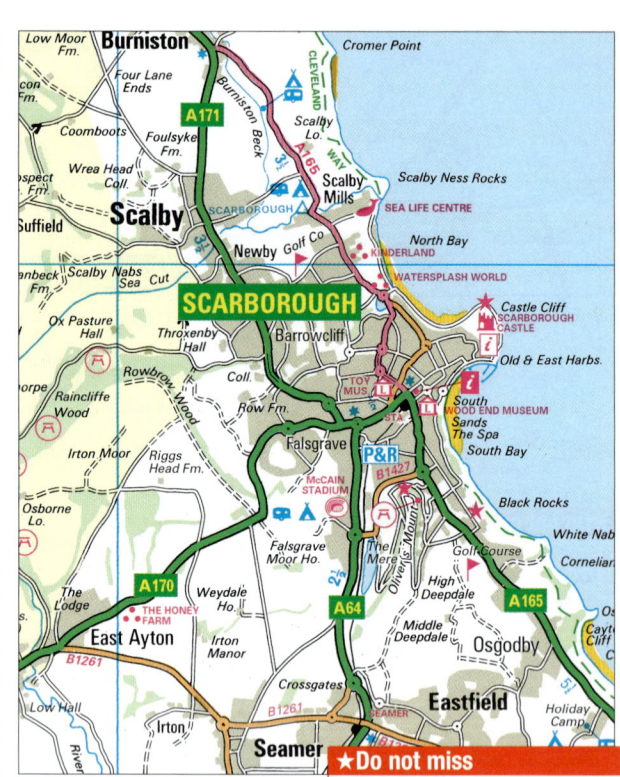

★ **Do not miss**
★ **Cleveland Way**, Scarborough to Filey
★ **Kinderland**, Burniston Road – play and activity park
★ **Sea Life Centre and Marine Sanctuary**, Scalby Mills Road

Scarborough

Aberdeen Walk ... B2
Albert Rd ... A2
Albion Rd ... C2
Alexandra
  Bowling Hall ... A1
Alexandra Gdns ... A1
Atlantis ✦ ... A1
Auborough St ... A2
Belle Vue St ... C1
Belmont Rd ... C2
Brunswick
  Shopping Ctr ... B2
Castle Dykes ... B3
Castlegate ... B3
Castle Holms ... A3
Castle Hill ... A3
Castle Rd ... A3
Castle Walls ... A3
Cemetery ... B1
Central Lift ✦ ... C2
Clarence Gardens ... A2
Coach Park ... B1
Columbus Ravine ... A1
Court ... B2
Cricket Ground ... A1
Cross St ... B2
Crown Terr ... C2
Dean Rd ... B1
Devonshire Dr ... A1
East Harbour ... B3
East Pier ... B3
Eastborough ... B2
Elmville Ave ... A1
Esplanade ... C2
Falconers Rd ... B2
Falsgrave Rd ... C1
Fire Station ... B2
Foreshore Rd ... B2
Friargate ... B2
Futurist ✦ ... B2
Gladstone Rd ... B1
Gladstone St ... B1
Hoxton Rd ... B1
Information
  Ctr ... B2/B3
King St ... B2
Londesborough
  Rd ... C1
Longwestgate ... B3
Marine Dr ... A3
Miniature
  Railway ... A1
Nelson St ... B1
Newborough ... B2
Nicolas St ... B2
North Marine Rd ... A1
North St ... B2
Northway ... B1
Old Harbour ... B3
Peasholm Park ... A1
Peasholm Rd ... A1
Plaza ... A1
Police Station ... B1
Post Office
  ... A2/B1/B2/C1
Princess St ... B3
Prospect Rd ... B1
Queen St ... B2
Queen's Parade ... A2
Queen's Tower
  (Remains) ... A3
Ramshill Rd ... C2
Roman Signal
  Station ... A3
Roscoe St ... C1
Rotunda ... C2
Royal Albert Dr ... A1
St Martin-on-
  the-Hill ... C2
St Martin's Ave ... C2
St Mary's ... B3
St Nicholas' Lift ✦ ... B2
St Thomas St ... B2
Sandside ... B3
Scarborough Art
  Gallery ... C2
Scarborough
  Castle ... A3
Scarborough ... C1
Somerset Terr ... C2
South Cliff Lift ✦ ... C2
Spa, The ✦ ... C2
Spa Theatre ... C2
Stephen Joseph
  Theatre ... B1
Tennyson Ave ... B1
The Crescent ... C2
Tollergate ... B2
Town Hall ... B2
Trafalgar Rd ... B1
Trafalgar Square ... B1
Trafalgar St West ... B1
Valley Bridge Pde ... C2
Valley Rd ... C1
Vernon Rd ... C1
Victoria Park Mt ... A1
Victoria Rd ... B1
West Pier ... B3
Westborough ... C1
Westover Rd ... C1
Westwood ... C1
Woodall Ave ... A1
Wood End ... C2
York Pl ... B2

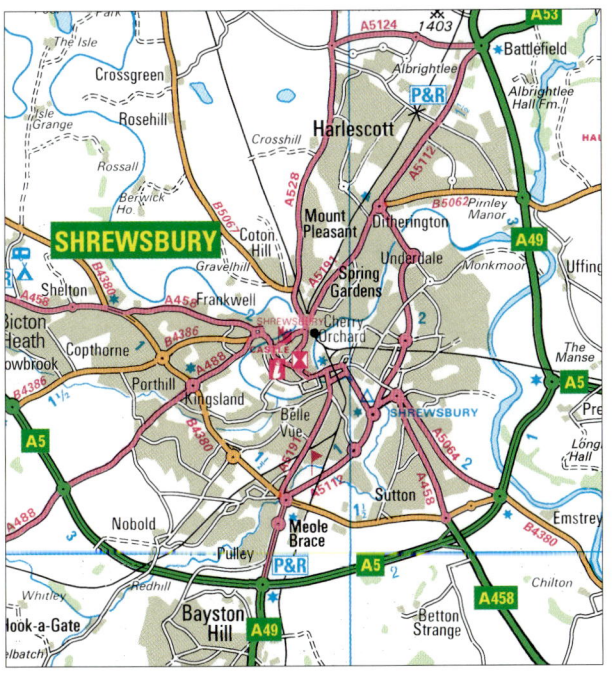

Shrewsbury

Shrewsbury is situated within a great loop of the River Severn with the sole land approach guarded by the castle. The original castle was built under the order of William the Conqueror and was rebuilt and enlarged by Edward II. The town is an important centre for artists and is home to many galleries from contemporary art to photography. There is a wealth of timber-framed and Georgian houses, steep narrow streets and little alleys with many independent shops as well as high street names, and an indoor market four days a week. The Music Hall incorporates a theatre and restaurant, and there are many other restaurants and pubs based in the centre of the town.

▲Shrewsbury from Coleham Head

★ Do not miss

- ★ Shrewsbury Castle (including Museum of Shropshire Regiments)
- ★ Shrewsbury Museum and Art Gallery, Barker Street
- ★ Coleham Pumping Station, Longden Road

Shrewsbury Tourist Information Centre, The Music Hall, The Square, Shrewsbury SY1 1LH
Tel 01743 281200

BBC Radio Shropshire 96.0 FM
Classic Gold 1017 AM
Beacon 97.2 and 103.1 FM

www.shrewsbury.gov.uk

Shrewsbury

Abbey Church ⛪ . . B3	Hills La B1	Town Walls C1	Victoria St B2
Abbey Foregate . . B3	Holywell St B3	Trinity St C2	Welsh Bridge B1
Abbey Lawn Business Park . . B3	Hunter St B1	Underdale Rd B3	Whitehall St B3
Abbots House 🏛 . B2	Information Ctr 🛈 . B1	Victoria Ave B1	Wood St A2
Agricultural Show Ground . . A1	Ireland's Mansion & Bear Steps B1	Victoria Quay B1	Wyle Cop B2
Albert St A2	John St A3
Alma St B3	Kennedy Rd C1
Ashley St A3	King St B3
Ashton Rd C1	Kingsland Br C1
Avondale Dr A3	Kingsland Br (toll) C1
Bage Way B3	Kingsland Rd C1
Barker St B1	Library B2
Beacall's La A2	Lime St C2
Beeches La C2	Longden Coleham C2
Belle Vue Gdns . . C2	Longden Rd C2
Belle Vue Rd C2	Longner St B1
Belmont Bank . . . C1	Luciefelde Rd C1
Berwick Ave A1	Mardol B1
Berwick Rd A1	Market B1
Betton St B2	Monkmoor Rd . . . B3
Bishop St B3	Moreton Cr C2
Bradford St B3	Mount St A1
Bridge St B2	Music Hall 🎭 B1
Bus Station B2	New Park Cl A3
Butcher Row B2	New Park Rd A2
Burton St B3	New Park St A3
Butler St C1	North St A2
Bynner St C2	Oakley St C1
Canon St B3	Old Coleham C2
Canonbury C1	Old Market Hall 🎭 B1
Castle Business Park, The A2	Old Potts Way . . . C3
Castle Foregate . . A2	Parade Centre . . . B2
Castle Gates B2	Police Station 🛡 . B1
Castle Museum 🏛 B2	Post Office ✉ A2/B1/B2/B3
Castle St B2	Pride Hill B1
Cathedral (RC) ✝ . C1	Pride Hill Centre . . B1
Chester St A2	Priory Rd B1
Cineworld 🎬 C3	Queen St A3
Claremont Bank . . B1	Raby Cr C2
Claremont Hill . . . B1	Rad Brook C1
Cleveland St B3	Rea Brook C3
Coleham Head . . . B2	Riverside B1
Coleham Pumping Station 🏛 . . . C2	Roundhill La C1
College Hill B1	Rowley's House 🏛 B1
Corporation La . . . A1	St Alkmund's ⛪ . . B2
Coton Cres A1	St Chad's ⛪ B1
Coton Hill A1	St Chad's Terr . . . B1
Coton Mount A1	St John's Hill B1
Crescent La A1	St Julians Friars . . C2
Crewe St A2	St Mary's ⛪ B2
Cross Hill B1	St Mary's St B2
Darwin Centre . . . B2	Scott St C3
Dingle, The ✿ . . . B1	Severn Bank A3
Dogpole B2	Severn St A2
Draper's Hall 🏛 . . B2	Shrewsbury 🚂 . . . B2
English Bridge . . . B2	Shrewsbury High School for Girls . C1
Fish St B2	Shrewsbury Sch ✝ C1
Frankwell A1	Shrewsbury Town F.C. B2
Gateway Ctr 🏛 . . B2	Shropshire Wildlife Trust ✿ . B3
Gravel Hill La A1	Smithfield Rd B1
Greyfriars Rd C2	South Hermitage C1
Guildhall 🏛 B1	Swan Hill B1
Hampton Rd A3	Sydney Ave A3
Haycock Way . . . C3	Tankerville St B3
HM Prison B2	The Dana B2
Hereford Rd C3	The Quarry B1
High St B1	The Square B1
	Tilbrook Dr A3

129

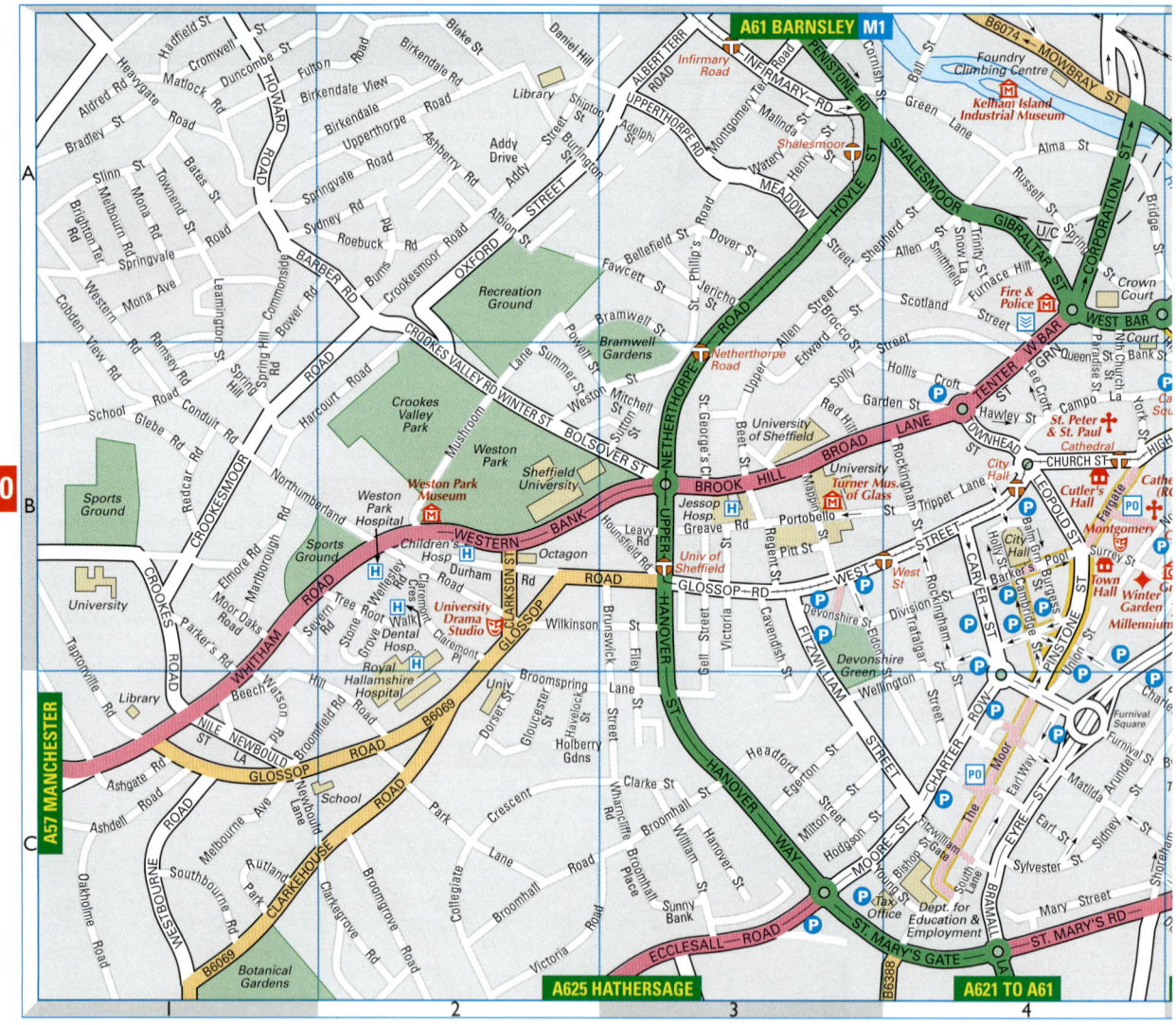

Sheffield

Addy Dr A2	Broad La B3	Collegiate Cr C2	Fargate B4	Heavygate Rd . . . A1	Milton St C3	Queen St B4		¼ mile
Addy St A2	Broad St B6	Commercial St . . B5	Farm Rd C5	Henry St A3	Mitchell St B3	Queen's Rd C5	¼	½ km
Adelphi St A3	Brocco St A3	Commonside A1	Fawcett St A3	High St B4	Mona Ave A1	Ramsey Rd B1	Showroom, The . . C5
Albert Terrace Rd . . A3	Brook Hill B3	Conduit Rd B1	Filey St B3	Hodgson St C3	Mona Rd A1	Red Hill B3	Shrewsbury Rd . . C5
Albion St A2	Broomfield Rd . . . C1	Cornish St A4	Fire & Police	Holberry Gdns . . . C2	Montgomery	Redcar Rd B1	Sidney St C5
Aldred Rd A1	Broomgrove Rd . . C2	Corporation St . . . A4	Museum A4	Hollis Croft B4	Terrace Rd A3	Regent St B3	Slinn St A1
Allen St A4	Broomhall Pl C3	Court B4	Fitzalan Sq/	Holly St B4	Montgomery	Rockingham St . . B4	Smithfield B3
Alma St A4	Broomhall St C3	Cricket Inn Rd . . . B6	Ponds Forge	Hounsfield Rd . . . C3	Theatre B4	Roebuck Rd A2	Snig Hill A5
Angel St B5	Broomspring La . . C2	Cromwell St A1	(Tram Station) . . B5	Howard St B5	Monument Gdns . C6	Royal Hallamshire	Snow La A4
Arundel Gate B5	Brown St C5	Crookes Rd B1	Fitzwater Rd C6	Hoyle St A3	Moor Oaks Rd . . . B1	Hospital C2	Solly St B3
Arundel St C4	Brunswick Rd . . . A5	Crookes Valley	Fitzwilliam Gate . . C4	Hyde Park	Moore St C3	Russell St A4	South La C4
Ashberry Rd A2	Brunswick St B3	Park B2	Fitzwilliam St . . . B3	(Tram Station) . . A6	Mowbray St A4	Rutland Park C1	South St B5
Ashdell Rd C1	Burgess St B4	Crookes Valley Rd . B2	Flat St B5	Infirmary Rd A3	Mushroom La . . . B2	St George's Cl . . . B3	Southbourne Rd . . C1
Ashgate Rd C1	Burlington St A2	Crookesmoor Rd . . A2	Foley St A6	Infirmary Rd	Netherthorpe Rd . . B3	St Mary's Gate . . . C3	Spital Hill A5
Attercliffe Rd A6	Burns Rd A2	Crown Court A4	Foundry Climbing	(Tram Station) . . A3	Netherthorpe Rd	St Mary's Rd . . C4/C5	Spital St A5
Ball St A4	Bus/Coach	Crucible	Centre A4	Jericho St A3	(Tram Station) . . B3	St Peter & St Paul	Spring Hill B1
Balm Green B4	Station B5	Theatre B5	Fulton Rd A1	Jessop Hospital . . B3	Newbould La C1	Cathedral B4	Spring Hill Rd . . . B1
Bank St B4	Cadman St A6	Cutlers Gate A6	Furnace Hill A4	Johnson St A5	Nile St C1	St Philip's Rd . . . A3	Spring St A4
Barber Rd A2	Cambridge St . . . B4	Cutler's Hall B4	Furnival Rd A5	Kelham Island	Norfolk Park Rd . . C6	Savile St B1	Springvale Rd . . . B1
Bard St B5	Campo La B4	Daniel Hill A2	Furnival Sq C4	Industrial	Norfolk Rd C6	School Rd B1	Stafford Rd C6
Barker's Pool B4	Carver St B4	Dental	Furnival St C4	Museum A4	North Church St . . B4	Scotland St A4	Stafford St B6
Bates St A1	Castle Market . . . B5	Hospital B3	Garden St B3	Leadmill Rd C5	Northumberland	Severn Rd B1	Stanley St A5
Beech Hill Rd . . . C1	Castle Square	Dept for Education	Gell St B3	Leadmill St C5	Rd B1	Shalesmoor A4	Stone Gr B2
Beet St B3	(Tram Station) . . B5	& Employment . . C4	Gibraltar St A4	Leamington St . . . A1	Nursery St A5	Shalesmoor	Suffolk Rd C5
Bellefield St A3	Castlegate A5	Destination	Glebe Rd B1	Leavy Rd B3	Oakholme Rd . . . C1	(Tram Station) . . A4	Summer St B2
Bernard Rd A6	Cathedral (RC) † . . B4	Sheffield B5	Glencoe Rd C6	Lee Croft B4	Octagon B3	Shalesmoor	Sunny Bank C3
Bernard St B6	Cathedral	Devonshire Green . B3	Glossop	Leopold St B4	Odeon B5	(Tram Station) . . A4	Surrey St B4
Birkendale A2	(Tram Station) . . B4	Devonshire St . . . B4	Rd B2/B3/C1	Leveson St A6	Old St B6	Sheaf Sq C5	Sussex St A6
Birkendale Rd . . . A1	Cavendish St B3	Division St B4	Gloucester St . . . C2	Library A1	Oxford St A3	Sheaf St B5	Sutton St B3
Birkendale View . . A1	Charles St C4	Dorset St C2	Granville Rd C5	Library B5	Paradise St B4	Sheffield Ice	Sydney Rd C4
Bishop St C4	Charter Row C4	Dover St A3	Granville Rd/	Library C1	Park La C5	Sports Centre . . C5	Sylvester St C4
Blackwell Pl B6	Children's	Duchess Rd C5	Sheffield College	Lyceum	Park Sq B5	Sheffield	Talbot St B5
Blake St A5	Hospital B2	Duke St B5	(Tram Station) . . C5	Theatre B5	Parker's Rd C1	Parkway A6	Taptonville Rd . . . B1
Blonk St A5	Church St B4	Duncombe St . . . A1	Graves Gallery . . . B5	Malinda St A3	Penistone Rd A3	Sheffield	Tax Office C4
Bolsover St B2	City Hall B4	Durham Rd B2	Greave Rd B3	Maltravers St A6	Pinstone St B4	Station B5	Tenter St A4
Botanical Gdns . . . C1	City Hall	Earl St C4	Green La A4	Manor Oaks Rd . . B6	Pitt St B3	Sheffield Station/	The Leadmill C5
Bower Rd A1	(Tram Station) . . B4	Earl Way C4	Hadfield St A1	Mappin St B4	Police	Sheffield Hallam	The Moor C4
Bradley St A1	City Rd C6	Ecclesall Rd C3	Hallam University . B5	Marlborough Rd . . B1	Station A4/B5	University	Town Hall B4
Bramall La C4	Claremont Cr B2	Edward St B3	Hanover St C3	Mary St C4	Pond Hill B5	(Tram Station) . . B5	Townend St A1
Bramwell Gdns . . . B3	Claremont Pl B2	Effingham La A6	Hanover Way C3	Matilda St C4	Pond St B5	Sheffield	Townhead St B4
Bramwell St A3	Clarke St C3	Effingham Rd . . . A6	Harcourt Rd C1	Matlock Rd A1	Ponds Forge	University B2	Trafalgar St C4
Bridge St A4/A5	Clarkegrove Rd . . C2	Egerton St C3	Harmer La C5	Meadow St A3	Sports Centre . . B5	Shepherd St A4	Tree Root Walk . . B2
Brighton Terrace	Clarkehouse Rd . . C1	Eldon St B3	Havelock St C2	Melbourn Rd C1	Portobello B3	Shipton St A2	Trinity St A4
Rd A1	Clarkson St B2	Elmore Rd B1	Hawley St B4	Melbourne Ave . . . C1	Post Office . . B5/C4	Shoreham St C4	Trippet La B4
	Cobden View Rd . . A1	Exchange St B5	Haymarket B5	Millennium	Powell St A2		
		Eyre St C4	Headford St C3	Galleries B5			

130

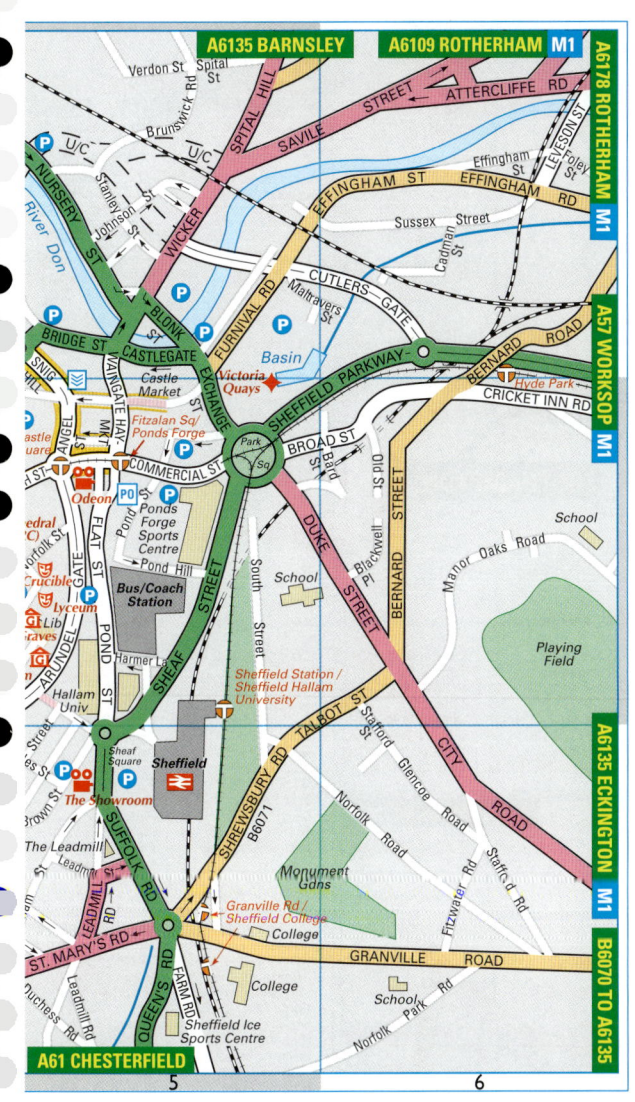

Sheffield

A former steel-producing and coal-mining city where industrial heritage rubs shoulders with a surprising array of green spaces, from Ecclesall Woods to the Botanical Gardens, Graves Park, with its bird and sculpture trail and animal farm, and Heeley City Farm and environmental study centre. Recent regeneration includes the creation of the award-winning Peace Garden public square. Museums and galleries include Graves Art Gallery (19th- and 20th-century modern art), Turner Museum of Glass, Weston Park Museum (reopening 2006), the Fire and Police Museum, the Kelham Island Museum and Traditional Heritage Museum of local history, and the Sheffield Bus Museum at Tinsley. Buildings of interest include the medieval cathedral, Sheffield Manor Lodge, where Mary Queen of Scots was held for 14 years, Bishop's House, the city's oldest surviving half-timbered house (with a museum), the remains of 12th-century Beauchief Abbey, the Victorian Birley Spa in Hackenthorpe, and the Abbeythorpe Industrial Hamlet, an 18th-century scythe works. The stunning Peak District National Park is a few miles away.

▲ Fargate

Destination Sheffield,
Tel 0114 221 1900

BBC Radio Sheffield 104.1, 88.6 FM
Hallam 97.4 FM • **Galaxy** 105.6 FM
Magic 990, 1305, 1548 AM
Real Radio Yorkshire 107.7 FM

www.sheffield.gov.uk

▲ Do not miss

★ **Hillsborough Walled and Wildlife Garden**, Middlewood Road, Hillsborough Park
★ **Millennium Galleries**, Arundel Gate – art and design
★ **Winter Garden**, Surrey Street – temperate glasshouse

Turner Museum of Glass B3
Union St B4
University Drama Studio B2
University of Sheffield (Tram Station) B3
Upper Allen St A3
Upper Hanover St B3
Upperthorpe Rd A2/A3
Verdon St A5
Victoria Quays ✦ B5
Victoria Rd C2
Victoria St B3
Waingate B5
Watery St A3
Watson Rd C1
Wellesley Rd B2
Wellington St L5
West Bar A4
West Bar Green ... A4
West St A3
West St (Tram Station) ... B4
Westbourne Rd ... C1
Western Bank B2
Western Rd A1
Weston Park B2
Weston Park Hospital B2
Weston Park Museum B2
Weston St B2
Wharncliffe Rd ... C3
Whitham Rd B1
Wicker A5
Wilkinson St B2
William St C3
Winter Garden ✦ ... B4
Winter St B2
York St B4
Young St C4

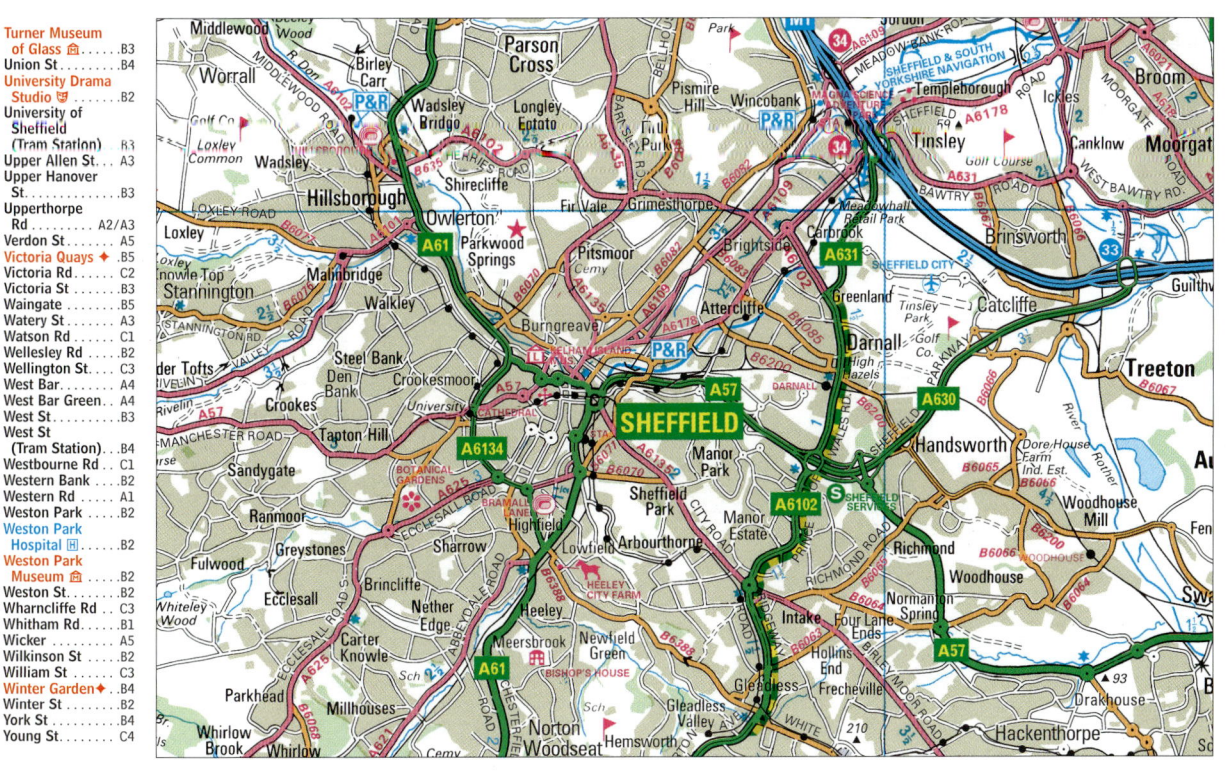

Southampton

A port of Saxon origins with some of the country's best-preserved medieval walls. It was through the Westgate that Henry V set out for Agincourt and the Pilgrim Fathers for America, while the Maritime Museum in a medieval warehouse charts Southampton's rich maritime history. Other sights include the Medieval Merchant's House, God's House Tower Museum of Archaeology, Hall of Aviation and the Millais and John Hansard art galleries. Shopping, from big retail stores to smaller independent outlets, is a high point and Ocean Village is one of the UK's biggest marina developments. Among nearby attractions are the New Forest and the ruins of 13th-century Netley Abbey.

▲ Queen Mary 2

Southampton City Information, 9 Civic Centre Road, Southampton SO14 7FJ Tel 02380 833 333

BBC Radio Solent 96.1 FM and 999 AM • **Capital Gold** 1447 AM • **Ocean** 97.5FM • **Power** 103.2 FM • **The Saint** 107.8 FM • **Wave** 105.2 FM

www.southampton.gov.uk

★ Do not miss
- ★ **Hall of Aviation**, Albert Road South
- ★ **Maritime Museum**, Town Quay
- ★ **Southampton City Art Gallery**, Civic Centre, Commercial Road
- ★ **Titanic Trail** – city centre

Southampton

Street	Grid
Above Bar St	A2
Albert Rd North	B3
Albert Rd South	C3
Anderson's Rd	B3
Argyle Rd	A2
Arundel Tower ✦	B1
Bargate, The ✦	B2
Bargate Centre	B2
BBC Regional Ctrl	A1
Bedford Pl	A1
Belvidere Rd	A3
Bernard St	C2
Blechynden Terr	A1
Brazil Rd	C3
Brinton's Rd	A2
Britannia Rd	A3
Briton St	C2
Brunswick Pl	A2
Bugle St	C1
Canute Rd	C3
Castle Way	C2
Catchcold Twr ✦	B1
Central Bridge	C3
Central Rd	C2
Channel Way	C3
Chapel Rd	B3
Cineworld	C2
City Art Gallery	A1
City College	B3
Civic Centre	A1
Civic Centre Rd	A1
Coach Station	B1
Commercial Rd	A1
Cumberland Pl	A1
Cunard Rd	C2
Derby Rd	A3
Devonshire Rd	A1
Dock Gate 4	C2
Dock Gate 8	B1
East Park	A2
East Park Terr	A2
East St	B2
East St Shopping Centre	B2
Endle St	B3
European Way	C2
Fire Station	A2
Floating Bridge Rd	C3
God's House Tower Museum of Archaeology	C2
Golden Gr	A3
Graham Rd	A2
Guildhall	A1
Hanover Bldgs	B2
Harbour Lights	C3
Harbour Pde	B1
Hartington Rd	A3
Havelock Rd	A1
Henstead Rd	A1
Herbert Walker Ave	B1
High St	B2
Hoglands Park	B2
Holy Rood (Rems), Merchant Navy Memorial ✦	B2
Hospital	A2
Houndwell Pl	B2
Hythe Ferry	C2
Information Ctr	A1
Isle of Wight Ferry Terminal	C1
James St	B3
Java Rd	C3
Kingsland Market	B2
Kingsway	A2
Leisure World	B1
Library	A1
Lime St	B2
London Rd	A1
Marine Pde	B3
Maritime	C1
Marsh La	B2
Mayflower Memorial ✦	C1
Mayflower Park	B1
Mayflower Theatre, The	A1
Medieval Merchant's House	C1
Melbourne St	B3
Millais	A1
Morris Rd	A1
Neptune Way	C2
New Rd	A2
Nichols Rd	A3
Northam Rd	A3
Ocean Dock	C2
Ocean Village Marina	C3
Ocean Way	C3
Odeon	B1
Ogle Rd	B1
Old Northam Rd	A2
Orchard La	B2
Oxford Ave	A2
Oxford St	B2
Palmerston Park	A2
Palmerston Rd	A2
Parsonage Rd	A3
Peel St	A3
Platform Rd	C2
Police Station	A1
Portland Terr	B1
Post Office	A2/A3/B2
Pound Tree Rd	B2
Quays Swimming & Diving Complex	B1
Queen's Park	C2
Queen's Peace Fountain ✦	A2
Queen's Terr	C2
Queen's Way	B2
Radcliffe Rd	A3
Rochester St	A3
Royal Pier	C1
St Andrew's Rd	A3
St Mary St	A2
St Mary's	B3
St Mary's Leisure Centre	A2
St Mary's Pl	B2
St Mary's Rd	A2
St Mary's Stadium (Southampton F.C.)	A3
St Michael's	C1
Solent Sky	C3
South Front	B2
Southampton Central	A1
Southampton Solent University	A2
Southhampton Oceanography Centre ✦	C3
SS Shieldhall	C2
Terminus Terr	C2
The Mall, Marlands	A1
The Polygon	A1
Threefield La	C1
Titanic Engineers' Memorial ✦	A2
Town Quay	C1
Town Walls	B2
Tudor House	B2
Vincent's Walk	B2
West Gate	C1
West Marlands	A1
West Park	A1
West Park Rd	A1
West Quay Rd	B1
West Quay Retail Park	B1
West Quay Shopping Ctr	B1
West Rd	C2
Western Esplanade	B1

132

Southend-on-Sea

A traditional seaside centre on the Thames Estuary in Essex, on a site inhabited during the Stone Age, Bronze Age and early Iron Age, and successively settled by the Romans, Saxons and Danes – a history that is traced at Prittlewell Priory Museum. The closest resort to London, it boasts the world's longest pleasure pier (2360 yards), built in 1835, parts of which are shut following a fire in 2005 although attractions near the shore are open. The Golden Mile of leisure attractions includes Adventure Island themepark, the Kursaal with 10-pin bowling and other activities, and Never Never Land fantasy park, and the Central Museum including a planetarium. Just outside town are the 14th-century remains of Hadleigh Castle.

▲ Southend beach huts

Southend Visitor Information Centre, The Pier Entrance, Southend Pier, Eastern Esplanade, Southend-on-Sea SS1 1EE Tel 01702 215620

BBC Essex 95.3 FM
Classic Gold Breeze 1431 AM
Essex 96.3, 102.6 FM

www.southend.gov.uk

★ Do not miss
- ★ **Jubilee Beach**, from Southend Pier to Thorpe Bay
- ★ **Sealife Adventure**, Eastern Esplanade
- ★ **Southend Pier**, Western Esplanade

133

Southend

Adventure Island ◆ C3	Milton Rd B1	Wesley Rd C3	Weston Rd C2
Albany Ave A1	Milton St B2	West Rd A1	Whitegate Rd ... B3
Albert Rd A3	Napier Ave B2	West St A1	Wilson Rd C1
Alexandra Rd ... C2	**Never Never Land** ◆ C2	Westcliff Parade . C1	Wimborne Rd ... B3
Alexandra St ... C1	North Ave A3	Western Espl C1	York Rd C3
Art Gallery ☐ ... C1	North Rd A1/B1		
Ashburnham Rd .. B2	**Odeon** ☐ B2		
Ave Rd B1	Osborne Rd B1		
Avenue Terr B1	Park Cres B1		
Balmoral Rd B1	Park Rd B1		
Baltic Ave B3	Park St B1		
Baxter Ave A2/B2	Park Terr B1		
Bircham Rd A2	**Peter Pan's Playground** ◆ .. C2		
Boscombe Rd ... B3	Pier Hill C3		
Boston Ave A1/B2	Pleasant Rd B1		
Bournemouth Park Rd A3	**Police Station** ☐ . A2		
Browning Ave ... A3	**Post Office** ☐ .. B2/B3		
Bus Station C3	Princes St B2		
Byron Ave A3	Queens Rd B2		
Cambridge Rd . C1/C2	Queensway ... B2/B3/C3		
Canewdon Rd ... B1	Rayleigh Ave A1		
Carnarvon Rd ... C2	Redstock Rd A2		
Central Ave A3	Rochford Ave A1		
Chelmsford Ave .. A1	Royal Mews C2		
Chichester Rd ... B2	Royal Terr C2		
Church Rd C3	Royals Shopping Precinct C3		
Civic Centre A2	Ruskin Ave A3		
Clarence Rd C2	St Ann's Rd B3		
Clarence St C2	St Helen's Rd ... B1		
Cliff Ave B1	St John's Rd ... B1		
Cliffs Pavilion ☐ .. C1	St Leonard's Rd .. C3		
Clifftown Parade . C1	St Lukes Rd A3		
Clifftown Rd C2	St Vincent's Rd .. C1		
Colchester Rd ... A1	Salisbury Ave .. A1/B1		
College Way B2	Scratton Rd B1		
County Court ... B3	Shakespeare Dr .. A1		
Cromer Rd B2	Short St A2		
Crowborough Rd . A2	South Ave A3		
Dryden Ave A3	Southchurch Rd .. B3		
East St A2	South East Essex College .. B2		
Elmer App B2	**Southend Central** ☒ B2		
Elmer Ave B2	**Southend Pier Railway** ☐ ... C3		
Gainsborough Dr . A1	Southend United F.C. .. A1		
Gayton Rd A2	**Southend Victoria** ☒ ... B2		
Glenhurst Rd A2	Stadium Rd A2		
Gordon Pl B2	Stanfield Rd A2		
Gordon Rd B2	Stanley Rd C3		
Grainger Rd B2	Sutton Rd A3/B3		
Greyhound Way .. A3	Swanage Rd B3		
Guildford Rd B3	Sweyne Ave A1		
Hamlet Ct Rd ... C1	Swimming Pool .. B3		
Hamlet Rd C1	Sycamore Gr ... A3		
Harcourt Ave ... A1	Tennyson Ave ... A3		
Hartington Rd ... C3	The Grove A3		
Hastings Rd B3	Tickfield Ave A2		
Herbert Gr C3	Tudor Rd A1		
Heygate Ave C3	Tunbridge Rd ... A2		
High St B2/C2	Tylers Ave B3		
Information Ctr ☐ . C3	Tyrrel Dr B3		
Kenway A2	Vale Rd A2		
Kilworth Ave B3	Victoria Ave A2		
Lancaster Gdns .. B3	Victoria Plaza Shopping Precinct .. B2		
Library B2	Warrior Sq B3		
London Rd B1			
Lucy Rd C3			
MacDonald Ave .. A1			
Magistrates Court A2			
Maldon Rd A2			
Marine Parade .. C3			

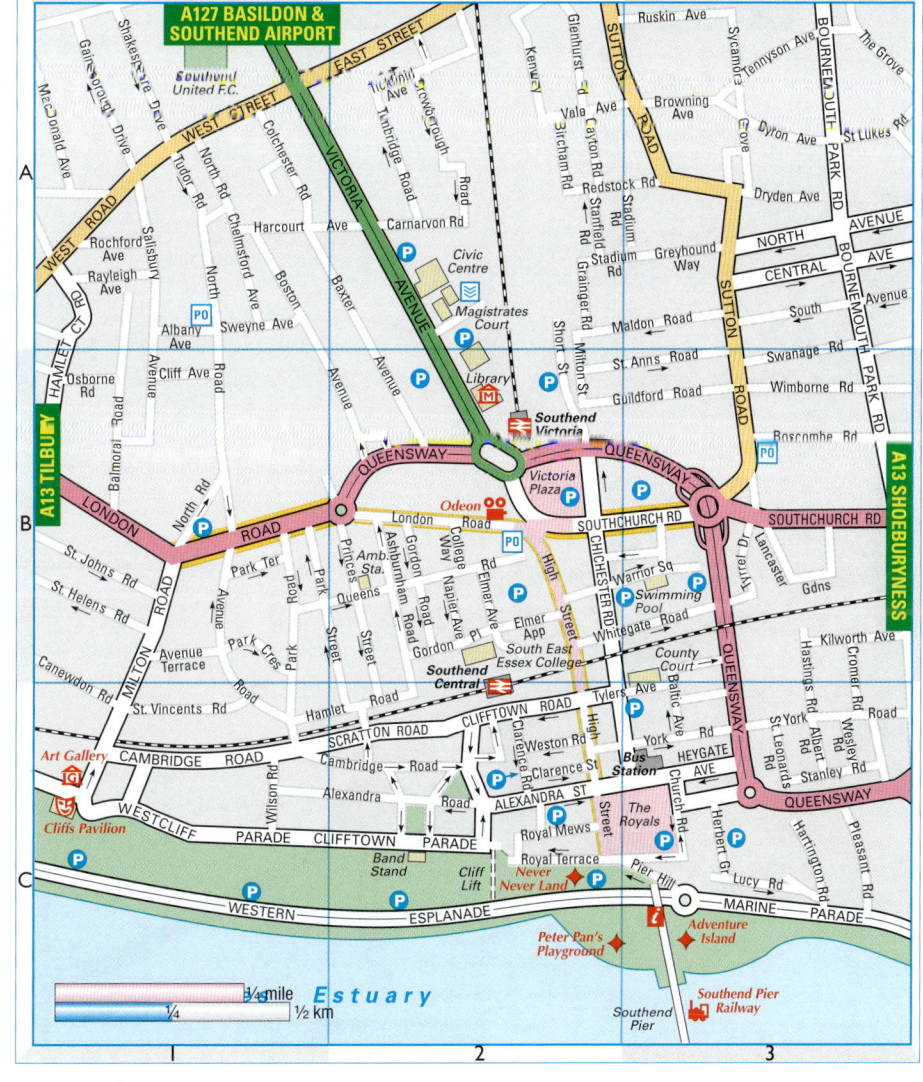

Stirling

A nucleus of Scottish heritage, with a large student population and good shopping amenities. Its superb castle, built during the reign of James VI, was a popular residence among Scottish monarchs. The Old Town has cobbled streets and some impressive architecture, including the medieval Church of the Holy Rude, where James VI was crowned and John Knox preached, and Argyll's Lodging, a restored 1570s mansion, while nearby ruined Cambuskenneth Abbey is where Robert the Bruce, victor of the nearby Battle of Bannockburn, held his parliament in 1326, and the National Wallace Memorial bears witness to William the Braveheart's battle for Scottish independence. This and other local history is charted in the Royal Burgh of Stirling Visitor Centre and the Smith Art Gallery and Museum. The city is well sited for visits to Loch Lomond and the Trossachs National Park, the Rob Roy & Trossachs Visitor Centre, and also handy for Gargunnock House and Garden, Blair Drummond Safari and Adventure Park, and the late-14th-century Doune Castle, used by Mary Queen of Scots.

Stirling Tourist Information Centre, Dumbarton Road, Stirling FK8 2QQ
Tel 01786 475019

BBC Radio Scotland 94.5 FM and 810 AM **Central** 103.1 FM
Xfm Scotland 106 FM

www.scottish.heartlands.org

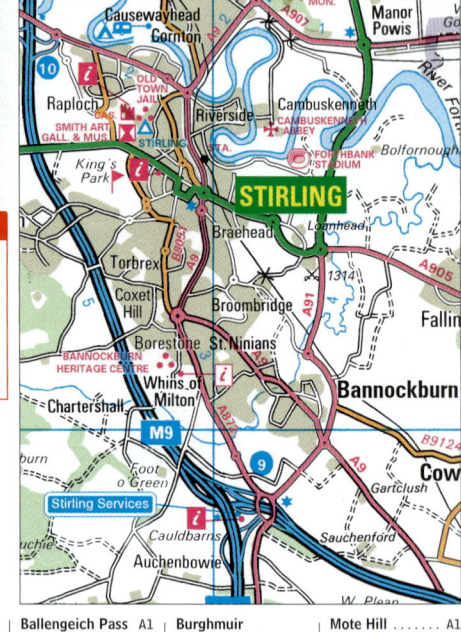

★ Do not miss
★ **Bannockburn Heritage Centre**, Glasgow Road
★ **Old Town Jail**, St John Street
★ **Stirling Castle and Regimental Museum of the Argyll and Sutherland Highlanders**, Castle Wynd

▲ Stirling Castle

Stirling

Abbey Rd	A3
Abbotsford Pl	A3
Abercromby Pl	C1
Albert Halls	B1
Albert Pl	B1
Alexandra Pl	A3
Allan Park	C2
Ambulance Station	A2
AMF Ten Pin Bowling ✦	B2
Argyll Ave	A3
Back O' Hill Industrial Estate	A1
Back O' Hill Rd	A1
Baker St	B2
Ballengeich Pass	A1
Balmoral Pl	B1
Barn Rd	B1
Barnton St	B2
Bow St	B1
Bruce St	A2
Burghmuir Industrial Estate	C2
Burghmuir Rd	A2/B2/C2
Bus Station	B2
Cambuskenneth Bridge	A3
Carlton ♨	C2
Castle Ct	B1
Causewayhead Rd	A2/B1
Cemetery	A2
Church of the Holy Rude ⛪	B1
Clarendon Pl	C1
Club House	B1
Colquhoun St	C3
Corn Exchange	B2
Council Offices	C2
Court	B2
Cowane ♨	A2
Cowane St	A2
Cowane's Hospital ⛪	B1
Crawford Shopping Arcade	B2
Crofthead Rd	A3
Dean Cres	A3
Douglas St	A2
Drip Rd	A1
Drummond La	C1
Drummond Pl	C1
Drummond Pl La	C1
Dumbarton Rd	C2
Eastern Access Rd	B2
Edward Ave	A3
Edward Rd	A2
Forrest Rd	A2
Fort	A1
Forth Cres	B2
Forth St	A2
Gladstone Pl	C1
Glebe Ave	C1
Glebe Cres	C1
Glendevon Dr	A1
Golf Course	C1
Goosecroft Rd	B2
Gowanhill	A1
Greenwood Ave	B1
Harvey Wynd	A1
Information Ctr ℹ	A1/C2
Irvine Pl	B2
James St	A2
John St	B1
Kerse Rd	C3
King's Knot ✦	B1
King's Park	C1
King's Park Rd	C1
Laurencecroft Rd	A2
Leisure Pool	B2
Library	B2
Linden Ave	C2
Lovers Wk	A2
Lower Back Walk	A2
Lower Bridge St	A2
Lower Castlehill	A1
Mar Pl	B1
Meadow Pl	A1
Meadowforth Rd	C3
Middlemuir Rd	C3
Millar Pl	A3
Morris Terr	B2
Mote Hill	A1
Murray Pl	B2
Nelson Pl	C2
Old Town Jail	B1
Orchard House Hospital (No A&E) H	A2
Park Terr	C1
Phoenix Industrial Estate	C3
Players Rd	C3
Port St	C2
Post Office ✉	A3/B1/B2/C2
Princes St	B2
Queen St	B2
Queen's Rd	C1
Queenshaugh Dr	A3
Rainbow Slides	B2
Ramsay Pl	A1
Riverside Dr	A3
Ronald Pl	A1
Rosebery Pl	A1
Royal Gardens	B1
Royal Gdns	B1
St Mary's Wynd	B1
St Ninian's Rd	C2
Scott St	A2
Seaforth Pl	C1
Shore Rd	A3
Smith Art Gallery & Museum 🏛	B1
Snowdon Pl	C1
Snowdon Pl La	C1
Spittal St	B2
Springkerse Industrial Estate	C3
Springkerse Rd	C3
Stirling Business Centre	C2
Stirling Castle 🏰	A1
Stirling County Rugby Football Club	A3
Stirling Enterprise Park	B3
Stirling Old Bridge	A2
Stirling 🚉	B2
Superstore	A2
Sutherland Ave	A3
TA Centre	C3
Tannery La	C1
Thistle Industrial Estate	C3
Thistles Shopping Centre, The	B2
Tollbooth, The ✦	B1
Town Wall	B1
Union St	B1
Upper Back Walk	A1
Upper Bridge St	A1
Upper Castlehill	B1
Upper Craigs	C2
Victoria Pl	C1
Victoria Rd	C1
Victoria Sq	B1/C1
Wallace St	A2
Waverley Cres	A3
Wellgreen Rd	C2
Windsor Pl	C1
YHA ▲	B1

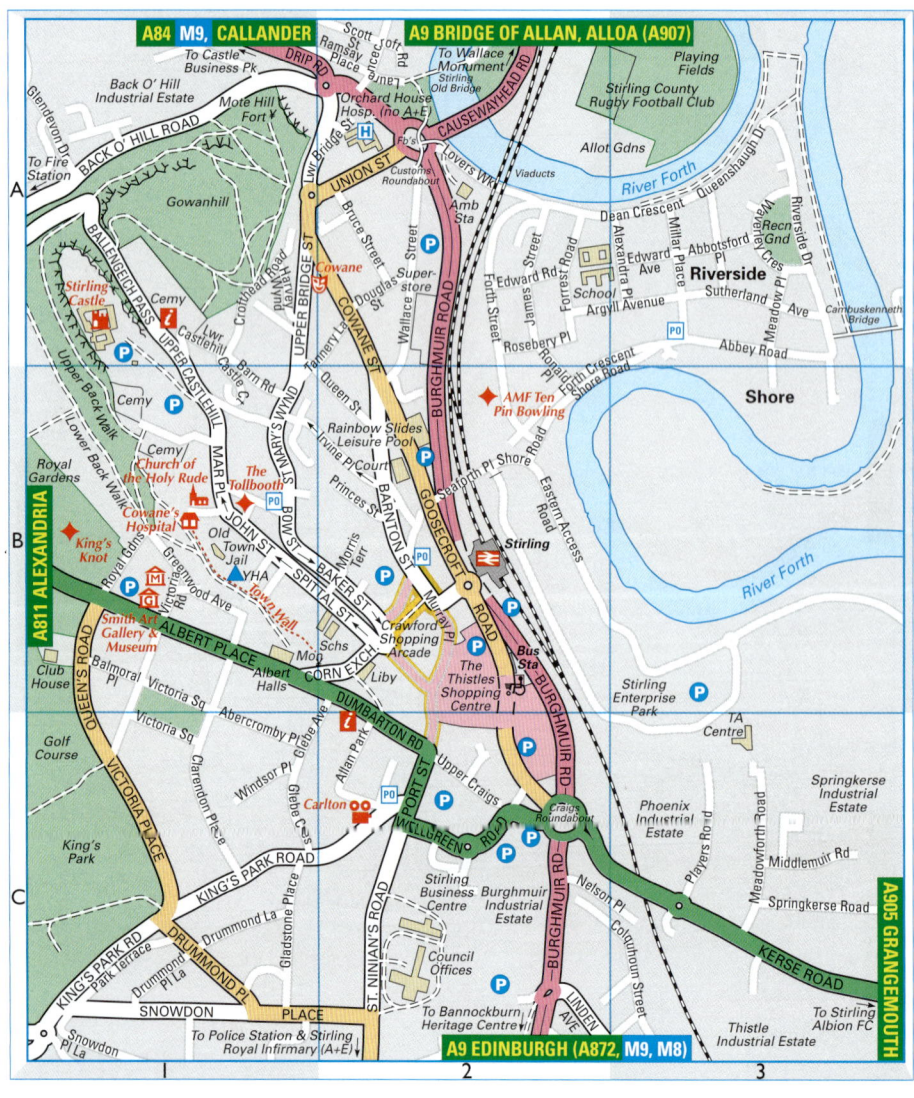

Stoke-on-Trent

Stoke is part of a city made up of six towns known collectively as The Potteries. The city is thus named as it is home to a host of world-renowned pottery manufacturers such as Aynsley, Portmeirion, Royal Doulton, Spode and Wedgwood. There are visitor centres, ceramic museums, and factory shops where you can buy direct from source. For your shopping requirements there are indoor and outdoor markets. Stoke is home to Staffordshire University and therefore a very vibrant town with its many theatres, pubs and restaurants. Festival Park has family attractions, including Waterworld theme park.

▲Gladstone Pottery Museum, Longton

Stoke-on-Trent Tourist Information Centre, Victoria Hall, Cultural Quarter, Stoke-on-Trent City Centre ST1 3AD
Tel 01782 236000

BBC Radio Stoke 94.6 FM • Signal 1 102.6 FM • Signal 2 1170 AM

www.visitstoke.co.uk

★ Do not miss
- ★ **The Courtyards at Spode**, Church Street – visitor centre and factory tour
- ★ **Churchill China**, Whielden Road – factory tour
- ★ **Gladstone Pottery Museum**, Uttoxeter Road, Longton

Stoke-on-Trent

Street	Ref	Street	Ref
Ashford St	A3	Lytton St	B3
Avenue Rd	A3	Market	C2
Aynsley Rd	A2	Mount School for the Deaf	B1
Barnfield	C1	Newcastle La	C1
Bath St	C2	Newlands St	A2
Beresford St	A3	Norfolk St	A2
Bilton St	C2	North St	A1/B2
Boon Ave	B2	North Staffordshire Royal Infirmary (A&E)	B1
Booth St	C2	Northcote Ave	C1
Boothen Rd	B2/B3	Oldmill St	C3
Boughey St	C2	Oriel St	B1
Boughley Rd	B3	Oxford St	B1
Brighton St	B1	Penkhull New Rd	C1
Campbell Rd	C2	Penkhull St	C1
Carlton Rd	B3	Police Station	C2
Cauldon Rd	A3	Portmeirion Pottery	C2
Cemetery	A2	Post Office	A3/B1/B3/C1/C2
Cemetery Rd	A2	Prince's Rd	B1
Chamberlain Ave	C1	Pump St	B2
Church (RC)	B2	Quarry Ave	B1
Church St	C2	Quarry Rd	B1
City Rd	C3	Queen Anne St	A3
Civic Centre	B3	Queen's Rd	C1
Cliff Vale Pk	A1	Queensway	A1/B2/C3
College Rd	A3	Richmond St	B1
Convent Cl	B2	Rothwell St	C1
Copeland St	B2	St Peter's	B3
Cornwallis St	C3	St Thomas Pl	C1
Corporation St	C2	Scrivenor Rd	A1
Crowther St	A3	Seaford St	A3
Dominic St	B2	Selwyn St	C3
Elenora St	B2	Shelton New Rd	A1
Elgin St	B2	Shelton Old Rd	B2
Epworth St	C1	Sheppard St	C2
Etruscan St	A1	Spark St	C2
Fleming Rd	C2	Spencer Rd	B3
Fletcher Rd	C2	Spode Museum & Visitor Centre	B2
Floyd St	B2	Spode St	C2
Foden St	C2	Squires View	B3
Frank St	C2	Staffordshire Univ	B3
Franklin Rd	C1	Stanley Matthews Sports Centre	B3
Frederick Ave	B1	Station Rd	B3
Garden St	C1	Stoke Business Park	C3
Garner St	A1	Stoke Film Theatre	B3
Gerrard St	B1	Stoke Rd	A2
Glebe St	B3	Stoke-on-Trent College	A3
Greatbach Ave	B1	Stoke-on-Trent Station	B3
Hanley Park	A3	Sturgess St	C2
Harris St	B1	The Villas	C1
Hartshill Rd	B1	Thistley Hough	C1
Hayward St	A2	Thornton Rd	B3
Hide St	B2	Tolkien Way	C1
Higson Ave	B2	Trent Valley Rd	C1
Hill St	B2	Vale St	B2
Honeywall	B2	Watford St	A3
Hunters Dr	C1	Wellesley St	B1
Hunters Way	C1	West Ave	B1
Keary St	C2	Westland St	B1
Kingsway	B2	Yeaman St	C2
Leek Rd	B3	Yoxall Ave	B1
Leisure Centre	C2		
Library	B1		
Lime St	B2		
Liverpool Rd	B2		
London Rd	C2		
Lonsdale St	C2		
Lovatt St	B2		

Stratford-upon-Avon

Historic medieval market town most famous as the birthplace of William Shakespeare in 1564, boasting several sites associated with the playwright, including Mary Arden's House, childhood home of his mother; Hall's Croft, a Tudor house inhabited by his daughter Susanna; Nash's House/New Place, a replica of an Elizabethan knot garden on the site of his retirement home; and his wife's pre-marital home. The Royal Shakespeare Company operates three venues here, including The Swan, a recreation of an Elizabethan galleried playouse, and there is a wide range of restaurants and specialist shops catering to theatregoers and tourists. Other sights include Harvard House, a largely 17th-century townhouse linked with the founder of Harvard University, the Shire Horse Centre and, a few miles away, the National Trust's Charlecote Park.

◀ The Swan Theatre

Stratford-upon-Avon Tourist Information Centre, Bridgefoot, Stratford CV37 6GW
Tel 0870 160 7930

BBC Coventry and Warwickshire
94.8, 103.7 FM • **102FM The Bear**
102 FM

www.shakespeare-country.co.uk

★ **Do not miss**
★ **Anne Hathaway's Cottage**, Shottery
★ **Shakespeare's Birthplace**, Henley Street
★ **The Swan Theatre**, Waterside

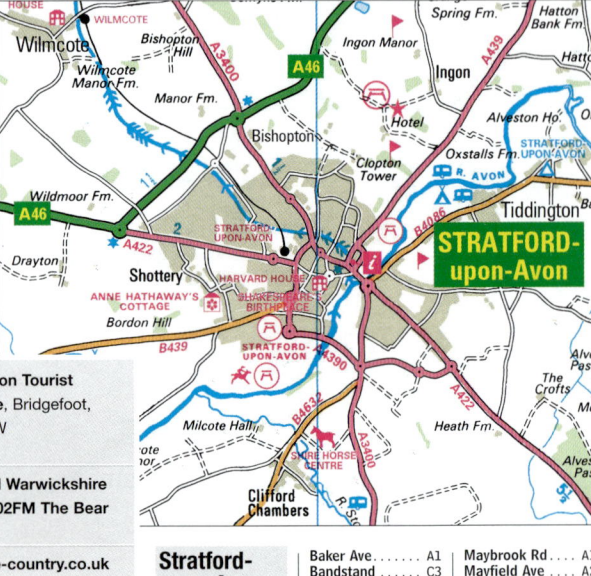

Stratford-upon-Avon

Albany Rd B1	Baker Ave A1
Alcester Rd B1	Bandstand C3
Ambulance Stn B1	Benson Rd A3
Arden St B2	Birmingham Rd . . . A2
Avenue Farm A1	Boat Club B3
Avenue Field Ind Est A1	Borden Pl C1
Avenue Rd A3	**Brass Rubbing Centre** ✦ C2
Avon Ind Est A2	Bridge St B2
	Bridgetown Rd . . . C3
	Bridgeway B3
	Broad St C2
	Broad Walk C2
	Brookvale Rd C1
	Bull St C2
	Butterfly Farm & Jungle Safari ✦ . . C3
	Bus Station B2
	Cemetery C1
	Chapel La B2
	Cherry Orchard . . . C1
	Chestnut Walk . . . B2
	Children's Playground C3
	Church St C2
	Civic Hall B2
	Clarence Rd B1
	Clopton Bridge ✦ . . B3
	Clopton Rd A2
	Coach Terminal & Park B3
	College B1
	College La C2
	College St C2
	Community Sports Centre . . B1
	Council Offices (District) B2
	Council Offices (Town) B2
	Courtyard ✦ C2
	Cox's Yard ✦ B3
	Cricket Ground . . . C3
	Ely Gdns B2
	Ely St B2
	Evesham Rd C1
	Fire Station B1
	Foot Ferry C3
	Football Ground . . A1
	Fordham Ave A2
	Gallery, The ✦ B3
	Garrick Way C1
	Gower Memorial ✦ . . . B3
	Great William St . . B2
	Greenhill St B2
	Grove Rd B2
	Guild St B2
	Guildhall & Sch ✦ . B2
	Hall's Croft ✦ C2
	Hartford Rd C1
	Harvard House ✦ . . B2
	Henley St B2
	High St B2
	Holton St C2
	Holy Trinity ✦ C2
	Information Ctr . . . B3
	Jolyffe Park Rd . . . A2
	Judith Shakespeare's House ✦ B2
	Kipling Rd C3
	Leisure & Visitor Centre B3
	Library B2
	Lodge Rd B1
	Maidenhead Rd . . . A3
	Mansell St B2
	Masons Court B1
	Masons Rd A1
	Maybird Retail Pk A2
Maybrook Rd A1
Mayfield Ave A2
Meer St B2
Mill La C2
Moat House Hotel . . B3
Narrow L C2
New Place & Nash's House ✦ . . B2
New St C2
Old Town C2
Orchard Way C1
Paddock La C1
Park Rd A1
Payton St B2
Percy St A2
Police Station ✦ B2
Post Office ✉ B2/B3/C2
Rec Grnd C2
Regal Rd A2
Regal Road Trading Estate . . A2
Rother St B2
Rowley Cr A3
Royal Shakespeare Theatre ✦ B3
Ryland St B3
Saffron Meadow . . C2
St Andrew's Cr . . . B1
St Gregory's ✦ A3
St Gregory's Rd . . . A3
St Mary's Rd B1
Sanctus Dr C2
Sanctus St C1
Sandfield Rd C2
Scholars La C2
Seven Meadows Rd C2
Shakespeare Ctr ✦ . B2
Shakespeare Inst . . C2
Shakespeare La . . . B2
Shakespeare's Birthplace ✦ . . . B2
Sheep St B2
Shelley Rd C3
Shipston Rd C3
Shottery Rd C1
Slingates Rd A2
Southern La C2
Station Rd B1
Stratford-upon-Avon Hospital ⊞ . B2
Stratford Sports Club B1
Stratford-upon-Avon Station ⇌ . . B1
Swan Theatre ✦ . . . B3
Talbot Rd A2
Teddy Bears Museum ✦ B2
The Greenway C1
The Willows B1
The Willows North . B1
Tiddington Rd B3
Timothy's Bridge Rd A1
Town Hall B2
Town Sq B2
Tramway Bridge . . B3
Trinity St C2
Tyler St B2
War Memorial Gdns B3
Warwick Rd B3
Waterside B3
Welcombe Rd B3
West St C2
Western Rd A2
Wharf Rd A2
Wood St B2

Sunderland

The port of Sunderland has a heritage going back over 800 years. By 1840 Sunderland was the biggest shipbuilding port in the world but by 1988 the last shipyard had closed. Meanwhile, location of a Nissan plant in Sunderland was a catalyst for new jobs in the automotive sector. The closure of the City's last coalmine, Wearmouth Colliery, in 1994 brought to an end the traditional industries. St Peter's Church founded in 674AD is one of the most important sites of early Christian history in England. Other places of interest include the Monkwearmouth Station Museum, Ryhope Engines Museum and Sunderland Museum and Winter Gardens. There's the beautiful fully restored Mowbray Park in the centre and Roker Beach on the coast. The Bridges Shopping centre boasts a wide selection of high street brands and there are many theatres, restaurants and pubs to choose from.

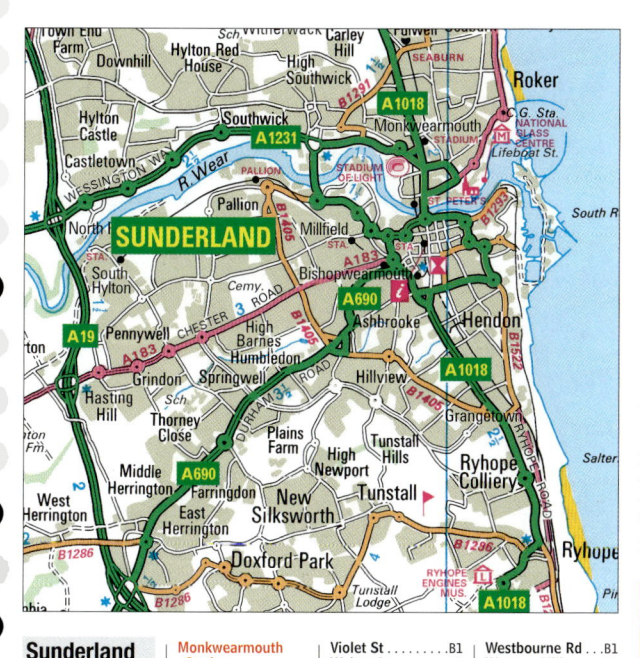

▲ St Peter's church

★ Do not miss:
- ★ National Glass Centre, Liberty Way
- ★ Northern Gallery for Contemporary Art, City Library and Arts Centre, Fawcett Street – new work by international artists
- ★ St Peter's Church, St Peter's Way

Tourist Information Centre, 50 Fawcett Street, Sunderland SR1 1RF Tel 0191 553 2000

BBC Radio Newcastle 95.4 FM and 1458 AM • Century 101.8 FM Galaxy 105.3 FM • Sun 103.4 FM

www.sunderland.gov.uk

137

Sunderland

Street	Grid
Albion Pl	C2
Alliance Pl	B1
Argyle St	C2
Ashwood St	C2
Athenaeum St	B2
Azalea Terr	C2
Beach St	A1
Bede Theatre	C3
Bedford St	B2
Beechwood Terr	C1
Belvedere Rd	C2
Blandford St	B2
Borough Rd	B3
Bridge Cr	B2
Bridge St	A2
Brooke St	A2
Brougham St	B2
Burdon Rd	C2
Burn Park	C1
Burn Park Rd	C1
Carol St	B1
Charles St	A3
Chester St	C1
Chester Terr	B1
Church St	A3
Cineworld	B2
Civic Centre	C2
Cork St	B3
Coronation St	B3
Cowan Terr	C2
Crowtree Rd	B2
Dame Dorothy St	A2
Deptford Rd	C1
Deptford Terr	A1
Derby St	C2
Derwent St	C2
Dock St	A3
Dundas St	A2
Durham Rd	C1
Easington St	A2
Egerton St	C3
Empire Theatre	B2
Farringdon Row	B1
Fawcett St	B2
Festival Park	B2
Fox St	C1
Foyle St	B3
Frederick St	B3
Gill Rd	B2
Hanover Pl	A1
Havelock Terr	C1
Hay St	A2
Headworth Sq	B3
Hendon Rd	B3
High St East	B3
High St West	B2/B3
Holmeside	B2
Hylton Rd	B1
Information Ctr	B2
John St	B3
Kier Hardie Way	A3
Lambton St	B3
Laura St	C3
Lawrence St	B3
Leisure Centre	B2
Library & Arts Centre	B3
Lily St	B1
Lime St	B1
Livingstone Rd	B2
Low Row	B2
Matamba Terr	B1
Millburn St	B1
Millennium Way	A2
Minster	B2
Monkwearmouth Station Museum	A2
Mowbray Park	C3
Mowbray Rd	C3
Murton St	C3
Museum	B3
National Glass Centre	A3
New Durham Rd	C1
Newcastle Rd	A2
Nile St	B3
Norfolk St	B3
North Bridge St	A2
Otto Terr	C1
Park La	C2
Park Lane (Metro Station)	C2
Park Rd	C2
Paul's Rd	B3
Peel St	C3
Police Station	B2
Post Office	B2
Priestly Cr	A1
Queen St	B2
Railway Row	B1
Retail Park	A1
Richmond St	C2
Roker Ave	A2
Royalty Theatre	B2
Ryhope Rd	C2
St Mary's Way	B2
St Michael's Way	B2
St Peter's	A3
St Peter's (Metro Station)	A2
St Peter's Way	A3
St Vincent St	C3
Salem Rd	C3
Salem St	C3
Salisbury St	C3
Sans St	C2
Silkworth Row	B1
Southwick Rd	A2
Stadium of Light (Sunderland A.F.C.)	A2
Stadium Way	A2
Stobart St	A2
Stockton Rd	C2
Suffolk St	C3
Sunderland (Metro Station)	B2
Sunderland	B3
Sunderland St	B3
Tatham St	C3
Tavistock Pl	B3
Technology Park	B2
The Bridges	B2
The Royalty	C1
Thelma St	C1
Thomas St North	A2
Thornholme Rd	C1
Toward Rd	C3
Transport Interchange	C2
Trimdon St Way	B1
Tunstall Rd	C2
University	A3/B1/C2
University (Metro Station)	C1
University Library	C1
Vaux Brewery Way	A2
Villiers St	B3
Villiers St South	B3
Vine Pl	C2
Violet St	B1
Walton La	B3
Waterworks Rd	B1
Wearmouth Bridge	B2
Wellington La	A1
West Sunniside	B3
West Wear St	B3
Westbourne Rd	C2
Western Hill	C1
Wharncliffe	B3
Whickham St	A3
White House Rd	A3
Wilson St North	A2
Winter Gdns	C3
Wreath Quay	A1

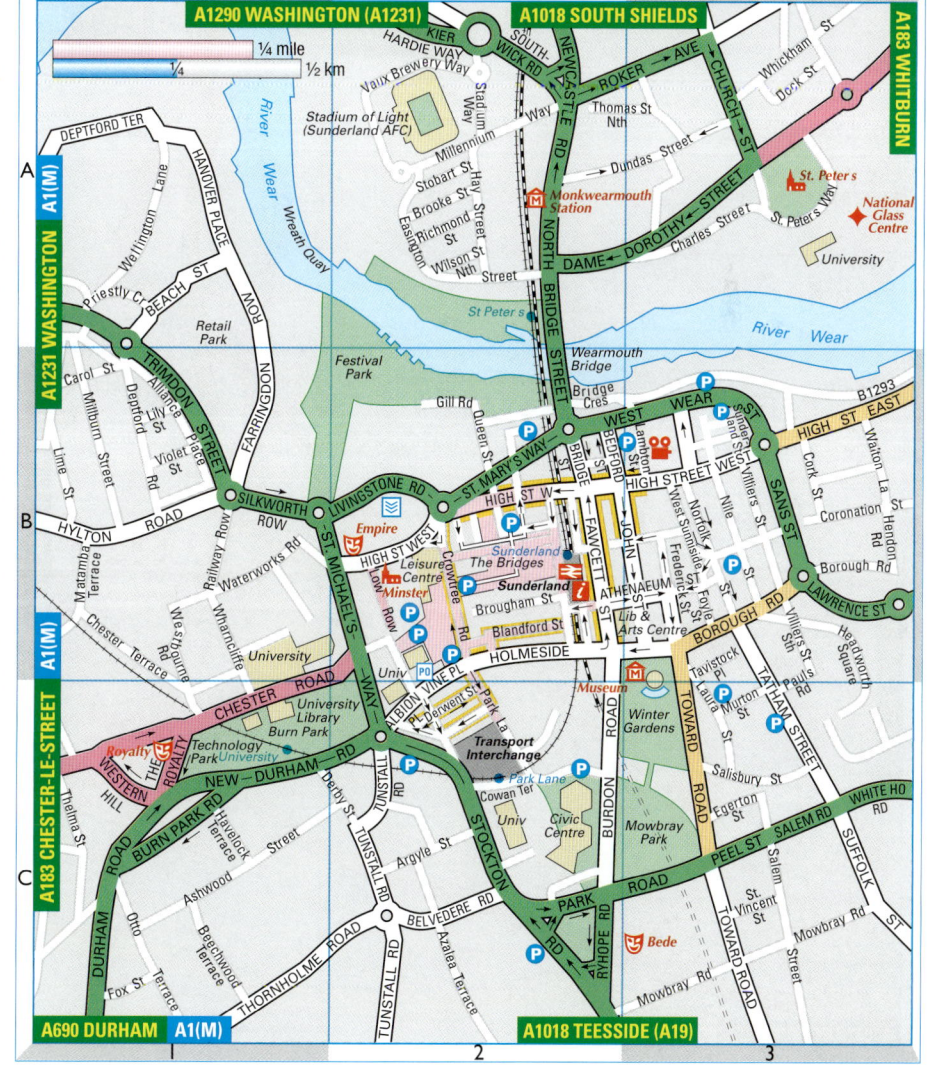

Swansea

▲ Swansea's Maritime Quarter

ℹ Tourist Information Centre, Plymouth St, Swansea SA1 3QG Tel 01792 468321

📡 BBC Radio Wales 93.9 FM • **Real Radio** 106.0 FM • **The Wave** 96.4 FM
Swansea Sound 1170 AM

🌐 www.swansea.gov.uk

Swansea was founded in the 10th century by the Vikings and named after the Danish king Swein Forkbeard. Extensively bombed in WWII there remains little physical evidence of the city's history. Swansea was one of the major smelting centres of the Industrial Revolution, but now as a 21st-century city it focuses on its literary and maritime heritage with the Dylan Thomas Centre and National Waterfront Museum. There is a wide array of shopping with both The Quadrant and St David's centres. There are also the Blue Flag beaches, Botanical Gardens – with Chyne Gardens, Singleton Botanical Garden and Plantasia, several theatres and a variety of pubs and restaurants.

★ Do not miss
- ★ **Glynn Vivian Art Gallery**, Alexandra Road – international fine art
- ★ **Swansea Museum**, Victoria Road, The Maritime Quarter – local history
- ★ **Plantasia**, Parc Tawe – hothouse garden with animals and plants

Swansea/Abertawe

Street	Grid
Adelaide St	C3
Albert Row	C3
Alexandra Rd	B3
Argyle St	C1
Baptist Well Pl	A2
Beach St	C1
Belle Vue Way	B3
Berw Rd	A1
Berwick Terr	A2
Bond St	C1
Brangwyn Concert Hall	A1
Bridge St	A3
Brookands Terr	B1
Brunswick St	C1
Bryn-Syfi Terr	A2
Bryn-y-Mor Rd	C1
Bullins La	B1
Burrows Rd	C1
Bus/Rail link	A3
Bus Station	C2
Cadfan Rd	A1
Cadrawd Rd	A1
Caer St	B3
Carig Cr	A1
Carlton Terr	B2
Carmarthen Rd	A3
Castle St	B3
Catherine St	C1
City & County of Swansea Offices (County Hall)	B3
City & County of Swansea Offices (Guildhall)	C1
Clarence St	C2
Colbourne Terr	A2
Constitution Hill	B1
Court	B3
Creidiol Rd	A2
Cromwell St	B2
Duke St	B1
Dunvant Pl	C2
Dyfatty Park	A3
Dyfatty St	A3
Dyfed Ave	A1
Dylan Thomas Centre ♦	B3
Dylan Thomas ⚓	C3
Eaton Cr	C1
Eigen Cr	A1
Elfed Rd	A1
Emlyn Rd	A1
Evans Terr	A3
Fairfield Terr	B1
Ffynone Dr	B1
Ffynone Rd	B1
Fire Station	B3
Firm St	A2
Fleet St	C1
Francis St	C1
Fullers Row	B1
George St	B2
Glamorgan St	C2
Glyndwr Pl	A1
Glynn Vivian 🖼	B3
Graig Terr	A3
Grand Theatre 🎭	C2
Granogwen Rd	A2
Guildhall Rd South	C1
Gwent Rd	C1
Gwynedd Ave	A1
Hafod St	A3
Hanover St	B1
Harcourt St	B2
Harries St	A2
Heathfield	B2
Henrietta St	B1
Hewson St	B1
High St	A3/B3
High View	B1
Hill St	A2
Historic Ships Berth ⚓	C3
HM Prison	C2
Information Ctr ℹ	C2
Islwyn Rd	A1
King Edward's Rd	C1
Law Courts	C1
Library	B3
Long Ridge	A2
Madoc St	C2
Mansel St	B2
Maritime Quarter	C3
Market	B3
Mayhill Gdns	B1
Mayhill Rd	A1
Mega Bowl ♦	B3
Milton Terr	A2
Mission Gallery 🖼	C3
Montpellier Terr	B1
Morfa Rd	A3
Mount Pleasant	B2
National Waterfront Museum 🖼	C3
Nelson St	C2
New Cut Rd	A3
New St	A3
Nicander Pde	A2
Nicander Pl	A2
Nicholl St	B2
Norfolk St	B2
North Hill Rd	A1
Northampton La	B2
Orchard St	B3
Oxford St	B2
Oystermouth Rd	C1
Page St	B2
Pant-y-Celyn Rd	B1
Parc Tawe North	B3
Parc Tawe Shopping & Leisure Ctr	B3
Patti Pavilion 🎭	C1
Paxton St	C2
Penmaen Terr	B1
Pen-y-Graig Rd	A1
Phillips Pde	C1
Picton Terr	B2
Plantasia ✿	B3
Police Station	B2
Post Office	A1/A2/A3/B2/C1/C2/C3
Powys Ave	A1
Primrose St	B2
Princess Way	B3
Promenade	A1
Pryder Gdns	A1
Quadrant Centre	C2
Quay Park	C3
Rhianfa La	B1
Rhondda St	B2
Richardson St	C2
Rodney St	C1
Rose Hill	B1
Rosehill Terr	B1
Russell St	B1
St David's Sq	C3
St Helen's Ave	C1
St Helen's Cr	C1
St Helen's Rd	C1
St James Gdns	B1
St James's Cr	B1
St Mary's	B3
Sea View Terr	A3
Singleton St	C2
South Dock	C3
Stanley Pl	B1
Strand	B3
Swansea Castle ♦	B3
Swansea College Arts Centre	C1
Swansea	C3
Swansea 🚉	A3
Taliesyn Rd	B1
Tan y Marian Rd	A1
Technical College	B2
Tegid Rd	A1
Teilo Cr	C1
Terrace Rd	B1/B2
The Kingsway	B2
Tontine St	A3
Tower of Eclipse ♦	C3
Townhill Rd	A1
Tram Museum 🚋	C3
Trawler Rd	C3
Union St	B2
Upper Strand	A3
Vernon St	A3
Victoria Quay	C3
Victoria Rd	C3
Vincent St	C1
Walter Rd	B1
Watkin St	A2
Waun-Wen Rd	A2
Wellington St	C2
Western St	C1
Westbury St	C1
Westway	C2
William St	C2
Wind St	B3
Woodlands Terr	B1
YMCA	B2
York St	C3

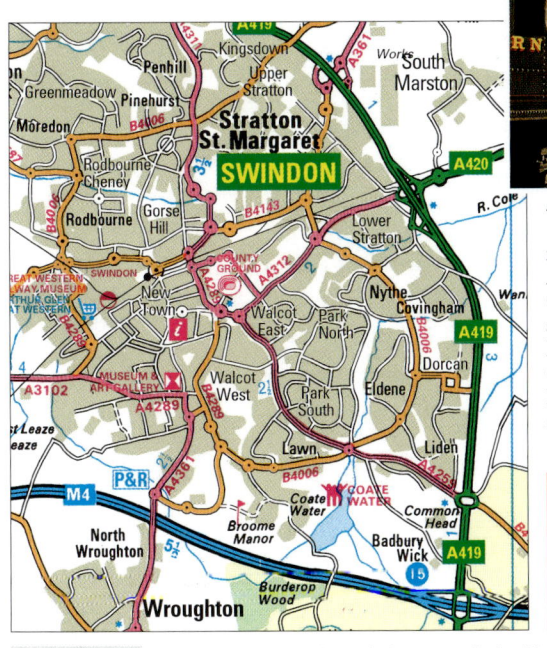

Swindon

▲ Swindon-built locomotive, *Nunney Castle*

A Saxon village that grew into a hilltop medieval market town and then into Wiltshire's biggest town with the arrival of the Great Western Railway in 1840 – the reconstructed Swindon and Cricklade Railway now offers steam-train trips. A thriving commercial centre, it has a number of small specialist shops in its Old Town and a designer clothes centre in restored railway buildings that also house the Great Western Railway museum. There's an important collection of 20th-century British works in its art gallery. Green spaces include Coate Water Country Park with its 56-acre lake, and, a few miles away, Barbury Castle, an Iron Age hillfort on the Ridgeway, surrounded by a 150-acre country park, Stanton Park, an area of 19th-century landscaped parkland.

★ Do not miss
- ★ **Lydiard House**, Park and Visitor Centre, Hook Street, Lydiard Tregoze
- ★ **Swindon Museum and Art Gallery**, Bath Road
- ★ **STEAM, Museum of the Great Western Railway**, Kemble Drive

ℹ Swindon Tourist Information Centre, 37 Regent St, Swindon SN1 1JL Tel 01793 530328

BBC Radio Wiltshire 103.5 FM
Classic Gold 936 and 1101 AM
GWR 97.2 and 102.2 FM

www.visitswindon.co.uk

139

Swindon

Albert St.	C3
Albion St.	C1
Alfred St.	A2
Alvescot Rd	C3
Art Gallery & Museum	C3
Ashford Rd.	C1
Aylesbury St.	A2
Bath Rd.	C1
Bathampton St.	B1
Bathurst Rd	B3
Beatrice St.	A2
Beckhampton St.	B3
Bowood Rd	C1
Bristol St.	A3
Broad St.	A3
Brunel Arcade	B2
Brunel Plaza	B2
Brunswick St.	C2
Bus Station	B2
Cambria Br Rd.	B1
Cambria Pl.	B1
Canal Walk	B2
Carfax St	B2
Carr St	B2
Cemetery	C1/C3
Chandler Cl	C3
Chapel	C2
Chester St	B1
Christ Church	C3
Church Pl	B1
Cirencester Way	A3
Clarence St	B2
Clifton St	C1
Cockleberry (r'about)	A2
Colbourne (r'about)	A3
Colbourne St	A3
College St	B2
Commercial Rd	B2
Corporation St	A2
Council Offices	B3
County Rd	A3
Courts	B2
Cricket Ground	A3
Cricklade St	C3
Crombey St	B1/B2
Cross St	C2
Curtis St	B1
Deacon St	C1
Designer Outlet (Great Western)	B1
Dixon St	C2
Dover St	C2
Dowling St	C2
Drove Rd	C3
Dryden St	C1
Durham St	C3
East St	B1
Eastcott Hill	C2
Eastcott Rd	C2
Edgeware Rd	B2
Elmina Rd.	A3
Emlyn Sq	B1
Euclid St	B3
Exeter St.	B1
Fairview	C1
Faringdon Rd.	B1
Farnsby St.	B1
Fire Station	B3
Fleet St	B2
Fleming Way	B2/B3
Florence St	A2
Gladstone St	A3
Gooch St	A2
Graham St	A3
Great Western Way	A1/A2
Groundwell Rd	B3
Hawksworth Way	A1
Haydon St	A2
Henry St	B2
Hillside Ave	C1
Holbrook Way	B2
Hunt St	C1
Hydro	B1
Hythe Rd	C2
Information Ctr	B2
Joseph St	C1
Kent Rd.	C2
King William St	C1
Kingshill Rd	C1
Lansdown Rd	C2
Leicester St	B3
Library	B2
Lincoln St	C3
Little London	C3
London St	B1
Magic R'about	A3
Maidstone Rd	C2
Manchester Rd	A3
Market Hall	B2
Maxwell St	B1
Milford St	B2
Milton Rd	B1
Morse St	C2
Nat Monuments Record Centre	B1
Newcastle St	B3
Newcombe Dr	A1
Newcombe Trading Estate	A1
Newhall St	C2
North St	C2
North Star (r'about)	A1
North Star Ave	A1
Northampton St	B3
Oasis Leisure Ctr.	A1
Ocotal Way	A3
Okus Rd	C1
Old Town	C3
Oxford St	B1
Park Lane	B1
Park Lane (r'about)	B1
Pembroke St	C2
Plymouth St	B3
Polaris House	A2
Polaris Way	A2
Police Station	B2
Ponting St	B1
Post Office	B1/B2/C1/C3
Poulton St	A3
Princes St	B2
Prospect Hill	C2
Prospect Pl	C2
Queen St	B2
Queen's Park	C3
Radnor St	C1
Railway Village	B1
Read St	C1
Reading St	B1
Regent St	B1
Retail Park	A2/A3/B3
Rosebery St	A3
St Mark's	B1
Salisbury St	A3
Savernake St	C2
Shelley St	C1
Sheppard St	B1
South St	C1
Southampton St	B3
Spring Gdns	B1
Stafford St	C1
Stanier St	C2
Station Rd	A2
Steam	B1
Swindon	B1
Swindon Coll.	A2/C2
Swindon Rd	C1
Swindon Town F.C.	A3
TA Centre	B1
Tennyson St	B1
The Lawn	C3
The Nurseries	C1
The Parade	B2
The Park	B1
Theobald St	B1
Town Hall	B2
Transfer Bridges (r'about)	A3
Union St	C2
Upham Rd	C3
Victoria Rd	C3
Walcot Rd	B3
War Memorial	B2
Wells St	B3
Western St	C2
Westmorland Rd	B3
Whalebridge (r'about)	B2
Whitehead St	C1
Whitehouse Rd	A3
William St	C1
Wood St	C3
Wyvern	B2
York Rd	B3

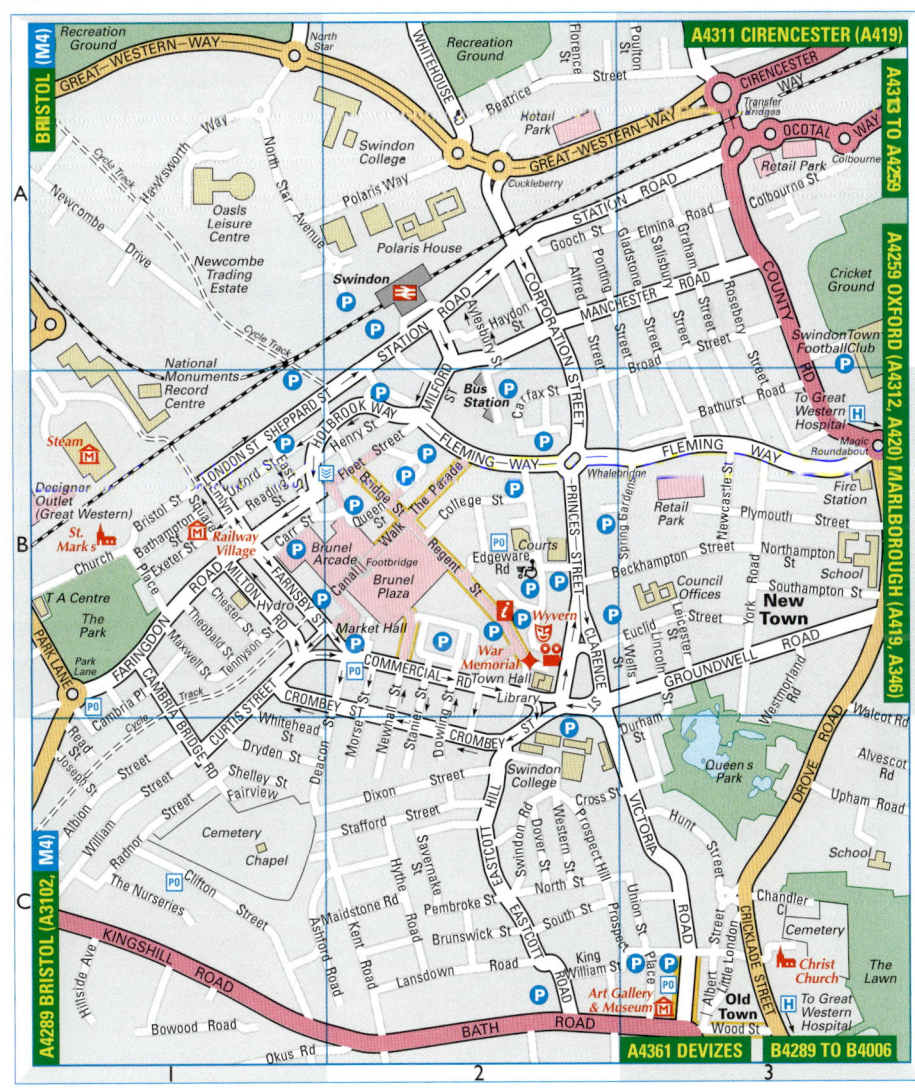

Taunton

Taunton Tourist Information Centre,
Paul Street, Taunton TA1 3PF
Tel 01823 336344

BBC Somerset Sound 1566 AM
Orchard 96.5, 102.6 FM

www.tauntondeane.gov.uk

★ Do not miss

- ★ **Hestercombe Gardens**, Cheddon Fitzpaine
- ★ **Sheppy's Cider Farm**, Three Bridges, Bradford-on-Tone
- ★ **Somerset Cricket Museum**, County Ground

Somerset's county town, on the site of a Saxon fortress, with a pre-Conquest Saturday market. Buildings of historic interest include the Perpendicular St Mary Magdalene with its splendid tower, and a grammar school founded in 1522. Taunton has a tradition of brewing dating back as far as the Romans and continued by medieval monks; in the 20th century this was overtaken by cider-making. Somerset County Museum in historic Taunton Castle has a toy and doll collection, plus archeological artefacts, some from Roman times. There's a Monday antiques market with around 130 stalls and a good range of shops. Sights in the immediate vicinity include Bishops Lydeard Mill with its 2-tonne waterwheel, and Blazes Fire Museum about humans' relationship with fire.

▲ Taunton Castle

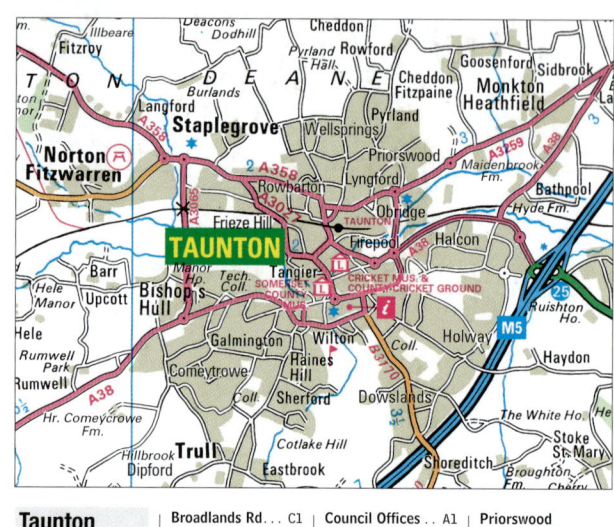

Street	Grid
Addison Gr.	A1
Albemarle Rd.	A1
Alfred St.	B3
Alma St.	C2
Bath Pl.	C1
Belvedere Rd.	A1
Billet St	B2
Billetfield	C2
Birch Gr	A1
Brewhouse Theatre ⚜	B2
Bridge St	B1
Bridgwater & Taunton Canal.	A2
Broadlands Rd.	C1
Burton Pl	C1
Bus Station	B1
Canal Rd.	A2
Cann St.	C1
Canon St.	B2
Castle ⚜	B1
Castle St.	B1
Cheddon Rd.	A2
Chip Lane	A1
Clarence St.	B1
Cleveland St.	B1
Coleridge Cres	C3
Compass Hill	C1
Compton Cl	A2
Corporation St	B1
Council Offices	A1
County Walk Shopping Ctr.	C2
Courtyard	B2
Cranmer Rd	B2
Cyril St	A1
Deller's Wharf	B1
Duke St.	B2
East Reach	B3
East St	B3
Eastbourne Rd.	A2
Eastleigh Rd	C3
Eaton Cres	A2
Elm Gr	A1
Elms Cl	A1
Fons George	C1
Fore St	B2
Fowler St	A1
French Weir Rec Grnd	B1
Geoffrey Farrant Wk.	A2
Gray's Almshouses ⚜	B2
Grays Rd.	B3
Greenway Ave	A1
Guildford Pl	C1
Hammet St.	B2
Haydon Rd	B3
Heavitree Way	A2
Herbert St	A1
High St	B2
Holway Ave	C3
Hugo St	B3
Huish's Almshouses ⚜	B2
Hurdle Way	C2
Information Ctr ℹ	C2
Jubilee St.	A1
King's College	C3
Kings Cl	C3
Laburnum St	B2
Lambrook Rd.	B3
Lansdowne Rd.	A2
Leslie Ave.	A1
Leycroft Rd	A3
Library	C2
Linden Gr	A1
Livestock Market.	A2
Magdalene St	B2
Magistrates Court.	B1
Malvern Terr	A2
Market House ⚜	B2
Mary St.	C2
Middle St	C2
Midford Rd.	B3
Mitre Court	B3
Mount Nebo	C1
Mount St	C1
Mountway	C2
North St	B2
Northfield Ave.	B1
Northfield Rd.	B1
Northleigh Rd	C3
Obridge Allotments	A3
Obridge Lane.	A3
Obridge Rd	A3
Obridge Viaduct	A3
Old Market Shopping Ctr.	C2
Osborne Way.	C1
Park St	C1
Paul St	C2
Plais St.	A2
Playing Field	C1
Police Station 🚔	C1
Portland St	B1
Post Office ✉	A1/B1/B2/C1
Priorswood Industrial Estate	A3
Priorswood Rd	A2
Priory Ave	B2
Priory Barn Cricket Museum ⚜	B1
Priory Bridge Rd.	B2
Priory Park	A2
Priory Way	A3
Queen St	B3
Railway St	A1
Records Office.	A2
Recreation Grd	A1
Riverside Place	B2
St Augustine St.	B2
St George's ⚜	C2
St Georges Sq	C2
St James ⚜	B2
St. James St	B2
St John's ⚜	C1
St John's Rd	B1
St Joseph's Field	C2
St Mary Magdalene's ⚜	B2
Samuels Ct.	A1
Shire Hall & Law Courts.	C1
Somerset County & Military Museum ⚜	B1
Somerset County Cricket Grnd	B2
Somerset County Hall	C1
South Rd	C3
South St	C3
Staplegrove Rd.	B1
Station Rd	A1
Stephen St.	B2
Swimming Pool.	A1
Tancred St.	B2
Tauntfield Cl	C3
Taunton Dean Cricket Club.	C2
Taunton 🚂	A2
The Avenue	A1
The Crescent	C1
The Mount	C2
Thomas St	A1
Toneway	A3
Tower St.	B1
Trevor Smith Pl.	C3
Trinity Rd	C2
Trinity St.	B3
Trull Rd	C1
Tudor House ⚜	B2
Upper High St	C1
Venture Way	A3
Victoria Gate	B3
Victoria Park	B3
Victoria St	B3
Viney St	B3
Vivary Park.	C2
Vivary Rd	C1
War Memorial ✦	C1
Yarde Pl	B1
Victoria Parkway.	B3
Wellesley St.	A2
Wheatley Cres	A3
Whitehall	A1
Wilfred Rd	B3
William St	A1
Wilton Church ⚜	C1
Wilton Cl	C1
Wilton Gr	C1
Wilton St	C1
Winchester St	B2
Winters Field.	B2
Wood St	B1
Yarde Pl	B1

Telford

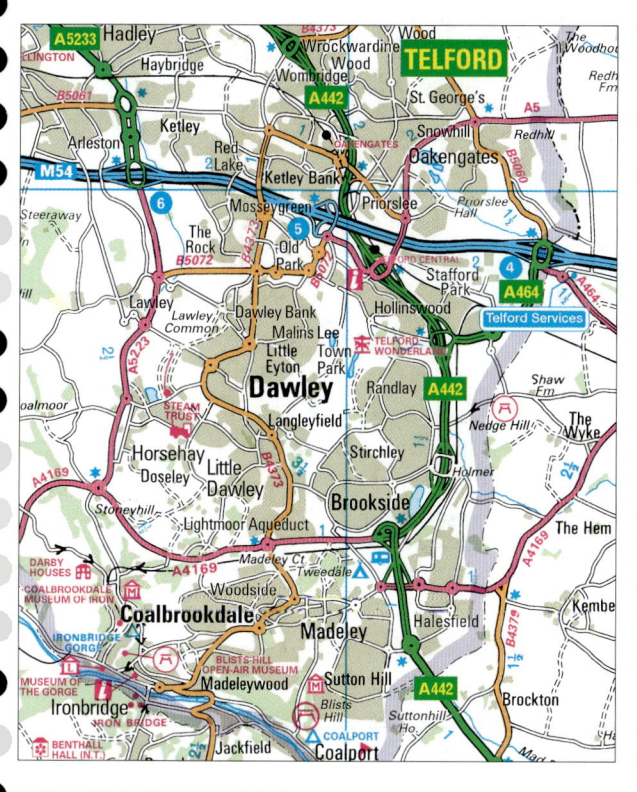

★ Do not miss
- **Benthall Hall (National Trust)**, Benthall
- ★ **Ironbridge Gorge Museums**, Ironbridge
- ★ **Wonderland**, Telford Town Park – animated nursery rhymes and fairytales for children

A hi-tech New Town, named after civil engineer Thomas Telford and adjoining Ironbridge, the birthplace of the Industrial Revolution and site of the world's first cast-iron bridge, built to span the River Severn and now a UNESCO World Heritage Site with a total of nine museums about different aspects of the gorge, from ironwork to orchids. Family attractions in Telford include the 450-acre Town Park, Granville Country Park, and a steam railway. Nearby lie the ruined Augustinian 12th–13th-century Lilleshall Abbey, Wenlock Priory, Boscobel House, Weston Park (1671) with its Capability Brown landscaped gardens, and Cosford Aerospace Museum.

▲ The iron bridge at Ironbridge

Telford Tourist Information Centre, Telford Shopping Centre, Telford TF3 4BX Tel 01952 230032

BBC Radio Shropshire 96 FM
Beacon 103.1 FM • **Classic Gold** 1017 AM • **Telford** 107.4 FM
www.ironbridge.ws

Telford

Alma Ave C1	Mount Rd C1
Amphitheatre C2	NFU Offices B1
Bowling Alley B2	Park Lane A1
Brandsfarm Way . . C3	Police Station . . . B1
Brunel Rd B1	Post Office B1
Bus Station B2	Priorslee Ave A3
Buxton Rd C1	Queen Elizabeth Ave C3
Castle Trading Estate A3	Queen Elizabeth Way B1
Central Park A2	Queensway . . . A2/B3
Civic Offices B2	Rampart Way A2
Coach Central . . . B1	Randlay Ave C3
Coachwell Cl B1	Randlay Wood . . . C3
Colliers Way A1	Rhodes Ave C1
Courts B2	Royal Way B1
Dale Acre Way . . . B3	St Leonards Rd . . . B1
Darliston C3	St Quentin Gate . . B2
Deepdale B3	Shifnal Rd A3
Deercote B3	Sixth Ave A1
Dinthill C3	Southwater Way . . B1
Doddington C3	Spout Lane C1
Dodmoor Grange . C3	Spout Mound B1
Downemead B3	Spout Way C1
Duffryn B3	Stafford Court . . . B3
Dunsheath B3	Stafford Park B3
Euston Way A1	Stirchley Ave C3
Eyton Mound C1	Stone Row C1
Eyton Rd C1	Telford Bridge Retail Park A1
Forge Retail Park . A1	Telford Central Station A3
Forgegate A2	Telford Centre, The B2
Grange Central . . B2	Telford International Ctr . C2
Hall Park Way . . . B1	
Hinkshay Rd C2	Telford Way A3
Hollinsworth Rd . . A2	Third Ave A2
Holyhead Rd A3	Town Park C2
Housing Trust . . . A1	Town Park Visitor Centre B2
Ice Rink B2	
Information Ctr . . B2	Town Sports Club . C2
Ironmasters Way . A2	Walker House . . . B2
Job Centre B1	Wellswood Ave . . A2
Land Registry . . . B1	West Centre Way . B1
Lawn Central . . . B2	Withywood Drive . C1
Lawnswood C1	Woodhouse Central B2
Library B2	
Malinsgate B1	Yates Way A1
Matlock Ave C1	
Moor Rd C1	

¼ mile / ½ km

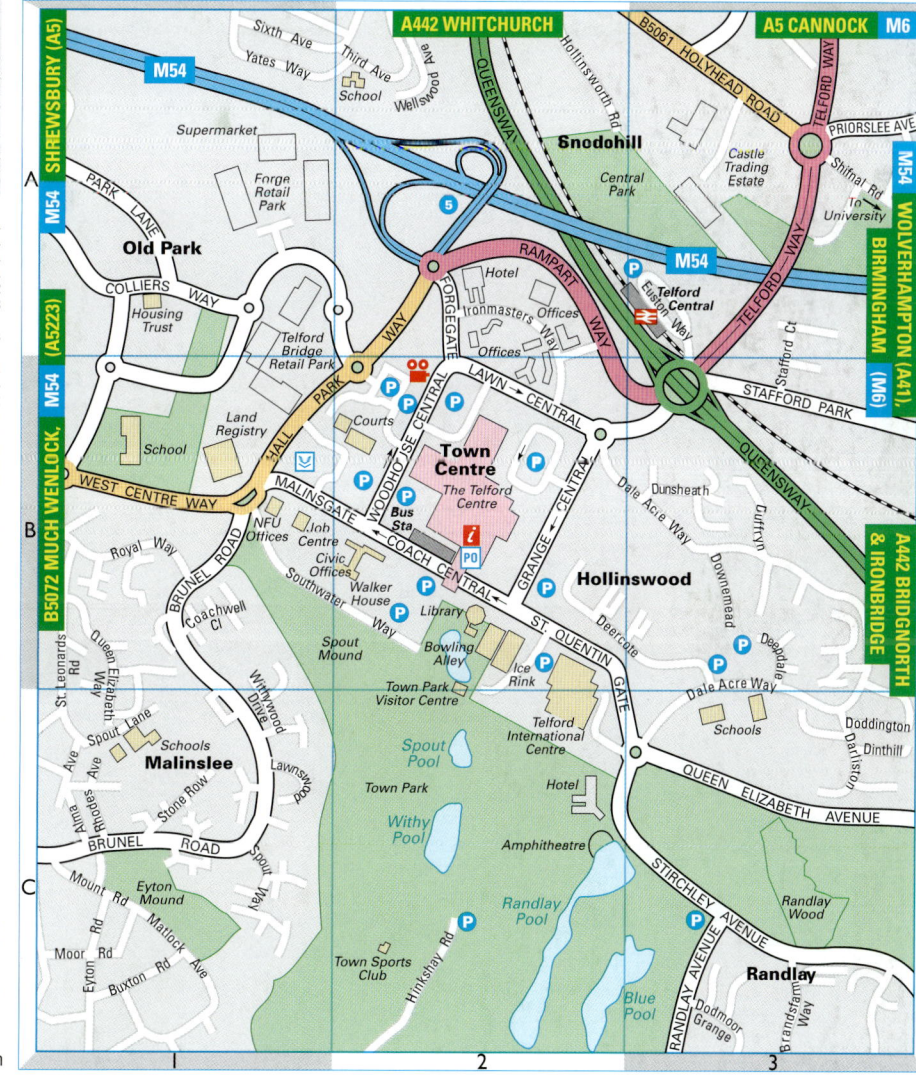

Torquay

A stylish Torbay town with a palm-fringed seafront, handsome Victorian terraces and white Italian-style villas dating from its time as a fashionable 19th-century health and leisure resort, plus a modern marina. Attractions include a the new Aqualand aquarium; Babbacombe Model Village; Kent Cavern with its prehistoric remains; Bygones, a re-created Victorian street with shops, period rooms, and toys and models; and the Agatha Christie Trail revisiting sites associated with the crime writer, including a special exhibition in Torquay Museum. Among beaches are the award-winning Corbyn Sands, also the town is on the South West Coast Path. Nearby are the 14th–16th century Compton Castle (National Trust), Plant World Gardens, Shaldon Wildlife Trust (a small-animal zoo) and Berry Head Country Park.

▲ Torquay at dusk

★ Do not miss
- ★ **Clifftop Railway**, Babbacombe to Oddicombe Beach
- ★ **Cockington Court and Country Park**, Cockington
- ★ **Torre Abbey and the Agatha Christie Memorial Room**, Kings Drive

Torquay Tourist Information Centre, Vaughan Parade, Torquay TQ2 5JG Tel 0870 7070010

BBC Radio Devon 104.3 FM and 1458 AM • **Classic Gold** 954 AM
Gemini 96.4 FM

www.torbay-online.co.uk/torquay

Torquay

Abbey Rd	B2
Alexandra Rd	A2
Alpine Rd	B3
Aqualand	C3
Ash Hill Rd	A2
Babbacombe Rd	B3
Bampfylde Rd	B1
Barton Rd	A1
Beacon Quay	C2
Belgrave Rd	A1/B1
Belmont Rd	A3
Berea Rd	A3
Braddons Hill Rd East	B3
Bronshill Rd	A2
Castle Rd	A2
Cavern Rd	A3
Central Cinema	B2
Chatsworth Rd	A2
Chestnut Ave	B1
Church St	A1
Civic Offices	A2
Coach Station	A1
Corbyn Head	C1
Croft Hill	B1
Croft Rd	B1
Daddyhole Plain	C3
East St	A1
Egerton Rd	A3
Ellacombe Church Rd	A3
Ellacombe Rd	A2
Falkland Rd	B1
Fleet St	B2
Fleet Walk Shopping Ctr	B2
Grafton Rd	B3
Haldon Pier	C2
Hatfield Rd	A2
Highbury Rd	A2
Higher Warberry Rd	A3
Hillesdon Rd	B3
Hollywood Bowl	C3
Hoxton Rd	A3
Hunsdon Rd	B3
Information Ctr	B2
Inner Harbour	C3
Kenwyn Rd	A3
Laburnum St	A1
Law Courts	A2
Library	A2
Lime Ave	B1
Living Coasts	C3
Lower Warberry Rd	B3
Lucius St	B1
Lymington Rd	A1
Magdalene Rd	A1
Marina	C2
Market St	B1
Meadfoot Lane	C3
Meadfoot Rd	C3
Melville St	B2
Middle Warberry Rd	B3
Mill Lane	A1
Montpellier Rd	B3
Morgan Ave	A1
Museum Rd	B3
Newton Rd	A1
Oakhill Rd	A1
Outer Harbour	C2
Parkhill Rd	C3
Pavilion	C2
Pimlico	B2
Police Station	A1
Post Office	A2/B1/B2
Princes Rd	A3
Princes Rd East	A3
Princes Rd West	A3
Princess	C2
Princess Gdns	C2
Princess Pier	C1
Rathmore Rd	B1
Recreation Grnd	B1
Riviera Centre International	B1
Rock End Ave	C3
Rock Rd	B2
Rock Walk	B2
Rosehill Rd	A3
St Efride's Rd	A1
St John's	B3
St Luke's Rd	B2
St Luke's Rd North	B2
St Luke's Rd South	B2
St Marychurch Rd	A2
Scarborough Rd	B1
Shedden Hill	B2
South Pier	C2
South St	A1
Spanish Barn	B1
Stitchill Rd	B3
Strand	B3
Sutherland Rd	B3
Teignmouth Rd	A1
Temperance St	B2
The King's Drive	B1
The Terrace	B3
Thurlow Rd	B1
Tor Bay	B1
Tor Church Rd	A1
Tor Hill Rd	A1
Torbay Rd	B2
Torquay Museum	B3
Torquay	C1
Torre Abbey Mansion	B1
Torre Abbey Meadows	B1
Torre Abbey Sands	B1
Torwood Gdns	B3
Torwood St	C3
Union Square	A2
Union St	A1
Upton Hill	A2
Upton Park	A2
Upton Rd	A1
Vanehill Rd	C3
Vansittart Rd	A1
Vaughan Parade	C2
Victoria Parade	C3
Victoria Rd	A2
Warberry Rd West	B2
Warren Rd	B2
Windsor Rd	A2/A3
Woodville Rd	A3

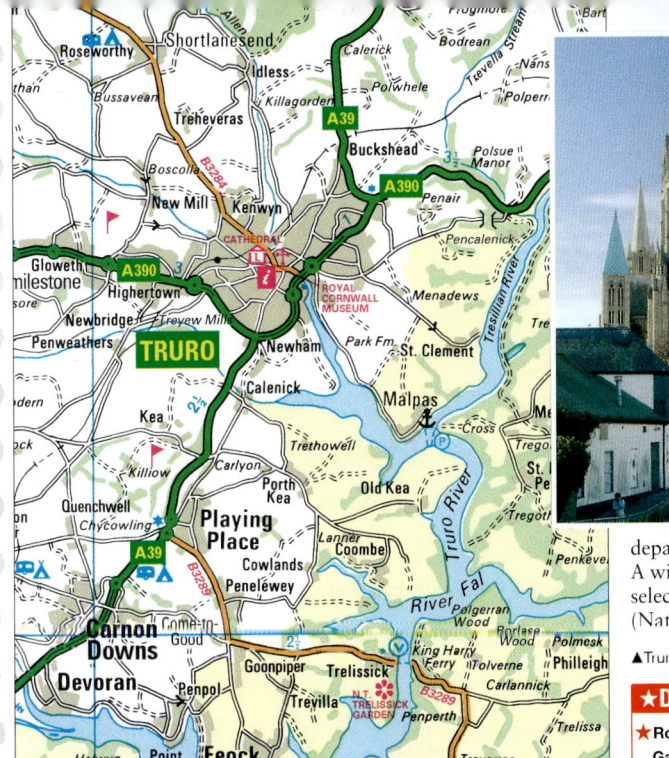

Truro

In the 19th and 20th centuries Truro was a very busy port and prior to this a large mining and agricultural area. Today Truro is the centre of Cornwall for trade and commerce. Truro Cathedral was built on the site of the 16th century St Mary the Virgin Parish Church with work starting in 1880. There are many beautiful parks and gardens and the granite viaduct is a good piece of industrial architecture. As the county town it is a major shopping centre with small independent shops as well as department stores, high street names and a regular farmers' market. A wide variety of international cuisines is on offer, as well as a good selection of pubs. Nearby attractions include Trelissick Garden (National Trust).

▲ Truro Cathedral

★ **Do not miss**
★ **Royal Cornwall Museum and Art Gallery**, River Street – Cornish history, art and mining heritage
★ **Truro Cathedral**, St Mary's Street

Tourist Information Centre, Municipal Buildings, Boscawen Street, Truro TR1 2NE
Tel 01872 274555

BBC Radio Cornwall 103.9 FM and 630 AM • **Pirate FM** 102.8 FM

www.truro.gov.uk

143

Truro

Street	Grid
Adelaide Ter.	B1
Agar Rd	B3
Arch Hill	C2
Arundell Pl.	C2
Avondale Rd.	B1
Back Quay	B3
Barrack La	C3
Barton Meadow	A1
Benson Rd	A2
Bishops Cl	B1
Bosvean Gdns	B1
Bosvigo Gardens	B1
Bosvigo La	A1
Bosvigo Rd.	B2
Broad St	A3
Burley Cl.	C3
Bus Station	B3
Calenick St.	B2
Campfield Hill	B3
Carclew St	B3
Carew Rd	A2
Carey Park	B2
Carlyon Rd	A2
Carvoza Rd.	A3
Castle St.	B2
Cathedral View	A2
Chainwalk Dr.	A2
Chapel Hill	B1
Charles St	B2
City Hall	B2
City Rd	B2
Coinage Hall	B3
Comprigney Hill	A1
Coosebean La	A1
Copes Gdns	A2
County Hall	B1
Courtney Rd.	C1
Crescent Rd.	B1
Crescent Rise	C1
Daniell Court.	C2
Daniell Rd	C2
Daniell St.	C2
Daubuz Cl.	A2
Dobbs La	B1
Edward St.	B2
Eliot Rd.	A2
Elm Court.	A3
Enys Cl	A1
Enys Rd.	A2
Fairmantle St.	B3
Falmouth Rd	C1
Ferris Town	B2
Fire Station	B2
Frances St	B2
George St.	B2
Green Cl.	B1
Green La.	C1
Grenville Rd.	A2
Hall For Cornwall	B3
Hendra Rd	A2
Hendra Vean	A1
High Cross	B3
Higher Newham La	C3
Higher Treheverne	A2
Hillcrest Ave	B1
Hospital	B2
Hunkin Cl	A2
Hurland Rd.	C3
Infirmary Hill	B2
James Pl	B3
Kenwyn Church Rd.	A1
Kenwyn Hill	A1
Kenwyn Rd.	A2
Kenwyn St	B2
Kerris Gdns	A1
King St	B3
Lemon Quay	B3
Lemon Street Gallery	B3
Library	B1/B3
Malpas Rd	B3
Market	B3
Memorial Gdns	B3
Merrifield Close	B1
Mitchell Hill	A3
Moresk Cl.	A3
Moresk Rd	A3
Morlaix Ave	C3
Nancemere Rd	A3
Newham Business Park	C3
Newham Industrial Estate	C3
Newham Rd.	C3
Northheld Dr	C3
Oak Way	A3
Pal's Terr.	A3
Park View	C2
Pendarves Rd	A2
Plaza Cinema	B3
Police Station	B2
Post Office	B2/B3
Prince's St	B3
Pydar St	A2
Quay St.	B3
Redannick Cres.	C2
Redannick La.	B2
Richard Lander Monument	C2
Richmond Hill	B1
River St.	B2
Rosedale Rd.	A2
Royal Cornwall Museum	B2
St Clement St	B3
St George's Rd	A1
School La	C2
Station Rd	B1
Stokes Rd	A2
Strangways Terr	C3
Tabernacle St	B3
The Avenue	A3
The Crescent	B1
The Leats	B2
The Spires	C1
Treharverne La	A2
Tremayne Rd	A2
Treseder's Gdns	A3
Treworder Rd.	B1
Treyew Rd.	B1
Truro Cathedral	B3
Truro Harbour Office	B3
Truro Station	B3
Union St	B2
Upper School La.	C2
Victoria Gdns	B2
Waterfall Gdns	B2

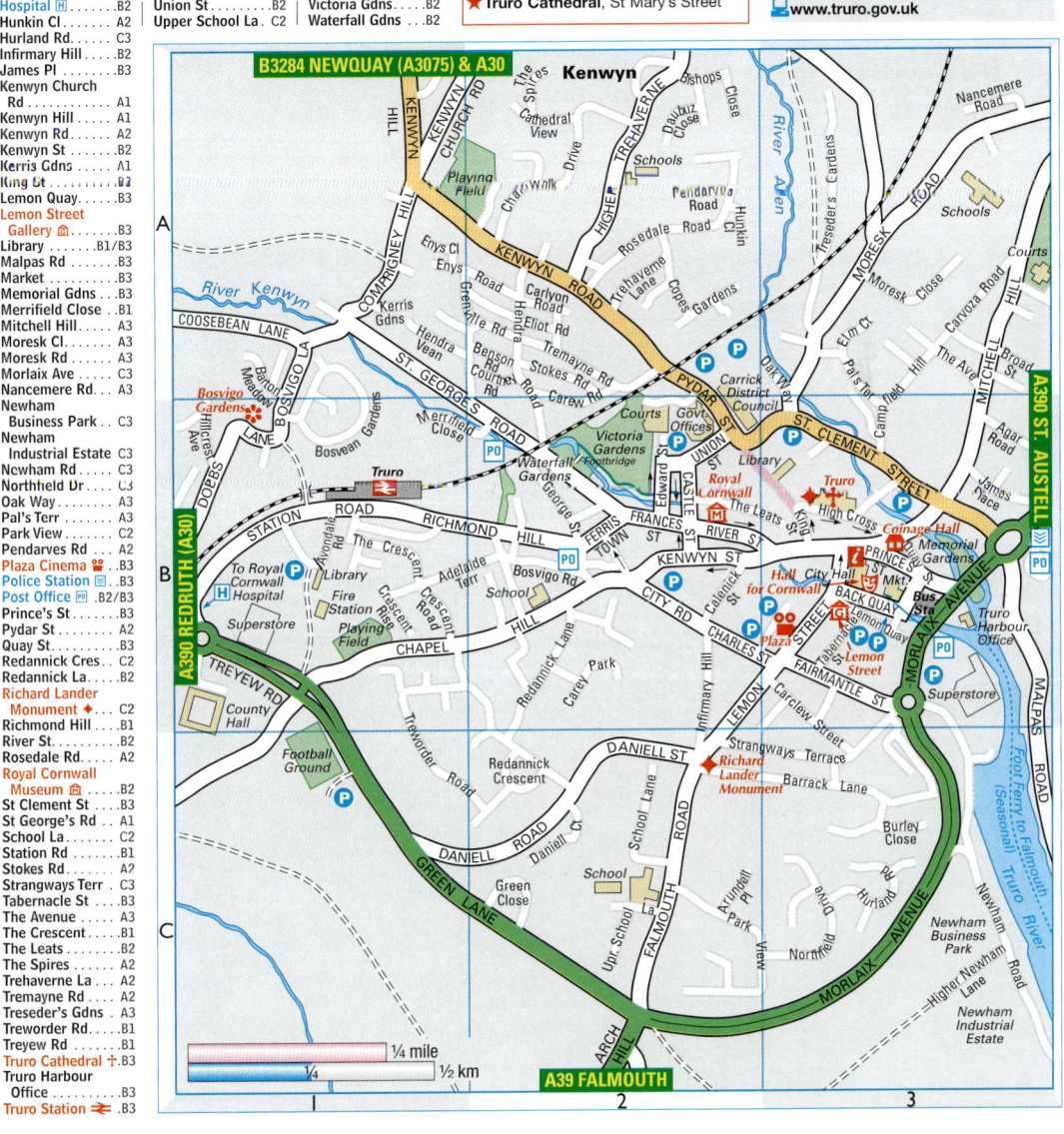

Wick

A Norse settlement on the far north-east coast of Scotland that became a royal burgh in 1589 and grew prosperous as a 19th-century herring 'boom town'. Of historical interest are the ruined castles of Girnigoe and Sinclair, separated by a rock-cut ravine, and clifftop Old Wick, one of the oldest remnants of a stone castle in Scotland, dating from the mid-12th century. Around Sinclair's Bay are two more ruined castles, Keiss and the Viking Bucholly, and a small museum on the history of the Norse settlers, while prehistoric remains in the area include the Cairn of Get, Hill O'Many Stanes and the Grey Cairns of Camster with their megaliths and stone circles. John O'Groats is 16 miles to the north.

▲ View over the bridge to Wick

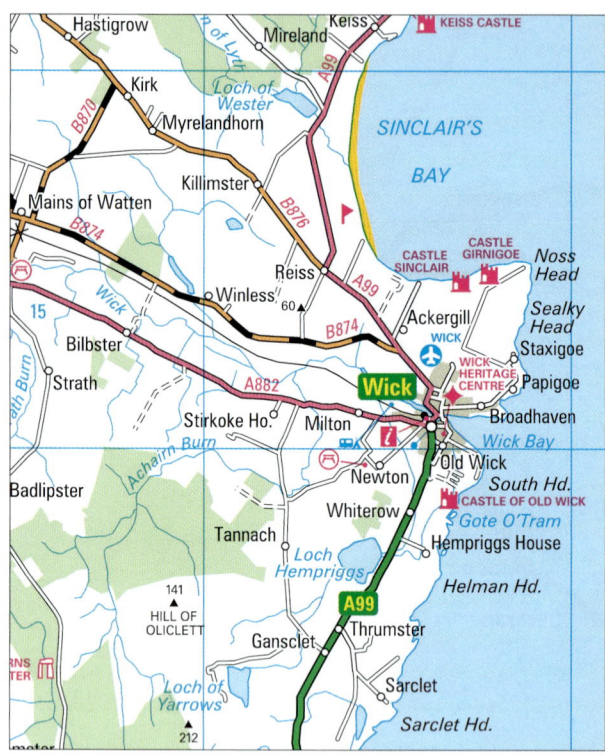

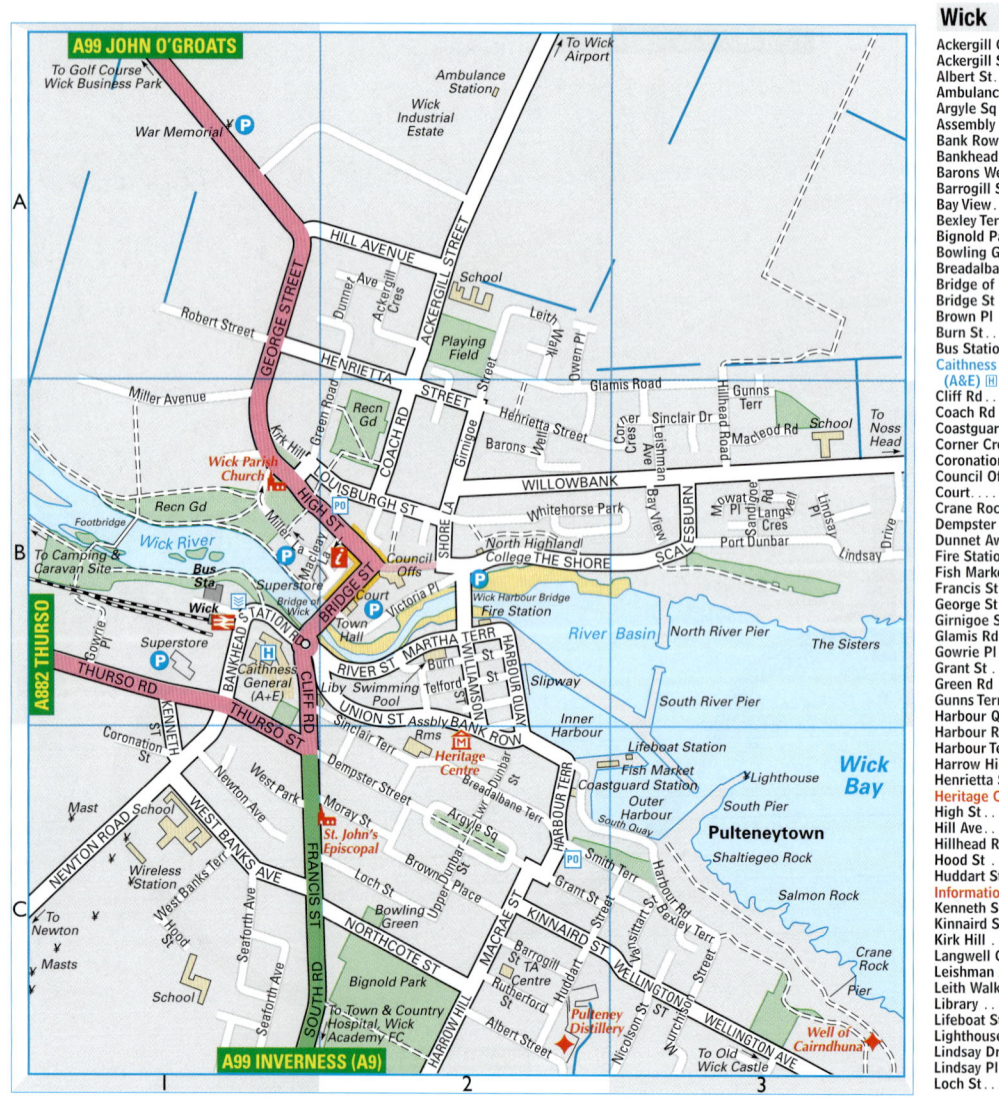

★ Do not miss
- ★ **Northlands Viking Centre**, Old School House, Auchengill
- ★ **Wick Heritage Centre**, Bank Row

Wick Tourist Information Centre,
Norseman Hotel, Riverside, Wick
KW1 4NL Tel 0845 2255121
BBC Radio Scotland 94.7 FM and 810 AM • **Caithness FM** 102.5 FM
www.caithness.org

Wick

Street	Grid
Ackergill Cres	A2
Ackergill St	A2
Albert St	C2
Ambulance Stn	A2
Argyle Sq	C2
Assembly Rooms	C2
Bank Row	C2
Bankhead	B1
Barons Well	B2
Barrogill St	C2
Bay View	B3
Bexley Terr	C3
Bignold Park	C2
Bowling Green	C2
Breadalbane Terr	C2
Bridge of Wick	B1
Bridge St	B2
Brown Pl	B2
Burn St	B2
Bus Station	B1
Caithness General (A&E)	B1
Cliff Rd	B1
Coach Rd	B2
Coastguard Stn	C3
Corner Cres	B3
Coronation St	C1
Council Offices	B2
Court	B2
Crane Rock	C3
Dempster St	B2
Dunnet Ave	A2
Fire Station	B2
Fish Market	C3
Francis St	C1
George St	A1
Girnigoe St	B2
Glamis Rd	B2
Gowrie Pl	B1
Grant St	C2
Green Rd	C2
Gunns Terr	B3
Harbour Quay	B2
Harbour Rd	C3
Harbour Terr	C2
Harrow Hill	C2
Henrietta St	A2/B2
Heritage Ctr	B2
High St	B2
Hill Ave	B2
Hillhead Rd	B3
Hood St	C1
Huddart St	C2
Information Ctr	B2
Kenneth St	C1
Kinnaird St	C2
Kirk Hill	B1
Langwell Cres	B3
Leishman Ave	A2
Leith Walk	A2
Library	B2
Lifeboat Stn	C3
Lighthouse	C3
Lindsay Dr	B3
Lindsay Pl	B3
Loch St	C2
Louisburgh St	B2
Lower Dunbar St	C2
Macleay La	B1
Macleod Rd	B3
MacRae St	C2
Martha Terr	B2
Miller Ave	B1
Miller La	B1
Moray St	C2
Mowat Pl	B3
Murchison St	C3
Newton Ave	C1
Newton Rd	C1
Nicolson St	C3
North Highland College	B2
North River Pier	B3
Northcote St	C2
Owen Pl	A2
Police Station	B1
Port Dunbar	B3
Post Office	B2/C2
Pulteney Distillery	C2
River St	B2
Robert St	A1
Rutherford St	C2
St John's Episcopal	C2
Sandigoe Rd	B3
Scalesburn	B3
Seaforth Ave	C1
Shore La	B2
Sinclair Dr	B3
Sinclair Terr	C2
Smith Terr	C3
South Pier	C3
South Quay	C3
South Rd	C1
South River Pier	B3
Station Rd	B1
Swimming Pool	B2
TA Centre	B2
Telford St	B2
The Shore	B2
Thurso Rd	B1
Thurso St	B1
Town Hall	B2
Union St	B2
Upper Dunbar St	C2
Vansittart St	C3
Victoria Pl	B2
War Memorial	A1
Well of Cairndhuna	C3
Wellington Ave	C3
Wellington St	C3
West Banks Ave	C1
West Banks Terr	C1
West Park	C1
Whitehorse Park	B2
Wick Harbour Br	B2
Wick Ind Est	A2
Wick Parish Church	B1
Wick	B1
Williamson St	B2
Willowbank	B2

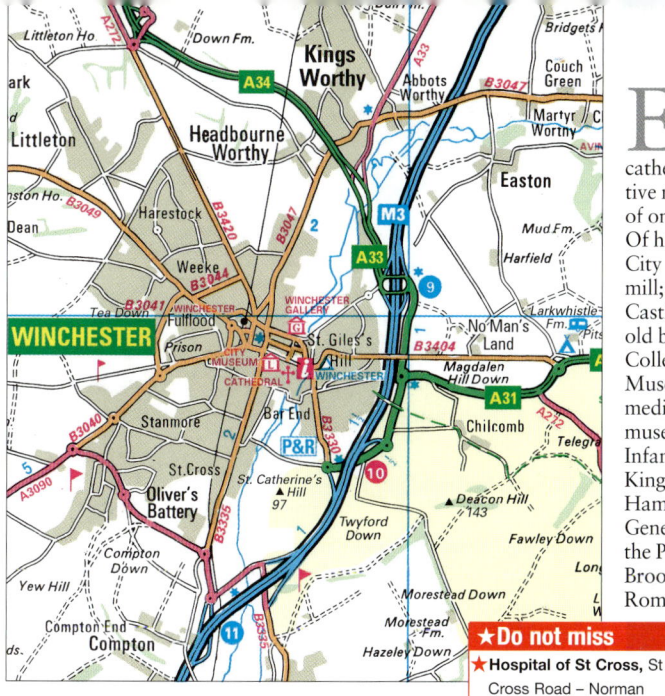

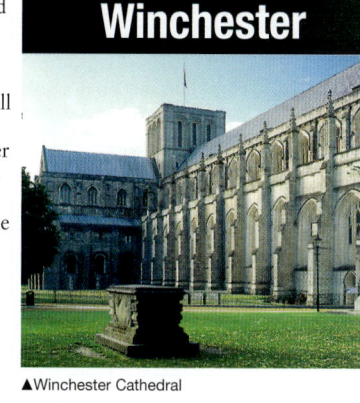

Winchester

England's ancient capital and the one-time seat of Alfred the Great, with a famous cathedral begun in 1079, attractive medieval streets and alleys full of one-off shops and boutiques. Of historic interest are Winchester City Mill, a working 1744 watermill; the remains of Winchester Castle and of Wolvesey Castle, the old bishops' palace; Winchester College, founded in 1382; City Museum; the Westgate fortified medieval gateway with its small museum; the Gurkha, Light Infantry, Royal Green Jackets, King's Royal Hussars, Royal Hampshire Regiment, Adjutant General's Corps museums in the Peninsula Barracks; and the Brooks Experience museum of Roman and medieval Winchester. INTECH is an interactive science and technology centre, while good green spaces include Queen Eleanor's Garden, a medieval herb garden. Nearby are Avington House and Park and Farley Mount Country Park, and the 100-mile South Downs Way of ancient routes and droveways runs from Winchester to Eastbourne.

▲ Winchester Cathedral

Tourist Information Centre, Guildhall, The Broadway, Winchester SO23 9LJ Tel 01962 840500

BBC Radio Solent 96.1 FM and 999 AM • **Win** 107.2 FM • **Capital Gold** 1557 AM • **Ocean** 96.7–97.5 FM • **Power** 103.2 FM

www.visitwinchester.co.uk

★ Do not miss

★ **Hospital of St Cross**, St Cross Road – Norman church, medieval hall
★ **Winchester Cathedral**, The Close
★ **Winchester Guildhall Gallery**, The Broadway

Winchester

Name	Grid
Andover Rd	A2
Andover Road Retail Park	A2
Archery La	C2
Arthur Rd	A2
Bar End Rd	C3
Beaufort Rd	C1
Beggar's La	B3
Bereweeke Ave	A1
Bereweeke Rd	A1
Boscobel Rd	A2
Brassey Rd	A2
Brooks Shopping Ctr, The	B3
Bus Station	B3
Butter Cross ✚	B2
Canon St	C2
Castle Wall	C2/C3
Castle, King Arthur's Round Table	B2
Cathedral ✚	C2
Cheriton Rd	A1
Chesil St	C3
Chesil Theatre	C3
Christchurch Rd	C1
City Museum	B2
City Offices	C3
City Rd	B2
Clifton Rd	B1
Clifton Terr	B2
Close Wall	C2
Coach Park	A2
Colebrook St	C3
College St	C3
College Walk	C3
Compton Rd	C1
County Council Offices	B2
Cranworth Rd	C1
Cromwell Rd	C1
Culver Rd	C3
Domum Rd	C3
Durngate Pl	B3
Eastgate St	B3
Edgar Rd	C2
Egbert Rd	A2
Elm Rd	B1
Fairfield Rd	A2
Fire Station	B3
Fordington Ave	B1
Fordington Rd	A1
Friarsgate	B3
Gordon Rd	B3
Greenhill Rd	B1
Guildhall	B3
HM Prison	B1
Hatherley Rd	A1
High St	B3
Hillier Way	A3
Hyde Abbey (Remains) ✚	A2
Hyde Abbey Rd	A2
Hyde Cl	A2
Hyde St	A2
Information Ctr	B3
Jewry St	B2
John Stripe	C1
King Alfred Pl	A2
Kingsgate Arch	C2
Kingsgate Rd	C2
Kingsgate Park	C2
Kingsgate St	C2
Lankhills Rd	A2
Library	B2
Lower Brook St	B3
Magdalen Hill	B3
Market La	B3
Mews La	B1
Middle Brook St	B3
Middle Rd	B1
Military Museums	B2
Milland Rd	C3
Milverton Rd	C1
Monks Rd	A3
North Hill Cl	A2
North Walls	B2
North Walls Rec Grnd	A3
Nuns Rd	A3
Oram's Arbour	B2
Owen's Rd	A2
Parchment St	C2
Park & Ride	C3
Park Ave	B2
Playing Field	A1
Police H.Q.	B1
Police Station	B3
Portal Rd	C3
Post Office	A2/B2/B3/C1/C2
Quarry Rd	C3
Ranelagh Rd	C1
River Park Leisure Centre	B3
Romans' Rd	C2
Romsey Rd	B1
Royal Hampshire County (A&E)	B1
St Cross Rd	C2
St George's St	B2
St Giles Hill	C3
St James' La	B1
St James' Terr	B1
St James Villas	C2
St John's	B3
St John's St	B3
St Michael's Rd	C2
St Paul's Hill	B1
St Peter St	B2
St Swithun St	C2
St Thomas St	C2
Saxon Rd	A1
School of Art	B3
Screen Cinema	B2
Sleepers Hill Rd	C1
Southgate St	B2
Sparkford Rd	C1
Staple Gdns	B2
Station Rd	B1
Step Terr	B1
Stockbridge Rd	A1
Stuart Cres	C1
Sussex St	B2
Swan Lane	B3
Tanner St	B3
The Square	B2
The Weirs	C3
Theatre Royal	B2
Tower St	B2
Town Hall	C3
Union St	B3
University of Winchester	C1
Upper Brook St	B3
Wales St	B3
Water Lane	B3
West End Terr	B1
West Gate	B2
Western Rd	B1
Wharf Hill	C3
Winchester Coll	C2
Winchester ⛭	A2
Wolvesey Castle	C3
Worthy Lane	A2
Worthy Rd	A2

Windsor

A royal borough on the River Thames, with a large castle that has been a royal residence for more than 900 years (making it the world's oldest in continuous occupation) and that contains the beautiful St George's Chapel, where 10 monarchs are buried (including Henry VIII), Frogmore House, a favourite retreat of Queen Victoria, and a farm shop. Other attractions include Guildhall Island, the town centre with its narrow cobbled streets and 17th-century buildings, including Sir Christopher Wren's Guildhall and his house, now a hotel; the vast Windsor Great Park, containing Savill Garden, a 35-acre woodland garden; and Dorney Court, a fine Tudor house (limited opening). A few miles to the south is prestigious Ascot Racecourse, and to the southeast is Runnymede, where King John sealed the Magna Carta in 1215, now home to memorials to JFK and Air Force personnel who died in WWII.

▼ Windsor Castle from The Home Park

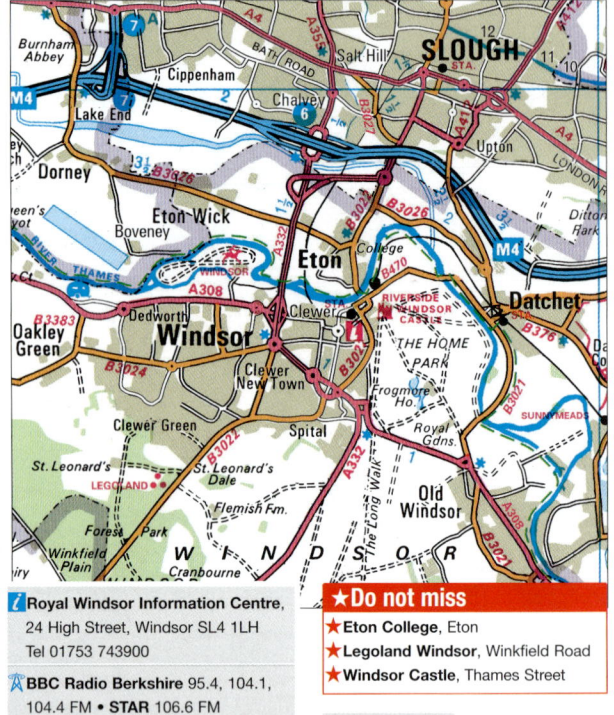

Royal Windsor Information Centre,
24 High Street, Windsor SL4 1LH
Tel 01753 743900

BBC Radio Berkshire 95.4, 104.1, 104.4 FM • **STAR** 106.6 FM

www.windsor.gov.uk

★ Do not miss
- ★ **Eton College**, Eton
- ★ **Legoland Windsor**, Winkfield Road
- ★ **Windsor Castle**, Thames Street

Windsor

Adelaide Sq	C3	King's Rd	C3
Albany Rd	C2	King Stable St	A2
Albert St	B1	Leisure Ctr & Pool	B1
Alexandra Gdns	B2	Library	C2
Alexandra Rd	C2	Maidenhead Rd	B1
Alma Rd	B2	Meadow La	C2
Ambulance Stn	B1	Municipal Offices	C3
Arthur Rd	B2	Nell Gwynne's House	B3
Bachelors Acre	B3	Osborne Rd	C2
Barry Ave	B2	Oxford Rd	B1
Beaumont Rd	C2	Park St	B3
Bexley St	B1	Peascod St	B2
Boat House	B2	Police Station	C2
Brocas St	B2	Post Office	A2/B2
Brook St	C3	Princess Margaret Hospital	C2
Bulkeley Ave	C1	Queen Victoria's Walk	B3
Castle Hill	B3	Queen's Rd	C1
Charles St	B2	River St	B2
Claremont Rd	B2	Romney Island	A3
Clarence Cr	B2	Romney Lock	A3
Clarence Rd	B1	Romney Lock Rd	A3
Clewer Court Rd	B1	Royal Mews Exhibition Ctr	B3
Coach Park	B2	Russell St	C2
College Cr	C1	St John's	B3
Courts	C2	St John's Chapel	A2
Cricket Ground	C3	St Leonards Rd	C2
Dagmar Rd	C2	St Mark's Rd	C2
Datchet Rd	B3	Sheet St	C3
Devereux Rd	C2	South Meadow	A2
Dorset Rd	C2	South Meadow La	A2
Duke St	B1	Springfield Rd	C1
Elm Rd	C1	Stovell Rd	B1
Eton College	A3	Sunbury Rd	A2
Eton Ct	A2	Tangier La	A2
Eton Sq	A2	Tangier St	A3
Eton Wick Rd	A2	Temple Rd	C2
Fire Station	C2	Thames St	B3
Farm Yard	B3	The Brocas	A2
Frances Rd	C2	The Home Pk	A3/B3
Frogmore Dr	B3	The Long Walk	C3
Gloucester Pl	C3	Theatre Royal	B3
Goslar Way	C1	Trinity Pl	C2
Goswell Hill	B2	Vansittart Rd	B1/C1
Goswell Rd	B2	Vansittart Rd Gdns	C1
Green La	C2	Victoria Barracks	C2
Grove Rd	C2	Victoria St	B2
Guildhall	B3	Ward Royal	B2
Helena Rd	C2	Westmead	C1
Helston La	B1	White Lilies Island	A1
High St	A2/B3	William St	B2
Holy Trinity	C2	Windsor Arts Centre	C2
Hospital (Private)	C2	Windsor Castle	B3
Household Cavalry	C2	Windsor & Eton Central	B2
Imperial Rd	C1	Windsor & Eton Riverside	A3
Information Ctr	B3	Windsor Bridge	B3
Keats La	A2	Windsor Great Pk	C3
King Edward Ct	B2	Windsor Relief Rd	A1
King Edward VII Ave	A3	York Ave	C1
King Edward VII Hospital	C2	York Rd	C1
King George V Memorial	B3		

¼ mile
½ km

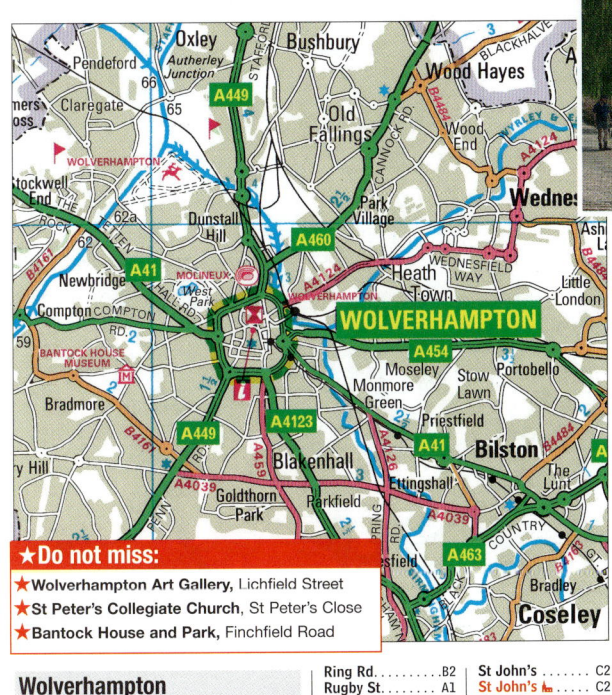

Wolverhampton

Wolverhampton has existed for over 1000 years and went from a wool-trade dominated town to a major centre of the Industrial Revolution. It is now a cultural centre with its galleries, museums and university, not to mention its football team Wolverhampton Wanderers. The Mander and Wulfrun shopping centres provide a wide range of shops and much of the city centre has been pedestrianised; Civic and Wulfrun halls are major concert venues for the Black Country; Light House Media Centre offers independent cinema; and the cosmopolitan population is reflected in the breadth of choice of bars, pubs and restaurants.

▲ Broad Street canal basin

Tourist Information Centre,
18 Queen Square, Wolverhampton
WV1 1TQ Tel 01902 556110

BBC WM 95.6 FM • **Beacon**
97.2 FM • **Classic Gold** 990 AM
Heart 100.7 FM • **Saga** 105.7 FM

www.wolverhampton.gov.uk

★ Do not miss:
- ★ **Wolverhampton Art Gallery,** Lichfield Street
- ★ **St Peter's Collegiate Church,** St Peter's Close
- ★ **Bantock House and Park,** Finchfield Road

Wolverhampton

Street	Grid
Albany Rd	B1
Albion St	B3
Alexandra St	C1
Gallery	B2
Ashland St	C1
Austin St	A1
Badger Dr	A3
Bailey St	B3
Bath Ave	B1
Bath Rd	B1
Bell St	C2
Berry St	B3
Bilston Rd	C3
Bilston St	C3
Birmingham Canal	A3
Bone Mill La	A2
Bright St	A1
Burton Cres	B3
Bus Station	B3
Cambridge St	A3
Camp St	C2
Cannock Rd	A3
Castle St	C2
Chapel Ash	C1
Cherry St	C1
Chester St	A1
Church La	C2
Church St	C2
Civic Centre	B2
Clarence Rd	C2
Cleveland Rd	C2
Cleveland St	C2
Clifton St	C1
Coach Station	C2
Compton Rd	B1
Corn Hill	B3
Coven St	A1
Craddock St	A1
Cross St North	A1
Crown & County Courts	C3
Crown St	A1
Culwell St	B3
Dale St	C1
Darlington St	C1
Dartmouth St	C3
Devon Rd	B2
Drummond St	B2
Dudley Rd	C3
Dudley St	B2
Duke St	C3
Dunkley St	B1
Dunstall Ave	A2
Dunstall Hill	A2
Dunstall Rd	A1/A2
Evans St	A1
Eye Infirmary	B2
Fawdry St	B2
Field St	B3
Fire Station	A1
Fiveways (r'about)	A2
Fowler Playing Fields	A3
Fox's La	A2
Francis St	A2
Fryer St	B3
Gloucester St	A1
Gordon St	C3
Graiseley St	C1
Grand	B3
Granville St	C3
Great Western St	B3
Great Brickkiln St	C1
Grimstone St	B3
Gt. Hampton St	A1
Harrow St	A1
Hilton St	A3
Horseley Fields	C3
Humber Rd	C1
Jack Hayward Wy	A2
Jameson St	A1
Jenner St	B3
Kennedy Rd	B3
Kimberley St	C1
King St	B2
Laburnum St	C1
Lansdowne Rd	B1
Leicester St	A1
Lever St	A1
Library	B2
Lichfield St	B2
Lighthouse	B3
Little's La	B3
Lock St	B3
Lord St	C1
Lowe St	A1
Lower Stafford St	A2
Magistrates Court	B2
Mander Centre	C2
Mander St	C1
Market St	B2
Market	C2
Melbourne St	C3
Merridale St	C1
Middlecross	C3
Molineux St	B2
Mostyn St	A1
New Hampton Rd East	A1
Nine Elms La	A3
North Rd	A2
Oaks Cres	C1
Oxley St	A2
Paget St	B1
Park Ave	B1
Park Rd East	A1
Park Rd West	B1
Paul St	C2
Pelham St	C1
Penn Rd	C2
Piper's Row	C2
Pitt St	C2
Police Station	C3
Pool St	C2
Poole St	A3
Post Office	A1/A2/B2/B2/C2
Powlett St	C2
Queen St	B2
Raby St	C3
Raglan St	C1
Railway Dr	B3
Red Hill St	A3
Red Lion St	B2
Retreat St	C1
Ring Rd	B2
Rugby St	A1
Russell St	C1
St Andrew's	B1
St David's	B3
St George's	C3
St James St	C3
St John's	C2
St John's	C2
St John's Retail Park	C2
St John's Square	C2
St Mark's	C1
St Marks Rd	C1
St Marks St	C1
St Patrick's	D2
St Peter's	B2
St Peter's	B2
Salisbury St	C1
Salop St	C2
School St	C2
Sherwood St	A2
Smestow St	A3
Snowhill	C2
Springfield Rd	A3
Stafford St	B2
Staveley Rd	A1
Steelhouse La	C3
Stephenson St	C1
Stewart St	C2
Sun St	B3
Sutherland Pl	C3
Tempest St	C2
Temple St	C2
Tettenhall Rd	B1
The Maltings	B2
The Royal (Metro)	C3
Thomas St	C2
Thornley St	B2
Tower St	C2
Town Hall	C2
University	B2
Upper Zoar St	C1
Vicarage Rd	C3
Victoria St	C2
Walpole St	A1
Walsall St	C3
Ward St	C3
Warwick St	C3
Water St	A3
Waterloo Rd	B2
Wednesfield Rd	B3
West Park (not A&E)	B1
West Park Swimming Pool	B1
Wolverhampton St Georges (Metro)	C2
Wharf St	C2
Whitmore Hill	B2
Wolverhampton	B3
Wolverhampton Wanderers Football Grnd (Molineux)	B2
Worcester St	C2
Wulfrun Centre	C2
Yarwell Cl	A3
York St	C2
Zoar St	C1

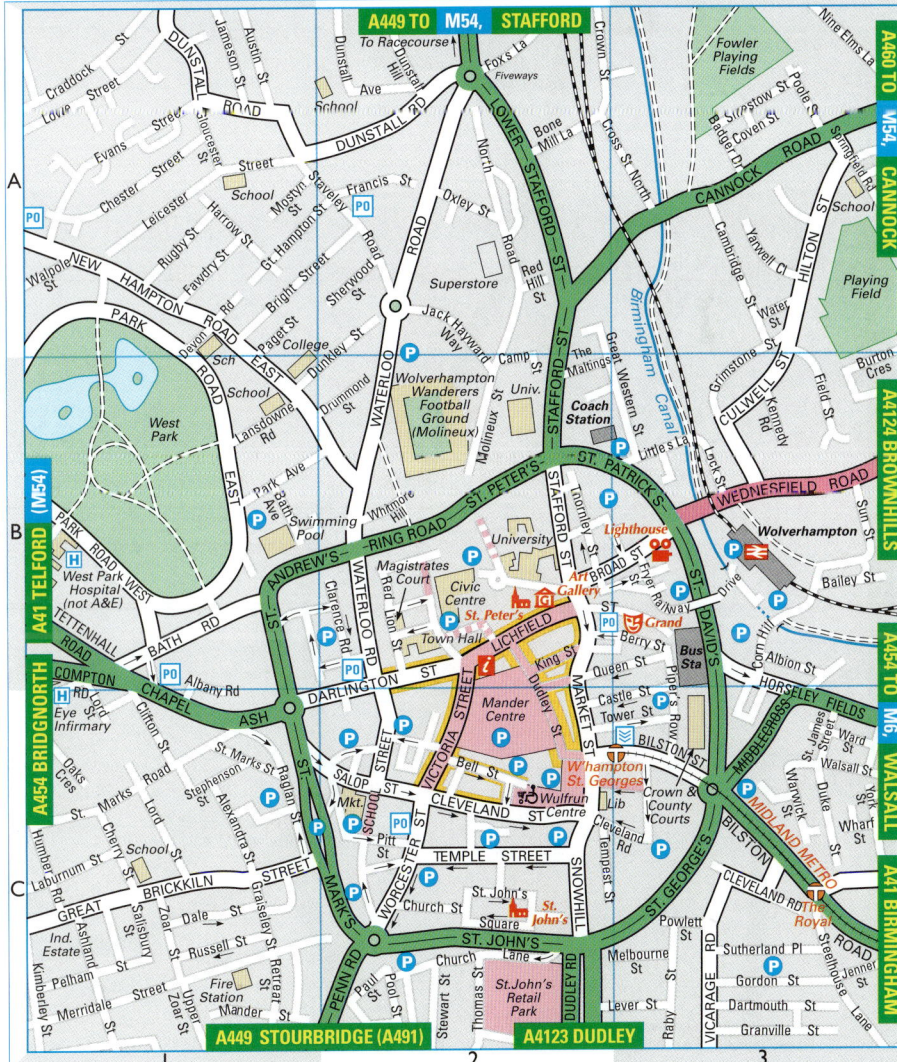

Worcester

▲ Worcester Cathedral

★ Do not miss:
- **Worcester Cathedral**, College Green
- **Worcester City Art Gallery and Museum**, Foregate Street
- **The Greyfriars**, Friar Street – medieval merchant's house

Worcester is a beautiful cathedral city on the River Severn with a history going back over 1,000 years. The city played an important part in the Civil War and The Commandery museum honours this heritage. Other notable places of interest include the Worcester Guildhall; City Museum and Art Gallery; The Greyfriars; and Royal Worcester, the porcelain manufacturer, with a factory tour, visitor centre and museum. There's a good range of spectator sport with Worcester Racecourse, Worcestershire County Cricket Club and Worcester Rugby Club all centrally located. The Crown Gate Centre offers a variety of well known stores, or there are specialist shops off the pedestrianised High Street. For entertainment there is a choice of cinema and theatre and a good range of restaurants and pubs, with cider being prevalent as a speciality to nearby Herefordshire. Nearby green spaces include Worcester Woods Country Park and Spetchley Park Gardens.

The Guildhall, High Street, Worcester WR1 2EY
Tel 01905 726211

BBC Radio Worcester 104.0 FM and 738 AM • **Classic Hits** 1530 AM
Wyvern 97.6, 102.8 FM

www.cityofworcester.gov.uk

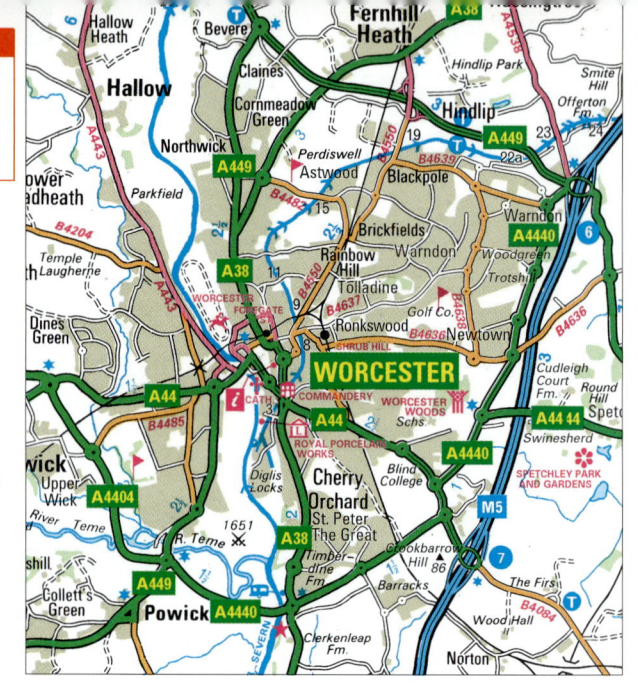

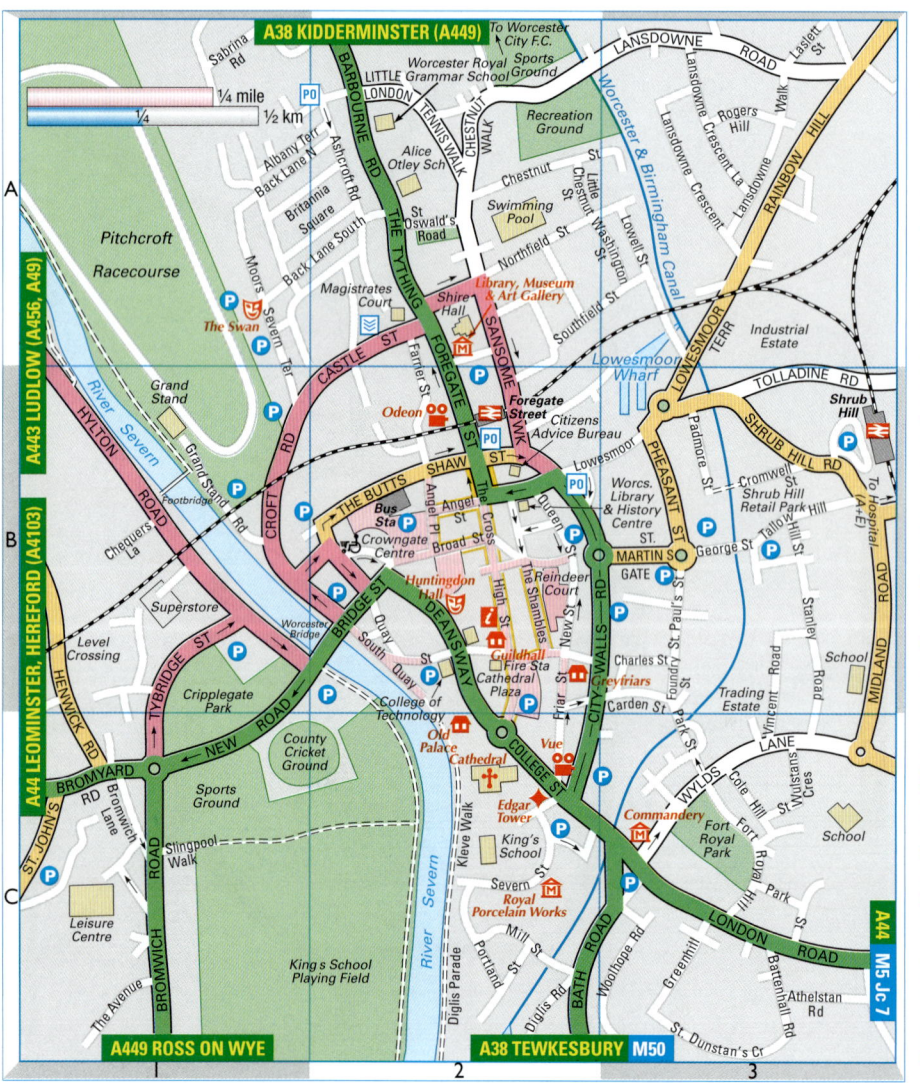

Worcester

Albany Terr	A1
Alice Otley Sch	A2
Angel Pl	B2
Angel St	B2
Ashcroft Rd	A2
Athelstan Rd	C3
Back Lane North	A1
Back Lane South	A1
Barbourne Rd	A1
Bath Rd	C2
Battenhall Rd	C3
Bridge St	B2
Britannia Sq	A1
Broad St	B2
Bromwich La	C1
Bromwich Rd	C1
Bromyard Rd	C1
Bus Station	B2
Carden St	B3
Castle St	A2
Cathedral †	C2
Cathedral Plaza	B2
Charles St	B3
Chequers La	B1
Chestnut St	A2
Chestnut Walk	A2
Citizens' Advice Bureau	B2
City Walls Rd	B2
Cole Hill	C3
Coll of Technology	B2
College St	C2
Commandery	C3
County Cricket Ground	C1
Cripplegate Park	B1
Croft Rd	B1
Cromwell St	C3
Crowngate Ctr	B2
Deansway	B2
Diglis Pde	C2
Diglis Rd	C2
Edgar Tower †	C2
Farrier St	A2
Fire Station	B2
Foregate St	B2
Foregate St ≋	B2
Fort Royal Hill	C3
Fort Royal Park	C3
Foundry St	B3
Friar St	C2
George St	B3
Grand Stand Rd	B1
Greenhill	C3
Greyfriars	B2
Guildhall	B2
Henwick Rd	B1
High St	B2
Hill St	B3
Huntingdon Hall	B2
Hylton Rd	B1
Information Ctr	B2
King's School	C2
King's School Playing Field	C2
Kleve Walk	C2
Lansdowne Cr	A3
Lansdowne Rd	A3
Lansdowne Walk	A3
Laslett St	A3
Leisure Centre	C1
Library, Museum & Art Gallery	A2
Little Chestnut St	A2
Little London	A2
London Rd	C3
Lowell St	A3
Lowesmoor	B2
Lowesmoor Terr	A3
Lowesmoor Wharf	A3
Magistrates Ct	A2
Midland Rd	B3
Mill St	C2
Moors Severn Terr	A1
New Rd	C1
New St	B2
Northfield St	A2
Odeon	B2
Old Palace	B2
Oswald's Rd	A2
Padmore St	B3
Park St	C3
Pheasant St	B3
Pitchcroft Racecourse	A1
Police Station	A2
Portland St	C1
Post Office	A1/A2/B2
Quay St	B2
Queen St	B2
Rainbow Hill	A3
Recreation Grnd	A2
Reindeer Court	B2
Rogers Hill	A3
Royal Worcester Factory Visitor Ctr & Mus	C2
Sabrina Rd	A1
St Dunstan's Cr	C3
St John's	C1
St Martin's Gate	B3
St Paul's St	B3
St Wulstans Cr	C3
Sansome Walk	A2
Severn St	C2
Shaw St	B2
Shire Hall	A2
Shrub Hill ≋	B3
Shrub Hill Retail Park	B3
Shrub Hill Rd	B3
Slingpool Walk	C1
South Quay	B2
Southfield St	A2
Sports Grnd	A2/C1
Stanley Rd	A3
Swan, The	A1
Swimming Pool	A2
Tallow Hill	B3
Tennis Walk	A2
The Avenue	C1
The Butts	B2
The Cross	B2
The Shambles	B2
The Tything	A2
Tolladine Rd	B3
Tybridge St	B1
Vincent Rd	C3
Vue Cinema	C2
Washington St	A3
Woolhope Rd	C3
Worcester Br	C2
Worcester Library & History Ctr	B3
Worcester Royal Grammar Sch	A2
Wylds La	C3

148

Wrexham

Scenically situated between the Cheshire plains and the Welsh hills, Wrexham is home to the magnificent St Giles' Church, with a Perpendicular tower dubbed one of the 'seven wonders of Wales', the County Borough Museum in a former militia barracks, and a contemporary arts centre. Nearby attractions include Chirk Castle (National Trust); the picturesque village of Bangor-on-Dee with its part-medieval, part-17th-century bridge; the unspoilt Ceiriog Valley, described by Lloyd George as 'a little bit of heaven on earth' and traversed by the Offa's Dyke Path and the former Glyn Valley Tramway; Farmworld dairy farm and adventure park; and Alyn Waters and Ty Mawr country parks. The 5-mile waymarked Clywedog Trail explores the industrial heritage of the town, starting at Minera Lead Mines and taking in Nant Mill, Bersham Ironworks and Heritage Centre and the Erddig estate on its way to Wrexham.

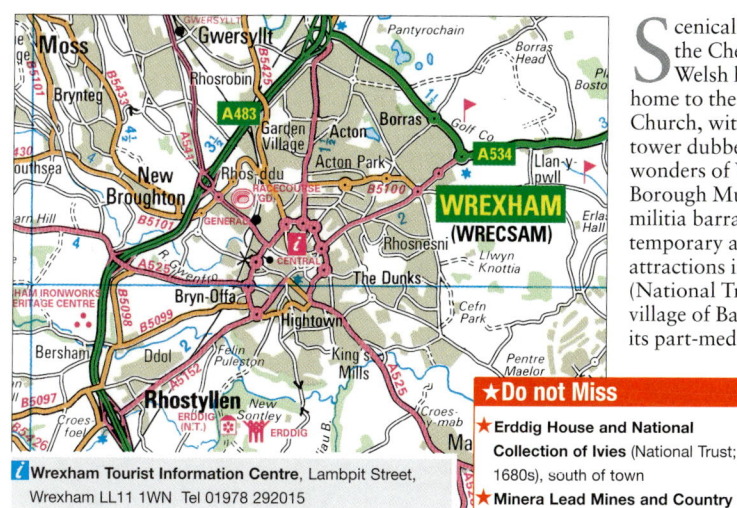

▲ Wrexham town centre

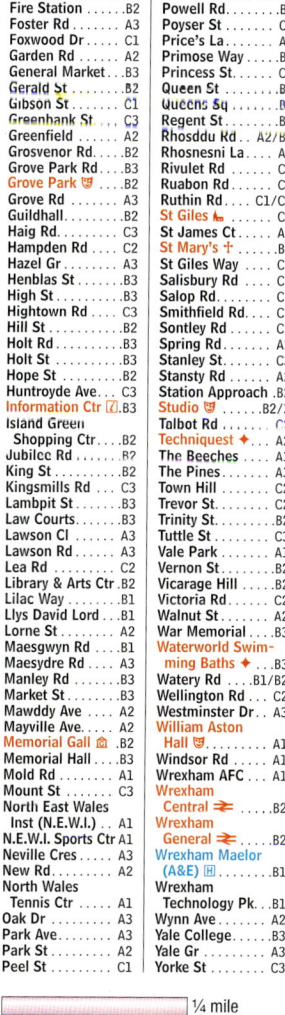

Wrexham Tourist Information Centre, Lambpit Street, Wrexham LL11 1WN Tel 01978 292345

BBC Radio Wales 95.4 FM
Classic Gold Marcher 1260 AM • MFM 103.4 FM

www.wrexham.gov.uk

★ Do not Miss

★ **Erddig House and National Collection of Ivies** (National Trust; 1680s), south of town

★ **Minera Lead Mines and Country Park**, Wern Road, Minera

★ **Pontcysyllte Aqueduct** (Thomas Telford, 1795), Froncysyllte, near Cefn-mwar

Wrexham/Wrecsam

Street	Grid
Abbot St	B2
Acton Rd	A3
Albert St	C3
Alexandra Rd	C1
Aran Rd	A3
Barnfield	C3
Bath Rd	C3
Beechley Rd	C3
Belgrave Rd	C2
Belle Vue Park	B3
Belle Vue Rd	C2
Belvedere Dr	A1
Bennion's Rd	A3
Berse Rd	A1
Bersham Rd	C1
Birch St	C3
Bodhyfryd	B3
Border Retail Park	B3
Bradley Rd	B2
Bright St	B1
Bron-y-Nant	B1
Brook St	C2
Bryn-y-Cabanau Rd	C3
Bury St	C3
Bus Station	B2
Butchers Market	B3
Citizens Advice Bureau	B2
Caia Rd	C3
Cambrian Ind Est	C3
Caxton Pl	B2
Cemetery	C1
Centenary Rd	C1
Chapel St	C2
Charles St	B3
Chester Rd	A3
Chester St	B3
Cilcen Gr	A3
Cobden Rd	B1
College of Art & Design	B2
Council Offices	B3
County	B2
Crescent Rd	C3
Crispin La	A2
Croesnewyth Rd	B1
Cross St	A2
Cunliffe St	A2
Derby Rd	C3
DHS	B2
Dolydd Rd	B1
Duke St	B2
Eagles Meadow	C3
Earle St	C2
East Ave	A2
Edward St	C2
Egerton St	B2
Empress Rd	C1
Erddig Rd	C2
Fairy Rd	C2
Fire Station	B2
Foster Rd	A3
Foxwood Dr	C1
Garden Rd	A2
General Market	B3
Gerald St	B2
Gibson St	C1
Greenbank St	C3
Greenfield	A2
Grosvenor Rd	B2
Grove Park Rd	A3
Grove Park	B2
Grove Rd	A3
Guildhall	B2
Haig Rd	C2
Hampden Rd	C2
Hazel Gr	A3
Henblas St	B3
High St	B3
Hightown Rd	C3
Hill St	B2
Holt Rd	B3
Hope St	B3
Huntroyde Ave	C3
Information Ctr	B3
Island Green Shopping Ctr	B2
Jubilee Rd	B2
King St	B2
Kingsmills Rd	C3
Lambpit St	B3
Law Courts	B3
Lawson Cl	A3
Lawson Rd	A3
Lea Rd	C2
Library & Arts Ctr	B2
Lilac Way	B1
Llys David Lord	B1
Lorne St	B2
Maesgwyn Rd	B1
Maesydre Rd	A3
Manley Rd	B3
Market St	B3
Mawddy Ave	A2
Mayville Ave	A2
Memorial Gall	B2
Memorial Hall	B3
Mold Rd	A1
Mount St	C3
North East Wales Inst (N.E.W.I.)	A1
N.E.W.I. Sports Ctr	A1
Neville Cres	A3
New Rd	A2
North Wales Tennis Ctr	A1
Oak Dr	A3
Park Ave	C3
Park St	A2
Peel St	C1
Pentre Felin	C2
Pen-y-Bryn	C2
Penymaes Ave	A3
Peoples Market	B3
Percy St	C3
Plas Coch Retail Park	A1
Plas Coch Rd	A1
Police Station	B3
Poplar Rd	C2
Post Office	A2/B2/C2/C3
Powell Rd	B3
Poyser St	C2
Price's La	C1
Primose Way	B1
Princess St	C1
Queen St	B3
Queens Sq	B2
Regent St	B2
Rhosddu Rd	A2/B2
Rhosnesni La	C3
Rivulet Rd	C3
Ruabon Rd	C3
Ruthin Rd	C1/C2
St Giles	C3
St James Ct	A2
St Mary's	B2
St Giles Way	C3
Salisbury Rd	C3
Salop Rd	C3
Smithfield Rd	C3
Sontley Rd	C2
Spring Rd	A2
Stanley St	A2
Stansty Rd	A2
Station Approach	B2
Studio	B2/3
Talbot Rd	C2
Techniquest	A2
The Beeches	A3
The Pines	A3
Town Hill	C2
Trevor St	C2
Trinity St	B2
Tuttle St	C3
Vale Park	A1
Vernon St	B2
Vicarage Hill	B2
Victoria Rd	C2
Walnut St	C2
War Memorial	B3
Waterworld Swimming Baths	B3
Watery Rd	B1/B2
Wellington Rd	C1
Westminster Dr	A3
William Aston Hall	A1
Windsor Rd	A1
Wrexham AFC	A1
Wrexham Central	B2
Wrexham General	B2
Wrexham Maelor (A&E)	B1
Wrexham Technology Pk	B1
Wynn Ave	A2
Yale College	B3
Yale Gr	A3
Yorke St	C3

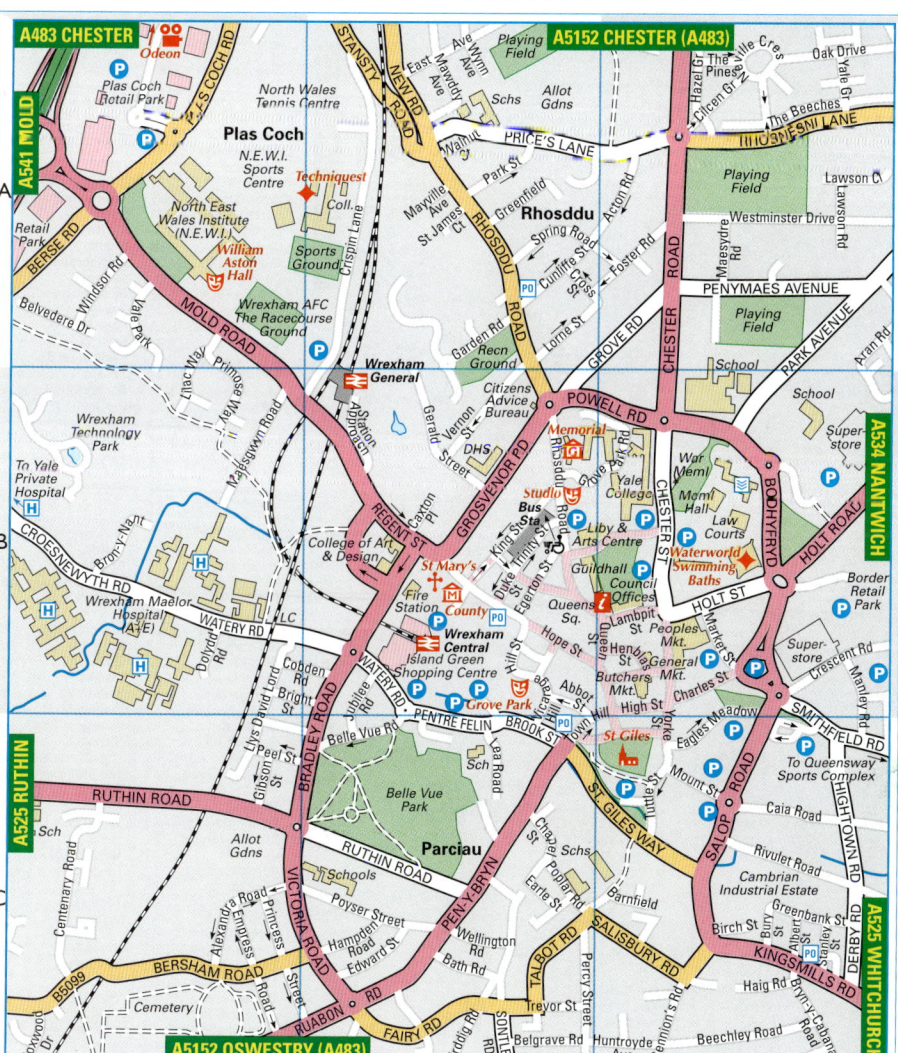

¼ mile / ½ km

York

An attractive city on the site of a major Roman settlement, subsequently occupied by the Anglo-Saxons, Vikings and Normans. The rebuilding of the Anglo-Saxon cathedral, which became York Minster (northern Europe's biggest medieval cathedral), began in the 11th century, and over the next 3 centuries York was transformed into the second largest city in the country. Its history can be explored in the Yorkshire Museum & Gardens; Treasurer's House; Barley Hall, a re-created medieval townhouse; Fairfax House, an 18th-century townhouse with a furniture collection; the Micklegate Bar Museum; the Richard III Museum; the Regimental Museum; the Castle Museum; and the York Dungeon. Other attractions include the York Art Gallery, York Brewery, National Centre for Early Music with its festivals, York Maze (the world's largest, grown each summer) and York Model Railway. New for 2006 is DIG, an interactive simulated archaeological excavation.

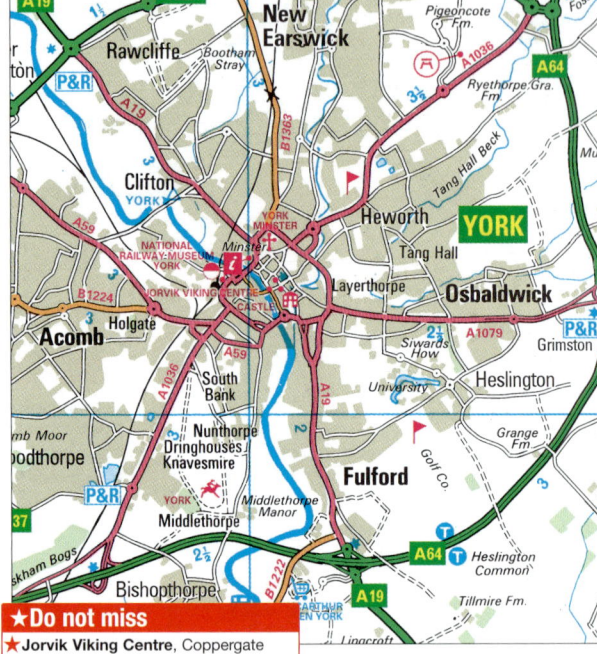

▲ York Minster

Tourist Information Centre,
De Grey Rooms, Exhibition Square,
York YO1 2HB Tel 01904 621756

BBC Radio York 103.7 FM and 666 AM • **Galaxy** 105 FM
Minster 104.7 FM

www.visityork.org

★ Do not miss
★ **Jorvik Viking Centre**, Coppergate
★ **National Railway Museum**, Leeman Road
★ **York Minster**, Minster Yard

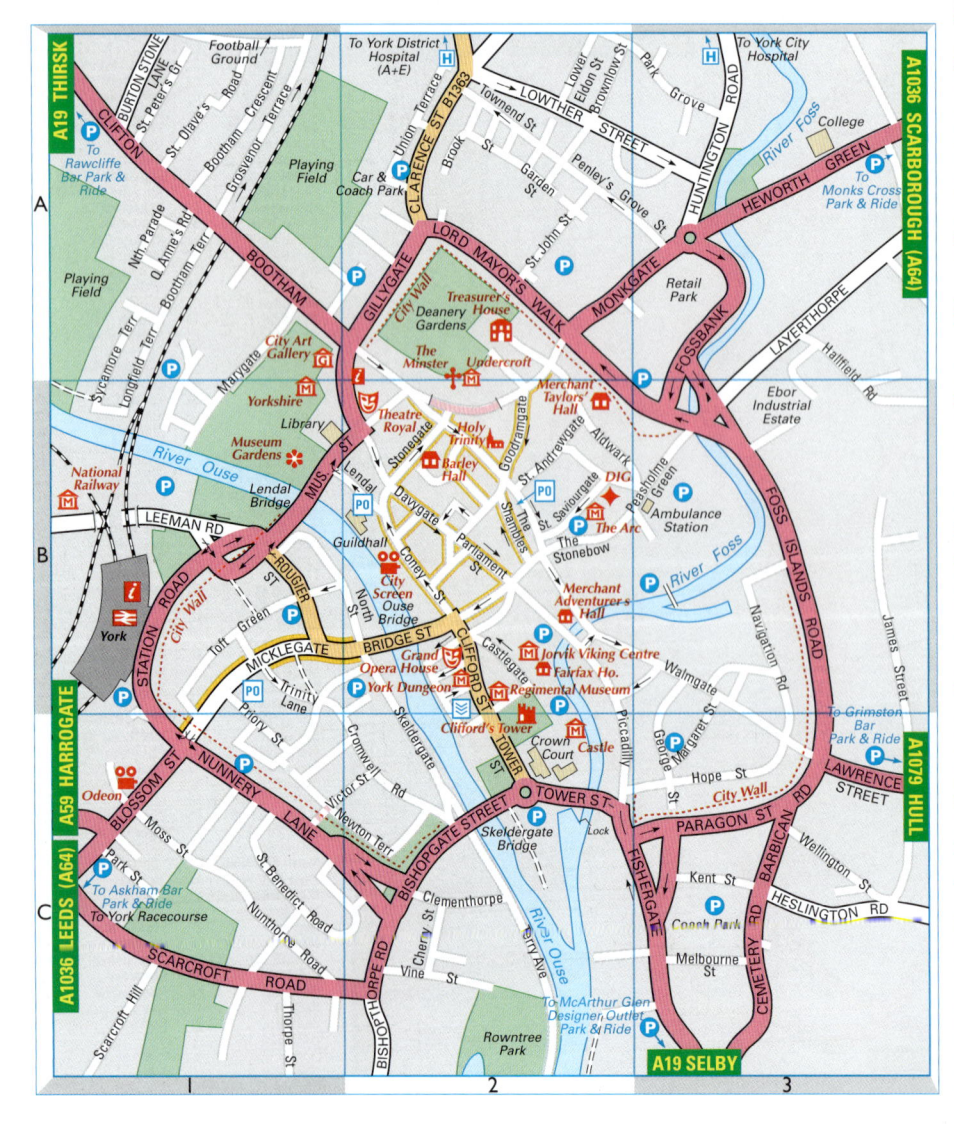

York

Aldwark	B2
Ambulance Stn	B3
Arc Museum, The	B2
Barbican Rd	C3
Barley Hall	B2
Bishopgate St	C2
Bishopthorpe Rd	C1
Blossom St	C1
Bootham	A1
Bootham Cr	A1
Bootham Terr	A1
Bridge St	B2
Brook St	A2
Brownlow St	A1
Burton Stone La	A1
Castle Museum	C2
Castlegate	B2
Cemetery Rd	C3
Cherry St	C1
City Art Gallery	B1
City Screen	B2
City Wall	A2/B1/C3
Clarence St	A2
Clementhorpe	C2
Clifford St	B2
Clifford's Tower	B2
Clifton	A1
Coach park	A2/C3
Coney St	B2
Cromwell Rd	C1
Crown Court	C2
Davygate	B2
Deanery Gdns	B1
DIG	B2
Ebor Ind Est	B3
Fairfax House	B2
Fishergate	C3
Foss Islands Rd	B3
Fossbank	A3
Garden St	A2
George St	C3
Gillygate	A2
Goodramgate	B2
Grand Opera House	B2
Grosvenor Terr	A1
Guildhall	B2
Hallfield Rd	A3
Heslington Rd	C3
Heworth Green	A3
Holy Trinity	B2
Hope St	C3
Huntington Rd	A3
Information Ctr	A2
James St	B3
Jorvik Viking Centre	B2
Kent St	C3
Lawrence St	C3
Layerthorpe	A3
Leeman Rd	B1
Lendal	B2
Lendal Bridge	B1
Library	B1
Longfield Terr	A1
Lord Mayor's Wlk	A2
Lower Eldon St	A1
Lowther St	A2
Margaret St	C3
Marygate	A1
Melbourne St	C3
Merchant Adventurers' Hall	B2
Merchant Taylors' Hall	B2
Micklegate	B1
Minster, The	A2
Monkgate	A2
Moss St	C1
Museum Gdns	B1
Museum St	B1
National Railway Museum	B1
Navigation Rd	B3
Newton Terr	C1
North Pde	A1
North St	B1
Nunnery La	C1
Nunthorpe Rd	C1
Odeon	C1
Ouse Bridge	B2
Paragon St	C3
Park Gr	A3
Park St	C1
Parliament St	B2
Peasholme Green	B3
Penley's Grove St	A2
Piccadilly	B2
Police Station	C1
Post Office	B1/B2
Priory St	B1
Queen Anne's Rd	A1
Regimental Museum	C2
Rowntree Park	C2
St Andrewgate	B2
St Benedict Rd	C1
St John St	A2
St Olave's Rd	A1
St Peter's Gr	A1
St Saviourgate	B2
Scarcroft Hill	C1
Scarcroft Rd	C1
Skeldergate	C2
Skeldergate Br	C2
Station Rd	B1
Stonegate	B2
Sycamore Terr	A1
Terry Ave	C2
The Shambles	B2
The Stonebow	B2
Theatre Royal	B2
Thorpe St	C1
Toft Green	B1
Tower St	C2
Townend St	A2
Treasurer's House	A2
Trinity Lu	B1
Undercroft Museum	A2
Union Terr	A2
Victor St	C2
Vine St	C2
Walmgate	B3
Wellington St	C3
York Dungeon	B2
York Station	B1
Yorkshire Museum	B1

150

Index to road maps

Abbreviations

Aberd C	Aberdeen City
Aberds	Aberdeenshire
Angl	Isle of Anglesey
Arg/Bute	Argyll & Bute
Bath/NE Som'set	Bath & North East Somerset
Beds	Bedfordshire
Bl Gwent	Blaenau Gwent
Blackb'n	Blackburn with Darwen
Blackp'l	Blackpool
Bournem'th	Bournemouth
Brackn'l	Bracknell Forest
Bridg	Bridgend
Brighton/Hove	City of Brighton and Hove
Bristol	City and County of Bristol
Bucks	Buckinghamshire
C/Edinb	City of Edinburgh
C/Glasg	Glasgow City
C/York	City of York
Caerph	Caerphilly
Cambs	Cambridgeshire
Card	Cardiff
Carms	Carmarthenshire
Ceredig'n	Ceredigion
Ches	Cheshire
Clack	Clackmannanshire
Cornw'l	Cornwall
Cumb	Cumbria
D'lington	Darlington
Denbs	Denbighshire
Derby	Derbyshire
Derby C	Derby City
Dumf/Gal	Dumfries & Galloway
Dundee C	Dundee City
E Ayrs	East Ayrshire
E Dunb	East Dunbartonshire
E Loth	East Lothian
E Renf	East Renfrewshire
ER Yorks	East Riding of Yorkshire
E Sussex	East Sussex
Falk	Falkirk
Flints	Flintshire
Glos	Gloucestershire
Gtr Man	Greater Manchester
Gwyn	Gwynedd
H'land	Highland
Hants	Hampshire
Hartlep'l	Hartlepool
Heref'd	Herefordshire
Herts	Hertfordshire
I/Man	Isle of Man
I/Scilly	Isles of Scilly
I/Wight	Isle of Wight
Invercl	Inverclyde
Kingston/Hull	Kingston upon Hull
Lancs	Lancashire
Leics	Leicestershire
Leics C	Leicester City
Lincs	Lincolnshire
London	Greater London
M/Keynes	Milton Keynes
Mersey	Merseyside
Merth Tyd	Merthyr Tydfil
Middlesbro	Middlesbrough
Midloth	Midlothian
Monmouths	Monmouthshire
N Ayrs	North Ayrshire
N Lanarks	North Lanarkshire
N Lincs	North Lincolnshire
N Som'set	North Somerset
N Yorks	North Yorkshire
NE Lincs	North East Lincolnshire
Neath P Talb	Neath Port Talbot
Newp	City and County of Newport
Northants	Northamptonshire
Northum	Northumberland
Nott'ham	City of Nottingham
Notts	Nottinghamshire
Oxon	Oxfordshire
Pembs	Pembrokeshire
Perth/Kinr	Perth and Kinross
Peterbro	Peterborough
Plym'th	Plymouth
Portsm'th	Portsmouth
Redcar/Clevel'd	Redcar and Cleveland
Renf	Renfrewshire
Rh Cyn Taff	Rhondda Cynon Taff
Rutl'd	Rutland
S'thampton	Southampton
S Ayrs	South Ayrshire
S Gloucs	South Gloucestershire
S Lanarks	South Lanarkshire
S Yorks	South Yorkshire
Scot Borders	Scottish Borders
Shetl'd	Shetland
Shrops	Shropshire
Som'set	Somerset
Southend	Southend-on-Sea
Staffs	Staffordshire
Stirl	Stirling
Stockton	Stockton on Tees
Stoke	Stoke-on-Trent
Swan	Swansea
Telford	Telford and Wrekin
Thurr'k	Thurrock
Torf	Torfaen
Tyne/Wear	Tyne and Wear
V/Glam	Vale of Glamorgan
W Berks	West Berkshire
W Dunb	West Dunbartonshire
W Isles	Western Isles
W Loth	West Lothian
W Midlands	West Midlands
W Sussex	West Sussex
W Yorks	West Yorkshire
Warwick	Warwickshire
Wilts	Wiltshire
Windsor	Windsor and Maidenhead
Worcs	Worcestershire
Wrex	Wrexham

A

Place	Page	Grid
Abbey Town Cumb	19	E9
Abbots Bromley Staffs	11	B7
Abbotsbury Dorset	4	G4
Aberaeron Ceredig'n	8	E5
Aberarth Ceredig'n	8	E5
Abercarn Caerph	4	B3
Aberchirder Aberds	29	D8
Abercrave Powys	9	H7
Aberdare Rh Cyn Taff	9	H7
Aberdaron Gwyn	8	B3
Aberdeen Aberd C	29	F9
Aberdour Fife	24	E4
Aberdulais Neath P Talb	9	H6
Aberdyfi Gwyn	8	D6
Aberfeldy Perth/Kinr	24	B3
Aberffraw Angl	14	G1
Aberfoyle Stirl	23	D9
Abergavenny Monmouths	10	H3
Abergele Conwy	14	G4
Abergwili Carms	9	G5
Abergwyngregyn Gwyn	14	G3
Abergynolwyn Gwyn	8	C6
Aberlady E Loth	25	E6
Abernethy Perth/Kinr	24	D4
Aberporth Ceredig'n	9	F4
Abersoch Gwyn	8	B4
Abersychan Torf	4	A3
Abertillery Bl Gwent	4	A3
Aberystwyth Ceredig'n	8	D5
Abingdon Oxon	5	B9
Abington S Lanarks	19	A8
Aboyne Aberds	29	G7
Accrington Lancs	15	D8
Acha Arg/Bute	22	B2
Achanalt H'land	27	C10
Achaphubuil H'land	27	H9
Acharacle H'land	22	A5
Achavanich H'land	31	F7
Achavraie H'land	27	A9
Achiemore H'land	30	E3
Achiltibuie H'land	27	A9
Achnacroish Arg/Bute	23	B6
Achnasheen H'land	27	D9
Achnashellach H'land	27	D9
Achosnich H'land	22	A4
Achriabhach H'land	23	A7
Acklam N Yorks	16	B5
Acle Norfolk	13	C9
Acomb C/York	16	C4
Acton Burnell Shrops	10	C2
Addingham W Yorks	16	C2
Adlington Lancs	15	E8
Adwick le Street S Yorks	16	E4
Affric Lodge H'land	27	E9
Ainsdale Mersey	15	E6
Aird Arg/Bute	22	D5
Aird a Mhulaidh W Isles	32	H3
Aird Asaig Tairbeart W Isles	26	A4
Aird Uig W Isles	32	G3
Airdrie N Lanarks	24	F2
Airor H'land	27	F7
Airth Falk	24	E3
Aisgill Cumb	20	H3
Aith Orkney	31	B10
Aith Shetl'd	32	D2
Akeley Bucks	11	G10
Albrighton Shrops	10	C6
Alcester Warwick	11	F7
Aldborough N Yorks	16	B4
Aldbourne Wilts	5	C8
Aldbrough ER Yorks	17	D8
Aldeburgh Suffolk	13	F10
Alderbury Wilts	5	E7
Alderley Edge Ches	15	G9
Aldermaston W Berks	5	C9
Aldershot Hants	6	D2
Aldridge W Midlands	11	C7
Aldsworth Glos	11	H7
Aldwick W Sussex	6	G2
Alexandria W Dunb	23	E8
Alford Aberds	29	F7
Alford Lincs	17	G9
Alfreton Derby	16	H4
Alfriston E Sussex	6	F5
Alkham Kent	7	D9
Allendale Town Northum	20	E4
Allenheads Northum	20	E4
Alloa Clack	24	E3
Allonby Cumb	19	E9
Almondsbury S Gloucs	4	B5
Alness H'land	28	C3
Alnmouth Northum	21	B6
Alnwick Northum	20	B5
Alphington Devon	3	D10
Alrewas Staffs	11	C7
Alsager Ches	15	H9
Alston Cumb	20	E3
Alt na h'Airbhe H'land	27	B9
Altandun Cornw'l	3	E7
Altass H'land	28	A2
Althorne Essex	7	B7
Althorpe N Lincs	17	E6
Altnaharra H'land	30	G4
Alton Hants	5	E10
Alton Staffs	11	A7
Altrincham Gtr Man	15	F8
Alva Clack	24	E3
Alvechurch Worcs	11	E7
Aveley Shrops	10	D5
Alveston S Gloucs	4	B5
Alvie H'land	28	F4
Alwinton Northum	20	B4
Alyth Perth/Kinr	24	B5
Amble Northum	21	B6
Ambleside Cumb	20	G1
Armathwaite Cumb	20	E2
Amersham Bucks	6	B2
Amesbury Wilts	5	D7
Amlwch Angl	14	F2
Ammanford Carms	9	H6
Ampleforth N Yorks	16	B4
Ampthill Beds	12	G3
Amulree Perth/Kinr	24	C3
An t-Ob W Isles	26	B4
Ancaster Lincs	12	A2
Ancroft Northum	25	G8
Ancrum Scot Borders	20	A3
Andover Hants	5	D8
Andoversford Glos	11	H7
Andreas I/Man	14	A2
Angle Pembs	9	H2
Angmering W Sussex	6	F3
Annan Dumf/Gal	19	D9
Annbank S Ayrs	19	A6
Annfield Plain Durham	20	E5
Anstey Leics	11	C9
Anstruther Fife	25	D6
Appleby-in-Westmorland Cumb	20	F3
Applecross H'land	27	D7
Appledore Devon	3	B8
Appledore Kent	7	E7
Arbroath Angus	25	B7
Archiestown Moray	29	D6
Ardarroch H'land	27	D8
Ardbeg Arg/Bute	22	G4
Ardcharnich H'land	27	B9
Ardchyle Stirl	23	C9
Ardentinny Arg/Bute	23	E7
Ardersier H'land	28	D3
Ardessie H'land	27	B9
Ardgay H'land	28	B3
Ardhasig W Isles	26	A4
Ardingly W Sussex	6	E4
Ardleigh Essex	13	G8
Ardley Oxon	11	G9
Ardlui Arg/Bute	23	D8
Ardlussa Arg/Bute	22	E5
Ardnave Arg/Bute	22	F3
Ardrishaig Arg/Bute	23	E6
Ardrossan N Ayrs	23	G8
Ardtalnaig Perth/Kinr	24	C2
Ardvasar H'land	27	F7
Ardwell Dumf/Gal	18	E4
Ardwell Moray	29	E6
Arinagour Arg/Bute	22	B3
Arisaig H'land	27	G7
Armadale H'land	27	F7
Armadale W Loth	24	F3
Armitage Staffs	11	C7
Armthorpe S Yorks	16	E5
Arncliffe N Yorks	15	B9
Arncott Oxon	11	H10
Arnisdale H'land	27	F8
Arnold Notts	11	A9
Arnside Cumb	15	B7
Arreton I/Wight	5	G9
Arrochar Arg/Bute	23	D8
Arundel W Sussex	6	F3
Ascot Windsor	6	C2
Asfordby Leics	11	B10
Ash Kent	7	D9
Ash Surrey	6	D2
Ashbourne Derby	11	A7
Ashburton Devon	3	E9
Ashbury Oxon	5	B8
Ashby de-la-Zouch Leics	11	C8
Ashchurch Glos	11	F6
Ashford Derby	16	G2
Ashford Kent	7	D8
Ashingdon Essex	7	B7
Ashington Northum	21	C6
Ashley Staffs	10	B5
Ashton Ches	15	G7
Ashton-in-Makerfield Gtr Man	15	F7
Ashton Keynes Wilts	5	B7
Ashton under Hill Worcs	11	G7
Ashton Under Lyne Gtr Man	15	F9
Ashurst Hants	5	F8
Ashwater Devon	3	D7
Ashwell Herts	12	G4
Ashwick Som'set	4	D5
Askam-in-Furness Cumb	15	B6
Askern S Yorks	16	E4
Askrigg N Yorks	20	H4
Aslackby Lincs	12	B3
Aspatria Cumb	19	E9
Asterton Warwick	11	E7
Atherstone Warwick	11	D8
Atherton Gtr Man	15	E8
Attleborough Norfolk	13	D8
Atworth Wilts	4	C6
Auchenblae Aberds	29	G8
Auchencairn Dumf/Gal	19	E7
Auchengray S Lanarks	24	G3
Auchinleck E Ayrs	19	A6
Auchronie Angus	29	G7
Auchterarder Perth/Kinr	24	D3
Auchterderran Fife	24	E5
Auchtermuchty Fife	24	D5
Auchtertyre H'land	27	E8
Audlem Ches	10	A5
Audley Staffs	15	H8
Auldearn H'land	28	D4
Aultbea H'land	27	B8
Austwick N Yorks	15	B8
Avebury Wilts	5	C7
Avening Glos	4	B6
Aveton Gifford Devon	3	F9
Aviemore H'land	28	F4
Avoch H'land	28	D3
Avonmouth Bristol	4	C4
Axbridge Som'set	4	D4
Axminster Devon	4	G3
Axmouth Devon	4	G3
Aylesbury Bucks	12	H2
Aylesford Kent	7	D6
Aylesham Kent	7	D9
Aylsham Norfolk	13	B8
Aynho Northants	11	G9
Ayr S Ayrs	18	A5
Aysgarth N Yorks	15	A9
Ayton N Yorks	17	A6
Ayton Scot Borders	25	F8

B

Place	Page	Grid
Bac W Isles	32	F5
Backwell N Som'set	4	C4
Bacton Norfolk	13	B9
Bacup Lancs	15	D9
Badenscoth Aberds	29	E8
Badenyon Aberds	29	F6
Badrallach H'land	27	B9
Bagh a Chaisteil W Isles	26	G2
Bagillt Flints	15	G6
Bagshot Surrey	6	C2
Baildon W Yorks	16	D2
Baile Ailein W Isles	32	G4
Bainbridge N Yorks	15	A9
Bainton ER Yorks	17	C6
Bakewell Derby	16	G3
Bala Gwyn	8	B7
Balbeggie Perth/Kinr	24	C4

Balblair *H'land* 28 C3
Balcombe *W Sussex* 6 E4
Balderton *Notts* 17 H6
Baldock *Herts* 12 G4
Balfour *Orkney* 31 C9
Balfron *Stirl* 23 E9
Balintore *H'land* 28 C4
Ballachulish *H'land* 23 B7
Ballantrae *S Ayrs* 18 C4
Ballasalla *I/Man* 14 B1
Ballater *Aberds* 29 G6
Ballaugh *I/Man* 14 A1
Ballinluig *Perth/Kinr* 24 B3
Balloch *H'land* 28 D3
Balloch *W Dunb* 23 E8
Ballochan *Aberds* 29 G7
Ballygrant *Arg/Bute* 22 F3
Balmaclellan *Dumf/Gal* 19 D7
Balmedie *Aberds* 29 F9
Balnapaling *H'land* 28 C3
Balquhidder *Stirl* 23 C9
Balsall *W Midlands* 11 E8
Balsham *Cambs* 12 F5
Baltasound *Shetl'd* 32 A4
Balvicar *Arg/Bute* 22 D5
Bamber Bridge *Lancs* 15 D7
Bamburgh *Northum* 25 H9
Bamford *Derby* 16 F3
Bampton *Devon* 3 B10
Bampton *Oxon* 5 A8
Banbury *Oxon* 11 F9
Banchory *Aberds* 29 G8
Banff *Aberds* 29 C8
Bangor *Gwyn* 14 G2
Bangor-is-y-coed *Wrex* 10 A3
Banham *Norfolk* 13 D8
Bankend *Dumf/Gal* 19 D9
Bankfoot *Perth/Kinr* 24 C4
Bankhead *Aberd C* 29 F9
Banks *Lancs* 15 D6
Bannockburn *Stirl* 24 E3
Banstead *Surrey* 6 D4
Banwell *N Som'set* 4 D3
Bar Hill *Cambs* 12 E4
Barabhas *W Isles* 32 F4
Barassie *S Ayrs* 23 H8
Barbon *Cumb* 15 A8
Bardney *Lincs* 17 G7
Barford *Warwick* 11 E8
Bargoed *Caerph* 4 A2
Bargrennan *Dumf/Gal* 18 D5
Barham *Kent* 7 D9
Barkway *Herts* 12 G4
Barlborough *Derby* 16 G4
Barlby *N Yorks* 16 D5
Barley *Herts* 12 G5
Barmby Moor *ER Yorks* 16 C5
Barmoor Castle *Northum* 25 H8
Barmouth *Gwyn* 8 C6
Barnard Castle *Durham* 20 G5
Barnet *London* 6 B4
Barnetby le Wold *N Lincs* 17 E7
Barnham *Suffolk* 13 E7
Barnhill *Moray* 28 D5
Barnoldswick *Lancs* 15 C9
Barnsley *S Yorks* 16 E3
Barnstaple *Devon* 3 B8
Barnt Green *Worcs* 11 E7
Barr *S Ayrs* 18 C5
Barrhead *E Renf* 23 G9
Barrhill *S Ayrs* 18 C5
Barrow-In-Furness *Cumb* 14 B5
Barrow upon Humber *N Lincs* 17 D7
Barrowford *Lancs* 15 D9
Barry *Angus* 25 C6
Barry *V/Glam* 4 C2
Barton *N Yorks* 21 G6
Barton-le-Clay *Beds* 12 G3
Barton upon Humber *N Lincs* 17 D7
Barwell *Leics* 11 D9
Baschurch *Shrops* 10 B4
Basildon *Essex* 7 B6
Basingstoke *Hants* 5 D10
Baslow *Derby* 16 G3
Baston *Lincs* 12 C3
Bath *Bath/NE Som'set* 4 C5
Bathford *Bath/NE Som'set* 4 C5
Bathgate *W Loth* 24 F3
Batley *W Yorks* 16 D3
Battle *E Sussex* 7 F6
Bawdeswell *Norfolk* 13 B8
Bawdsey *Suffolk* 13 F9
Bawtry *S Yorks* 16 F5
Bayston Hill *Shrops* 10 C4
Beachley *Glos* 4 B4
Beaconsfield *Bucks* 6 B2
Beadnell *Northum* 21 A6
Beaminster *Dorset* 4 F4
Bearsden *E Dunb* 23 F9
Bearsted *Kent* 7 D6
Beattock *Dumf/Gal* 19 B9
Beaufort *Bl Gwent* 10 H2
Beaulieu *Hants* 5 F8
Beauly *H'land* 28 D2
Beaumaris *Angl* 14 G2
Bebington *Mersey* 15 F6
Beccles *Suffolk* 13 D10
Beck Row *Suffolk* 12 E6
Beckermet *Cumb* 19 G9
Beckfoot *Cumb* 19 E9
Beckhampton *Wilts* 5 C7
Beckingham *Notts* 16 F5
Beckington *Som'set* 4 D6
Bedale *N Yorks* 16 A3
Beddgelert *Gwyn* 8 A5
Bedford *Beds* 12 F3
Bedlington *Northum* 21 C6
Bedwas *Caerph* 4 B2
Bedworth *Warwick* 11 D8
Beeford *ER Yorks* 17 C7
Beer *Devon* 4 G3
Beeston *Notts* 11 B9
Beeswing *Dumf/Gal* 19 D8
Begelly *Pembs* 9 H3
Beguildy *Powys* 10 E2
Beighton *S Yorks* 16 F4
Beith *N Ayrs* 23 G8
Belbroughton *Worcs* 11 E6
Belchford *Lincs* 17 G8
Belford *Northum* 25 H9
Bellingham *Northum* 20 C4
Bellsbank *E Ayrs* 19 B6
Bellshill *N Lanarks* 24 F2
Belmont *Blackb'n* 15 E8
Belmont *Shetl'd* 32 A3
Belper *Derby* 11 A8
Belsay *Northum* 20 D5
Beltinge *Kent* 7 C8
Belton *N Lincs* 16 E5
Belton *Norfolk* 13 C10
Bembridge *I/Wight* 5 G10
Benington *Lincs* 12 A5
Benllech *Angl* 14 F2
Benson *Oxon* 5 B10
Bentley *Hants* 5 D10
Bentley *S Yorks* 16 E4
Benwick *Cambs* 12 D4
Bere Alston *Devon* 3 E8
Bere Regis *Dorset* 4 G6
Berkeley *Glos* 4 B5
Berkhamsted *Herts* 6 A2
Berriedale *H'land* 31 G7
Berriew *Powys* 10 C2
Berrow *Som'set* 4 D3
Berwick *E Sussex* 6 F5
Berwick-Upon-Tweed *Northum* 25 G8
Bethersden *Kent* 7 E7
Bethesda *Gwyn* 14 G3
Bettws Bledrws *Ceredig'n* 9 F6
Bettyhill *H'land* 30 E5
Betws *Bridg* 9 J7
Betws-y-Coed *Conwy* 8 A6
Beulah *Powys* 9 F7
Beverley *ER Yorks* 17 D7
Bewcastle *Cumb* 20 D2
Bewdley *Worcs* 10 E5
Bexhill *E Sussex* 7 F6
Bexley *London* 6 C5
Bibury *Glos* 5 A7
Bicester *Oxon* 11 G9
Bickington *Devon* 3 E9
Bicton *Shrops* 10 C4
Biddenden *Kent* 7 E7
Biddulph *Staffs* 15 H9
Bideford *Devon* 3 B8
Bidford-on-Avon *Warwick* 11 F7
Bigbury *Devon* 3 F9
Biggar *S Lanarks* 24 H4
Biggin Hill *London* 6 D5
Biggleswade *Beds* 12 F4
Bildeston *Suffolk* 13 F7
Billericay *Essex* 6 B6
Billesdon *Leics* 11 C10
Billingborough *Lincs* 12 B3
Billingham *Stockton* 21 F7
Billinghay *Lincs* 17 H7
Billingshurst *W Sussex* 6 E3
Bilston *W Midlands* 11 D6
Binbrook *Lincs* 17 F8
Bingham *Notts* 11 B10
Bingley *W Yorks* 16 D2
Birchgrove *Swan* 9 J6
Birchington *Kent* 7 C9
Birdlip *Glos* 11 H6
Birkdale *Mersey* 15 E6
Birkenhead *Mersey* 15 F6
Birmingham *W Midlands* 11 D7
Birtley *Northum* 20 D4
Birtley *Tyne/Wear* 21 E6
Bishop Auckland *Durham* 21 F6
Bishop Monkton *N Yorks* 16 B3
Bishopbriggs *E Dunb* 24 F2
Bishop's Castle *Shrops* 10 D3
Bishop's Cleeve *Glos* 11 G6
Bishop's Frome *Heref'd* 10 F5
Bishops Lydeard *Som'set* 4 E2
Bishop's Nympton *Devon* 3 B9
Bishop's Stortford *Herts* 12 G5
Bishop's Tawton *Devon* 3 B8
Bishop's Waltham *Hants* 5 F9
Bishopsteignton *Devon* 3 E10
Bishopstoke *Hants* 5 F9
Bishopston *Swan* 9 J5
Bitton *S Gloucs* 4 C5
Blaby *Leics* 11 D9
Blackburn *Blackb'n* 15 D8
Blackford *Cumb* 20 D1
Blackford *Perth/Kinr* 24 D3
Blackpool *Blackp'l* 15 D6
Blackridge *W Loth* 24 F3
Blackwaterfoot *N Ayrs* 18 A3
Blackwood *Caerph* 4 B2
Blackwood *S Lanarks* 24 G2
Blaenau Ffestiniog *Gwyn* 8 A6
Blaenavon *Torf* 4 A3
Blagdon *N Som'set* 4 D4
Blaina *Bl Gwent* 4 A3
Blair Atholl *Perth/Kinr* 24 A3
Blairgowrie *Perth/Kinr* 24 B4
Blakeney *Glos* 4 A5
Blakeney *Norfolk* 13 A8
Blanchand *Northum* 20 E4
Blandford Forum *Dorset* 4 F6
Blaydon *Tyne/Wear* 20 D5
Bleadon *N Som'set* 4 D3
Blean *Kent* 7 C8
Bletchingdon *Oxon* 11 H9
Bletchley *M/Keynes* 12 G2
Blewbury *Oxon* 5 B9
Blidworth *Notts* 16 H5
Blisworth *Northants* 11 F10
Blockley *Glos* 11 G7
Blofield *Norfolk* 13 C9
Bloxham *Oxon* 11 G9
Blubberhouses *N Yorks* 16 C2
Blundeston *Norfolk* 13 D10
Blyth *Northum* 21 C6
Blyth *Notts* 16 F5
Blyth Bridge *Scot Borders* 24 G4
Blythburgh *Suffolk* 13 E10
Blythe Bridge *Staffs* 11 A6
Blyton *Lincs* 17 F6
Boat of Garten *H'land* 28 F4
Boddam *Aberds* 29 D10
Boddam *Shetl'd* 32 F2
Bodedern *Angl* 14 G1
Bodenham *Heref'd* 10 F4
Bodiam *E Sussex* 7 E6
Bodinnick *Cornw'l* 3 F6
Bodmin *Cornw'l* 2 E6
Bognor Regis *W Sussex* 6 G2
Boldon *Tyne/Wear* 21 D6
Bollington *Ches* 15 G9
Bolney *W Sussex* 6 E4
Bolsover *Derby* 16 G4
Bolton *Gtr Man* 15 E8
Bolton Abbey *N Yorks* 16 C2
Bolton Bridge *N Yorks* 16 C2
Bolton by Bowland *Lancs* 15 C8
Bolton le Sands *Lancs* 15 B7
Bonarbridge *H'land* 28 B3
Bonby *N Lincs* 17 E6
Bonchester Bridge *Scot Borders* 20 B2
Bonchurch *I/Wight* 5 H9
Bo'ness *Falk* 24 E3
Bonhill *W Dunb* 23 E8
Bonnybridge *Falk* 24 E3
Bonnyrigg *Midloth* 24 F5
Bonvilston *V/Glam* 4 C2
Boot *Cumb* 19 G9
Bootle *Cumb* 14 A5
Bootle *Mersey* 15 F6
Bordon *Hants* 6 E2
Borehamwood *Herts* 6 B4
Boreland *Dumf/Gal* 19 C9
Borgh *W Isles* 32 F4
Borgue *Dumf/Gal* 19 E7
Borough Green *Kent* 6 D6
Boroughbridge *N Yorks* 16 B3
Borrowdale *Cumb* 19 G10
Borth *Ceredig'n* 8 D6
Bosbury *Heref'd* 10 F5
Boscastle *Cornw'l* 2 D6
Bosham *W Sussex* 6 F2
Boston *Lincs* 12 A4
Boston Spa *W Yorks* 16 C4
Botesdale *Suffolk* 13 E8
Bothel *Cumb* 19 E9
Bothenhampton *Dorset* 4 G4
Botley *Oxon* 5 A9
Bottesford *Leics* 12 B2
Bottisham *Cambs* 12 E5
Botwnnog *Gwyn* 8 B4
Bourne *Lincs* 12 B3
Bourne End *Bucks* 6 B2
Bournemouth *Bournem'th* 5 G7
Bourton-on-the-Water *Glos* 11 G7
Bovey Tracey *Devon* 3 E10
Bow *Devon* 3 C9
Bowes *Durham* 20 G5
Bowmore *Arg/Bute* 22 G3
Bowness-on-Solway *Cumb* 19 D10
Bowness-on-Windermere *Cumb* 20 H2
Box *Wilts* 4 C6
Bozeat *Northants* 12 E2
Brabourne *Kent* 7 D8
Brabourne Lees *Kent* 7 E8
Bracadale *H'land* 26 E5
Bracebridge Heath *Lincs* 17 G6
Bracklesham *W Sussex* 6 G2
Brackley *Northants* 11 G9
Bracknell *Brackn'l* 6 C2
Braco *Perth/Kinr* 24 D3
Bradford *W Yorks* 16 D2
Bradford on Avon *Wilts* 4 C6
Brading *I/Wight* 5 G10
Bradpole *Dorset* 4 G4
Bradwell-on-Sea *Essex* 7 A8
Bradworthy *Devon* 3 C7
Brae *Shetl'd* 32 C2
Brae Roy Lodge *H'land* 28 G1
Braemar *Aberds* 28 G5
Braemore *H'land* 27 C9
Braemore *H'land* 31 G7
Brailsford *Derby* 11 A8
Braintree *Essex* 13 G6
Bramford *Suffolk* 13 F8
Bramhall *Gtr Man* 15 F9
Bramhope *W Yorks* 16 C3
Brampton *Cambs* 12 E4
Brampton *Cumb* 20 D2
Brancaster *Norfolk* 13 A6
Branderburgh *Moray* 29 C6
Brandon *Durham* 21 E6
Brandon *Suffolk* 13 D6
Branston *Lincs* 17 G7
Brantham *Suffolk* 13 G8
Bratton Fleming *Devon* 3 B9
Braunston *Northants* 11 E9
Braunton *Devon* 3 B8
Bray *Windsor* 6 C2
Breage *Cornw'l* 2 G4
Breakish *H'land* 27 E7
Bream *Glos* 4 A5
Breanais *W Isles* 32 G2
Brechfa *Carms* 9 G5
Brechin *Angus* 25 A7
Brecon *Powys* 10 G2
Brede *E Sussex* 7 F7
Bredenbury *Heref'd* 10 F5
Brent *London* 6 B4
Brentwood *Essex* 6 B6
Bretforton *Worcs* 11 F7
Brewood *Staffs* 10 C6
Bride *I/Man* 19 G6
Bridestowe *Devon* 3 D8
Bridge *Kent* 7 D8
Bridge of Allan *Stirl* 24 E2
Bridge of Balgie *Perth/Kinr* 23 B9
Bridge of Cally *Perth/Kinr* 24 B4
Bridge of Don *Aberd C* 29 F9
Bridge of Earn *Perth/Kinr* 24 D4
Bridge of Orchy *Arg/Bute* 23 B8
Bridge of Weir *Renf* 23 F8
Bridgend *Arg/Bute* 22 F3
Bridgend *Bridg* 9 K7
Bridgnorth *Shrops* 10 D5
Bridgwater *Som'set* 4 E3
Bridlington *ER Yorks* 17 B7
Bridport *Dorset* 4 G4
Brierfield *Lancs* 15 D9
Brierley Hill *W Midlands* 11 D6
Brigg *N Lincs* 17 E7
Brighouse *W Yorks* 16 D2
Brighstone *I/Wight* 5 G9
Brightlingsea *Essex* 13 H8
Brighton *Brighton/Hove* 6 F4
Brigstock *Northants* 12 D2
Brill *Bucks* 11 H10
Brimfield *Heref'd* 10 E4
Brinklow *Warwick* 11 D9
Brinkworth *Wilts* 5 B7
Brinyan *Orkney* 31 B9
Bristol *Bristol* 4 C4
Briston *Norfolk* 13 B8
Briton Ferry *Neath P Talb* 9 J6
Brixham *Torbay* 3 F10
Brixton *Devon* 3 F8
Brixworth *Northants* 11 E10
Brize Norton *Oxon* 5 A8
Broad Chalke *Wilts* 5 E7
Broad Haven *Pembs* 9 H2
Broad Hinton *Wilts* 5 C7
Broadclyst *Devon* 3 D10
Broadford *H'land* 27 E7
Broadhembury *Devon* 4 F2
Broadmayne *Dorset* 4 G5
Broadstairs *Kent* 7 C10
Broadstone *Poole* 5 G6
Broadwas *Worcs* 10 F5
Broadway *Worcs* 11 G7
Broadwey *Dorset* 4 G5
Broadwindsor *Dorset* 4 F4
Brochel *H'land* 27 D6
Brockenhurst *Hants* 5 F8
Brockworth *Glos* 11 H6
Brocton *Staffs* 11 B6
Brodick *N Ayrs* 23 H7
Bromfield *Shrops* 10 E4
Bromham *Beds* 12 F2
Bromham *Wilts* 5 C6
Bromley *London* 6 C5
Bromley Green *Kent* 7 E8
Brompton *N Yorks* 21 H6
Brompton Regis *Som'set* 3 B10
Bromsgrove *Worcs* 11 E6
Bromyard *Heref'd* 10 F5
Brooke *Norfolk* 13 D9
Broomfield *Essex* 13 H6
Broomhaugh *Northum* 20 D5
Broomhill *Northum* 21 B6
Brora *H'land* 28 A4
Broseley *Shrops* 10 C5
Brothertoft *Lincs* 12 A4
Brotton *Redcar/Clevel'd* 21 F8
Brough *Cumb* 20 G4
Brough *ER Yorks* 17 D6
Brough *H'land* 31 E8
Broughton *Cumb* 19 F9
Broughton *Hants* 5 E8
Broughton *Lancs* 15 D7
Broughton *N Lincs* 17 E6
Broughton *Northants* 12 E2
Broughton *Scot Borders* 24 H4
Broughton Astley *Leics* 11 D9
Broughton-in-Furness *Cumb* 15 A6
Broughty Ferry *Dundee C* 25 C6
Brownhills *W Midlands* 11 C7
Broxburn *W Loth* 24 F4
Broxton *Ches* 15 H7
Bruichladdich *Arg/Bute* 22 F3
Brundall *Norfolk* 13 C9
Brunton *Northum* 20 D4
Brunton *Northum* 21 A6
Bruton *Som'set* 4 E5
Brymbo *Wrex* 15 H6
Brynamman *Carms* 9 H6
Bryncrug *Gwyn* 8 C6
Brynmawr *Bl Gwent* 10 H2
Brynsiencyn *Angl* 14 G2
Bubwith *ER Yorks* 16 D5
Buchlyvie *Stirl* 23 E9
Buckden *Cambs* 12 E3
Buckden *N Yorks* 15 B9
Buckfast *Devon* 3 E9
Buckfastleigh *Devon* 3 E9
Buckhaven *Fife* 24 E5
Buckie *Moray* 29 C7
Buckingham *Bucks* 11 G10
Buckland *Oxon* 5 B8
Buckland Brewer *Devon* 3 C8
Buckland Newton *Dorset* 4 F5
Buckley *Flints* 15 G6
Buck's Cross *Devon* 3 B7
Bucksburn *Aberd C* 29 F9
Bude *Cornw'l* 3 C6
Budleigh Salterton *Devon* 4 G2
Bugbrooke *Northants* 11 F10
Bugle *Cornw'l* 2 F6
Builth Wells *Powys* 10 F2
Bulford *Wilts* 5 D7
Bulkington *Warwick* 11 D8
Bulwell *Nott'ham* 11 A9
Bunbury *Ches* 15 H7
Bunessan *Arg/Bute* 22 C3
Bungay *Suffolk* 13 D9
Bunnahabhain *Arg/Bute* 22 F4
Buntingford *Herts* 12 G4
Bunwell *Norfolk* 13 D8
Burbage *Derby* 16 G2
Burbage *Leics* 11 D9
Burbage *Wilts* 5 C8
Bures *Suffolk* 13 G7
Burford *Oxon* 11 H8
Burgess Hill *W Sussex* 6 F4
Burgh-by-Sands *Cumb* 20 E1
Burgh le Marsh *Lincs* 17 G9
Burghclere *Hants* 5 C9
Burghead *Moray* 28 C5
Burghfield Common *W Berks* 5 C10
Burley *Hants* 5 F8
Burley *W Yorks* 16 C2
Burlton *Shrops* 10 B4
Burneside *Cumb* 20 H2
Burness *Orkney* 31 A10
Burnham *Bucks* 6 B2
Burnham Market *Norfolk* 13 A7
Burnham-on-Crouch *Essex* 7 B7
Burnham-on-Sea *Som'set* 4 D3
Burniston *N Yorks* 21 H10
Burnley *Lancs* 15 D9
Burnmouth *Scot Borders* 25 G8
Burntisland *Fife* 24 E5
Burntwood *Staffs* 11 C7
Burravoe *Shetl'd* 32 B3
Burrelton *Perth/Kinr* 24 C4
Burry Port *Carms* 9 H5
Burscough Bridge *Lancs* 15 E7
Burstwick *ER Yorks* 17 D8
Burton *Cumb* 15 B7
Burton Agnes *ER Yorks* 17 B7
Burton Bradstock *Dorset* 4 G4

Burton Fleming *ER Yorks* 17 B7
Burton in Lonsdale *N Yorks* 15 B8
Burton Latimer *Northants* 12 E2
Burton upon Stather *N Lincs* 17 E6
Burton Upon Trent *Staffs* 11 B8
Burwash *E Sussex* 6 E6
Burwell *Cambs* 12 E5
Burwick *Orkney* 31 D9
Bury *Gtr Man* 15 E9
Bury St. Edmunds *Suffolk* 13 E7
Bushey *Herts* 6 B3
Buttermere *Cumb* 19 G9
Buxted *E Sussex* 6 E5
Buxton *Derby* 16 G2
Byfield *Northants* 11 F9
Byfleet *Surrey* 6 C3
Bylchau *Conwy* 14 G4

C

Cabrach *Moray* 29 E6
Caenby Corner *Lincs* 17 F6
Caergwrle *Flints* 15 H6
Caerleon *Newp* 4 B3
Caernarfon *Gwyn* 14 G2
Caerphilly *Caerph* 4 B2
Caersws *Powys* 10 D2
Caerwent *Monmouths* 4 B4
Cairinis *W Isles* 26 D3
Cairndow *Arg/Bute* 23 D7
Cairnryan *Dumf/Gal* 18 D4
Caister-on-Sea *Norfolk* 13 C10
Caistor *Lincs* 17 E7
Calanais *W Isles* 32 G4
Caldbeck *Cumb* 20 E1
Calder Bridge *Cumb* 19 G9
Caldercruix *N Lanarks* 24 F3
Caldicot *Monmouths* 4 B4
Calfsound *Orkney* 31 B9
Calgary *Arg/Bute* 22 B3
Callander *Stirl* 24 D2
Callington *Cornw'l* 3 E7
Calne *Wilts* 5 C7
Calshot *Hants* 5 F9
Calstock *Cornw'l* 3 E8
Calverton *Notts* 11 A10
Cam *Glos* 4 D5
Camber *E Sussex* 7 F7
Camberley *Surrey* 6 C2
Cambo *Northum* 20 C5
Camborne *Cornw'l* 2 G4
Cambridge *Cambs* 12 F5
Camden *London* 6 B4
Camelford *Cornw'l* 2 D6
Cammachmore *Aberds* 29 G9
Campbeltown *Arg/Bute* 18 A2
Camrose *Pembs* 9 H2
Canisbay *H'land* 31 E8
Cannich *H'land* 28 E1
Cannington *Som'set* 4 E3
Cannock *Staffs* 11 C6
Canonbie *Dumf/Gal* 20 D1
Canterbury *Kent* 7 D8
Canvey *Essex* 7 B7
Caol *H'land* 27 H9
Caolas Stocinis *W Isles* 26 B4
Caoles *Arg/Bute* 22 B2
Capel *Surrey* 6 D3
Capel Curig *Conwy* 14 H3
Capel St. Mary *Suffolk* 13 G8
Carbis Bay *Cornw'l* 2 G3
Carbost *H'land* 26 E5
Carbost *H'land* 27 D6
Cardiff *Card* 4 C2
Cardigan *Ceredig'n* 9 F3
Cardington *Beds* 12 F3
Cardross *Arg/Bute* 23 F8
Cargill *Perth/Kinr* 24 C4
Carhampton *Som'set* 4 D2
Carisbrooke *I/Wight* 5 G9
Cark *Cumb* 15 B6
Carlabhagh *W Isles* 32 F3
Carleton Rode *Norfolk* 13 D8
Carlisle *Cumb* 20 E2
Carlops *Scot Borders* 24 G4
Carlton *N Yorks* 16 D5
Carlton *Notts* 11 A10
Carlton Colville *Suffolk* 13 D10
Carlton-in-Lindrick *Notts* 16 F4
Carlton Miniott *N Yorks* 16 A4
Carluke *S Lanarks* 24 G3
Carmarthen *Carms* 9 G5
Carmyllie *Angus* 25 B6
Carnachuin *H'land* 28 G4
Carnforth *Lancs* 15 B7
Carno *Powys* 8 D7
Carnoustie *Angus* 25 C6
Carnwath *S Lanarks* 24 G3
Carradale *Arg/Bute* 23 H6
Carrbridge *H'land* 28 E4
Carrick *Arg/Bute* 23 E8
Carronbridge *Dumf/Gal* 19 C8
Carsaig *Arg/Bute* 22 C4
Carsphairn *Dumf/Gal* 19 C6
Carstairs *S Lanarks* 24 G3
Carterton *Oxon* 5 A8
Cartmel *Cumb* 15 B6
Castle Acre *Norfolk* 13 C7
Castle Cary *Som'set* 4 E5
Castle Donington *Leics* 11 B9
Castle Douglas *Dumf/Gal* 19 D7
Castleford *W Yorks* 16 D4
Castlemartin *Pembs* 9 J2
Castleside *Durham* 20 E5
Castleton *Derby* 16 F2
Castleton *N Yorks* 21 G8
Castletown *H'land* 31 E8
Castletown *I/Man* 14 B1
Caston *Norfolk* 13 D7
Castor *Peterbro* 12 D3
Catcleugh *Northum* 20 B3
Caterham *Surrey* 6 D4
Caton *Lancs* 15 B7
Catrine *E Ayrs* 19 A6
Catsfield *E Sussex* 7 F6
Catterall *Lancs* 15 C7
Catterick *N Yorks* 21 H6
Catterick Camp *N Yorks* 20 H5
Catton *Northum* 20 E4
Caulkerbush *Dumf/Gal* 19 E8
Cawdor *H'land* 28 D4
Cawood *N Yorks* 16 D4
Cawston *Norfolk* 13 B8
Caythorpe *Lincs* 12 A2
Cefn-mawr *Wrex* 10 A3
Cemaes *Angl* 14 F1
Cemmaes Road *Powys* 8 C7
Cenarth *Carms* 9 F4
Ceres *Fife* 25 D6
Cerne Abbas *Dorset* 4 F5
Cerrigydrudion *Conwy* 8 A7
Chacewater *Cornw'l* 2 F4
Chaddesley Corbet *Worcs* 10 E6
Chadwell St. Mary *Thurr'k* 6 C6
Chagford *Devon* 3 D9
Chalfont St. Giles *Bucks* 6 B2
Chalford *Glos* 5 A6
Chalgrove *Oxon* 5 B10
Challacombe *Devon* 3 A9
Challock *Kent* 7 D8
Chandler's Ford *Hants* 5 E9
Chapel en le Frith *Derby* 16 F2
Chapel St. Leonards *Lincs* 17 G9
Chapeltown *S Lanarks* 24 G2
Chapeltown *S Yorks* 16 F3
Chard *Som'set* 4 F3
Charing *Kent* 7 D7
Charlbury *Oxon* 11 H8
Charlestown of Aberlour *Moray* 29 D6
Charlton *Wilts* 5 B6
Charlton Horethorne *Som'set* 4 E5
Charlton Kings *Glos* 11 G6
Charlwood *Surrey* 6 D4
Charminster *Dorset* 4 G5
Charmouth *Dorset* 4 G3
Chartham *Kent* 7 D8
Chatham *Medway* 7 C6
Chathill *Northum* 20 A5
Chatteris *Cambs* 12 D4
Chatton *Northum* 20 A5
Chawleigh *Devon* 3 C9
Cheadle *Gtr Man* 15 F9
Cheadle *Staffs* 11 A7
Chedburgh *Suffolk* 13 F6
Cheddar *Som'set* 4 D4
Cheddleton *Staffs* 15 H9
Chellaston *Derby C* 11 B8
Chelmarsh *Shrops* 10 D5
Chelmsford *Essex* 7 A6
Cheltenham *Glos* 11 G6
Chepstow *Monmouths* 4 B4
Cherhill *Wilts* 5 C7
Cheriton *Hants* 5 E10
Cheriton Fitzpaine *Devon* 3 C10
Chertsey *Surrey* 6 C3
Chesham *Bucks* 6 A2
Cheshunt *Herts* 6 A4
Chester *Ches* 15 G6
Chester-le-Street *Durham* 21 E6
Chesterfield *Derby* 16 G3
Chew Magna *Bath/NE Som'set* 4 C4
Chewton Mendip *Som'set* 4 D4
Chichester *W Sussex* 6 F2
Chiddingfold *Surrey* 6 E2
Chideock *Dorset* 4 G4
Chigwell *Essex* 6 B5
Chilcompton *Som'set* 4 D5
Chilham *Kent* 7 D8
Chillington *Devon* 3 F9
Chilton *Durham* 21 F6
Chingford *London* 6 B4
Chinnor *Oxon* 5 A10
Chippenham *Wilts* 5 C6
Chipping Campden *Glos* 11 G7
Chipping Norton *Oxon* 11 G8
Chipping Ongar *Essex* 6 A5
Chipping Sodbury *S Gloucs* 4 B5
Chirbury *Shrops* 10 D3
Chirk *Wrex* 10 B3
Chirnside *Scot Borders* 25 G8
Chiseldon *Swindon* 5 C7
Chitterne *Wilts* 5 D6
Chobham *Surrey* 6 C2
Chollerton *Northum* 20 D4
Cholsey *Oxon* 5 B9
Chorley *Lancs* 15 E7
Chorleywood *Herts* 6 B3
Christchurch *Cambs* 12 D5
Christchurch *Dorset* 5 G7
Christow *Devon* 3 D10
Chudleigh *Devon* 3 E10
Chulmleigh *Devon* 3 C9
Church Stretton *Shrops* 10 D4
Church Village *Rh Cyn Taff* 4 B2
Churchdown *Glos* 10 G6
Churchill *Oxon* 11 G8
Churchstow *Devon* 3 F9
Chwilog *Gwyn* 8 B5
Cilgerran *Pembs* 9 F3
Cille Bhrighde *W Isles* 26 F2
Cilycwm *Carms* 9 G6
Cinderford *Glos* 10 H5
Cirencester *Glos* 5 A7
Clabhach *Arg/Bute* 22 B2
Clachan *Arg/Bute* 22 G5
Clachan *H'land* 27 E6
Clachan na Luib *W Isles* 26 C3
Clackmannan *Clack* 24 E3
Clacton-on-Sea *Essex* 13 H8
Cladich *Arg/Bute* 23 C7
Claggan *H'land* 22 B5
Claigan *H'land* 26 D5
Clanfield *Hants* 5 F10
Claonaig *Arg/Bute* 23 G6
Clapham *Beds* 12 F3
Clapham *N Yorks* 15 B8
Clare *Suffolk* 13 F6
Clashmore *H'land* 28 B3
Clavering *Essex* 12 G5
Claverley *Shrops* 10 D5
Clawton *Devon* 3 D7
Clay Cross *Derby* 16 G3
Claydon *Suffolk* 13 F8
Claypole *Lincs* 12 A2
Cleadale *H'land* 27 G6
Cleat *Orkney* 31 D9
Cleator Moor *Cumb* 19 G9
Cleethorpes *NE Lincs* 17 E8
Cleeve Prior *Warwick* 11 F7
Clehonger *Heref'd* 10 G4
Cleobury Mortimer *Shrops* 10 E5
Clevedon *N Som'set* 4 C4
Cleveleys *Lancs* 15 C6
Cley *Norfolk* 13 A8
Cliffe *Medway* 7 C6
Clifford *Heref'd* 10 F3
Clipston *Northants* 11 D10
Clitheroe *Lancs* 15 C8
Clive *Shrops* 10 B4
Clophill *Beds* 12 G3
Closeburn *Dumf/Gal* 19 C8
Cloughton *N Yorks* 21 H10
Clova *Angus* 29 H6
Clovelly *Devon* 3 B7
Clovenfords *Scot Borders* 25 H6
Clowne *Derby* 16 G4
Clun *Shrops* 10 D3
Clunbury *Shrops* 10 D3
Clunes *H'land* 27 G9
Clungunford *Shrops* 10 E3
Clutton *Bath/NE Som'set* 4 D5
Clydach *Swan* 9 H6
Clydebank *W Dunb* 23 F9
Clynnog-fawr *Gwyn* 8 A5
Clyro *Powys* 10 F3
Coalbrookdale *Telford* 10 C5
Coalburn *S Lanarks* 24 H3
Coalville *Leics* 11 C9
Coatbridge *N Lanarks* 24 F2
Cobham *Kent* 6 C6
Cobham *Surrey* 6 D3
Cock Bridge *Aberds* 29 F6
Cockburnspath *Scot Borders* 25 F7
Cockenzie *E Loth* 25 F6
Cockerham *Lancs* 15 C7
Cockermouth *Cumb* 19 F9
Cockfield *Durham* 20 F5
Cockfield *Suffolk* 13 F7
Cockshutt *Shrops* 10 B4
Coddenham *Suffolk* 13 F8
Codford St. Mary *Wilts* 5 D6
Coggeshall *Essex* 13 G7
Coignafearn Lodge *H'land* 28 F3
Coille Mhorgil *H'land* 27 F9
Coillore *H'land* 26 E5
Colby *I/Man* 14 B1
Colchester *Essex* 13 G8
Cold Ashton *S Gloucs* 4 C5
Coldingham *Scot Borders* 25 F8
Coldstream *Scot Borders* 25 H8
Colebrooke *Devon* 3 D9
Coleford *Glos* 10 H4
Coleshill *Warwick* 11 D8
Colinton *C/Edinb* 24 F5
Colintraive *Arg/Bute* 23 F7
Collin *Dumf/Gal* 19 D9
Collingbourne Kingston *Wilts* 5 D8
Collingham *Notts* 17 G6
Collingham *W Yorks* 16 C3
Colmonel *S Ayrs* 18 C4
Colne *Lancs* 15 D9
Colpy *Aberds* 29 E8
Colsterworth *Lincs* 12 B2
Coltishall *Norfolk* 13 B9
Colwell *Northum* 20 D4
Colwich *Staffs* 11 B7
Colwyn Bay *Conwy* 14 G4
Colyton *Devon* 4 G3
Combe Martin *Devon* 3 A8
Comberton *Cambs* 12 F4
Combwich *Som'set* 4 D3
Compton *W Berks* 5 C9
Compton *W Sussex* 5 F10
Compton Martin *Bath/NE Som'set* 4 D4
Comrie *Perth/Kinr* 24 C2
Condover *Shrops* 10 C4
Congleton *Ches* 15 G9
Congresbury *N Som'set* 4 C4
Coningsby *Lincs* 17 H8
Conisbrough *S Yorks* 16 F4
Coniston *Cumb* 19 H10
Connah's Quay *Flints* 15 G6
Connel *Arg/Bute* 23 C6
Connel Park *E Ayrs* 19 B7
Cononbridge *H'land* 28 D2
Consett *Durham* 20 E5
Contin *H'land* 28 D2
Conwy *Conwy* 14 G3
Cookham *Windsor* 6 B2
Coolham *W Sussex* 6 E3
Coombe Bissett *Wilts* 5 E7
Copplestone *Devon* 3 C9
Coppull *Lancs* 15 E7
Copthorne *W Sussex* 6 E4
Corbridge *Northum* 20 D4
Corby *Northants* 12 D2
Corby Glen *Lincs* 12 B3
Corfe Castle *Dorset* 5 G6
Corfe Mullen *Dorset* 5 G6
Cornhill on Tweed *Northum* 25 H8
Corpach *H'land* 27 H9
Corran *H'land* 23 A7
Corrie *N Ayrs* 23 G7
Corringham *Lincs* 17 F6
Corringham *Thurr'k* 7 B6
Corris *Gwyn* 8 C6
Corsham *Wilts* 4 C6
Corsley *Wilts* 4 D6
Corsock *Dumf/Gal* 19 D7
Corton *Norfolk* 13 D10
Corwen *Denbs* 10 A2
Coseley *W Midlands* 11 D6
Cosham *Portsm'th* 5 F10
Costessey *Norfolk* 13 C8
Cotgrave *Notts* 11 B10
Cotherstone *Durham* 20 F5
Cottenham *Cambs* 12 E5
Cottered *Herts* 12 G4
Cottesmore *Rutl'd* 12 C2
Cottingham *ER Yorks* 17 D7
Coulags *H'land* 27 D8
Coulport *Arg/Bute* 23 E8
Countesthorpe *Leics* 11 D9
Coupar Angus *Perth/Kinr* 24 B5
Cove *Arg/Bute* 23 E8
Cove *H'land* 27 B8
Cove Bay *Aberd C* 29 F9
Coventry *W Midlands* 11 D8
Coverack *Cornw'l* 2 H4
Cowbit *Lincs* 12 C4
Cowbridge *V/Glam* 9 K7
Cowdenbeath *Fife* 24 E4
Cowes *I/Wight* 5 G9
Cowfold *W Sussex* 6 E4
Cowpen *Northum* 21 C6
Cowplain *Hants* 5 F10
Coxheath *Kent* 7 D6
Coylton *S Ayrs* 19 A6
Craggie *H'land* 28 E3
Crai *Powys* 9 G7
Craibstone *Moray* 29 D7
Craigellachie *Moray* 29 D6
Craighouse *Arg/Bute* 22 F4
Craigmore *Arg/Bute* 23 F7
Craignure *Arg/Bute* 22 C5
Craigtown *H'land* 31 F6
Crail *Fife* 25 D7
Cramlington *Northum* 21 D6
Cranborne *Dorset* 5 F7
Cranbrook *Kent* 7 E6
Cranleigh *Surrey* 6 E3
Cranmore *Som'set* 4 D5
Cranwell *Lincs* 12 A3
Crathie *Aberds* 29 G6
Craven Arms *Shrops* 10 D4
Crawford *S Lanarks* 19 A8
Crawfordjohn *S Lanarks* 19 A8
Crawley *W Sussex* 6 E4
Creag Ghoraidh *W Isles* 26 D3
Creake *Norfolk* 13 B7
Credenhill *Heref'd* 10 F4
Crediton *Devon* 3 D10
Creetown *Dumf/Gal* 19 E6
Cressage *Shrops* 10 C4
Cresselly *Pembs* 9 H3
Crewe *Ches* 15 H8
Crewkerne *Som'set* 4 F4
Crianlarich *Stirl* 23 C8
Criccieth *Gwyn* 8 B5
Crick *Northants* 11 E9
Crickhowell *Powys* 10 H3
Cricklade *Wilts* 5 B7
Crieff *Perth/Kinr* 24 C3
Crimond *Aberds* 29 D10
Crinan *Arg/Bute* 22 E5
Crocketford *Dumf/Gal* 19 D8
Croggan *Arg/Bute* 22 C5
Croglin *Cumb* 20 E2
Croick *H'land* 28 B2
Cromarty *H'land* 28 C3
Cromer *Norfolk* 13 A9
Cromor *W Isles* 32 G4
Crondall *Hants* 5 D10
Crook *Durham* 20 F5
Crookham *Northum* 25 H8
Crooklands *Cumb* 15 A7
Crosbost *W Isles* 32 G4
Crosby *Cumb* 19 E9
Crosby Ravensworth *Cumb* 20 G3
Cross-Hands *Carms* 9 H5
Crosshill *S Ayrs* 18 B5
Crossmichael *Dumf/Gal* 19 D7
Croston *Lancs* 15 E7
Crowborough *E Sussex* 6 E5
Crowland *Lincs* 12 C4
Crowle *N Lincs* 16 E5
Crowthorne *Wokingham* 6 C2
Croxton Kerrial *Leics* 12 B2
Croyde *Devon* 3 B8
Croydon *London* 6 C4
Cruden Bay *Aberds* 29 E10
Crudgington *Telford* 10 C5
Crymych *Pembs* 9 G3
Cuckfield *W Sussex* 6 E4
Cuddington *Bucks* 11 H10
Cuddington *Ches* 15 G7
Cudworth *S Yorks* 16 E3
Cuffley *Herts* 6 A4
Culgaith *Cumb* 20 F3
Culkein *H'land* 30 G2
Cullen *Moray* 29 C7
Cullicudden *H'land* 28 C3
Cullivoe *Shetl'd* 32 A3
Culloden *H'land* 28 D3
Cullompton *Devon* 4 F2
Culmazie *Dumf/Gal* 18 E5
Culmington *Shrops* 10 D4
Culmstock *Devon* 4 F2
Culrain *H'land* 28 B2
Culross *Fife* 24 E3
Cults *Aberd C* 29 F9
Cumbernauld *N Lanarks* 24 F2
Cuminestown *Aberds* 29 D9
Cummertrees *Dumf/Gal* 19 D9
Cumnock *E Ayrs* 19 A6
Cumnor *Oxon* 5 A9
Cumwhinton *Cumb* 20 E2
Cupar *Fife* 24 D5
Currie *C/Edinb* 24 F4
Curry Rivel *Som'set* 4 E3
Cwmafan *Neath P Talb* 9 J6
Cwmann *Carms* 9 F5
Cwmbran *Torf* 4 B3
Cwrt *Gwyn* 8 C6
Cymmer *Neath P Talb* 9 J7
Cynwyl Elfed *Carms* 9 G4

D

Dagenham *London* 6 B5
Dail bho Dheas *W Isles* 32 E5
Daily *S Ayrs* 18 B5
Dalabrog *W Isles* 26 E2
Dalbeattie *Dumf/Gal* 19 D8
Dale *Pembs* 9 H2
Dale *Shetl'd* 32 D1
Dalguise *Perth/Kinr* 24 B3
Dalhalvaig *H'land* 31 F6
Dalkeith *Midloth* 24 F5
Dallas *Moray* 28 D5
Dalleagles *E Ayrs* 19 B6
Dalmally *Arg/Bute* 23 C7
Dalmellington *E Ayrs* 19 B6
Dalnaspidal *Perth/Kinr* 28 H3
Dalnessie *H'land* 30 H5
Dalry *Dumf/Gal* 19 C7

Dalry *N Ayrs* 23 G8
Dalrymple *E Ayrs* 18 B5
Dalston *Cumb* 20 E1
Dalton *Dumf/Gal* 19 D9
Dalton *N Yorks* 21 G6
Dalton-in-Furness *Cumb* 15 B6
Dalwhinnie *H'land* 28 G3
Damerham *Hants* 5 F7
Danbury *Essex* 7 A7
Darlington *D'lington* 21 G6
Dartford *Kent* 6 C5
Dartington *Devon* 3 E9
Dartmouth *Devon* 3 F10
Darton *S Yorks* 16 E3
Darvel *E Ayrs* 23 H9
Darwen *Blackb'n* 15 D8
Daventry *Northants* 11 E9
Davington *Dumf/Gal* 19 B10
Dawlish *Devon* 3 E10
Deal *Kent* 7 D9
Dearham *Cumb* 19 F9
Dearne *S Yorks* 16 E4
Debenham *Suffolk* 13 E8
Deddington *Oxon* 11 G9
Deeping St. Nicholas *Lincs* 12 C4
Deerness *Orkney* 31 C9
Deganwy *Conwy* 14 G3
Delabole *Cornw'l* 2 D6
Delchirach *Moray* 28 E5
Delves *Durham* 20 E5
Denbigh *Denbs* 14 G5
Denby Dale *W Yorks* 16 E3
Denholm *Scot Borders* 20 B2
Denny *Falk* 24 E3
Dent *Cumb* 15 A8
Denton *Gtr Man* 15 F9
Denton *Lincs* 12 B2
Derby *Derby C* 11 B8
Dereham *Norfolk* 13 C7
Dersingham *Norfolk* 12 B6
Dervaig *Arg/Bute* 22 B4
Desborough *Northants* 12 D2
Desford *Leics* 11 C9
Devil's Bridge *Ceredig'n* 8 E6
Devizes *Wilts* 5 C7
Devonport *Plym'th* 3 F8
Dewsbury *W Yorks* 16 D3
Diabaig *H'land* 27 C7
Dibden Purlieu *Hants* 5 F9
Dickleborough *Norfolk* 13 D8
Didcot *Oxon* 5 B9
Digby *Lincs* 17 H7
Dinas Mawddwy *Gwyn* 8 C7
Dinas Powis *V/Glam* 4 C2
Dingwall *H'land* 28 D2
Dinnington *S Yorks* 16 F4
Dinton *Wilts* 5 E7
Dippen *N Ayrs* 18 A4
Dirleton *E Loth* 25 E6
Diss *Norfolk* 13 D8
Distington *Cumb* 19 F9
Ditchingham *Norfolk* 13 D9
Ditchling *E Sussex* 6 F4
Dittisham *Devon* 3 F10
Ditton Priors *Shrops* 10 D5
Dobwalls *Cornw'l* 3 E7
Docking *Norfolk* 13 B6
Dockray *Cumb* 20 F1
Doddinghurst *Essex* 6 B5
Doddington *Cambs* 12 D4
Doddington *Northum* 25 H8
Dolanog *Powys* 10 C2
Dolfor *Powys* 10 D2
Dolgarrog *Conwy* 14 G3
Dolgellau *Gwyn* 8 C6
Dollar *Clack* 24 E3
Dolphinton *S Lanarks* 24 G4
Dolton *Devon* 3 C8
Dolwyddelan *Conwy* 8 A6
Doncaster *S Yorks* 16 E4
Donhead St.Andrew *Wilts* 5 E6
Donington *Lincs* 12 B4
Donnington *Telford* 10 C5
Dorchester *Dorset* 4 G5
Dorchester *Oxon* 5 B9
Dores *H'land* 28 E3
Dorking *Surrey* 6 D3
Dornie *H'land* 27 E8
Dornoch *H'land* 28 B3
Dorridge *W Midlands* 11 E7
Dorstone *Heref'd* 10 F3
Douglas *I/Man* 14 B1
Douglas *S Lanarks* 24 H3
Dounby *Orkney* 31 B8
Doune *Stirl* 24 D2
Dounreay *H'land* 31 E6
Dove Holes *Derby* 16 G2
Dover *Kent* 7 D9
Doveridge *Derby* 11 B7
Downham *Cambs* 12 D5
Downham Market *Norfolk* 12 C6
Downton *Wilts* 5 E7
Drayton *Norfolk* 13 C8
Dreghorn *N Ayrs* 23 H8
Drem *E Loth* 25 F6
Driffield *ER Yorks* 17 C7
Drigg *Cumb* 19 G9
Drimnin *H'land* 22 B4
Droitwich *Worcs* 10 E6
Dronfield *Derby* 16 G3
Drongan *E Ayrs* 19 B6
Druid *Denbs* 10 A2
Drumbeg *H'land* 30 G2
Drumgask *H'land* 28 G3
Drumjohn *Dumf/Gal* 19 C6
Drummore *Dumf/Gal* 18 F4
Drumnadrochit *H'land* 28 E2
Drymen *Stirl* 23 E9
Drynoch *H'land* 26 E5
Duchally *H'land* 30 H3
Duddington *Northants* 12 C2
Dudley *W Midlands* 11 D6
Duffield *Derby* 11 A8
Dufftown *Moray* 29 E6
Dukinfield *Gtr Man* 15 F9
Dullingham *Cambs* 12 F6
Dulnain Bridge *H'land* 28 E4
Duloe *Cornw'l* 3 F7
Dulverton *Som'set* 3 B10
Dumbarton *W Dunb* 23 F9
Dumfries *Dumf/Gal* 19 D8
Dunans *Arg/Bute* 23 E7
Dunbar *E Loth* 25 F7
Dunbeath *H'land* 31 G7
Dunblane *Stirl* 24 D2
Duncansby *H'land* 31 E8
Dunchurch *Warwick* 11 E9
Dundee *Dundee C* 24 C5
Dundonald *S Ayrs* 23 H8
Dundrennan *Dumf/Gal* 19 E7
Dunecht *Aberds* 29 F8
Dunfermline *Fife* 24 E4
Dunino *Fife* 25 D6
Dunipace *Falk* 24 E3
Dunkeld *Perth/Kinr* 24 B4
Dunlop *E Ayrs* 23 G9
Dunnet *H'land* 31 E8
Dunning *Perth/Kinr* 24 D4
Dunnington *C/York* 16 C5
Dunoon *Arg/Bute* 23 F7
Dunragit *Dumf/Gal* 18 E4
Duns *Scot Borders* 25 G7
Dunsby *Lincs* 12 B3
Dunscore *Dumf/Gal* 19 C8
Dunsford *Devon* 3 D10
Dunstable *Beds* 12 G3
Dunster *Som'set* 3 A10
Dunston *Staffs* 11 C6
Dunsyre *S Lanarks* 24 G4
Dunure *S Ayrs* 18 B5
Dunvegan *H'land* 26 D5
Durham *Durham* 21 E6
Durness *H'land* 30 E4
Durrington *Wilts* 5 D7
Dursley *Glos* 4 B5
Dyce *Aberd C* 29 F9
Dykehead *Angus* 24 A5
Dymchurch *Kent* 7 E8
Dymock *Glos* 10 G5
Dysart *Fife* 24 E5
Dyserth *Denbs* 14 G5

E

Eaglescliffe *Stockton* 21 G7
Eaglesfield *Dumf/Gal* 19 D10
Eaglesham *E Renf* 23 G9
Eakring *Notts* 16 G5
Ealing *London* 6 B3
Earby *Lancs* 15 C9
Eardisley *Heref'd* 10 F3
Earith *Cambs* 12 E4
Earl Shilton *Leics* 11 D9
Earl Soham *Suffolk* 13 E9
Earls Barton *Northants* 12 E2
Earl's Colne *Essex* 13 G7
Earlsferry *Fife* 25 D6
Earlston *Scot Borders* 25 H6
Earsdon *Tyne/Wear* 21 D6
Easebourne *W Sussex* 6 E2
Easington *Durham* 21 E7
Easington *ER Yorks* 17 E8
Easington Colliery *Durham* 21 E7
Easingwold *N Yorks* 16 B4
East Bergholt *Suffolk* 13 G8
East Boldre *Hants* 5 G8
East Brent *Som'set* 4 D3
East Bridgford *Notts* 11 A10
East Calder *W Loth* 24 F4
East Cowes *I/Wight* 5 G9
East Cowton *N Yorks* 21 G6
East Dean *E Sussex* 6 G5
East Grinstead *W Sussex* 6 E5
East Harling *Norfolk* 13 D7
East Horsley *Surrey* 6 D3
East Ilsley *W Berks* 5 B9
East Kilbride *S Lanarks* 24 G2
East Leake *Notts* 11 B9
East Linton *E Loth* 25 F6
East Looe *Cornw'l* 3 F7
East Markham *Notts* 16 G5
East Norton *Leics* 11 C10
East Oakley *Hants* 5 D9
East Wemyss *Fife* 24 E5
East Wittering *W Sussex* 6 G2
East Witton *N Yorks* 16 A2
East Woodhay *Hants* 5 C9
Eastbourne *E Sussex* 6 G6
Eastchurch *Kent* 7 C8
Easter Skeld *Shetl'd* 32 D2
Eastfield *N Yorks* 17 A7
Eastleigh *Hants* 5 F9
Eastnor *Heref'd* 10 G5
Easton *Dorset* 4 H5
Easton *Northants* 12 C3
Easton-in-Gordano *N Som'set* 4 C4
Eastry *Kent* 7 D9
Eastwood *Notts* 11 A9
Eaton *Leics* 11 B10
Eaton Socon *Cambs* 12 F3
Ebberston *N Yorks* 17 A6
Ebbw Vale *Bl Gwent* 4 A2
Ecclaw *Scot Borders* 25 F7
Ecclefechan *Dumf/Gal* 19 D9
Eccleshall *Staffs* 10 B6
Echt *Aberds* 29 F8
Eckington *Derby* 16 G4
Eckington *Worcs* 11 F6
Edderton *H'land* 28 B3
Edenbridge *Kent* 6 D5
Edgmond *Telford* 10 C5
Edinburgh *C/Edinb* 24 F5
Edington *Wilts* 5 D6
Edmundbyers *Durham* 20 E5
Edwinstowe *Notts* 16 G5
Edzell *Angus* 25 A7
Egham *Surrey* 6 C3
Eglwyswrw *Pembs* 9 G3
Egremont *Cumb* 19 G9
Egton *N Yorks* 21 G9
Eilean Iarmain *H'land* 27 F7
Elan Village *Powys* 8 E7
Elgin *Moray* 29 C6
Elgol *H'land* 27 F6
Elham *Kent* 7 D8
Elie *Fife* 25 D6
Elishaw *Northum* 20 C4
Elland *W Yorks* 16 D2
Ellesmere *Shrops* 10 B4
Ellesmere Port *Ches* 15 G6
Ellington *Northum* 21 C6
Ellon *Aberds* 29 E9
Elmswell *Suffolk* 13 E7
Elphin *H'land* 30 H3
Elsdon *Northum* 20 C4
Elsenham *Essex* 12 G5
Elstead *Surrey* 6 D2
Elston *Notts* 11 A10
Elvanfoot *S Lanarks* 19 B8
Elveden *Suffolk* 13 E7
Elvington *C/York* 16 C5
Elworth *Ches* 15 G8
Ely *Cambs* 12 D5
Embleton *Northum* 21 A6
Embo *H'land* 28 B4
Empingham *Rutl'd* 12 C2
Emsworth *Hants* 5 F10
Enderby *Leics* 11 D9
Endon *Staffs* 15 H9
Enfield *London* 6 B4
Enstone *Oxon* 11 G8
Enterkinfoot *Dumf/Gal* 19 B8
Epping *Essex* 6 A5
Epsom *Surrey* 6 D4
Epworth *N Lincs* 16 E5
Eriboll *H'land* 30 F4
Errogie *H'land* 28 E2
Errol *Perth/Kinr* 24 C5
Erskine *Renf* 23 F9
Escrick *N Yorks* 16 C5
Esh Winning *Durham* 20 E5
Esher *Surrey* 6 C3
Eskdalemuir *Dumf/Gal* 19 C10
Eston *Redcar/Clevel'd* 21 F7
Etchingham *E Sussex* 7 E6
Eton *Windsor* 6 C2
Ettington *Warwick* 11 F8
Etwall *Derby* 11 B8
Euxton *Lancs* 15 D7
Evanton *H'land* 28 C3
Evercreech *Som'set* 4 E5
Everleigh *Wilts* 5 D8
Evershot *Dorset* 4 F4
Evesham *Worcs* 11 F7
Ewell *Surrey* 6 C4
Ewhurst *Surrey* 6 D3
Ewyas Harold *Heref'd* 10 G3
Exbourne *Devon* 3 C8
Exeter *Devon* 3 D10
Exford *Som'set* 3 B10
Exminster *Devon* 3 D10
Exmouth *Devon* 3 D10
Exton *Rutl'd* 12 C2
Eyam *Derby* 16 G3
Eye *Peterbro* 12 C4
Eye *Suffolk* 13 E8
Eyemouth *Scot Borders* 25 F8
Eynsford *Kent* 6 C5
Eynsham *Oxon* 5 A9

F

Faddiley *Ches* 15 H7
Fairbourne *Gwyn* 8 C6
Fairford *Glos* 5 A7
Fairlie *N Ayrs* 23 G8
Fairlight *E Sussex* 7 F7
Fakenham *Norfolk* 13 B7
Fala *Midloth* 25 F6
Faldingworth *Lincs* 17 F7
Falkirk *Falk* 24 E3
Falkland *Fife* 24 D5
Falmer *E Sussex* 6 F4
Falmouth *Cornw'l* 2 G5
Falstone *Northum* 20 C3
Fareham *Hants* 5 F9
Faringdon *Oxon* 5 B8
Farnborough *Hants* 6 D2
Farnborough *W Berks* 5 B9
Farndon *Ches* 15 H7
Farnham *Surrey* 6 D2
Farnworth *Gtr Man* 15 E8
Farr *H'land* 28 E3
Fasag *H'land* 27 D8
Faslane *Arg/Bute* 23 E8
Fauldhouse *W Loth* 24 F3
Faversham *Kent* 7 C8
Fawley *Hants* 5 F9
Fazeley *Staffs* 11 C8
Fearn *H'land* 28 C4
Fearnan *Perth/Kinr* 24 B2
Feckenham *Worcs* 11 E7
Felixstowe *Suffolk* 13 G9
Felton *Northum* 20 B5
Feltwell *Norfolk* 13 D6
Fenny Bentley *Derby* 16 H2
Fenny Compton *Warwick* 11 F9
Fenny Stratford *M/Keynes* 12 G2
Fenwick *E Ayrs* 23 G9
Feock *Cornw'l* 2 G5
Feolin Ferry *Arg/Bute* 22 F4
Ferndown *Dorset* 5 F7
Ferness *H'land* 28 D4
Fernhurst *W Sussex* 6 E2
Fernilea *H'land* 26 E5
Ferryhill *Durham* 21 F6
Ferryside *Carms* 9 H4
Fettercairn *Aberds* 29 H8
Ffestiniog *Gwyn* 8 A6
Filby *Norfolk* 13 C10
Filey *N Yorks* 17 A7
Fillongley *Warwick* 11 D8
Filton *S Glouc* 4 C5
Fincham *Norfolk* 12 C6
Finchingfield *Essex* 12 G6
Finchley *London* 6 B4
Findhorn *Moray* 28 C5
Findochty *Moray* 29 C7
Findon *W Sussex* 6 F3
Finedon *Northants* 12 E2
Finningley *S Yorks* 16 F5
Finstown *Orkney* 31 C8
Fintry *Stirl* 24 E2
Fionnphort *Arg/Bute* 22 C3
Fishbourne *I/Wight* 5 G9
Fishguard *Pembs* 9 G2
Fishnish *Arg/Bute* 22 B5
Fishtoft *Lincs* 12 A4
Flamborough *ER Yorks* 17 B8
Fleet *Hants* 6 D2
Fleetwood *Lancs* 15 C6
Flimby *Cumb* 19 F9
Flint *Flints* 15 G6
Flitwick *Beds* 12 G3
Flodden *Northum* 25 H8
Flookburgh *Cumb* 15 B6
Fochabers *Moray* 29 D6
Foel *Powys* 10 C2
Folkestone *Kent* 7 E9
Fontmell Magna *Dorset* 4 F6
Ford *Arg/Bute* 23 D6
Forden *Powys* 10 C3
Fordham *Cambs* 12 E6
Fordingbridge *Hants* 5 F7
Fordyce *Aberds* 29 C7
Forest Row *E Sussex* 6 E5
Forfar *Angus* 25 B6
Formby *Mersey* 15 E6
Forres *Moray* 28 D5
Forsinain *H'land* 31 F6
Forsinard *H'land* 31 F6
Fort Augustus *H'land* 28 F1
Fort William *H'land* 27 H9
Forth *S Lanarks* 24 G3
Fortrie *Aberds* 29 D8
Fortrose *H'land* 28 D3
Fortuneswell *Dorset* 4 H5
Fothergill *Cumb* 19 F9
Fotheringhay *Northants* 12 D3
Foulden *Scot Borders* 25 G8
Foulsham *Norfolk* 13 B8
Fountainhall *Scot Borders* 25 G6
Fovant *Wilts* 5 E7
Fowey *Cornw'l* 3 F6
Fownhope *Heref'd* 10 G4
Foxdale *I/Man* 14 B1
Foyers *H'land* 28 E2
Fraddon *Cornw'l* 2 F5
Framlingham *Suffolk* 13 E9
Frampton on Severn *Glos* 4 A5
Frant *E Sussex* 6 E5
Fraserburgh *Aberds* 29 C9
Freckleton *Lancs* 15 D7
Freethorpe *Norfolk* 13 C10
Fremington *Devon* 3 B8
Frensham *Surrey* 6 D2
Freshwater *I/Wight* 5 G8
Fressingfield *Suffolk* 13 E9
Freswick *H'land* 31 E8
Freuchie *Fife* 24 D5
Friday Bridge *Cambs* 12 C5
Fridaythorpe *ER Yorks* 17 B6
Frimley *Surrey* 6 D2
Frinton-on-Sea *Essex* 13 H9
Friockheim *Angus* 25 B6
Frizington *Cumb* 19 G9
Frodsham *Ches* 15 G7
Frome *Som'set* 4 D5
Frongoch *Gwyn* 8 B7
Froxfield *Wilts* 5 C8
Fulbourn *Cambs* 12 F5
Fulford *C/York* 16 C5
Fulwood *Lancs* 15 D7
Funzie *Shetl'd* 32 B4
Furnace *Arg/Bute* 23 D7
Fyfield *Essex* 6 A5
Fyvie *Aberds* 29 E8

G

Gaerwen *Angl* 14 G2
Gaick Lodge *H'land* 28 G3
Gailey *Staffs* 11 C6
Gainford *Durham* 20 G5
Gainsborough *Lincs* 17 F6
Gairloch *H'land* 27 C8
Gairlochy *H'land* 27 G9
Galashiels *Scot Borders* 25 H6
Galgate *Lancs* 15 C7
Galmisdale *H'land* 27 G6
Galmpton *Torbay* 3 F10
Galston *E Ayrs* 23 H9
Gamlingay *Cambs* 12 F4
Garbhallt *Arg/Bute* 23 E7
Garboldisham *Norfolk* 13 D8
Gardenstown *Aberds* 29 C9
Garelochhead *Arg/Bute* 23 E8
Garforth *W Yorks* 16 D4
Gargrave *N Yorks* 15 C9
Gargunnock *Stirl* 24 E2
Garlieston *Dumf/Gal* 19 E6
Garmouth *Moray* 29 C6
Garrow *Perth/Kinr* 24 B3
Garsdale Head *Cumb* 20 H3
Garstang *Lancs* 15 C7
Garston *Mersey* 15 F6
Garton-on-the-Wolds *ER Yorks* 17 B6
Garvald *E Loth* 25 F6
Garve *H'land* 28 C1
Gatehouse of Fleet *Dumf/Gal* 19 E6
Gateshead *Tyne/Wear* 21 D6
Gatley *Gtr Man* 15 F9
Gawthwaite *Cumb* 15 A6
Gaydon *Warwick* 11 F8
Gayton *Norfolk* 13 B6
Gaywood *Norfolk* 12 B6
Gearraidh na h-Aibhne *W Isles* 32 G4
Geary *H'land* 26 C5
Geddington *Northants* 12 D2
Gedney *Lincs* 12 B5
Georgeham *Devon* 3 B8
Gerrards Cross *Bucks* 6 B3
Gifford *E Loth* 25 F6
Giggleswick *N Yorks* 15 B9
Gillingham *Dorset* 4 E5
Gillingham *Medway* 7 C6
Gilmerton *Perth/Kinr* 24 C3
Gilsland *Northum* 20 D3
Gilwern *Monmouths* 10 H3
Giosla *W Isles* 32 G3
Girton *Cambs* 12 E5
Girvan *S Ayrs* 18 C4
Gisburn *Lancs* 15 C9
Gladestry *Powys* 10 F3
Glamis *Angus* 24 B5
Glanaman *Carms* 9 H6
Glanton *Northum* 20 B5
Glasbury *Powys* 10 G2
Glasgow *Glasg C* 23 F9
Glasserton *Dumf/Gal* 19 F6
Glasson *Lancs* 15 C7
Glastonbury *Som'set* 4 E4
Glemsford *Suffolk* 13 F7
Glenbarr *Arg/Bute* 22 H5
Glenborrodale *H'land* 22 A5
Glenbrittle *H'land* 27 E6
Glencaple *Dumf/Gal* 19 D8
Glencarse *Perth/Kinr* 24 C5
Glencoe *H'land* 23 B7
Glendoll Lodge *Angus* 29 H6

Gleneagles *Perth/Kinr* 24 D3
Glenelg *H'land* 27 F8
Glenfinnan *H'land* 27 G8
Glenluce *Dumf/Gal* 18 E5
Glenmaye *I/Man* 14 B1
Glenmore Lodge *H'land* 28 F4
Glenprosen Lodge *Angus* 24 A5
Glenrothes *Fife* 24 D5
Glenstriven *Arg/Bute* 23 F7
Glentrool Village *Dumf/Gal* 18 D5
Glenwhilly *Dumf/Gal* 18 D4
Glinton *Peterbro* 12 C3
Glossop *Derby* 16 F2
Gloucester *Glos* 10 H6
Glusburn *N Yorks* 16 C2
Glyn Ceiriog *Wrex* 10 B2
Glyn Neath *Neath P Talb* 9 H7
Glyncorrwg *Neath P Talb* 9 J7
Glynde *E Sussex* 6 F5
Glyndyfrdwy *Denbs* 10 A2
Gnosall *Staffs* 10 B6
Goathland *N Yorks* 21 G9
Gobowen *Shrops* 10 B3
Godalming *Surrey* 6 D2
Godmanchester *Cambs* 12 E4
Godshill *I/Wight* 5 G9
Godstone *Surrey* 6 D4
Goldhanger *Essex* 7 A7
Golspie *H'land* 28 B4
Goodrich *Heref'd* 10 H4
Goodwick *Pembs* 9 G2
Goodwood *W Sussex* 6 F2
Goole *ER Yorks* 16 D5
Goonhavern *Cornw'l* 2 F4
Gordon *Scot Borders* 25 G7
Gorebridge *Midloth* 24 F5
Goring *Oxon* 5 B10
Goring-by-Sea *W Sussex* 6 F3
Gorleston-on-Sea *Norfolk* 13 C10
Gorran Haven *Cornw'l* 2 F6
Gorseinon *Swan* 9 J5
Gorslas *Carms* 9 H5
Gosberton *Lincs* 12 B4
Gosfield *Essex* 13 G6
Gosforth *Cumb* 19 G9
Gosport *Hants* 5 G10
Goswick *Northum* 25 G9
Gotham *Notts* 11 B9
Goudhurst *Kent* 7 E6
Gourdon *Aberds* 29 H9
Gourock *Invercl* 23 F8
Gowerton *Swan* 9 J5
Grabhair *W Isles* 32 H4
Grain *Medway* 7 C7
Grainthorpe *Lincs* 17 F8
Grampound *Cornw'l* 2 F5
Gramsdal *W Isles* 26 D3
Grange-over-Sands *Cumb* 15 B7
Grangemouth *Falk* 24 E3
Grantham *Lincs* 12 B2
Grantown-on-Spey *H'land* 28 E5
Grantshouse *Scot Borders* 25 F8
Grasby *Lincs* 17 E7
Grasmere *Cumb* 20 G1
Grassington *N Yorks* 16 B2
Grateley *Hants* 5 D8
Gravesend *Kent* 6 C6
Grayrigg *Cumb* 20 H2
Grays *Thurr'k* 6 C6
Grayshott *Hants* 6 E2
Great Ayton *N Yorks* 21 G7
Great Baddow *Essex* 7 A6
Great Badminton *S Gloucs* 4 B6
Great Barford *Beds* 12 F3
Great Bentley *Essex* 13 G8
Great Bridgeford *Staffs* 10 B6
Great Broughton *N Yorks* 21 G7
Great Chesterford *Essex* 12 F5
Great Clifton *Cumb* 19 F9
Great Dunmow *Essex* 12 G6
Great Eccleston *Lancs* 15 C7
Great Ellingham *Norfolk* 13 D8
Great Gidding *Cambs* 12 D3
Great Harwood *Lancs* 15 D8
Great Horwood *Bucks* 11 G10
Great Malvern *Worcs* 10 F5
Great Massingham *Norfolk* 13 B7
Great Missenden *Bucks* 6 A2
Great Oakley *Essex* 13 G9
Great Sampford *Essex* 12 G6
Great Shefford *W Berks* 5 C8
Great Shelford *Cambs* 12 F5
Great Somerford *Wilts* 5 B6
Great Staunton *Cambs* 12 E3
Great Torrington *Devon* 3 C8
Great Wakering *Essex* 7 B7
Great Waltham *Essex* 13 H6
Great Witley *Worcs* 10 E5
Great Yarmouth *Norfolk* 13 C10
Greatham *Hartlep'l* 21 F7
Greatstone-on-Sea *Kent* 7 E8
Green Hammerton *N Yorks* 16 C4
Greenhead *Northum* 20 D3
Greenholm *E Ayrs* 23 H9
Greenlaw *Scot Borders* 25 G7
Greenloaning *Perth/Kinr* 24 D3
Greenock *Invercl* 23 F8
Greenodd *Cumb* 15 A6
Greenway *Pembs* 9 G3
Greenwich *London* 6 C4
Gretna *Dumf/Gal* 20 D1
Gretna Green *Dumf/Gal* 20 D1
Gretton *Northants* 12 D2
Greystoke *Cumb* 20 F2
Grimsby *NE Lincs* 17 E8
Gritley *Orkney* 31 C9
Grizebeck *Cumb* 15 A6
Groby *Leics* 11 C9
Grove *Oxon* 5 B9
Grundisburgh *Suffolk* 13 F9
Guard Bridge *Fife* 25 D6
Guestling Green *E Sussex* 7 F7
Guildford *Surrey* 6 D3
Guildtown *Perth/Kinr* 24 C4
Guilsfield *Powys* 10 C3
Guisborough *Redcar/Clevel'd* 21 G8
Guiseley *W Yorks* 16 C2
Gullane *E Loth* 25 E6
Gunnerside *N Yorks* 20 H4
Gunnislake *Cornw'l* 3 E8
Gunnista *Shetl'd* 32 D3
Gutcher *Shetl'd* 32 B3
Gwalchmai *Angl* 14 G1
Gwaun-Cae-Gurwen *Neath P Talb* 9 H6
Gwbert-on-Sea *Ceredig'n* 9 F3
Gweek *Cornw'l* 2 G4
Gwennap *Cornw'l* 2 G4
Gwyddelwern *Denbs* 10 A2
Gwytherin *Conwy* 14 G4

H

Hackney *London* 6 B4
Hackthorpe *Cumb* 20 F2
Haddenham *Bucks* 5 A10
Haddenham *Cambs* 12 E5
Haddington *E Loth* 25 F6
Haddiscoe *Norfolk* 13 D10
Hadleigh *Essex* 7 B7
Hadleigh *Suffolk* 13 F8
Hadlow *Kent* 6 D6
Hadnall *Shrops* 10 B4
Hagworthingham *Lincs* 17 G8
Hailsham *E Sussex* 6 F5
Hainton *Lincs* 17 F7
Halberton *Devon* 4 F2
Halesowen *W Midlands* 11 D6
Halesworth *Suffolk* 13 E9
Halford *Warwick* 11 F8
Halifax *W Yorks* 16 D2
Halkirk *H'land* 31 F7
Halland *E Sussex* 6 F5
Hallow *Worcs* 10 F6
Hallworthy *Cornw'l* 3 D6
Halstead *Essex* 13 G7
Halton *Lancs* 15 B7
Haltwhistle *Northum* 20 D3
Halwill Junction *Devon* 3 D8
Hamble-le-Rice *Hants* 5 F9
Hambledon *Hants* 5 F10
Hambleton *Lancs* 15 C6
Hambleton *N Yorks* 16 D4
Hamerton *Cambs* 12 D3
Hamilton *S Lanarks* 24 G2
Hammersmith & Fulham *London* 6 C4
Hamnavoe *Shetl'd* 32 C3
Hamnavoe *Shetl'd* 32 E2
Hampstead Norreys *W Berks* 5 C9
Hampton in Arden *W Midlands* 11 D8
Hamstreet *Kent* 7 E8
Handcross *W Sussex* 6 E4
Hannington *Hants* 5 D9
Harbury *Warwick* 11 E8
Harby *Leics* 11 B10
Hardingstone *Northants* 11 F10
Harewood *W Yorks* 16 C3
Haringey *London* 6 B4
Harlech *Gwyn* 8 B5
Harleston *Norfolk* 13 D9
Harlow *Essex* 6 A5
Haroldswick *Shetl'd* 32 A4
Harpenden *Herts* 12 H3
Harrietfield *Perth/Kinr* 24 C3
Harrietsham *Kent* 7 D7
Harrington *Cumb* 19 F8
Harris *H'land* 26 G5
Harrogate *N Yorks* 16 C3
Harrold *Beds* 12 F2
Harrow *London* 6 B3
Harston *Cambs* 12 F5
Hartburn *Northum* 20 C5
Hartest *Suffolk* 13 F7
Hartfield *E Sussex* 6 E5
Harthill *N Lanarks* 24 F3
Hartington *Derby* 16 G2
Hartland *Devon* 3 B7
Hartlebury *Worcs* 10 E6
Hartlepool *Hartlep'l* 21 F7
Hartley *Kent* 6 C6
Hartley *Northum* 21 D6
Hartley Wintney *Hants* 5 D10
Hartpury *Glos* 10 G5
Hartshill *Warwick* 11 D8
Harvington *Worcs* 11 F7
Harwell *Oxon* 5 B9
Harwich *Essex* 13 G9
Harworth *Notts* 16 F5
Haselbury Plucknett *Som'set* 4 F4
Haslemere *Surrey* 6 E2
Haslingden *Lancs* 15 D8
Hassocks *W Sussex* 6 F4
Hastigrow *H'land* 31 E8
Hastings *E Sussex* 7 F7
Haswell *Durham* 21 E6
Hatch Beauchamp *Som'set* 4 F3
Hatfield *Herts* 6 A4
Hatfield *S Yorks* 16 E5
Hatfield Heath *Essex* 12 H5
Hatfield Peverel *Essex* 13 H7
Hatherleigh *Devon* 3 C8
Hathersage *Derby* 16 F3
Hatton *Aberds* 29 E10
Hatton *Derby* 11 B8
Haugh of Urr *Dumf/Gal* 19 D7
Haughley *Suffolk* 13 E8
Haughton *Staffs* 10 B6
Havant *Hants* 5 F10
Haverfordwest *Pembs* 9 H2
Haverhill *Suffolk* 12 F6
Haverigg *Cumb* 14 A5
Havering *London* 6 B5
Hawarden *Flints* 15 G6
Hawes *N Yorks* 15 A9
Hawick *Scot Borders* 20 B2
Hawkchurch *Devon* 4 G3
Hawkesbury Upton *S Gloucs* 4 B5
Hawkhurst *Kent* 7 E6
Hawkinge *Kent* 7 E9
Hawkshead *Cumb* 20 H1
Hawnby *N Yorks* 21 H7
Haworth *W Yorks* 16 D2
Hawsker *N Yorks* 21 G9
Haxby *C/York* 16 C5
Haxey *N Lincs* 16 E5
Hay-on-Wye *Powys* 10 F3
Haydon Bridge *Northum* 20 D4
Hayfield *Derby* 16 F2
Hayle *Cornw'l* 2 G3
Hayton *Cumb* 20 E2
Hayton *ER Yorks* 17 C6
Haywards Heath *W Sussex* 6 E4
Hazel Grove *Gtr Man* 15 F9
Hazlemere *Bucks* 6 B2
Heacham *Norfolk* 12 B6
Headcorn *Kent* 7 D7
Headley *Hants* 6 E2
Heanor *Derby* 11 A9
Heath End *Hants* 5 C9
Heathfield *E Sussex* 6 F5
Hebburn *Tyne/Wear* 21 D6
Hebden Bridge *W Yorks* 15 D9
Heckington *Lincs* 12 A3
Hedge End *Hants* 5 F9
Hednesford *Staffs* 11 C7
Hedon *ER Yorks* 17 D7
Heighington *D'lington* 21 F6
Heilam *H'land* 30 E4
Helensburgh *Arg/Bute* 23 E8
Hellifield *N Yorks* 15 C9
Helmsdale *H'land* 31 H7
Helmsley *N Yorks* 16 A5
Helperby *N Yorks* 16 B4
Helpringham *Lincs* 12 A3
Helsby *Ches* 15 G7
Helston *Cornw'l* 2 G4
Hemel Hempstead *Herts* 6 A3
Hemingbrough *N Yorks* 16 D5
Hempnall *Norfolk* 13 D9
Hempton *Norfolk* 13 B7
Hemsby *Norfolk* 13 C10
Hemsworth *W Yorks* 16 E4
Hemyock *Devon* 4 F2
Henfield *W Sussex* 6 F4
Hengoed *Caerph* 4 B2
Henley-in-Arden *Warwick* 11 E7
Henley-on-Thames *Oxon* 5 B10
Henllan *Denbs* 14 G5
Henlow *Beds* 12 G3
Henstridge *Som'set* 4 F5
Herbrandston *Pembs* 9 H2
Hereford *Heref'd* 10 F4
Heriot *Scot Borders* 25 G6
Hermitage *W Berks* 5 C9
Herne Bay *Kent* 7 C8
Herstmonceux *E Sussex* 6 F6
Hertford *Herts* 12 H4
Hessle *Kingston/Hull* 17 D7
Heswall *Mersey* 15 F6
Hethersett *Norfolk* 13 C8
Hetton-le-Hole *Tyne/Wear* 21 E6
Hexham *Northum* 20 D4
Heybridge *Essex* 7 A7
Heysham *Lancs* 15 B7
Heytesbury *Wilts* 5 D6
Heywood *Gtr Man* 15 E9
Hibaldstow *N Lincs* 17 E6
High Bentham *N Yorks* 15 B8
High Bickington *Devon* 3 C8
High Ercall *Telford* 10 C5
High Hesket *Cumb* 20 E2
High Legh *Ches* 15 F8
High Wycombe *Bucks* 6 B2
Higham *Kent* 7 C6
Higham Ferrers *Northants* 12 E2
Highbridge *Som'set* 4 D3
Highclere *Hants* 5 D9
Highley *Shrops* 10 D5
Hightae *Dumf/Gal* 19 D9
Highworth *Swindon* 5 B8
Hilborough *Norfolk* 13 C7
Hildenborough *Kent* 6 D5
Hilgay *Norfolk* 12 D6
Hillingdon *London* 6 B3
Hillington *Norfolk* 13 B6
Hillswick *Shetl'd* 32 C2
Hilmarton *Wilts* 5 C7
Hilton *Derby* 11 B8
Hinckley *Leics* 11 D9
Hinderwell *N Yorks* 21 G9
Hindhead *Surrey* 6 E2
Hindley *Gtr Man* 15 E8
Hindon *Wilts* 5 E6
Hingham *Norfolk* 13 C8
Hinstock *Shrops* 10 B5
Hirwaun *Rh Cyn Taff* 9 H7
Histon *Cambs* 12 E5
Hitchin *Herts* 12 G3
Hockley *Essex* 7 B7
Hockliffe *Beds* 12 G2
Hoddesdon *Herts* 6 A4
Hodnet *Shrops* 10 B5
Hoff *Cumb* 20 G3
Holbeach *Lincs* 12 B4
Holbrook *Suffolk* 13 G8
Holbury *Hants* 5 F9
Holford *Som'set* 4 D2
Holkham *Norfolk* 13 A7
Holland on Sea *Essex* 13 H9
Hollandstoun *Orkney* 31 A10
Hollym *ER Yorks* 17 D8
Holme-on-Spalding-moor *ER Yorks* 17 D6
Holmer *Heref'd* 10 F4
Holmes Chapel *Ches* 15 G8
Holmfirth *W Yorks* 16 E2
Holsworthy *Devon* 3 C7
Holt *Norfolk* 13 B8
Holt *Wrex* 15 H7
Holyhead *Angl* 14 F1
Holywell *Flints* 14 G5
Honington *Lincs* 12 A2
Honiton *Devon* 4 G2
Hoo *Medway* 7 C6
Hook *Hants* 5 D10
Hook Norton *Oxon* 11 G8
Hope *Flints* 15 H6
Hope under Dinmore *Heref'd* 10 F4
Hopeman *Moray* 28 C5
Horam *E Sussex* 6 F5
Horden *Durham* 21 E7
Horley *Surrey* 6 D4
Horncastle *Lincs* 17 G8
Horndean *Hants* 5 F10
Horningsham *Wilts* 4 D6
Hornsea *ER Yorks* 17 C7
Horrabridge *Devon* 3 E8
Horringer *Suffolk* 13 E7
Horsey *Norfolk* 13 B10
Horsford *Norfolk* 13 C8
Horsforth *W Yorks* 16 D3
Horsham *W Sussex* 6 E3
Horsham St. Faith *Norfolk* 13 C9
Horsted Keynes *W Sussex* 6 E4
Horton *Northants* 12 F2
Horton *Som'set* 4 F3
Horton in Ribblesdale *N Yorks* 15 B9
Horwich *Gtr Man* 15 E8
Hoswick *Shetl'd* 32 E3
Houghton *Cumb* 20 E2
Houghton-le-Spring *Tyne/Wear* 21 E6
Houghton Regis *Beds* 12 G3
Hounslow *London* 6 C3
Hove *Brighton/Hove* 6 F4
Hoveton *Norfolk* 13 C9
Hovingham *N Yorks* 16 B5
Howden *ER Yorks* 16 D5
Howpasley *Scot Borders* 20 B1
Hoxne *Suffolk* 13 E8
Hoylake *Mersey* 15 F6
Hucknall *Notts* 11 A9
Huddersfield *W Yorks* 16 E2
Hugh Town *I/Scilly* 2 J12
Hulland Ward *Derby* 11 A8
Hullavington *Wilts* 4 B6
Hullbridge *Essex* 7 B7
Hulme End *Staffs* 16 H2
Humberston *NE Lincs* 17 E8
Humshaugh *Northum* 20 D4
Hundred House *Powys* 10 F2
Hungerford *W Berks* 5 C8
Hunmanby *N Yorks* 17 B7
Hunstanton *Norfolk* 12 A6
Hunterston *N Ayrs* 23 G7
Huntford *Scot Borders* 20 B3
Huntingdon *Cambs* 12 E4
Huntley *Glos* 10 H5
Huntly *Aberds* 29 D7
Hurlford *E Ayrs* 23 H9
Hurliness *Orkney* 31 D8
Hurn *Dorset* 5 G7
Hursley *Hants* 5 E9
Hurstbourne Tarrant *Hants* 5 D8
Hurstpierpoint *W Sussex* 6 F4
Hurworth-on-Tees *Durham* 21 G6
Husbands Bosworth *Leics* 11 D10
Husinish *W Isles* 32 H2
Huttoft *Lincs* 17 G9
Hutton Cranswick *ER Yorks* 17 C7
Hutton-le-Hole *N Yorks* 21 H8
Hutton Rudby *N Yorks* 21 G7
Huyton *Mersey* 15 F7
Hyde *Gtr Man* 15 F9
Hynish *Arg/Bute* 22 C1
Hythe *Hants* 5 F9
Hythe *Kent* 7 E8

I

Ibsey *Hants* 5 F7
Ibstock *Leics* 11 C8
Icklingham *Suffolk* 13 E6
Idmiston *Wilts* 5 E8
Ilchester *Som'set* 4 E4
Ilderton *Northum* 20 A5
Ilfracombe *Devon* 3 A8
Ilkeston *Derby* 11 A9
Ilkley *W Yorks* 16 C2
Illogan *Cornw'l* 2 F4
Ilminster *Som'set* 4 F3
Immingham *NE Lincs* 17 E7
Inchnadamph *H'land* 30 G3
Inchture *Perth/Kinr* 24 C5
Ingatestone *Essex* 6 B6
Ingleton *N Yorks* 15 B8
Ingoldmells *Lincs* 17 G9
Ingram *Northum* 20 B5
Ingrave *Essex* 6 B6
Inkberrow *Worcs* 11 F7
Innellan *Arg/Bute* 23 F7
Innerleithen *Scot Borders* 24 H5
Innermessan *Dumf/Gal* 18 D4
Insch *Aberds* 29 E8
Instow *Devon* [illegible]
Inverallochy *Aberds* 29 C10
Inveran *H'land* 28 B2
Inveraray *Arg/Bute* 23 D7
Inverarity *Angus* 25 B6
Inverbervie *Aberds* 29 H9
Invergarry *H'land* 28 F1
Invergordon *H'land* 28 C3
Invergowrie *Dundee C* 24 C5
Inverie *H'land* 27 F7
Inverinate *H'land* 27 E8
Inverkeilor *Angus* 25 B7
Inverkeithing *Fife* 24 E4
Inverkirkaig *H'land* 30 G2
Inverlochlarig *Stirl* 23 D9
Invermoriston *H'land* 28 F2
Inverness *H'land* 28 D3
Inversnaid *Stirl* 23 D8
Inverurie *Aberds* 29 E8
Ipswich *Suffolk* 13 F8
Irchester *Northants* 12 E2
Irlam *Gtr Man* 15 F8
Ironbridge *Telford* 10 C5
Irthlingborough *Northants* 12 E2
Irvine *N Ayrs* 23 H8
Isbister *Shetl'd* 32 B2
Isle of Whithorn *Dumf/Gal* 19 F6
Isleham *Cambs* 12 E6
Islington *London* 6 B4
Islip *Oxon* 11 H9
Ivinghoe *Bucks* 12 H2
Ivybridge *Devon* 3 F9
Iwerne Minster *Dorset* 4 F6
Ixworth *Suffolk* 13 E7

J

Jamestown *W Dunb* 23 E8
Jarrow *Tyne/Wear* 21 D6
Jaywick *Essex* 13 H8
Jedburgh *Scot Borders* 20 A3
Jervaulx *N Yorks* 16 A2
John o'Groats *H'land* 31 E8
Johnshaven *Aberds* 25 A8
Johnston *Pembs* 9 H2
Johnstone *Renf* 23 F9

K

Kames *Arg/Bute* 23 F6
Kea *Cornw'l* 2 F4
Kedington *Suffolk* 13 F6
Keelby *Lincs* 17 E7
Keele *Staffs* 10 A6
Kegworth *Leics* 11 B9
Keighley *W Yorks* 16 C2
Keillmore *Arg/Bute* 22 E5
Keiss *H'land* 31 E8
Keith *Moray* 29 D7
Keld *N Yorks* 20 G4
Kellas *Moray* 28 D5
Kelsale *Suffolk* 13 E9
Kelsall *Ches* 15 G7
Kelso *Scot Borders* 25 H7
Keltneyburn *Perth/Kinr* 24 B2
Kelty *Fife* 24 E4
Kelvedon *Essex* 13 H7
Kelynack *Cornw'l* 2 G2
Kemble *Glos* 5 B7
Kemnay *Aberds* 29 F8
Kempsey *Worcs* 10 F6
Kempston *Beds* 12 F3
Kemsing *Kent* 6 D5
Kendal *Cumb* 20 H2
Kenilworth *Warwick* 11 E8
Kenmore *Perth/Kinr* 24 B2
Kennacraig *Arg/Bute* 23 F6
Kennethmont *Aberds* 29 E7
Kennford *Devon* 3 D10
Kenninghall *Norfolk* 13 D8
Kennington *Oxon* 5 A9
Kensington & Chelsea *London* 6 C4
Kentford *Suffolk* 13 E6
Kentisbeare *Devon* 4 F2
Kerry *Powys* 10 D2
Kerrysdale *H'land* 27 C8
Kershopefoot *Scot Borders* 20 C2
Kesgrave *Suffolk* 13 F9
Kessingland *Suffolk* 13 D10
Keswick *Cumb* 19 F10
Kettering *Northants* 12 E2
Kettletoft *Orkney* 31 B10
Kettlewell *N Yorks* 15 B9
Ketton *Rutl'd* 12 C2
Kexby *Lincs* 17 F6
Keyingham *ER Yorks* 17 D8
Keymer *W Sussex* 6 F4
Keynsham *Bath/NE Som'set* 4 C5
Keysoe *Beds* 12 E3
Keyworth *Notts* 11 B10
Kibworth Beauchamp *Leics* 11 D10
Kidderminster *Worcs* 10 E6
Kidlington *Oxon* 11 H9
Kidsgrove *Staffs* 15 H9
Kidstones *N Yorks* 15 A9
Kidwelly *Carms* 9 H5
Kielder *Northum* 20 C3
Kilberry *Arg/Bute* 22 F5
Kilbirnie *N Ayrs* 23 G8
Kilbride *Arg/Bute* 23 C6
Kilcadzow *S Lanarks* 24 G3
Kilchattan *Arg/Bute* 23 G7
Kilchenzie *Arg/Bute* 18 A2
Kilchiaran *Arg/Bute* 22 F2
Kilchoan *H'land* 22 A4
Kilchrenan *Arg/Bute* 23 C7
Kilcreggan *Arg/Bute* 23 E8
Kildonan *H'land* 31 G6
Kilfinan *Arg/Bute* 23 F6
Kilham *ER Yorks* 17 B7
Kilkhampton *Cornw'l* 3 C7
Killamarsh *Derby* 16 F4
Killean *Arg/Bute* 22 G5
Killearn *Stirl* 23 E9
Killin *Stirl* 23 C9
Killinghall *N Yorks* 16 C3
Kilmacolm *Invercl* 23 F8
Kilmaluag *H'land* 27 C6
Kilmany *Fife* 24 C5
Kilmarnock *E Ayrs* 23 H9
Kilmartin *Arg/Bute* 23 E6
Kilmaurs *E Ayrs* 23 G9
Kilmelford *Arg/Bute* 23 D6
Kilmory *Arg/Bute* 22 F5
Kilmory *H'land* 26 F5
Kilmory *H'land* 27 H6
Kilmuir *H'land* 28 C3
Kilninver *Arg/Bute* 23 C6
Kilnsea *ER Yorks* 17 E9
Kilrenny *Fife* 25 D6
Kilsby *Northants* 11 E9
Kilsyth *N Lanarks* 24 F2
Kilwinning *N Ayrs* 23 G8
Kimbolton *Cambs* 12 E3
Kimpton *Herts* 12 H3
Kinbrace *H'land* 31 G6
Kinbuck *Stirl* 24 D2
Kincardine *Fife* 24 E3
Kincardine *H'land* 28 B3
Kincraig *H'land* 28 F4
Kineton *Warwick* 11 F8
Kingarth *Arg/Bute* 23 G7
Kinghorn *Fife* 24 E5
King's Cliffe *Northants* 12 D3
Kings Langley *Herts* 6 A3
King's Lynn *Norfolk* 12 C6
King's Somborne *Hants* 5 E8
King's Sutton *Northants* 11 G9
King's Thorn *Heref'd* 10 G4
King's Worthy *Hants* 5 E9
Kingsbarns *Fife* 25 D6
Kingsbridge *Devon* 3 F9
Kingsbury *Warwick* 11 D8
Kingsclere *Hants* 5 D9
Kingsdown *Kent* 7 D9
Kingskerswell *Devon* 3 E10
Kingsland *Heref'd* 10 E4
Kingsley *Hants* 5 E10
Kingsley *Staffs* 11 A7
Kingsteignton *Devon* 3 E10
Kingston *Devon* 3 F9
Kingston *London* 6 C3
Kingston Bagpuize *Oxon* 5 B9
Kingston Upon Hull *Kingston/Hull* 17 D7
Kingswear *Devon* 3 F10
Kingswood *S Gloucs* 4 C5
Kington *Heref'd* 10 F3
Kingussie *H'land* 28 F3
Kinloch *H'land* 26 G5
Kinloch *H'land* 30 G3
Kinloch Rannoch *Perth/Kinr* 24 B2
Kinlochbervie *H'land* 30 F3
Kinlocheil *H'land* 27 G8
Kinlochewe *H'land* 27 C9
Kinlochleven *H'land* 23 A7
Kinlochmoidart *H'land* 27 H7
Kinloss *Moray* 28 C5
Kinmel Bay *Conwy* 14 F4
Kinross *Perth/Kinr* 24 D4
Kintarvie *W Isles* 32 H4
Kintore *Aberds* 29 F8
Kinuachdrachd *Arg/Bute* 22 E5
Kinver *Staffs* 10 D6
Kippax *W Yorks* 16 D4
Kippen *Stirl* 24 E2
Kirk Michael *I/Man* 14 A1
Kirkabister *Shetl'd* 32 E3
Kirkbean *Dumf/Gal* 19 E8
Kirkbride *Cumb* 19 E10
Kirkburton *W Yorks* 16 E2
Kirkby *Mersey* 15 F7
Kirkby-in-Ashfield *Notts* 16 H4
Kirkby-in-Furness *Cumb* 15 A6
Kirkby Lonsdale *Cumb* 15 B8
Kirkby Malzeard *N Yorks* 16 B3
Kirkby Stephen *Cumb* 20 G3
Kirkby Thore *Cumb* 20 F3
Kirkbymoorside *N Yorks* 16 A5
Kirkcaldy *Fife* 24 E5
Kirkcolm *Dumf/Gal* 18 D4
Kirkconnel *Dumf/Gal* 19 B7
Kirkcowan *Dumf/Gal* 18 D5
Kirkcudbright *Dumf/Gal* 19 E7
Kirkham *Lancs* 15 D7
Kirkinner *Dumf/Gal* 19 E6
Kirkintilloch *E Dunb* 24 F2
Kirkland *Dumf/Gal* 19 C8
Kirkliston *C/Edinb* 24 F4
Kirkmichael *Perth/Kinr* 24 A4
Kirkmichael *S Ayrs* 18 B5
Kirknewton *Northum* 25 H8
Kirkoswald *Cumb* 20 E2
Kirkoswald *S Ayrs* 18 B5
Kirkpatrick Durham *Dumf/Gal* 19 D7
Kirkpatrick Fleming *Dumf/Gal* 19 D10
Kirkton of Glenisla *Angus* 24 A5
Kirkton of Largo *Fife* 25 D6
Kirkwall *Orkney* 31 C9
Kirkwhelpington *Northum* 20 C5
Kirriemuir *Angus* 24 B5
Kirtling *Cambs* 12 F6
Kirtlington *Oxon* 11 G9
Kirton *Lincs* 12 B4
Kirton in Lindsey *N Lincs* 17 E6
Knaresborough *N Yorks* 16 C3
Knayton *N Yorks* 16 A4
Knebworth *Herts* 12 G4
Knighton *Powys* 10 E3
Knott End-on-Sea *Lancs* 15 C6
Knottingley *W Yorks* 16 D4
Knowle *W Midlands* 11 E7
Knutsford *Ches* 15 G8
Kyle of Lochalsh *H'land* 27 E7
Kyleakin *H'land* 27 E7
Kylerhea *H'land* 27 E7
Kylestrome *H'land* 30 G3

L

Laceby *NE Lincs* 17 E8
Lacock *Wilts* 5 C6
Ladock *Cornw'l* 2 F5
Ladybank *Fife* 24 D5
Lagg *Arg/Bute* 22 F4
Laggan *H'land* 27 G10
Laggan *H'land* 28 G3
Laggan *Moray* 29 E6
Laide *H'land* 27 B8
Lairg *H'land* 28 A2
Lakenheath *Suffolk* 13 D6
Lamberhurst *Kent* 6 E6
Lambeth *London* 6 C4
Lambley *Northum* 20 E3
Lambourn *W Berks* 5 C8
Lamlash *N Ayrs* 23 H7
Lampeter *Ceredig'n* 9 F5
Lanark *S Lanarks* 24 G3
Lancaster *Lancs* 15 B7
Lanchester *Durham* 20 E5
Lancing *W Sussex* 6 F3
Landkey *Devon* 3 B8
Landrake *Cornw'l* 3 E7
Langford Budville *Som'set* 4 E2
Langham *Rutl'd* 12 C2
Langholm *Dumf/Gal* 20 C1
Langport *Som'set* 4 E4
Langsett *S Yorks* 16 E3
Langtoft *ER Yorks* 17 B7
Langtoft *Lincs* 12 C3
Langton Matravers *Dorset* 5 H6
Langtree *Devon* 3 C8
Langwathby *Cumb* 20 F2
Langwell *H'land* 28 A3
Lanivet *Cornw'l* 2 E6
Lapford *Devon* 3 C9
Larbert *Falk* 24 E3
Largs *N Ayrs* 23 G8
Larkhall *S Lanarks* 24 G2
Larkhill *Wilts* 5 D7
Lasswade *Midloth* 24 F5
Latchingdon *Essex* 7 A7
Latheron *H'land* 31 G8
Lauder *Scot Borders* 25 G6
Laugharne *Carms* 9 H4
Launceston *Cornw'l* 3 D7
Laurencekirk *Aberds* 29 H8
Laurieston *Dumf/Gal* 19 D7
Lavendon *M/Keynes* 12 F2
Lavenham *Suffolk* 13 F7
Lawers *Perth/Kinr* 24 C2
Laxey *I/Man* 14 A2
Laxfield *Suffolk* 13 E9
Laxford Bridge *H'land* 30 F3
Laxton *Notts* 16 G5
Layer de la Haye *Essex* 13 G7
Lazonby *Cumb* 20 E2
Lea *Lincs* 17 F6
Leadburn *Midloth* 24 G5
Leaden Roding *Essex* 12 H6
Leadenham *Lincs* 17 H6
Leadgate *Durham* 20 E5
Leadhills *S Lanarks* 19 B8
Leasingham *Lincs* 12 A3
Leatherhead *Surrey* 6 D3
Lechlade-on-Thames *Glos* 5 B8
Ledbury *Heref'd* 10 G5
Ledmore *H'land* 30 H3
Lee-on-the-Solent *Hants* 5 F9
Leeds *W Yorks* 16 D3
Leedstown *Cornw'l* 2 G4
Leek *Staffs* 15 H9
Leeming Bar *N Yorks* 21 H6
Legbourne *Lincs* 17 F8
Leicester *Leics C* 11 C9
Leigh *Gtr Man* 15 E8
Leigh *Worcs* 10 F5
Leighton Buzzard *Beds* 12 G2
Leintwardine *Heref'd* 10 E4
Leiston *Suffolk* 13 E10
Leith *C/Edinb* 24 F5
Leitholm *Scot Borders* 25 G7
Lelant *Cornw'l* 2 G3
Lendalfoot *S Ayrs* 18 C4
Lenham *Kent* 7 D7
Lennoxtown *E Dunb* 24 F2
Leominster *Heref'd* 10 F4
Lephin *H'land* 26 D4
Lerwick *Shetl'd* 32 D3
Lesbury *Northum* 21 B6
Leslie *Fife* 24 D5
Lesmahagow *S Lanarks* 24 G3
Leswalt *Dumf/Gal* 18 D4
Letchworth *Herts* 12 G4
Letterston *Pembs* 9 G2
Lettoch *H'land* 28 E5
Leuchars *Fife* 25 C6
Leumrabhagh *W Isles* 32 H4
Leven *ER Yorks* 17 C7
Leven *Fife* 24 D5
Lewes *E Sussex* 6 F5
Lewisham *London* 6 C4
Lewiston *H'land* 28 E2
Leyburn *N Yorks* 20 H5
Leyland *Lancs* 15 D7
Leysdown on Sea *Kent* 7 C8
Lhanbryde *Moray* 29 C6
Liatrie *H'land* 27 E10
Lichfield *Staffs* 11 C7
Lidgate *Suffolk* 13 F6
Lifton *Devon* 3 D7
Lilleshall *Telford* 10 C5
Lincoln *Lincs* 17 G6
Lindale *Cumb* 15 A7
Lingfield *Surrey* 6 D4
Linkinhorne *Cornw'l* 3 E7
Linksness *Orkney* 31 C8
Linlithgow *W Loth* 24 F3
Linslade *Beds* 12 G2
Linton *Cambs* 12 F5
Liphook *Hants* 6 E2
Liskeard *Cornw'l* 3 E7
Liss *Hants* 5 E10
Lissett *ER Yorks* 17 C7
Litcham *Norfolk* 13 C7
Litherland *Mersey* 15 F6
Little Shelford *Cambs* 12 F5
Little Stukeley *Cambs* 12 E4
Little Walsingham *Norfolk* 13 B7
Littleborough *Gtr Man* 15 E9
Littlehampton *W Sussex* 6 F3
Littlemill *H'land* 28 D4
Littleport *Cambs* 12 D5
Littlestone-on-Sea *Kent* 7 E8
Liverpool *Mersey* 15 F6
Livingston *W Loth* 24 F4
Lizard *Cornw'l* 2 H4
Llanaber *Gwyn* 8 C5
Llanaelhaiarn *Gwyn* 8 A4
Llanafan-fawr *Powys* 9 F7
Llanarmon *Denbs* 15 H5
Llanarmon Dyffryn Ceiriog *Wrex* 10 B2
Llanarth *Ceredig'n* 9 F5
Llanarthney *Carms* 9 H5
Llanbadarn Fynydd *Powys* 10 E2
Llanbedr *Gwyn* 8 B5
Llanbedrog *Gwyn* 8 B4
Llanberis *Gwyn* 14 G2
Llanbister *Powys* 10 E2
Llanbrynmair *Powys* 8 C7
Llanddewi-Brefi *Ceredig'n* 9 F6
Llanddulas *Conwy* 14 G4
Llandeilo *Carms* 9 G6
Llandinam *Powys* 10 D2
Llandissilio *Pembs* 9 G3
Llandogo *Monmouths* 4 A4
Llandovery *Carms* 9 G6
Llandrillo *Denbs* 10 B2
Llandrindod Wells *Powys* 10 E2
Llandudno *Conwy* 14 F3
Llandybie *Carms* 9 H6
Llandyfriog *Ceredig'n* 9 F4
Llandygwydd *Ceredig'n* 9 F4
Llandyrnog *Denbs* 14 G5
Llandysul *Ceredig'n* 9 F5
Llanelidan *Denbs* 10 A2
Llanelli *Carms* 9 H5
Llanelltyd *Gwyn* 8 B6
Llanenddwyn *Gwyn* 8 B5
Llanerchymedd *Angl* 14 F2
Llanerfyl *Powys* 10 C2
Llanfaethlu *Angl* 14 F1
Llanfair Caereinion *Powys* 10 C2
Llanfair Talhaiarn *Conwy* 14 G4
Llanfairfechan *Conwy* 14 G3
Llanfairpwllgwngyll *Angl* 14 G2
Llanfechain *Powys* 10 B2
Llanfechell *Angl* 14 F1
Llanfihangel-ar-arth *Carms* 9 G5
Llanfrynach *Powys* 10 G2
Llanfyllin *Powys* 10 C2
Llangadfan *Powys* 10 C2
Llangadog *Carms* 9 G6
Llangammarch Wells *Powys* 9 F7
Llangefni *Angl* 14 G2
Llangeitho *Ceredig'n* 9 F6
Llangelynin *Gwyn* 8 C5
Llangennech *Carms* 9 H5
Llangernyw *Conwy* 14 G4
Llangoed *Angl* 14 G3
Llangollen *Denbs* 10 A3
Llangorse *Powys* 10 G2
Llangranog *Ceredig'n* 9 F4
Llangunllo *Powys* 10 E3
Llangurig *Powys* 8 D7
Llangwm *Conwy* 8 A7
Llangwm *Monmouths* 4 A4
Llangybi *Ceredig'n* 9 F6
Llangynidr *Powys* 10 H2
Llangynog *Powys* 10 B2
Llanharan *Rh Cyn Taff* 9 J7
Llanidloes *Powys* 8 D7
Llanilar *Ceredig'n* 8 E6
Llanllyfni *Gwyn* 8 A5
Llannor *Gwyn* 8 B4
Llanon *Ceredig'n* 8 E5
Llanpumsaint *Carms* 9 G5
Llanrhaeadr-ym-Mochnant *Powys* 10 B2
Llanrhian *Pembs* 9 G2
Llanrhidian *Swan* 9 J5
Llanrhystyd *Ceredig'n* 8 E5
Llanrug *Gwyn* 14 G2
Llanrwst *Conwy* 14 G3
Llansannan *Conwy* 14 G4
Llansawel *Carms* 9 G6
Llanstephan *Carms* 9 H4
Llanthony *Monmouths* 10 G3
Llantrisant *Rh Cyn Taff* 4 B2
Llantwit-Major *V/Glam* 9 K7
Llanuwchllyn *Gwyn* 8 B7
Llanvihangel Crucorney *Monmouths* 10 G3
Llanwddyn *Powys* 10 C2
Llanwenog *Ceredig'n* 9 F5
Llanwrda *Carms* 9 G6
Llanwrtyd Wells *Powys* 9 F7
Llanyblodwel *Shrops* 10 B3
Llanybydder *Carms* 9 F5
Llanymynech *Powys* 10 B3
Llanystumdwy *Gwyn* 8 B5
Llay *Wrex* 15 H6
Lledrod *Ceredig'n* 8 E6
Llithfaen *Gwyn* 8 A4
Llwyngwril *Gwyn* 8 C6
Llyswen *Powys* 10 G2
Loanhead *Midloth* 24 F5
Loch Baghasdail *W Isles* 26 F2
Loch nam Madadh *W Isles* 26 C3
Lochailort *H'land* 27 G7
Lochaline *H'land* 22 B5
Lochans *Dumf/Gal* 18 E4
Locharbriggs *Dumf/Gal* 19 C8
Lochbuie *Arg/Bute* 22 C5
Lochcarron *H'land* 27 D8
Lochdon *Arg/Bute* 22 C5
Lochearnhead *Stirl* 23 C9
Lochgair *Arg/Bute* 23 E6
Lochgelly *Fife* 24 E4
Lochgilphead *Arg/Bute* 23 E6
Lochgoilhead *Arg/Bute* 23 D8
Lochinver *H'land* 30 G2
Lochmaben *Dumf/Gal* 19 C9
Lochranza *N Ayrs* 23 G6
Lochwinnoch *Renf* 23 F8
Lockerbie *Dumf/Gal* 19 C9
Lockton *N Yorks* 21 H9
Loddiswell *Devon* 3 F9
Loddon *Norfolk* 13 D9
Loftus *Redcar/Clevel'd* 21 G8
Logan *E Ayrs* 19 A6
London *London* 6 B4
London Colney *Herts* 6 A3
Long Ashton *Bristol* 4 C4
Long Bennington *Lincs* 12 A2
Long Clawson *Leics* 11 B10
Long Compton *Warwick* 11 G8
Long Crendon *Bucks* 5 A10
Long Eaton *Derby* 11 B9
Long Itchington *Warwick* 11 E9
Long Melford *Suffolk* 13 F7
Long Preston *N Yorks* 15 C9
Long Stratton *Norfolk* 13 D8
Long Sutton *Lincs* 12 B5
Longbenton *Tyne/Wear* 21 D6
Longbridge Deverill *Wilts* 4 D6
Longdon *Worcs* 10 G6
Longford *Glos* 10 G6
Longforgan *Perth/Kinr* 24 C5
Longformacus *Scot Borders* 25 G7
Longframlington *Northum* 20 B5
Longhope *Orkney* 31 D8
Longhorsley *Northum* 20 C5
Longhoughton *Northum* 21 B6
Longnor *Staffs* 16 G2
Longridge *Lancs* 15 D8
Longside *Aberds* 29 D10
Longton *Lancs* 15 D7
Longtown *Cumb* 20 D1
Longtown *Heref'd* 10 G3
Loose *Kent* 7 D6
Lossiemouth *Moray* 29 C6
Lostock Gralam *Ches* 15 G8
Lostwithiel *Cornw'l* 2 F6
Loughborough *Leics* 11 B9
Loughor *Swan* 9 J5
Loughton *Essex* 6 B5
Louth *Lincs* 17 F8
Lowdham *Notts* 11 A10
Lower Beeding *W Sussex* 6 E4
Lower Killeyan *Arg/Bute* 22 G3
Lower Langford *N Som'set* 4 C4
Lower Mayland *Essex* 7 A7
Lower Shiplake *Oxon* 5 C10
Lowestoft *Suffolk* 13 D10

Lowick *Northum* 25 H9
Loxwood *W Sussex* 6 E3
Lubcroy *H'land* 28 A1
Lucker *Northum* 25 H9
Ludborough *Lincs* 17 F8
Ludford *Lincs* 17 F7
Ludgershall *Wilts* 5 D8
Ludgvan *Cornw'l* 2 G3
Ludham *Norfolk* 13 C9
Ludlow *Shrops* 10 E4
Lugton *E Ayrs* 23 G9
Lugwardine *Heref'd* 10 F4
Lumphanan *Aberds* 29 F7
Lumsden *Aberds* 29 E7
Luss *Arg/Bute* 23 E8
Lusta *H'land* 26 D5
Luton *Luton* 12 G3
Lutterworth *Leics* 11 D9
Lutton *Northants* 12 D3
Lybster *H'land* 31 G8
Lydd *Kent* 7 F8
Lydford *Devon* 3 D8
Lydham *Shrops* 10 D3
Lydney *Glos* 4 A5
Lyme Regis *Dorset* 4 G3
Lyminge *Kent* 7 D8
Lymington *Hants* 5 G8
Lymm *Warrington* 15 F8
Lympne *Kent* 7 E8
Lympstone *Devon* 3 D10
Lyndhurst *Hants* 5 F8
Lyneham *Wilts* 5 C7
Lyness *Orkney* 31 D8
Lynmouth *Devon* 3 A9
Lynton *Devon* 3 A9
Lytchett Minster *Dorset* 5 G6
Lytham St. Anne's *Lancs* 15 D6
Lythe *N Yorks* 21 G9

M

Mablethorpe *Lincs* 17 F9
Macclesfield *Ches* 15 G9
Macduff *Aberds* 29 C8
Machen *Caerph* 4 B3
Machrihanish *Arg/Bute* 18 B2
Machynlleth *Powys* 8 C6
Macmerry *E Loth* 25 F6
Madeley *Staffs* 10 A5
Madley *Heref'd* 10 G4
Maentwrog *Gwyn* 8 B6
Maesteg *Bridg* 9 J7
Maghull *Mersey* 15 E6
Magor *Monmouths* 4 B4
Maiden Bradley *Wilts* 4 E6
Maiden Newton *Dorset* 4 G4
Maidenhead *Windsor* 6 B2
Maidstone *Kent* 7 D6
Maldon *Essex* 7 A7
Malham *N Yorks* 15 B9
Mallaig *H'land* 27 G7
Mallwyd *Gwyn* 8 C7
Malmesbury *Wilts* 5 B6
Malpas *Ches* 10 A4
Maltby *S Yorks* 16 F4
Maltby le Marsh *Lincs* 17 F9
Malton *N Yorks* 16 B5
Manafon *Powys* 10 C2
Manby *Lincs* 17 F9
Manchester *Gtr Man* 15 F9
Manea *Cambs* 12 D5
Mangotsfield *S Gloucs* 4 C5
Manningtree *Essex* 13 G8
Manorbier *Pembs* 9 J3
Mansfield *Notts* 16 G4
Mansfield Woodhouse *Notts* 16 G4
Manton *Rutl'd* 12 C2
Marazion *Cornw'l* 2 G3
March *Cambs* 12 D5
Marden *Heref'd* 10 F4
Marden *Kent* 7 D6
Mareham le Fen *Lincs* 17 G8
Maresfield *E Sussex* 6 E5
Marfleet *Kingston/Hull* 17 D7
Margam *Neath P Talb* 9 J6
Margate *Kent* 7 C9
Marham *Norfolk* 13 C6
Market Bosworth *Leics* 11 C9
Market Deeping *Lincs* 12 C3
Market Drayton *Shrops* 10 B5
Market Harborough *Leics* 11 D10
Market Lavington *Wilts* 5 D7
Market Rasen *Lincs* 17 F7
Market Warsop *Notts* 16 G4
Market Weighton *ER Yorks* 17 C6
Markfield *Leics* 11 C9
Markinch *Fife* 24 D5
Marks Tey *Essex* 13 G7
Markyate *Herts* 12 H3
Marlborough *Devon* 3 G9
Marlborough *Wilts* 5 C7
Marlow *Bucks* 6 B2
Marnhull *Dorset* 4 F5
Marple *Gtr Man* 15 F9
Marshchapel *Lincs* 17 E8
Marshfield *S Gloucs* 4 C5
Marske by the Sea *Redcar/Clevel'd* 21 F8
Marston Magna *Som'set* 4 E4
Martham *Norfolk* 13 C10
Martin *Hants* 5 F7
Martley *Worcs* 10 E5
Martock *Som'set* 4 F4
Marton *Lincs* 17 F6
Marykirk *Aberds* 25 A7
Marypark *Moray* 28 E5
Maryport *Cumb* 19 F9
Marytavy *Devon* 3 E8
Marywell *Aberds* 29 G7
Marywell *Angus* 25 B7
Masham *N Yorks* 16 A3
Mathry *Pembs* 9 G2
Matlock *Derby* 16 G3
Mattishall *Norfolk* 13 C8
Mauchline *E Ayrs* 19 A6
Maud *Aberds* 29 D9
Maughold *I/Man* 14 A2
Mawgan *Cornw'l* 2 G4
Maxwellheugh *Scot Borders* 25 H7
Maybole *S Ayrs* 18 B5
Mayfield *E Sussex* 6 E5
Mayfield *Staffs* 11 A7
Mealabost *W Isles* 32 G5
Mealsgate *Cumb* 19 E10
Measham *Leics* 11 C8
Medstead *Hants* 5 E10
Meidrim *Carms* 9 H4
Meifod *Powys* 10 C2
Meigle *Perth/Kinr* 24 B5
Melbourn *Cambs* 12 F4
Melbourne *Derby* 11 B8
Melksham *Wilts* 5 C6
Mellon Charles *H'land* 27 B8
Mellor *Lancs* 15 D8
Melmerby *Cumb* 20 F3
Melrose *Scot Borders* 25 H6
Melsonby *N Yorks* 20 G5
Meltham *W Yorks* 16 E2
Melton *Suffolk* 13 F9
Melton Constable *Norfolk* 13 B8
Melton Mowbray *Leics* 11 B10
Melvaig *H'land* 27 B7
Melvich *H'land* 31 E6
Menai Bridge *Angl* 14 G2
Mendlesham *Suffolk* 13 E8
Mennock *Dumf/Gal* 19 B8
Menston *W Yorks* 16 C2
Menstrie *Clack* 24 E3
Meonstoke *Hants* 5 F10
Meopham *Kent* 6 C6
Mere *Wilts* 4 E6
Mere Brow *Lancs* 15 E7
Meriden *W Midlands* 11 D8
Merriott *Som'set* 4 F4
Merthyr Tydfil *Merth Tyd* 4 A2
Merton *London* 6 C4
Meshaw *Devon* 3 C9
Messingham *N Lincs* 17 E6
Metfield *Suffolk* 13 D9
Metheringham *Lincs* 17 G7
Methil *Fife* 24 D5
Methlick *Aberds* 29 E9
Methven *Perth/Kinr* 24 C4
Methwold *Norfolk* 13 D6
Mevagissey *Cornw'l* 2 F6
Mexborough *S Yorks* 16 E4
Mey *H'land* 31 E8
Micheldever *Hants* 5 D9
Michelmersh *Hants* 5 E8
Mickleover *Derby C* 11 B8
Mickleton *Durham* 20 F4
Mickleton *Glos* 11 F7
Mid Lavant *W Sussex* 6 F2
Mid Yell *Shetl'd* 32 B3
Midbea *Orkney* 31 A9
Middle Barton *Oxon* 11 G9
Middleham *N Yorks* 16 A2
Middlemarsh *Dorset* 4 F5
Middlesbrough *Middlesbro* 21 F7
Middleton *Arg/Bute* 22 B1
Middleton *Gtr Man* 15 E9
Middleton *Norfolk* 12 C6
Middleton Cheney *Northants* 11 F9
Middleton in Teesdale *Durham* 20 F4
Middleton-on-Sea *W Sussex* 6 F2
Middleton on the Wolds *ER Yorks* 17 C6
Middlewich *Ches* 15 G8
Middlezoy *Som'set* 4 E3
Midhurst *W Sussex* 6 E2
Midsomer Norton *Bath/NE Som'set* 4 D5
Milborne Port *Som'set* 4 F5
Mildenhall *Suffolk* 13 E6
Milford *Surrey* 6 D2
Milford Haven *Pembs* 9 H2
Milford on Sea *Hants* 5 G8
Millbrook *Cornw'l* 3 F8
Millom *Cumb* 14 A5
Millport *N Ayrs* 23 G7
Milnathort *Perth/Kinr* 24 D4
Milngavie *E Dunb* 23 F9
Milnthorpe *Cumb* 15 A7
Milovaig *H'land* 26 D4
Milton *H'land* 28 D1
Milton Abbot *Devon* 3 E7
Milton Keynes *M/Keynes* 12 G2
Milverton *Som'set* 4 E2
Minchinhampton *Glos* 4 A6
Minehead *Som'set* 3 A10
Minera *Wrex* 15 H6
Minety *Wilts* 5 B7
Mingary *H'land* 22 A4
Minnigaff *Dumf/Gal* 19 D6
Minstead *Hants* 5 F8
Minster *Kent* 7 C7
Minster *Kent* 7 C9
Minsterley *Shrops* 10 C3
Mintlaw *Aberds* 29 D9
Mirfield *W Yorks* 16 E3
Misterton *Notts* 16 F5
Misterton *Som'set* 4 F4
Mistley *Essex* 13 G8
Mitchel Troy *Monmouths* 4 A4
Mitcheldean *Glos* 10 H5
Modbury *Devon* 3 F9
Moelfre *Angl* 14 F2
Moffat *Dumf/Gal* 19 B9
Mold *Flints* 15 G6
Monar Lodge *H'land* 27 D9
Moniaive *Dumf/Gal* 19 C7
Monifieth *Angus* 25 C6
Monikie *Angus* 25 C6
Monkland *Heref'd* 10 F4
Monkokehampton *Devon* 3 C8
Monkton *S Ayrs* 18 A5
Monmouth *Monmouths* 10 H4
Montacute *Som'set* 4 F4
Montgomery *Powys* 10 D3
Montrose *Angus* 25 B7
Monymusk *Aberds* 29 F8
Morar *H'land* 27 G7
Morchard Bishop *Devon* 3 C9
Mordiford *Heref'd* 10 G4
Morebattle *Scot Borders* 20 A3
Morecambe *Lancs* 15 B7
Moreton-in-Marsh *Glos* 11 G8
Moretonhampstead *Devon* 3 D9
Morley *W Yorks* 16 D3
Morpeth *Northum* 21 C6
Mortehoe *Devon* 3 A8
Mortimer's Cross *Heref'd* 10 F4
Morwenstow *Cornw'l* 3 C7
Mossley *Gtr Man* 15 E9
Mostyn *Flints* 14 G5
Motcombe *Dorset* 4 E6
Motherwell *N Lanarks* 24 G2
Mottisfont *Hants* 5 E8
Moulton *Lincs* 12 B4
Moulton *Northants* 12 E2
Moulton *Suffolk* 13 E6
Mountain Ash *Rh Cyn Taff* 4 B2
Mountsorrel *Leics* 11 C9
Mousehole *Cornw'l* 2 G3
Mouswald *Dumf/Gal* 19 D9
Moy *H'land* 28 E3
Much Dewchurch *Heref'd* 10 G4
Much Marcle *Heref'd* 10 G5
Much Wenlock *Shrops* 10 C5
Muchalls *Aberds* 29 G9
Muir of Ord *H'land* 28 D2
Muirdrum *Angus* 25 C6
Muirhead *N Lanarks* 24 F2
Muirkirk *E Ayrs* 19 A7
Muker *N Yorks* 20 H4
Mulben *Moray* 29 D6
Mullion *Cornw'l* 2 H4
Mundesley *Norfolk* 13 B9
Mundford *Norfolk* 13 D7
Munlochy *H'land* 28 D3
Murlaggan *H'land* 27 G9
Murton *Durham* 21 E7
Musbury *Devon* 4 G3
Musselburgh *E Loth* 24 F5
Muthill *Perth/Kinr* 24 D3
Mybster *H'land* 31 F7
Myddfai *Carms* 9 G6
Myddle *Shrops* 10 B4
Mydroilyn *Ceredig'n* 9 F5
Mynydd Isa *Flints* 15 G6

N

Nafferton *ER Yorks* 17 C7
Nailsea *N Som'set* 4 C4
Nailsworth *Glos* 4 B6
Nairn *H'land* 28 D4
Nannerch *Flints* 14 G5
Nantwich *Ches* 15 H8
Nappa *N Yorks* 15 C9
Narberth *Pembs* 9 H3
Narborough *Leics* 11 D9
Naseby *Northants* 11 E10
Navenby *Lincs* 17 H6
Neap *Shetl'd* 32 D3
Neath *Neath P Talb* 9 J6
Necton *Norfolk* 13 C7
Needham Market *Suffolk* 13 F8
Needingworth *Cambs* 12 E4
Nefyn *Gwyn* 8 B4
Neilston *E Renf* 23 G9
Nelson *Lancs* 15 D9
Nenthead *Cumb* 20 E3
Neston *Ches* 15 G6
Nether Stowey *Som'set* 4 E2
Netheravon *Wilts* 5 D7
Netherbury *Dorset* 4 G4
Netherton *Northum* 20 B4
Nethy Bridge *H'land* 28 E5
Netley *Hants* 5 F9
Nettlebed *Oxon* 5 B10
Nettleham *Lincs* 17 G7
Nettleton *Lincs* 17 F7
Nevern *Pembs* 9 F3
New Abbey *Dumf/Gal* 19 D8
New Aberdour *Aberds* 29 C9
New Alresford *Hants* 5 E10
New Buckenham *Norfolk* 13 D8
New Clipstone *Notts* 16 G4
New Costessey *Norfolk* 13 C8
New Cumnock *E Ayrs* 19 B7
New Deer *Aberds* 29 D9
New Earswick *C/York* 16 C5
New Edlington *S Yorks* 16 F4
New Galloway *Dumf/Gal* 19 D7
New Holland *N Lincs* 17 D7
New Luce *Dumf/Gal* 18 D4
New Mills *Derby* 16 F2
New Milton *Hants* 5 G8
New Pitsligo *Aberds* 29 D9
New Quay *Ceredig'n* 9 F4
New Radnor *Powys* 10 E3
New Romney *Kent* 7 E8
New Rossington *S Yorks* 16 F5
New Scone *Perth/Kinr* 24 C4
New Tredegar *Caerph* 4 A2
New Waltham *NE Lincs* 17 E8
Newark-on-Trent *Notts* 17 H6
Newbiggin-by-the-Sea *Northum* 21 C6
Newbigging *S Lanarks* 24 G4
Newborough *Angl* 14 G2
Newbridge *Caerph* 4 B3
Newbridge on Wye *Powys* 10 F2
Newbrough *Northum* 20 D4
Newburgh *Aberds* 29 E9
Newburgh *Fife* 24 D5
Newburn *Tyne/Wear* 20 D5
Newbury *W Berks* 5 C9
Newby Bridge *Cumb* 15 A6
Newbyth *Aberds* 29 D9
Newcastle *Shrops* 10 D3
Newcastle Emlyn *Carms* 9 F4
Newcastle-Under-Lyme *Staffs* 10 A6
Newcastle-Upon-Tyne *Tyne/Wear* 21 D6
Newcastleton *Scot Borders* 20 C2
Newchurch *Powys* 10 F3
Newdigate *Surrey* 6 D4
Newent *Glos* 10 G5
Newgale *Pembs* 9 G2
Newham *London* 6 B5
Newhaven *E Sussex* 6 F5
Newick *E Sussex* 6 E5
Newington *Kent* 7 C7
Newington *Kent* 7 E8
Newlyn *Cornw'l* 2 G3
Newmachar *Aberds* 29 F9
Newmarket *Suffolk* 12 E6
Newmarket *W Isles* 32 G5
Newmill *Moray* 29 D7
Newmilns *E Ayrs* 23 H9
Newnham *Glos* 10 H5
Newport *Essex* 12 G5
Newport *I/Wight* 5 G9
Newport *Newp* 4 B3
Newport *Pembs* 9 G3
Newport *Telford* 10 B5
Newport-on-Tay *Fife* 25 C6
Newport Pagnell *M/Keynes* 12 F2
Newquay *Cornw'l* 2 E4
Newton *Lancs* 15 C8
Newton Abbot *Devon* 3 E10
Newton Arlosh *Cumb* 19 E9
Newton Aycliffe *Durham* 21 F6
Newton Ferrers *Devon* 3 F8
Newton le Willows *Mersey* 15 F7
Newton Mearns *E Renf* 23 G9
Newton Poppleford *Devon* 4 G2
Newton St. Cyres *Devon* 3 D10
Newton Stewart *Dumf/Gal* 19 D6
Newtongrange *Midloth* 24 F5
Newtonhill *Aberds* 29 G9
Newtonmore *H'land* 28 G3
Newtown *Heref'd* 10 F5
Newtown *Powys* 10 D2
Newtown St. Boswells *Scot Borders* 25 H6
Neyland *Pembs* 9 H2
Ninfield *E Sussex* 7 F6
Niton *I/Wight* 5 H9
Nordelph *Norfolk* 12 C5
Norham *Northum* 25 G8
Normanby le Wold *Lincs* 17 F7
Normanton *W Yorks* 16 D4
North Baddesley *Hants* 5 E8
North Berwick *E Loth* 25 E6
North Cerney *Glos* 5 A7
North Charlton *Northum* 20 A5
North Elmham *Norfolk* 13 B7
North Ferriby *ER Yorks* 17 D6
North Frodingham *ER Yorks* 17 C7
North Hill *Cornw'l* 3 E7
North Hykeham *Lincs* 17 G6
North Kessock *H'land* 28 D3
North Molton *Devon* 3 B9
North Newbald *ER Yorks* 17 D6
North Petherton *Som'set* 4 E3
North Queensferry *Fife* 24 E4
North Somercotes *Lincs* 17 F9
North Sunderland *Northum* 25 H10
North Tawton *Devon* 3 C9
North Thoresby *Lincs* 17 F8
North Tidworth *Wilts* 5 D8
North Walsham *Norfolk* 13 B9
North Wingfield *Derby* 16 G4
Northallerton *N Yorks* 21 H6
Northam *Devon* 3 B8
Northampton *Northants* 11 E10
Northchapel *W Sussex* 6 E2
Northfleet *Kent* 6 C6
Northiam *E Sussex* 7 E7
Northleach *Glos* 11 H7
Northop *Flints* 15 G6
Northpunds *Shetl'd* 32 E3
Northrepps *Norfolk* 13 B9
Northwich *Ches* 15 G8
Northwold *Norfolk* 13 D6
Northwood *London* 6 B3
Northwood *I/Wight* 5 G9
Norton *Glos* 10 G6
Norton *N Yorks* 16 B5
Norton *Suffolk* 13 E7
Norton *Worcs* 10 F6
Norton Fitzwarren *Som'set* 4 E2
Norwich *Norfolk* 13 C9
Norwick *Shetl'd* [illegible] A4
Nottingham *Nott'ham* 11 B9
Nuneaton *Warwick* 11 D8
Nunney *Som'set* 4 D5
Nutley *E Sussex* 6 E5
Nybster *H'land* 31 E8

O

Oadby *Leics* 11 C10
Oakdale *Caerph* 4 B2
Oakengates *Telford* 10 C5
Oakham *Rutl'd* 12 C2
Oban *Arg/Bute* 23 C6
Ochiltree *E Ayrs* 19 A6
Ockley *Surrey* 6 D3
Odie *Orkney* 31 B10
Odiham *Hants* 5 D10
Offord D'Arcy *Cambs* 12 E4
Ogbourne St. George *Wilts* 5 C7
Okehampton *Devon* 3 D8
Old Basing *Hants* 5 D10
Old Bolingbroke *Lincs* 17 G8
Old Colwyn *Conwy* 14 G4
Old Deer *Aberds* 29 D9
Old Fletton *Peterbro* 12 D3
Old Leake *Lincs* 12 A4
Old Radnor *Powys* 10 F3
Oldbury *S Gloucs* 4 B5
Oldham *Gtr Man* 15 E9
Oldmeldrum *Aberds* 29 E9
Olgrinmore *H'land* 31 F7
Ollerton *Notts* 16 G5
Olney *M/Keynes* 12 F2
Ombersley *Worcs* 10 E6
Onchan *I/Man* 14 B1
Onich *H'land* 23 A7
Ordhead *Aberds* 29 F8
Ordie *Aberds* 29 F7
Orford *Suffolk* 13 F10
Orleton *Heref'd* 10 E4
Ormesby St. Margaret *Norfolk* 13 C10
Ormiston *E Loth* 25 F6
Ormskirk *Lancs* 15 E7
Orphir *Orkney* 31 C8
Orpington *London* 6 C5
Orton *Cumb* 20 G3
Osbournby *Lincs* 12 B3
Oskamull *Arg/Bute* 22 B4
Osmotherley *N Yorks* 21 H7
Ossett *W Yorks* 16 D3
Oswaldtwistle *Lancs* 15 D8
Oswestry *Shrops* 10 B3
Otford *Kent* 6 D5
Othery *Som'set* 4 E3

Otley *W Yorks* 16 C2
Otter Ferry *Arg/Bute* 23 E6
Otterburn *Northum* 20 C4
Otterton *Devon* 4 G2
Ottery St. Mary *Devon* 4 G2
Oulton *Norfolk* 13 D10
Oulton Broad *Suffolk* 13 D10
Oundle *Northants* 12 D3
Ousdale *H'land* 31 G7
Outwell *Norfolk* 12 C5
Over *Cambs* 12 E4
Over Wallop *Hants* 5 E8
Overbister *Orkney* 31 A10
Overseal *Derby* 11 C8
Overstrand *Norfolk* 13 A9
Overton *Hants* 5 D9
Overton *Wrex* 10 A3
Owston Ferry *N Lincs* 17 F6
Oxenholme *Cumb* 15 A7
Oxford *Oxon* 5 A9
Oxnam *Scot Borders* 20 B3
Oxted *Surrey* 6 D4
Oykel Bridge *H'land* 28 A1

P

Pabail *W Isles* 32 G5
Paddock Wood *Kent* 6 D6
Padiham *Lancs* 15 D9
Padstow *Cornw'l* 2 E5
Paibeil *W Isles* 26 C2
Paignton *Torbay* 3 E10
Pailton *Warwick* 11 D9
Painscastle *Powys* 10 F2
Painshawfield *Northum* 20 E5
Painswick *Glos* 10 H6
Paisley *Renf* 23 F9
Palgrave *Suffolk* 13 E8
Palnackie *Dumf/Gal* 19 E8
Pangbourne *W Berks* 5 C10
Papworth Everard *Cambs* 12 E4
Parkeston *Essex* 13 G9
Parkhurst *I/Wight* 5 G9
Parracombe *Devon* 3 A9
Partney *Lincs* 17 G9
Parton *Cumb* 19 F8
Pateley Bridge *N Yorks* 16 B2
Pathhead *Midloth* 25 F5
Patna *E Ayrs* 19 B6
Patrick Brompton *N Yorks* 21 H6
Patrington *ER Yorks* 17 D8
Patterdale *Cumb* 20 G1
Paull *ER Yorks* 17 D7
Paulton *Bath/NE Som'set* 4 D5
Peacehaven *E Sussex* 6 F5
Peak Forest *Derby* 16 G2
Peasedown St. John *Bath/NE Som'set* 4 D5
Peasenhall *Suffolk* 13 E9
Peasmarsh *E Sussex* 7 E7
Peebles *Scot Borders* 24 G5
Peel *I/Man* 14 A1
Pegswood *Northum* 21 C6
Pembrey *Carms* 9 H5
Pembridge *Heref'd* 10 F4
Pembroke *Pembs* 9 H2
Pembroke Dock *Pembs* 9 H2
Pembury *Kent* 6 E6
Penally *Pembs* 9 J3
Penarth *V/Glam* 4 C2
Pencader *Carms* 9 G5
Pencoed *Bridg* 9 J7
Pendeen *Cornw'l* 2 G2
Penderyn *Rh Cyn Taff* 9 H7
Pendine *Carms* 9 H4
Penicuik *Midloth* 24 F5
Penistone *S Yorks* 16 E3
Penkridge *Staffs* 11 C6
Penmachno *Conwy* 8 A6
Penmaenmawr *Conwy* 14 G3
Pennan *Aberds* 29 C9
Pennyghael *Arg/Bute* 22 C4
Penpont *Dumf/Gal* 19 C8
Penrhyndeudraeth *Gwyn* 8 B6
Penrith *Cumb* 20 F2
Penryn *Cornw'l* 2 G4
Pensford *Bath/NE Som'set* 4 C5
Penshaw *Tyne/Wear* 21 E6
Penshurst *Kent* 6 D5
Pensilva *Cornw'l* 3 E7
Pentraeth *Angl* 14 G2
Pentrefoelas *Conwy* 8 A7
Penwortham *Lancs* 15 D7
Penybont *Powys* 10 E2
Penybontfawr *Powys* 10 B2
Penygroes *Carms* 9 H5
Penygroes *Gwyn* 8 A5
Penysarn *Angl* 14 F2
Penzance *Cornw'l* 2 G3
Perranporth *Cornw'l* 2 F4
Perranzabuloe *Cornw'l* 2 F4
Pershore *Worcs* 11 F6
Perth *Perth/Kinr* 24 C4
Peterborough *Peterbro* 12 D3
Peterchurch *Heref'd* 10 G3
Peterculter *Aberd C* 29 F9
Peterhead *Aberds* 29 D10
Peterlee *Durham* 21 E7
Petersfield *Hants* 5 E10
Petham *Kent* 7 D8
Petworth *W Sussex* 6 E2
Pevensey *E Sussex* 6 F6
Pewsey *Wilts* 5 C7
Pickering *N Yorks* 16 A5
Piddletrenthide *Dorset* 4 G5
Pidley *Cambs* 12 E4
Pierowall *Orkney* 31 A9
Pilling *Lancs* 15 C7
Pilton *Som'set* 4 D4
Pinchbeck *Lincs* 12 B4
Pinhoe *Devon* 3 D10
Pinmore Mains *S Ayrs* 18 C5
Pinwherry *S Ayrs* 18 C5
Pirbright *Surrey* 6 D2
Pirnmill *N Ayrs* 23 G6
Pitlochry *Perth/Kinr* 24 B3
Pittenweem *Fife* 25 D6
Plean *Stirl* 24 E3
Plockton *H'land* 27 E7
Pluckley *Kent* 7 D7
Plumpton *Cumb* 20 F2
Plymouth *Plym'th* 3 F8
Plympton *Plym'th* 3 F8
Plymstock *Plym'th* 3 F8
Pocklington *ER Yorks* 17 C6
Polegate *E Sussex* 6 F5
Polesworth *Warwick* 11 C8
Polloch *H'land* 22 A5
Polperro *Cornw'l* 3 F6
Polruan *Cornw'l* 3 F6
Polwarth *Scot Borders* 25 G7
Polzeath *Cornw'l* 2 E5
Pontardawe *Neath P Talb* 9 H6
Pontardulais *Swan* 9 H5
Pontefract *W Yorks* 16 D4
Ponteland *Northum* 20 D5
Ponterwyd *Ceredig'n* 8 D6
Pontesbury *Shrops* 10 C4
Pontrhydfendigaid *Ceredig'n* 8 E6
Pontrilas *Heref'd* 10 G4
Pontyates *Carms* 9 H5
Pontyberem *Carms* 9 H5
Pontycymer *Bridg* 9 J7
Pontypool *Torf* 4 A3
Pontypridd *Rh Cyn Taff* 4 B2
Pool *Cornw'l* 2 F4
Poole *Poole* 5 G7
Poolewe *H'land* 27 C8
Pooley Bridge *Cumb* 20 F2
Porlock *Som'set* 3 A10
Port Askaig *Arg/Bute* 22 F4
Port Bannatyne *Arg/Bute* 23 F7
Port Carlisle *Cumb* 19 D10
Port Charlotte *Arg/Bute* 22 G3
Port Ellen *Arg/Bute* 22 G3
Port Erin *I/Man* 14 B1
Port Eynon *Swan* 9 J5
Port Glasgow *Invercl* 23 F8
Port Henderson *H'land* 27 C7
Port Isaac *Cornw'l* 2 E5
Port Logan *Dumf/Gal* 18 E4
Port Nan Giuran *W Isles* 32 G5
Port Nis *W Isles* 32 E5
Port St. Mary *I/Man* 14 B1
Port Talbot *Neath P Talb* 9 J6
Port William *Dumf/Gal* 18 E5
Portavadie *Arg/Bute* 23 F6
Portgordon *Moray* 29 C6
Porth *Rh Cyn Taff* 4 B2
Porthcawl *Bridg* 9 K7
Porthleven *Cornw'l* 2 G4
Porthmadog *Gwyn* 8 B5
Portishead *N Som'set* 4 C4
Portknockie *Moray* 29 C7
Portlethen *Aberds* 29 G9
Portmahomack *H'land* 28 B4
Portnacroish *Arg/Bute* 23 B6
Portnahaven *Arg/Bute* 22 G2
Porton *Wilts* 5 E7
Portpatrick *Dumf/Gal* 18 E4
Portreath *Cornw'l* 2 F4
Portree *H'land* 27 D6
Portskerra *H'land* 31 E6
Portslade *Brighton/Hove* 6 F4
Portsmouth *Portsm'th* 5 G10
Portsoy *Aberds* 29 C7
Postbridge *Devon* 3 E9
Potter Heigham *Norfolk* 13 C10
Potterne *Wilts* 5 D6
Potters Bar *Herts* 6 A4
Potterspury *Northants* 11 F10
Potton *Beds* 12 F4
Poulton-le-Fylde *Lancs* 15 D6
Poundstock *Cornw'l* 3 D6
Powick *Worcs* 10 F6
Poynton *Ches* 15 F9
Praa Sands *Cornw'l* 2 G3
Prees *Shrops* 10 B4
Preesall *Lancs* 15 C6
Presbury *Ches* 15 G9
Prescot *Mersey* 15 F7
Prestatyn *Denbs* 14 F5
Prestbury *Glos* 11 G6
Presteigne *Powys* 10 E3
Preston *Dorset* 4 G5
Preston *ER Yorks* 17 D7
Preston *Kent* 7 C9
Preston *Lancs* 15 D7
Preston *Scot Borders* 25 G7
Preston Candover *Hants* 5 D10
Prestonpans *E Loth* 24 F5
Prestwich *Gtr Man* 15 E9
Prestwick *S Ayrs* 18 A5
Prestwood *Bucks* 6 A2
Princes Risborough *Bucks* 6 A2
Princetown *Devon* 3 E8
Probus *Cornw'l* 2 F5
Prudhoe *Northum* 20 D5
Pucklechurch *S Gloucs* 4 C5
Puddletown *Dorset* 4 G5
Pudsey *W Yorks* 16 D3
Pulborough *W Sussex* 6 F3
Pulham Market *Norfolk* 13 D8
Pulham St. Mary *Norfolk* 13 D9
Pumpsaint *Carms* 9 F6
Purfleet *Thurr'k* 6 C5
Purley *London* 6 C4
Purley *W Berks* 5 C10
Purton *Wilts* 5 B7
Puttenham *Surrey* 6 D2
Pwllheli *Gwyn* 8 B4
Pyle *Bridg* 9 J7

Q

Quadring *Lincs* 12 B4
Quainton *Bucks* 11 H10
Quedgeley *Glos* 10 H6
Queenborough *Kent* 7 C7
Queensbury *W Yorks* 16 D2
Queensferry *Flints* 15 G6
Quorndon *Leics* 11 C9

R

Rackenford *Devon* 3 C10
Rackheath *Norfolk* 13 C9
Rackwick *Orkney* 31 D8
Radcliffe *Gtr Man* 15 E8
Radcliffe-on-Trent *Notts* 11 B10
Radlett *Herts* 6 B3
Radley *Oxon* 5 B9
Radstock *Bath/NE Som'set* 4 D5
Radyr *Card* 4 B2
Raglan *Monmouths* 4 A4
Rainham *Medway* 7 C7
Rainworth *Notts* 16 H5
Rampside *Cumb* 15 B6
Ramsbottom *Gtr Man* 15 E8
Ramsbury *Wilts* 5 C8
Ramsey *Cambs* 12 D4
Ramsey *Essex* 13 G9
Ramsey *I/Man* 14 A2
Ramseycleuch *Scot Borders* 19 B10
Ramsgate *Kent* 7 C9
Rannoch Station *Perth/Kinr* 23 B9
Rapness *Orkney* 31 A9
Rathen *Aberds* 29 C10
Rattray *Perth/Kinr* 24 B4
Raunds *Northants* 12 E2
Ravenglass *Cumb* 19 H9
Ravenshead *Notts* 16 H4
Ravenstonedale *Cumb* 20 G3
Rawcliffe *C/York* 16 C4
Rawmarsh *S Yorks* 16 F4
Rawtenstall *Lancs* 15 D9
Rayleigh *Essex* 7 B7
Reading *Reading* 5 C10
Reay *H'land* 31 E6
Red Dial *Cumb* 19 E10
Red Point *H'land* 27 C7
Redbourn *Herts* 12 H3
Redbridge *London* 6 B5
Redcar *Redcar/Clevel'd* 21 F8
Redditch *Worcs* 11 E7
Redesmouth *Northum* 20 C4
Redhill *Surrey* 6 D4
Redland *Orkney* 31 B8
Redlynch *Wilts* 5 E8
Redmile *Leics* 12 B2
Redmire *N Yorks* 20 H5
Redruth *Cornw'l* 2 F4
Reedham *Norfolk* 13 C10
Reepham *Norfolk* 13 B8
Reeth *N Yorks* 20 H5
Reiff *H'land* 30 H1
Reigate *Surrey* 6 D4
Reiss *H'land* 31 F8
Renfrew *Renf* 23 F9
Rennington *Northum* 21 B6
Repton *Derby* 11 B8
Resolven *Neath P Talb* 9 H7
Reston *Scot Borders* 25 F8
Retford *Notts* 16 F5
Reydon *Suffolk* 13 E10
Rhayader *Powys* 8 E7
Rhewl *Denbs* 14 G5
Rhiconich *H'land* 30 F3
Rhiw *Gwyn* 8 B4
Rhondda *Rh Cyn Taff* 9 J7
Rhoose *V/Glam* 4 C2
Rhos-on-Sea *Conwy* 14 F4
Rhoslan *Gwyn* 8 A5
Rhosllanerchrugog *Wrex* 10 A3
Rhosneigr *Angl* 14 G1
Rhossili *Swan* 9 J5
Rhostryfan *Gwyn* 8 A5
Rhubodach *Arg/Bute* 23 F7
Rhuddlan *Denbs* 14 G5
Rhyd-Ddu *Gwyn* 8 A5
Rhyl *Denbs* 14 F5
Rhymney *Caerph* 4 A2
Rhynie *Aberds* 29 E7
Riccall *N Yorks* 16 D5
Richmond *London* 6 C3
Richmond *N Yorks* 20 G5
Rickmansworth *Herts* 6 B3
Ridsdale *Northum* 20 C4
Rievaulx *N Yorks* 16 A4
Rigside *S Lanarks* 24 H3
Rillington *N Yorks* 17 B6
Ringford *Dumf/Gal* 19 E7
Ringmer *E Sussex* 6 F5
Ringwood *Hants* 5 F7
Ripley *Derby* 16 H4
Ripley *N Yorks* 16 B3
Ripley *Surrey* 6 D3
Ripon *N Yorks* 16 B3
Ripponden *W Yorks* 16 D2
Risca *Caerph* 4 B3
Rishton *Lancs* 15 D8
Roade *Northants* 11 F10
Roadhead *Cumb* 20 D2
Roberton *Scot Borders* 20 B2
Robertsbridge *E Sussex* 7 E6
Robin Hood's Bay *N Yorks* 21 G9
Rocester *Staffs* 11 B7
Rochdale *Gtr Man* 15 E9
Roche *Cornw'l* 2 F5
Rochester *Medway* 7 C6
Rochester *Northum* 20 C4
Rochford *Essex* 7 B7
Rockcliffe *Cumb* 20 D1
Rockcliffe *Dumf/Gal* 19 E8
Rockingham *Northants* 12 D2
Rogart *H'land* 28 A3
Rogate *W Sussex* 6 E2
Roghadal *W Isles* 26 B4
Rolvenden *Kent* 7 E7
Romford *London* 6 B5
Romsey *Hants* 5 E8
Ropsley *Lincs* 12 B3
Rosedale Abbey *N Yorks* 21 H8
Rosehall *H'land* 28 A2
Rosehearty *Aberds* 29 C9
Rosemarket *Pembs* 9 H2
Rosemarkie *H'land* 28 D3
Roskhill *H'land* 26 D5
Roslin *Midloth* 24 F5
Rosneath *Arg/Bute* 23 E8
Ross *Northum* 25 H9
Ross-on-Wye *Heref'd* 10 G5
Rossett *Wrex* 15 H6
Rosyth *Fife* 24 E4
Rothbury *Northum* 20 B5
Rotherham *S Yorks* 16 F4
Rothes *Moray* 29 D6
Rothesay *Arg/Bute* 23 F7
Rothienorman *Aberds* 29 E8
Rothiesholm *Orkney* 31 B10
Rothwell *Northants* 12 D2
Rothwell *W Yorks* 16 D3
Rottal *Angus* 24 A5
Rottingdean *Brighton/Hove* 6 F4
Rowanburn *Dumf/Gal* 20 D2
Rowlands Gill *Tyne/Wear* 20 E5
Roxburgh *Scot Borders* 25 H7
Roxby *N Lincs* 17 E6
Royal Leamington Spa *Warwick* 11 E8
Royal Tunbridge Wells *Kent* 6 E5
Roybridge *H'land* 27 G10
Royston *Herts* 12 F4
Royston *S Yorks* 16 E3
Royton *Gtr Man* 15 E9
Ruabon *Wrex* 10 A3
Ruan Minor *Cornw'l* 2 H4
Ruardean *Glos* 10 H5
Rubery *Worcs* 11 E6
Rudston *ER Yorks* 17 B7
Rufford *Lancs* 15 E7
Rugby *Warwick* 11 E9
Rugeley *Staffs* 11 C7
Ruislip *London* 6 B3
Rumburgh *Suffolk* 13 D9
Rumney *Card* 4 C3
Runcorn *Halton* 15 F7
Rushden *Northants* 12 E2
Rushwick *Worcs* 10 F6
Ruskington *Lincs* 12 A3
Rutherglen *S Lanarks* 24 F2
Ruthin *Denbs* 14 H5
Ruthven *H'land* 28 G3
Ruthwell *Dumf/Gal* 19 D9
Ryal *Northum* 20 D5
Rydal *Cumb* 20 G1
Ryde *I/Wight* 5 G9
Rye *E Sussex* 7 E7
Ryhall *Rutl'd* 12 C3
Ryhope *Tyne/Wear* 21 E7
Ryton *Warwick* 11 E8

S

Sacriston *Durham* 21 E6
Saddell *Arg/Bute* 22 H5
Saffron Walden *Essex* 12 G5
Sageston *Pembs* 9 H3
St. Abb's *Scot Borders* 25 F8
St. Agnes *Cornw'l* 2 F4
St. Albans *Herts* 6 A3
St. Andrews *Fife* 25 D6
St. Ann's *Dumf/Gal* 19 C9
St. Arvans *Monmouths* 4 B4
St. Asaph *Denbs* 14 G5
St. Athan *V/Glam* 4 C2
St. Austell *Cornw'l* 2 F6
St. Bees *Cumb* 19 G8
St. Blazey *Cornw'l* 2 F6
St. Breward *Cornw'l* 2 E6
St. Briavels *Glos* 4 A4
St. Bride's Major *V/Glam* 9 K7
St. Buryan *Cornw'l* 2 G2
St. Clears *Carms* 9 H4
St. Columb Major *Cornw'l* 2 E5
St. Columb Minor *Cornw'l* 2 E5
St. Combs *Aberds* 29 C10
St. Cyrus *Aberds* 25 A7
St. David's *Pembs* 9 G1
St. Day *Cornw'l* 2 F4
St. Dennis *Cornw'l* 2 F5
St. Dogmaels *Ceredig'n* 9 F3
St. Dominick *Cornw'l* 3 E7
St. Enoder *Cornw'l* 2 F5
St. Erth *Cornw'l* 2 G3
St. Fergus *Aberds* 29 D10
St. Fillans *Perth/Kinr* 24 C2
St. Germans *Cornw'l* 3 F7
St. Harmon *Powys* 8 E7
St. Helens *Mersey* 15 F7
St. Issey *Cornw'l* 2 E5
St. Ives *Cambs* 12 E4
St. Ives *Cornw'l* 2 F3
St. John's *I/Man* 14 A1
St. Johns Chapel *Durham* 20 F4
St. Just *Cornw'l* 2 G2
St. Keverne *Cornw'l* 2 G4
St. Leonards *E Sussex* 7 F7
St. Levan *Cornw'l* 2 G2
St. Mabyn *Cornw'l* 2 E6
St. Margaret's-at-Cliffe *Kent* 7 D9
St. Margaret's Hope *Orkney* 31 D9
St. Mary Bourne *Hants* 5 D9
St. Mary's *Orkney* 31 C9
St. Mary's Bay *Kent* 7 E8
St. Mawes *Cornw'l* 2 G5
St. Mellons *Card* 4 B3
St. Merryn *Cornw'l* 2 E5
St. Minver *Cornw'l* 2 E5
St. Monance *Fife* 25 D6
St. Neots *Cambs* 12 E3
St. Newlyn East *Cornw'l* 2 F5
St. Olaves *Norfolk* 13 C10
St. Osyth *Essex* 13 H8
St. Stephen *Cornw'l* 2 F5
St. Teath *Cornw'l* 2 E6
St. Tudy *Cornw'l* 2 E6
Salcombe *Devon* 3 G9
Sale *Gtr Man* 15 F8
Salen *Arg/Bute* 22 B4
Salen *H'land* 22 A5
Salford *Gtr Man* 15 F9
Salford Priors *Warwick* 11 F7
Saline *Fife* 24 E4
Salisbury *Wilts* 5 E7
Sallachy *H'land* 28 A2
Saltash *Cornw'l* 3 F8
Saltburn-by-the-Sea *Redcar/Clevel'd* 21 F8
Saltcoats *N Ayrs* 23 G8
Saltfleet *Lincs* 17 F9
Saltfleetby *Lincs* 17 F9
Saltwood *Kent* 7 E8
Sampford Courtenay *Devon* 3 C9
Sanaigmore *Arg/Bute* 22 F3
Sandbach *Ches* 15 G8
Sandbank *Arg/Bute* 23 F7
Sandgate *Kent* 7 E9
Sandhead *Dumf/Gal* 18 E4
Sandhurst *Brackn'l* 6 C2
Sandleigh *Oxon* 5 A9
Sandness *Shetl'd* 32 D1
Sandown *I/Wight* 5 G9
Sandringham *Norfolk* 12 B6
Sandwich *Kent* 7 D9
Sandy *Beds* 12 F3
Sanquhar *Dumf/Gal* 19 B7
Sarnau *Ceredig'n* 9 F4
Sarnesfield *Heref'd* 10 F3

Sarre *Kent* 7 C9
Satterthwaite *Cumb* 20 H1
Saundersfoot *Pembs* 9 H3
Sawbridgeworth *Herts* 12 H5
Sawston *Cambs* 12 F5
Sawtry *Cambs* 12 D3
Saxilby *Lincs* 17 G6
Saxlingham Nethergate *Norfolk* 13 D9
Saxmundham *Suffolk* 13 E9
Saxthorpe *Norfolk* 13 B8
Scalasaig *Arg/Bute* 22 E3
Scalby *N Yorks* 17 A7
Scalloway *Shetl'd* 32 E2
Scamblesby *Lincs* 17 G8
Scarborough *N Yorks* 17 A7
Scardoy *H'land* 27 D10
Scarinish *Arg/Bute* 22 B2
Scarning *Norfolk* 13 C7
Scole *Norfolk* 13 E8
Sconser *H'land* 27 E6
Scopwick *Lincs* 17 H7
Scorton *N Yorks* 21 G6
Scotch Corner *N Yorks* 21 G6
Scotter *Lincs* 17 E6
Scourie *H'land* 30 F2
Scousburgh *Shetl'd* 32 F2
Scrabster *H'land* 31 E7
Scremerston *Northum* 25 G9
Scunthorpe *N Lincs* 17 E6
Sea Palling *Norfolk* 13 B10
Seaford *E Sussex* 6 G5
Seaham *Durham* 21 E7
Seahouses *Northum* 25 H10
Seamer *N Yorks* 17 A7
Seascale *Cumb* 19 G9
Seaton *Cumb* 19 F9
Seaton *Devon* 4 G3
Seaton Delaval *Northum* 21 D6
Sebergham *Cumb* 20 E1
Sedbergh *Cumb* 20 H3
Sedgefield *Durham* 21 F6
Seend *Wilts* 5 C6
Selborne *Hants* 5 E10
Selby *N Yorks* 16 D5
Selkirk *Scot Borders* 20 A2
Sellafield *Cumb* 19 G9
Selsey *W Sussex* 6 G2
Sennen *Cornw'l* 2 G2
Sennybridge *Powys* 9 G7
Settle *N Yorks* 15 B9
Seven Sisters *Neath P Talb* 9 H7
Sevenoaks *Kent* 6 D5
Severn Beach *S Gloucs* 4 B4
Severn Stoke *Worcs* 10 F6
Sgarasta Mhor *W Isles* 26 B4
Shaftesbury *Dorset* 4 E6
Shalcombe *I/Wight* 5 G8
Shaldon *Devon* 3 E10
Shalford *Surrey* 6 D3
Shanklin *I/Wight* 5 G9
Shap *Cumb* 20 G2
Sharnbrook *Beds* 12 E2
Sharpness *Glos* 4 A5
Shawbury *Shrops* 10 B4
Shawford *Hants* 5 E9
Shebbear *Devon* 3 C8
Sheerness *Kent* 7 C7
Sheffield *S Yorks* 16 F3
Shefford *Beds* 12 G3
Sheigra *H'land* 30 E2
Shenfield *Essex* 6 B6
Shepherdswell *Kent* 7 D9
Shepley *W Yorks* 16 E2
Shepshed *Leics* 11 B9
Shepton Mallet *Som'set* 4 D5
Sherborne *Dorset* 4 F5
Sherborne St. John *Hants* 5 D10
Sherburn *N Yorks* 17 B6
Sherburn in Elmet *N Yorks* 16 D4
Shere *Surrey* 6 D3
Sherfield English *Hants* 5 E8
Sherfield on Lodden *Hants* 5 D10
Sheriff Hutton *N Yorks* 16 B5
Sheringham *Norfolk* 13 A8
Sherston *Wilts* 4 B6
Shiel Bridge *H'land* 27 F8
Shieldaig *H'land* 27 D8
Shifnal *Shrops* 10 C5
Shilbottle *Northum* 21 B6
Shildon *Durham* 21 F6
Shillingstone *Dorset* 4 F6
Shillington *Beds* 12 G3
Shinfield *Wokingham* 5 C10
Shipdham *Norfolk* 13 C7
Shipley *W Yorks* 16 D2
Shipston-on-Stour *Warwick* 11 G8
Shipton under Wychwood *Oxon* 11 H8
Shirebrook *Notts* 16 G4
Shoeburyness *Southend* 7 B7
Shoreham by Sea *W Sussex* 6 F4
Shorwell *I/Wight* 5 G9
Shotley Gate *Suffolk* 13 G9
Shottermill *Surrey* 6 E2
Shottisham *Suffolk* 13 F9
Shotts *N Lanarks* 24 F3
Shrewsbury *Shrops* 10 C4
Shrewton *Wilts* 5 D7
Shrivenham *Oxon* 5 B8
Siabost *W Isles* 32 F4
Sible Hedingham *Essex* 13 G6
Sibsey *Lincs* 17 H8
Sidbury *Devon* 4 G2
Sidford *Devon* 4 G2
Sidlesham *W Sussex* 6 G2
Sidmouth *Devon* 4 G2
Silloth *Cumb* 19 E9
Silsden *W Yorks* 16 C2
Silver End *Essex* 13 G7
Silverdale *Lancs* 15 B7
Silverstone *Northants* 11 F10
Silverton *Devon* 3 C10
Simonsbath *Som'set* 3 B9
Singleton *W Sussex* 6 F2
Sittingbourne *Kent* 7 C7
Sixpenny Handley *Dorset* 5 F7
Sizewell *Suffolk* 13 E10
Skegness *Lincs* 17 G9
Skellingthorpe *Lincs* 17 G6
Skelmersdale *Lancs* 15 E7
Skelmorlie *N Ayrs* 23 F7
Skelton *Cumb* 20 F2
Skelton *Redcar/Clevel'd* 21 G8
Skinburness *Cumb* 19 E9
Skipness *Arg/Bute* 23 G6
Skipsea *ER Yorks* 17 C7
Skipton *N Yorks* 15 C9
Skirlaugh *ER Yorks* 17 D7
Slaidburn *Lancs* 15 C8
Slaithwaite *W Yorks* 16 E2
Slaley *Northum* 20 E4
Slamannan *Falk* 24 F3
Sleaford *Lincs* 12 A3
Sledmere *ER Yorks* 17 B6
Sleights *N Yorks* 21 G9
Sligachan *H'land* 27 E6
Slough *Slough* 6 C2
Smailholm *Scot Borders* 25 H7
Smarden *Kent* 7 D7
Smethwick *W Midlands* 11 D7
Smithfield *Cumb* 20 D2
Snainton *N Yorks* 17 A6
Snaith *ER Yorks* 16 D5
Snape *Suffolk* 13 F9
Sneaton *N Yorks* 21 G9
Snettisham *Norfolk* 12 B6
Snodland *Kent* 7 C6
Soham *Cambs* 12 E5
Solas *W Isles* 26 C3
Solihull *W Midlands* 11 D7
Solva *Pembs* 9 G1
Somerby *Leics* 11 C10
Somercotes *Derby* 16 H4
Somersham *Cambs* 12 E4
Somerton *Som'set* 4 E4
Sonning *Wokingham* 5 C10
Sonning Common *Oxon* 5 C10
Sopley *Hants* 5 G7
Sorbie *Dumf/Gal* 19 E6
Sordale *H'land* 31 E7
Sorisdale *Arg/Bute* 22 A3
Sorn *E Ayrs* 19 A6
Sortat *H'land* 31 E8
Soulby *Cumb* 20 G3
South Anston *S Yorks* 16 F4
South Benfleet *Essex* 7 B6
South Brent *Devon* 3 F9
South Cave *ER Yorks* 17 D6
South Cerney *Glos* 5 B7
South Elkington *Lincs* 17 F8
South Harting *W Sussex* 5 F10
South Hayling *Hants* 5 G10
South Kelsey *Lincs* 17 F7
South Kirkby *W Yorks* 16 E4
South Molton *Devon* 3 B9
South Ockendon *Thurr'k* 6 B6
South Otterington *N Yorks* 16 A3
South Petherton *Som'set* 4 F4
South Petherwin *Cornw'l* 3 D7
South Queensferry *C/Edinb* 24 F4
South Shields *Tyne/Wear* 21 D6
South Tawton *Devon* 3 D9
South Walsham *Norfolk* 13 C9
South Warnborough *Hants* 5 D10
South Woodham Ferrers *Essex* 7 B7
South Wootton *Norfolk* 12 B6
South Zeal *Devon* 3 D9
Southam *Warwick* 11 E9
Southampton *S'thampton* 5 F9
Southborough *Kent* 6 D5
Southend *Arg/Bute* 18 B2
Southend-on-Sea *Southend* 7 B7
Southery *Norfolk* 12 D6
Southminster *Essex* 7 B7
Southport *Mersey* 15 E6
Southwark *London* 6 C4
Southwell *Notts* 16 H5
Southwick *W Sussex* 6 F4
Southwold *Suffolk* 13 E10
Sowerby *N Yorks* 16 A4
Sowerby Bridge *W Yorks* 16 D2
Spalding *Lincs* 12 B4
Spaldwick *Cambs* 12 E3
Sparkford *Som'set* 4 E5
Spean Bridge *H'land* 27 G10
Speke *Mersey* 15 F7
Spennymoor *Durham* 21 F6
Spilsby *Lincs* 17 G9
Spittal *Pembs* 9 G2
Spittal of Glenmuick *Aberds* 29 G6
Spittle of Glenshee *Perth/Kinr* 28 H5
Spixworth *Norfolk* 13 C9
Spofforth *N Yorks* 16 C3
Spott *E Loth* 25 F7
Spreyton *Devon* 3 D9
Sproatley *ER Yorks* 17 D7
Stadhampton *Oxon* 5 B10
Staffin *H'land* 27 C6
Stafford *Staffs* 11 B6
Staindrop *Durham* 20 F5
Staines *Surrey* 6 C3
Stainforth *N Yorks* 15 B9
Stainforth *S Yorks* 16 E5
Stainton *Lincs* 17 G7
Stainton *Middlesbro* 21 G7
Staintondale *N Yorks* 21 H9
Staithes *N Yorks* 21 G8
Stalbridge *Dorset* 4 F5
Stalham *Norfolk* 13 B9
Stallingborough *NE Lincs* 17 E7
Stalybridge *Gtr Man* 15 F9
Stamford *Lincs* 12 C3
Stamford Bridge *ER Yorks* 16 C5
Stamfordham *Northum* 20 D5
Standish *Gtr Man* 15 E7
Standlake *Oxon* 5 A8
Stanford le Hope *Thurr'k* 6 B6
Stanford on Teme *Worcs* 10 E5
Stanhope *Durham* 20 F4
Stanley *Durham* 21 E6
Stanley *Perth/Kinr* 24 C4
Stannington *Northum* 21 D6
Stansted Mountfitchet *Essex* 12 G5
Stanton *Suffolk* 13 F7
Stanton Harcourt *Oxon* 5 A9
Stanton St. John *Oxon* 5 A9
Stanway *Glos* 11 G7
Stanwix *Cumb* 20 E2
Stapleford *Notts* 11 B9
Staplehurst *Kent* 7 D6
Starcross *Devon* 3 D10
Staunton *Glos* 10 G5
Staunton on Wye *Heref'd* 10 F3
Staveley *Cumb* 20 H2
Staveley *Derby* 16 G4
Staxigoe *H'land* 31 F8
Staxton *N Yorks* 17 B7
Steeple Bumpstead *Essex* 12 F6
Steeple Claydon *Bucks* 11 G10
Stein *H'land* 26 D5
Stenhousemuir *Falk* 24 E3
Stevenage *Herts* 12 G4
Stevenston *N Ayrs* 23 G8
Stewarton *E Ayrs* 23 G9
Steyning *W Sussex* 6 F3
Stibb Cross *Devon* 3 C8
Stichill *Scot Borders* 25 H7
Stickford *Lincs* 17 G8
Stickney *Lincs* 17 H8
Stillington *N Yorks* 16 B4
Stilton *Cambs* 12 D3
Stirling *Stirl* 24 E2
Stobbs *Scot Borders* 20 B2
Stobo *Scot Borders* 24 H4
Stock *Essex* 7 B6
Stockbridge *Hants* 5 E8
Stockport *Gtr Man* 15 F9
Stocksbridge *S Yorks* 16 F3
Stockton *Warwick* 11 E9
Stockton-on-Tees *Stockton* 21 F7
Stoer *H'land* 30 G2
Stoke *Medway* 7 C7
Stoke Albany *Northants* 12 D2
Stoke Ferry *Norfolk* 13 D6
Stoke Fleming *Devon* 3 F10
Stoke Gabriel *Devon* 3 F10
Stoke Mandeville *Bucks* 6 A2
Stoke-on-Trent *Stoke* 10 A6
Stoke Poges *Bucks* 6 B2
Stoke Prior *Worcs* 11 E6
Stokenchurch *Bucks* 5 B10
Stokesley *N Yorks* 21 G7
Stone *Bucks* 11 H10
Stone *Glos* 4 B5
Stone *Staffs* 11 B6
Stonehaven *Aberds* 29 G9
Stonehouse *Glos* 4 A6
Stonehouse *S Lanarks* 24 G2
Stoneykirk *Dumf/Gal* 18 E4
Stonham Aspal *Suffolk* 13 F8
Stony Stratford *M/Keynes* 12 G2
Store *Orkney* 31 B10
Stornoway *W Isles* 32 G5
Storrington *W Sussex* 6 F3
Stotfold *Beds* 12 G4
Stourbridge *W Midlands* 10 D6
Stourpaine *Dorset* 4 F6
Stourport-on-Severn *Worcs* 10 E6
Stow *Scot Borders* 25 G6
Stow Bardolph *Norfolk* 12 C6
Stow-on-the-Wold *Glos* 11 G8
Stowmarket *Suffolk* 13 F8
Strachan *Aberds* 29 G8
Strachur *Arg/Bute* 23 D7
Stradbroke *Suffolk* 13 E9
Straiton *S Ayrs* 18 B5
Stranraer *Dumf/Gal* 18 D4
Stratford St. Mary *Suffolk* 13 G8
Stratford-Upon-Avon *Warwick* 11 F8
Strathan *H'land* 30 E4
Strathaven *S Lanarks* 24 G2
Strathblane *Stirl* 23 F9
Strathdon *Aberds* 29 F6
Strathkanaird *H'land* 27 A9
Strathpeffer *H'land* 28 D2
Strathy *H'land* 31 E6
Strathyre *Stirl* 23 D9
Stratmiglo *Fife* 24 D5
Stratton *Cornw'l* 3 C7
Stratton *Glos* 5 A7
Stratton St. Margaret *Swindon* 5 B7
Streatley *W Berks* 5 B9
Street *Som'set* 4 E4
Strensall *C/York* 16 B5
Stretford *Gtr Man* 15 F9
Stretham *Cambs* 12 E5
Stretton *Rutl'd* 12 C2
Stretton *Staffs* 11 B8
Stretton *Warrington* 15 F8
Strichen *Aberds* 29 D9
Stromeferry *H'land* 27 E8
Stromemore *H'land* 27 E8
Stromness *Orkney* 31 C8
Stronachlachar *Stirl* 23 D9
Strone *Arg/Bute* 23 E7
Strontian *H'land* 23 A6
Stroud *Glos* 4 A6
Struy *H'land* 28 D1
Stubbington *Hants* 5 F9
Studland *Dorset* 5 G7
Studley *Warwick* 11 E7
Sturminster Marshall *Dorset* 5 G6
Sturminster Newton *Dorset* 4 F5
Sturry *Kent* 7 D8
Sturton *Lincs* 17 F6
Sudbury *Derby* 11 B7
Sudbury *Suffolk* 13 F7
Sulby *I/Man* 14 A2
Sullom *Shetl'd* 32 C2
Sully *V/Glam* 4 C2
Sunderland *Tyne/Wear* 21 E7
Sunk Island *ER Yorks* 17 E8
Sunninghill *Windsor* 6 C2
Sutterton *Lincs* 12 B4
Sutton *Cambs* 12 D5
Sutton *London* 6 C4
Sutton Bridge *Lincs* 12 B5
Sutton Coldfield *W Midlands* 11 D7
Sutton Courtenay *Oxon* 5 B9
Sutton-in-Ashfield *Notts* 16 G4
Sutton Lane Ends *Ches* 15 G9
Sutton-on-Sea *Lincs* 17 F9
Sutton-on-Trent *Notts* 16 G5
Sutton Scotney *Hants* 5 E9
Sutton-under-Whitestonecliffe *N Yorks* 16 A4
Sutton Valence *Kent* 7 D7
Swadlincote *Derby* 11 C8
Swaffham *Norfolk* 13 C7
Swalcliffe *Oxon* 11 G8
Swalecliffe *Kent* 7 C8
Swanage *Dorset* 5 H7
Swanley *Kent* 6 C5
Swansea *Swan* 9 J6
Sway *Hants* 5 G8
Swindon *Swindon* 5 B7
Swinefleet *ER Yorks* 16 D5
Swineshead *Lincs* 12 A4
Swinton *Gtr Man* 15 E8
Swinton *S Yorks* 16 F4
Swinton *Scot Borders* 25 G8
Symbister *Shetl'd* 32 C3
Symington *S Lanarks* 24 H3
Symonds Yat *Heref'd* 10 H4
Syresham *Northants* 11 F10
Syston *Leics* 11 C10

T

Tadcaster *N Yorks* 16 C4
Tadley *Hants* 5 C10
Tain *H'land* 28 B3
Tal-y-llyn *Gwyn* 8 C6
Talgarth *Powys* 10 G2
Talladale *H'land* 27 C8
Talley *Carms* 9 G6
Talsarnau *Gwyn* 8 B6
Talybont *Ceredig'n* 8 D6
Talysarn *Gwyn* 8 A5
Tamerton Foliot *Plym'th* 3 E8
Tamworth *Staffs* 11 C8
Tangmere *W Sussex* 6 F2
Tannadice *Angus* 25 B6
Tanworth-in-Arden *Warwick* 11 E7
Taobh Tuath *W Isles* 26 B3
Tarbert *Arg/Bute* 23 F6
Tarbet *Arg/Bute* 23 D8
Tarbet *H'land* 27 G7
Tarbolton *S Ayrs* 19 A6
Tarland *Aberds* 29 F7
Tarleton *Lancs* 15 D7
Tarporley *Ches* 15 G7
Tarrant Hinton *Dorset* 5 F6
Tarskavaig *H'land* 27 F6
Tarves *Aberds* 29 E9
Tarvin *Ches* 15 G7
Tattenhall *Ches* 15 H7
Tattersett *Norfolk* 13 B7
Taunton *Som'set* 4 E3
Tavistock *Devon* 3 E8
Tayinloan *Arg/Bute* 22 G5
Taynuilt *Arg/Bute* 23 C7
Tayport *Fife* 25 C6
Teangue *H'land* 27 F7
Tebay *Cumb* 20 G3
Tedburn St Mary *Devon* 3 D10
Teesside 21 F7
Teignmouth *Devon* 3 E10
Telford *Telford* 10 C5
Temple Combe *Som'set* 4 E5
Temple Ewell *Kent* 7 D9
Temple Sowerby *Cumb* 20 F3
Templeton *Pembs* 9 H3
Tenbury Wells *Heref'd* 10 E4
Tenby *Pembs* 9 H3
Tenterden *Kent* 7 E7
Terrington *N Yorks* 16 B5
Terrington St. Clement *Norfolk* 12 B5
Tetbury *Glos* 4 B6
Tetney *Lincs* 17 E8
Tetsworth *Oxon* 5 A10
Teviothead *Scot Borders* 20 B2
Tewkesbury *Glos* 10 G6
Teynham *Kent* 7 C7
Thame *Oxon* 5 A10
Thatcham *W Berks* 5 C9
Thaxted *Essex* 12 G6
The Barony *Orkney* 31 B8
The Mumbles *Swan* 9 J6
Theale *W Berks* 5 C10
Thetford *Norfolk* 13 D7
Thirsk *N Yorks* 16 A4
Thornaby on Tees *Stockton* 21 G7
Thornbury *S Gloucs* 4 B5
Thorndon *Suffolk* 13 E8
Thorne *S Yorks* 16 E5
Thorney *Peterbro* 12 C4
Thornham *Norfolk* 13 A6
Thornhill *Dumf/Gal* 19 C8
Thornhill *Stirl* 24 D2
Thornthwaite *Cumb* 19 F10
Thornton *Lancs* 15 C6
Thornton-le-Dale *N Yorks* 17 A6
Thorpe *Norfolk* 13 C9
Thorpe le Soken *Essex* 13 G8
Thorverton *Devon* 3 C10
Thrapston *Northants* 12 E3
Three Legged Cross *Dorset* 5 F7
Threlkeld *Cumb* 20 F1
Threshfield *N Yorks* 15 B9
Thrumster *H'land* 31 F8
Thurcroft *S Yorks* 16 F4
Thurlby *Lincs* 12 C3
Thurlestone *Devon* 3 F9
Thurmaston *Leics* 11 C10
Thursby *Cumb* 20 E1
Thurso *H'land* 31 E7
Ticehurst *E Sussex* 7 E6
Tickhill *S Yorks* 16 F4
Tideswell *Derby* 16 G2
Tighnabruaich *Arg/Bute* 23 F6
Tilbury *Thurr'k* 6 C6
Tillicoultry *Clack* 24 E3
Tillingham *Essex* 7 A8
Tilmanstone *Kent* 7 D9
Timberscombe *Som'set* 3 A10
Timsbury *Bath/NE Som'set* 4 D5
Tingewick *Bucks* 11 G10
Tintagel *Cornw'l* 2 D6
Tintern *Monmouths* 4 A4
Tipton *W Midlands* 11 D6
Tiptree *Essex* 13 H7
Tisbury *Wilts* 5 E6
Titchfield *Hants* 5 F9
Tiverton *Devon* 3 C10
Tobermory *Arg/Bute* 22 B4
Toberonochy *Arg/Bute* 22 D5

Place	County	Page	Grid
Tobha Mor	W Isles	26	E2
Toddington	Beds	12	G3
Todmorden	W Yorks	15	D9
Tolastadh bho Thuath	W Isles	32	F5
Tollesbury	Essex	7	A7
Tolob	Shetl'd	32	F2
Tolpuddle	Dorset	4	G5
Tomatin	H'land	28	E4
Tomdoun	H'land	27	F9
Tomintoul	Moray	28	F5
Tomnavoulin	Moray	29	E6
Tonbridge	Kent	6	D5
Tondu	Bridg	9	J7
Tong	Shrops	10	C6
Tongue	H'land	30	F4
Tonyrefail	Rh Cyn Taff	4	B2
Topcliffe	N Yorks	16	B4
Topsham	Devon	3	D10
Torbay	Torbay	3	E10
Torcross	Devon	3	F10
Torness	H'land	28	E2
Torphins	Aberds	29	F8
Torpoint	Cornw'l	3	F8
Torquay	Torbay	3	E10
Torridon	H'land	27	D8
Torroble	H'land	28	A2
Torthorwald	Dumf/Gal	19	D9
Torver	Cumb	19	H10
Toscaig	H'land	27	E7
Totland	I/Wight	5	G8
Totley	S Yorks	16	F3
Totnes	Devon	3	F9
Totton	Hants	5	F8
Tow Law	Durham	20	F5
Towcester	Northants	11	F10
Tower Hamlets	London	6	B4
Town Yetholm	Scot Borders	20	A4
Trafford Park	Gtr Man	15	F8
Tranent	E Loth	25	F6
Trawsfynydd	Gwyn	8	B6
Trecastle	Powys	9	G7
Tredegar	Bl Gwent	10	H2
Trefeglwys	Powys	8	D7
Trefnant	Denbs	14	G5
Trefriw	Conwy	14	G3
Tregaron	Ceredig'n	8	E6
Tregony	Cornw'l	2	F5
Tregynon	Powys	10	D2
Treharris	Merth Tyd	4	B2
Trelech	Carms	9	G4
Tremadog	Gwyn	8	B5
Trenance	Cornw'l	2	E5
Trentham	Stoke	10	A6
Treorchy	Rh Cyn Taff	9	J7
Tresilian	Cornw'l	2	F5
Tretower	Powys	10	G2
Treuddyn	Flints	15	H6
Trimdon	Durham	21	F6
Trimley	Suffolk	13	G9
Tring	Herts	12	H2
Troon	S Ayrs	23	H8
Troutbeck	Cumb	20	G2
Trowbridge	Wilts	4	D6
Trull	Som'set	4	E3
Trumpington	Cambs	12	F5
Trunch	Norfolk	13	B9
Truro	Cornw'l	2	F5
Tuddenham	Suffolk	13	E6
Tudweiliog	Gwyn	8	B4
Tullynessle	Aberds	29	F7
Tummel Bridge	Perth/Kinr	24	B2
Tunstall	Suffolk	13	F9
Turnberry	S Ayrs	18	B5
Turriff	Aberds	29	D8
Turvey	Beds	12	F2
Tutbury	Staffs	11	B8
Tuxford	Notts	16	G5
Twatt	Orkney	31	B8
Tweedmouth	Northum	25	G8
Tweedshaws	Scot Borders	19	B9
Tweedsmuir	Scot Borders	19	A9
Twenty	Lincs	12	B3
Twyford	Hants	5	E9
Twyford	Leics	11	C10
Twyford	Wokingham	6	C2
Tydd St. Giles	Cambs	12	C5
Tydd St. Mary	Lincs	12	C5
Tylorstown	Rh Cyn Taff	9	J7
Ty'n-y-groes	Conwy	14	G3
Tyndrum	Stirl	23	C8
Tynemouth	Tyne/Wear	21	D6
Tywardreath	Cornw'l	2	F6
Tywyn	Gwyn	8	C5

U

Place	County	Page	Grid
Uckfield	E Sussex	6	E5
Uddingston	S Lanarks	24	F2
Uffculme	Devon	4	F2
Uffington	Oxon	5	B8
Ufford	Suffolk	13	F9
Ugborough	Devon	3	F9
Uig	H'land	26	C5
Ulbster	H'land	31	F8
Ulceby	N Lincs	17	E7
Ulceby Cross	Lincs	17	G9
Uley	Glos	4	B5
Ullapool	H'land	27	B9
Ulsta	Shetl'd	32	B3
Ulverston	Cumb	15	B6
Unapool	H'land	30	G3
Upavon	Wilts	5	D7
Uphill	N Som'set	4	D3
Upper Chapel	Powys	10	F2
Upper Heyford	Oxon	11	G9
Upper Hindhope	Scot Borders	20	B3
Upper Poppleton	C/York	16	C4
Upper Tean	Staffs	11	B7
Uppingham	Rutl'd	12	C2
Upton	Ches	15	G7
Upton Snodsbury	Worcs	11	F6
Upton-upon-Severn	Worcs	10	F6
Upwey	Dorset	4	G5
Urchfont	Wilts	5	D7
Urmston	Gtr Man	15	F8
Usk	Monmouths	4	A3
Usselby	Lincs	17	F7
Uttoxeter	Staffs	11	B7
Uyeasound	Shetl'd	32	A3

V

Place	County	Page	Grid
Valley	Angl	14	G1
Veness	Orkney	31	B9
Ventnor	I/Wight	5	H9
Verwood	Dorset	5	F7
Veryan	Cornw'l	2	G5
Vickerstown	Cumb	14	B5
Vidlin	Shetl'd	32	C3
Virginia Water	Surrey	6	C3
Voe	Shetl'd	32	C2
Voy	Orkney	31	C8

W

Place	County	Page	Grid
Waddesdon	Bucks	11	H10
Waddingham	Lincs	17	F6
Waddington	Lincs	17	G6
Wadebridge	Cornw'l	2	E5
Wadhurst	E Sussex	6	E6
Wainfleet All Saints	Lincs	17	G9
Wakefield	W Yorks	16	D3
Walberswick	Suffolk	13	E10
Walcott	Lincs	17	H7
Walderslade	Medway	7	C6
Waldron	E Sussex	6	F5
Walford	Heref'd	10	G3
Walkerburn	Scot Borders	24	H5
Walkeringham	Notts	16	F5
Wallasey	Mersey	15	F6
Wallingford	Oxon	5	B10
Walls	Shetl'd	32	D2
Wallsend	Tyne/Wear	21	D6
Walmer	Kent	7	D9
Walpole Norfolk		12	C5
Walsall	W Midlands	11	D7
Walsham le Willows	Suffolk	13	E8
Walsoken	Cambs	12	C5
Waltham	NE Lincs	17	E8
Waltham Abbey	Essex	6	A4
Waltham Forest	London	6	B4
Waltham on the Wolds	Leics	12	B2
Walton	Cumb	20	D2
Walton-on-Thames	Surrey	6	C3
Walton-on-the-Naze	Essex	13	G9
Wanborough	Swindon	5	B8
Wandsworth	London	6	C4
Wangford	Suffolk	13	E10
Wansford	Peterbro	12	D3
Wantage	Oxon	5	B9
Warboys	Cambs	12	D4
Wardington	Oxon	11	F9
Wardle	Ches	15	H8
Ware	Herts	12	H4
Wareham	Dorset	5	G6
Wargrave	Wokingham	5	C10
Wark	Northum	20	D4
Warkworth	Northum	21	B6
Warley	W Midlands	11	D7
Warminster	Wilts	4	D6
Warrington	Warrington	15	F8
Warton	Lancs	15	B7
Warwick	Warwick	11	E8
Wasbister	Orkney	31	B8
Washaway	Cornw'l	2	E6
Washford	Som'set	4	D2
Washingborough	Lincs	17	G7
Washington	Tyne/Wear	21	E6
Washington	W Sussex	6	F3
Watchet	Som'set	4	D2
Watchfield	Oxon	5	B8
Waterbeach	Cambs	12	E5
Waterhead	Angus	29	H7
Waterhouses	Staffs	16	H2
Wateringbury	Kent	6	D5
Waterlooville	Hants	5	F10
Watford	Herts	6	B3
Wath upon Dearne	S Yorks	16	F4
Watlington	Norfolk	12	C6
Watlington	Oxon	5	B10
Watten	H'land	31	F8
Watton	Norfolk	13	C7
Waunfawr	Gwyn	14	H2
Weachyburn	Aberds	29	D8
Wearhead	Durham	20	F4
Weasenham	Norfolk	13	B7
Weaverham	Ches	15	G8
Weaverthorpe	N Yorks	17	B6
Wedmore	Som'set	4	D4
Wednesbury	W Midlands	11	D6
Wednesfield	W Midlands	11	C6
Weedon Bec	Northants	11	E10
Weeley	Essex	13	G8
Welbourn	Lincs	17	H6
Weldon	Northants	12	D2
Weldon	Northum	20	C5
Welford	Northants	11	D10
Welford	W Berks	5	C9
Wellesbourne	Warwick	11	F8
Wellingborough	Northants	12	E2
Wellington	Som'set	4	E2
Wellington	Telford	10	C5
Wellow Bath/NE Som'set		4	D5
Wells	Som'set	4	D4
Wells-next-the-Sea	Norfolk	13	A7
Welney	Norfolk	12	D5
Welshampton	Shrops	10	B4
Welshpool	Powys	10	C3
Welton	Lincs	17	G7
Welwyn Garden City	Herts	12	H4
Wem	Shrops	10	B4
Wembury	Devon	3	F8
Wemyss Bay	Inverc'l	23	F7
Wendover	Bucks	6	A2
Wensley	N Yorks	20	H5
Wenvoe	V/Glam	4	C2
Weobley	Heref'd	10	F4
Werrington	Cornw'l	3	D7
West Auckland	Durham	20	F5
West Bergholt	Essex	13	G7
West Bridgford	Notts	11	B9
West Bromwich	W Midlands	11	D7
West Burton	N Yorks	16	A2
West Calder	W Loth	24	F4
West Coker	Som'set	4	F4
West Dean	Wilts	5	E8
West End	Hants	5	F9
West Felton	Shrops	10	B3
West Grinstead	W Sussex	6	E3
West Haddon	Northants	11	E10
West Kilbride	N Ayrs	23	G8
West Kingsdown	Kent	6	C5
West Kirby	Mersey	15	F6
West Linton	Scot Borders	24	G4
West Looe	Cornw'l	3	F7
West Lulworth	Dorset	4	H6
West Malling	Kent	6	D6
West Meon	Hants	5	E10
West Mersea	Essex	13	H8
West Moors	Dorset	5	F7
West Rasen	Lincs	17	F7
West Thorney	W Sussex	5	F10
West Wellow	Hants	5	F8
West Woodburn	Northum	20	C4
Westbourne	W Sussex	5	F10
Westbury	Shrops	10	C3
Westbury	Wilts	4	D6
Westbury-on-Severn	Glos	10	H5
Westbury-sub-Mendip	Som'set	4	D4
Westcott	Surrey	6	D3
Westerham	Kent	6	D5
Westfield	E Sussex	7	F7
Westhill	Aberds	29	F9
Westhoughton	Gtr Man	15	E8
Westleton	Suffolk	13	E10
Westminster	London	6	B4
Weston	Staffs	11	B6
Weston-Super-Mare	N Som'set	4	C3
Westonzoyland	Som'set	4	E3
Westruther	Scot Borders	25	G7
Westward Ho!	Devon	3	B8
Wetheral	Cumb	20	E2
Wetherby	W Yorks	16	C4
Wetwang	ER Yorks	17	C6
Weybourne	Norfolk	13	A8
Weybridge	Surrey	6	C3
Weyhill	Hants	5	D8
Weymouth	Dorset	4	H5
Whaley Bridge	Derby	16	F2
Whalley	Lancs	15	D8
Whalton	Northum	20	C5
Whaplode	Lincs	12	C4
Whatton	Notts	11	B10
Whauphill	Dumf/Gal	18	E5
Wheathampstead	Herts	12	H3
Wheatley	Notts	16	F5
Wheatley	Oxon	5	A10
Wheatley Hill	Durham	21	F6
Wheaton Aston	Staffs	10	C6
Wheldrake	C/York	16	C5
Whicham	Cumb	14	A5
Whickham	Tyne/Wear	21	D6
Whimple	Devon	4	G2
Whipsnade	Beds	12	H3
Whissendine	Rutl'd	12	C2
Whitburn	W Loth	24	F3
Whitby	N Yorks	21	G9
Whitchurch	Bristol	4	C5
Whitchurch	Bucks	12	G2
Whitchurch	Devon	3	E8
Whitchurch	Hants	5	D9
Whitchurch	Heref'd	10	H4
Whitchurch	Shrops	10	A4
White Bridge	H'land	28	F2
Whitehall	Orkney	31	B10
Whitehaven	Cumb	19	G8
Whitehouse	Arg/Bute	23	F6
Whitekirk	E Loth	25	E7
Whiteparish	Wilts	5	E8
Whitfield	Kent	7	D9
Whithorn	Dumf/Gal	19	F6
Whitland	Carms	9	H3
Whitley Bay	Tyne/Wear	21	D6
Whitsome	Scot Borders	25	G8
Whitstable	Kent	7	C8
Whitstone	Cornw'l	3	D7
Whittington	Derby	16	G3
Whittington	Lancs	15	B8
Whittington	Shrops	10	B3
Whittington	Staffs	11	C7
Whittlebury	Northants	11	F10
Whittlesey	Cambs	12	D4
Whittlesford	Cambs	12	F5
Whitwell	Derby	16	G4
Whitwell	I/Wight	5	H9
Whitwick	Leics	11	C9
Whitworth	Lancs	15	E9
Whixley	N Yorks	16	C4
Wick	H'land	31	F8
Wick	S Gloucs	4	C5
Wick	V/Glam	9	K7
Wick	Wilts	5	E7
Wicken	Cambs	12	E5
Wickford	Essex	7	B6
Wickham	Hants	5	F9
Wickham Market	Suffolk	13	F9
Wickwar	S Gloucs	4	B5
Widdrington	Northum	21	C6
Wide Open	Tyne/Wear	21	D6
Widecombe	Devon	3	E9
Widemouth	Cornw'l	3	C8
Widnes	Halton	15	F7
Wigan	Gtr Man	15	E7
Wigmore	Heref'd	10	E4
Wigmore	Medway	7	C7
Wigston	Leics	11	D10
Wigton	Cumb	19	E10
Wigtown	Dumf/Gal	19	E6
Willand	Devon	4	F2
Willaston	Ches	15	G6
Willenhall	W Midlands	11	D6
Willersley	Heref'd	10	F3
Willesborough	Kent	7	D8
Willingdon	E Sussex	6	F6
Willington	Beds	12	F3
Willington	Durham	20	F5
Williton	Som'set	4	D2
Willoughby	Lincs	17	G9
Wilmington	Devon	4	G3
Wilmslow	Ches	15	F9
Wilnecote	Staffs	11	C8
Wilton	Wilts	5	E7
Wimblington	Cambs	12	D5
Wimborne Minster	Dorset	5	F7
Wincanton	Som'set	4	E5
Winchcombe	Glos	11	G7
Winchelsea	E Sussex	7	F7
Winchester	Hants	5	E9
Windermere	Cumb	20	H2
Windsor	Windsor	6	C2
Windygates	Fife	24	D5
Wing	Bucks	12	G2
Wingate	Durham	21	F7
Wingham	Kent	7	D9
Winkleigh	Devon	3	C9
Winscombe	N Som'set	4	D4
Winsford	Ches	15	G8
Winslow	Bucks	11	G10
Winster	Derby	16	G3
Winston	Durham	20	G5
Winterborne Abbas	Dorset	4	G5
Winterborne Stickland	Dorset	4	F6
Winterton	N Lincs	17	E6
Winterton	Norfolk	13	B10
Wirksworth	Derby	16	H3
Wisbech	Cambs	12	D5
Wisbech St. Mary	Cambs	12	C5
Wisborough Green	W Sussex	6	E3
Wishaw	N Lanarks	24	F2
Witchampton	Dorset	5	F7
Witchford	Cambs	12	E5
Witham	Essex	13	H7
Witheridge	Devon	3	C9
Withern	Lincs	17	F9
Withernsea	ER Yorks	17	D9
Withington	Glos	11	H7
Witley	Surrey	6	D2
Witnesham	Suffolk	13	F8
Witney	Oxon	11	H8
Wiveliscombe	Som'set	4	E2
Wivelsfield	E Sussex	6	F4
Wivenhoe	Essex	13	G8
Wix	Essex	13	G8
Woburn	Beds	12	G2
Woburn Sands	M/Keynes	12	G2
Woking	Surrey	6	D3
Wokingham	Wokingham	6	C2
Wolf's Castle	Pembs	9	G2
Wollaston	Northants	12	E2
Wolsingham	Durham	20	F5
Wolverhampton	W Midlands	11	D6
Wolverton	M/Keynes	12	F2
Wolviston	Stockton	21	F7
Wombwell	S Yorks	16	E3
Wonersh	Surrey	6	D3
Wonston	Hants	5	E9
Woodbridge	Suffolk	13	F9
Woodbury	Devon	4	G2
Woodchester	Glos	4	A6
Woodchurch	Kent	7	E7
Woodcote	Oxon	5	B10
Woodgreen	Hants	5	F7
Woodhall Spa	Lincs	17	G8
Woodhouse	S Yorks	16	F4
Woodhouse Eaves	Leics	11	C9
Woodley	Wokingham	5	C10
Woodstock	Oxon	11	H9
Woofferton	Shrops	10	E4
Wookey	Som'set	4	D4
Wookey Hole	Som'set	4	D4
Wool	Dorset	4	G6
Woolacombe	Devon	3	A8
Woolavington	Som'set	4	D3
Wooler	Northum	20	A4
Woolwich	London	6	C5
Wooperton	Northum	20	A5
Woore	Shrops	10	A5
Wootton Bassett	Wilts	5	B7
Wootton Bridge	I/Wight	5	G9
Wootton Wawen	Warwick	11	E7
Worcester	Worcs	10	F6
Worfield	Shrops	10	D5
Workington	Cumb	19	F8
Worksop	Notts	16	G4
Wormit	Fife	24	C5
Worsbrough	S Yorks	16	E3
Wortham	Suffolk	13	E8
Worthing	W Sussex	6	F3
Wotton under Edge	Gloucs	4	B5
Wragby	Lincs	17	G7
Wrangle	Lincs	17	H9
Wrea Green	Lancs	15	D8
Wrentham	Suffolk	13	D10
Wretham	Norfolk	13	D7
Wrexham	Wrex	15	H6
Writtle	Essex	6	A6
Wroughton	Swindon	5	B7
Wroxham	Norfolk	13	C9
Wroxton	Oxon	11	F9
Wyberton	Lincs	12	A4
Wye	Kent	7	D8
Wylye	Wilts	5	E7
Wymondham	Leics	12	C2
Wymondham	Norfolk	13	C8

Y

Place	County	Page	Grid
Y Felinheli	Gwyn	14	G2
Yalding	Kent	7	D6
Yarcombe	Devon	4	F3
Yardley Hastings	Northants	12	F2
Yarm	Stockton	21	G7
Yarmouth	I/Wight	5	G8
Yarnton	Oxon	11	H9
Yarrow	Scot Borders	20	A1
Yate	S Gloucs	4	B5
Yatton	N Som'set	4	C4
Yaxley	Cambs	12	D3
Yeadon	W Yorks	16	C2
Yealmpton	Devon	3	F8
Yelverton	Devon	3	E8
Yeovil	Som'set	4	F4
Yetminster	Dorset	4	F4
York	C/York	16	C4
Youlgreave	Derby	16	G3
Yoxall	Staffs	11	C7
Yoxford	Suffolk	13	E10
Ysbyty Ifan	Conwy	8	A7
Ysbyty Ystwyth	Ceredig'n	8	E6
Ystalyfera	Neath P Talb	9	H6
Ystradgynlais	Powys	9	H6

Z

Place	County	Page	Grid
Zennor	Cornw'l	2	G3